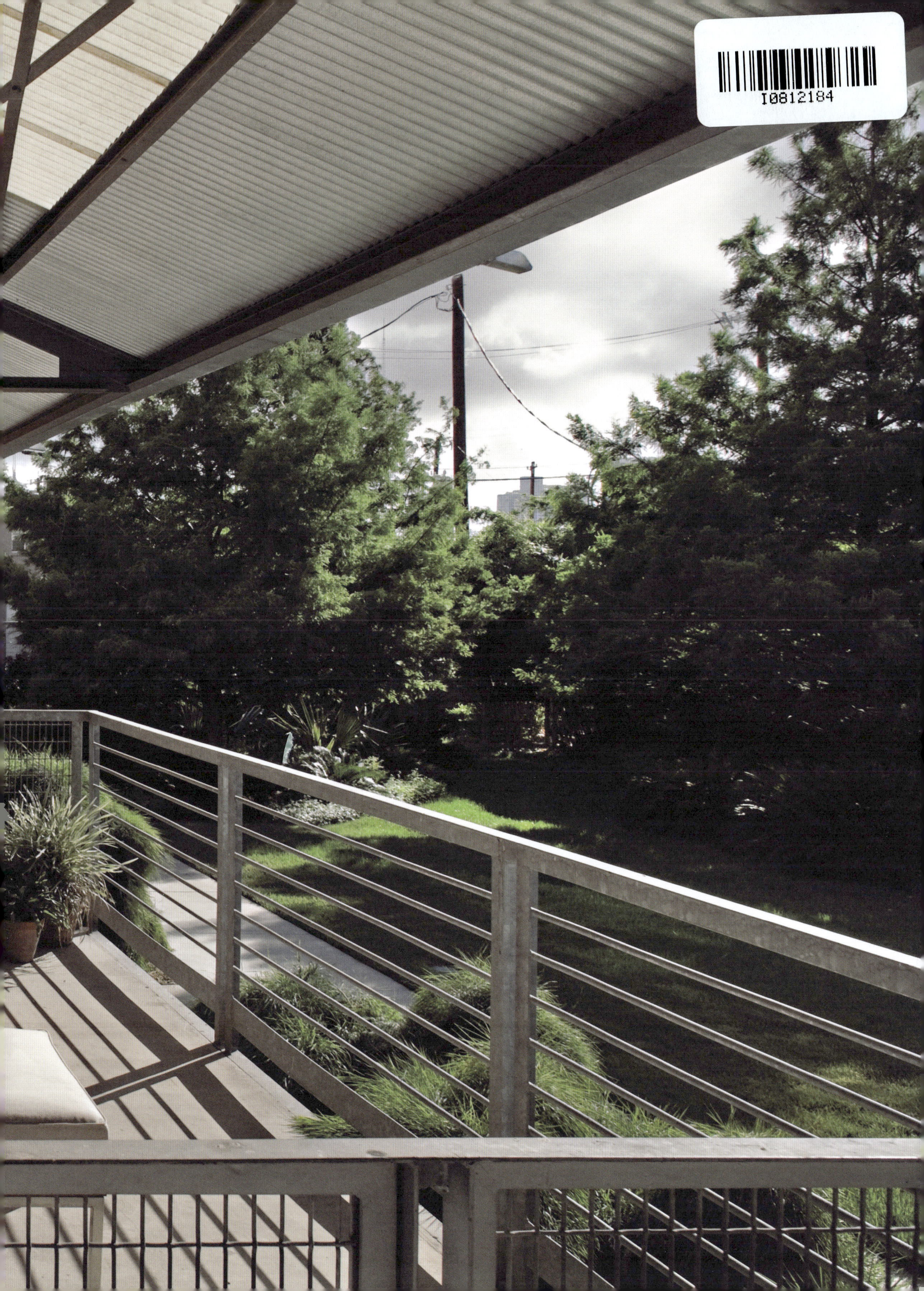

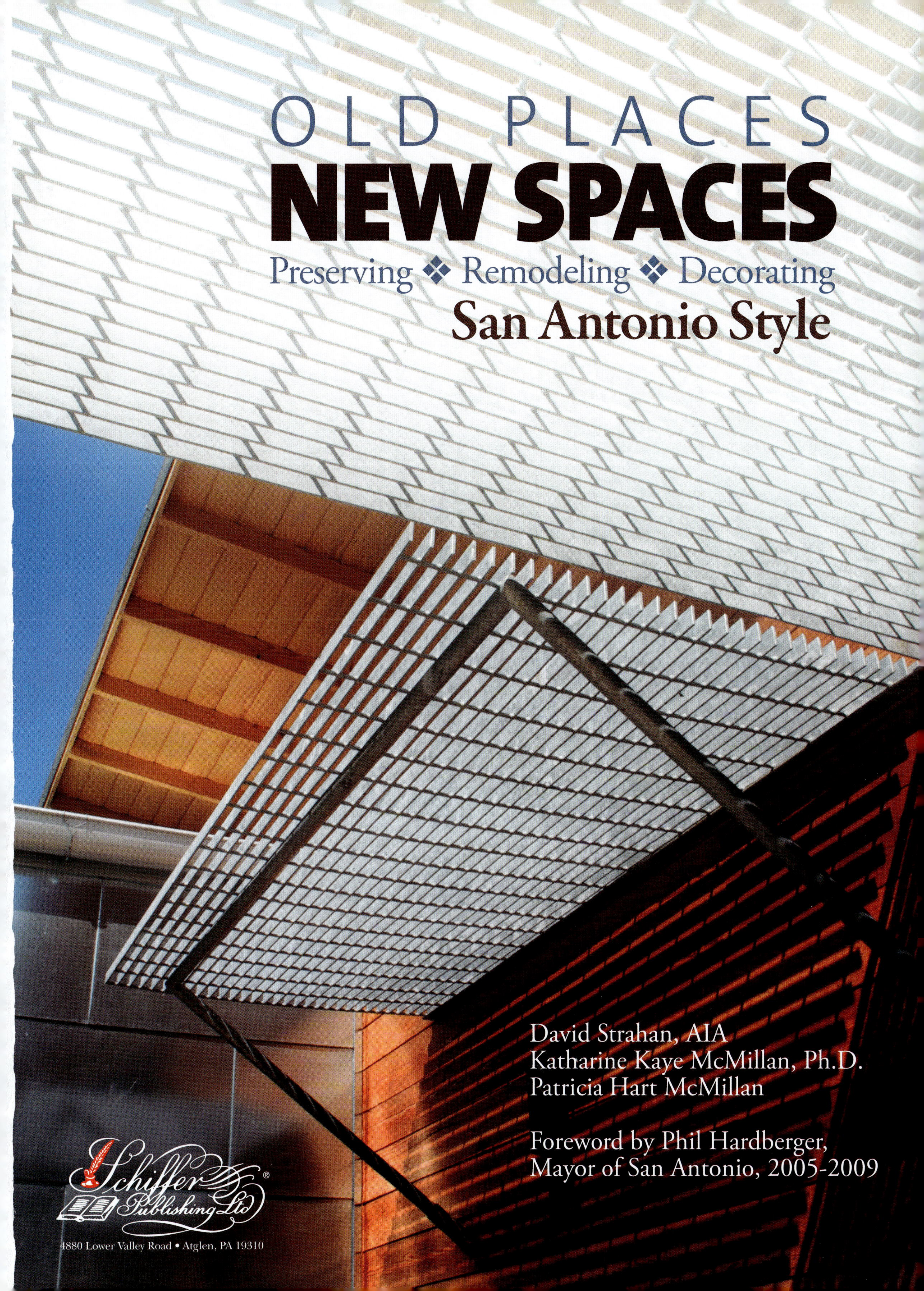

OLD PLACES NEW SPACES

Preserving ❖ Remodeling ❖ Decorating

San Antonio Style

David Strahan, AIA
Katharine Kaye McMillan, Ph.D.
Patricia Hart McMillan

Foreword by Phil Hardberger,
Mayor of San Antonio, 2005-2009

Schiffer Publishing Ltd
4880 Lower Valley Road • Atglen, PA 19310

Acknowledgments

Special thanks to Architectural Photographer Chris Cooper, whose talent is admired and appreciated by architects nationwide, and whose wonderful images of San Antonio homes make up much of this book.

Our gratitude to all the architects, builders, and interior designers, whose projects are featured.

Thanks to the homeowners who welcomed us and our readers into their unique residences.

—The Authors

Other Schiffer Books by the Authors:
Christmas at Historic Houses. ISBN: 9780764335594. $45.00
Contemporary Villas. ISBN: 9780764337741. $59.99
Decorating for Christmas at Historic Houses. ISBN: 9780764338397. $45.00
Glass Tile Inspirations for Kitchens and Baths. ISBN: 0764325094. $19.95

Other Schiffer Books on Related Subjects:
Eco-House Renovations: 45 Green Home Conversions. Lucy D. Rosenfeld. ISBN: 9780764339295. $49.99
Green Homes: Dwellings for the 21st Century. E. Ashley Rooney David Hartke and John C. McConnell. ISBN: 9780764330339. $39.99
Historic Doorways of San Antonio, Texas. Frederick R. Preston, Ed.D. Foreword by Judge Nelson W. Wolff. ISBN: 9780764331671. $19.99
Yesterday's Structures: Today's Homes. Lucy D. Rosenfeld. ISBN: 0764310143. $39.95

Library of Congress Control Number: 2012939959

Type set in The Sans Light-Plain & Black/Adobe Garamond Pro/Zurich BT

ISBN: 978-0-7643-4170-0
Printed in China

Published by Schiffer Publishing, Ltd.
4880 Lower Valley Road
Atglen, PA 19310
Phone: (610) 593-1777; Fax: (610) 593-2002
E-mail: Info@schifferbooks.com

In Europe, Schiffer books are distributed by
Bushwood Books
6 Marksbury Ave.
Kew Gardens
Surrey TW9 4JF England
Phone: 44 (0) 20 8392 8585; Fax: 44 (0) 20 8392 9876
E-mail: info@bushwoodbooks.co.uk
Website: www.bushwoodbooks.co.uk

Dedication

Founders of The San Antonio Conservation Society:

Mrs. Fannie Applewhite, Mrs. E. C. Branch, Mrs. Esther P. Carvajal, Mrs. Henry Drought, Miss Emily Edwards, Miss Anna Ellis, Mrs. Jules W. Fontaine, Mrs. Rena M. Green, Miss Eleanor Onderdonk, Mrs. W. P. Rote, Mrs. Conrad Schasse, Mrs. Lane Taylor, Mrs. R. O. Van Horn

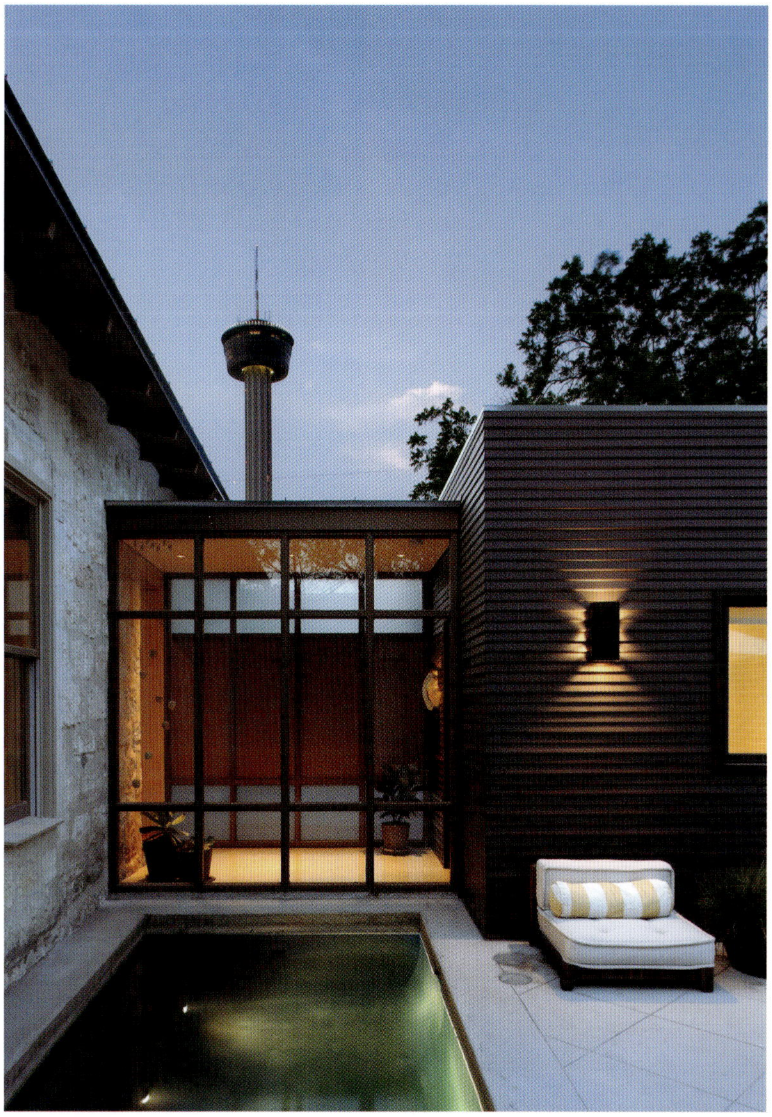

Foreword

—Phil Hardberger,
Mayor of San Antonio,
2005-2009

San Antonio is blessed with an abundance of beautiful historic homes. This may be understandable given that San Antonio itself has a rich history that is not surpassed by any American city. After all, there have been Europeans here since 1691 (and Indians for 10,000 years before that.) We are an old culture by New World standards. But not all old cities have been able to preserve their homes as has San Antonio.

There are several reasons for our wealth of historic homes. The Spaniards, who considered many of their buildings an homage to God, gave us graceful arches, extravagant artistic flourishes, and a sense of harmony with the land of South Texas. This European influence was a good foundation. And then some truly master home builders settled in San Antonio—the Germans.

The Germans built houses for the ages. Master stonecutters went to work with Texas limestone to build homes that were virtually indestructible by forces of wind, overabundant sunshine, rain, droughts, and even fires. Carpenters did magical things with wood that lightened the look of massive limestone, building overhanging or wrap-around porches, decorative gingerbread, generous windows, and high ceilings. What outside air there was became a captive of the house and moved easily from room to room. (Yes, there was life before air-conditioning.) Examples of this German craftsmanship are found in King William and Monte Vista—and in this book.

We had wonderful architects that took this merging of cultures and created beauty in our living spaces: Atlee Ayers, Alfred Giles, and O'Neil Ford are all departed architects that forever impacted our sense of beauty and the way we live. This tradition of talented architects and their timeless architecture continues to this day. We have more than our share of architects who are nationally, and even internationally famous, who live among us and continue to build homes for the ages.

We, as a people, cherish our community of architects and the historic houses that are their legacy. Books such as this lovely volume by David Strahan, Katharine Kaye McMillan, and Patricia Hart McMillan, with photographs by Barbara Justice, Chris Cooper, and other talented photographers, educate our eye and mind—and contribute to continuing the tradition of a city of beautiful homes. Read, look, and enjoy.

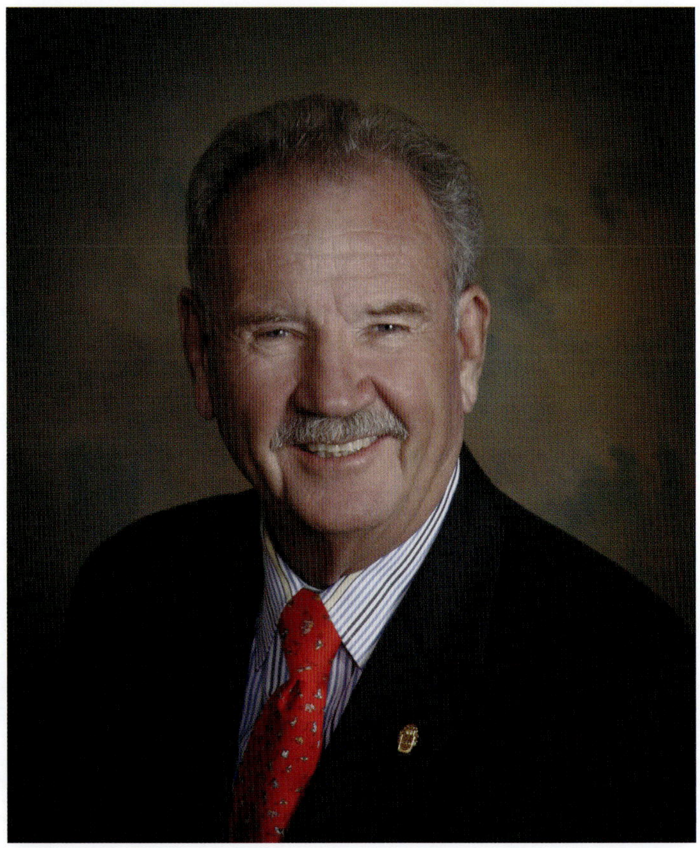

Contents

Introduction:
INSPIRING VINTAGE

—Katharine Kaye McMillan, Ph.D.

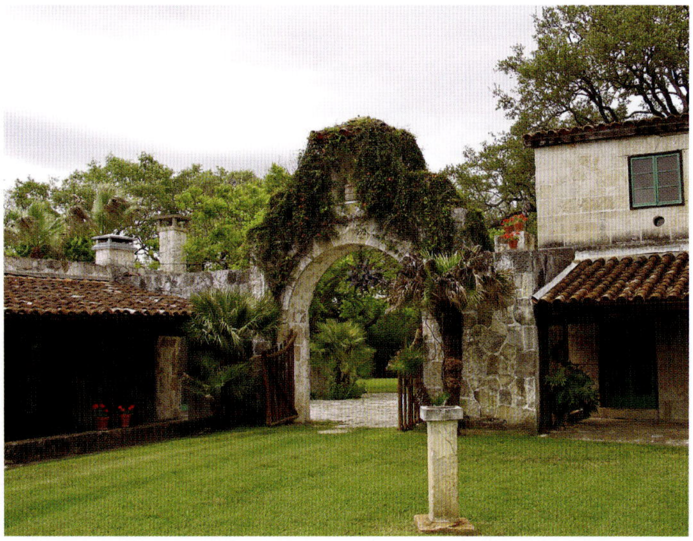

Gallagher Ranch—originally a working ranch, then a dude ranch, and occasionally a movie set—has been restored by Architect Chris Hill as his private residence. *Photograph by David Strahan, AIA*

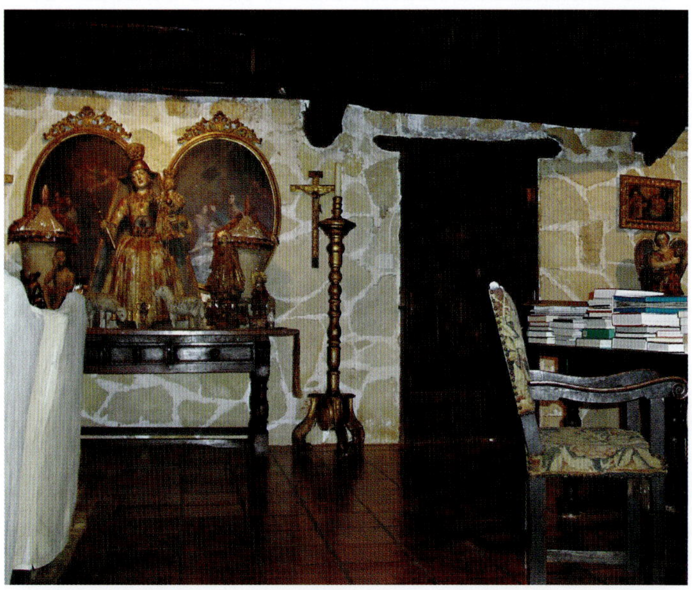

Elegant furnishings mingle with élan at the Gallagher Ranch, representing diverse cultural influences that contribute to San Antonio's rich history and vibrant present. *Photograph by David Strahan, AIA*

San Antonians, long steeped in the city's diverse cultural traditions, embrace time honored style and modern innovation. Our day and age has granted us a keen sense of awareness that pulls our attention to revering our past (Remember the Alamo!) and pushes our focus toward present day technology and sustainability. San Antonio's sustainability initiative for green living and green industry owes a great deal to the vision of Mayor Hardberger.

Fortunately, our quest to incorporate the past with the present opens the door to new possibilities. Much in the way Parisians fought to protect the iconic Eiffel Tower (built for a World Fair as the tallest structure on the globe at the time and repurposed as a transmission tower), San Antonians have battled to save its iconic sites of the Alamo, the Missions, and a host of commercial and residential architectural treasures. Our area architects, including co-author David Strahan, have toiled diligently to restore the glories of the past and incorporate the advancements of the present.

One champion of San Antonio is O'Neil Ford mastermind of the Hemisphere Tower. He battled to protect houses at HemisFair Park from demolition by moving as many houses as allowed by the City to new sites, while some (repurposed) remain in the Park today. Ford was unable to sway the City's decision to demolish the great homes designed by Atlee B. Ayres and Alfred Giles in the area now occupied by the winding U.S. 281. Routing the highway parallel to the straight north-south existing railroad tracks to the west would have spared these remarkable structures. We are fortunate to include some of their work—houses which exists in other areas.

Old Places New Spaces presents a broad sampling (including some repurposed commercial sites), but a mere fraction, of residences that embody a living and evolving history of the Alamo City. Some of these structures are grand in their own right, others modest. Different in size, style, and location, these spaces for living share a similar sensitivity to the past and dynamic engagement in San Antonio's future.

Notably, those who painstakingly and patiently refurbished these structures did not view them as frozen-in-time period pieces to double as museums or movie sets. Rather, they chose to breathe new life and livability into these places in a number of remarkable and time-honoring ways.

Two houses in the historic King William district shown in this book are excellent examples of once-grand structures restored for living elegantly in the present. The exquisite Chabot House received a great deal of attention from preservationist Walter Nold Mathis, a ninth generation Texan, who was responsible for pioneering the revitalization of the district. Mathis's own home, Villa Finale, a National Historic Preservation Site open to the public, is featured in another of our books, *Decorating for Christmas in Historic Houses* (Schiffer 2011).

The late nineteenth century Nix House is the city's and perhaps the nation's first designated Leadership in Energy and Environmental Design (LEED)/Platinum historic home preservation site. It was rebuilt by architect Roy Pachecano and his father, Omar Pachecano, to meet the highest standards of sustainability. LEED Platinum certification denotes that the structure was designed and built to achieve the highest levels of sustainable site development, water savings, energy efficiency, materials selection, and indoor environmental quality to protect human and environmental health, according to the U.S. Green Building Council.

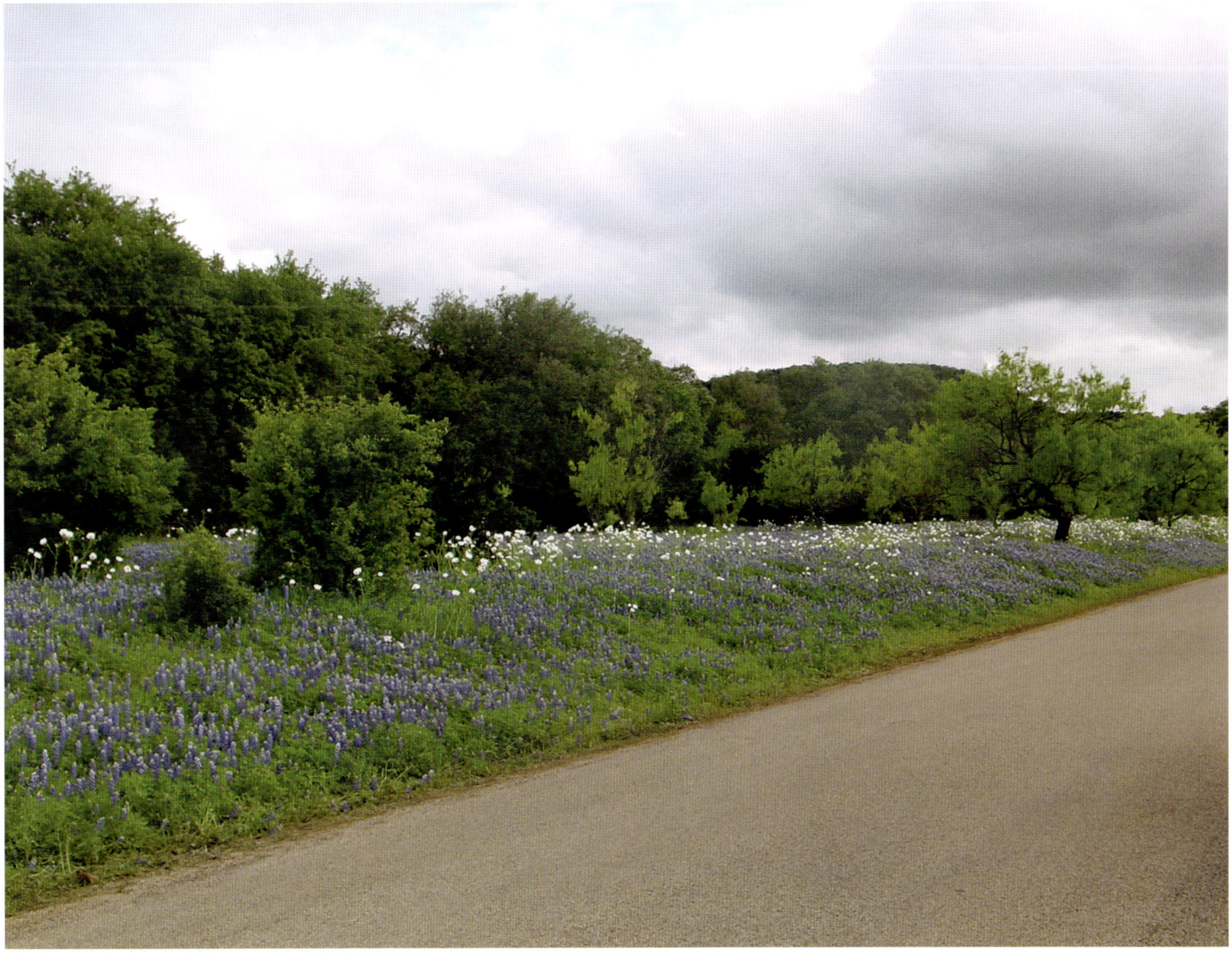

San Antonians roam—across the range, along byways when bluebonnets are in bloom, and around the globe at home with diverse styles.
Photograph by David Strahan, AIA

In vivid contrast to revitalized historic houses that have retained all the characteristics of their times stands Artpace, an exhibition and living/working space for artists. The mid-1950s downtown car dealership is both laboratory and temporary home for artists-in-residence. Artists own their artwork created during their brief two-month stay at Artpace—work often inspired by San Antonio—and it returns with them to their permanent residences. In this unique way, Artpace, which aims to diffuse its influence worldwide, simultaneously creates and promotes awareness of the unique culture of San Antonio.

The homes shown in *Old Places New Spaces* stand—like Architect John Grable's "Lantern House"—as beacons. They are shining examples of how people shape and re-shape older structures for living and working in the current age. Painstaking efforts to restore houses that are a vital part of San Antonio's history form a narrative of the past that continues to shape our present. Endeavors by those who have chosen to do this are rewarded with unique homes. To the San Antonians who restored, repurposed, and rejuvenated forgotten places, citizens of the city owe a great debt. They have preserved the life stories of those who came before us for those who come after us. They inspire us all. r

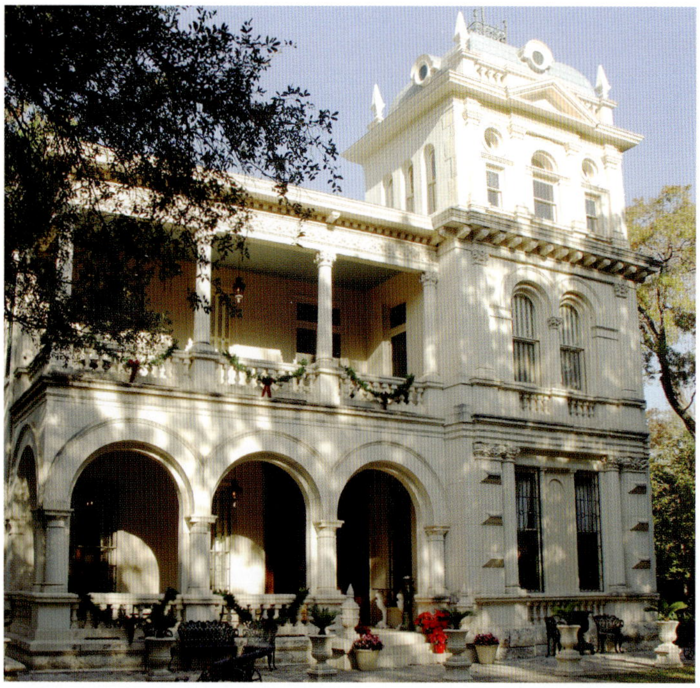

San Antonio's pioneer preservationist, Walter Nold Mathis, who restored fourteen houses in the King William district, willed his home, Villa Finale, to the National Trust for Historic Preservation, which opened the house as a museum in 2009.

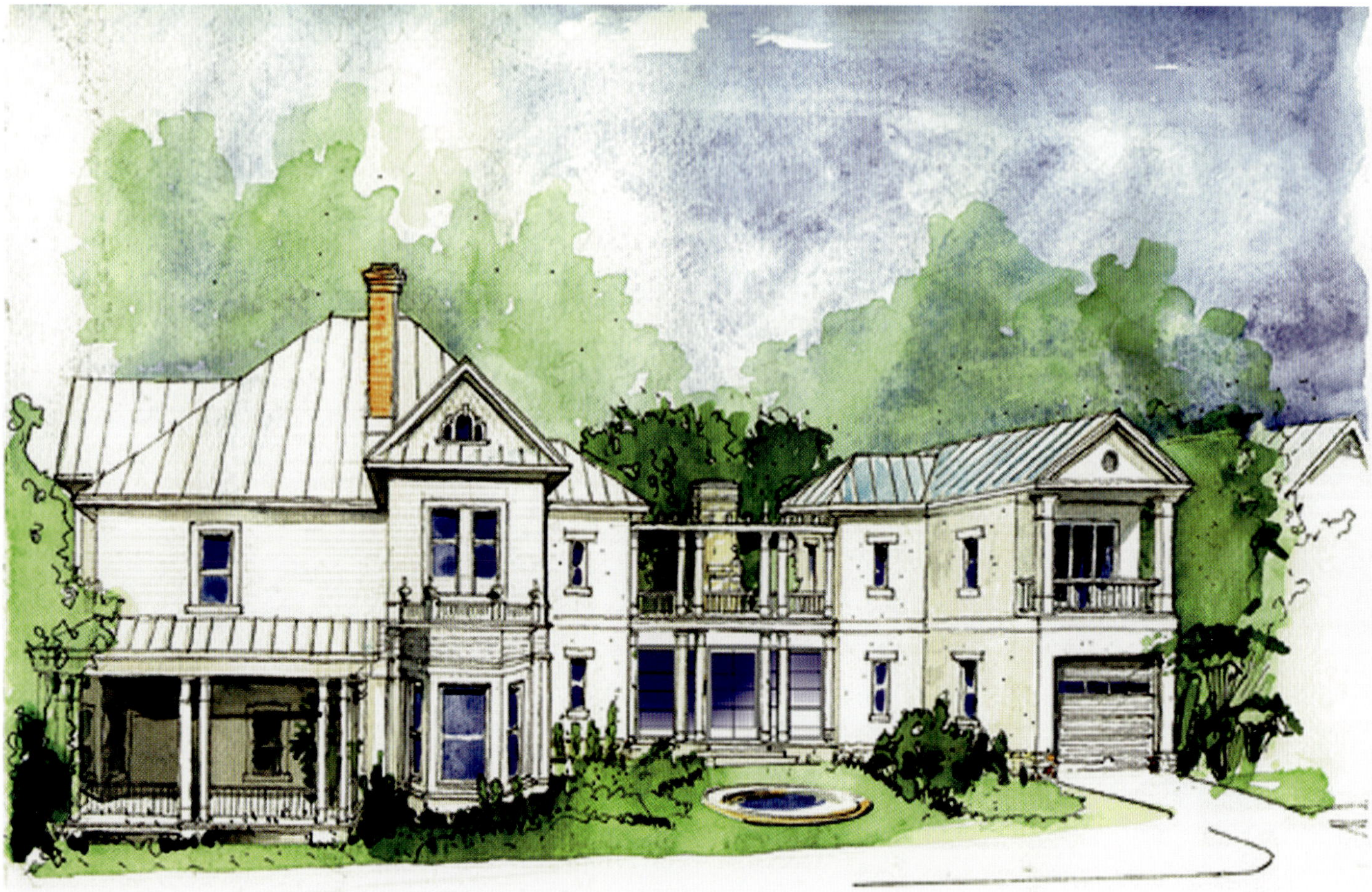

Roy Pachecano's watercolor of the restored Nix House—a job well done!

1
San Antonio Style Influences

—David Strahan, AIA

When I became an architect, I began to appreciate the wonderfully preserved, centuries-old details that visually define my hometown's past lifestyles. Most associate San Antonio with the image of a foot-bridge arching over a river, the beautiful Rose Window of Mission San Jose, or the infamous half circle crown of the Alamo, which was added by the military years after the battle. These are the iconic images of San Antonio's history.

San Antonio, like other American cities, has been and is growing with immigrants. The community was and continues to be shaped by the iconic architecture of their various cultures. Architects, craftsmen, and engineers brought their knowledge of materials and methods to the area to produce lasting structures; homes that have become the tactile connection to a certain period of history. They are a static historic legacy of bygone lifestyles, even though they have been transformed over time to sustain their occupants. Throughout the years, many families occupied the houses selected for this book. In each house, a change took place to meet the needs of the resident. Walls were knocked out or porches enclosed to create a gourmet kitchen. Chase walls or dropped ceilings were installed to hide air conditioning ducts. Bathrooms were remodeled to incorporate a larger tub. Some houses were left abandoned for years before someone recognized a diamond in the rough. Time has seen many influences that created the homes discussed in *Old Places New Spaces.*

Water Influence: The San Antonio River crosses six miles of city blocks and is the focus of the city. Early on tribes such as the Coahuitecan and Payaya camped on the place of restful waters known as Yanaguana near the head waters of the river. The year 1691 was the time of the first recorded visit by Europeans. On June 13, a day devoted to Saint Anthony of Padua, a group of Spanish missionaries first came upon the river; thus, the river became known as San Antonio River. In 1718, a new mission known as Mission San Antonio de Valero, and a town, Villa de Bexar, was established. In 1724, the town and mission were destroyed by a hurricane and rebuilt on the current location of the Alamo. The Alamo was the nickname given Mission San Antonio de Valero around 1800 by those settling near the groves of cottonwood trees (*alamos).* This and four other missions built along the path of the San Antonio River were the early roots of the city of San Antonio. Their influence can be seen in many of the homes built today.

San Antonio's layout is directly related to the San Antonio River and the man-made *acequias* (irrigation ditches) constructed to distribute water to the missions. These *acequias* are recognized as one of the most important civil engineering achievements of the Americas. Properties were formed that accessed the banks of these water paths, which in turn formed the street system of the inner city. The early eighteenth century suburb properties contained small houses built using either the Spanish *palisado* construction of vertical cedar posts or poles placed side by side or caliche (soft clay) plaster with thatched roofs to form huts or *jacales* (pronounced ha-kal). These are the earliest vernacular structures and some of the homes that remain today could have been built around remnants of this early construction.

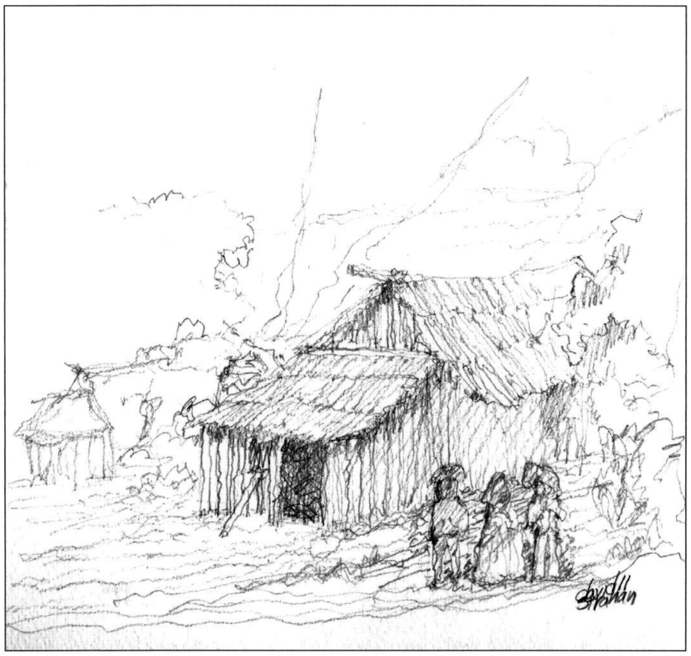

Early *Jacale* construction. *Sketch by David Strahan, AIA*

Immigrant Influence: Each decade saw immigrants from different countries change the image of San Antonio. From the first Canary Islanders to latter day European and American continent migration, San Antonio style has exemplified the culture, tastes, and architectural construction techniques of the times.

To quote the nineteenth-century landscape architect Frederick Law Olmsted on his 1854 visit: *"We have no city, except, perhaps, New Orleans, that can vie, in point of the picturesque interest that attaches to odd and antiquated foreignness, with San Antonio. Its jumble of races, costumes, languages, and buildings... its religious ruins, holding to an antiquity, for us, are indistinct enough to breed an unaccustomed solemnity."*

He further described San Antonio by narrowing this image to three styles. *"From the bridge we enter Commerce Street, the narrow principal thoroughfare, and here are American houses, and the triple nationalities break out into the most amusing display, till we reach Main Plaza. The sauntering Mexicans prevail on the pavements, but the bearded Germans and the sallow Yankees furnish their proportion. The signs are German by all odds, and perhaps the houses, trim-built, with pink window-blinds. The American dwellings stand back, with galleries and jalousies and a garden picket-fence against the walk, or rise, next door, in three-story brick to respectable city fronts. The Mexican buildings are stronger than those we saw before, but still of all sorts, and now put to all sorts of new uses. They are all low, of adobe or stone, washed blue and yellow, with flat roofs close down upon their single story."*

Olmsted left out one of the most influential immigrant groups, the Alsatians from France, who ten years earlier arrived in the area. They brought a simple rectangle structure with sloped roof-forming gabled ends. A combination of squares formed into cubes or boxes connected to triangles, which formed solids that became the basic form of these early structures. Shed roofs were common as expansions and porches. Two story houses became popular as construction technology progressed away from the palisado construction. This form would become the iconic image of a typical South Texas house.

The first San Antonio neighborhood, known as *La Villita*, contained a variety of architectural styles and construction. It is the beginning of a change from palisado construction to walls of thick stacked stone with one door and few windows that housed immigrants from Germany and France. *La Villita* became a cultural mix as described by Olmsted. This diverse neighborhood in terms of ethnicities and trades portrays the architectural evolution from palisade to Victorian houses.

The German immigrant craftsmen were known for their fine stone work and decorative "ginger bread" carvings. They influenced many of the preserved historic Victorian, Greek Revival, and Italianate style homes in a late nineteenth century suburb known as King William, adjacent to and south of *La Villita*. This area became the first upscale suburb, housing successful immigrant merchants from Europe. Many of these homes still exist today, and have undergone restorations and renovations as time progressed. The Chabot residence (chapter three) is an example of a Victorian-Italianate style house that was changed but has been restored to reflect only minor interior changes.

Migration continued into San Antonio and as more people moved in, more suburbs were established. This contributed to the King William area decline as a fashionable neighborhood. Bigger and better homes were built to the north and east of downtown. Suburbs known as Dignowity Hill, Monte Vista, and Monticello Park continued to expand northward. Broadway at one time was lined with stately manors that have vanished, giving way to commercial expansion. Even new towns, such as Alamo Heights and Olmos Park, became destinations for the affluent.

Later Architectural Influences: In each of these migratory areas, San Antonio has been shaped by several design influences and historical forces that contribute to the urban form and architecture. There are several historical context influences. Two have been discussed; Settlement to Spanish Colonial Period (1691-1845) and Gilded Age (1845-1900). The other two are Early Twentieth Century Urbanism (1900-1932) and Modernism (1932 to present).

With the early twentieth century, urbanism brought new technologies such as electricity used for lighting instead of gas or candles. Transportation changed from horse and buggy to streetcars and automobiles, increasing the distance one could travel in a half hour. New subdivisions grew—Monte Vista and Monticello Park. These new neighborhoods displayed the era's style of architectural range, consisting of Tudor, Craftsman, Spanish/Mission Revival, Art Moderne, and Classical Revival. The new homes ranged from small scale, simple vernacular styles to large scale, elegant mansions. From the early 1900s to the Great Depression, these houses represented the growth and success of San Antonio's economy.

San Antonio grew with a keen sense of the past, even into the Modernism of today. Shapes, materials, and construction methods simplified the building form and eliminated or covered up decorative ornaments so prevalent in earlier styles. Covering up the old, in some cases, would protect the beautiful craftsmanship to be discovered at a later date.

During the depression years, several key projects were started which defined the San Antonio of today. The restoration of *La Villita* and the creation of the River Walk (sometimes written Riverwalk) have led the way for advocacy of protection of historic resources. However, the development of HemisFair Plaza for the 1968 World's Fair would change the course of downtown and wipe out over 100 historic homes and buildings.

The Community Influences: During the 1920s, a group of thirteen socially prominent women founded an organization—The San Antonio Conservation Society—whose sole purpose is to preserve and encourage the preservation of historic buildings, objects, places, and customs relating to the history of Texas. Today, the San Antonio Conservation Society is one of the oldest and most active preservation groups involved in saving San Antonio's tactile past. The organization founded by those farsighted women is the reason The Alamo City or River City has become one of the top tourist destinations in Texas. Their efforts in preventing historic structures from being razed (and further, providing the funding for restoration) have led to the

La Villita, Missions, and numerous other restorations of much-visited historical sites, and to the River Walk, all of which define San Antonio. I am truly grateful to these thirteen ladies.

San Antonio has to-date twenty-seven designated historic districts, of which nineteen have National Register Historic District designations. Each of these districts is associated with a certain time period and a dominant architectural style popular at that time. The communities' acceptance of these historic district designations preserves the styles in each district.

The Architects, Builders, and Craftsmen Influences: Architecture is art created in most cases by unknown artists. (How many of us experience a building or a space and know the name of the planner, architect, contractor, interior designer or craftsman who created it?) From the detail to the whole, many known and unknown artists contribute to the creation of a client's vision for their house. San Antonio is no exception. Some historic houses have been documented, noting the artists who collaborated, working with wood, adobe, stone, plaster, and brick to create the preserved residences that stand today. Yet undocumented workmen have added to these originals, modifying structures to meet inhabitants' needs.

Atlee B. Ayers is one of the finest early twentieth century architects of San Antonio. If one architect could be chosen as the main influence of San Antonio style, it would be Atlee B. Ayers. Along with his son, Robert M. Ayers, Ayers senior designed houses, municipal buildings, and even the buildings at the historical "air city" of Randolph Air Force Base. His first commission was the two Nix Houses, one of which is included in this book as the flagship home. Trained at Columbia University in New York City, Mr. Ayers would design some of the city's best residences in the styles of Colonial Revival, Mission, Prairie, Tudor Revival, Arts and Crafts, Italian Renaissance, and Spanish Revival. His works are in King William, Monte Vista, Olmos Park, Alamo Heights, and Terrell Hills.

Other notable Architects are Francois Giraud, Henry Castro, Alfred Giles, James Wahrenberger, Tom Ryan, Reginald Roberts, Bartlette Cocke, and O'Neil Ford. There were craftsman such as O'Neil's brother, Lynn Ford, who was a master wood carver and home builder. Jerry Bywaters and Thomas M. Stell also contributed to the works of Ford.

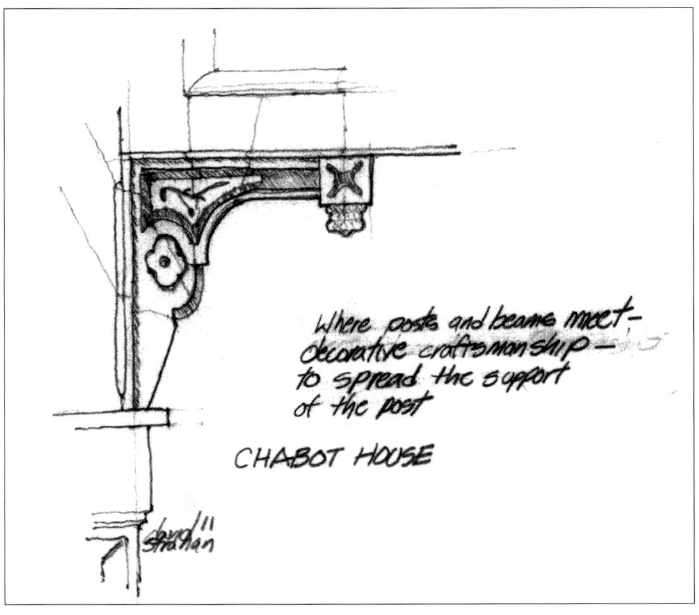

Chabot House bracket, a Victorian era detail. *Sketch by David Strahan, AIA*

From its Old World Spanish origins to today's Moderne continuance, San Antonio remains a city that honors the old and beautiful buildings of architects, builders, and craftsmen—artists known and unknown who shaped San Antonio as one of the most distinctive cities in Texas and America.

The Properties: The prodigious uniqueness of San Antonio's architectural and archaeological resources is due to the preservation efforts of its citizens. Some structures appear on the exterior to have been restored to their original time period; but, many have been transformed over the years to sustain the lives of inhabitants within the context of their lifestyles. But whether both exterior and interior are authentically restored, or the exterior restored and the interior changed, the basic function remains the same—to provide shelter. Only, due to the incorporation of new technologies, the way in which the occupants utilize and interact in these shelters has changed.

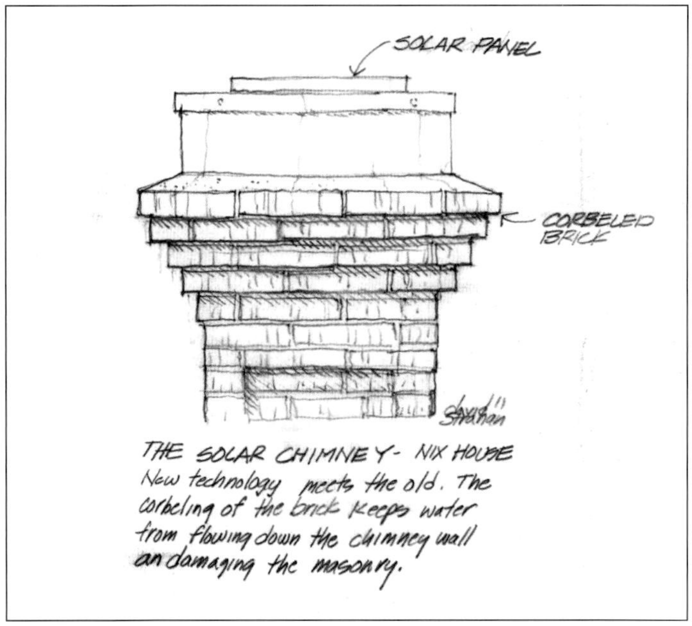

Old and new construction and technology meet in the Nix House solar chimney—an innovation by Architect Roy Pachecano. *Sketch by David Strahan, AIA*

The properties that are presented in this publication define and recognize the impact of the occupant's lifestyle on the historic function of the structure itself. From the urban advanced technology of the restored Nix House, to the rural retreat craftsmanship preserved at the Gallagher Ranch, to the remodeling of old commercial structures such as Camp Street Residences into contemporary residences, each tells of transformation to meet the needs of the current occupant's lifestyle. And while the structures in this book are historic for a variety of reasons (they are old and still exist, are of a noteworthy style, are in a particular historical district, or represent a major societal shift), changed and changing, each continues to provide the simple function of shelter—to be a *home*.

2

Nix House

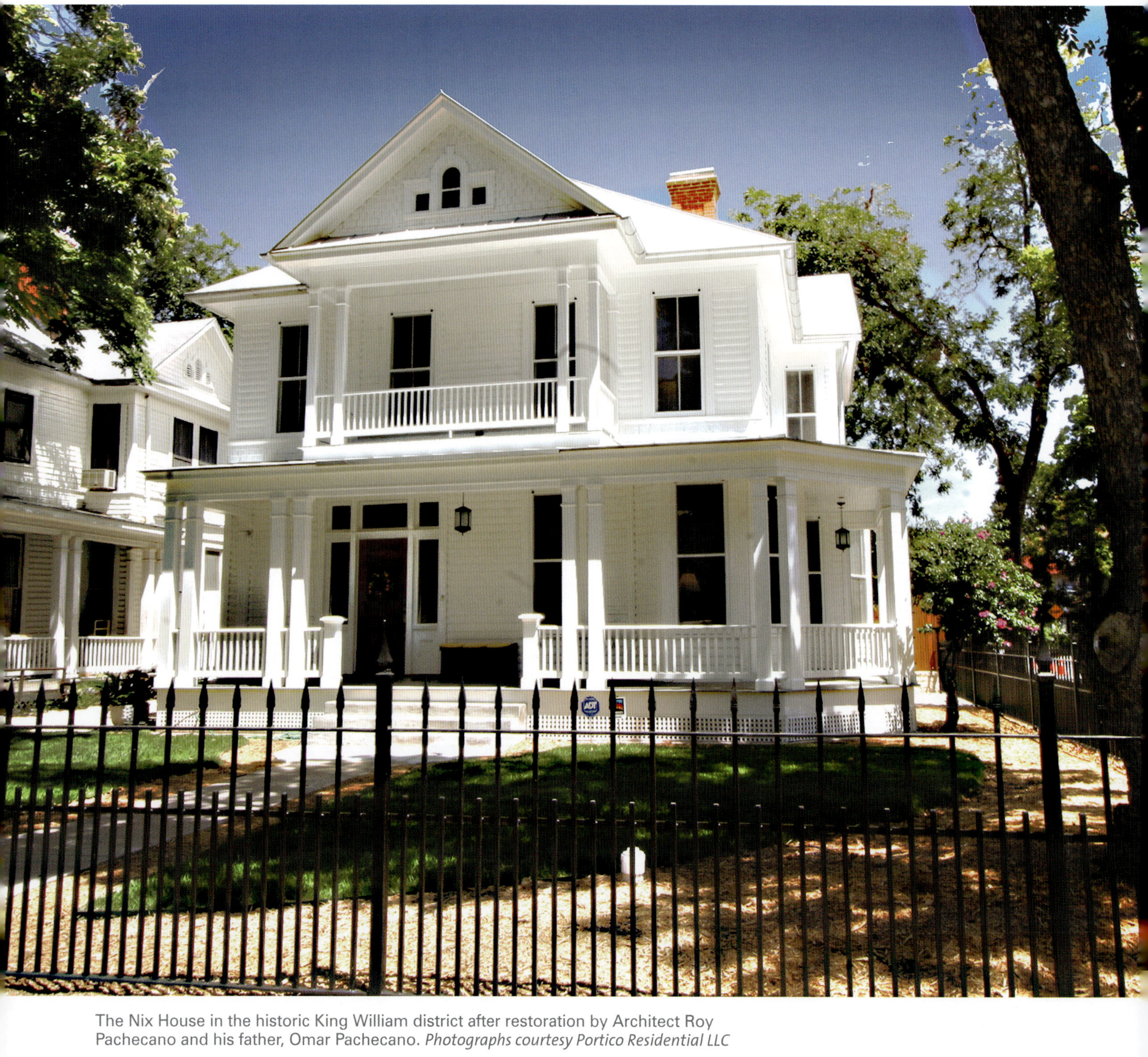

The Nix House in the historic King William district after restoration by Architect Roy Pachecano and his father, Omar Pachecano. *Photographs courtesy Portico Residential LLC*

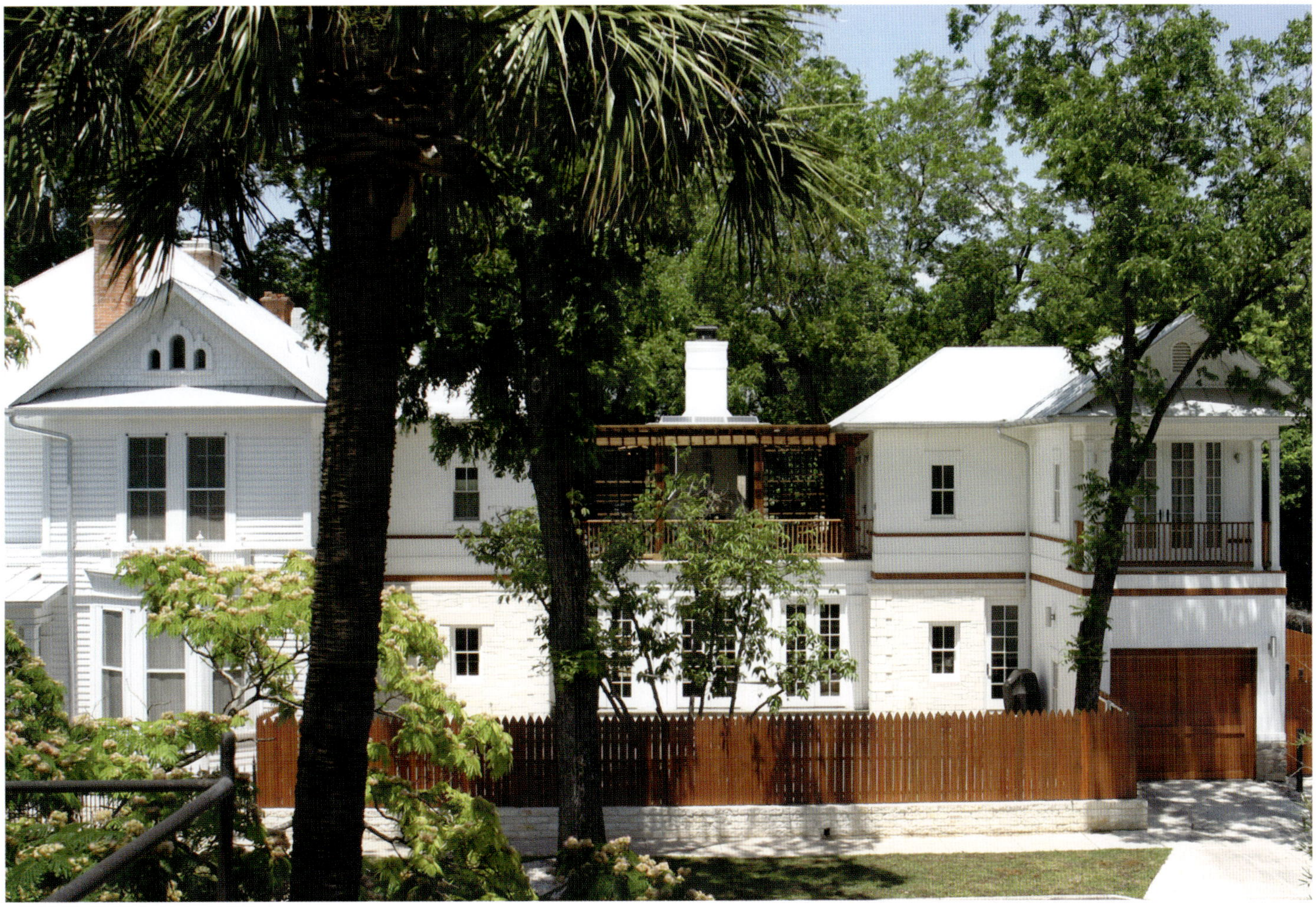

A new terrace with open-air fireplace and private balcony joins the main house with a second-story addition that can function as a studio or guest quarters.

When Architect Roy Pachecano talks about San Antonio, he speaks of patron families who built the city. He specifically cites J. M. and Birdie Nix—outsiders from Tennessee who arrived in San Antonio and called it their home in the late nineteenth century. "To say the Nix family elevated the stature of this once sleepy Spanish village is an understatement. Over a span of thirty years—the Nix family left behind a string of prominent downtown landmarks that now intermingle with the culture and fabric of the city," says Pachecano. "Recent research uncovered the significance of their work. The story of the Nix family's entrepreneurship and real estate development origins begin with twin dwellings, now called the 'Nix Houses,' located in the present-day King William Historic District. In 1899, the Nixes orchestrated a development team, which also sparked the origins of the Atlee B. Ayres architectural prominence that would shine in the mid-twentieth century. Ayres, another newcomer to town who had just completed architectural studies in New York City, was eager to turn his first commission—the Nix Houses—into a success. W.B. Massey, the builder, was given a tall-task—to build two prominent residences in two-and-one-half months along side the stately row of mansions on King William Street."

In 2005, Roy Pachecano was seeking to expand advisory work and moved his young family to his native San Antonio. It was in this town where generations of Pachecanos had operated a concrete construction business. Like Ayres, Pachecano was following the same path from New York City to the same corner—only separated by 100 years. Ayres attended classes at Columbia University and graduated in 1893. Pachecano graduated from Columbia University in 1993. Both architects had English mentors early in their careers. Upon finding the decaying Nix Houses that fronted on what has been referred to as "the Fifth Avenue" of the oldest historic district in Texas, Pachecano asked: "Can a drafty old house become state-of-the-art and incorporate today's energy-efficient materials and designs without losing its intrinsic historic character? Could anyone remake a classic?"

Some philosophers say that those who frame a question possess the answer. The answer—yes—had only to be proven by Roy and his father, Omar Pachecano, the former head of the family-owned concrete business. In 2008, when they completed the historic remaking of the Nix House, the project became the first 1890s LEED-Platinum historic recorded landmark dwelling in the United States. (LEED is the acronym for Leadership in Energy and Environmental Design.)

The restoration of the Nix House also received recognition by former Vice President Al Gore, The National Trust for Historic Preservation, Preservation Texas, and was featured on the Discovery Channel's *Renovation Nation* with Steve Thomas in 2010. The father-and-son team, Omar and Roy Pachecano, thus joined the ranks of contemporary patron families who are keeping San Antonio at the same time romantically old and vitally young.

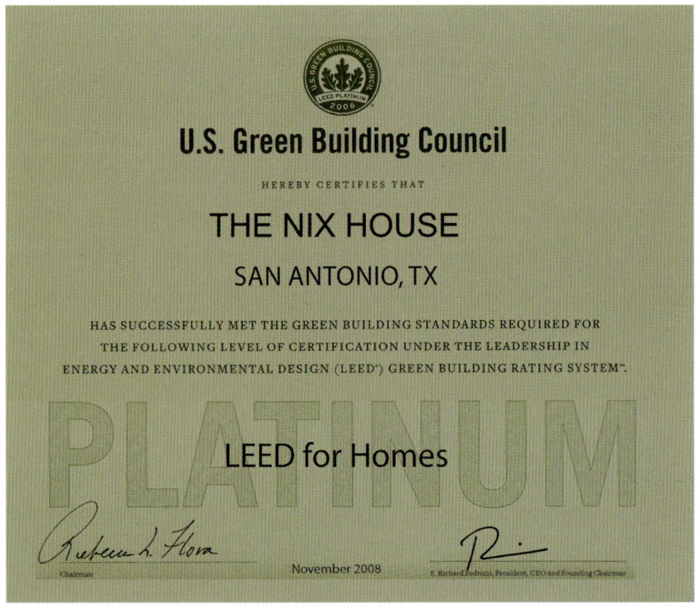
U.S. Green Building Council

HEREBY CERTIFIES THAT

THE NIX HOUSE

SAN ANTONIO, TX

HAS SUCCESSFULLY MET THE GREEN BUILDING STANDARDS REQUIRED FOR THE FOLLOWING LEVEL OF CERTIFICATION UNDER THE LEADERSHIP IN ENERGY AND ENVIRONMENTAL DESIGN (LEED®) GREEN BUILDING RATING SYSTEM™.

PLATINUM

LEED for Homes

November 2008

The project earned a LEEDS Platinum certificate in recognition of environmentally responsible construction techniques and materials used in revitalizing this structure.

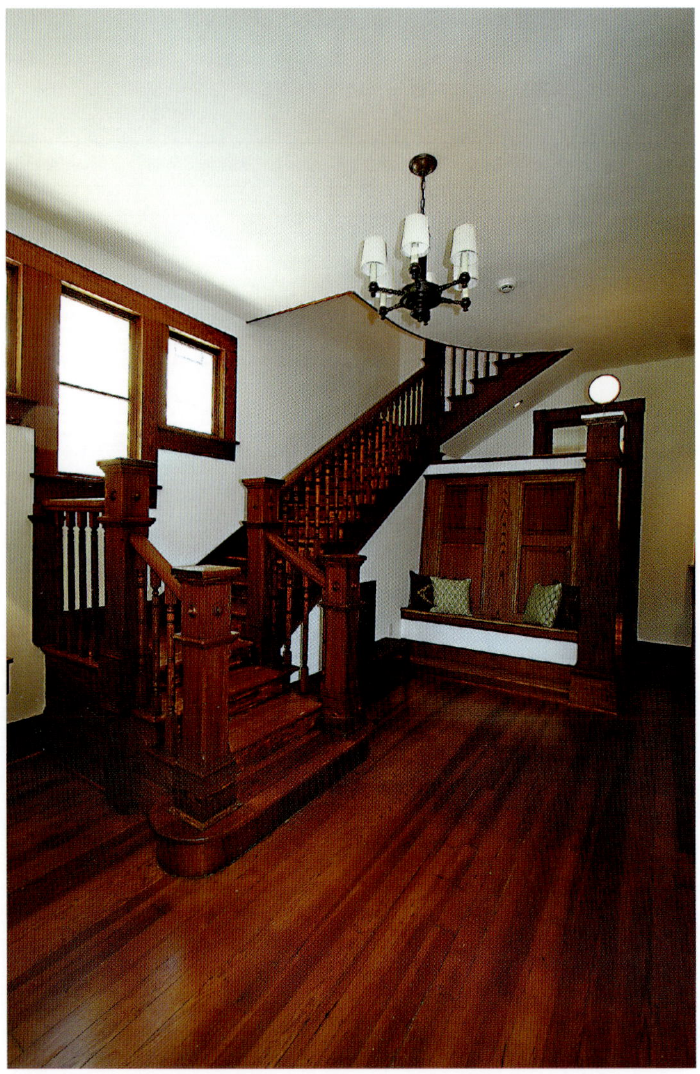

Interior views of the Palladian window shows the unusual arrangement of hanging the large middle window lower than the two smaller flanking windows.

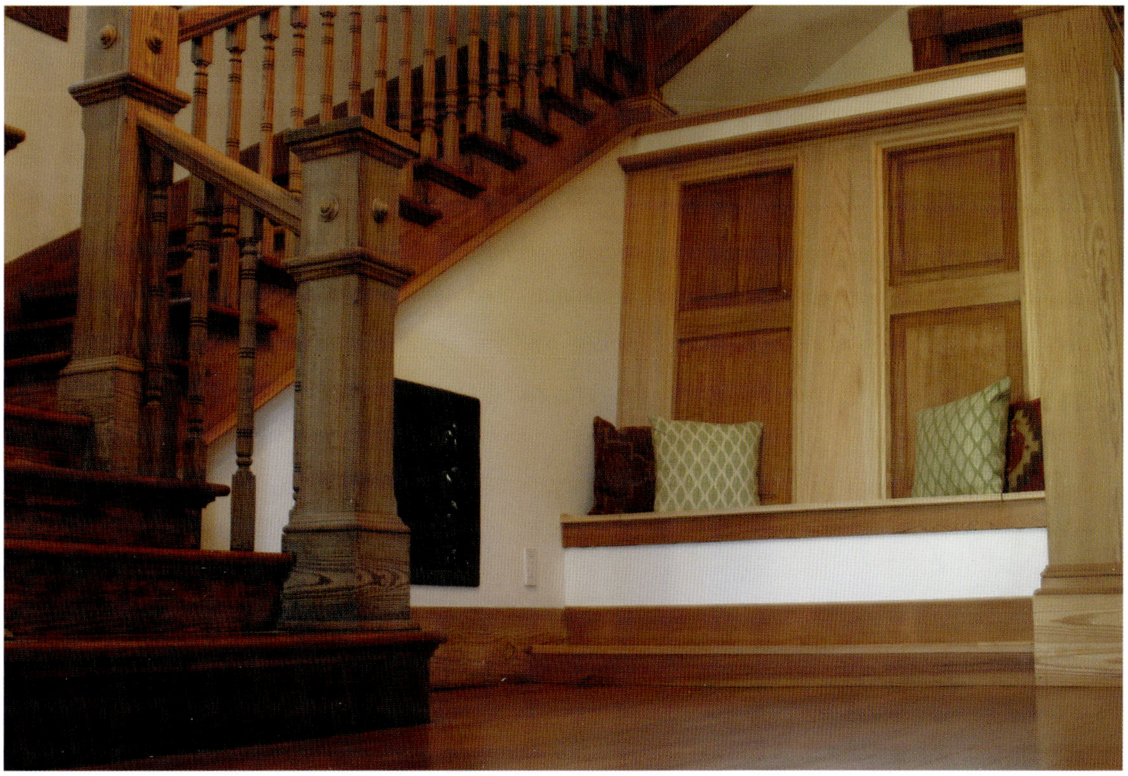

A handsomely designed carved wood staircase moves traffic from the entry to the second story.

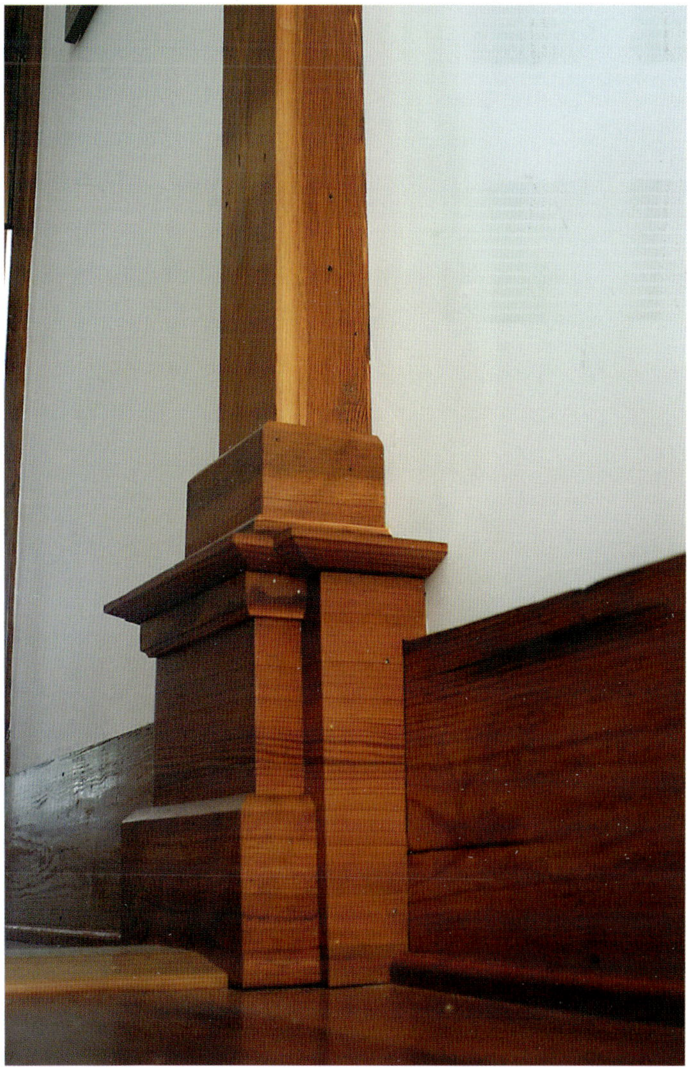

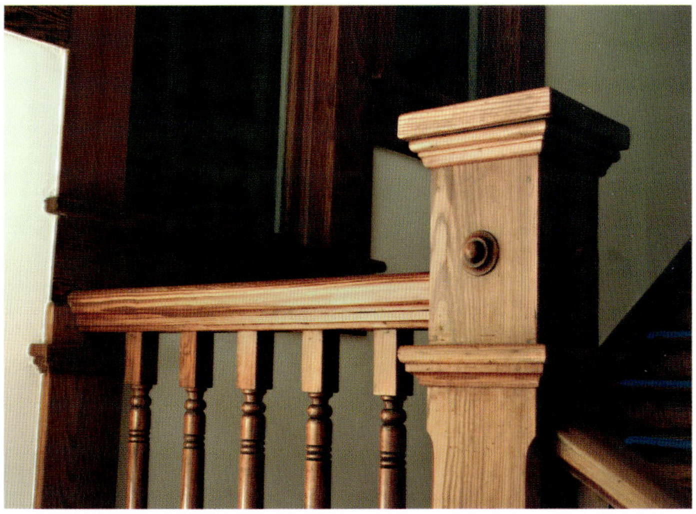

The Preservation Game Plan: A Pachecano company, Portico Residential LLC, undertook the challenge to rescue the Nix House at 434 King William. Work began by addressing two key issues: First, the dwelling had to be "reverted" from an SRO (single room occupancy) to single-family dwelling status. Like many grand old houses in this area, when this once desirable neighborhood declined in the 1950s, No. 434 became an apartment house with an Single Room Occupancy (SRO) addition. In September 2005, the City of San Antonio's Historic and Design Review Commission (HDRC) granted permission to dismantle the architecturally inappropriate SRO section.

Secondly, the dwelling lacked sufficient infrastructure. By bringing inadequate city utilities up to date, this offered an opportunity to bury 2,000 linear feet (10,000, counting cable redundancy) of overhead utility lines while simultaneously enhancing the historic nature of the streetscape. The utility pilot project, funded entirely by Portico, opened view corridors to the Edward Steves Museum and the East Johnson Street Footbridge across the San Antonio River only steps away. The new infrastructure work permitted laying empty conduit for future fiber optics to bring high bandwidth to the dwellings. Achieving this formidable task encouraged the King William Association to consider expanding the buried cable project throughout this picturesque historic area, now a major tourist attraction. By 2011, a public-private-partnership begun with Portico's efforts had completed Phase One of utility conversion at the cherished public space on the other end (The King William Park along with its restored gazebo).

Revising the Plot Plan: Lot area and new allowable density provided the impetus of a new plot plan for No. 434. Today, an intimate courtyard is flanked by a new addition designed to complement the Ayres-designed main house. "The whole composition (old and new) is a fusion of New England with South Texas," says Pachecano. Built to National Historic Preservation Guidelines and approved by the City of San Antonio's Historic Design and Review Commission, the new addition exterior incorporates elements found in South Texas vernacular architecture—cut limestone, stucco, and natural wood. Beautifully integrated classic trellis covers part of the addition, which includes a second floor private terrace with an open-air wood-burning fireplace. A terrace and a private balcony overlook East Johnson Street, providing a glimpse of the footbridge across the glamorous San Antonio River Walk. A new room serves as either studio or quarters for another family member. "In this way, the restoration project reflects a growing trend back toward multi-generational family living," says Pachecano.

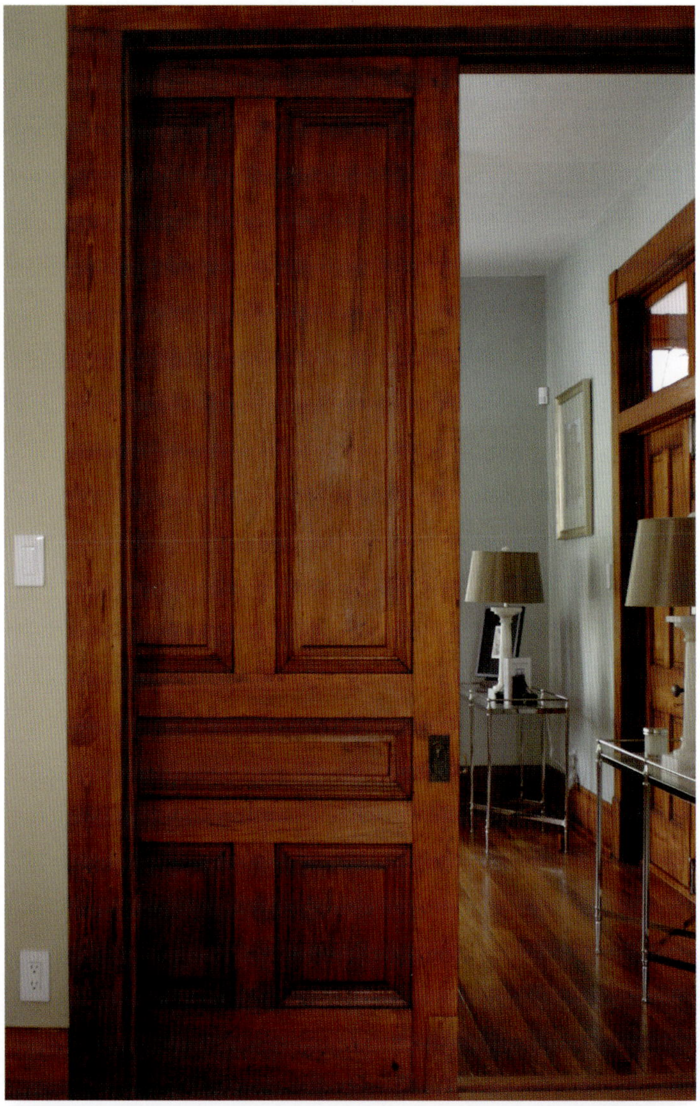

A pocket door opens into the spacious parlor, where tiles and finely carved woodwork surrounding the fireplace were refinished. (Above and opposite page)

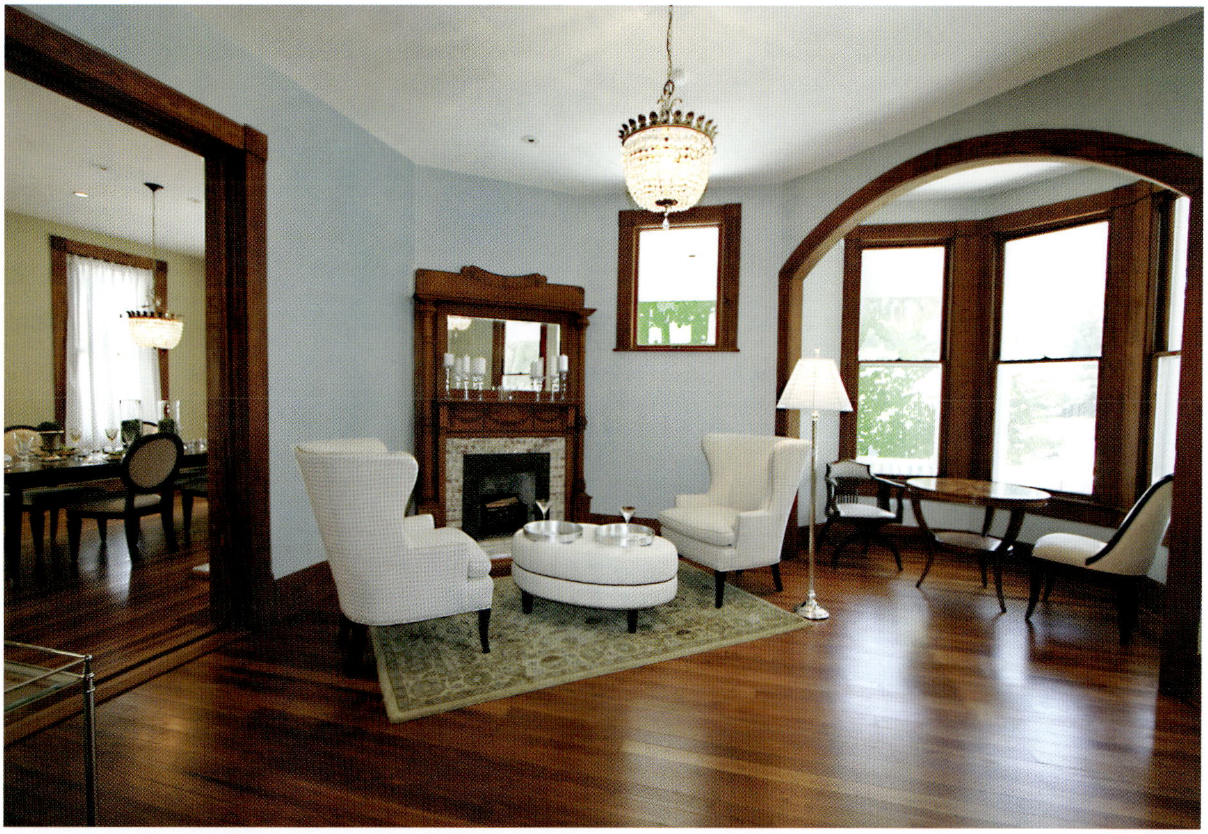

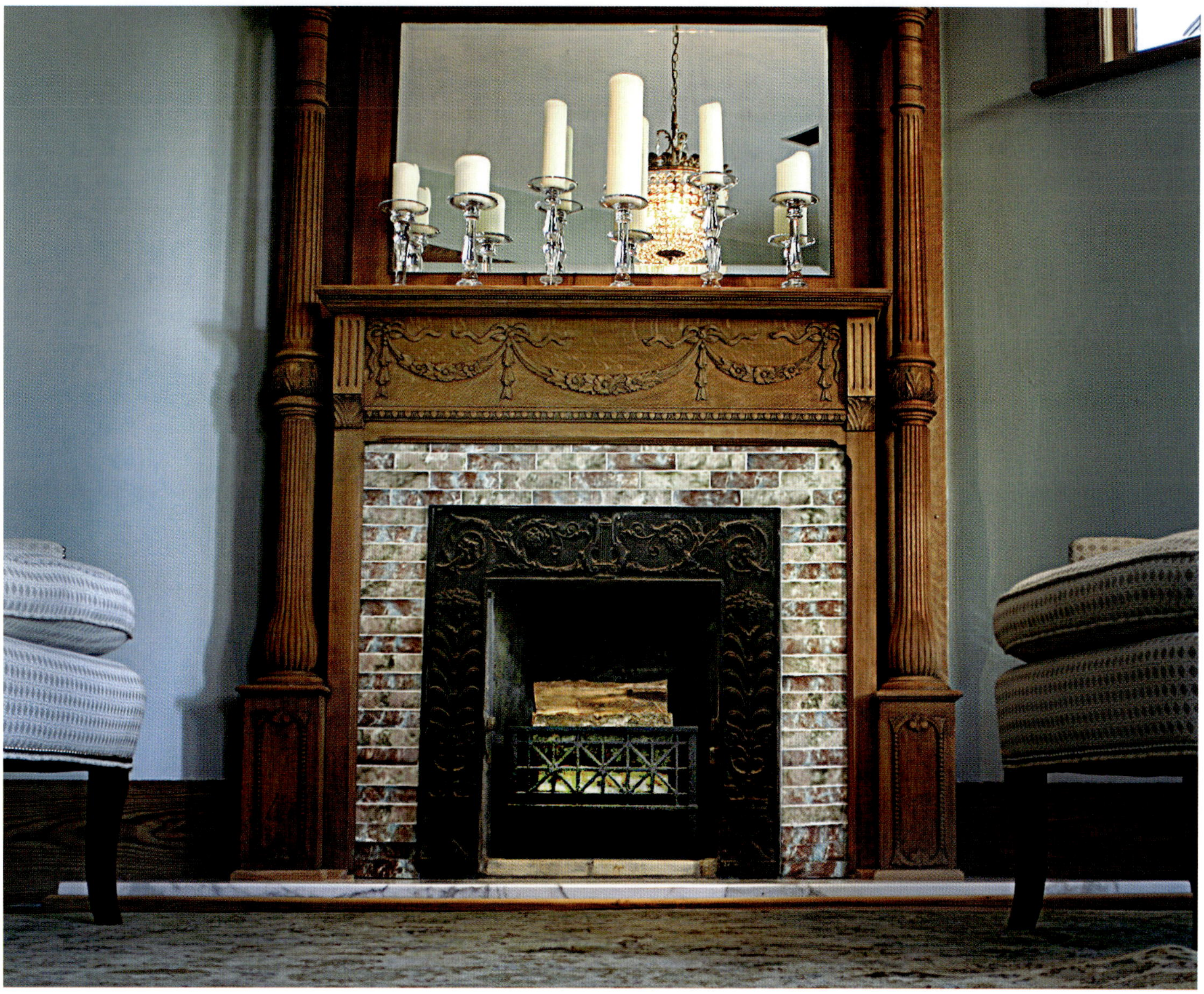

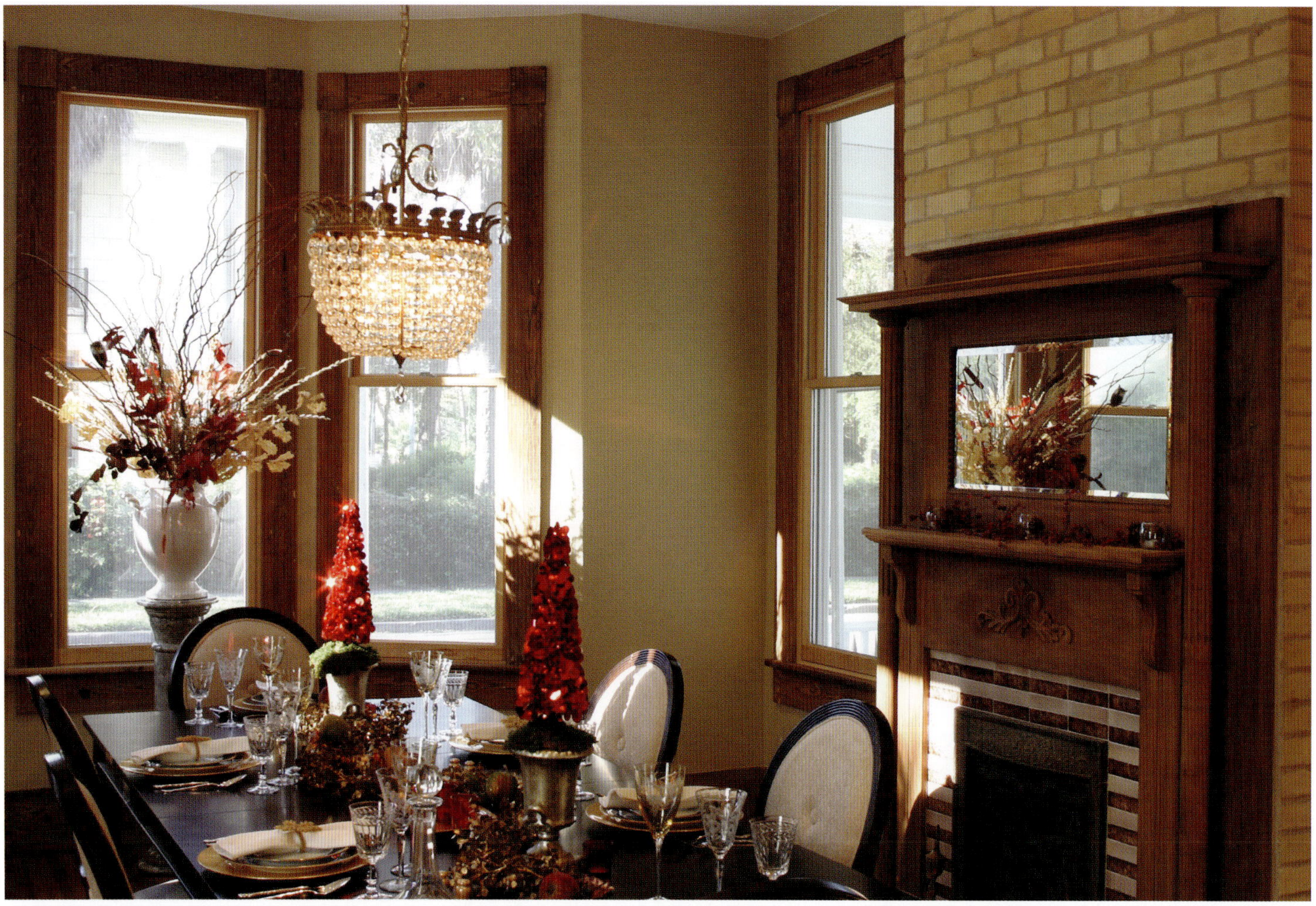

Generous windows and a handsome fireplace with overmantel add elegance to the dining room.

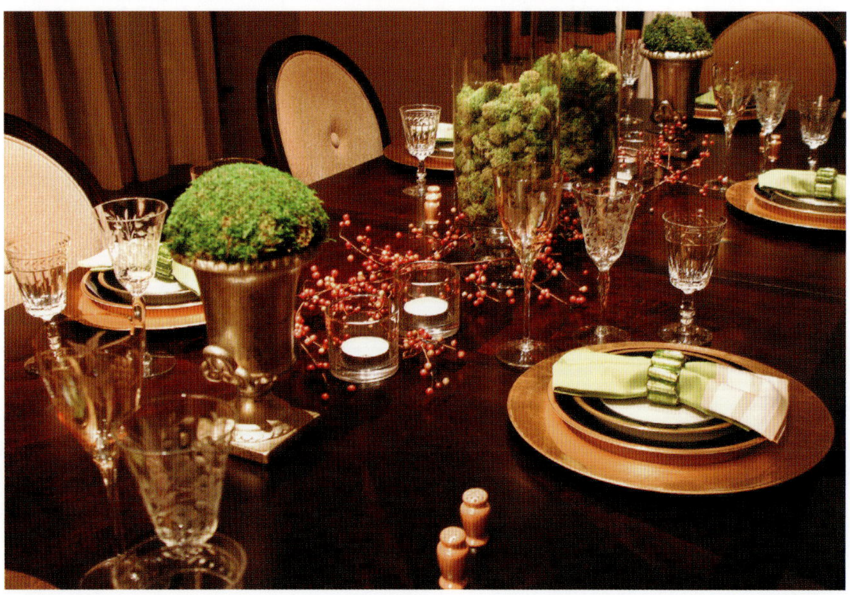

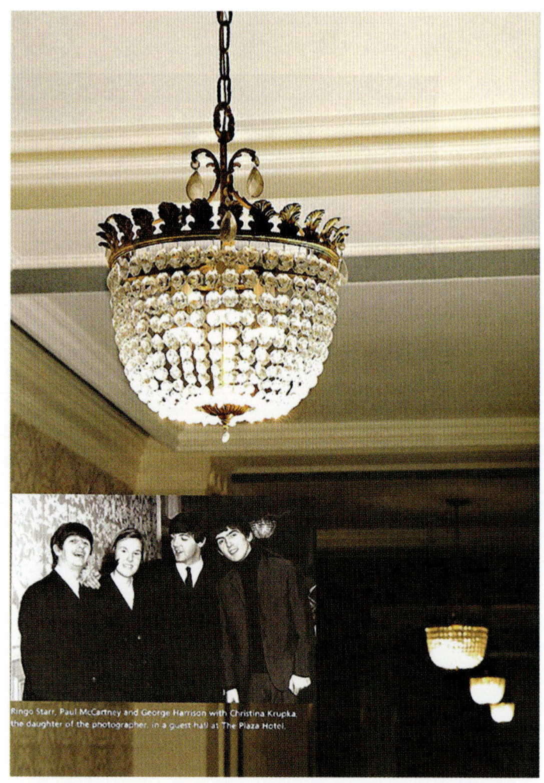

The crystal chandelier once hung in New York City's Plaza Hotel.

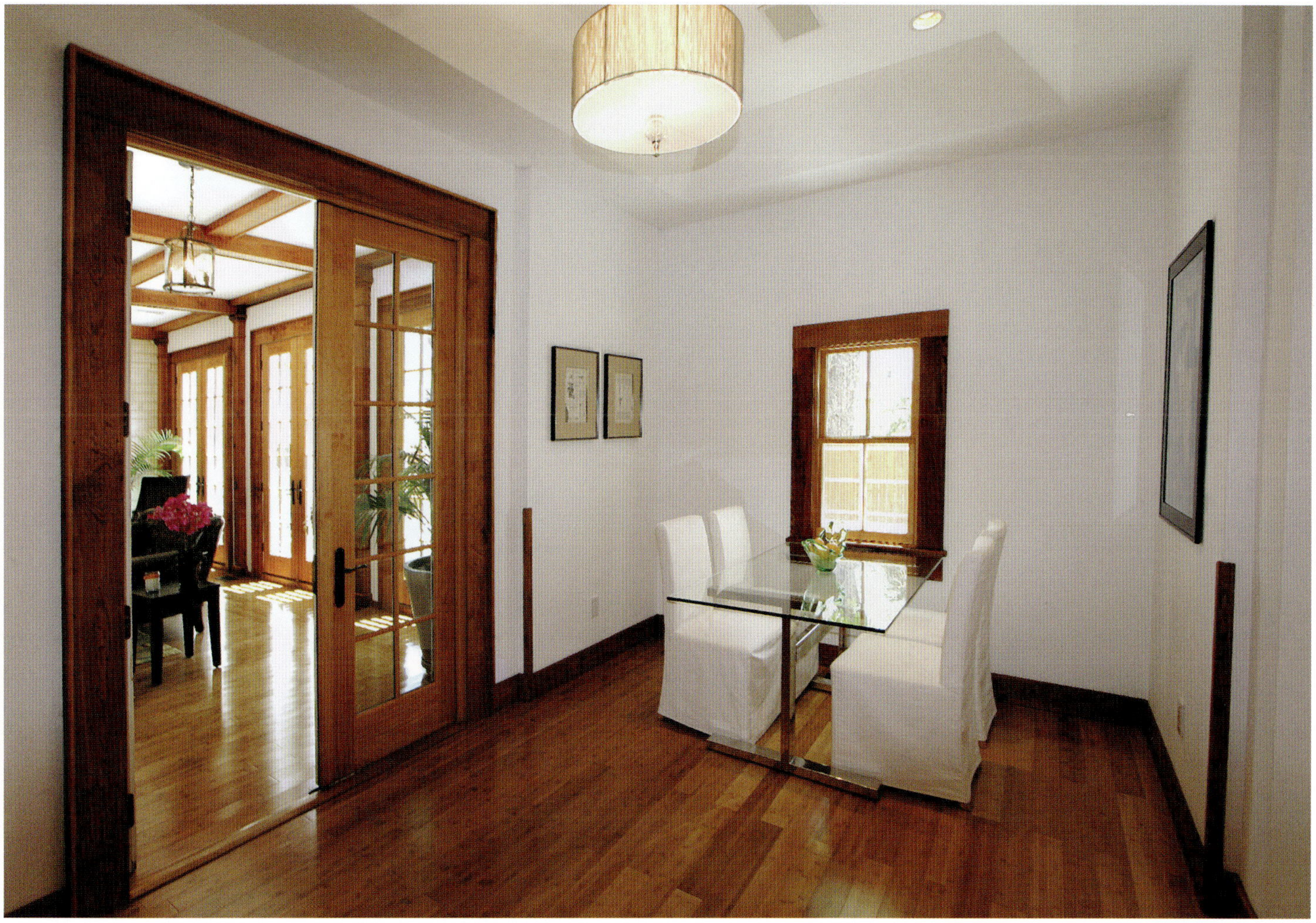

French doors open from the dining room into the breakfast room.

Engaging the Four Rs: This preservation involved all of the four Rs—restoration, rehabilitation, renovation, and remodeling. "The exterior of the house has been wholly restored," comments Pachecano. This meant restoring longleaf cedar and yellow pine siding—a feat undertaken with care—material whose strength is derived from milled lumber from trees that were saplings in the 1790s.

In restoring the exterior, care was taken to not disturb any of the original New England "free Classic, post-Victorian" character. "The style eliminates excessive ornamentation and moves away from Gothic-inspired eclecticism, opting for clean, crisp lines," Pachecano explains, adding, "....the houses, Nix I and II, are a break from all the surrounding gingerbread." Pachecano, trained as a modern architect, often dismisses as a waste of time modernist and preservationists argumentative posturing. "Why can't both styles live together?" he asks rhetorically. Indeed they do in the Nix House. While the Nix House style with its symmetrical façade and wrap-around veranda was a departure from high-Gothic asymmetry, it did not ignore the neighboring houses. "Both Nix Houses set on adjoining lots at 434 and 432 and successfully 'mirror' in scale and proportion, larger dwellings sited on two- and three-lot parcels across the street. This astute manipulation of economy of scale created cost-effective, elegant houses that felt as grand as neighboring structures such as the Steves family mansion built a decade earlier," Pachecano points out. He notes that the Nix Houses are examples of high quality upper middle-income housing that incorporate factory-produced elements that look handmade, a late Victorian era innovation in manufacturing.

The interior floor plan of the main house is as it was over a century ago, with a first floor entry hall, parlor, dining room, and second floor bedrooms. Millwork throughout has been preserved, doors and windows redone, and hardware refinished. The four 1899 fireplaces with hand-carved wood and ceramic art tile surrounds were restored. Deviations from the original plan occurred when necessary to accommodate twenty-first century technology. For example, fireboxes were electrified and overmantels outfitted with flat panel LED TVs.

Nothing could be salvaged in bathrooms or kitchens, so these spaces were outfitted with all-new fixtures and appliances.

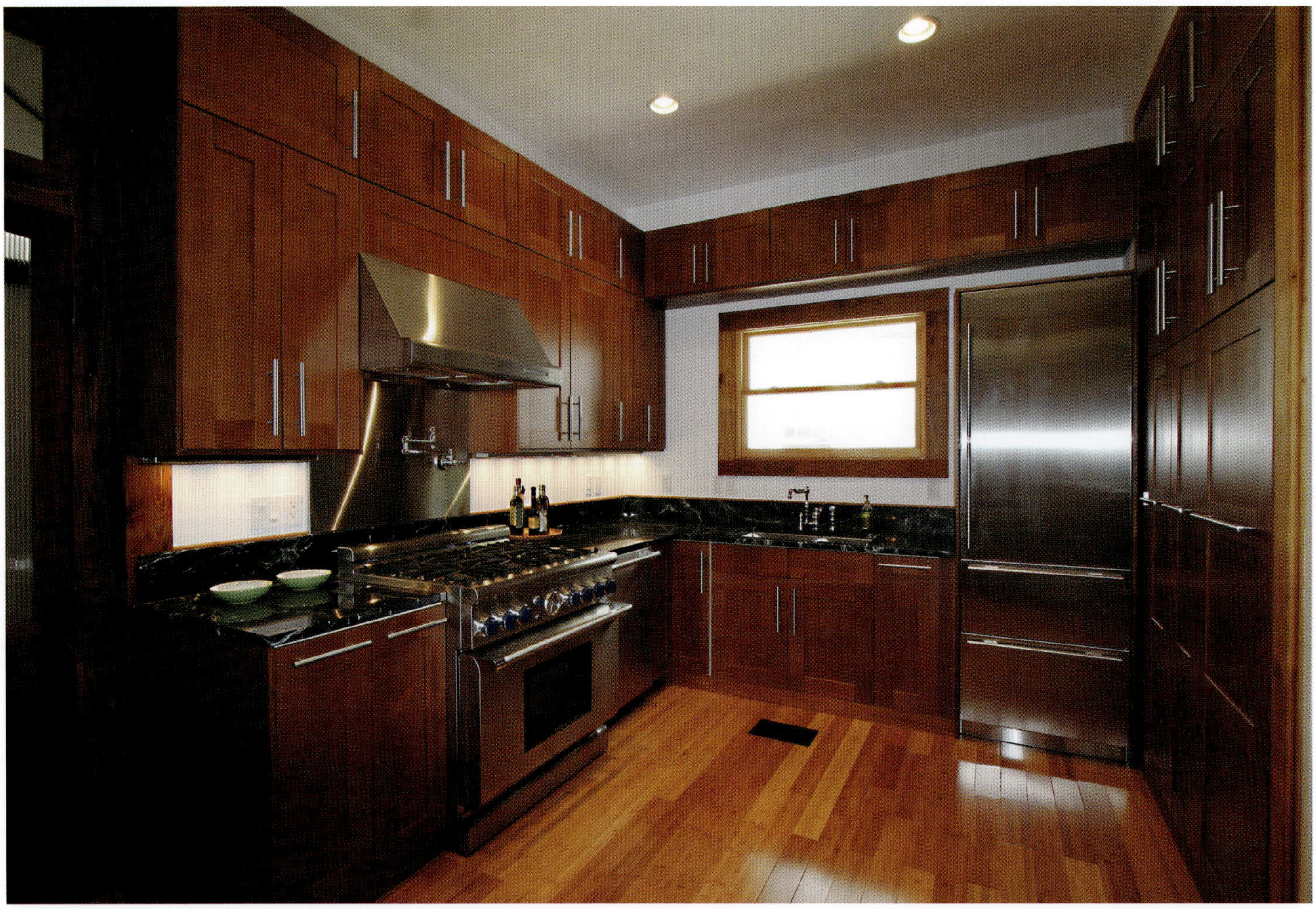

The kitchen was completely remodeled and fitted with state-of-the-art appliances. (Above and opposite page, top)

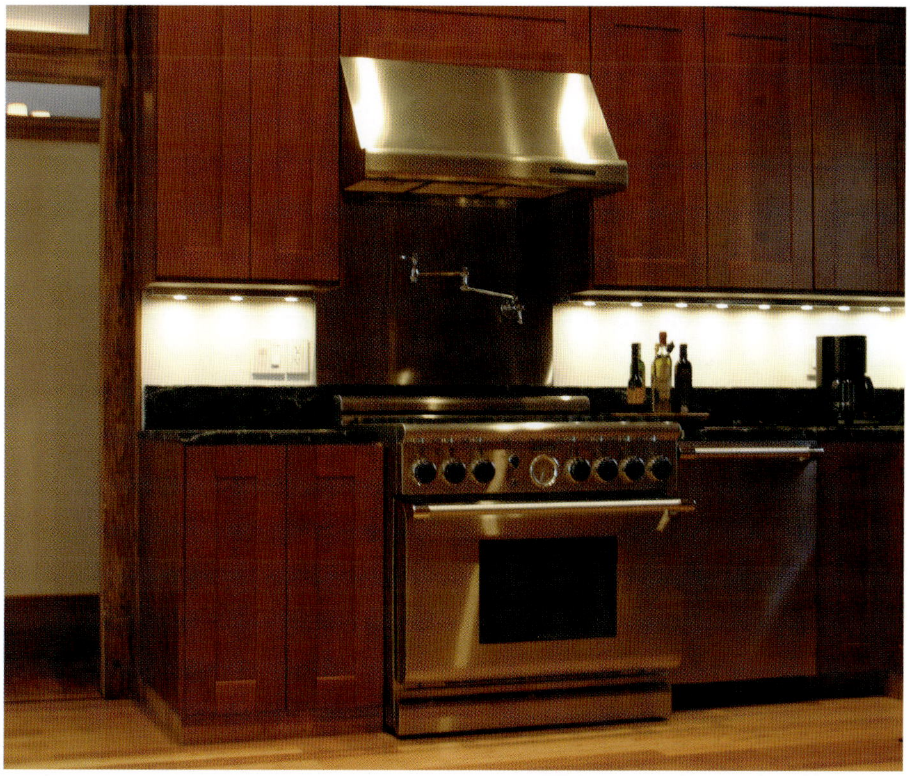

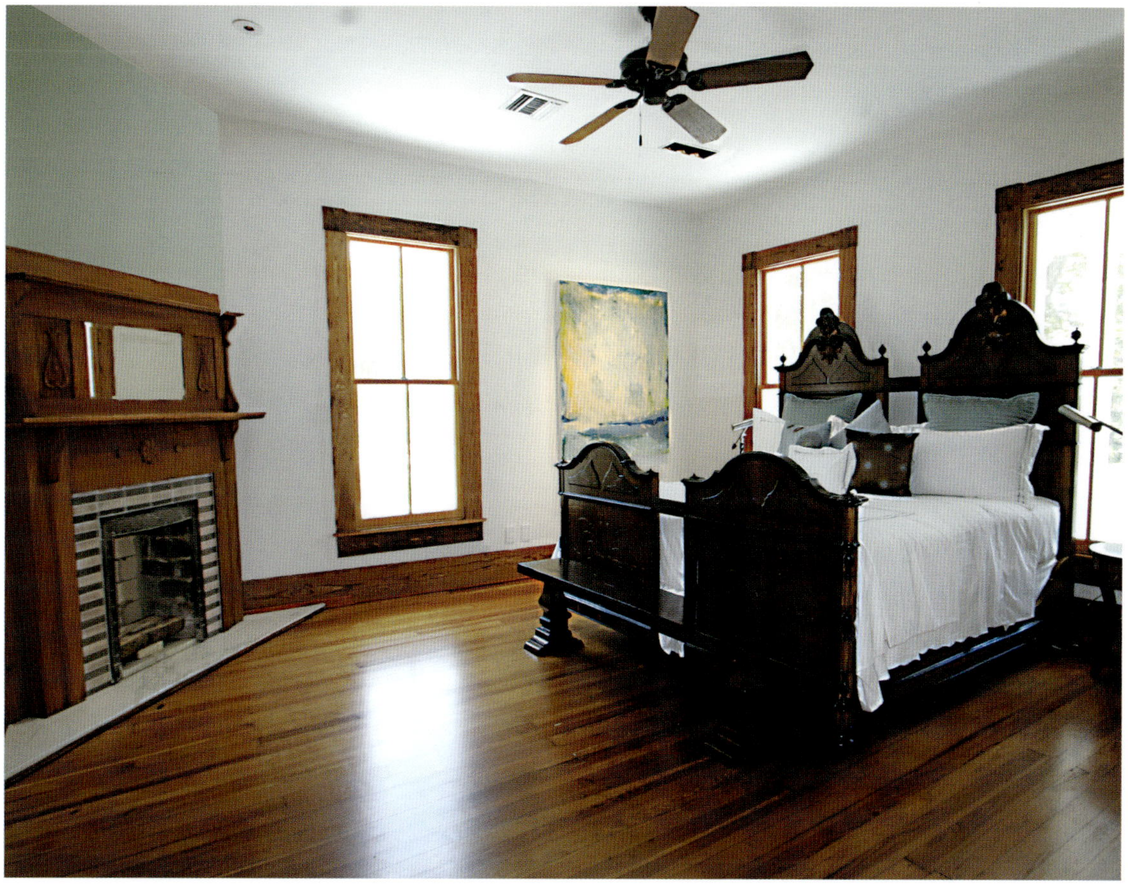

In the master bedroom, wood trim, floors, and the original fireplace were refurbished.

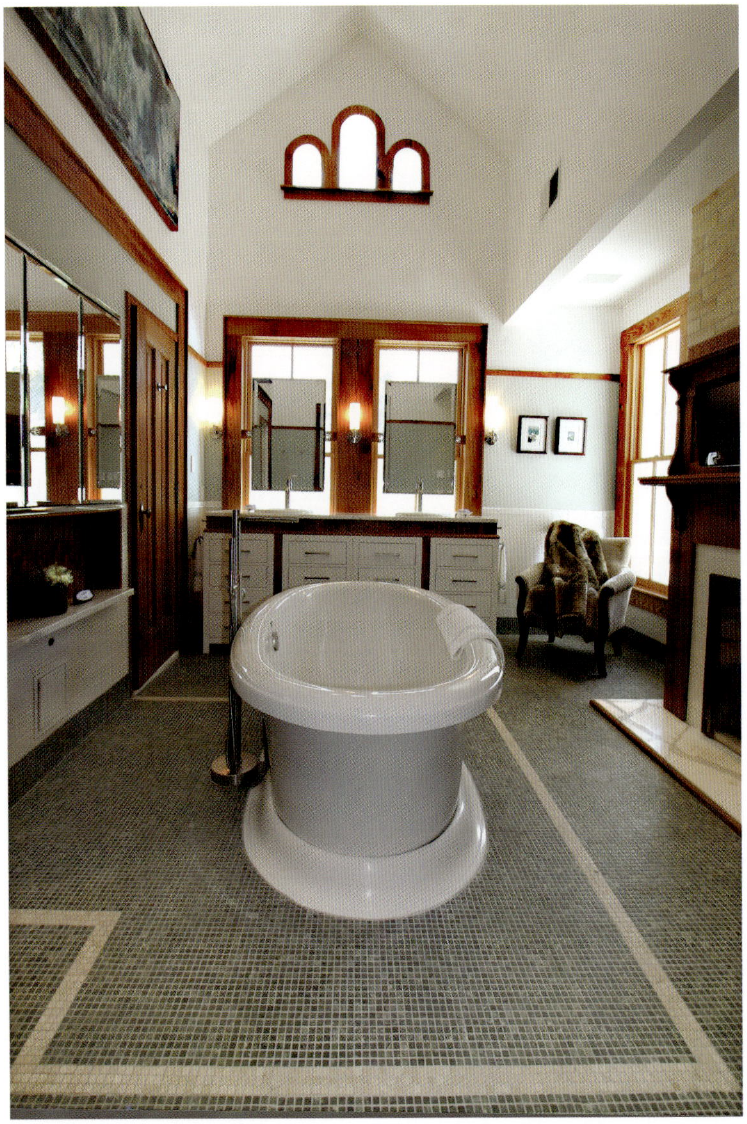

The restored structure houses a contemporary-style master bathroom.

The window behind a vanity provides a sweeping view of the city.

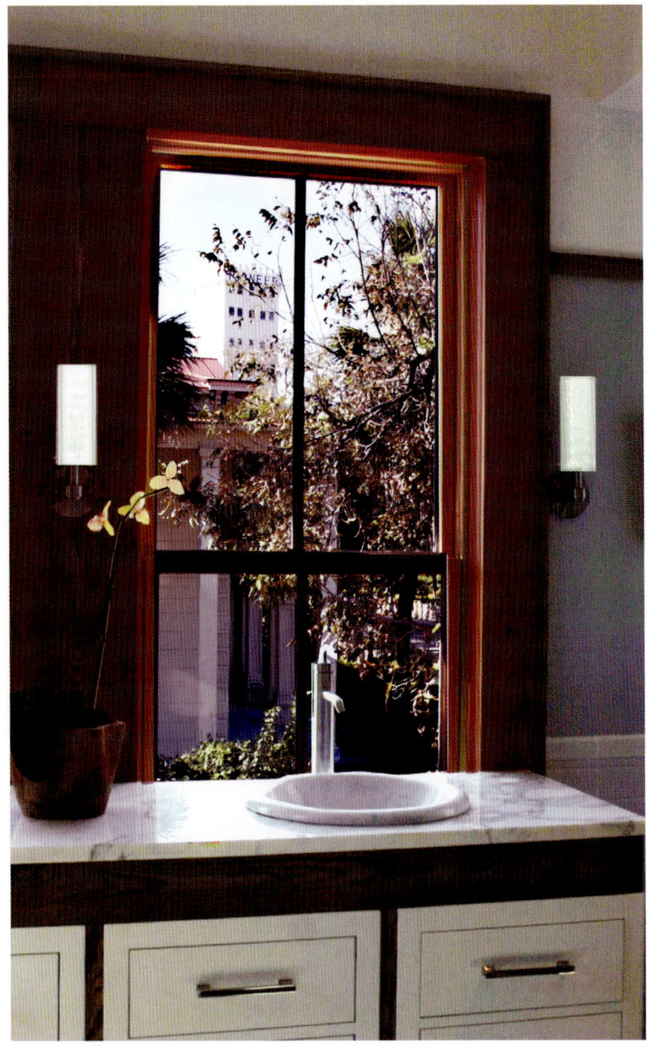

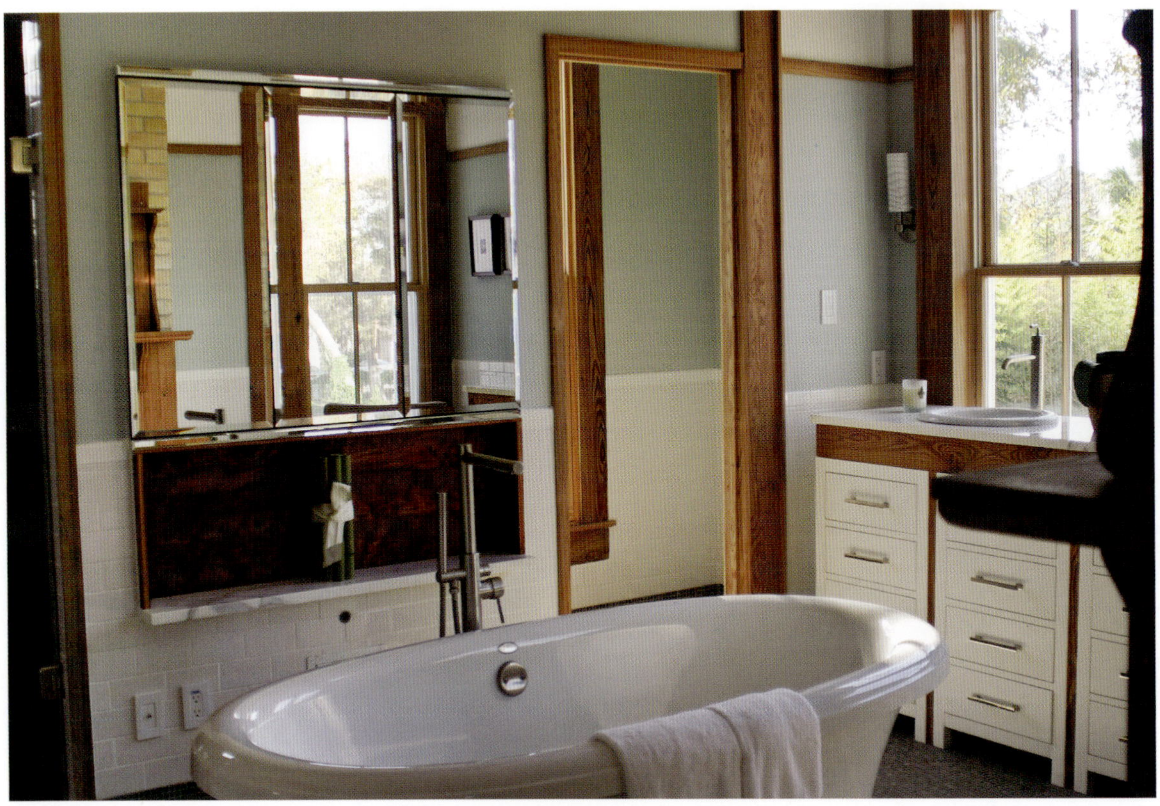

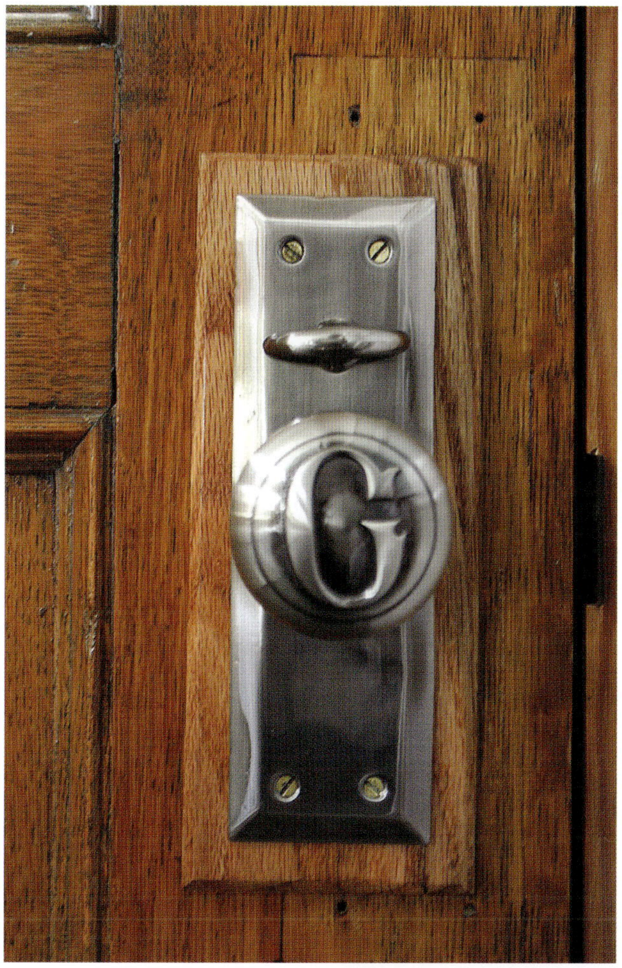

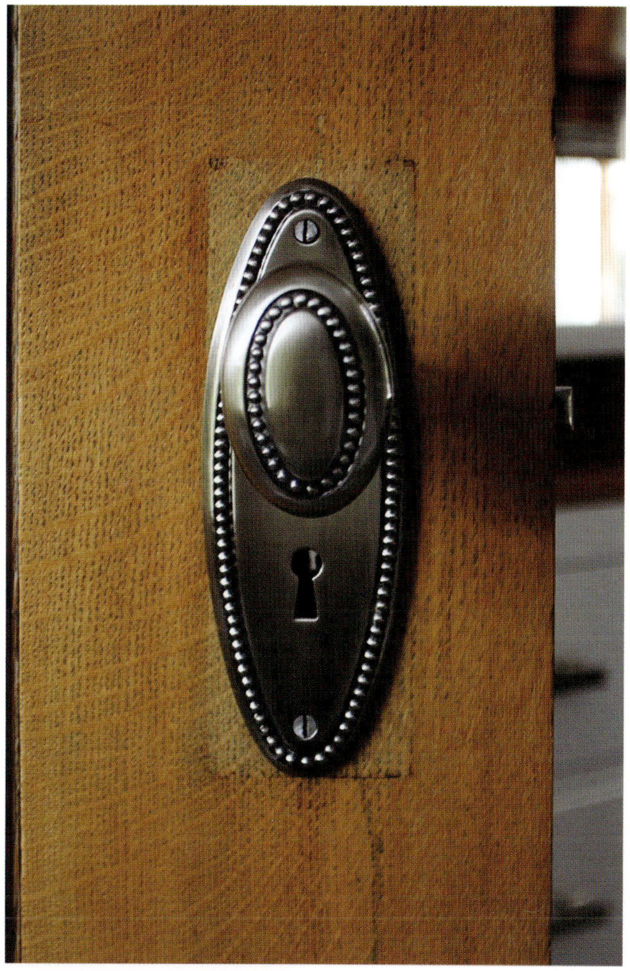

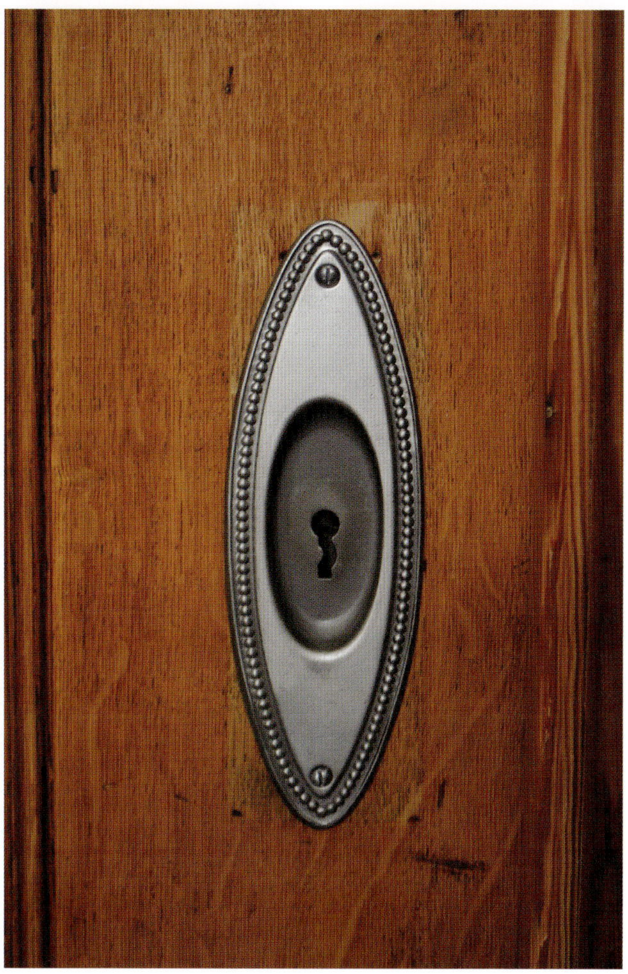

Original hardware in the master bathroom was refinished.

High Tech Innovations: Renovation opened the door to innovation in the form of utilizing the latest technology—state-of-the-art automation, for example. "It has the capacity to control/monitor air conditioning, lighting, security, and a variety of media," says Pachecano. "Using an internal computer network, the entire system is capable of programming from any location in the world." Does high tech compete with historic? "No. A 'hub wall' hides the automation system. Adaptive-reuse of historic chimneys gave rise to the 'Solar Chimney' that was featured in the *Wall Street Journal*. Old flues were adapted as vertical chases to run fiber optics, HDMI, and category 6 twisted copper for data transmission. The flat panel LED TVs are wired to the home automation system so that the interface allows downloading a movie without inserting a DVD into any player," says Pachecano. "At the time of construction, DVDs were already becoming passé and we did not want to have a digital infrastructure that was outdated once we finished the project. This is why Portico researched and embraced a new automation system that utilizes ZigBee mesh networks—a pioneering technology Portico installed at the Nix House years ahead of SmartGrid technology found in today's cutting edge utility metering systems."

A new type of building envelope and solar energy were two sustainable strategies incorporated into the preservation effort. "Arguments regarding environmental emissions and global warming may continue, but one thing seems sure: a kilo-watt hour does not care how you vote. The energy return on investment will pay for itself," says Pachecano, who invented a unique hybrid building envelope designed for historic and older buildings. "The net present value alone on the energy savings at No. 434 will pay for itself in less than 5 years," he says.

Pachecano concludes: "It seems that the Nix House at No. 434 is ready for its next 100 years. And restoration of No. 432, Nix House II, is on the drawing boards."

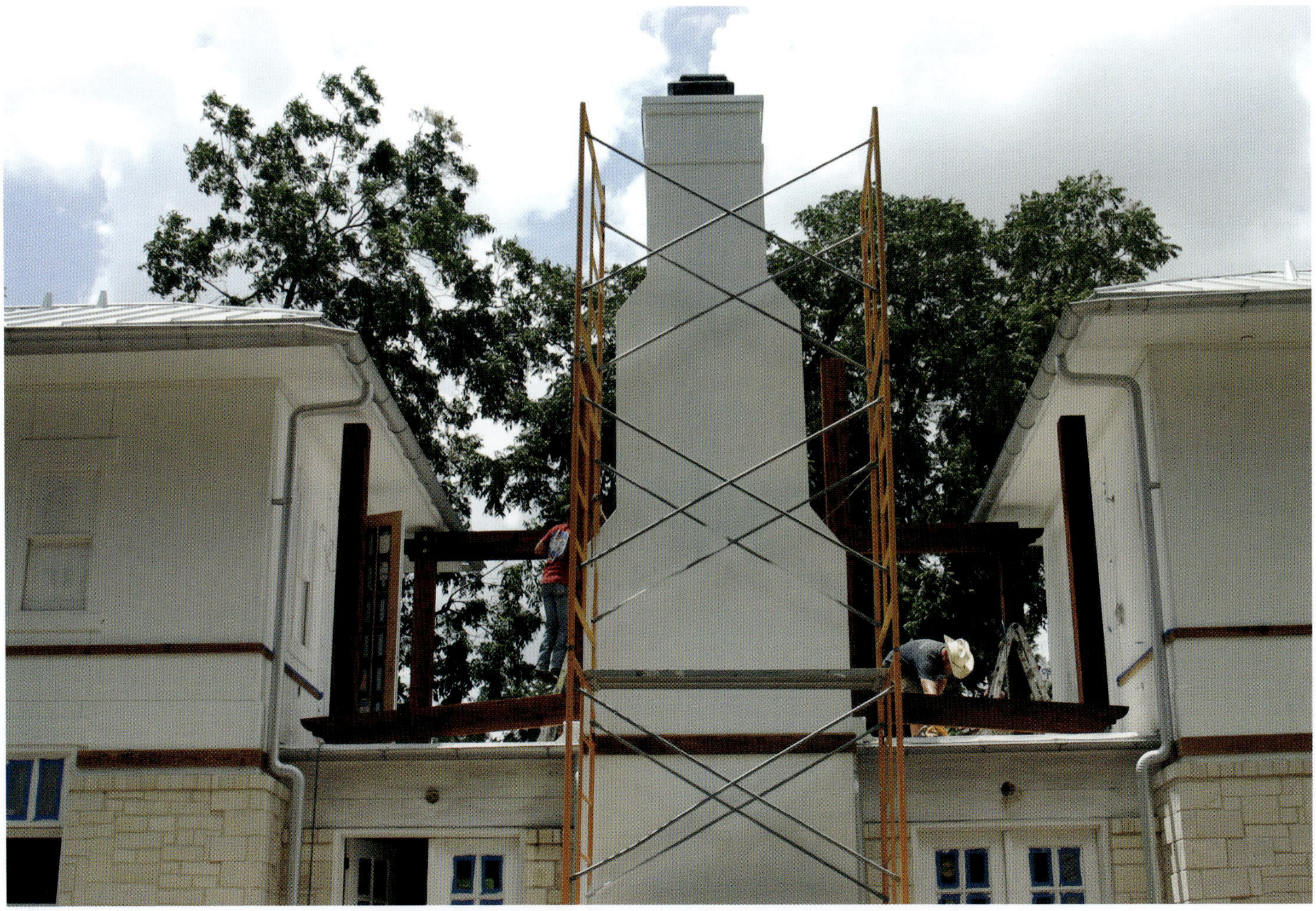

A new terrace with open-air fireplace and private balcony joins the main house with a second-story addition that can function as a studio or guest quarters.

Going Green

In his book, *The Nix Houses, Innovation and Style in Texas' Oldest Historic District,* (The Watercress Press, San Antonio, 2007), Architect Roy Pachecano describes in detail all the research and work that went into re-doing 434 King William, now even more remarkable because of efforts by him and his father, Omar, to preserve it. Here—as a guide to those who are considering re-doing a vintage house "green"—are the twenty items on Portico Residential's checklist of environmentally conscious green musts. These key considerations earned the Nix House a distinguished LEED-Platinum designation by the US Green Building Council:

1. Spray foam insulation to achieve high R values
2. Foam liners at all sole plates and stud wall joints to eliminate air infiltration
3. Insulated foundation walls and adjoining crawl spaces
4. Non-vented roof attic
5. Hybrid building envelop allowing breathing walls without losing insulation
6. Energy efficient air-conditioning system
7. Installation of state-of-the-art home automation and monitoring
8. Incorporation of solar photovoltaics for direct current electricity
9. Highly reflective metal roofing above the primary structure
10. Acrylic (non-petroleum based) roofing at open balconies and roof terraces
11. Tankless water heating system
12. Site design to enhance prevailing winds for cross breezes
13. Thermal glass for greater reduction in heat gain at windows and doors
14. Preservation of 1899 windows with upgrades to decrease air infiltration
15. Tandem car garage, for efficient compact garage and more courtyard/garden space
16. Solar shading at exterior of historic single-paned windows
17. Recycling wood from demolished sheds as new construction framing
18. Restoration of 95 percent of 1890s interior and exterior
19. 2,500 gallon rain water harvesting system (for irrigating plants and trees)
20. Use of native plants and minimal landscaping for water conservation

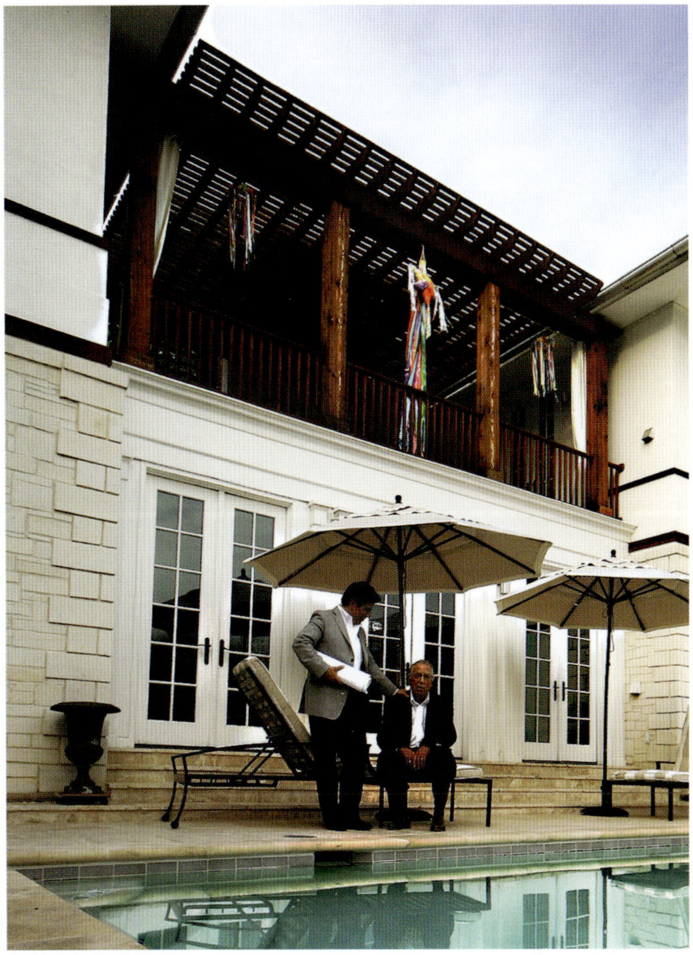

The Pachecanos by the new Nix House Courtyard pool during San Antonio's famous Fiesta.

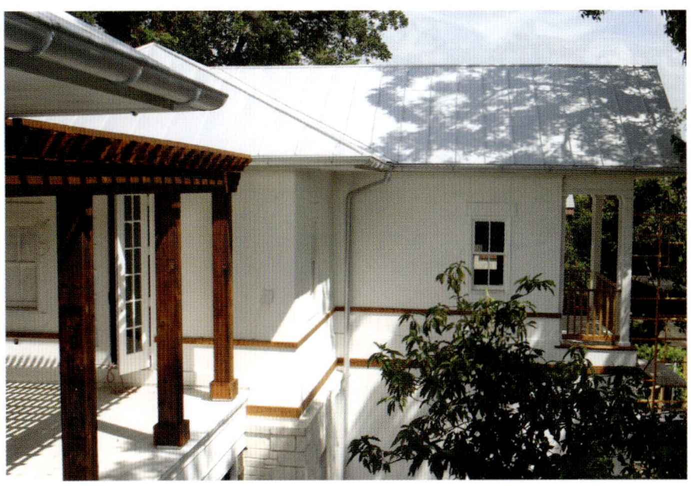

The new addition flanks a small courtyard.

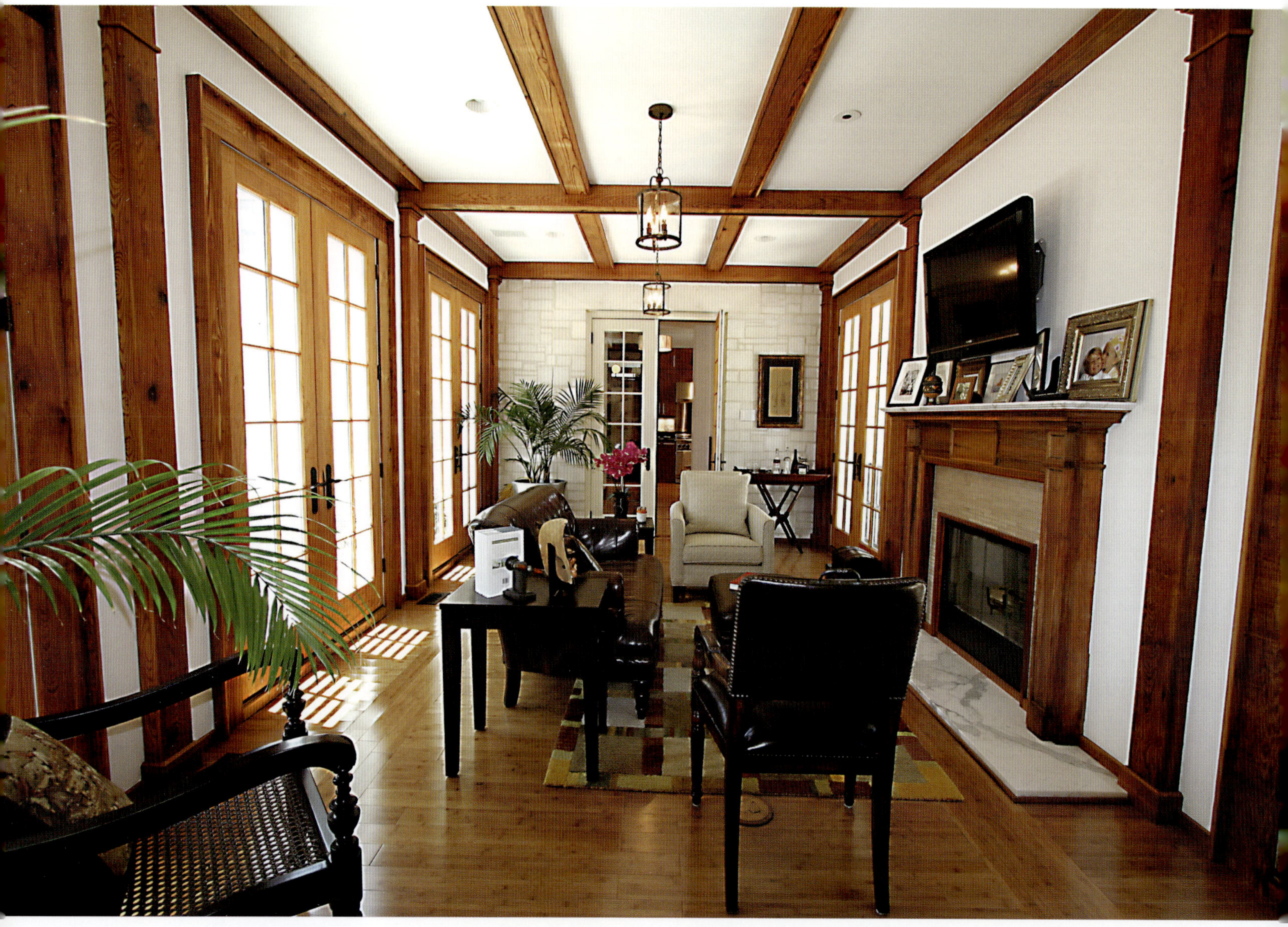

The trellis-covered open air terrace greatly expands second-floor living and entertaining areas.
(Above, below, and opposite page)

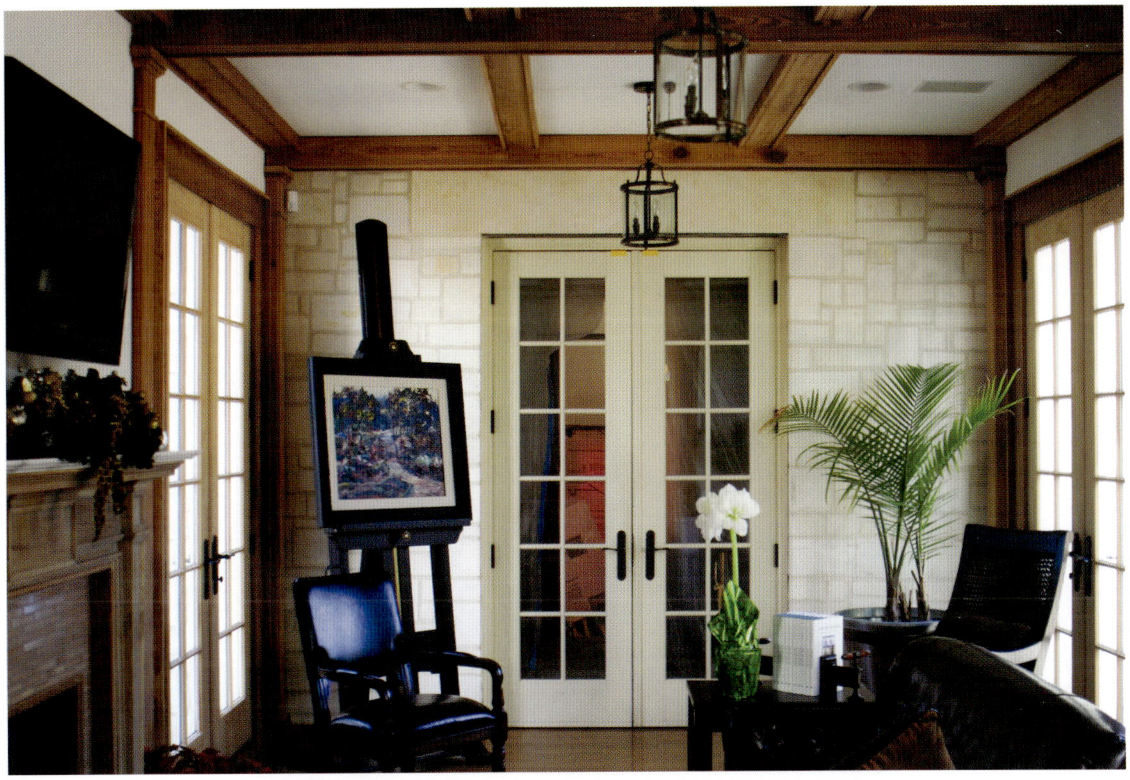

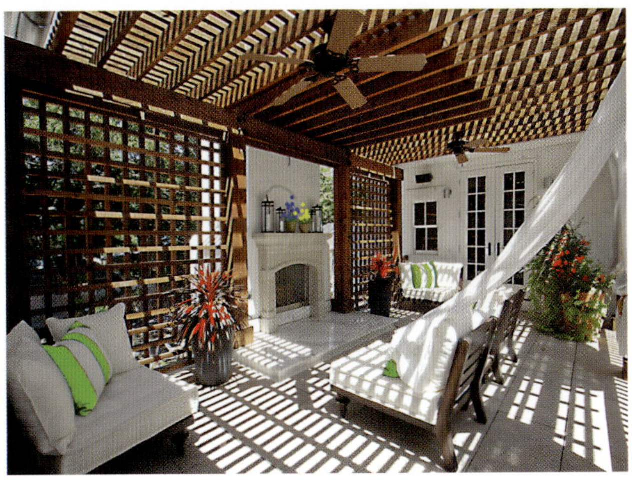

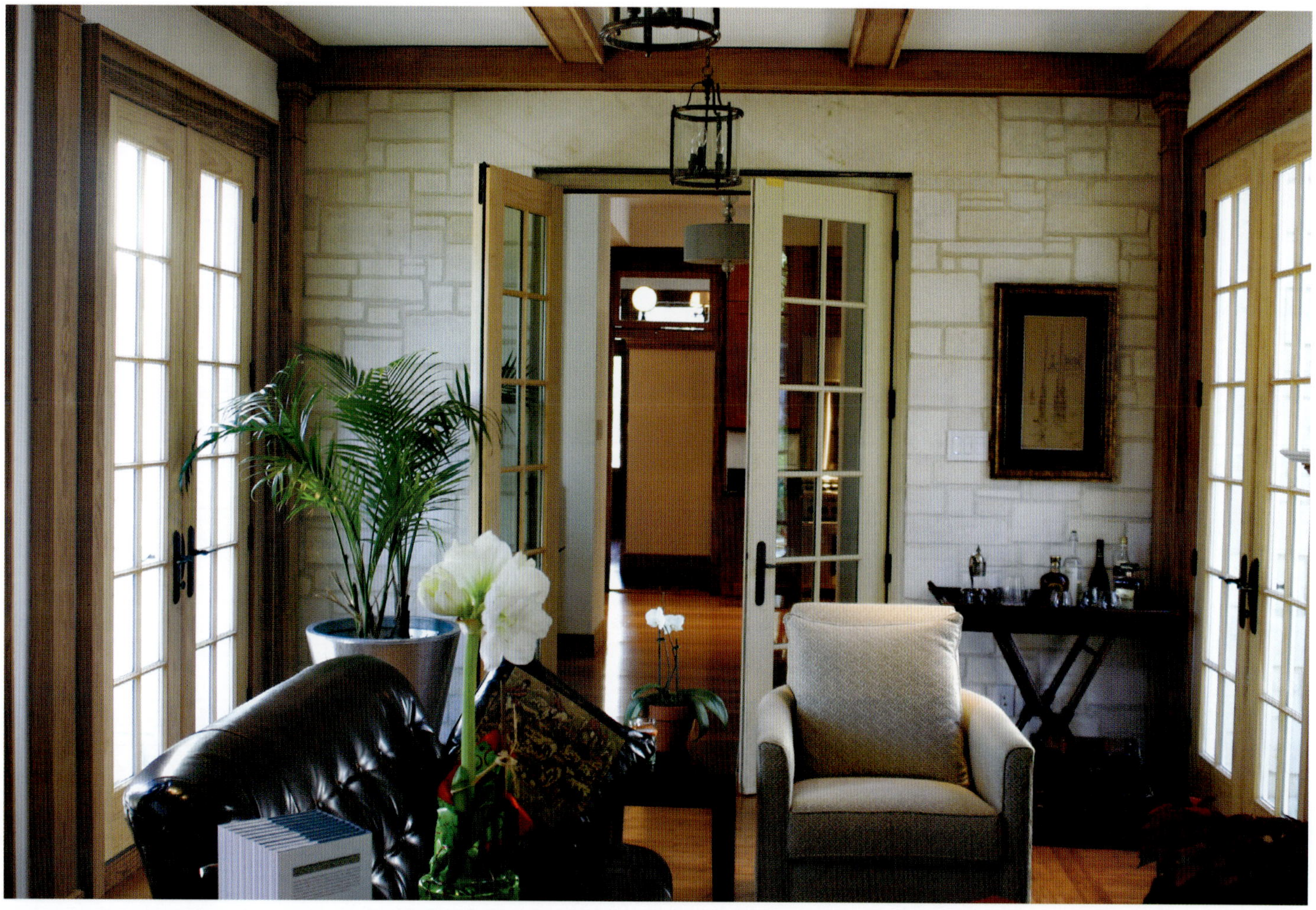

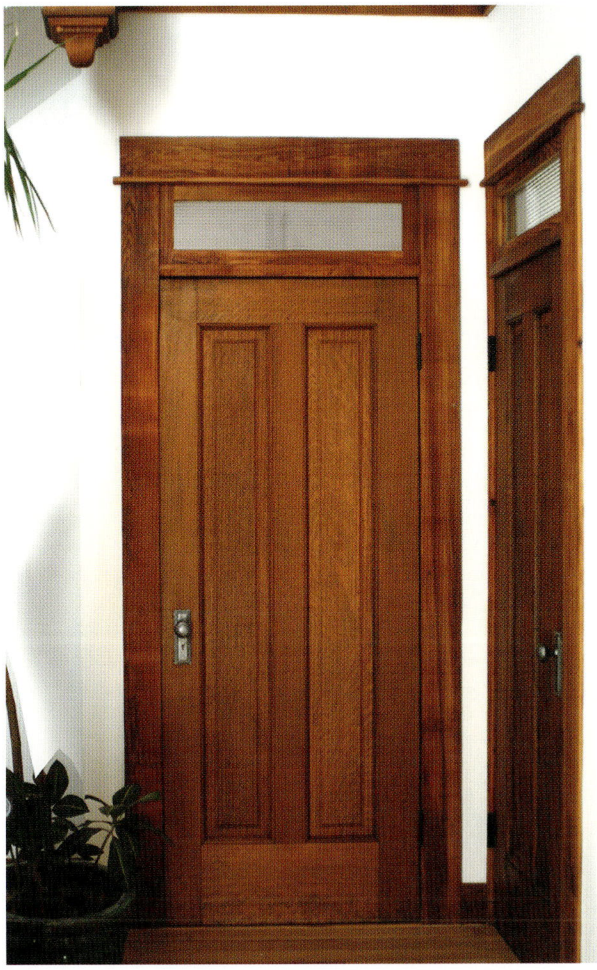

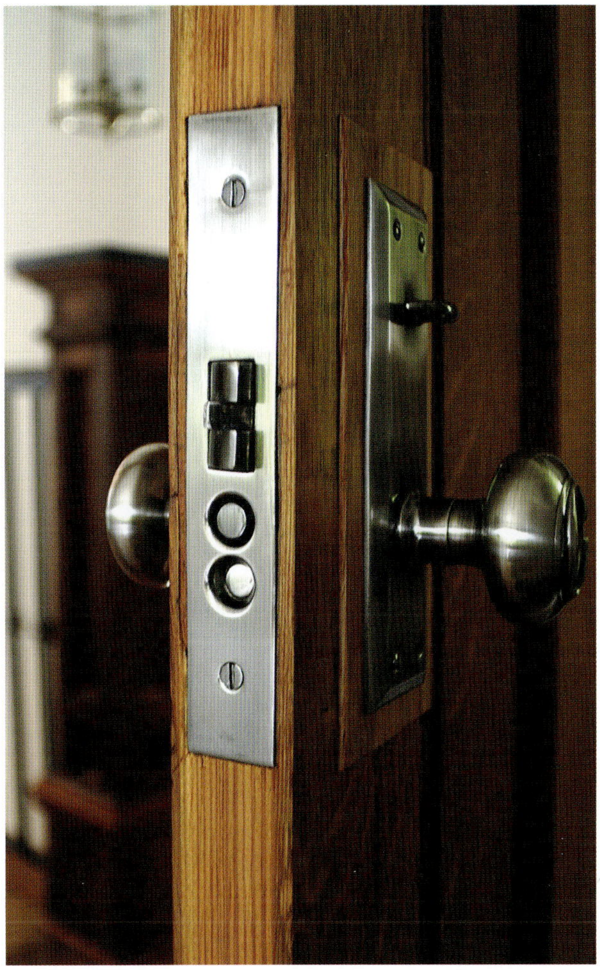

Refinished oak studio doors with transoms boast refinished hardware.

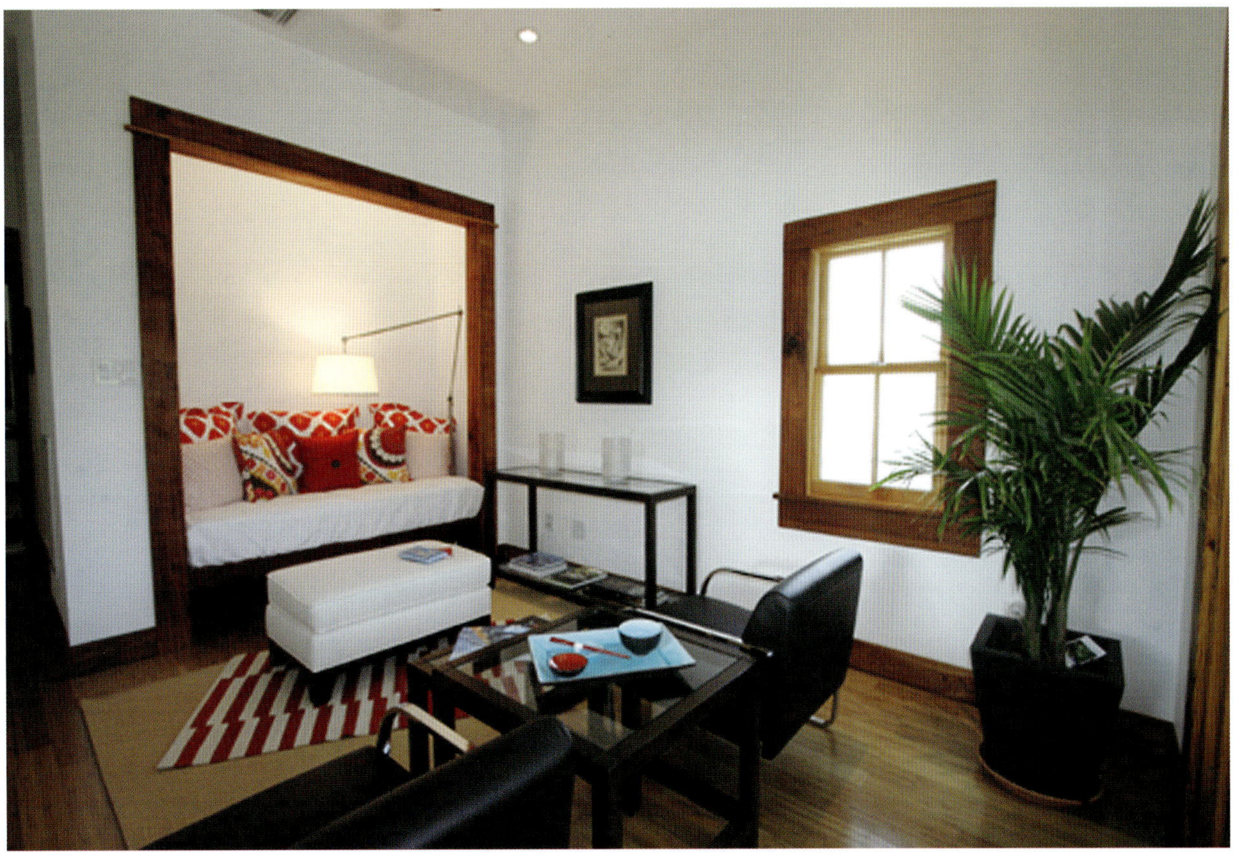

Wood trim in the new studio resembles that found in the old house.

Original fireplaces were carefully restored, calling new attention to the beauty of decorative surrounds and finely carved wood mantels.

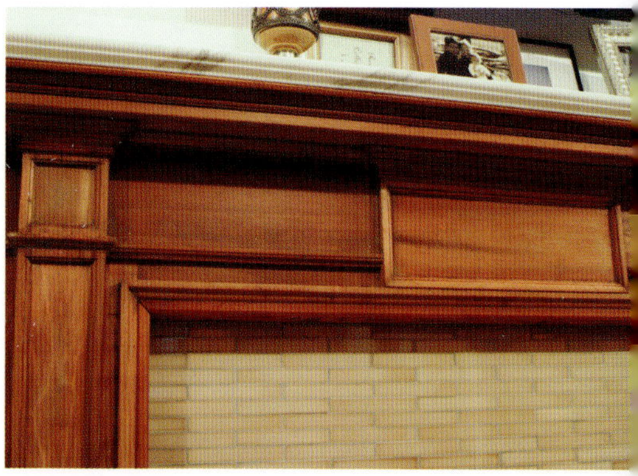

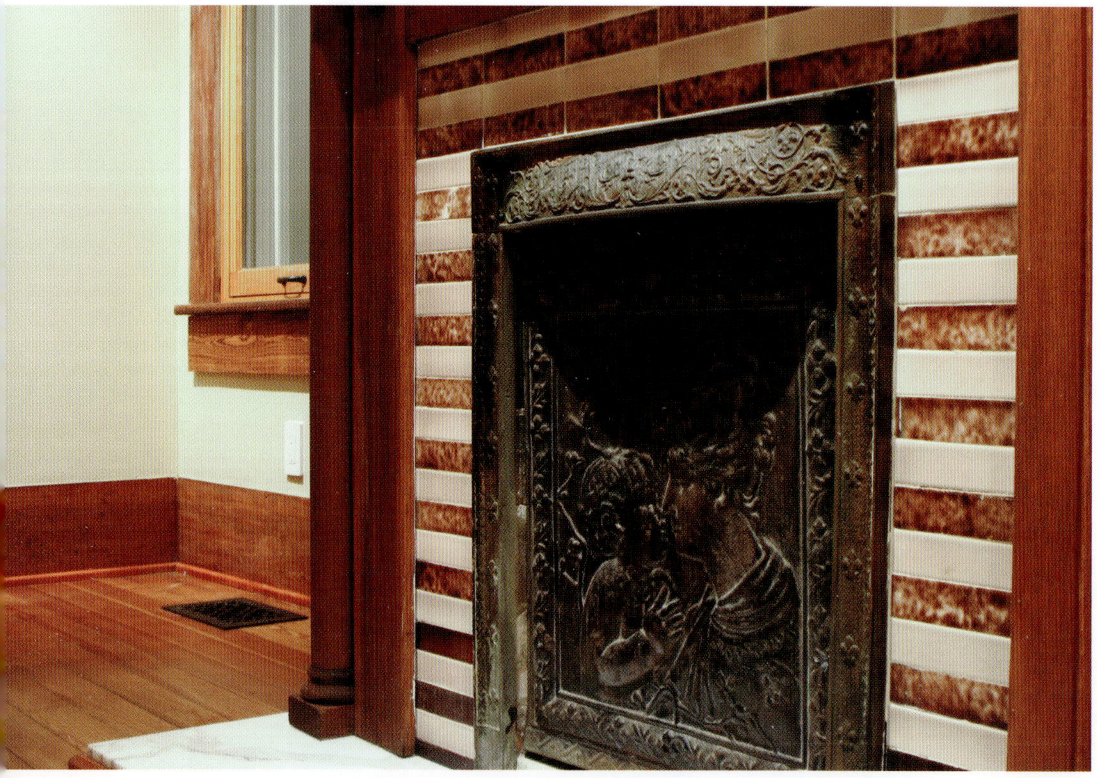

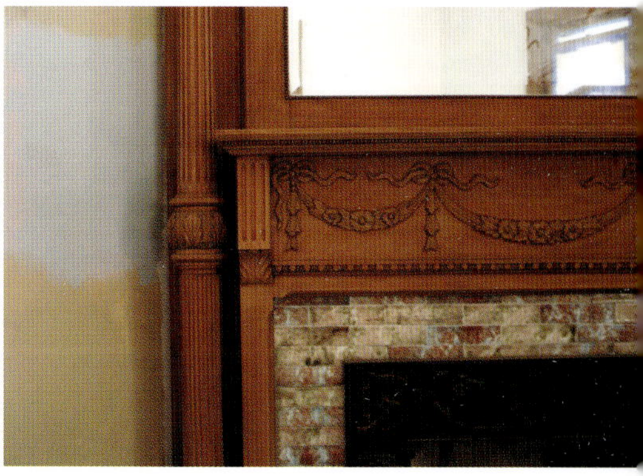

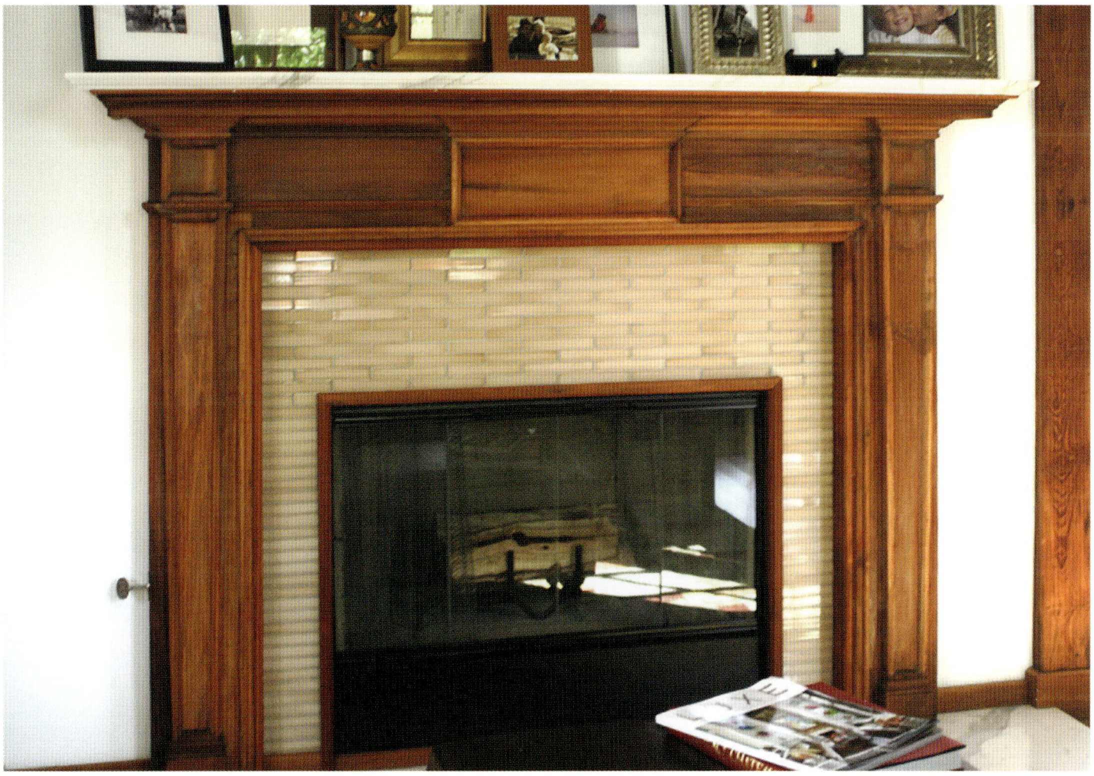

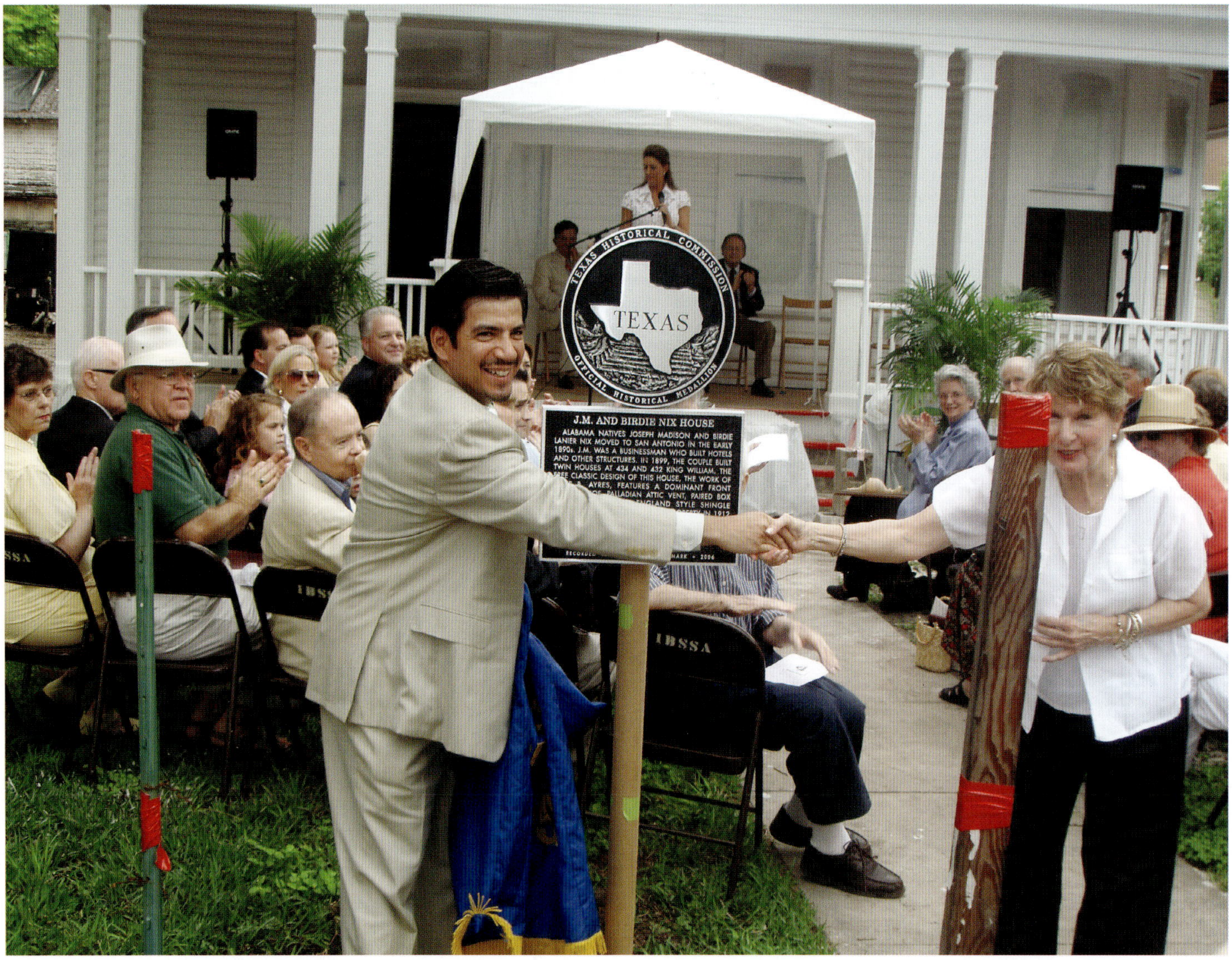

The new historic plaque was unveiled in May 2007.

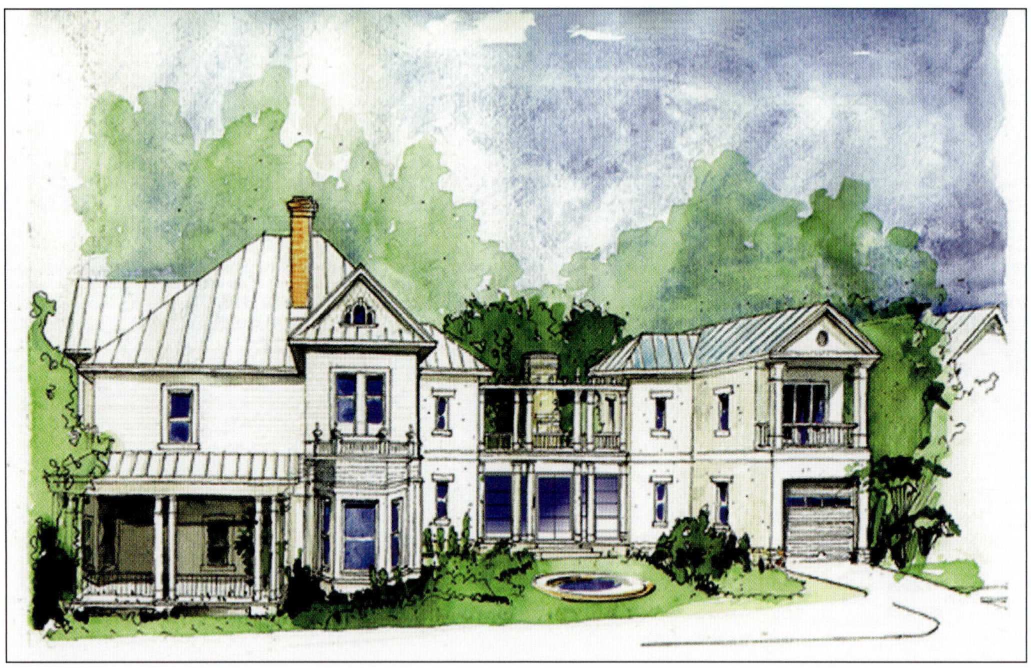

Roy Pachecano's watercolor of the restored Nix House—a job well done!

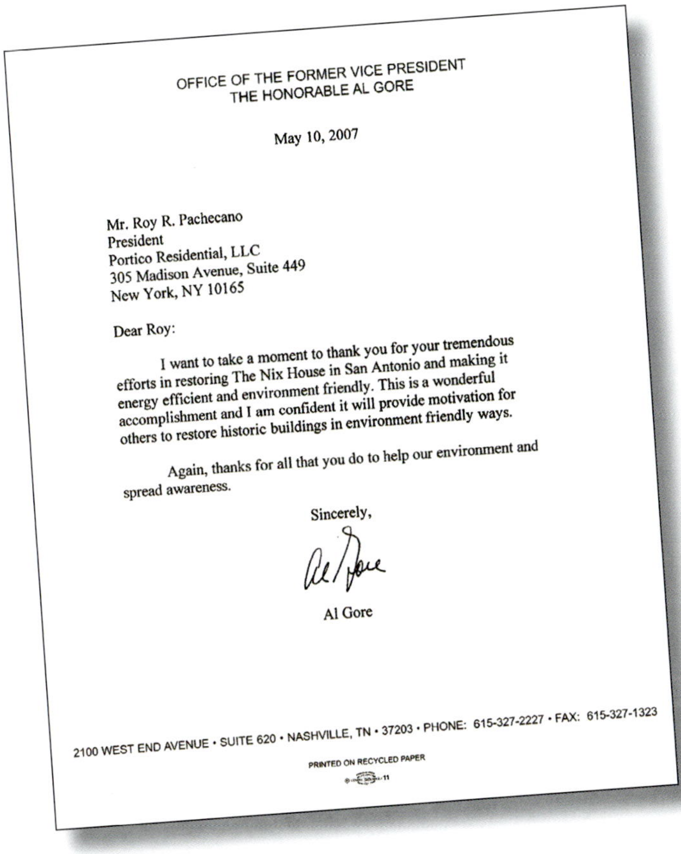

OFFICE OF THE FORMER VICE PRESIDENT
THE HONORABLE AL GORE

May 10, 2007

Mr. Roy R. Pachecano
President
Portico Residential, LLC
305 Madison Avenue, Suite 449
New York, NY 10165

Dear Roy:

I want to take a moment to thank you for your tremendous efforts in restoring The Nix House in San Antonio and making it energy efficient and environment friendly. This is a wonderful accomplishment and I am confident it will provide motivation for others to restore historic buildings in environment friendly ways.

Again, thanks for all that you do to help our environment and spread awareness.

Sincerely,

Al Gore

Al Gore

2100 WEST END AVENUE • SUITE 620 • NASHVILLE, TN • 37203 • PHONE: 615-327-2227 • FAX: 615-327-1323

PRINTED ON RECYCLED PAPER

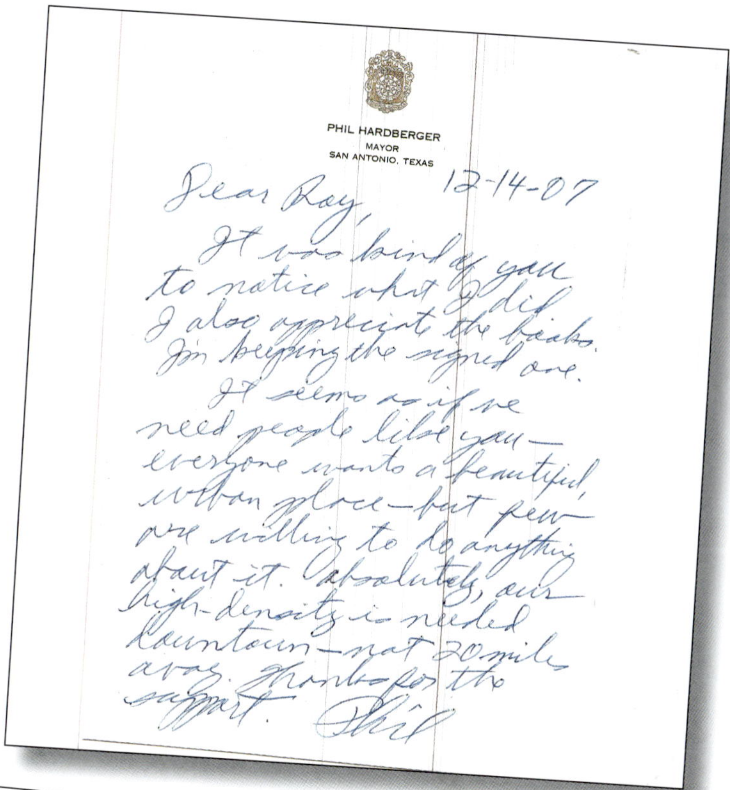

PHIL HARDBERGER
MAYOR
SAN ANTONIO, TEXAS

Dear Ray, 12-14-07

It was kind of you to notice what I did. I also appreciate the books. I'm keeping the signed one.

It seems as if we need people like you — everyone wants a beautiful urban place — but few are willing to do anything about it. Absolutely, our high-density is needed downtown — not 20 miles away. Thanks for the support. Phil

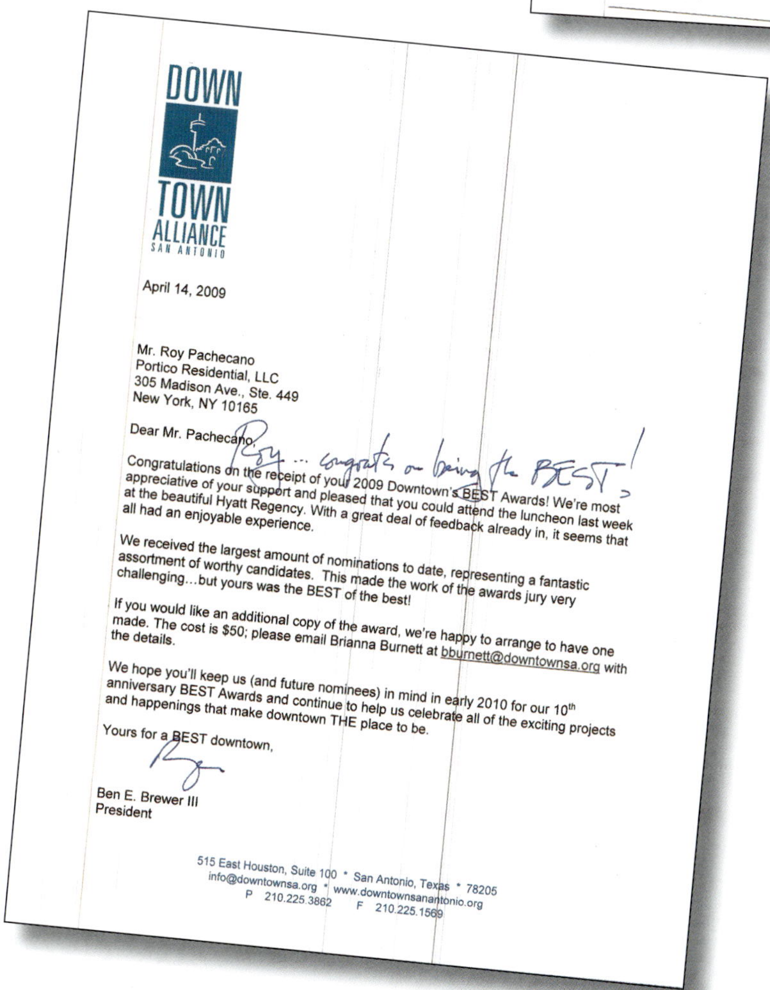

DOWN TOWN ALLIANCE
SAN ANTONIO

April 14, 2009

Mr. Roy Pachecano
Portico Residential, LLC
305 Madison Ave., Ste. 449
New York, NY 10165

Dear Mr. Pachecano,

Roy... congrats on being the BEST!

Congratulations on the receipt of your 2009 Downtown's BEST Awards! We're most appreciative of your support and pleased that you could attend the luncheon last week at the beautiful Hyatt Regency. With a great deal of feedback already in, it seems that all had an enjoyable experience.

We received the largest amount of nominations to date, representing a fantastic assortment of worthy candidates. This made the work of the awards jury very challenging…but yours was the BEST of the best!

If you would like an additional copy of the award, we're happy to arrange to have one made. The cost is $50; please email Brianna Burnett at bburnett@downtownsa.org with the details.

We hope you'll keep us (and future nominees) in mind in early 2010 for our 10th anniversary BEST Awards and continue to help us celebrate all of the exciting projects and happenings that make downtown THE place to be.

Yours for a BEST downtown,

Ben E. Brewer III
President

515 East Houston, Suite 100 * San Antonio, Texas * 78205
info@downtownsa.org * www.downtownsanantonio.org
P 210.225.3862 F 210.225.1569

Letters of congratulation.

3
Chabot House

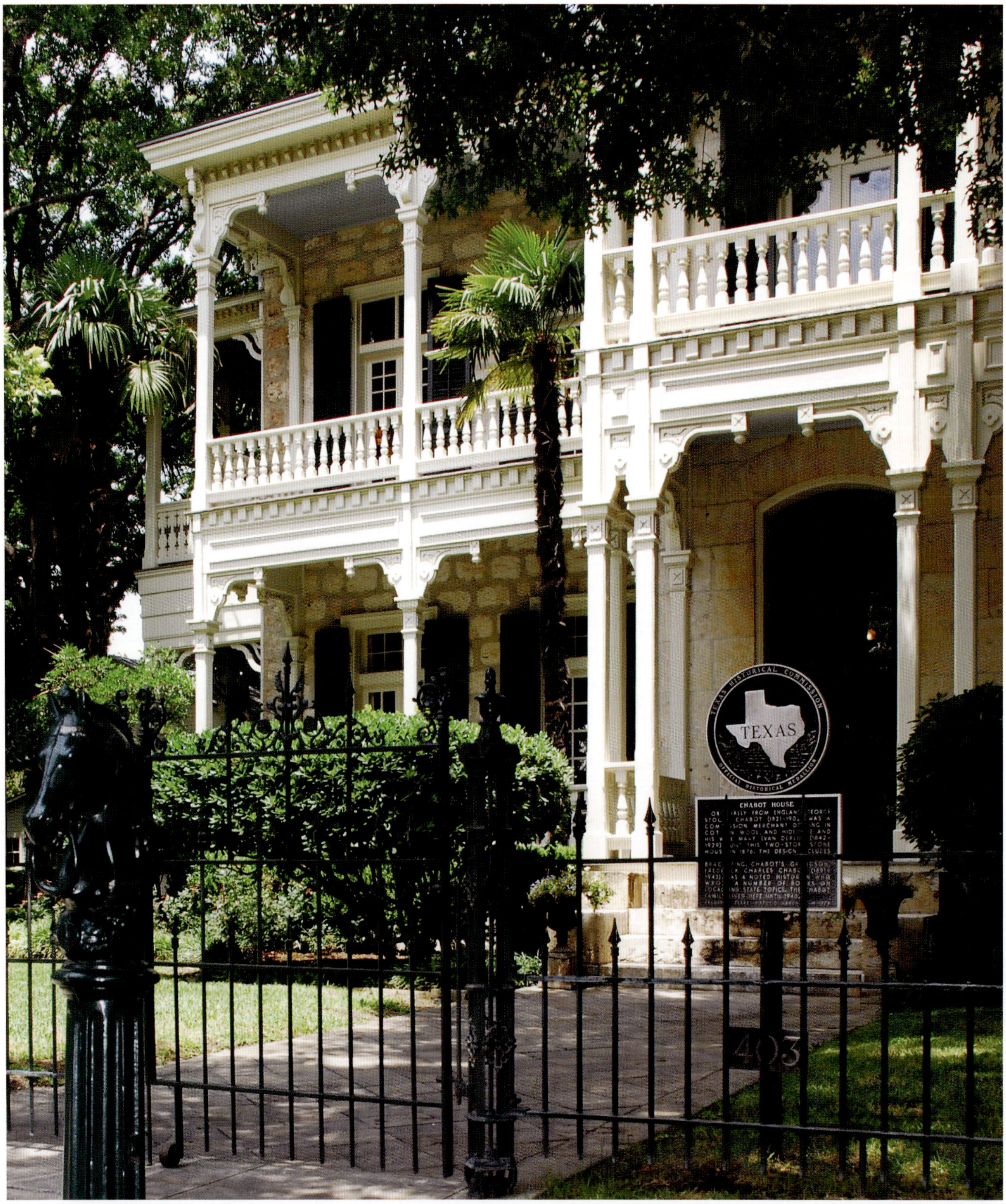

A plaque designates the Chabot House a historic landmark site—a favorite of visitors who stroll the historic King William district. *Photographs by Barbara Justice*

The elegant Chabot House behind a handsome bottle green wrought iron fence elicits oohs and aahs from tourists in horse-drawn carriages that pause before the gate. Curtis Johnson, a young San Antonio businessman who purchased the house at 403 Madison in 2006 says, "We are fortunate to have the original fence and gate. A Chabot family member had removed them to New Mexico. They were retrieved in the 1970s by Walter Mathis, who had purchased the property and was restoring the grounds and house. As a result of his efforts, the Texas Historical Commission granted the house Landmark status in 1978, and a Texas Historical Building marker was placed near the gate."

Style and Substance: In 1977, Joan Mondale (wife of then U.S. vice-president Walter Mondale) toured the picturesque King William area, declaring the house at 403 Madison her favorite. The architect and builder of this impressive dwelling are unknown, but the house they designed and constructed is testimony to taste, talent, and George Stooks Chabot's skills as a businessman. As a British Foreign Service officer, Chabot had served for 10 years in Mexico before moving to Texas with his wife, Mary Van Derlip Chabot and their two sons, George A. and Charles J. In San Antonio, he established a wool commission business with partners P. J. Moss and Charles Cresson, his wife's brother-in-law. In 1875, Chabot purchased a lot from Thomas J. Devine, built a house on it, and moved with Mary and their sons into the family's new home in San Antonio's desirable King William neighborhood.

The Italianate Chabot house exemplifies the popular Victorian-era Italian Villa style, with its graceful verticality and romantic embellishments. The house beautifully interprets the mood. Highly visible are distinguishing ornately trimmed galleries (porches) at first- and second-floor levels that span the façade and occur on all sides of the house. Covered porches were a natural cooling device that shielded the house from the hot sun. They also provided a spot in cool shade for social gathering. Generously sized porches were both practical and indicators of social status. Obvious to passersby, the more lavish and intricately detailed the trim—in this case, an outstanding example of carpenters' art—the wealthier the owner.

The main body of the house is constructed of smooth, articulated limestone. Walls of the wing to the left of the main structure of less refined caliche block (a soft limestone indigenous to South Texas and probably locally dug) suggest that it was a later addition. Indeed, over the years, owners modified the house to meet altered circumstances and changing times that brought about a decline to this house and its once-wonderful neighborhood.

Restoration, Renovation, and Remodeling: When Walter Nold Mathis bought Chabot House in 1974, he restored the original look of the landscape by demolishing a 1917 two-story apartment house and several small rental units. He renovated the charming stone carriage house at the rear of the property, and then sold it to his sister (whose house was directly behind it) for use as a guest house.

Work on the main house was more challenging. "Over the years, the house had been greatly altered from its original design," says Johnson. "The galleries had been enclosed, obliterating the most arresting feature of the house. And Mary Chabot had divided the interior to create apartments for three generations of family members, some of whom lived in the house until 1940."

Johnson pulls from his files the copy of a letter dated November 6, 1978, to the Texas Historical Commission, in which Mathis notes various features of the house:

- Encircling galleries (all across the front, with smaller galleries [porches] on three other sides).
- Interior walls are plaster on stone (15-inch thick hand-cut limestone block); the ceiling is plaster on wood lath.
- The front doors (imposingly tall, since interior ceilings are 16-feet high) and stair are of walnut (the only places in which this wood is visible).
- Floors and the rear stair are pine (long-leaf, popular in this area); exterior porch floors are cypress.
- Functioning fireplaces and their mantels (three each on first and second floors) are original.
- Windows (36-in. x 100-in.) are fitted with working cypress shutters
- All windows and doors were fitted with cypress shutters (except the front doors, which Mathis carefully replaced with matching cypress shutters)
- Several original chandeliers were in place

Mathis began work on the house by removing porch enclosures to painstakingly restore the galleries so that the exterior looked exactly as it did originally.

Thoughtful and carefully done work on the interior was a *renovation,* not a restoration, for Mathis reconfigured the interior to form three luxurious apartments, furnished them with antiques and fine art, and rented them out. Still, his effort was a monumental achievement. It earned him considerable recognition and credit as a major force for the re-gentrification of the newly prestigious King William area.

Complete *restoration* of the Chabot House was the work of Peter and Sister Reed, the couple who purchased the main house in 1985. They acquired the carriage house in 1986, so that it is once again part of the Chabot House property. Today, Johnson's partner, Leland Stone uses the ground floor as his office. The smartly furnished second floor is elegant guest quarters.

The Reeds teamed with Mike Hilger, a noted restoration architect, and over a two-year period returned the house to its original nineteenth century appearance. At this time, remodeling added up-to-date wiring, plumbing, and zoned central air-conditioning (retrofitted unobtrusively). A delightful surprise during the restoration occurred when old linoleum in the dining room was removed to reveal a beautiful oak floor with an inlay border.

Since every home owner leaves a personal stamp, what has Johnson, who has lived at 403 Madison since 2006, contributed to the house that he loves? "Very little was necessary," he says.

"A new serene taupe color scheme throughout seems both classic and contemporary. In the second-floor master suite, wall-to-wall carpeting was pulled up to reveal original longleaf pine floors in nearly pristine condition. All we had to do was have them refinished. In the bath, we installed quarter-sawn oak flooring to match that in the downstairs powder room and library. In the kitchen (small by today's standards but wonderfully adequate), installing bead board to certain wall areas adds an appropriate period look that is warmly inviting, once again popular, and sophisticated."

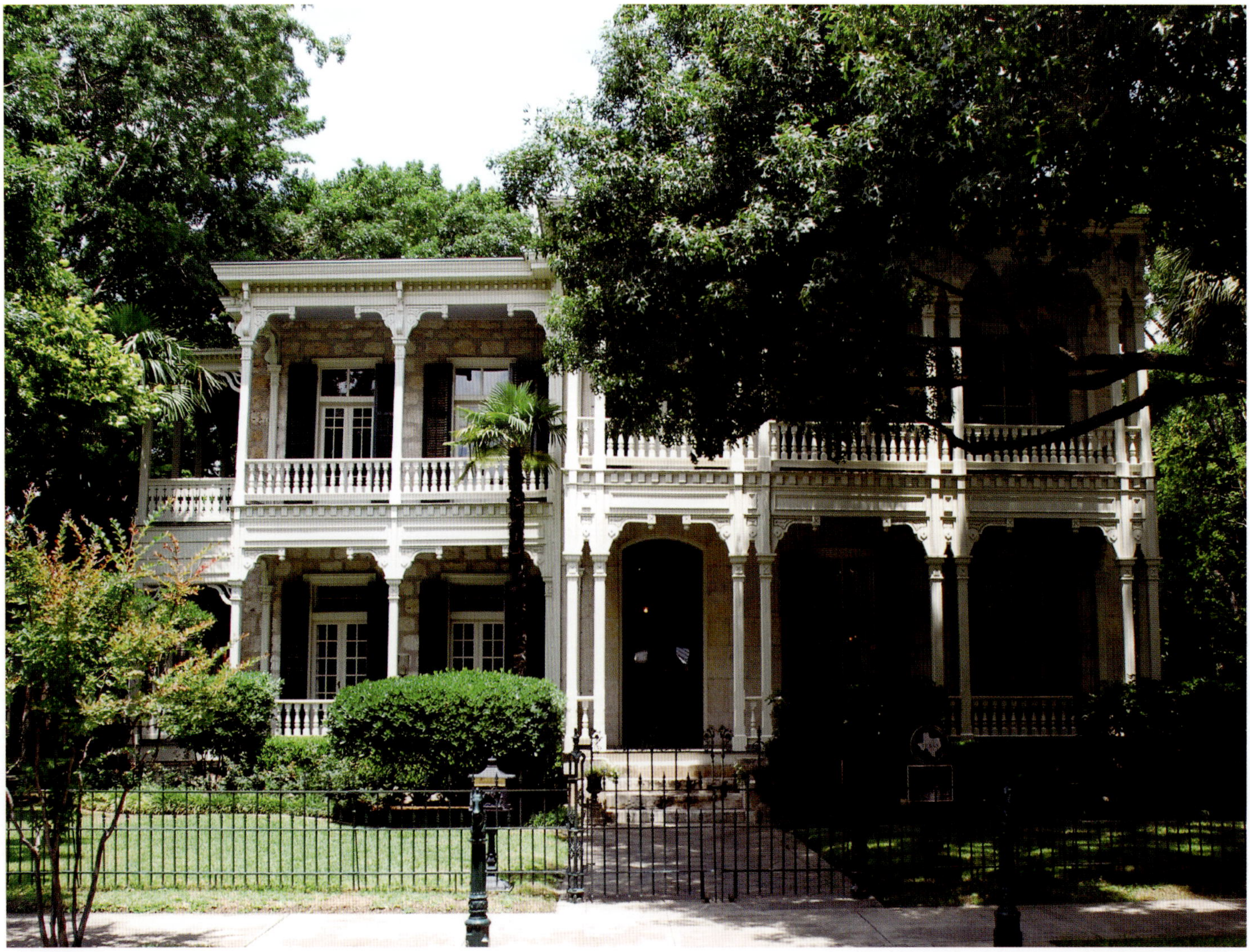

At one period in the history of this Italianate-style house, the porches—a sign of wealth when the house was built—were enclosed to create living space and the house was divided into apartments.

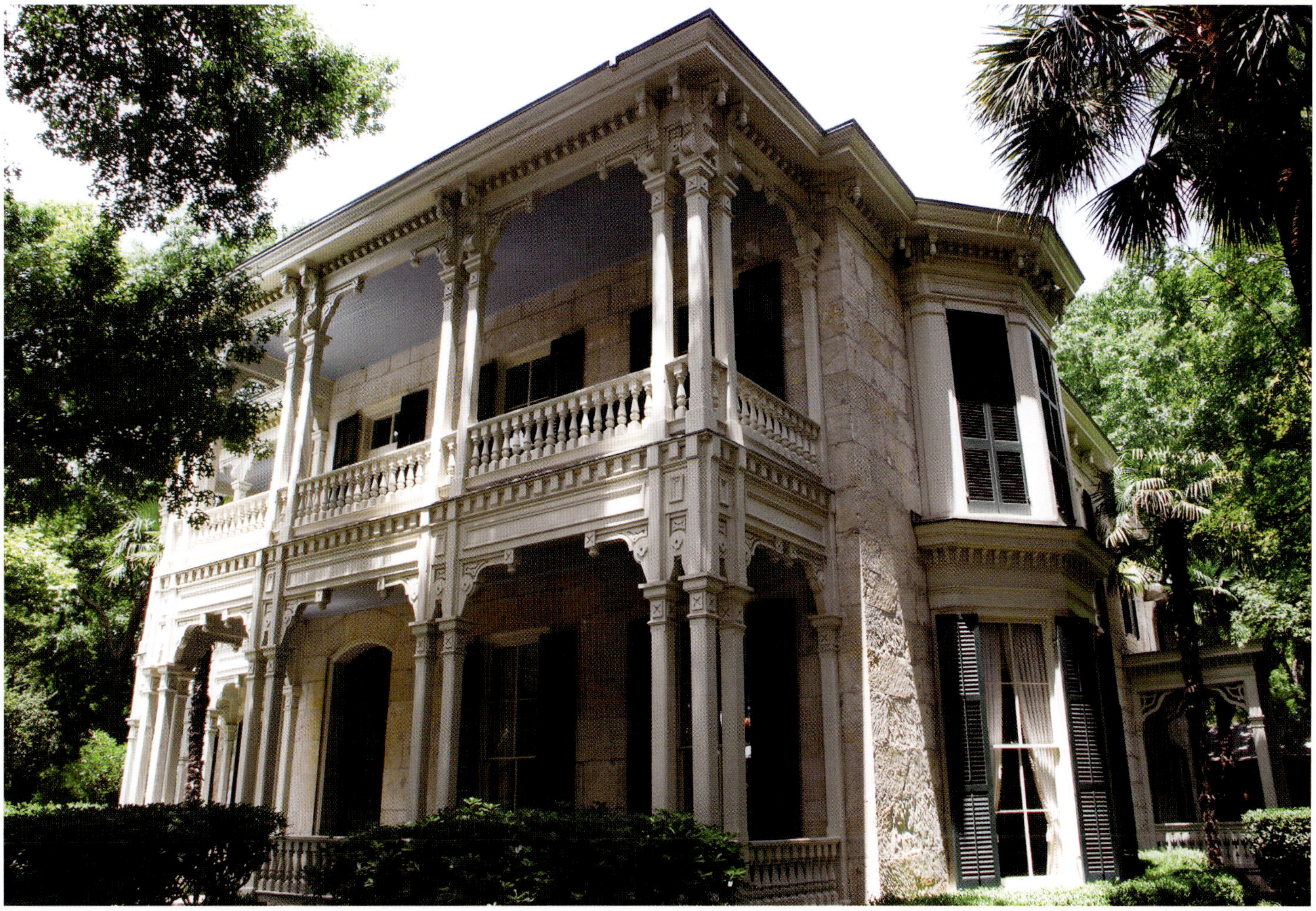

It was a common practice during the Victorian era to paint the underside of porch roofs sky-blue, a ploy to trick wasps into *not* building nests.

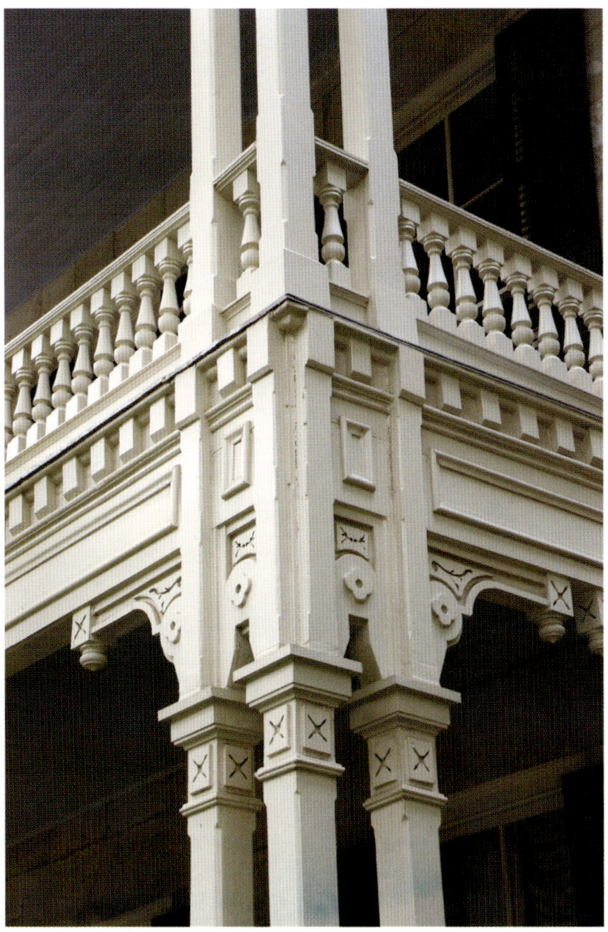

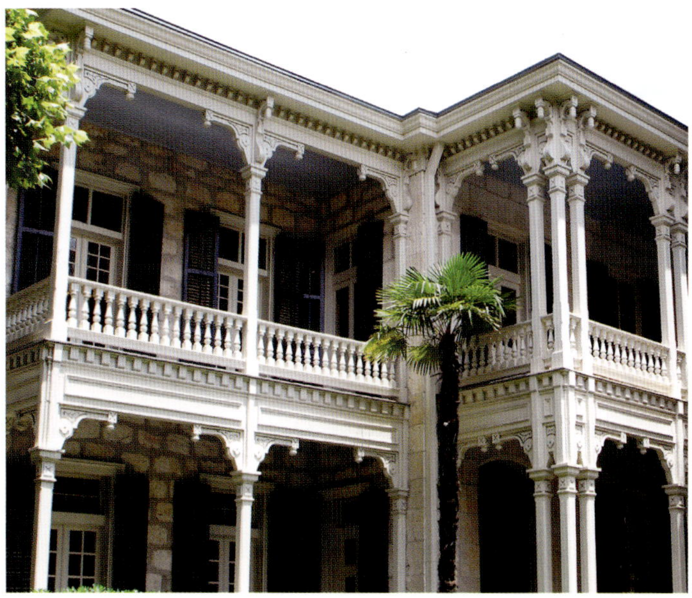

In a move to restore the house to its original grandeur, porch enclosures were removed, revealing the elaborate gingerbread ornamentation prized during the late Victorian period.

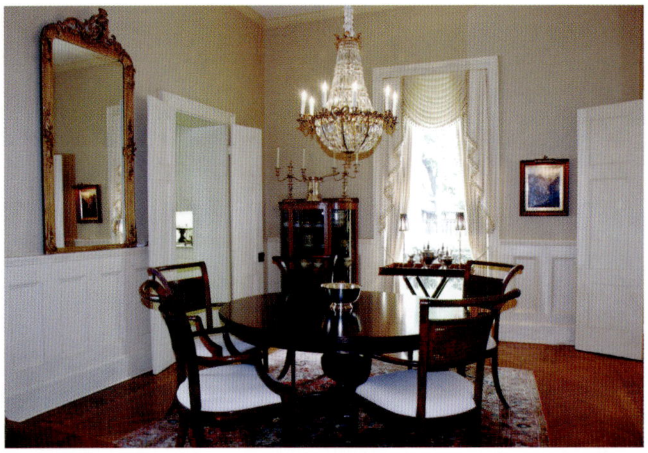

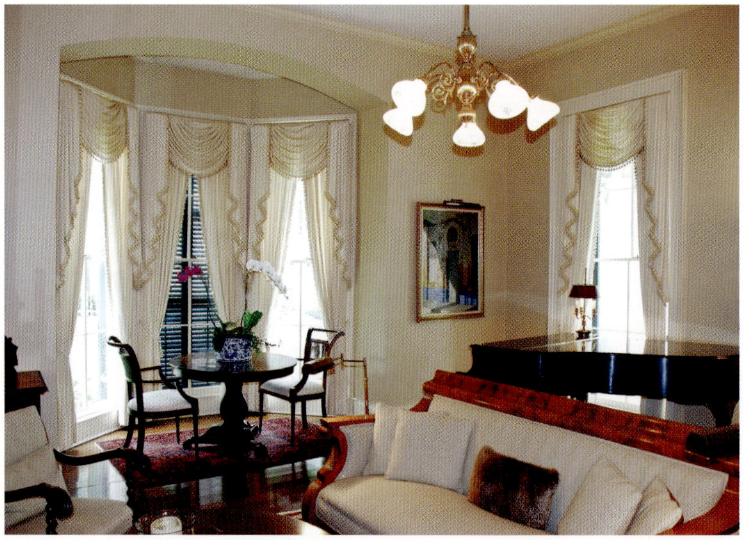

A light neutral color scheme adds fresh new sophistication to the living room and adjoining dining room.

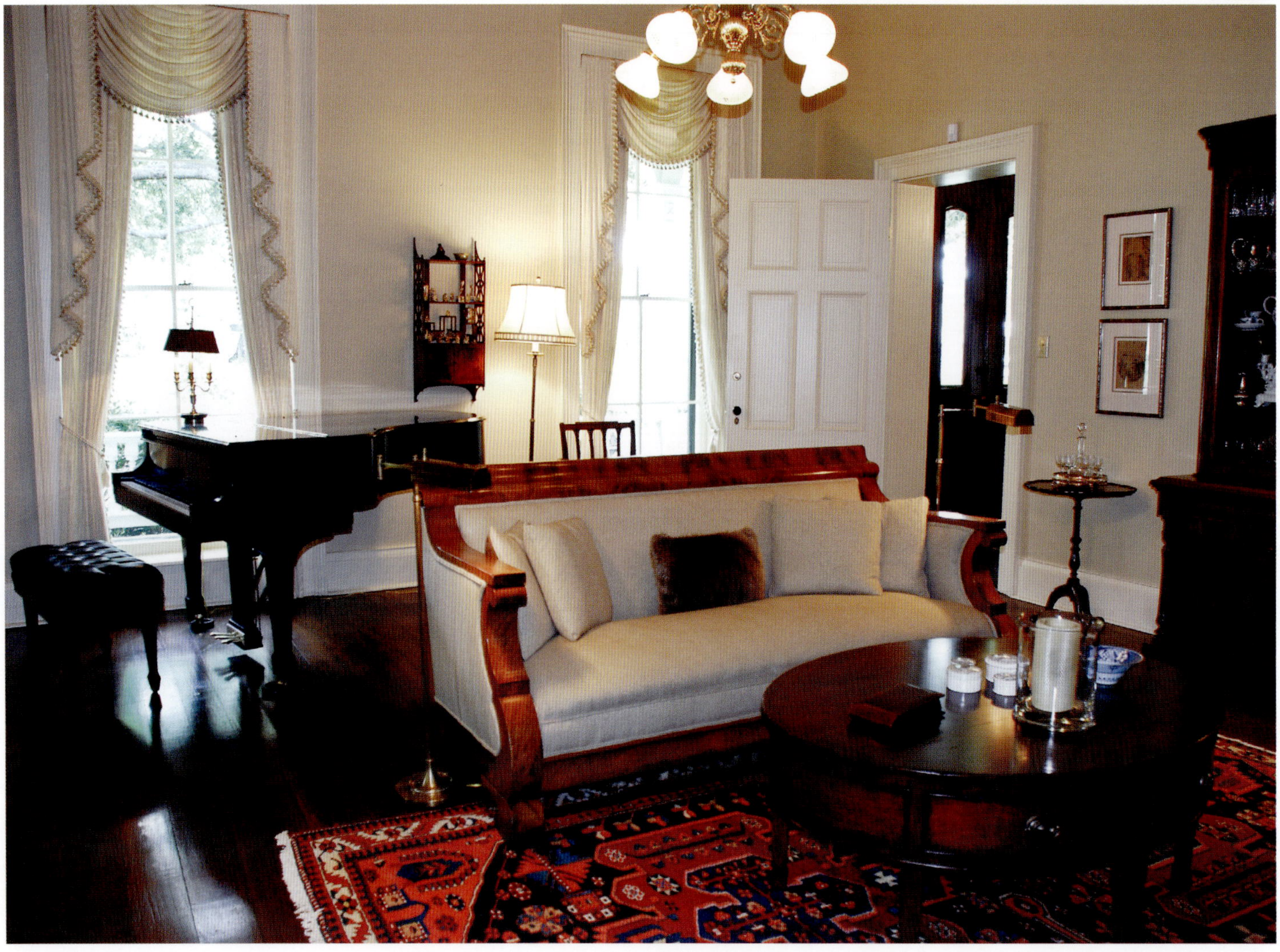

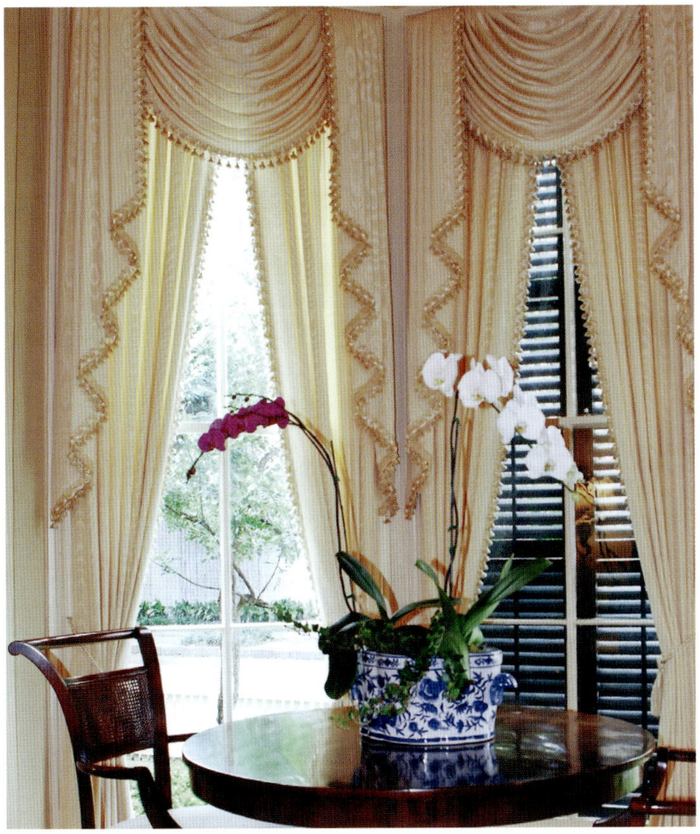

A bay window in the living room is a cozy spot for tea.

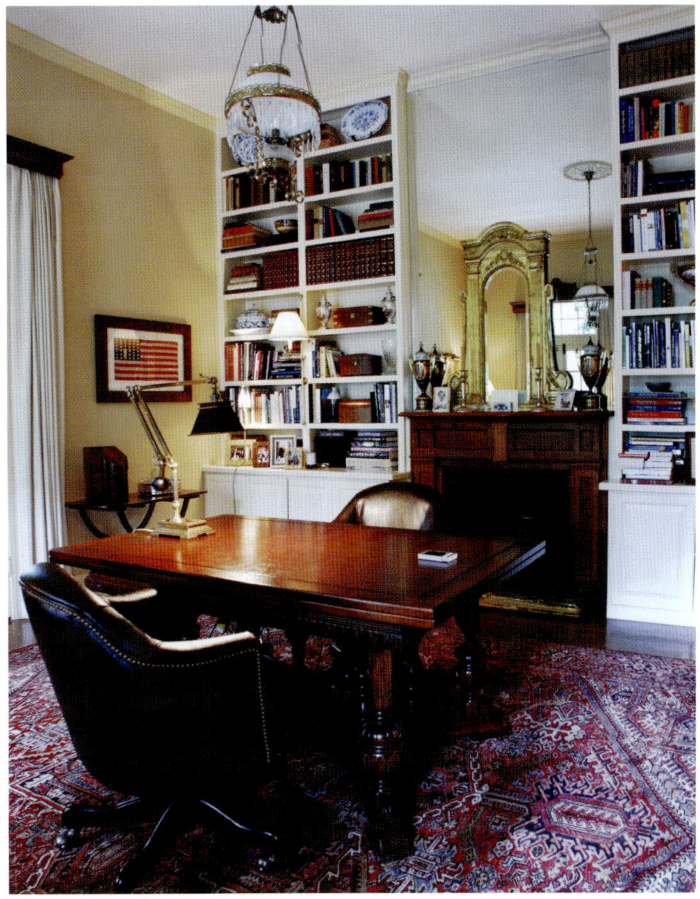

A framed antique American flag adorns a wall in the library. Built-in bookcases flank the original mantel.

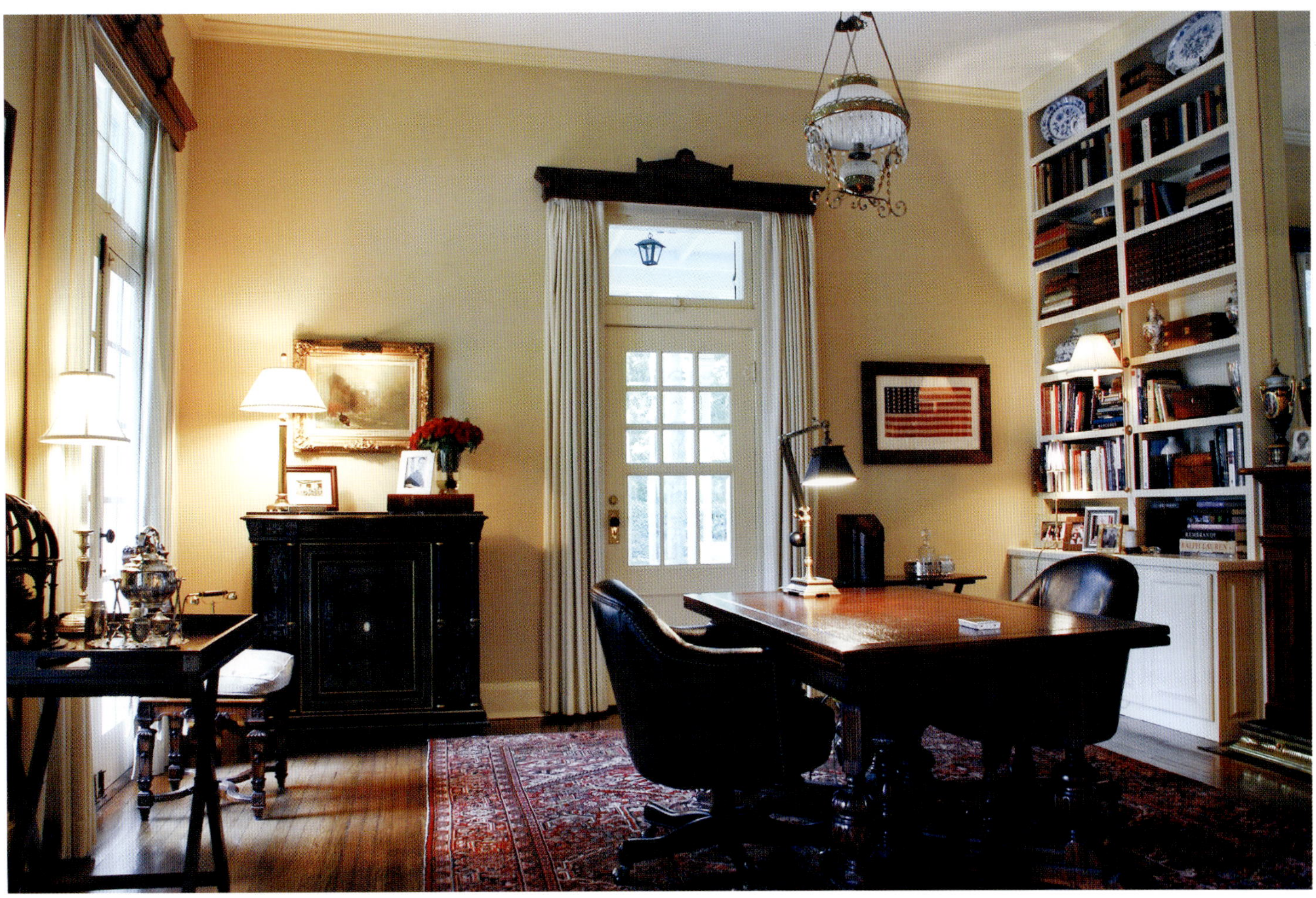

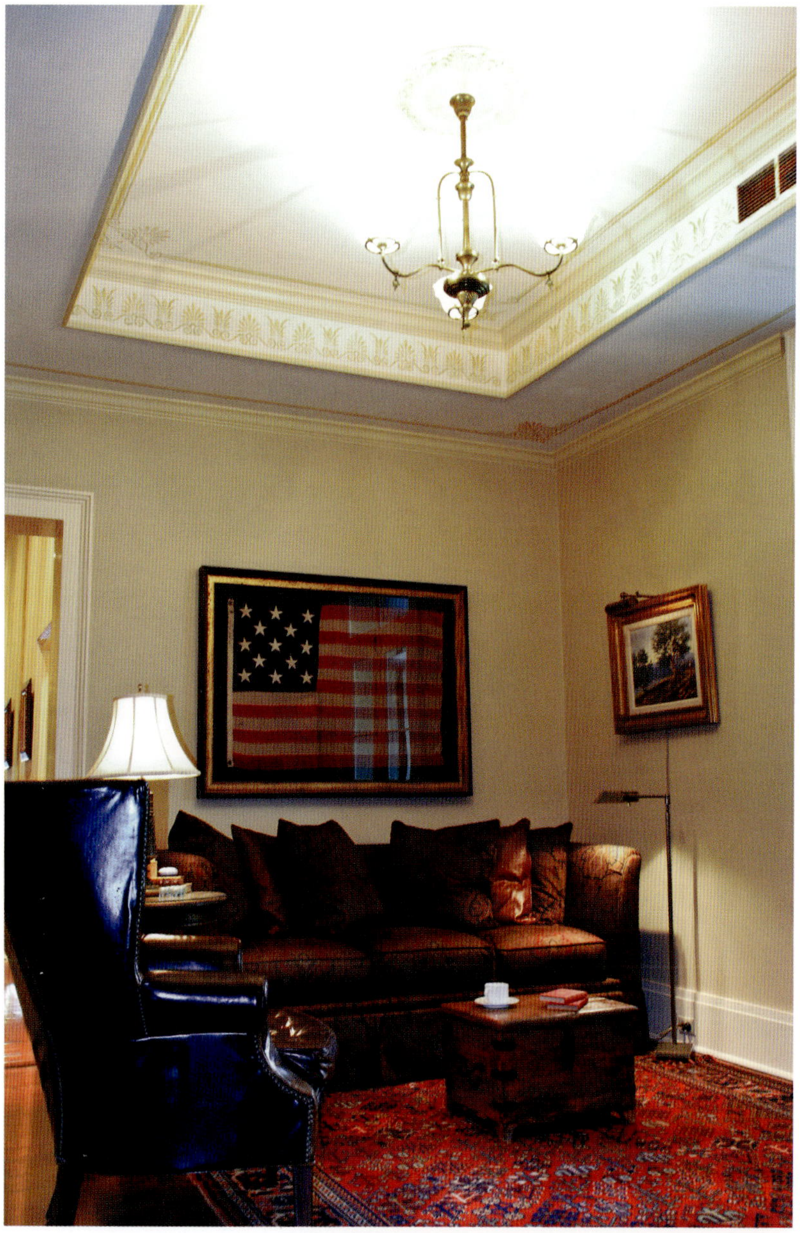

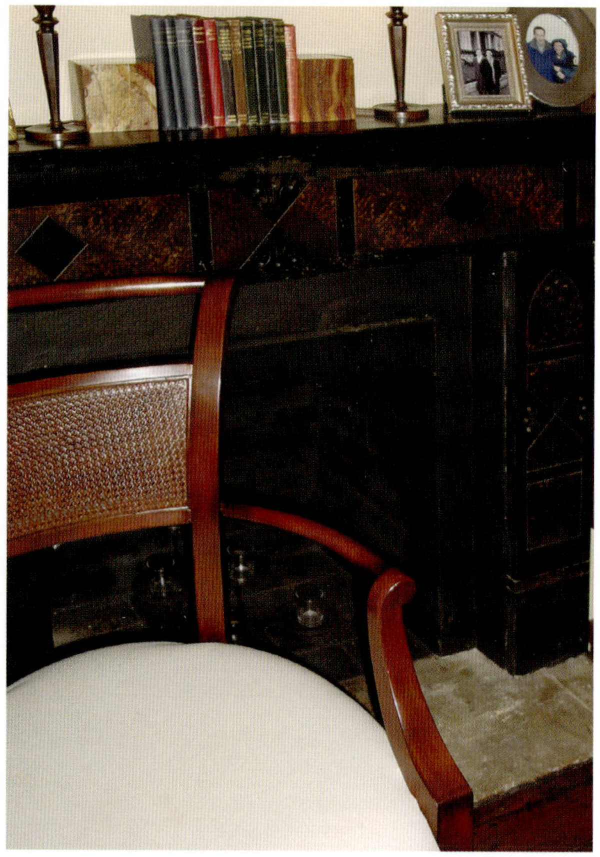

A giant antique flag graces the wall of a sitting room. Overhead, the recessed ceiling is decorated with stenciling. The fireplace mantel with art tile surround is original.

Rococo-style stenciling in a guest bedroom was so delightful that the current owner decided to keep it.

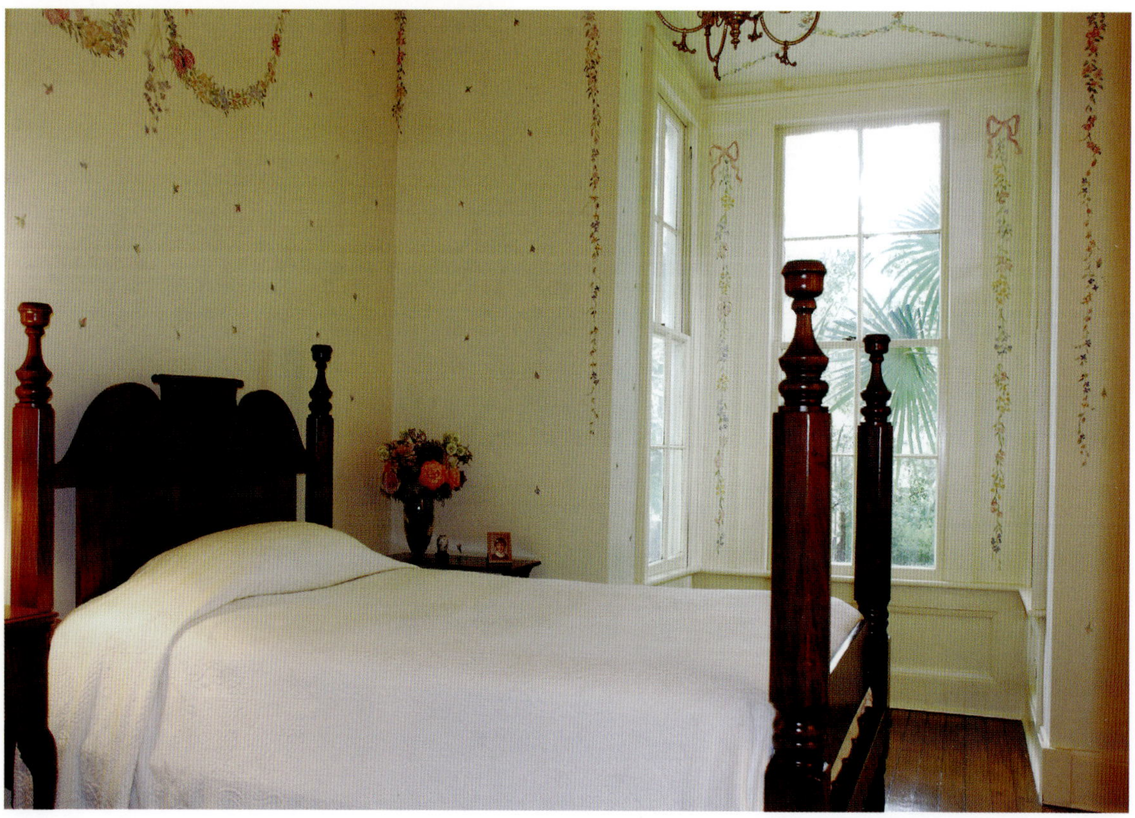

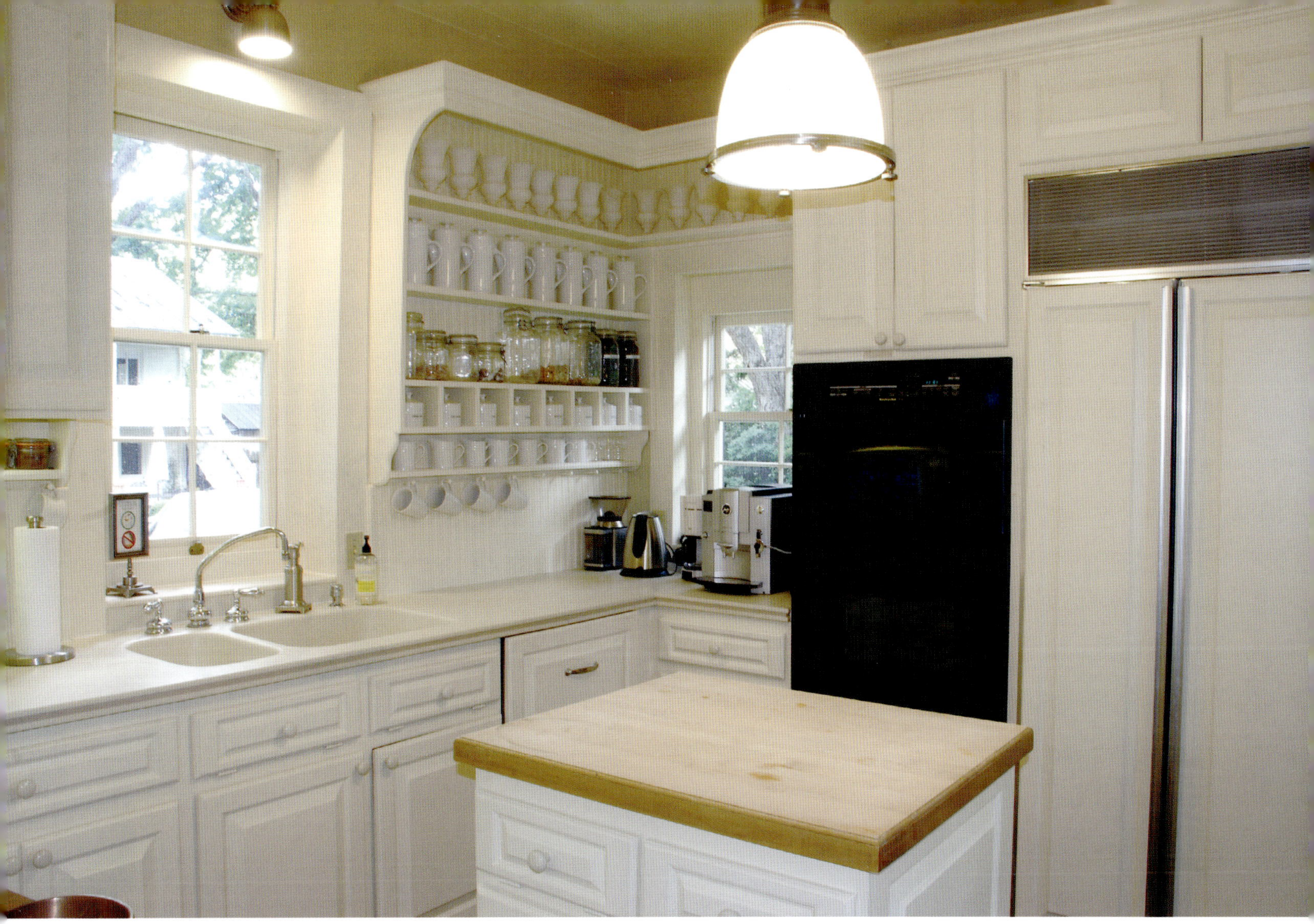

A light color scheme and open shelving create an airy mood in the cheerful, efficient kitchen.

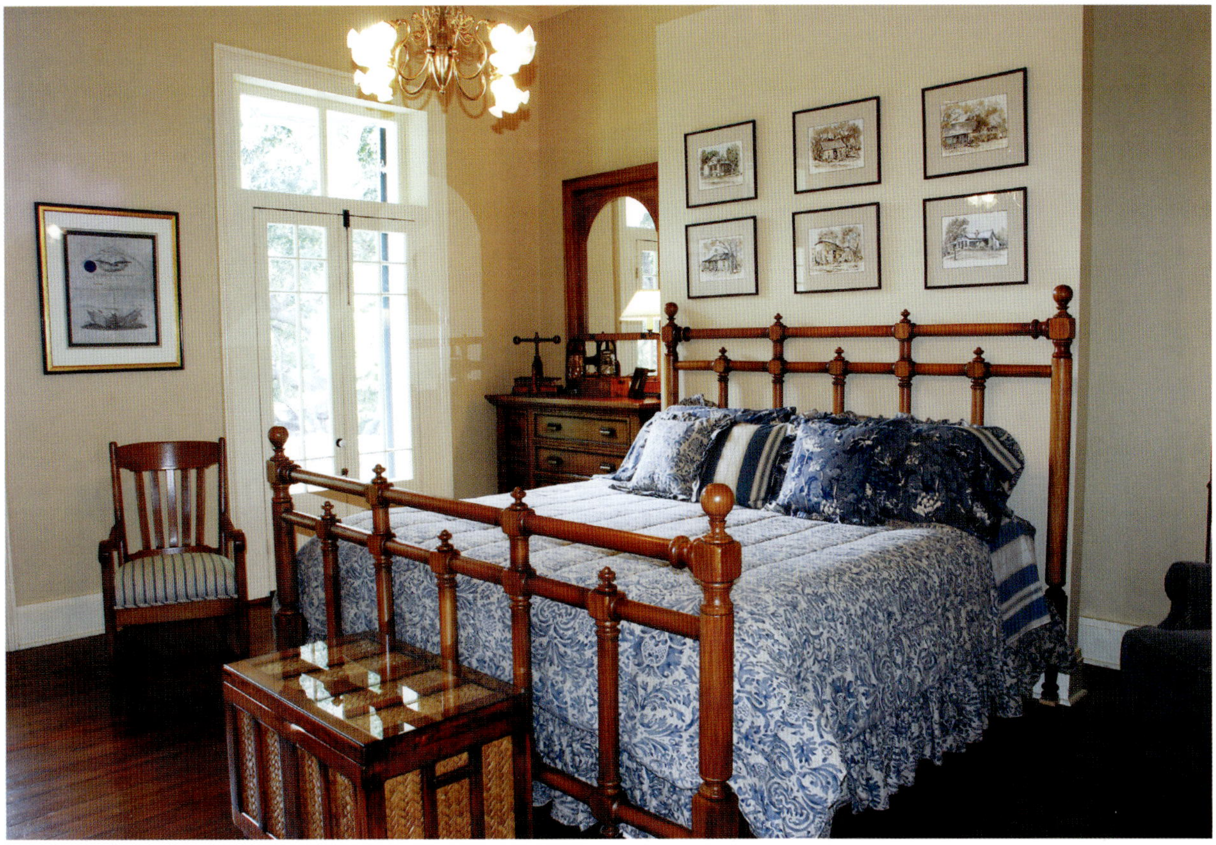

The bed in a guestroom backs up to a wall installed by an earlier owner to shield still-accessible French doors that open onto the second-story verandah.

Owner Curtis Johnson & his partner Leland Stone

Curtis Johnson, the owner of Chabot House. On the mantel is a photograph of his grandmother, Irma Gugenheim Oppenheim, who was born in a house nearby in 1910.

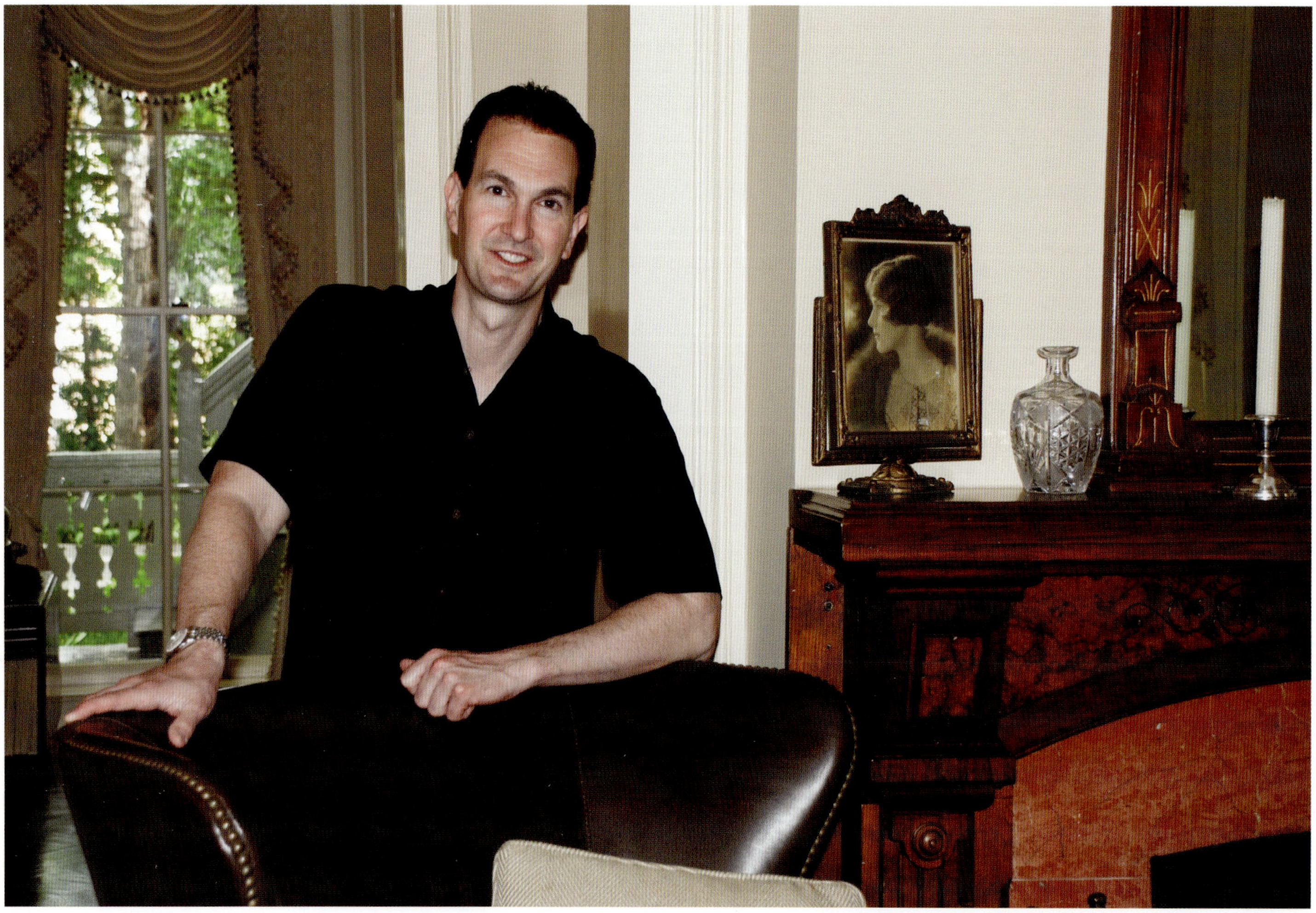

A portrait of the owner by a friend adorns a chest in the second-story hallway.

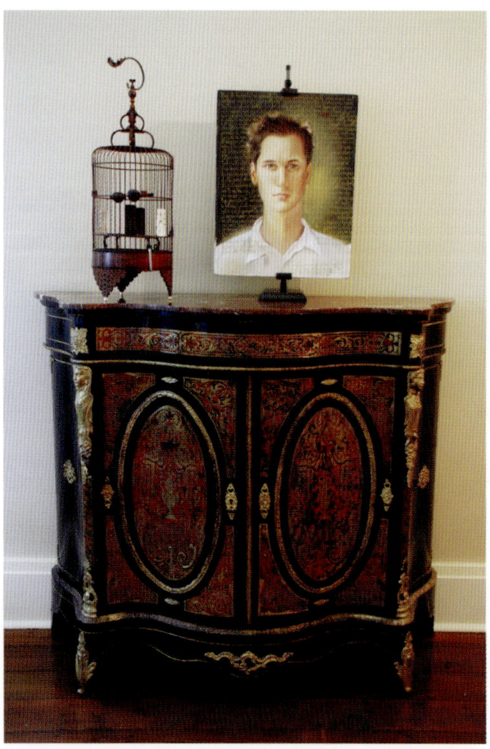

Right: Owner Curtis Johnson and his partner, Leland Stone, examine old books from their library. One—written by the son of the couple who built Chabot House, Frederick Charles Chabot—is ***With the Makers of San Antonio***, a history of the city's founding families.

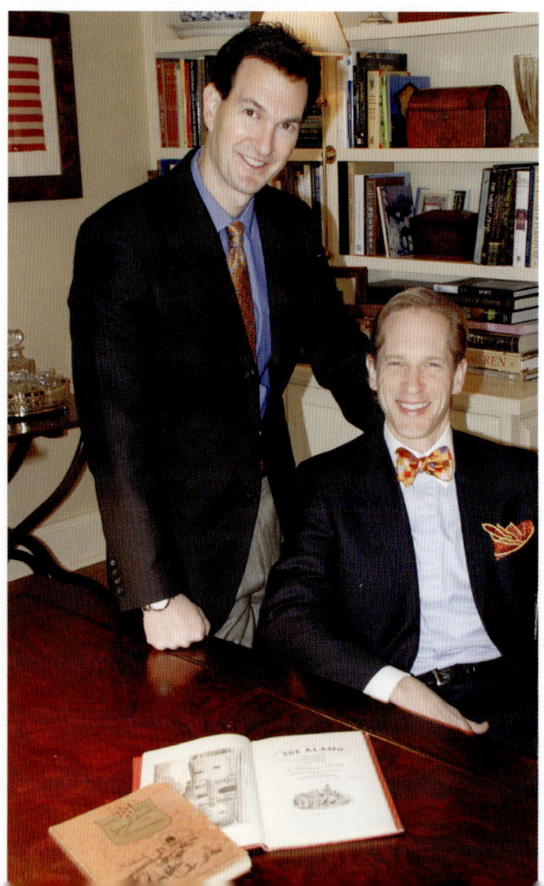

The Guesthouse

Enterprising Walter Mathis converted the carriage house at the rear of 403 Madison in the 1970s to a dwelling. His sister, Agnes Bain, who lived in the Ellis-Meusebach House at 414 King William Street—directly behind the carriage house—bought it and made it her guesthouse. In 1986, new owners of the Chabot House purchased it, restoring it to Chabot House property.

Curtis Johnson says, "When we bought the property in 2006, we removed the shag carpet in the lower level and replaced it with slate flooring. We added a pro-style *kitchenette* where all the cooking is done for major events held in the main house. Upstairs, the longleaf pine floor was refinished, using a natural stain that reveals the beauty of this wood. We installed slate floors in the second-story kitchen and bath. Like Chabot, all sinks and bathroom hardware are English imports." The carriage house is once again a Chabot House guesthouse.

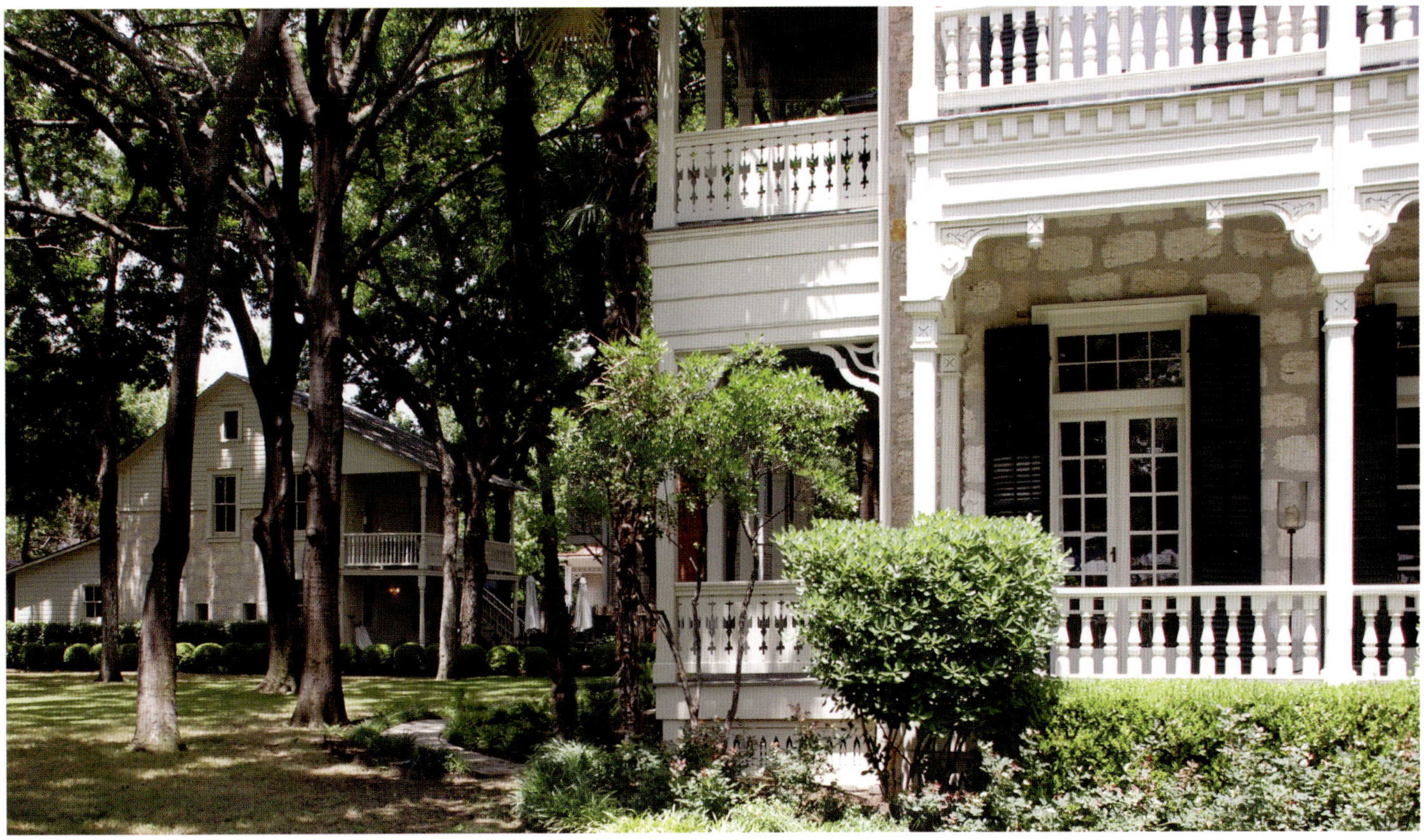

At the rear of the property stands a charming guest house, with its own patio. On the ground floor is a home office. (Above and following page)

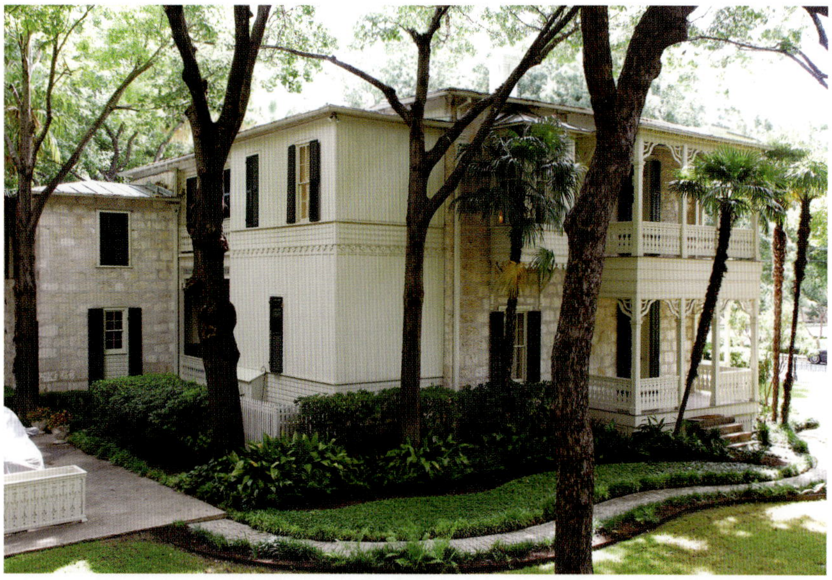

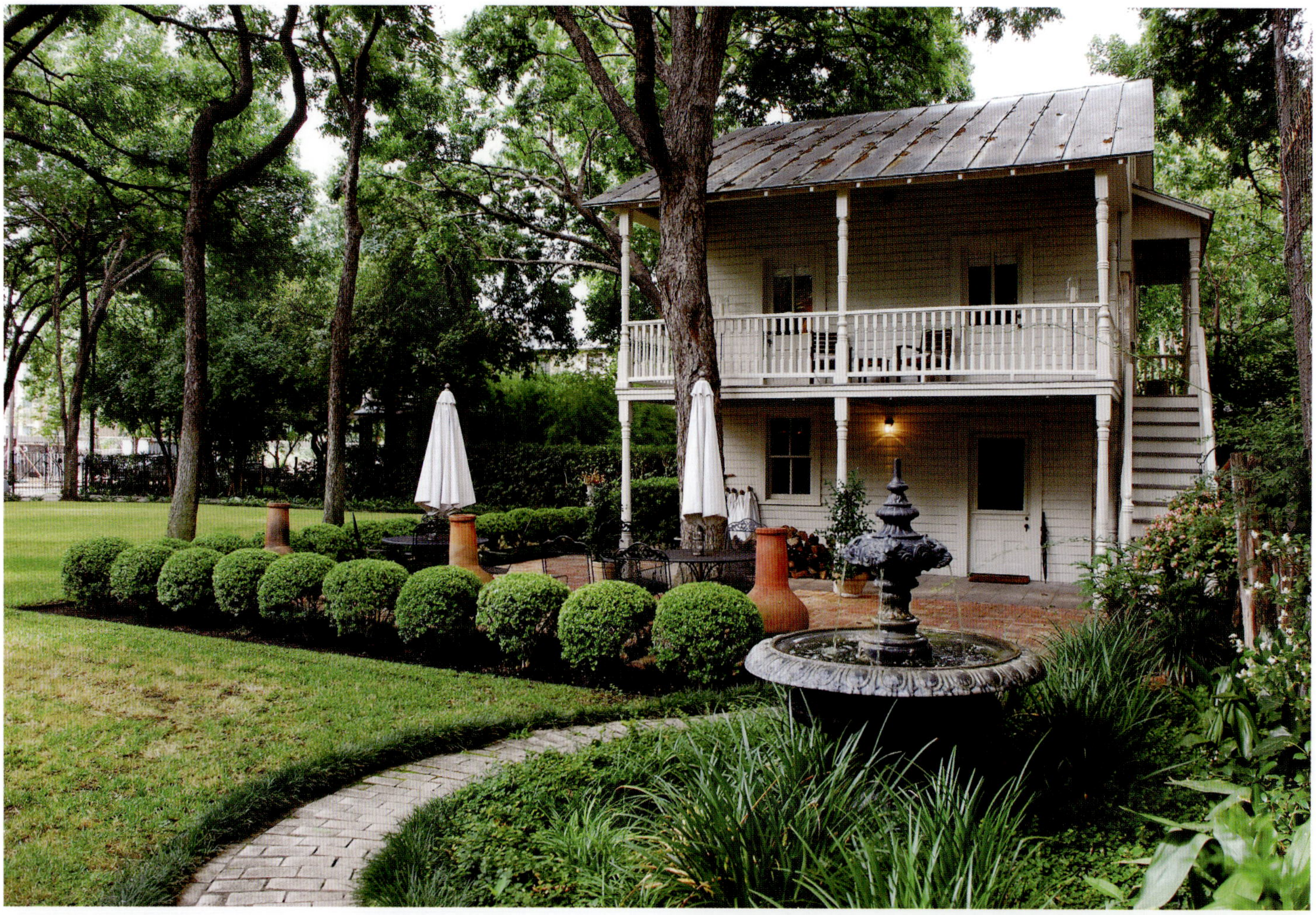

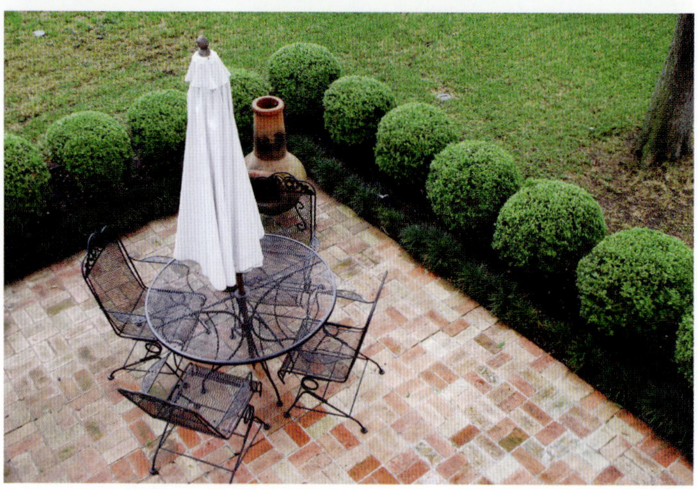

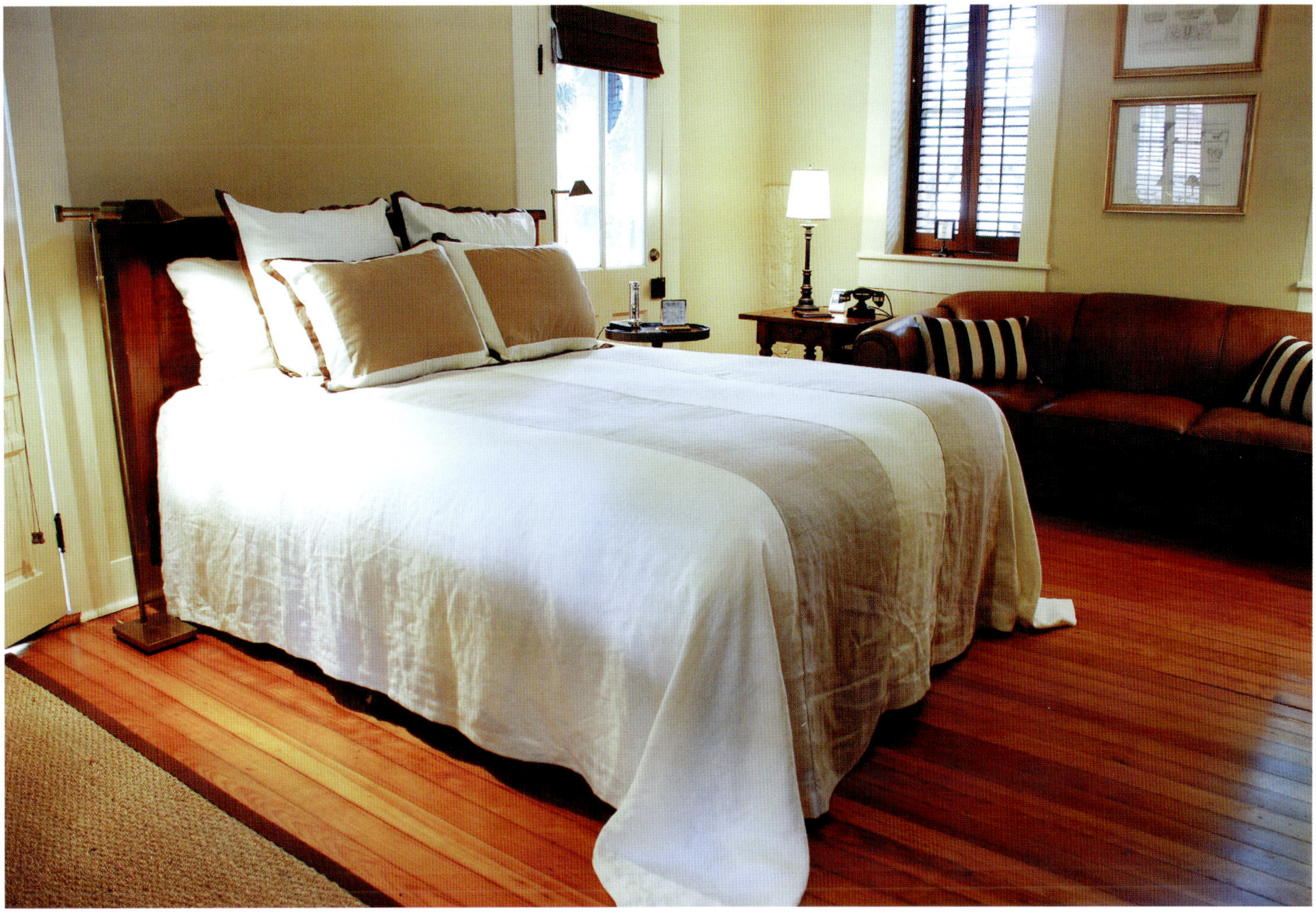

A guest suite—bedroom, bathroom, and kitchen—occupies the second story. The table-and-chairs double for games and dining.

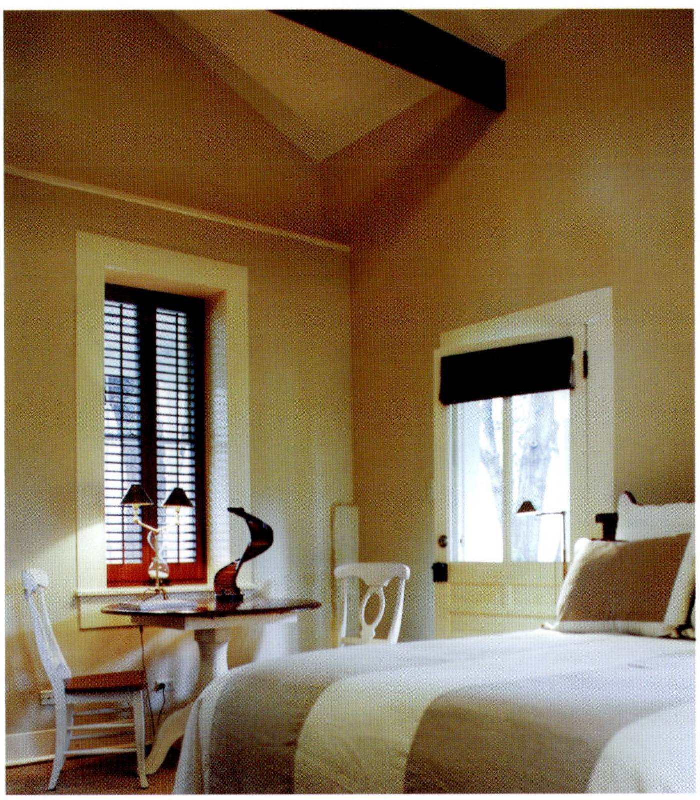

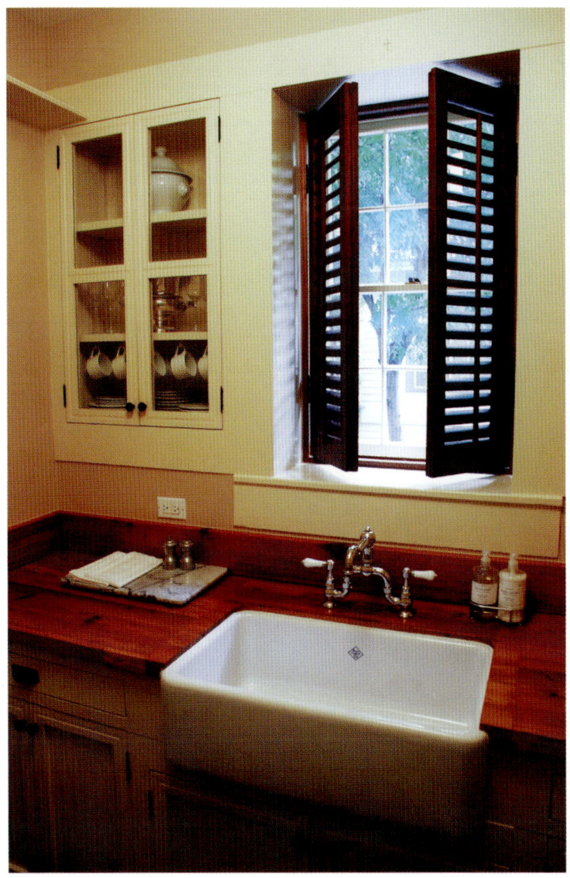

The chic compact kitchen is fully equipped and furnished.

4
Gallagher Ranch

Architect Christopher C. Hill's historic Gallagher Ranch in the Texas Hill Country is just a hop and a skip from San Antonio's bustling, downtown tourist-attracting River Walk. Technically in San Antonio, with its still wooded inner-city remnants of old ranches, the authentically old Gallagher Ranch seems worlds away, especially in the springtime. Then, the drive from the main road to the ranch house passes through fields carpeted with bright yellow flowers and beautiful bluebonnets—the distinctive flower extolled in countless Texas landscape paintings and photographs. The Lady Byrd Johnson Wildflower Center keeps attention focused on these and other treasured native wildflowers that are to Texans what turning autumn leaves are to New Englanders. The late President Lyndon Johnson called national attention time and again to the scenic Texas Hill Country which he loved. *Architectural Digest* quotes Chris Hill as pronouncing it "a very comfortable place in which to be."

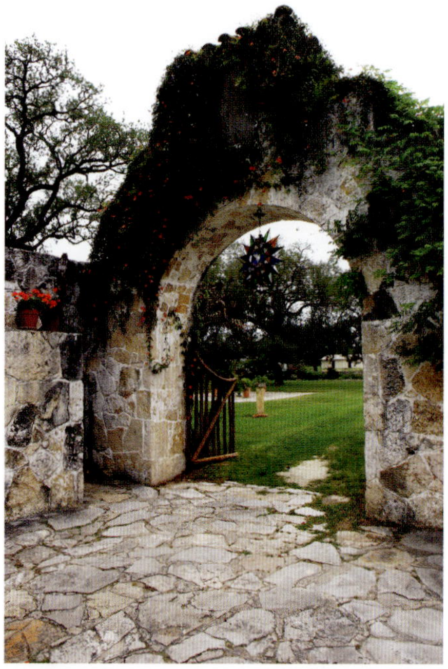

A handsome arched gateway opens onto an expansive rear garden.

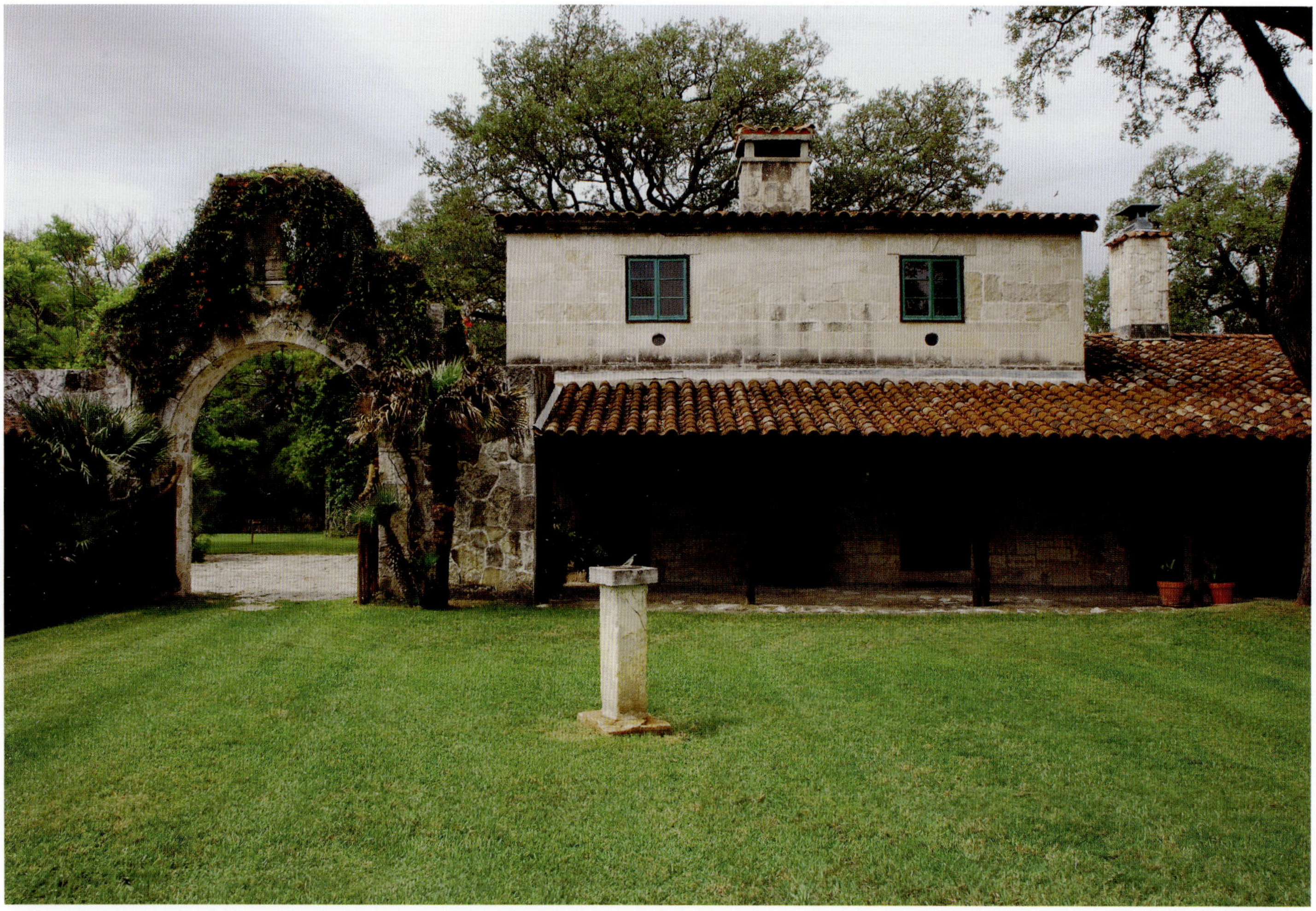

The original ranch house dominates the courtyard at the Gallagher Ranch, restored by Architect Christopher Hill. *Photographs by Barbara Justice*

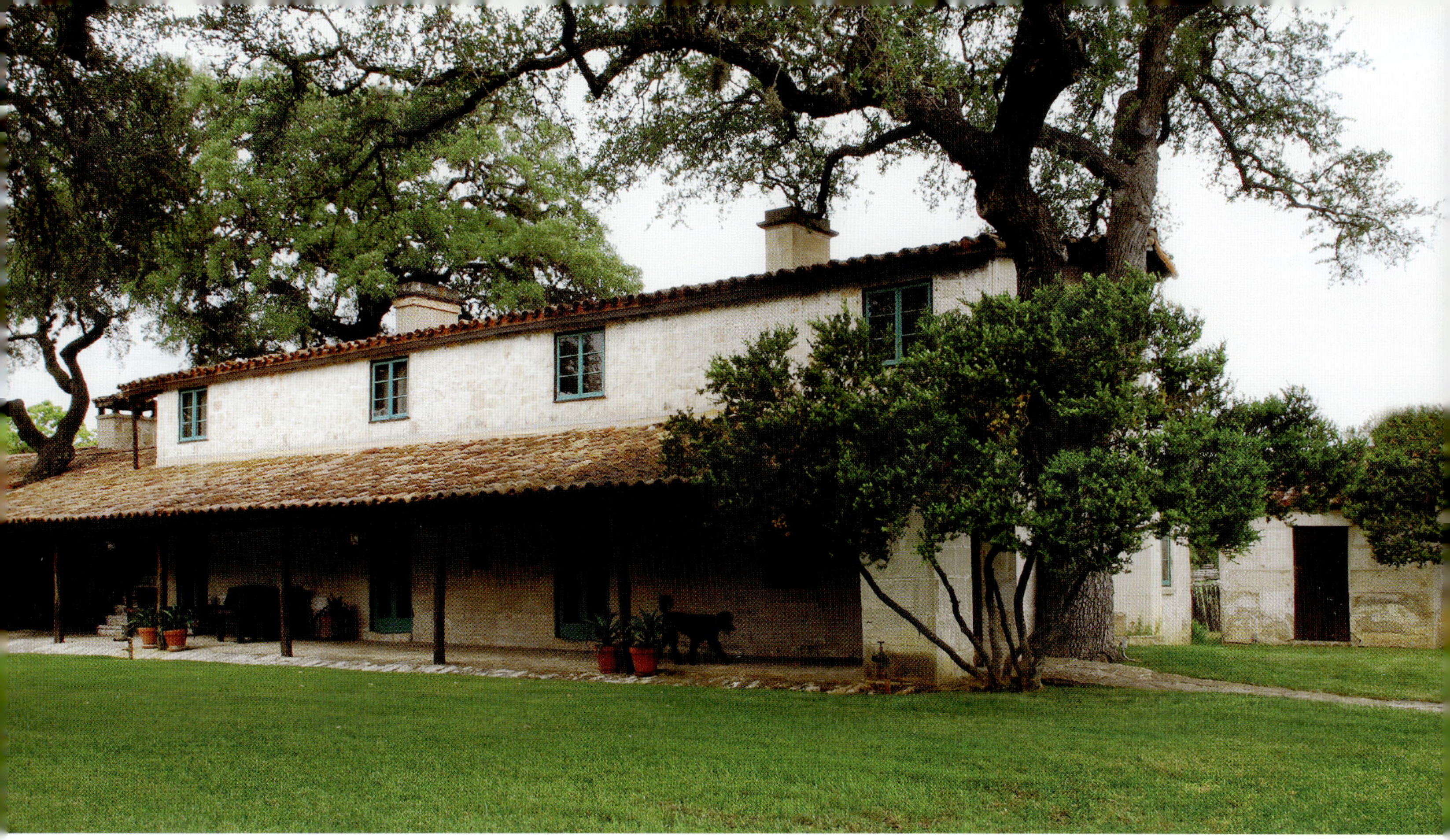

Bunkhouses in the hacienda style were added to the left and right of the original main house when earlier owners decided to create a dude ranch. Porches were added in the 1930s.

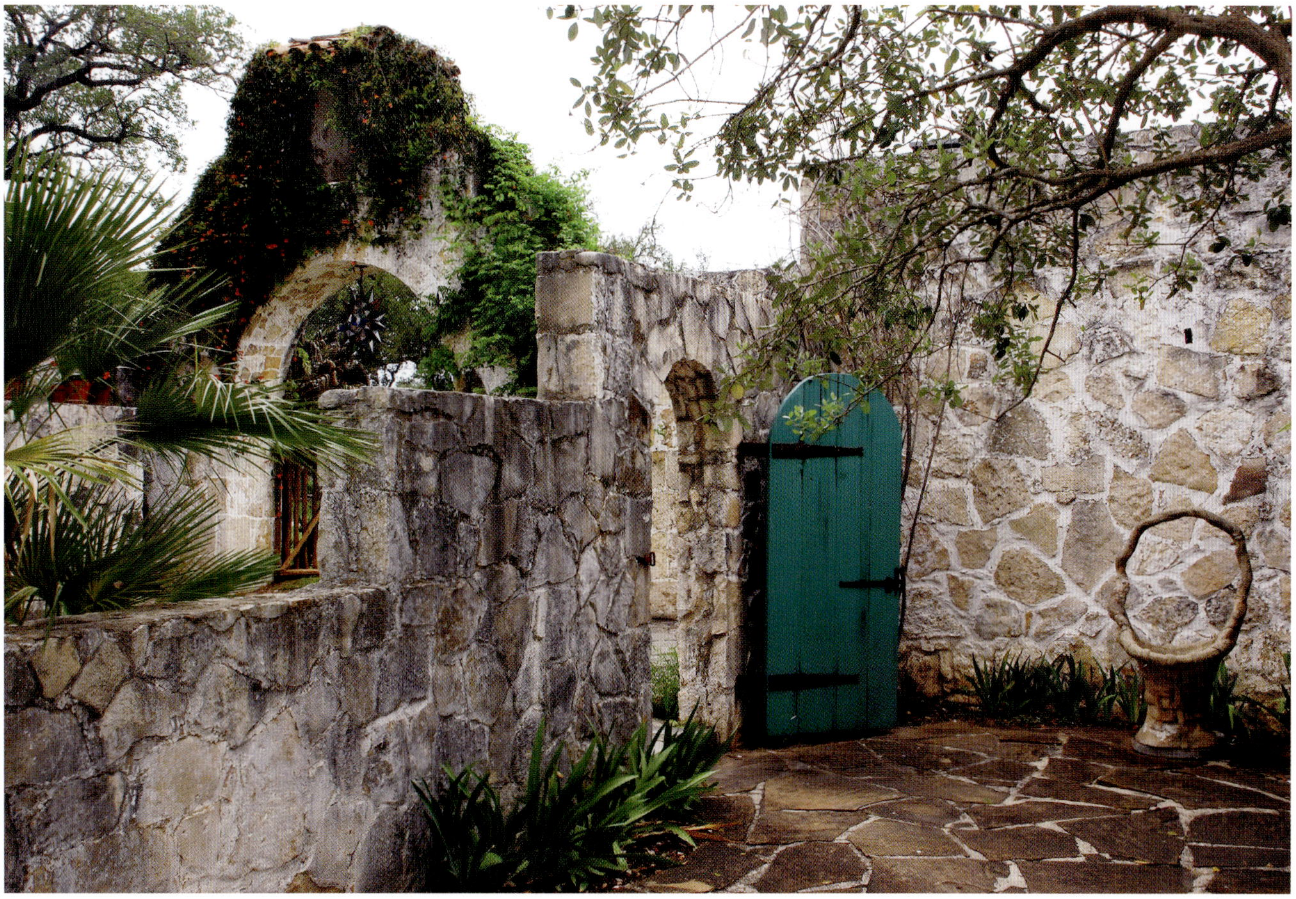

A brightly painted gate adds color to a small courtyard.

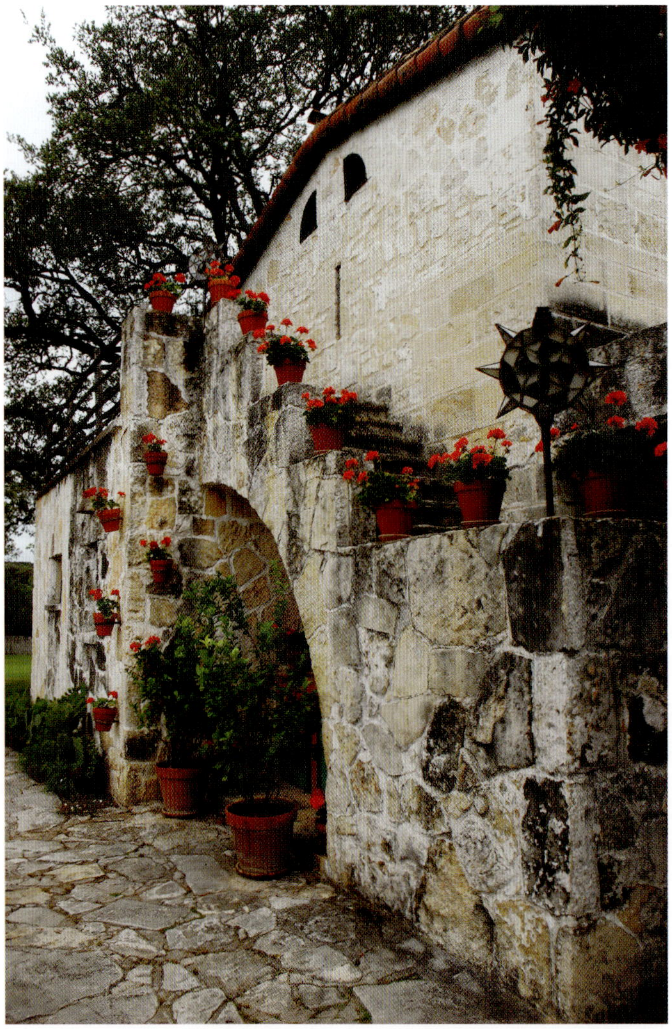

Pots of geranium highlight stairs leading to a second story guest suite.

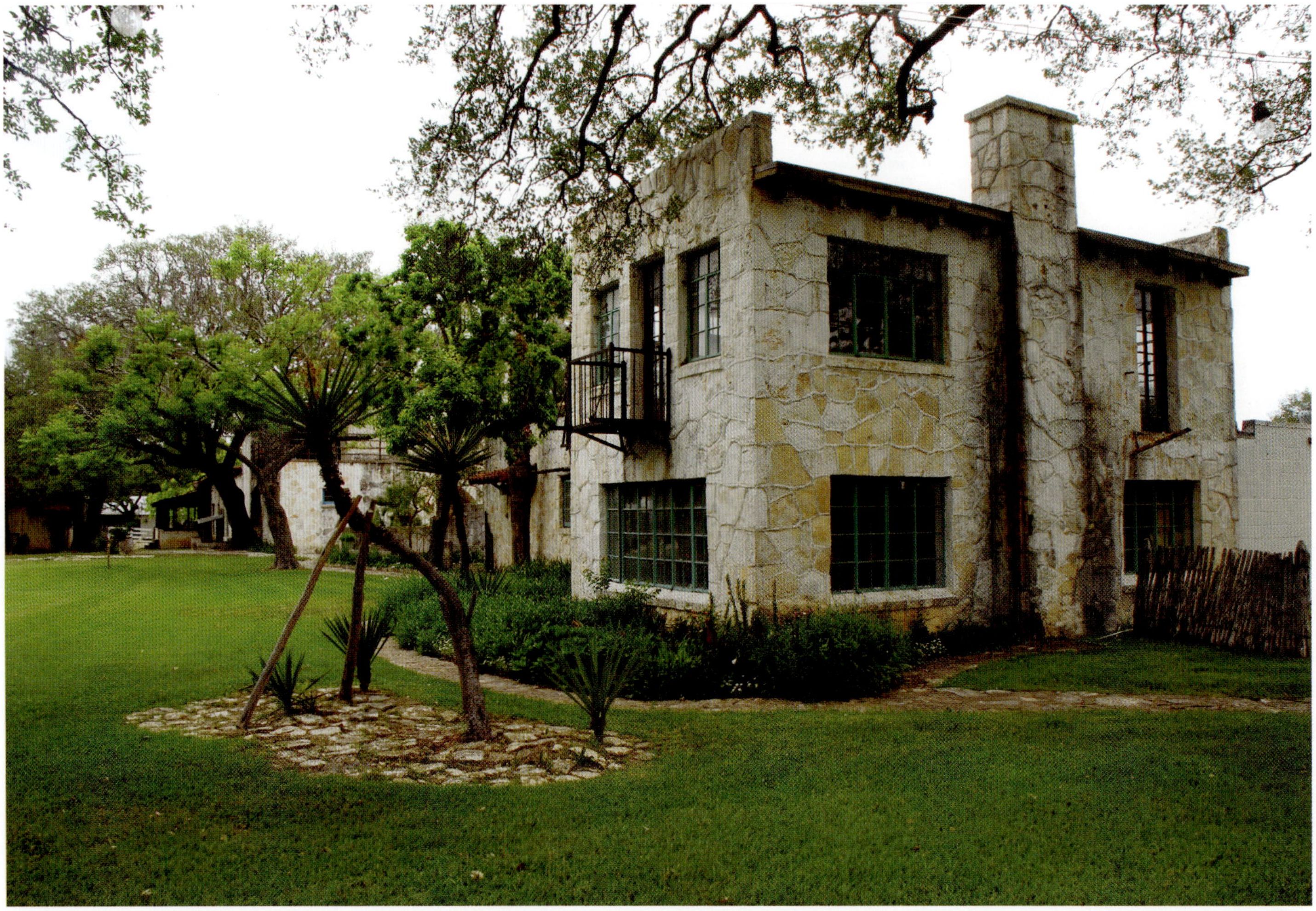

An addition, possibly dating to the 1940s, seamlessly fits in with the older structures.

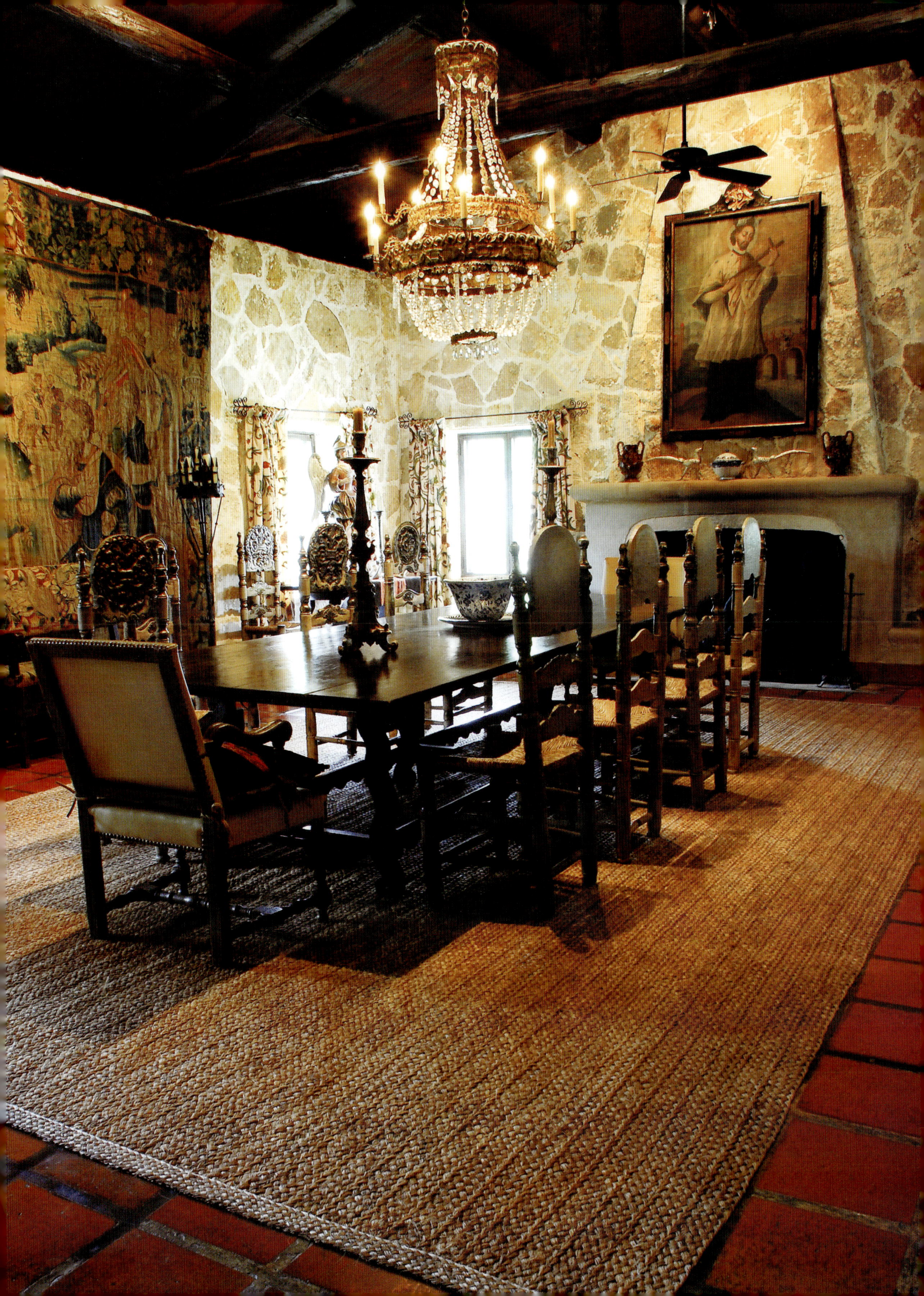

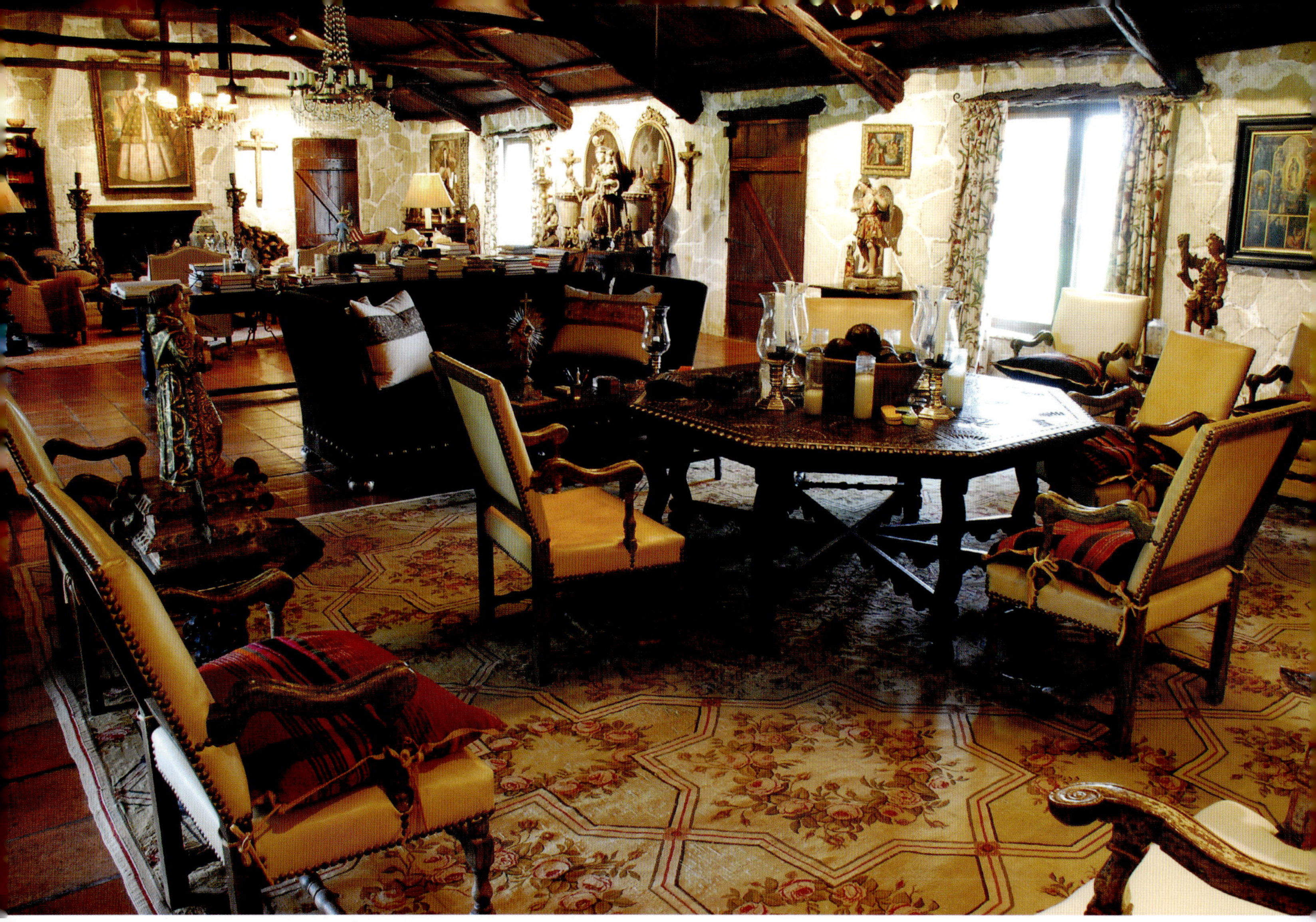

The living room occupies a great portion of the original hacienda. Floors are Mexican Saltillo tile. A discerning mix of Italian, French, and Mexican antique furnishings contrasts chicly with peeled cedar beams and rafters.

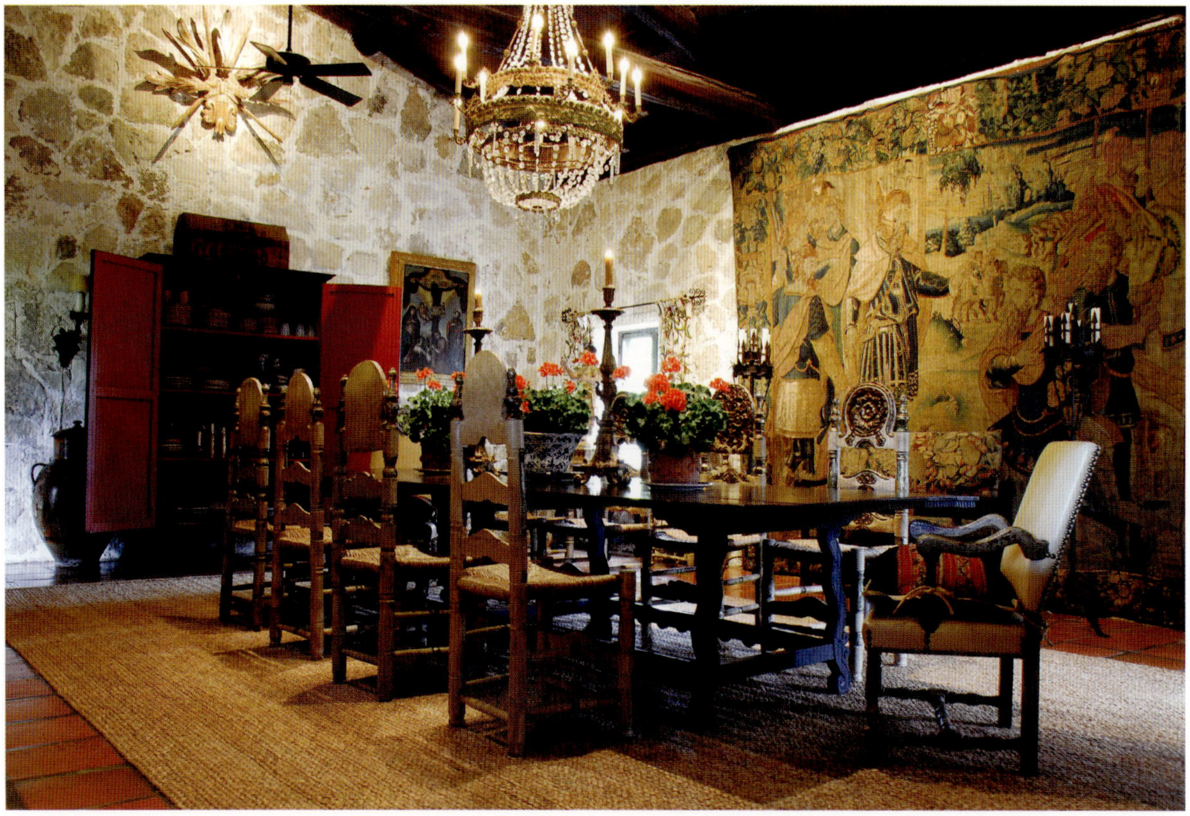

Native timbers and caliche (limestone) stone walls add a baronial air to the dining room. An antique tapestry hangs against an exterior wall. A large-scaled painted cabinet stores dinnerware at one end of the room. On the opposite wall is a commanding fireplace. Overhead hangs an eighteenth century Italian chandelier.

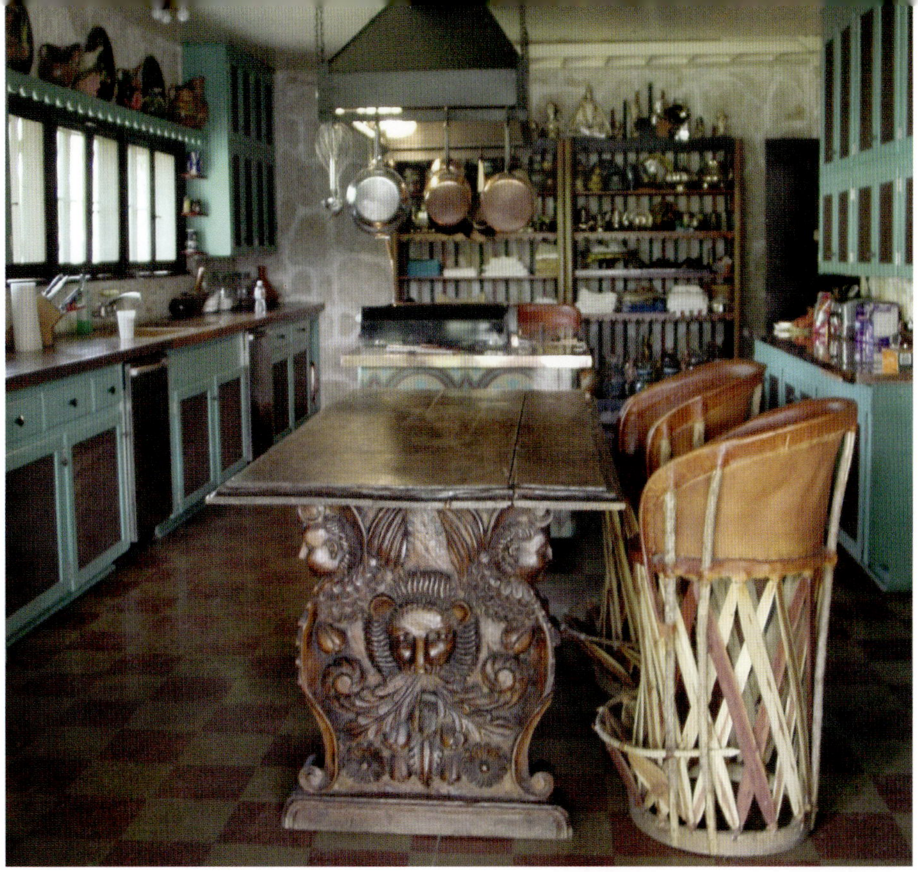

In the kitchen, cabinets are painted a turquoise color discovered by Hill during the renovation. Old tile marks guided the painting of the floor.

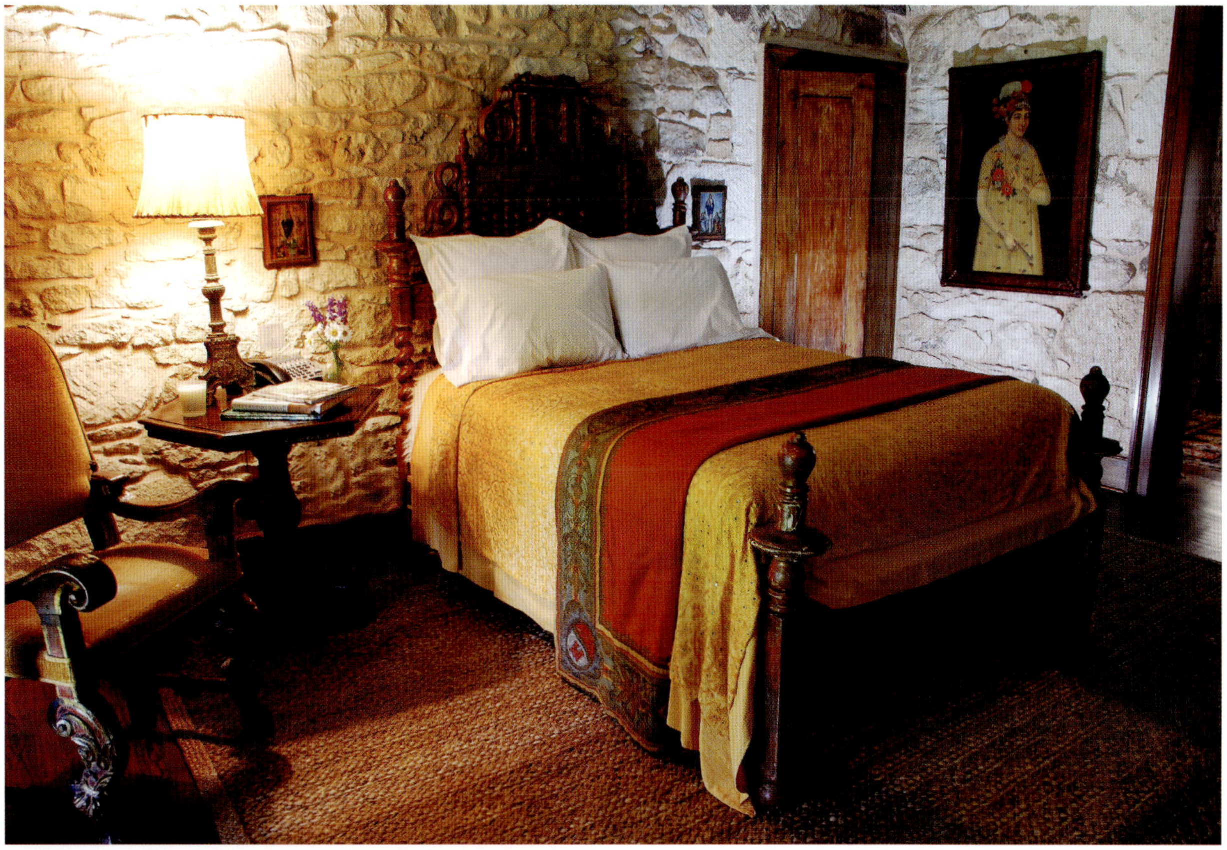

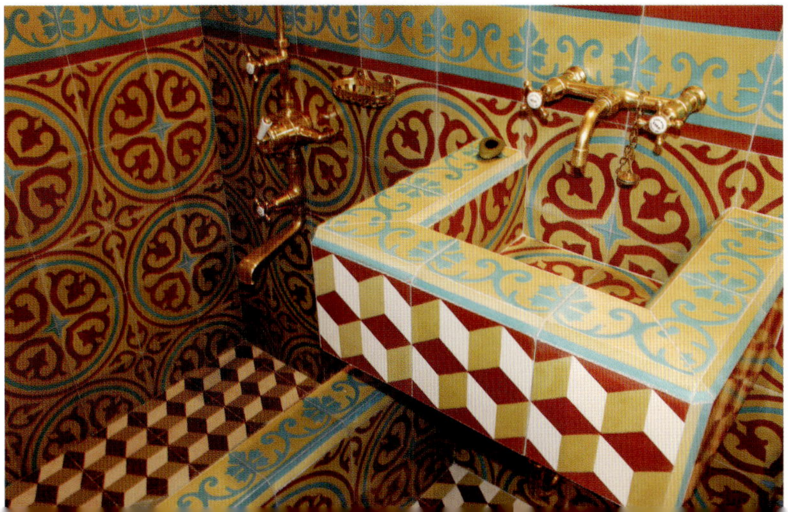

Typical of the gracious guest bedroom suites in the bunkhouses is this room, color-coordinated with its handsomely tiled bathroom.

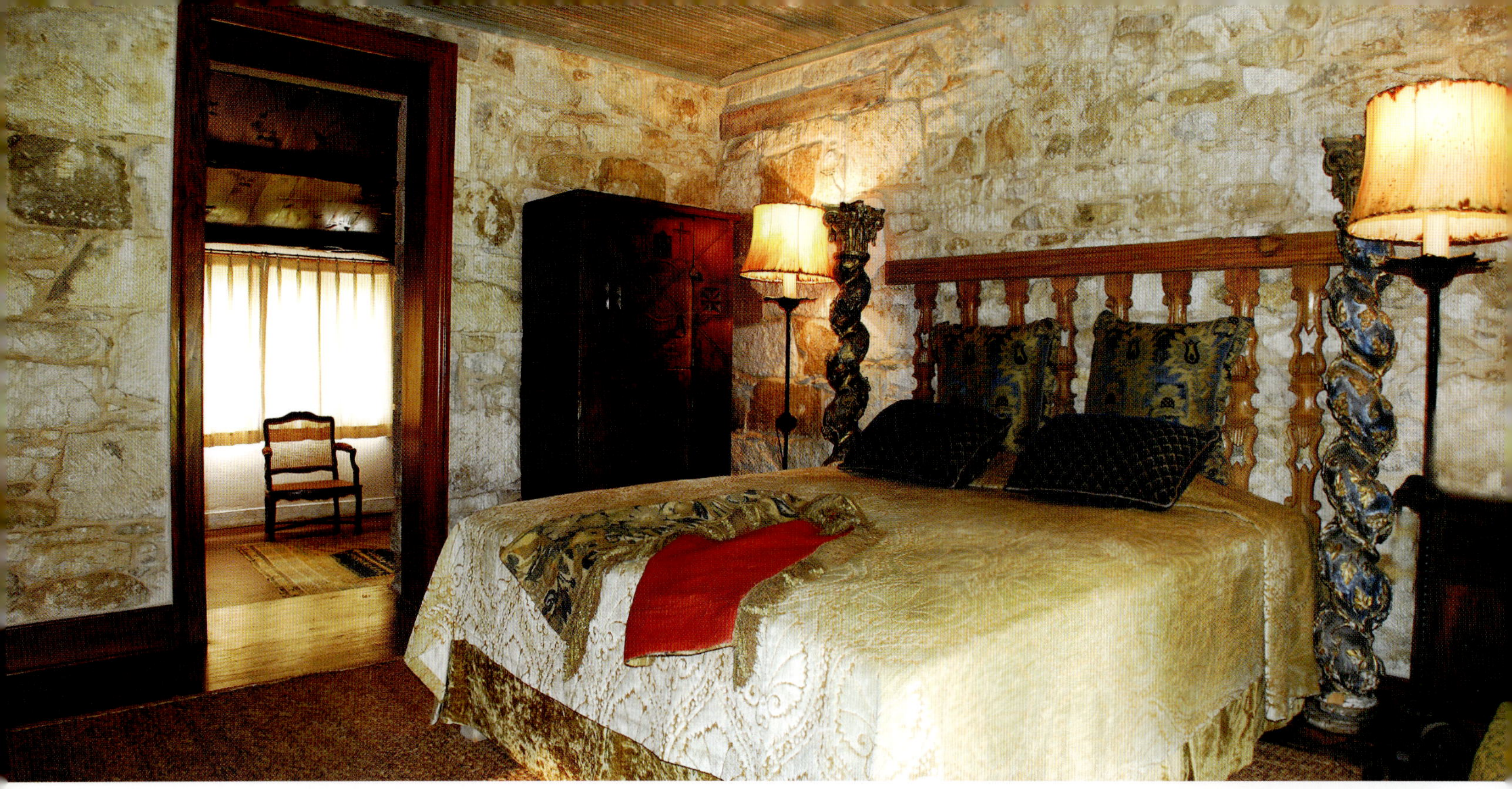

Each guestroom suite is uniquely decorated, and en suite bathroom tiles are different colors and patterns.

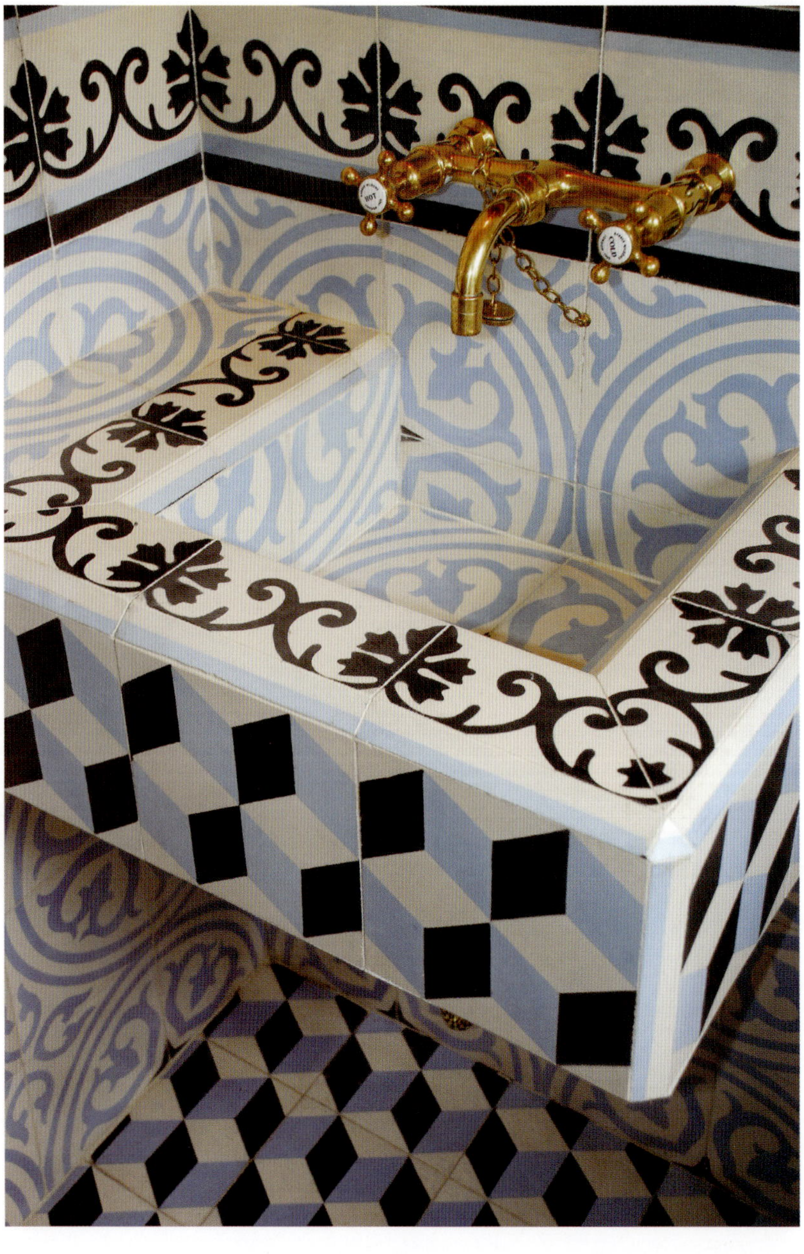

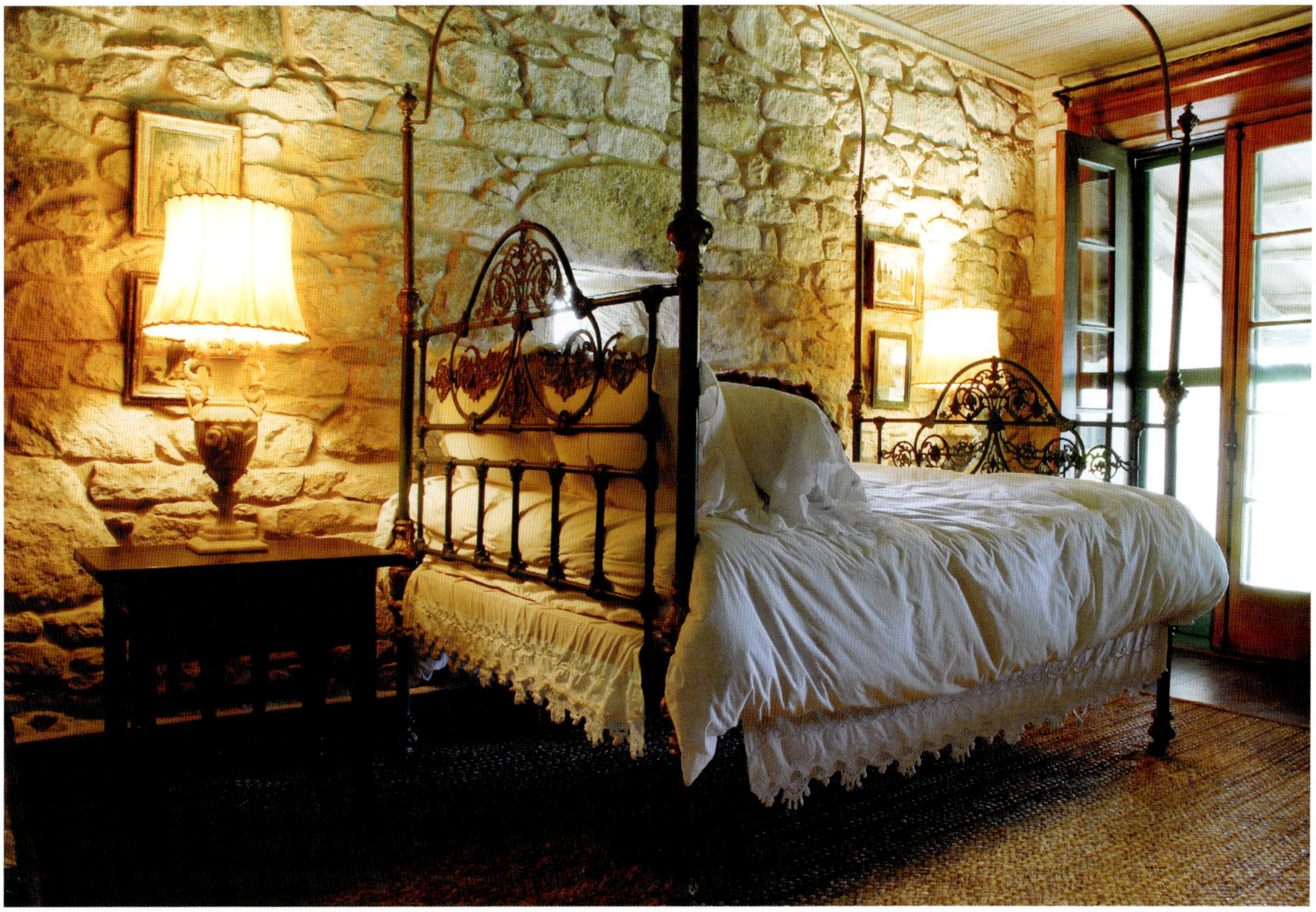

In one guestroom, a tall-poster wrought iron bed is placed campaign-style along one wall, leaving ample walking space. It almost obscures the small slit-like opening in the wall—an opening for a rifle when roving Indian bands attacked.

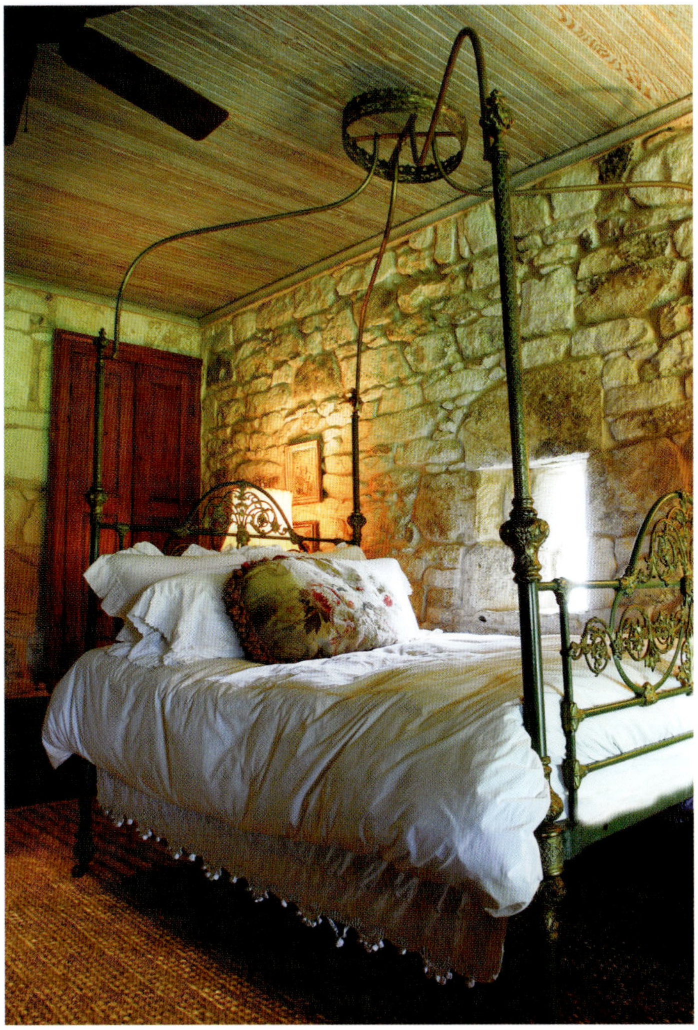

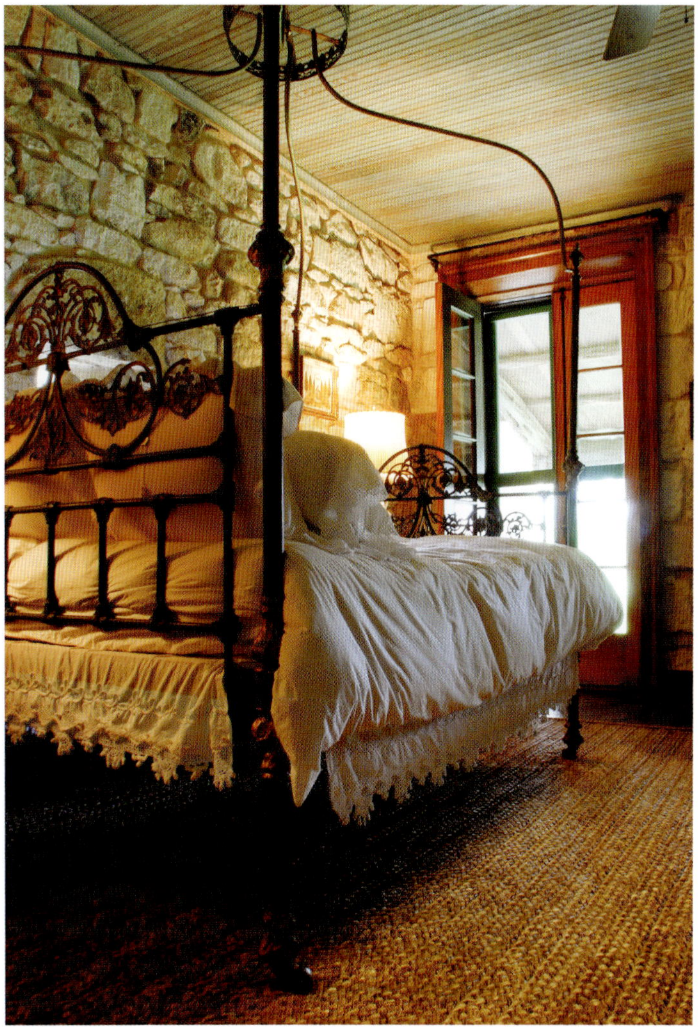

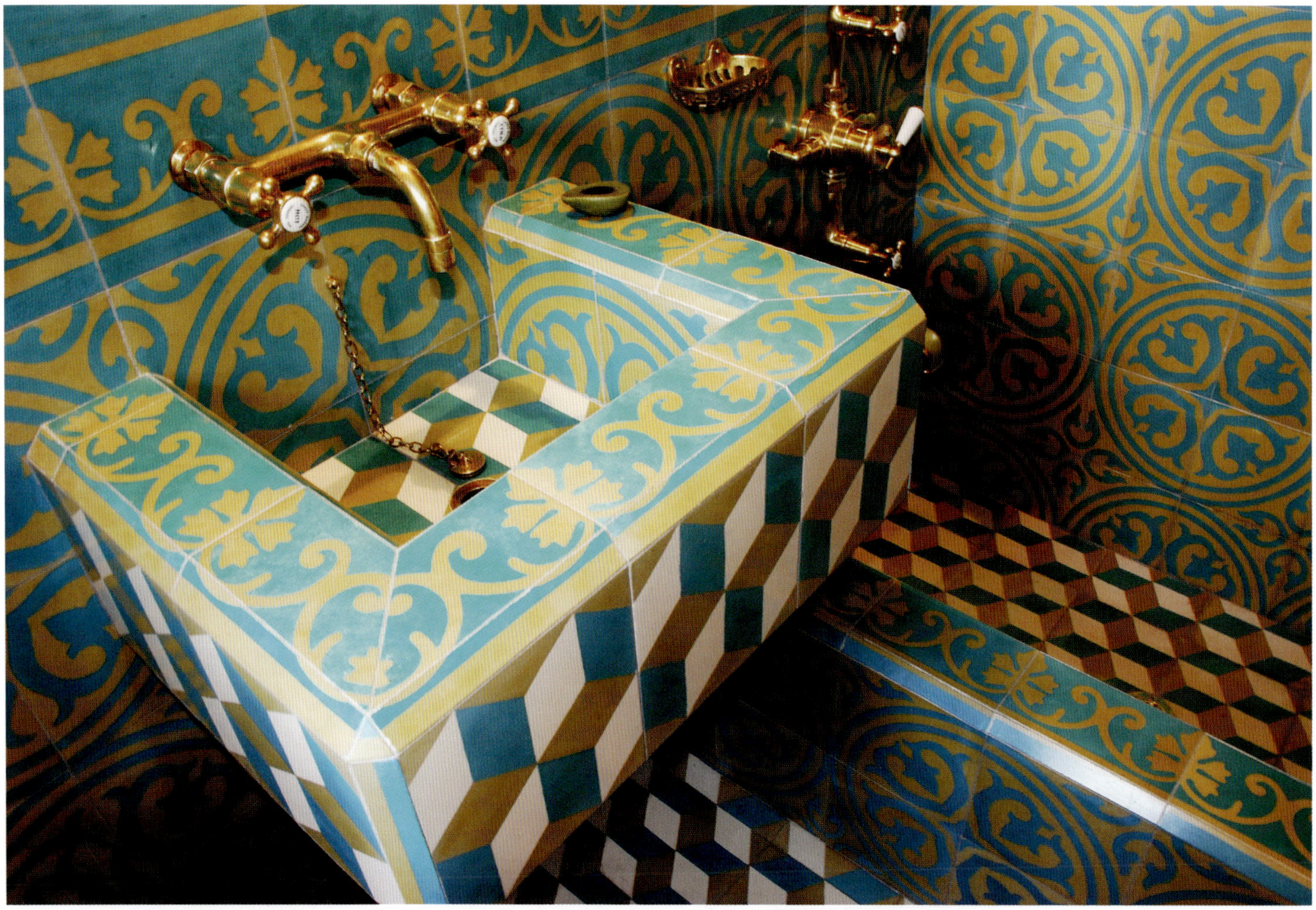

Antique cement tiles in the guest bathrooms were inspired by ancient Spanish-Moorish patterns.

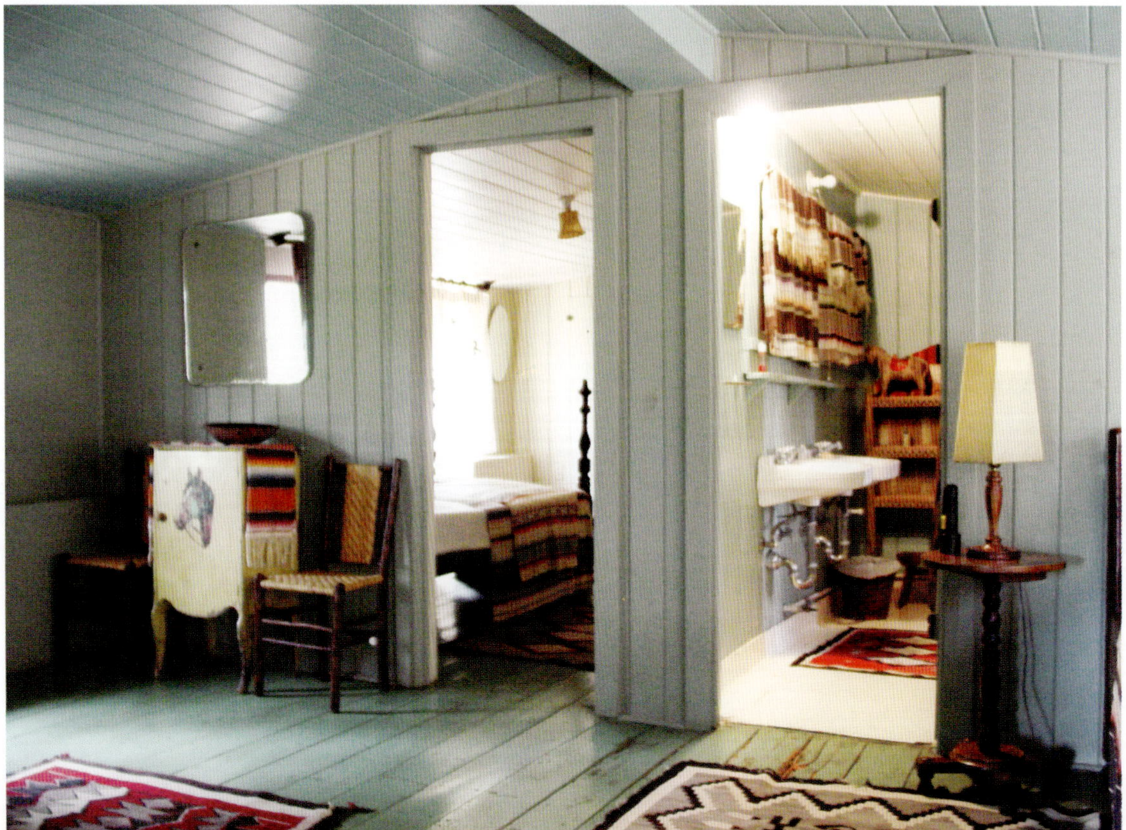

On the second floor of one of the bunkhouses is a suite designed for children, replete with cowboy motifs galore. (Above and opposite page)

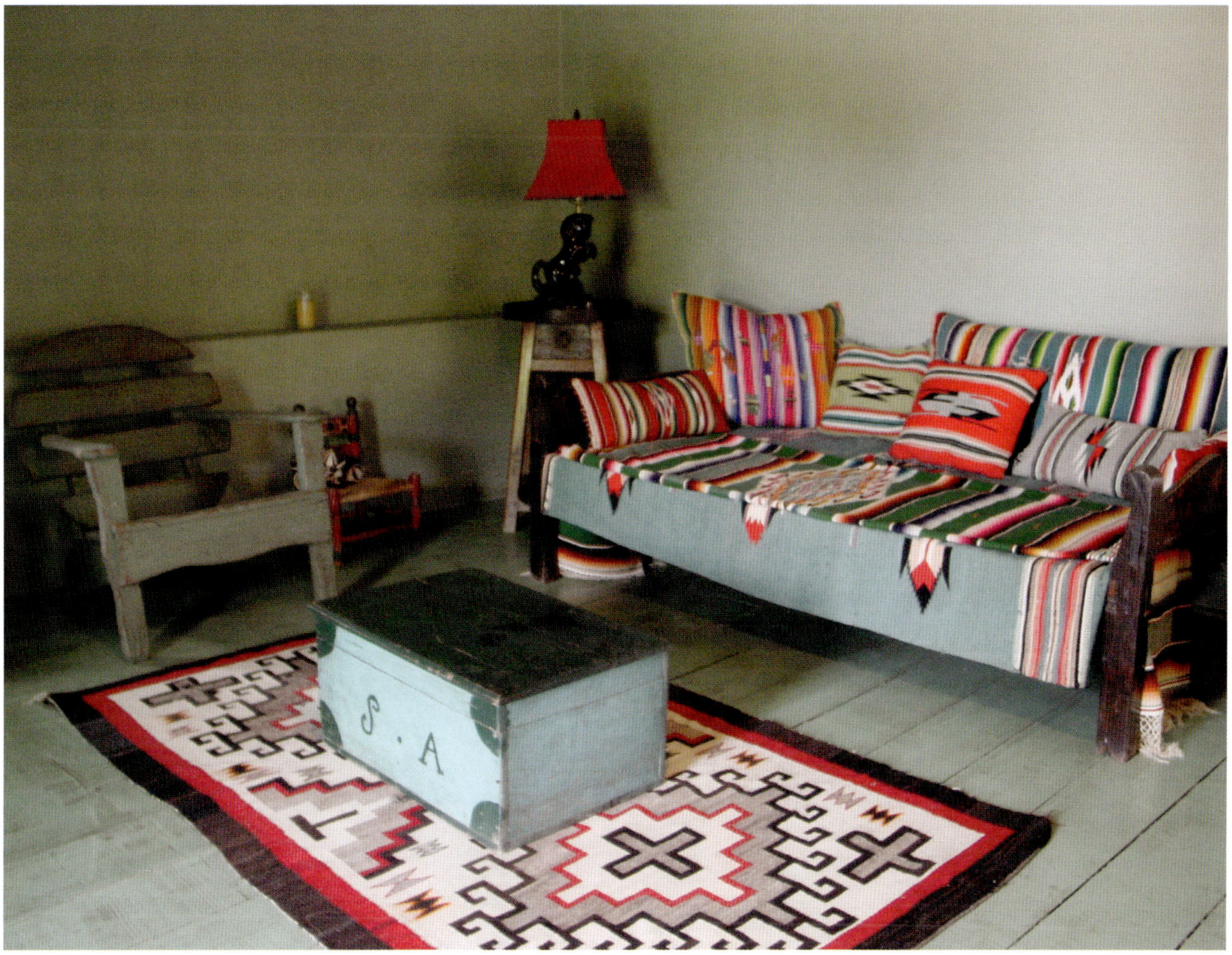
S . A

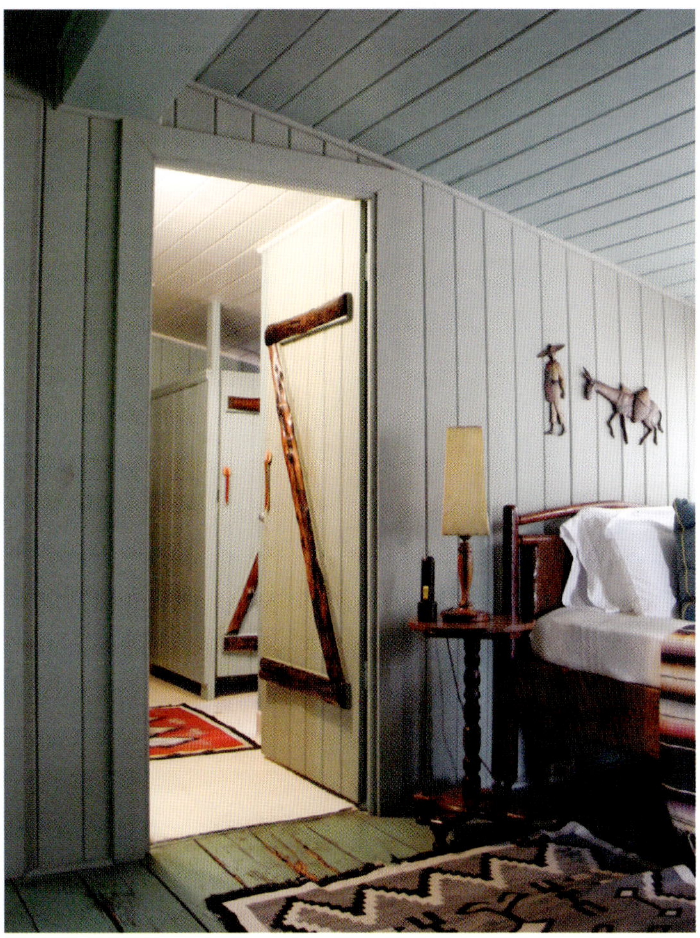

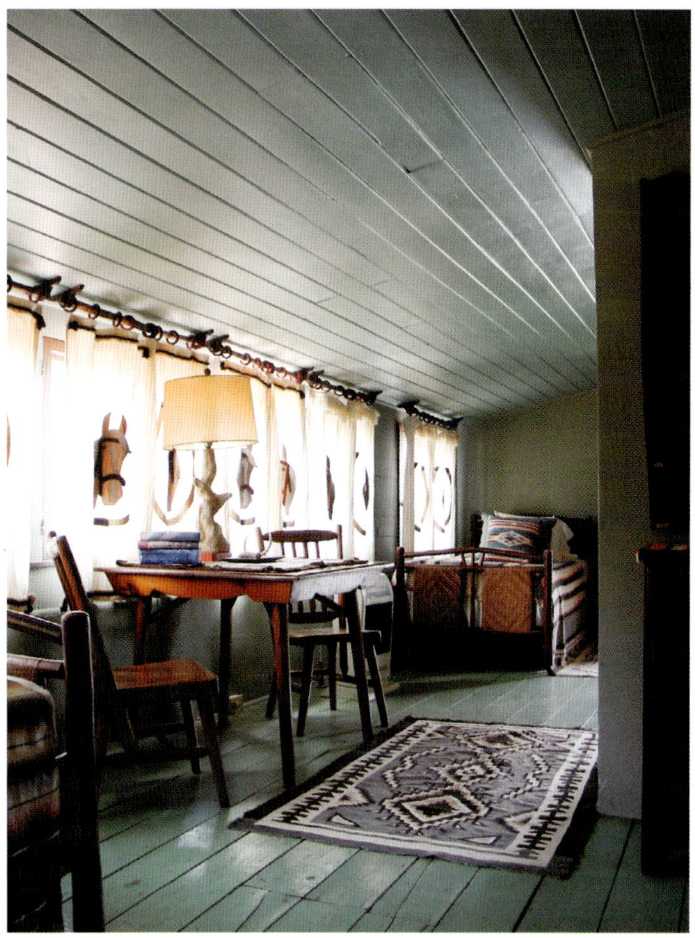

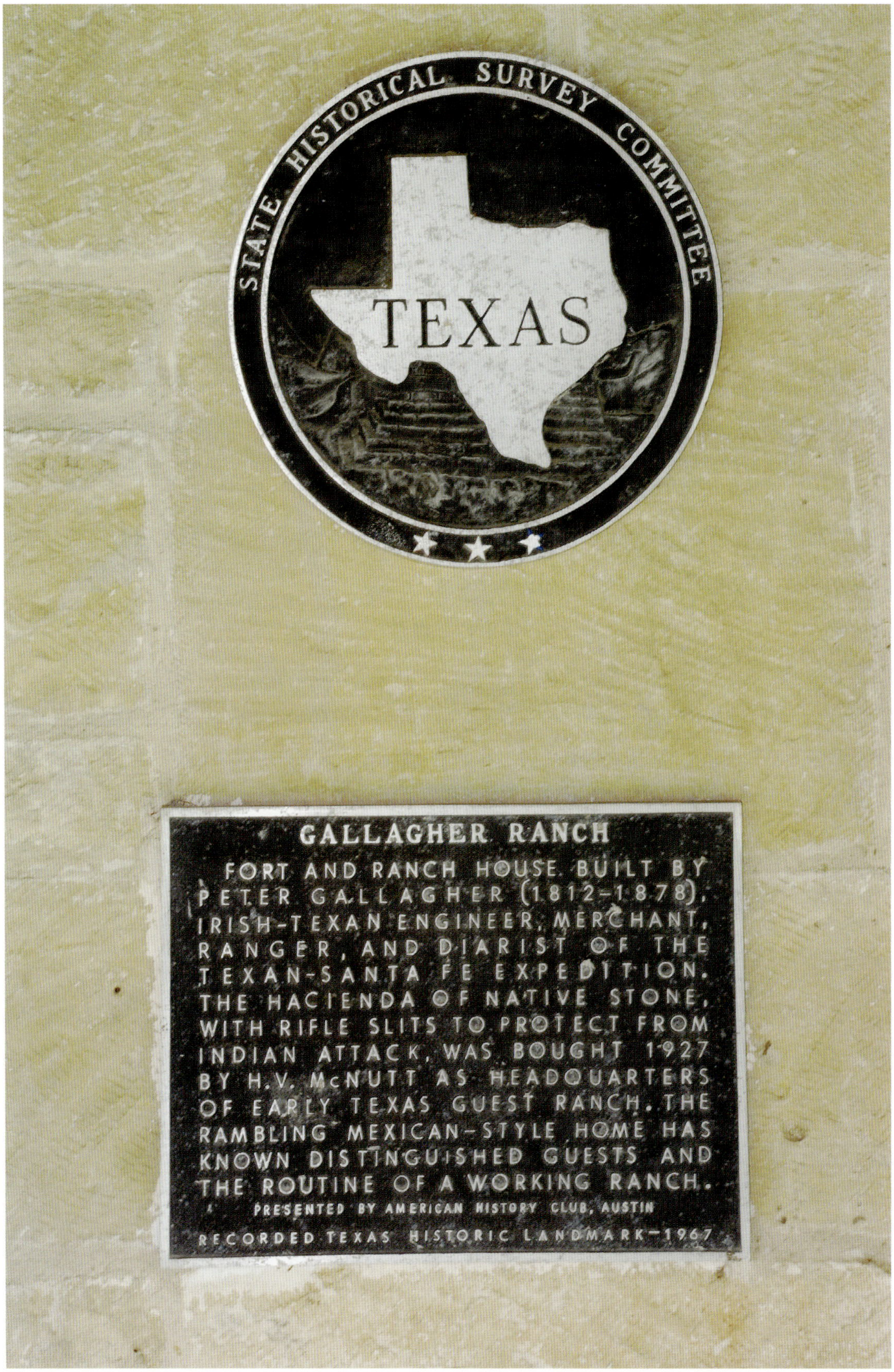

A plaque designates the Gallagher Ranch a landmark site.

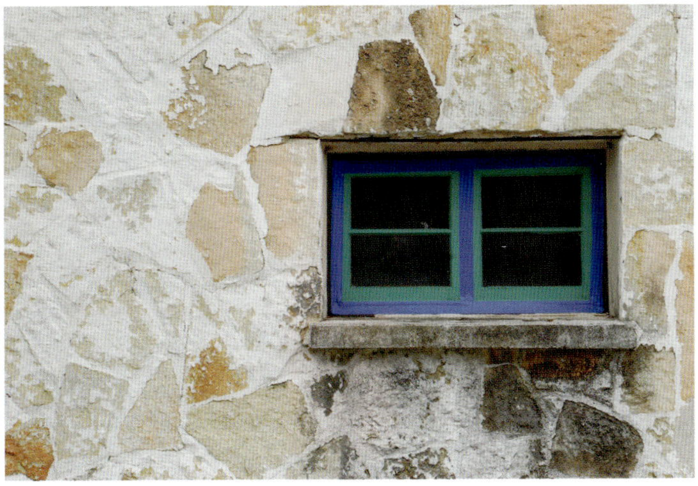

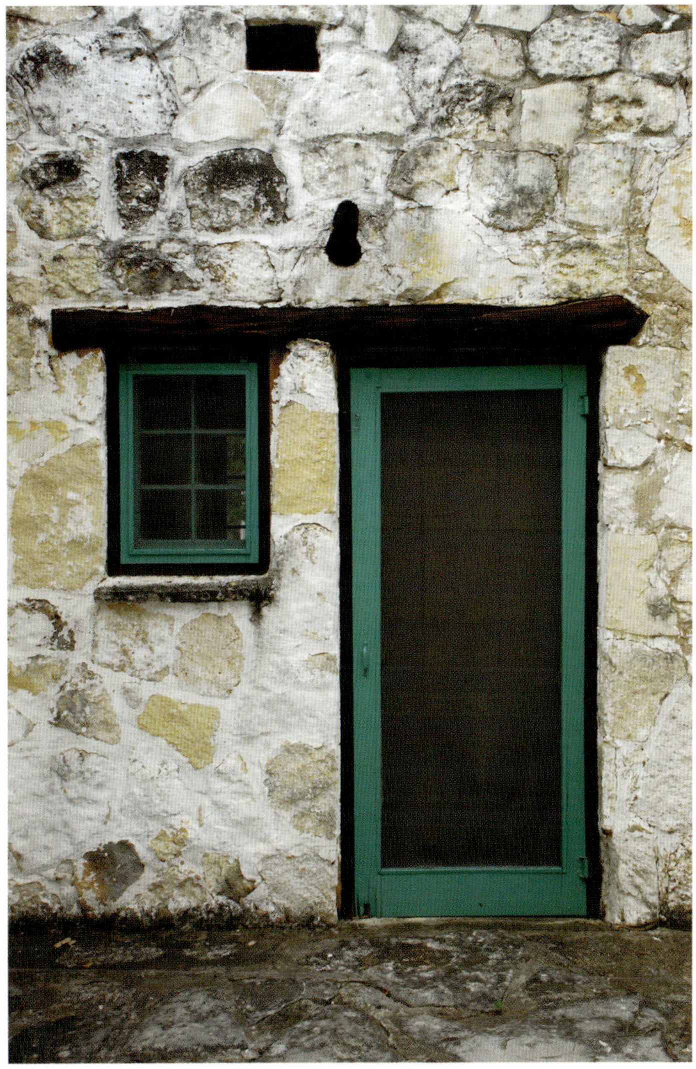

Bright paint accentuates doors and windows, contrasting vividly with the native caliche stone walls.

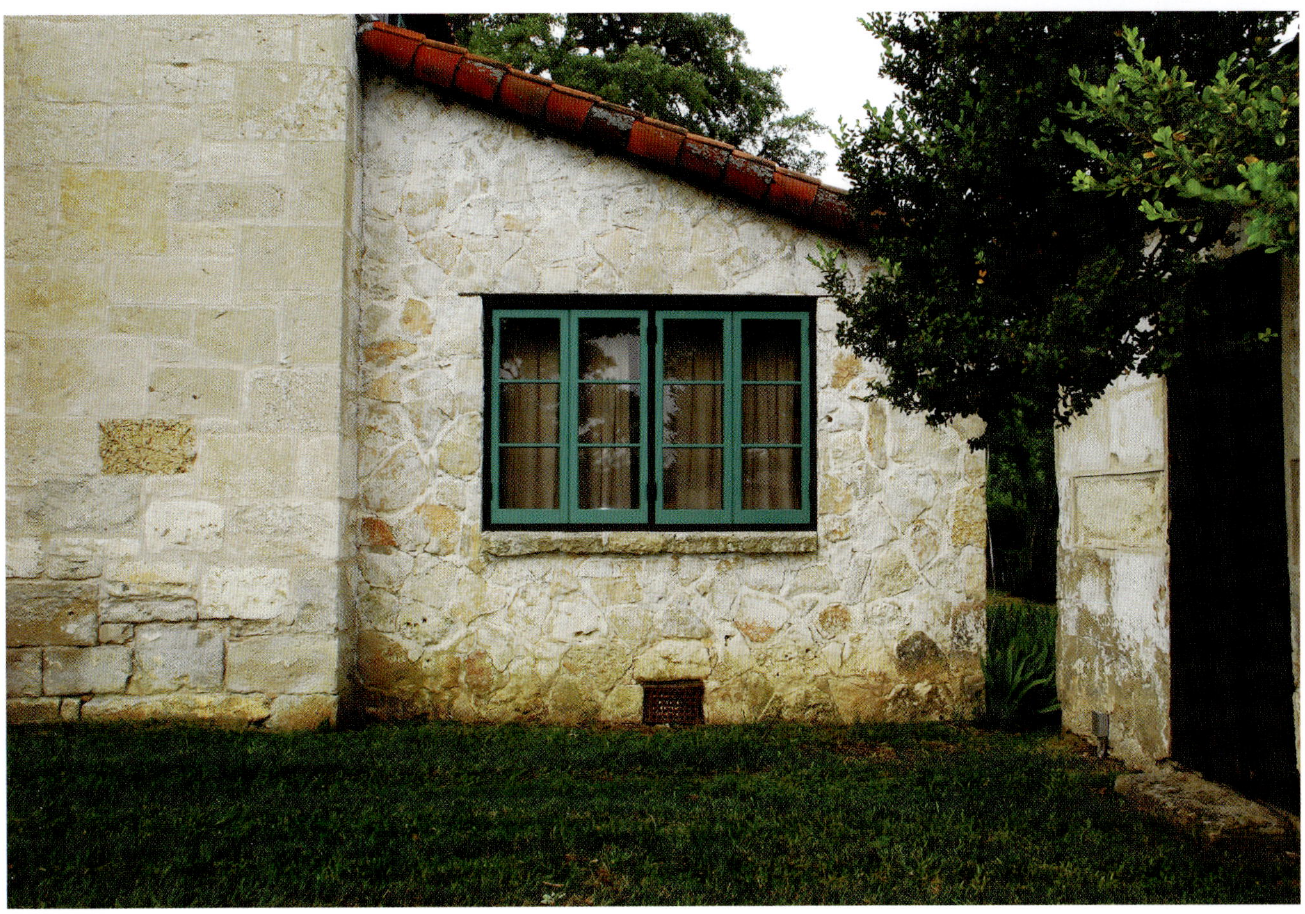

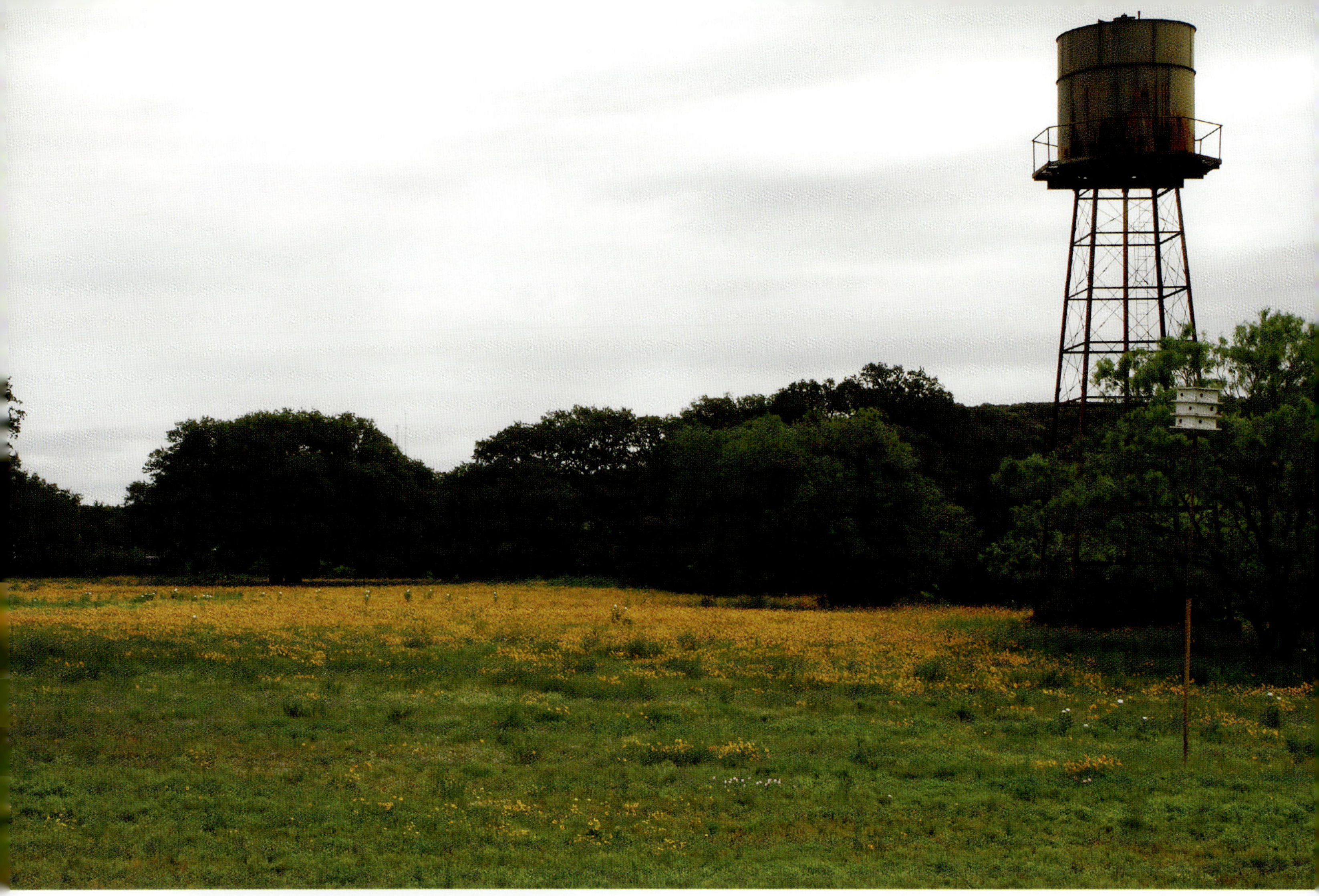

Across the courtyard and an adjoining field filled with wildflowers, the old water tower stands guard.

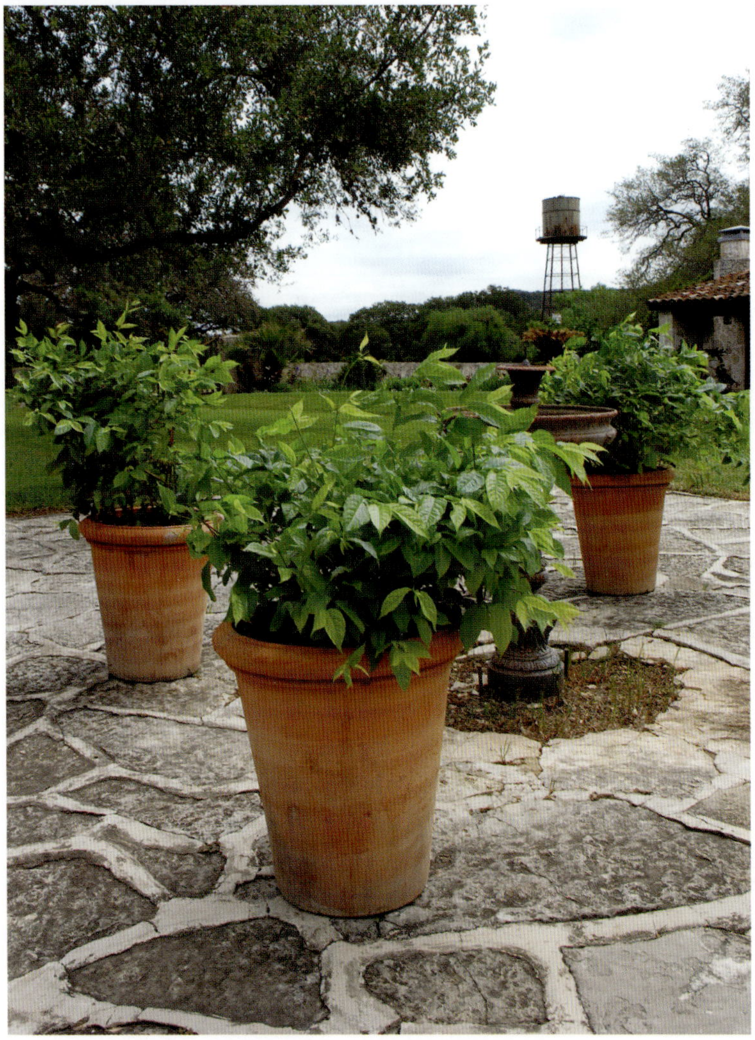

Potted plants adorn the paved area in the center of the enormous entry courtyard.

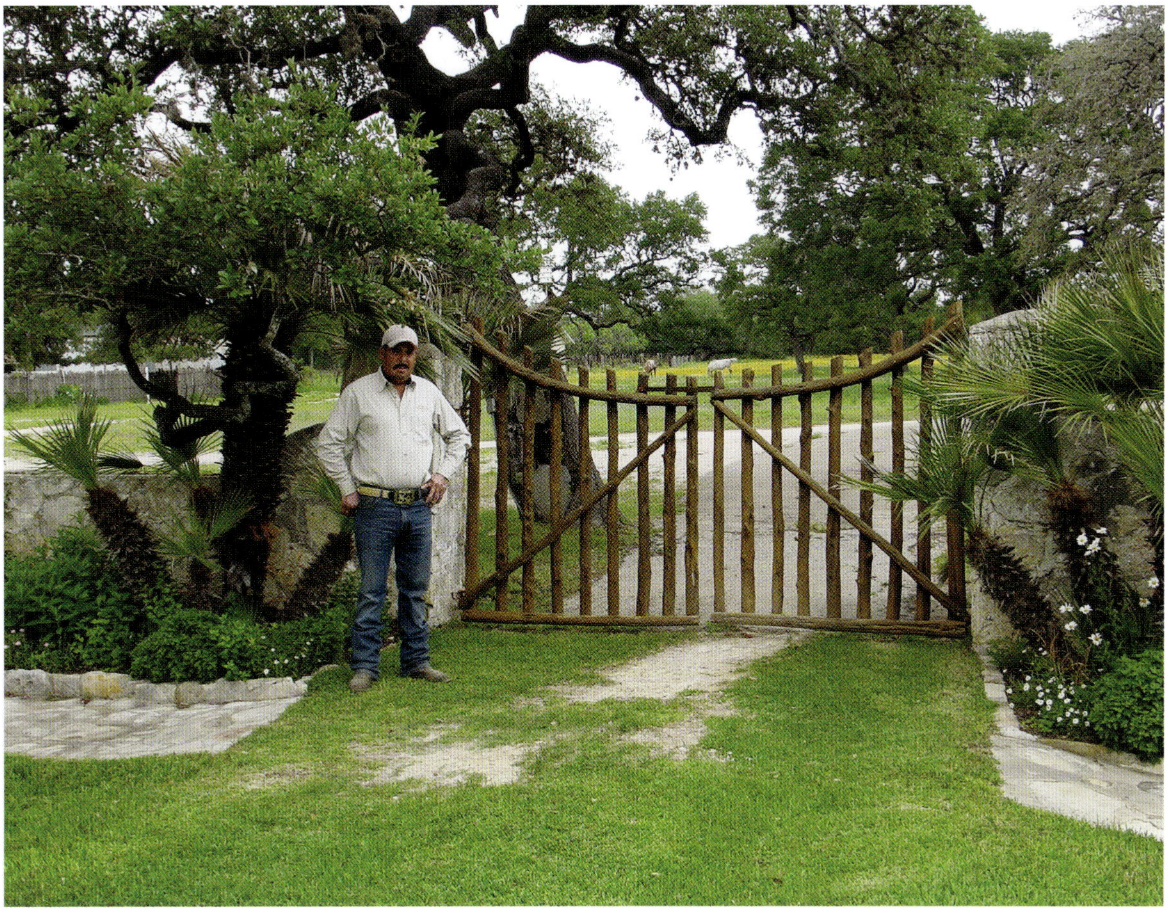

Ranch hand Tony Cosio stands beside the entry gate, which he fabricated from local cedar poles.

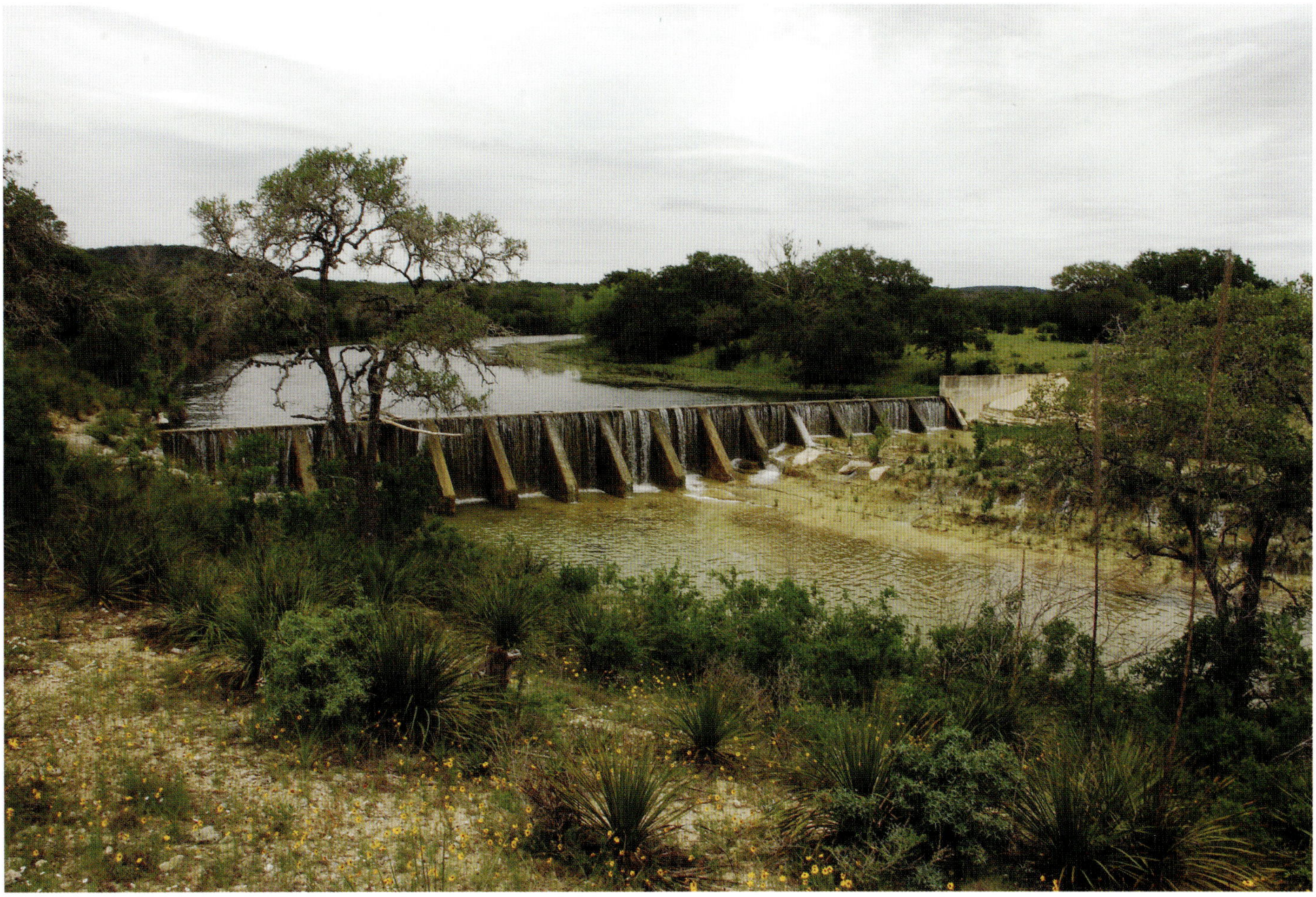

The long drive from the main road to the ranch house passes along a river, by a musical dam, and across fields of wildflowers.

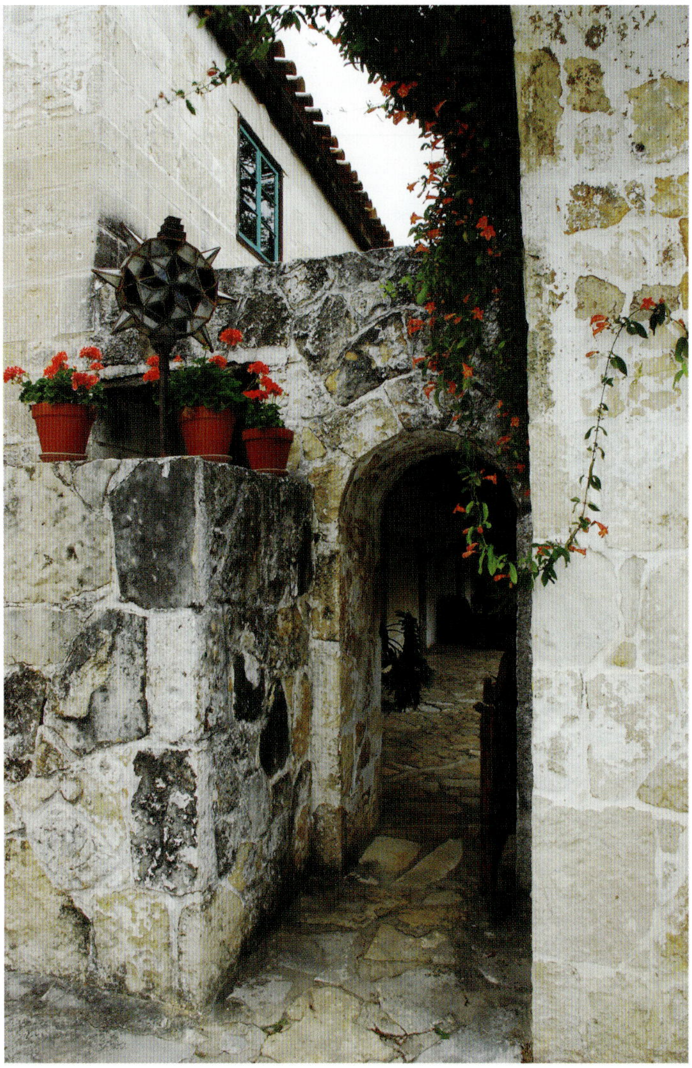

A peeled cedar pole gate opens into a porch.

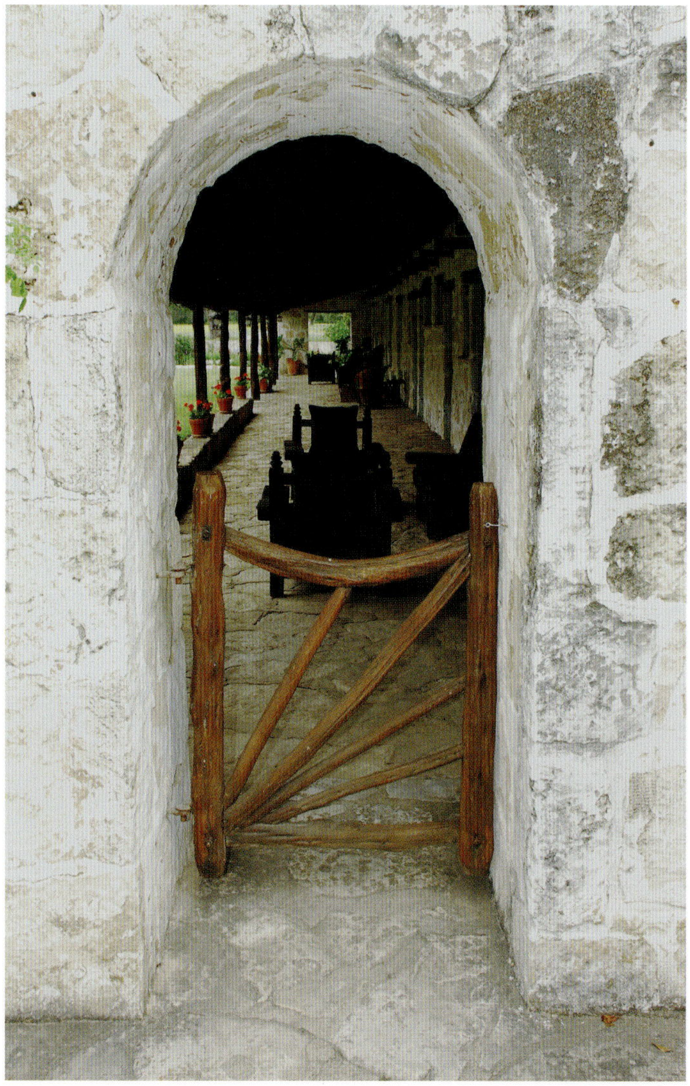

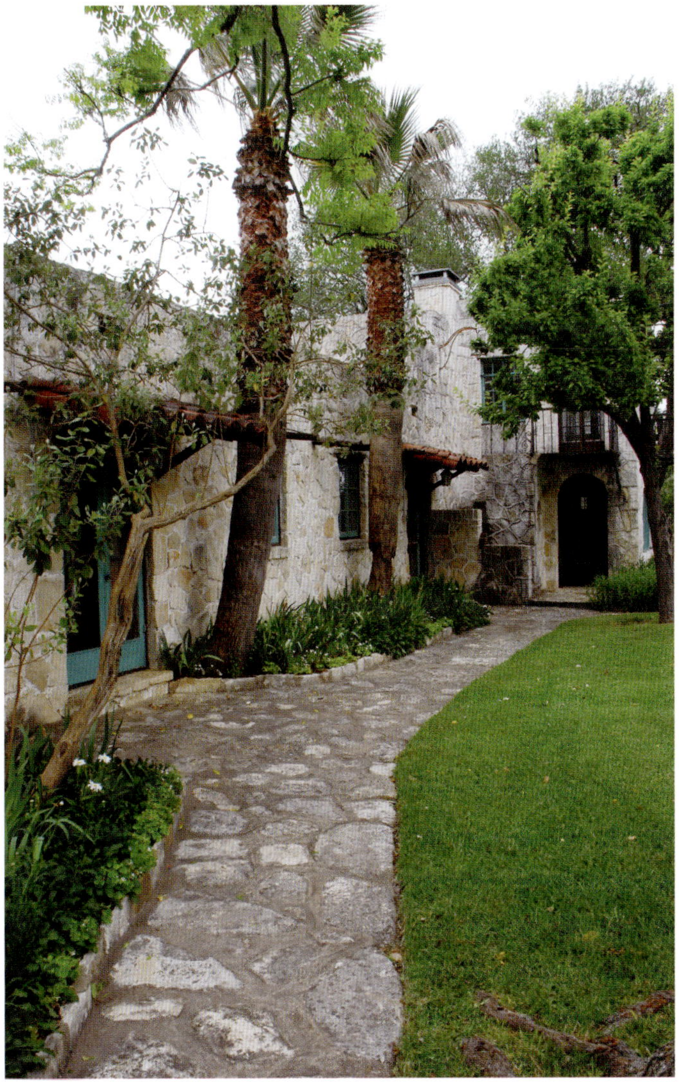

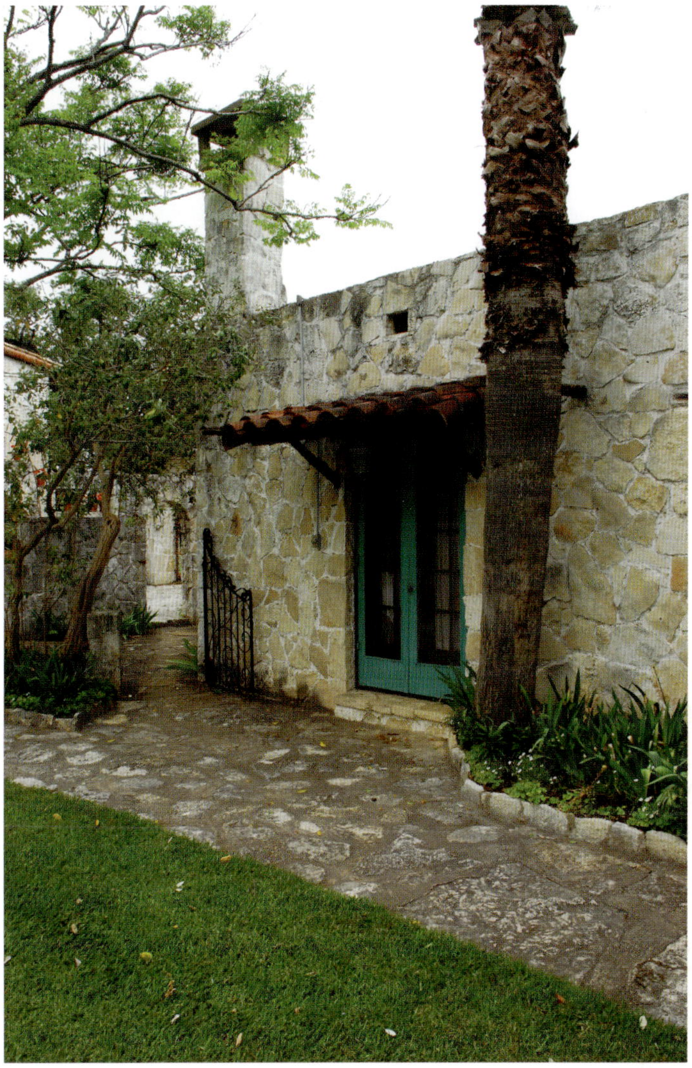

The walkway leading to the pool is made of the same native stone as walls of the house.

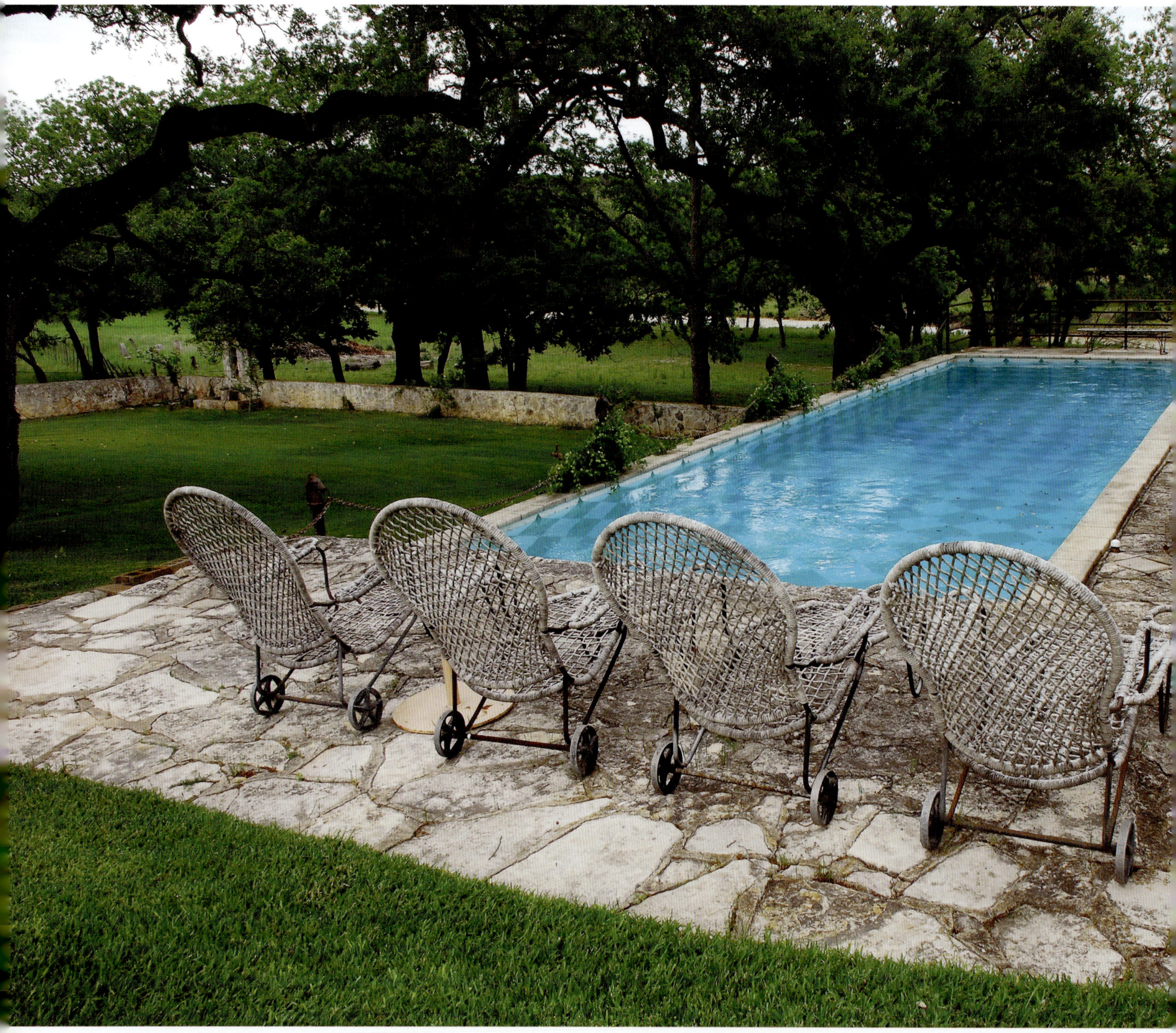

The pool at the rear of the east bunkhouse is a stone's throw from the river below. From the pool patio, looking toward the back of the east bunk-house, is a glimpse of wildflowers visible from the entry gate to the main courtyard.

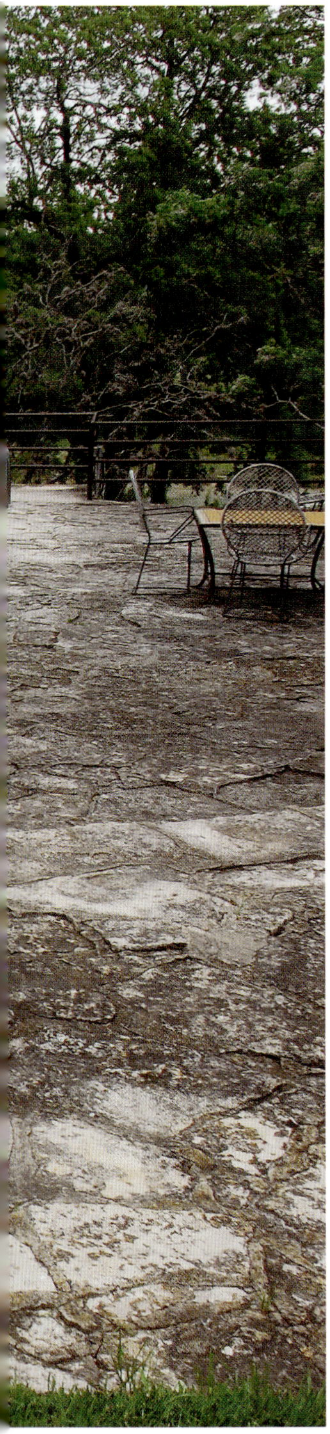

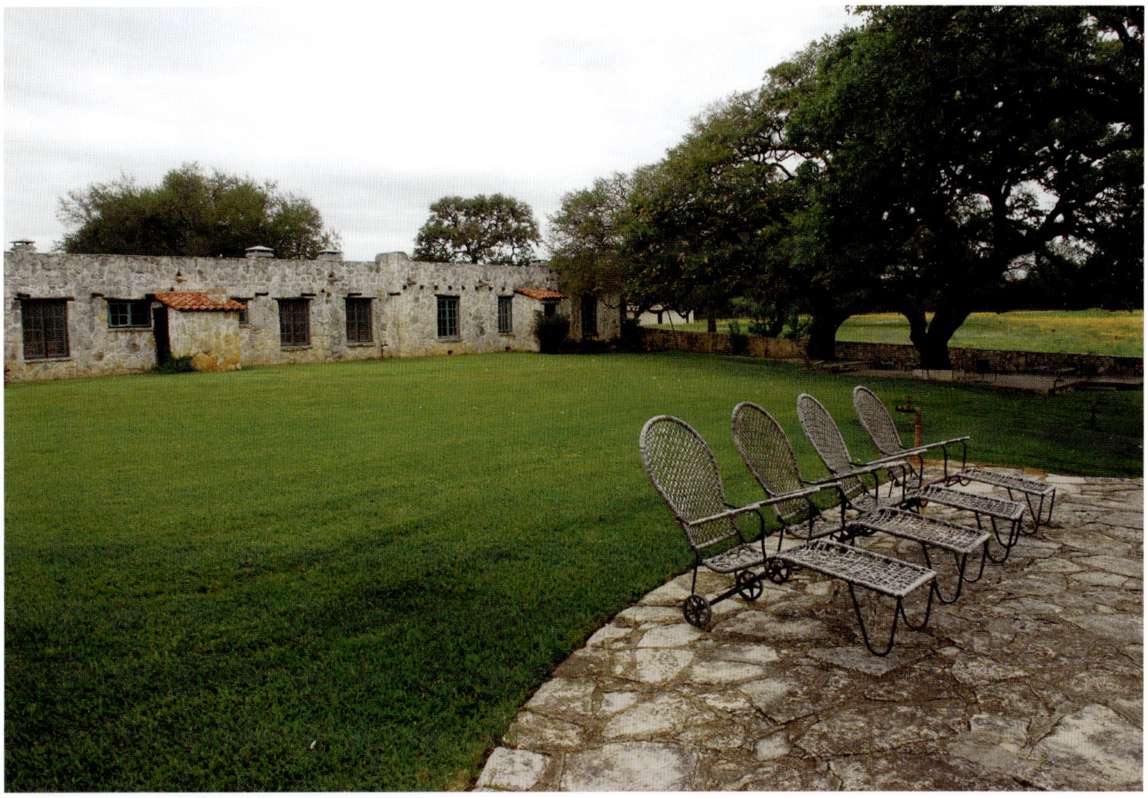

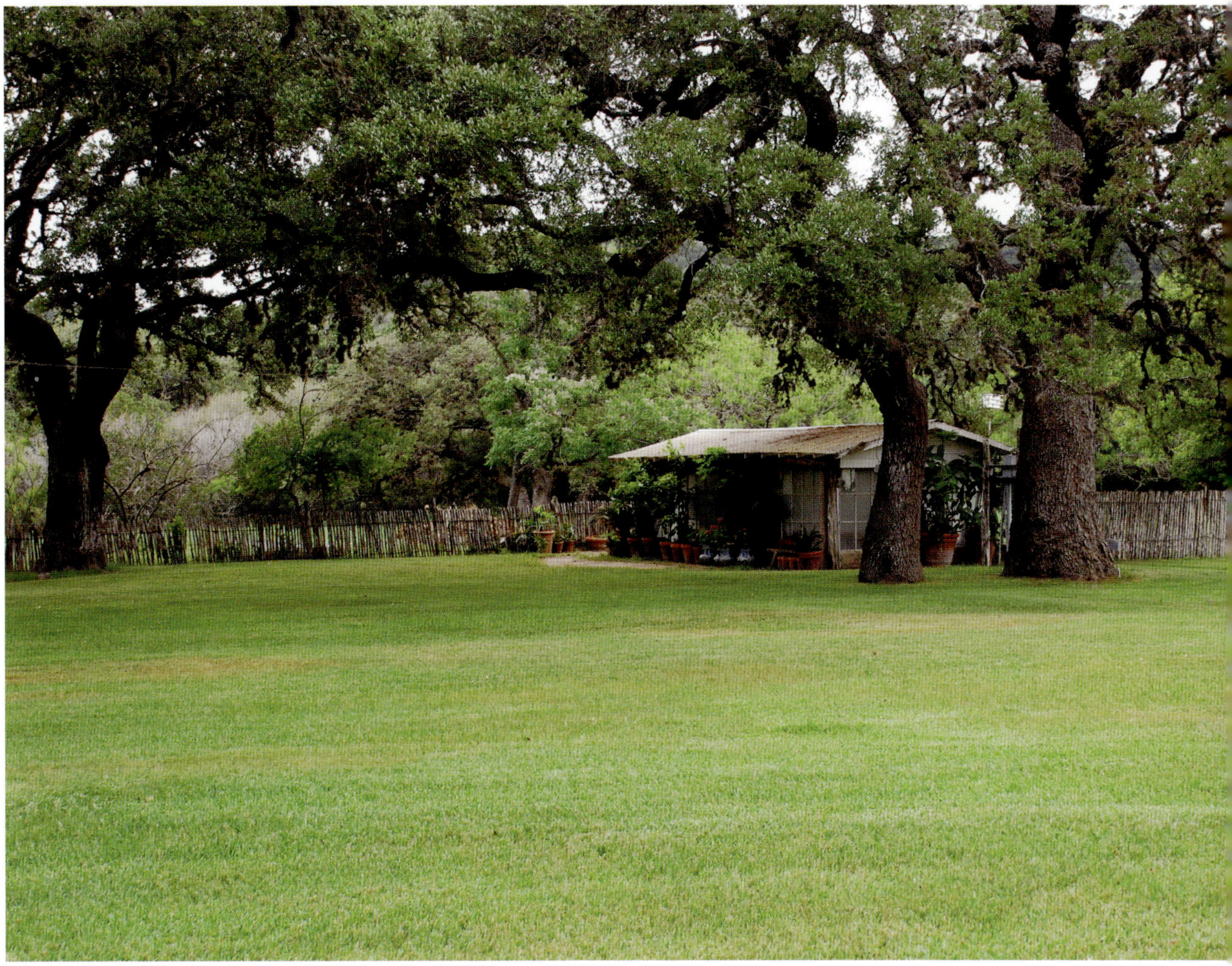

At the far side of the rear garden is a picturesque gardening shed.

Blue Bonnets

Hill was not considering buying a ranch when he learned that the once high-profile Gallagher Ranch was for sale. "I was developing Hill Country property. I didn't need more land. I decided to look only when told there was 'a really cool' house," he recalls.

On arrival, Hill saw a very large ranch. "The original 10,000-acre ranch was assembled by Peter Gallagher who bought up the property in one-quarter and one-half sections. That land had been given in the form of land patents by Sam Houston, President of the Republic of Texas, to men who had fought in the Battle of Jacinto," says Hill. "A piece of land once owned by Robert E. Lee became a part of the ranch."

At the end of a long, scenic winding drive, Hill saw not one, but three buildings—a large main house with long flanking ells. "There were 25 rooms—including 19 bedrooms—and 22 fireplaces. Both the large 30-foot by 60-foot living room and 30-foot by 16-foot dining room featured elegant 15-foot high ceilings," Hill says.

Deciding to buy the historic ranch—and all those glorious rooms—was easy. "Determining how to finance the deal required some thought," said the architect *cum* developer. "After about a year and a half, I figured out how best to buy the property," he says. "I also decided to work with The Nature Conservancy, preserving 1,800 acres from future development in honor of my mother, Elizabeth Potter Hill."

Once he had purchased the property, Hill turned his attention to the buildings, which had been vacant fifteen years. "They were not abandoned, just vacant," he says. The two-story high main house dates from the 1850s. A State Historical Survey Committee plaque affixed to one wall states:

> ***Presented by American History Club, Austin.***
> ***Recorded Texas Historic Landmark – 1967***
>
> *Fort and ranch house built by Peter Gallagher (1812-1878), Irish-Texas engineer, merchant, rancher, and diarist of the Texas-Santa Fe Expedition. The hacienda of native stone, with rifle slits to protect from Indian attack, was bought in 1927 by H.V. McNutt, as headquarters of an early Texas guest ranch. The rambling Mexican-style home has known distinguished guests and the routine of a working ranch.*

One-story high ells flank the fort/hacienda. Together, the three structures embrace an expansive courtyard enclosed by a cut-stone wall. The wall is fitted with a new peeled-pole gate, hand-crafted in the traditional way by ranch hand Tony Cosio. Hill says, "It is likely that the porches for all three sections were added in the 1930s by a colorful couple, H.V. (Vachel) and Amy (called Mama Mac) McNutt. They bought the ranch in 1927 and then turned their working spread into a dude ranch."

"Peter Gallagher built a lot of buildings around the Alamo and hired Santa Anna to come to San Antonio and build a depot. I like to say that Santa Anna slept here!" Hill says. Certainly, the McNutt's dude ranch attracted the stars of the day. Humorist Will Rogers and Orson Welles of movie and radio fame came. So did Lily Pons of the Metropolitan Opera. Prince Rainier and Princess Grace (nee Grace Kelly, movie legend) of Monaco arrived—to be feted at a party in their honor by the McNutts. "Purportedly, behavior at the party by famous South Texas guests was scandalous, although I doubt that the Rainiers were scandalized," Hill notes. If walls could talk, the walls of Hill's ranch would have volumes to say!

In the years that Hill has called the Gallagher Ranch home since buying it in 1996, a great deal of work has been done. "We've tried to bring the nineteenth century house with its twentieth century dude ranch innovations into the twenty-first century," he says. Care has been taken to not alter but to reveal its historic, charmingly rustic character. Walls cannot speak, but Hill couldn't avoid noticing immediately that stone walls in the dining room had been painted! "We removed the paint," he says with decided emphasis. Now, the full beauty of native stone is revealed. Walls in the master bedroom were stripped of plaster to reveal hand-quarried native stone; and the wood ceiling was stripped of many layers of paint to get to the pleasing1930s color that remains. In the kitchen, turquoise kitchen cabinets re-state an antique color discovered during cabinet repair work. Old tile colors, sizes, and shapes inspired the painted kitchen floor.

Furnishings throughout are a masterful collection of museum-quality pieces and other treasures from many eras and around the globe. Delightfully diverse, they live together with great ease and total élan, even as restoration and improvements to Gallagher Ranch—seemingly unending—continue apace.

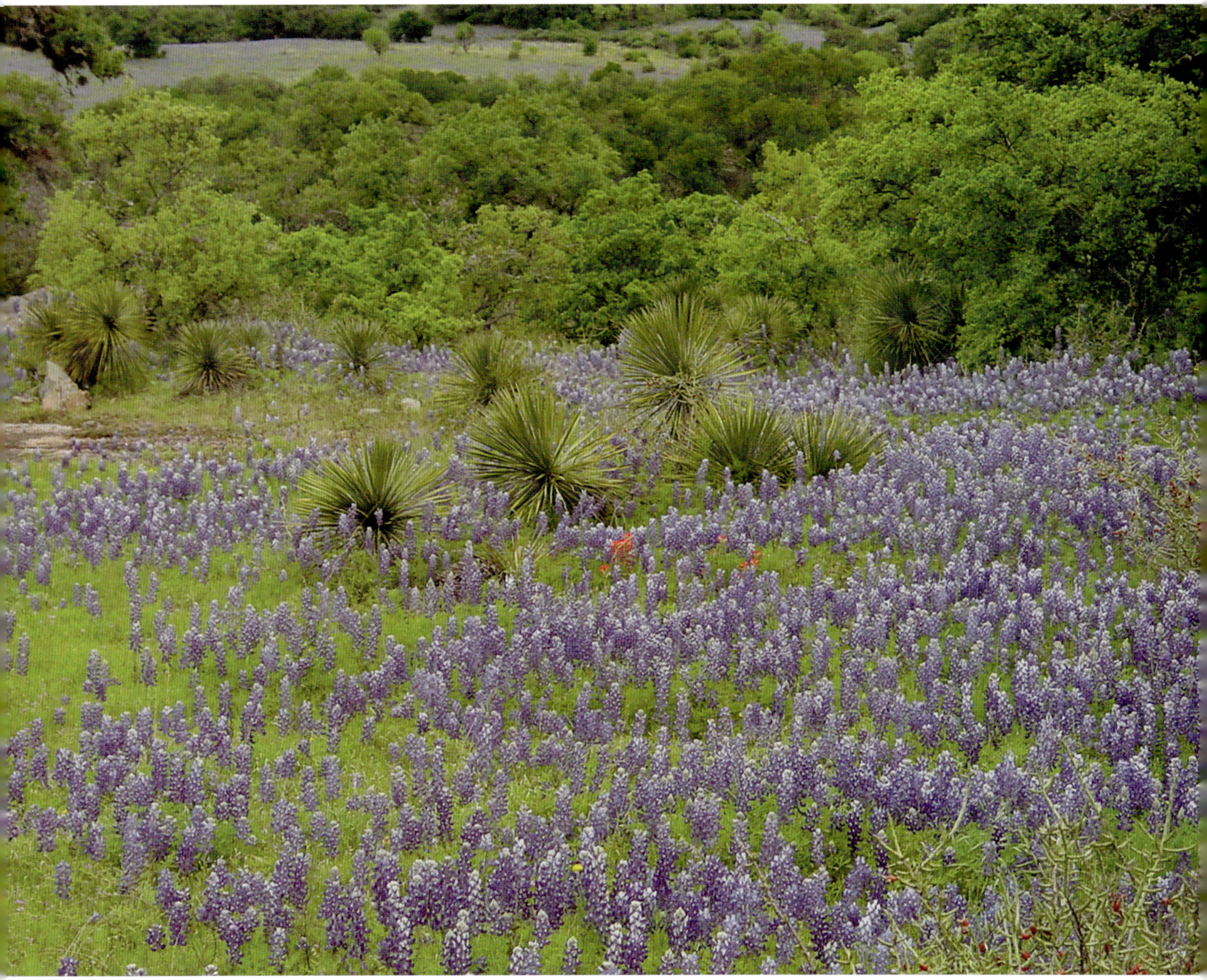

Texas bluebonnets. *Photograph by David Strahan, AIA*

5
The Collins House

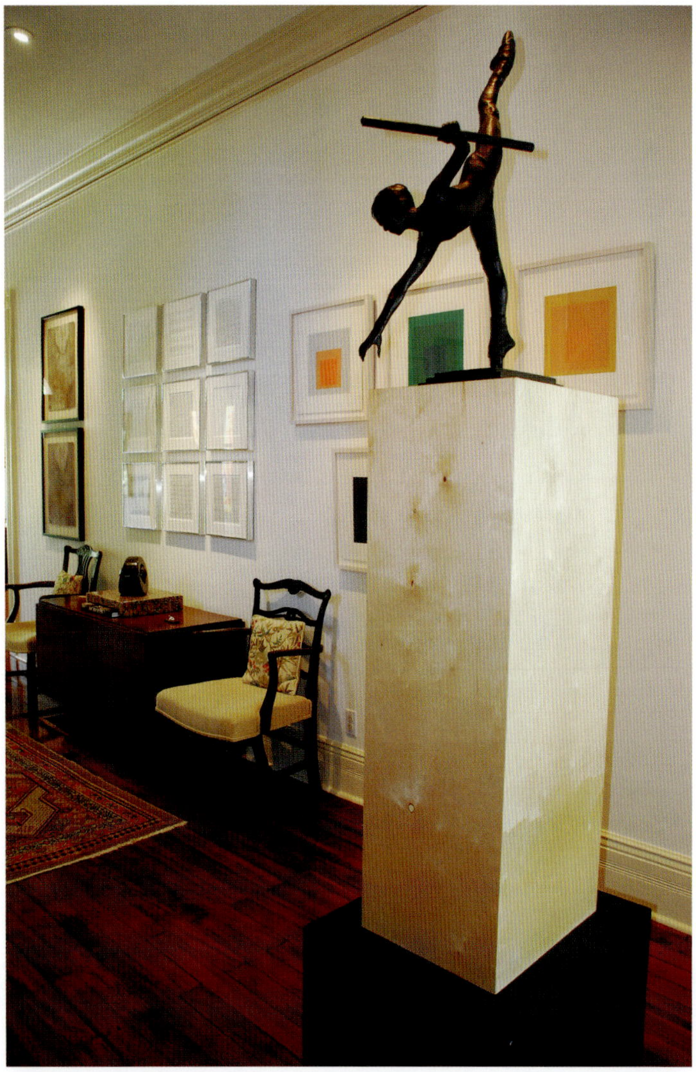

The welcoming entry hall, running the width of the house, is a gallery for wall-hung art and standing sculpture. *Photographs by Barbara Justice* (Above and opposite page)

Edward E. (Sonny) Collins' large house on Madison Street in the historic King William district is imposing, befitting a native son who retired to San Antonio following a successful financial career in New York City. One, who on arriving home again, took up the leadership of the San Antonio River Foundation, the civic group responsible for San Antonio's glamorous River Walk.

A visitor arriving at this Madison Street address climbs a handsome flight of wide stairs that rises to the large entry. The oversized entry door opens onto what in Italian architecture is called the *piano nobile* (noble floor), the floor of elegant, high-ceilinged main reception rooms immediately above the raised basement or ground floor. This architectural design was seen in buildings of the English Palladian style of the eighteenth century and in those built in Great Britain and the United States during the Renaissance Revival in the mid- and late nineteenth century. It is uncommon in San Antonio and therefore all the more impressive.

One enters a wide, high-ceilinged hallway that runs unimpeded from the front to the back of the building. *Feng Shui* may deplore this design, which lets chi (energy) rush out; but, Italian design says bravo to the tantalizing glimpse of an intriguing garden with its monumental sculpture.

On the left of the entry, the elegant living room parallels the hallway, running the width of the house. To the right of the entry is a spacious dining room, and beyond the dining room a butler's pantry followed by a jewel-box kitchen. Surprisingly for such an elegant, old traditionally designed structure, the partition between kitchen and hallway was removed, creating the kind of openness found in contemporary residences. This inventive remodeling was the work of the previous owner, Jill Giles, head of her well known eponymous graphic design firm. Giles says that she had tile-setters install her personal collection of beautiful hand-crafted glazed tiles in the kitchen backsplash.

Large-scale sculpture and walls hung gallery-fashion with fascinating framed art in every medium transform the entry hall, and indeed the entire house, into an art gallery.

Despite its grandeur, this is a friendly house. In the living room, comfortable seating gathers round and focuses on an elegant fireplace with a mantel from Mexico installed by Giles. In the dining room, the window that opened onto the too-close neighboring house was closed with a plywood panel. Now, the neighbors see what looks like a very real-looking drapery that is actually a *faux* painting. Inside, the paneling is covered with mirror that sparkles from the light of a gorgeous chandelier by glass artist Gini Garcia, making the room seem lighter and larger. New built-in shelves artfully displaying an extensive collection of porcelain statuary surround the walls of this inviting room clearly designed to encourage lingering.

Collins has some Texas-style tall-tales to tell about this intriguing house. "It was built around the turn of the century (some say 1896, others 1905) for I. B. Henyan, who bought the lot from the estate of Michael Eckenroth around 1899. Reportedly, it was the last legal brothel in San Antonio," he says with a grin. "See that long gouge in the living room floor? Some say it was made by the spur of a drunken cowboy as he was dragged out and off the premises."

To underscore this colorful version of the history of his house, Collins points out multiple doors on the lower level. "They provided discreet and hasty departure routes for clients wishing to avoid meeting the local law—and perhaps one another." He says: "I think that the girls used twelve rooms in the basement. Alan Cash told me that there were rooms one through six on one side, and seven through twelve on the other; each room signified by a black tile with a green numeral. The girls lived on the third floor of the four-story (including the basement) building. Their Madam lived on the fourth; although the old stairway to the third floor is no longer there and there's little evidence as to exactly where it was. Some of the information I have is contradictory so I don't know for sure what is accurate, but it does make the house fun and interesting." Whether this is real history or not, the story—like the paintings throughout—is colorful.

Any partitions on the ground floor (partially above-grade basement) were removed long before Collins arrived and made this space his warm, appealing, memorabilia-filled library. Locating the library here was no small undertaking, since there was a water problem. A new drainage system removed the threat of water, the walls were plastered, and shelving for an extensive library was installed. Just around the corner is Collins' very handy home office. Across the hall is a cozy guest room.

The floor above the *piano nobile* now is largely an expansive master suite. Notable are the carefully designed and installed closets that provide ample storage but look original to the space. The thoughtfully updated master bath in a sophisticated black-and-white scheme boasts a new floor of antique-design penny-round tiles. "It would appear that each owner has done a lot of work on the house to maintain the dignity and honesty of the original. Jill Giles probably did more than most, but everyone has accomplished something to improve the house," says Collins.

The elegant and colorful house on Madison and its extraordinary owner continue to contribute vitally to San Antonio's present and to ensure its future as a leading American city.

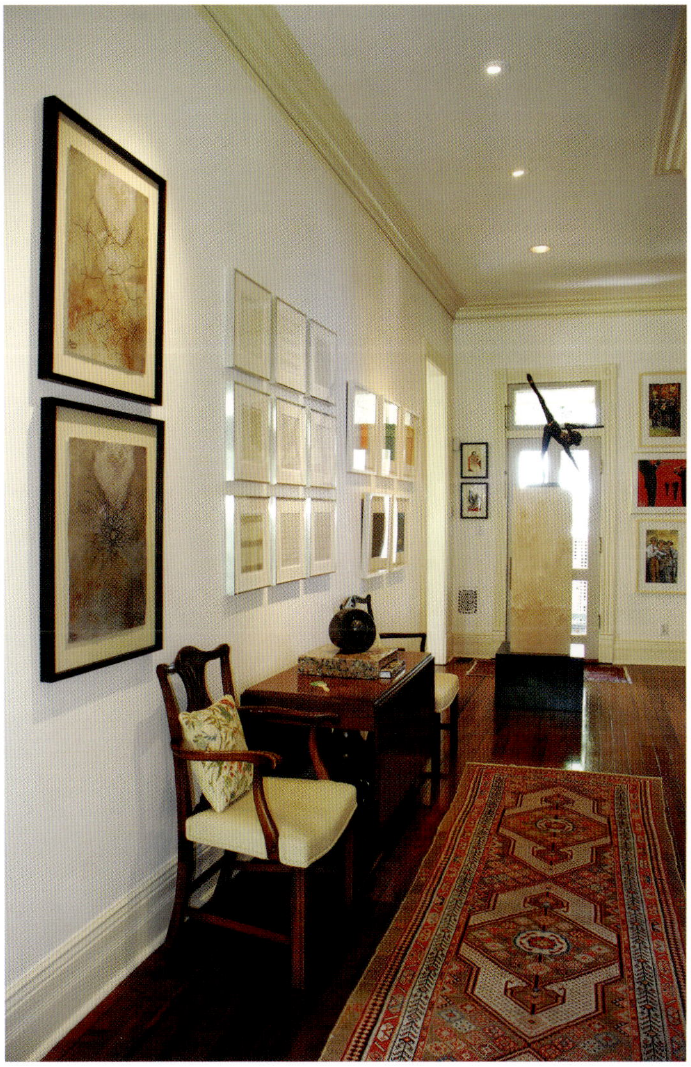

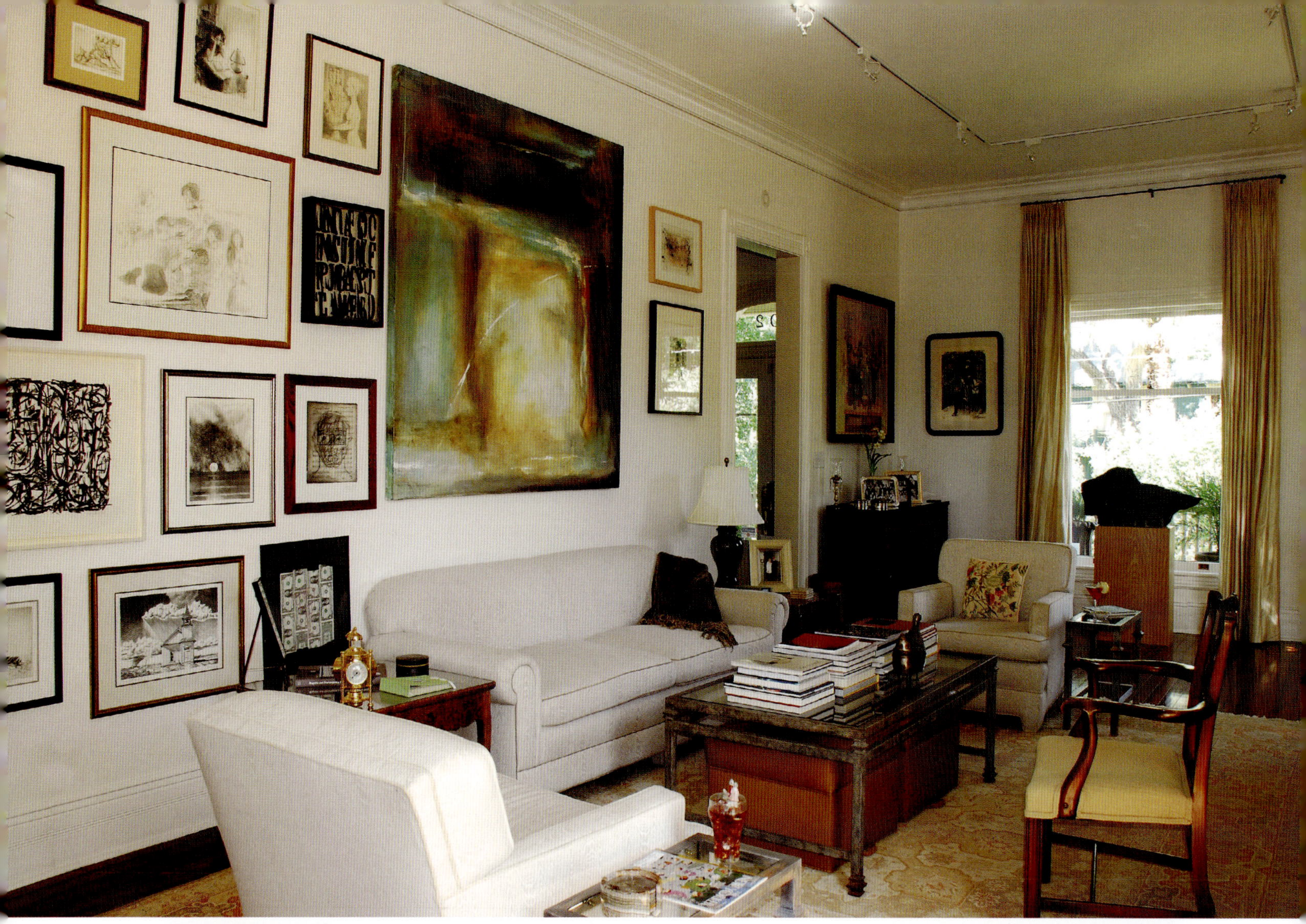

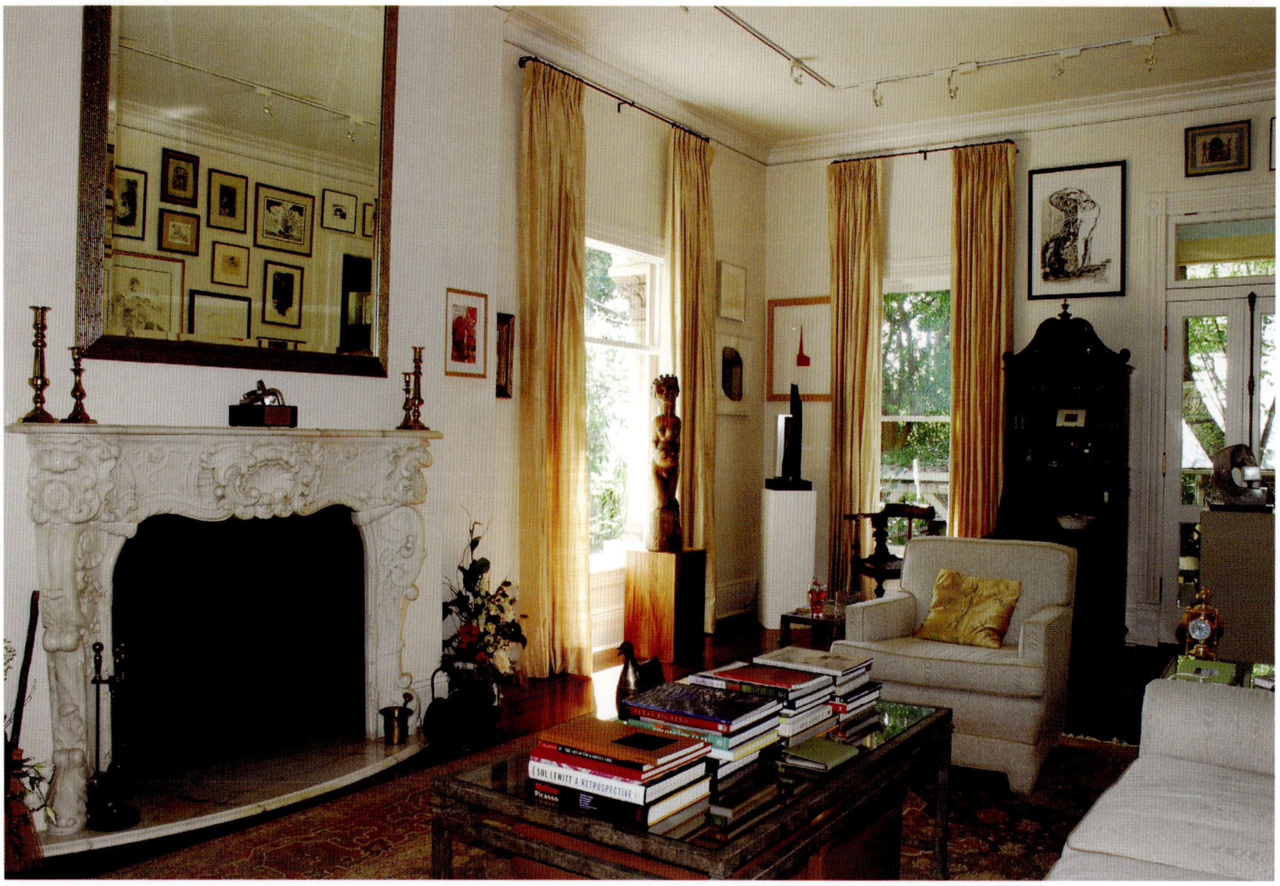

The living room, like the parallel hallway, displays a wonderful collection of art. Comfortable seating faces a French-style mantel imported from Mexico by an earlier owner.

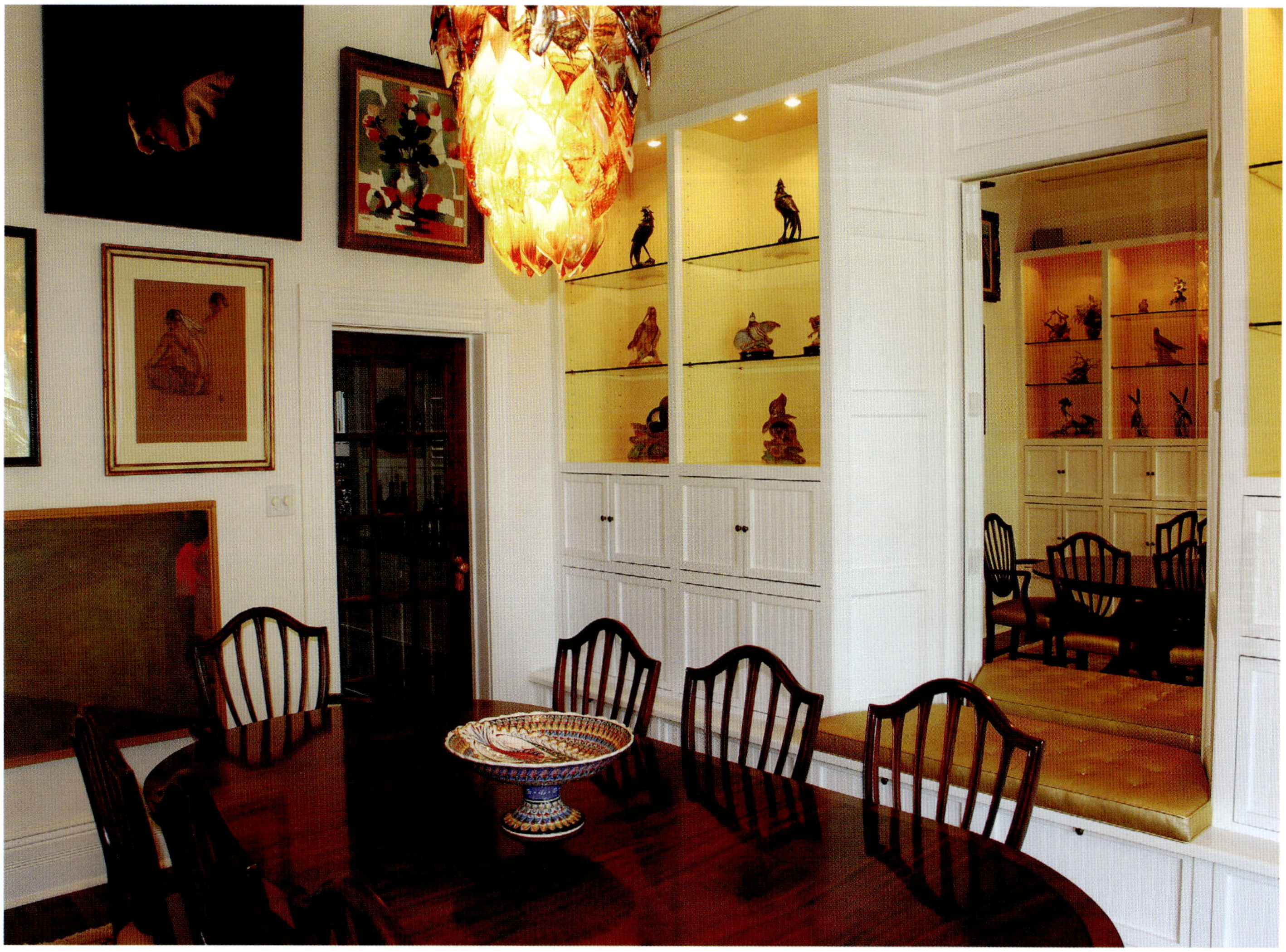

The mirrored niche in the dining room was originally a window with a view of a too-near neighboring house. New shelving displays sculpture.

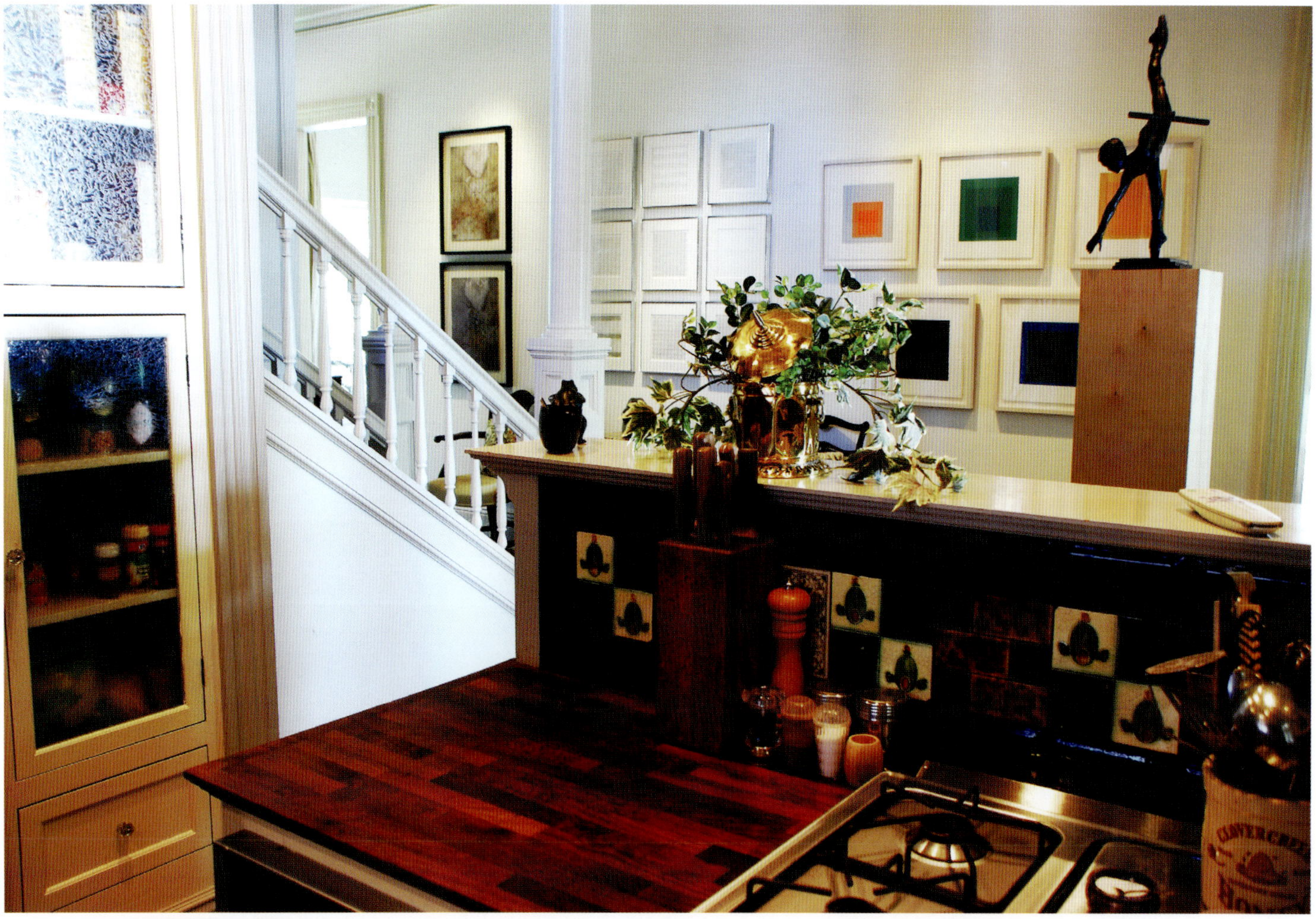

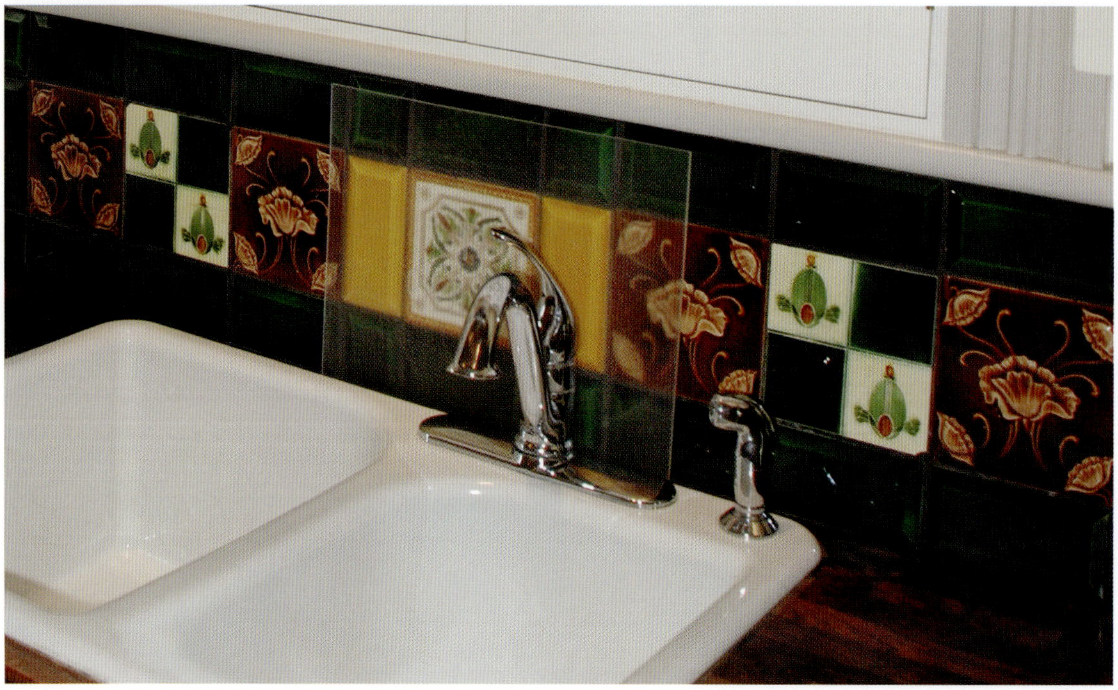

The updated kitchen opens to the rear of the entry hall. Art tiles in the backsplash were installed by noted designer Jill Giles. (Above and opposite page)

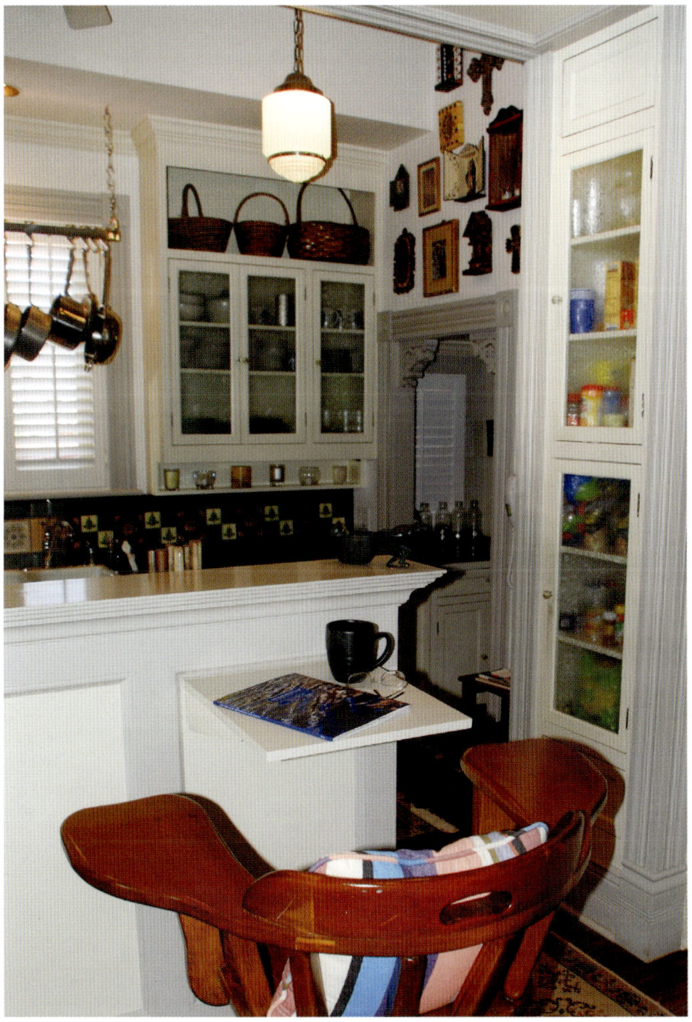

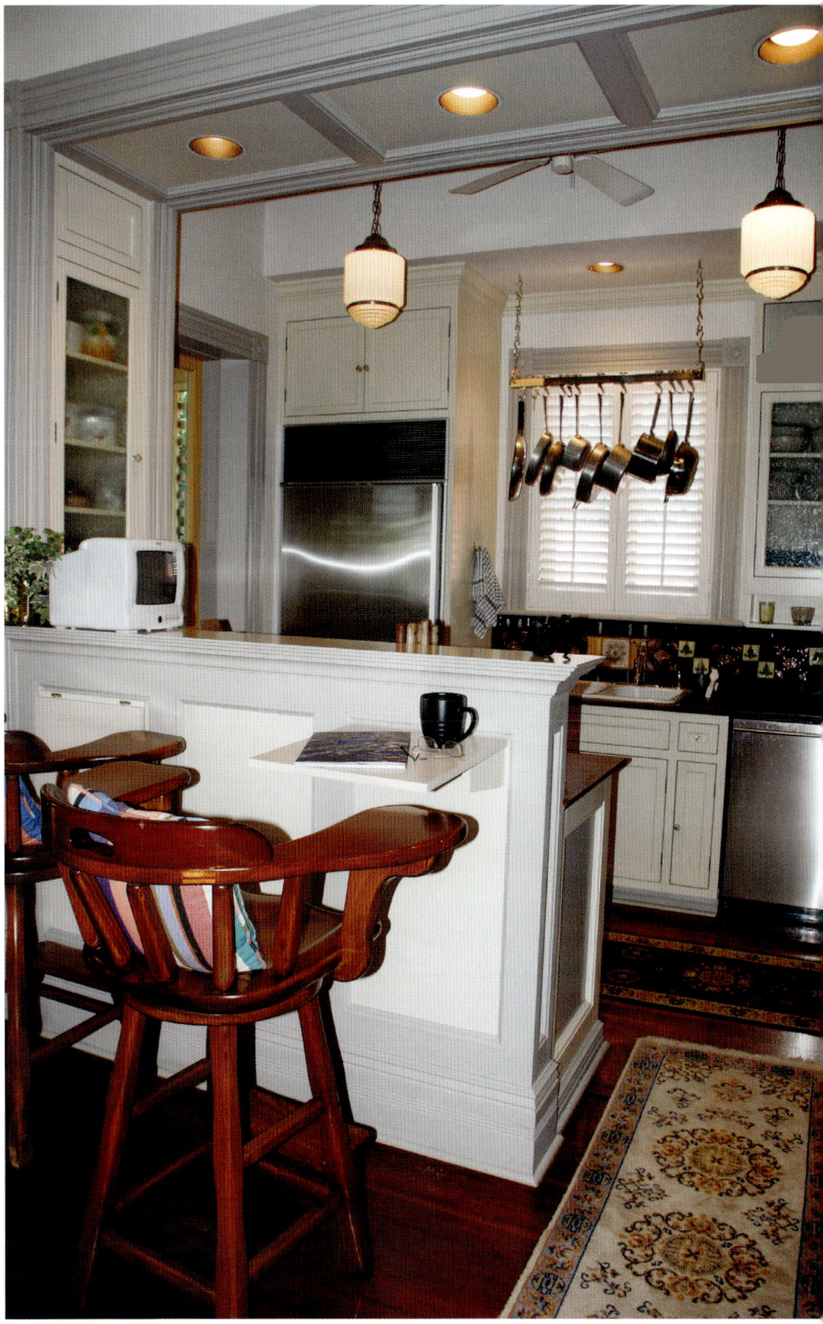

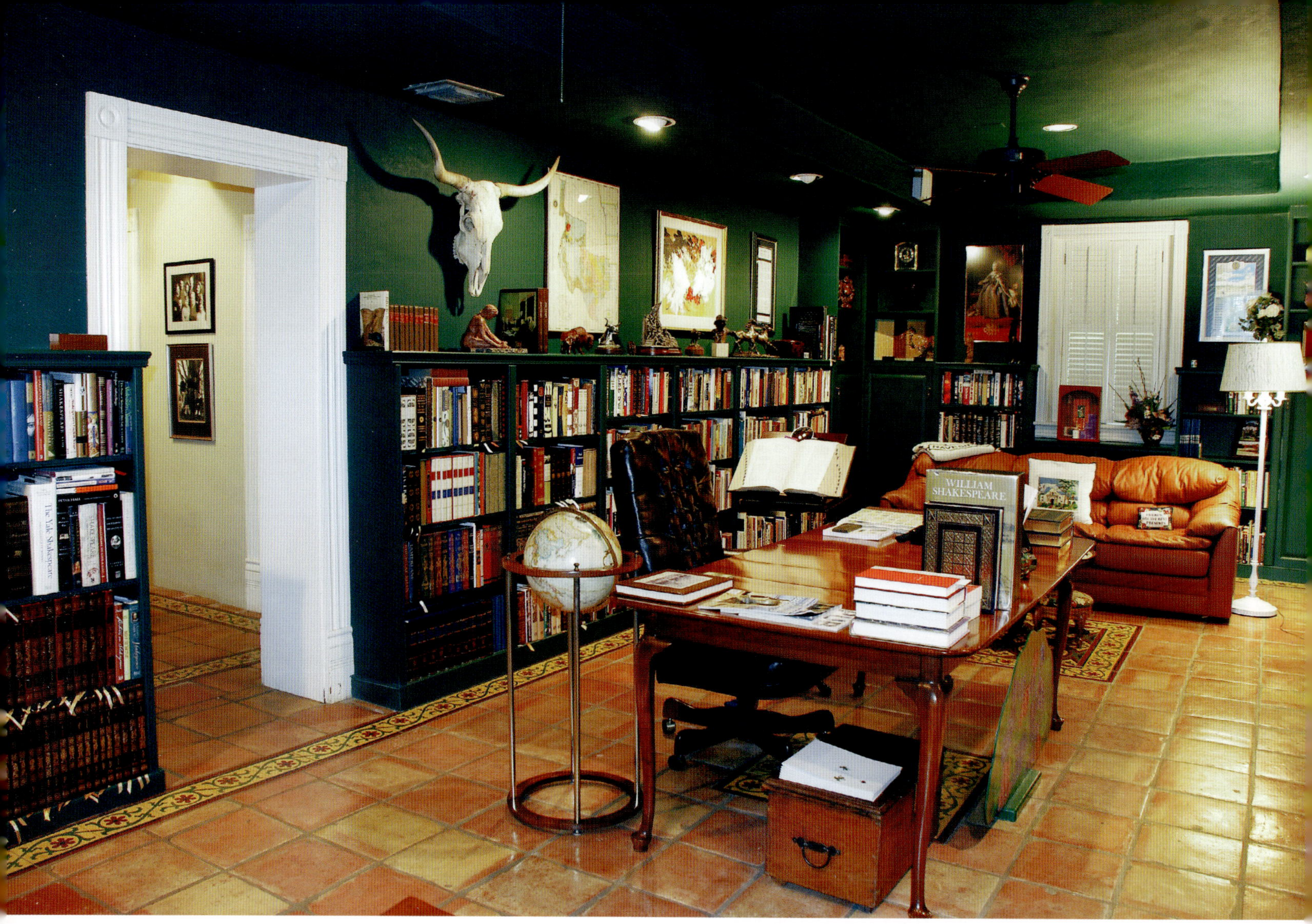

After removing the threat of water, a large room was fitted out as a library.

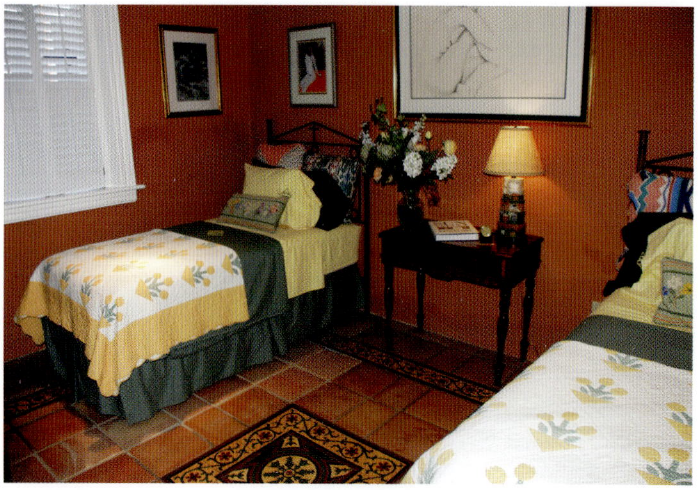

The ground level of this four-story home is a partially above-grade basement—unusual for San Antonio. A guestroom is on this floor.

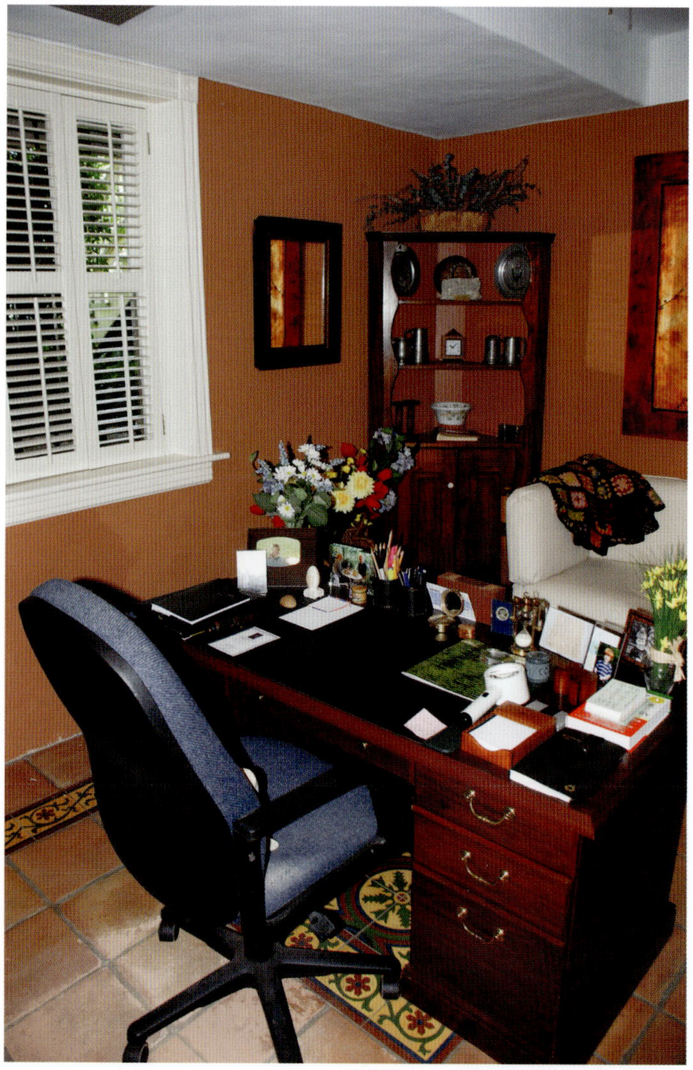

The owner's home office is located on the ground level.

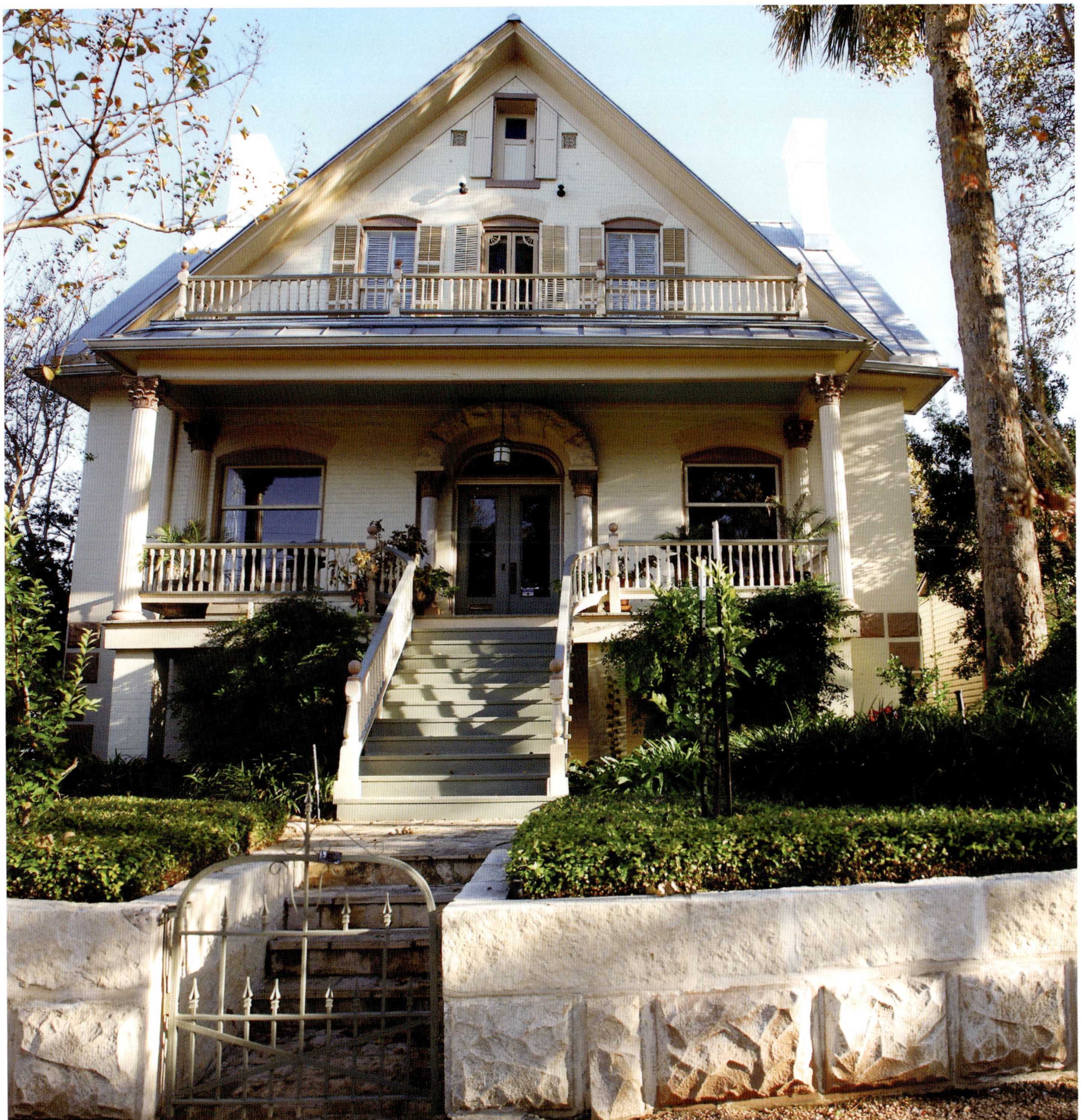

Exterior of the Collins House.

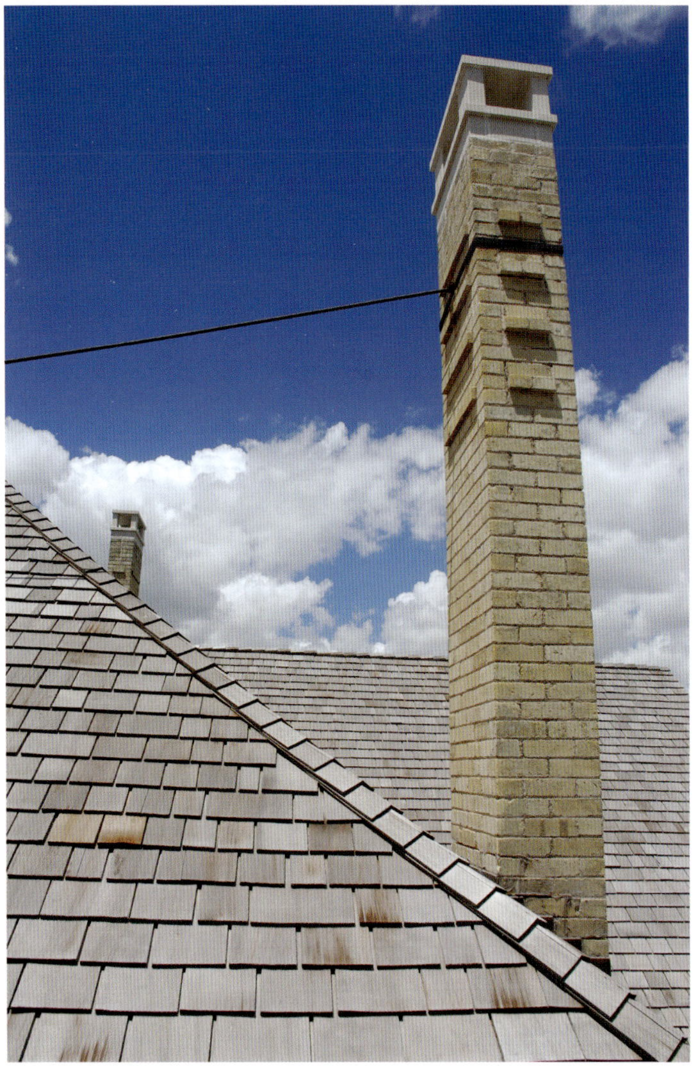

Decaying chimneys were rebuilt and new supports added.

general contractor for such a project. I knew from my initial evaluations and inspection reports that the house needed updated electrical, plumbing, roofing, and heating/air conditioning—all this in addition to repairing and restoring floors, walls, and trim. I did not want to extend the restoration over a long period of time.

I decided to reconstruct the property to the point where it would qualify as a Texas Historic Landmark. The City of San Antonio Historic Design and Review Department informed me that this house was considered a *special* historic landmark in the city within the King William Historic District.

I interviewed and contracted with Mainstreet Architects' Sue Ann Pemberton to draw up the plan for this massive project. We began work in September of 2007. Initial site reviews and plans for outbuilding new construction, main house, and carriage house developed over the next six months. After interviewing contractors, Rubiola Construction Company was selected to be the general contractor.

First things first: I needed a nearby place to live during the restoration. So, the initial phase of the work plan was the restoration/renovation of the carriage house, which would be my residence throughout the project. This involved demolition of the piecemeal, old uneven slab floor that had been poured in stages. The original walls were cleared of old drywall and insulation. The entire wooden superstructure was lifted, a reinforced concrete slab was poured, the old structure securely supported and rebuilt—preserving as much old material as possible—and the structure placed on the new slab.

A small one-car garage-sized building constructed in the late 1920s was similarly re-constructed to serve as a future workshop. Next, a three-car garage with a loft apartment—the only new structure—was built on the eastern part of the property where the original horse barn had been located.

The big house—a very big job: The majority of work in restoring *San Souci* centered around the restoration and renovation of the main house. We wanted to bring the house back to its original glory architecturally but modernize with up-to-date conveniences.

We had the great fortune to have access to several old photographs of the house as it appeared immediately after its construction. We were able to design many of the replacement architectural details *to match those original details* shown in the photographs. This helped us to get approval from the Historic Design and Review Committee.

Discovery—an exciting process: Demolition had to come first in order for us to determine the scope of work. We learned that the old original cedar shake roofing remained under later composition shingles. We replaced the roof with new fireproof cedar shake roofing.

Although the brick structure remained well intact, the porches were in great disrepair. Supports beneath the porches were all replaced. The third floor porch was reconstructed, supported within with engineered steel girders and plates. The original built-in gutter system was reconstructed.

The 1920s or '30s addition on the rear of the house was revised to retain the upper porch but open up the first floor.

Exterior brick and mortar were steam cleaned and mortar re-pointed.

All exterior painted surfaces were sanded, prepped, and painted with historic colors.

All of the original columns were re-used. The plaster capitals were cleaned and painted.

We retained all of the original windows, re-glazing where necessary and repairing all of the old sash cords.

The house had seven fireplaces—all were returned to functioning condition.

Retrofitting creature comfort: In order to update the heating/ventilation, electrical, and plumbing, interior walls and ceilings were exposed. The old and still-functioning knob and tube wiring was removed and replaced with all new electrical circuits. Similarly, all the old cast iron and galvanized pipe was removed and new modern plumbing (including a circulating hot water system) installed. The challenge of heating and air conditioning was significant. The house had an old non-functioning boiler and radiator system in the basement that we removed. The house had no air conditioning (except for

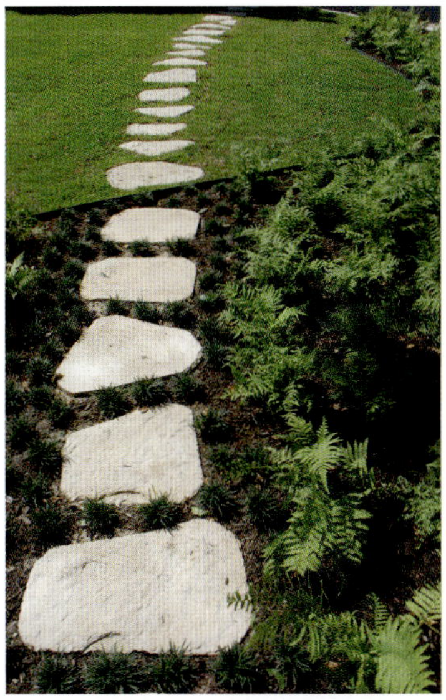
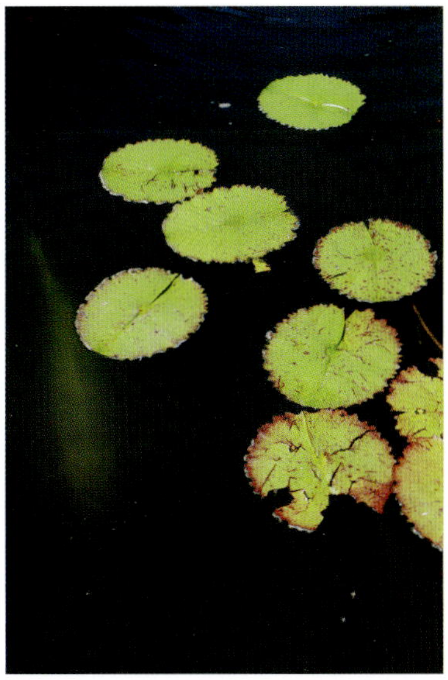
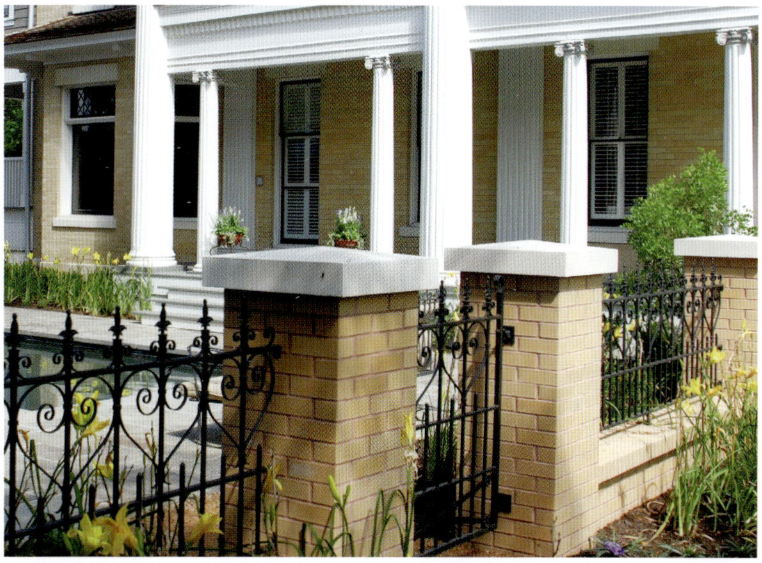
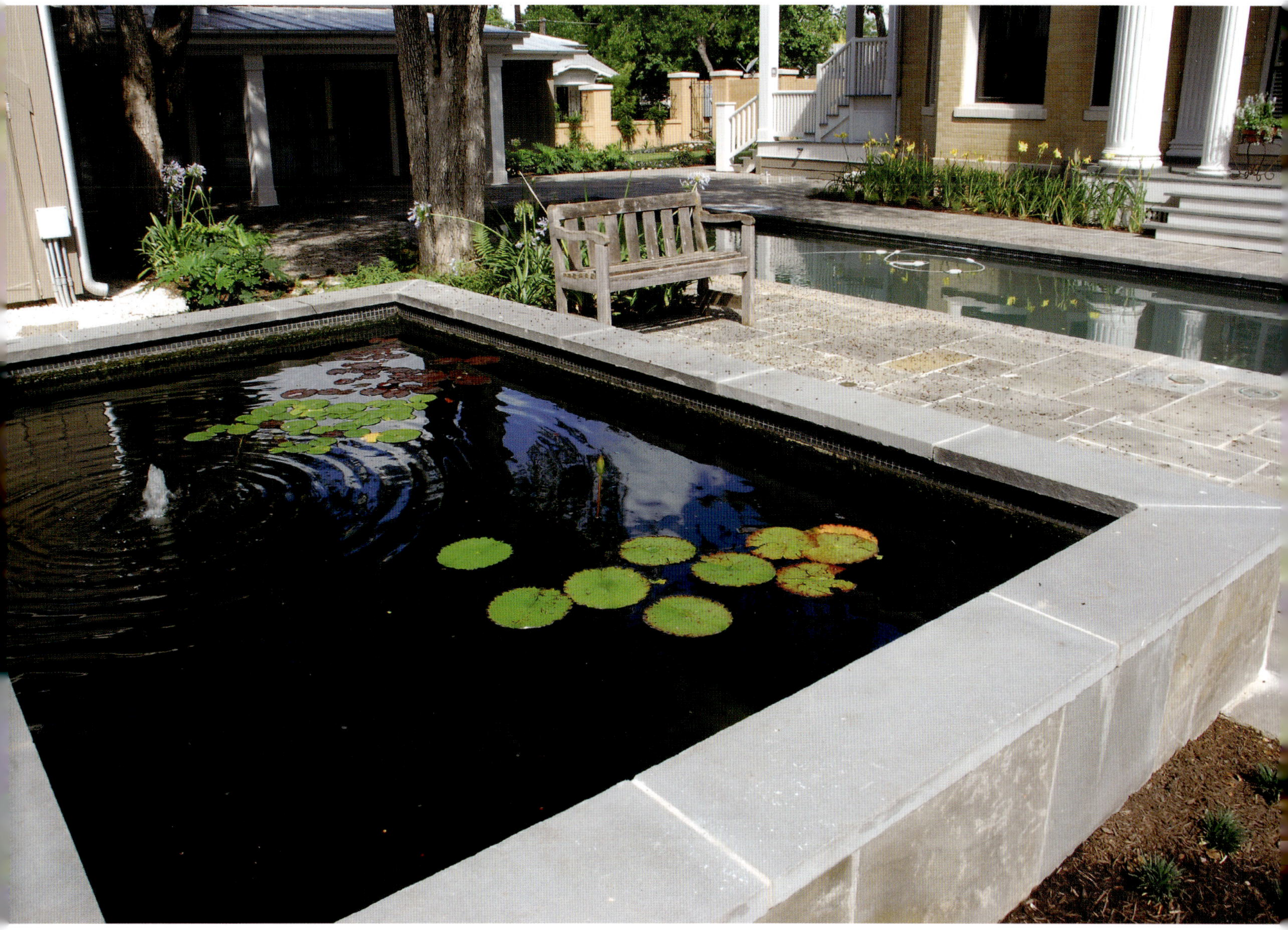

The gardens were newly landscaped and a pool added.

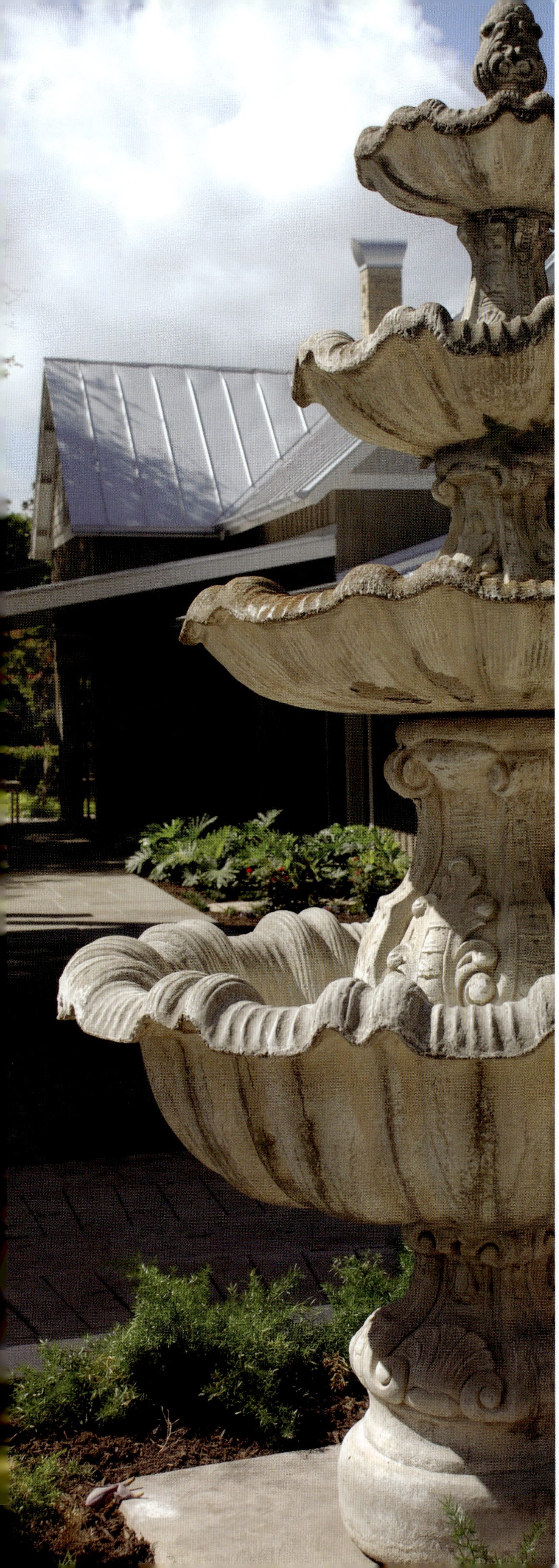

window units). We were able to find areas on, under or above each floor in which to place air handlers and furnaces. Duct work was hidden—creatively placed to avoid any exposed fur downs for duct work.

As much insulation as possible was installed. In many areas, new drywall was placed. The process of refinishing all of the original trim and bead board followed.

Updating kitchen and baths: A new, fully updated kitchen with soapstone counters, pecan cabinets, and new appliances replaced the original kitchen. We kept the original built-in cabinets in the butler's pantry and designed the new kitchen trim to match.

We retained the original bathroom on the second floor, including the old tub, toilet, and sink. A new master bath was constructed in what had been a bedroom on the second floor.

Interior touches: Virtually all of the original trim and molding as well as the doors were re-used and repainted. The house was essentially built of longleaf pine and every effort was made to retain as much as we could. All of the floors were long leaf pine, which we refinished, restoring them to excellent condition. The entire house was repainted, new light fixtures installed, and all the original hardware for doors and windows was re-plated and reinstalled.

Viola—San Souci* is *très magnifique: In March 2010, the main house was finished. Landscaping—including a swimming pool and Koi pond, new fencing, an irrigation system, and new lawn—was next.

On June 15, 2010, the restoration of San Souci, the Luby-Shaffer House was complete.

On June 19, 2010—on the porch overlooking the courtyard—I, Kevin Browne, wed Jody Stern, who has added gracious finishing touches to the beautiful interiors of the historic Luby-Shaffer-Browne House.

Arched openings in the spacious entry lead to a hallway and up the handsome staircase. The fireplace was original to the house.

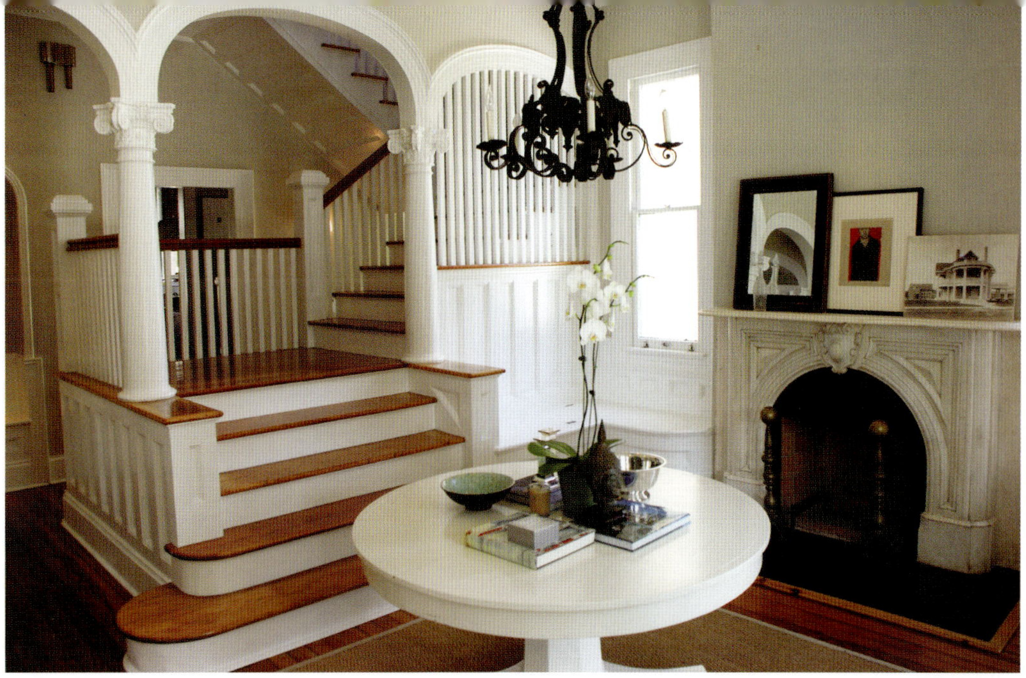

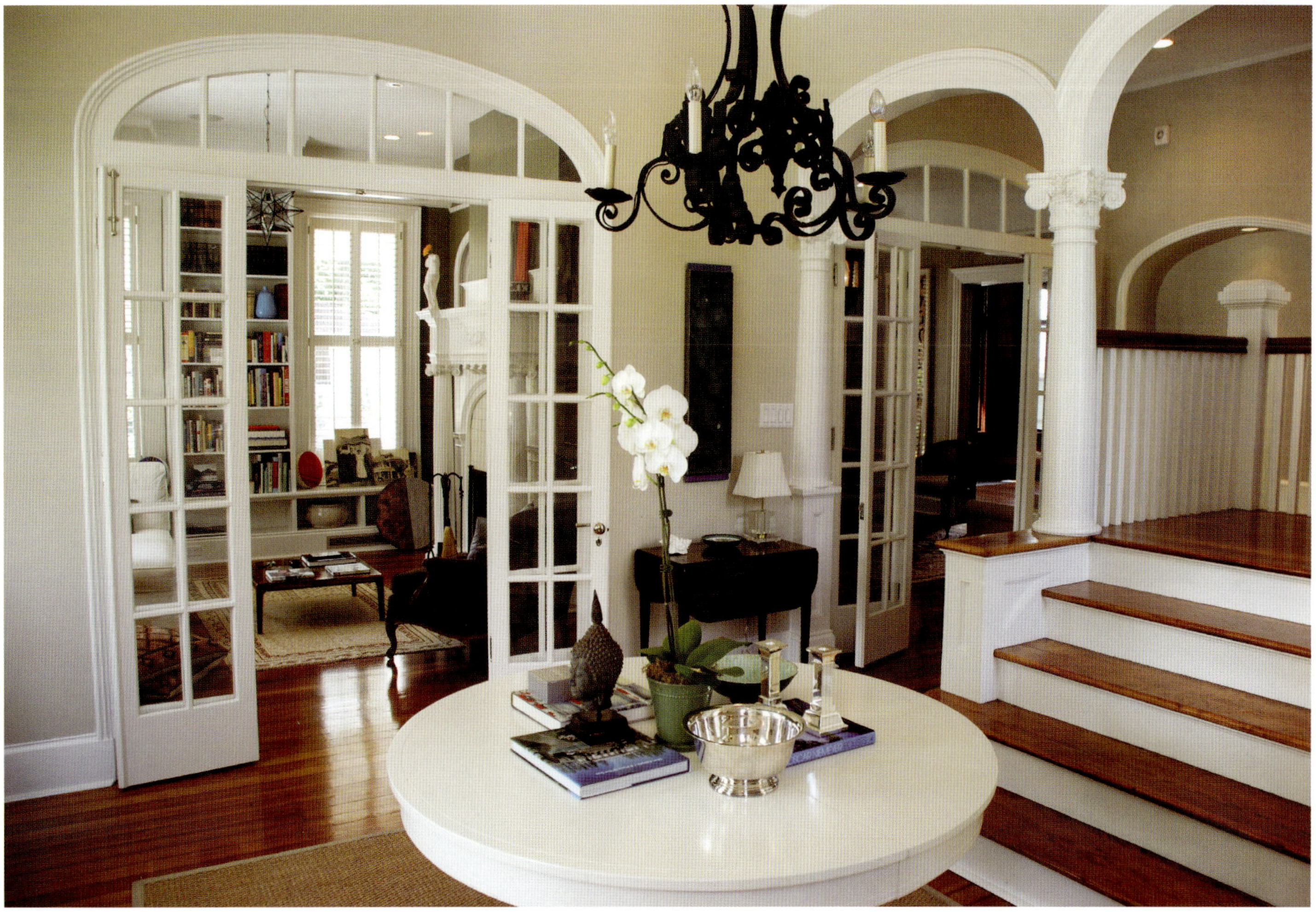

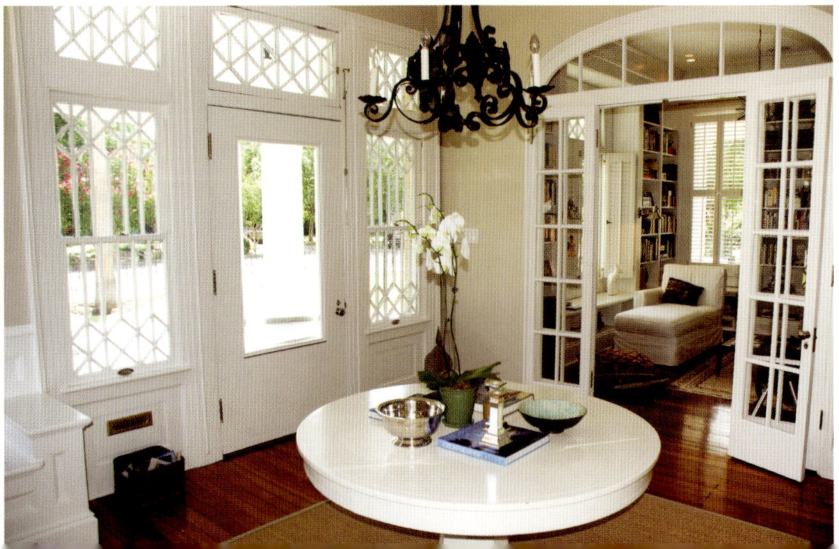

To the left of the entry door, French doors lead into a sitting room/library.

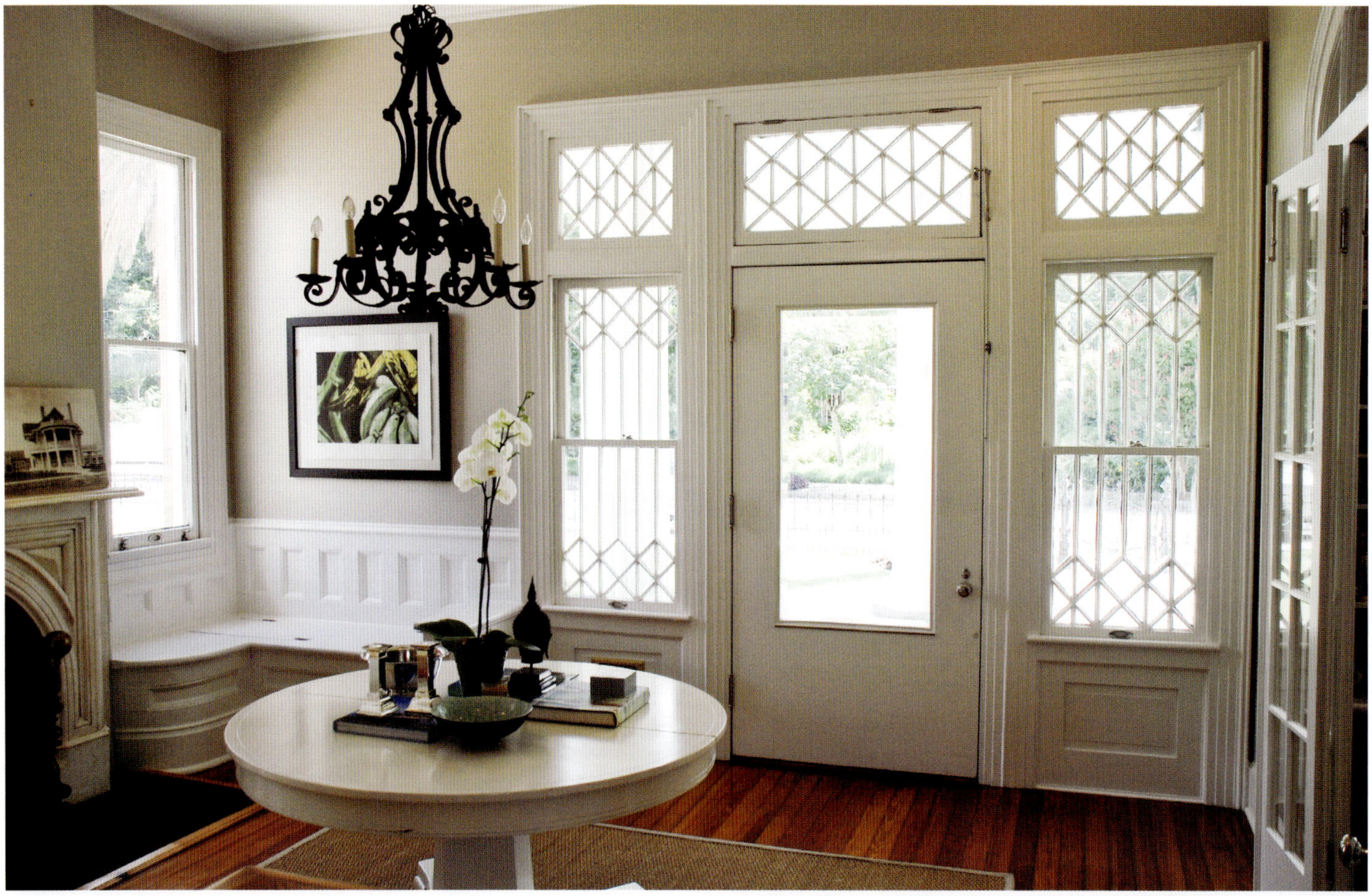

The gracious entry is composed of glass door, matching sidelights, and transoms with diamond panes. The window seat to the right of the fireplace is new, but looks original to the space.

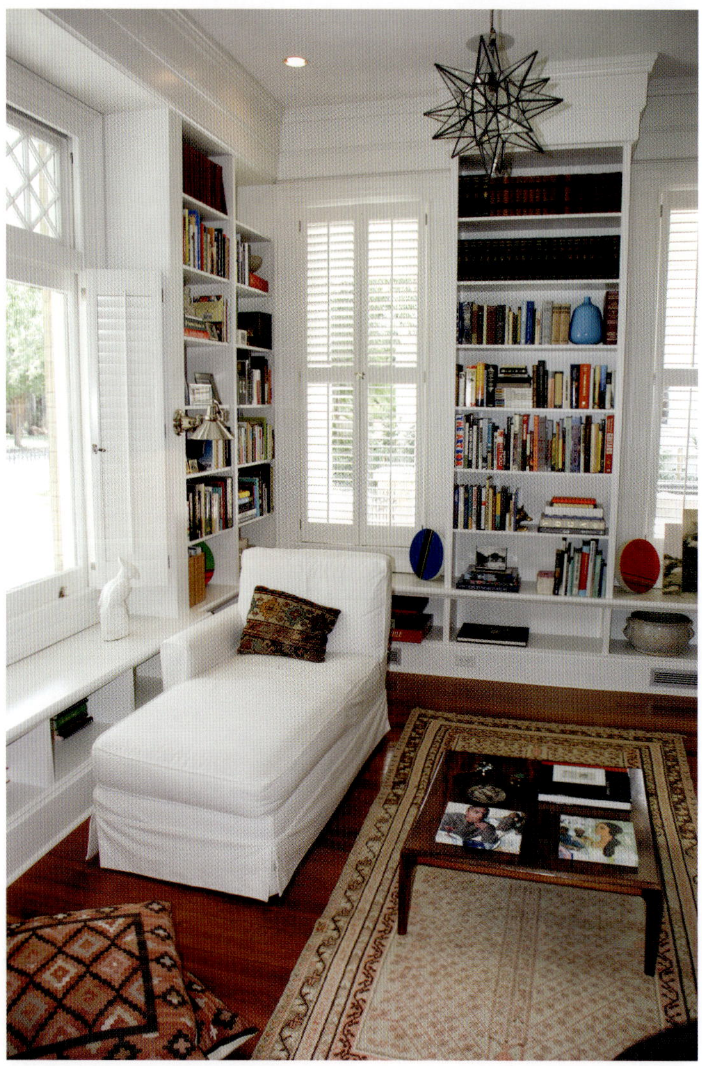

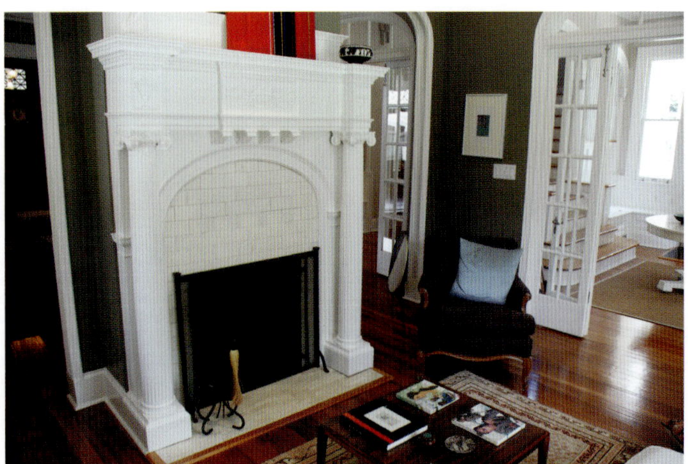

A chaise lounge provides comfortable seating in the sitting room/library, with its handsome fireplace.

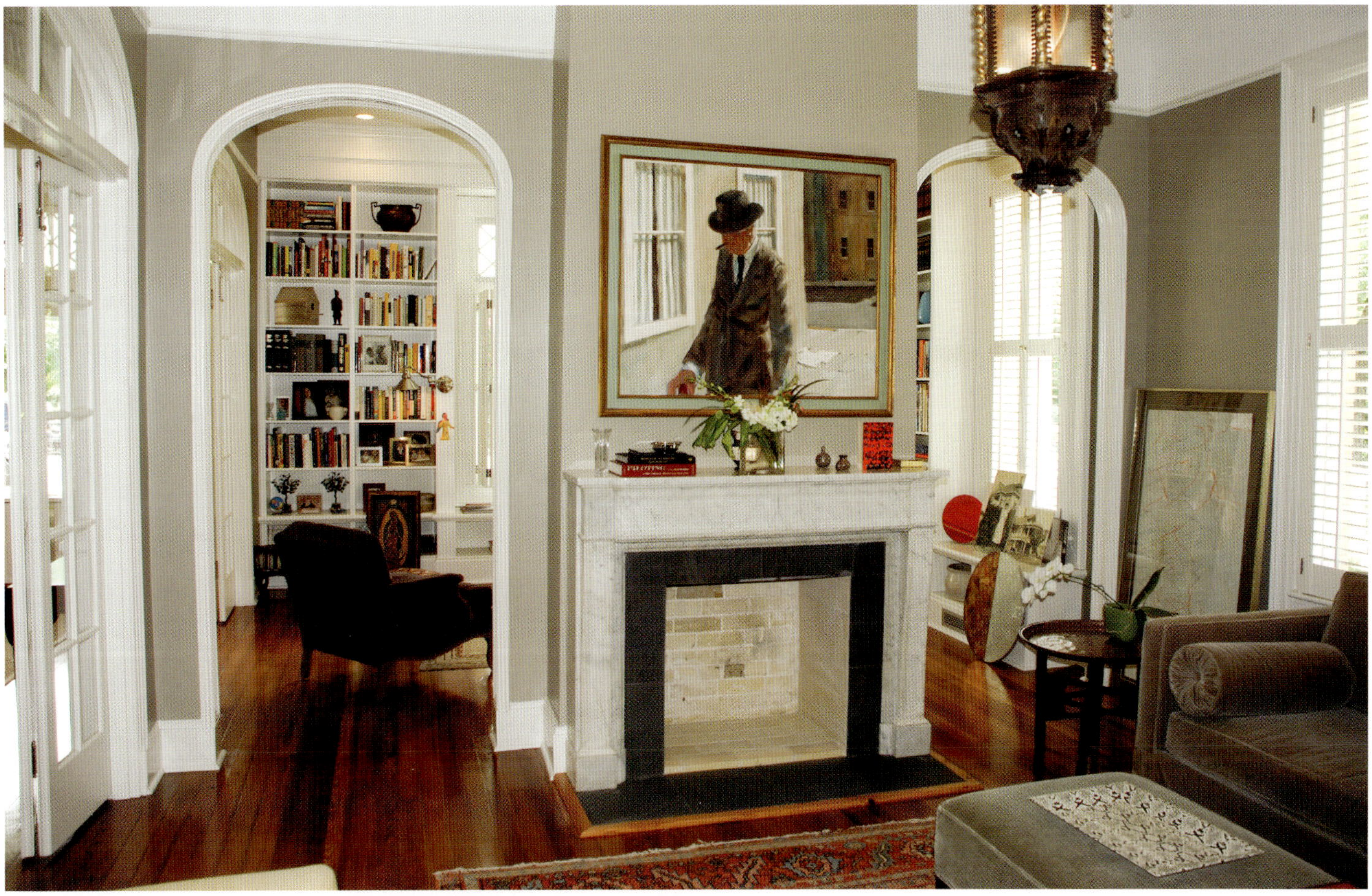

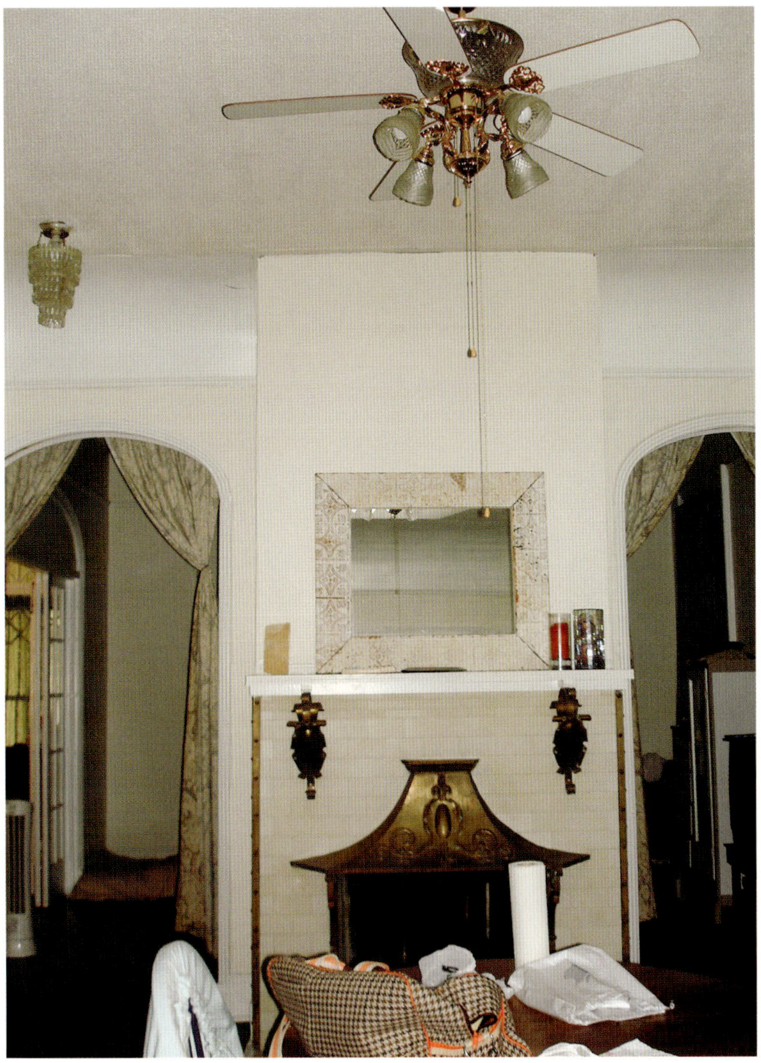

Adjacent to the sitting room/library is a comfortable living room with a fireplace that backs to the fireplace in the library. A classic mantel replaces the old copper pagoda-style.

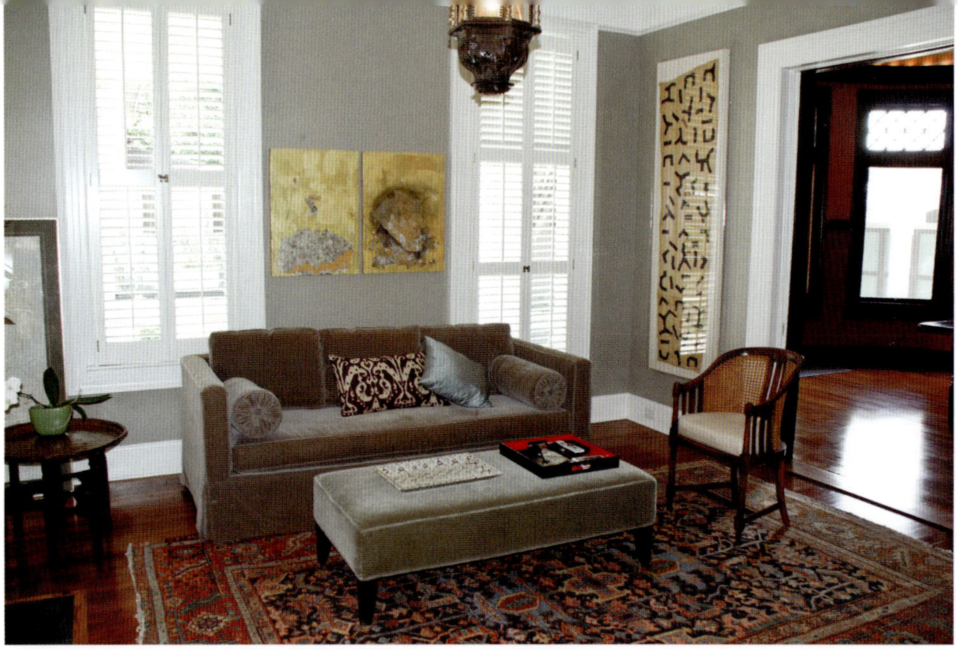

In the living room, muted colors and comfortable seating invite lingering.

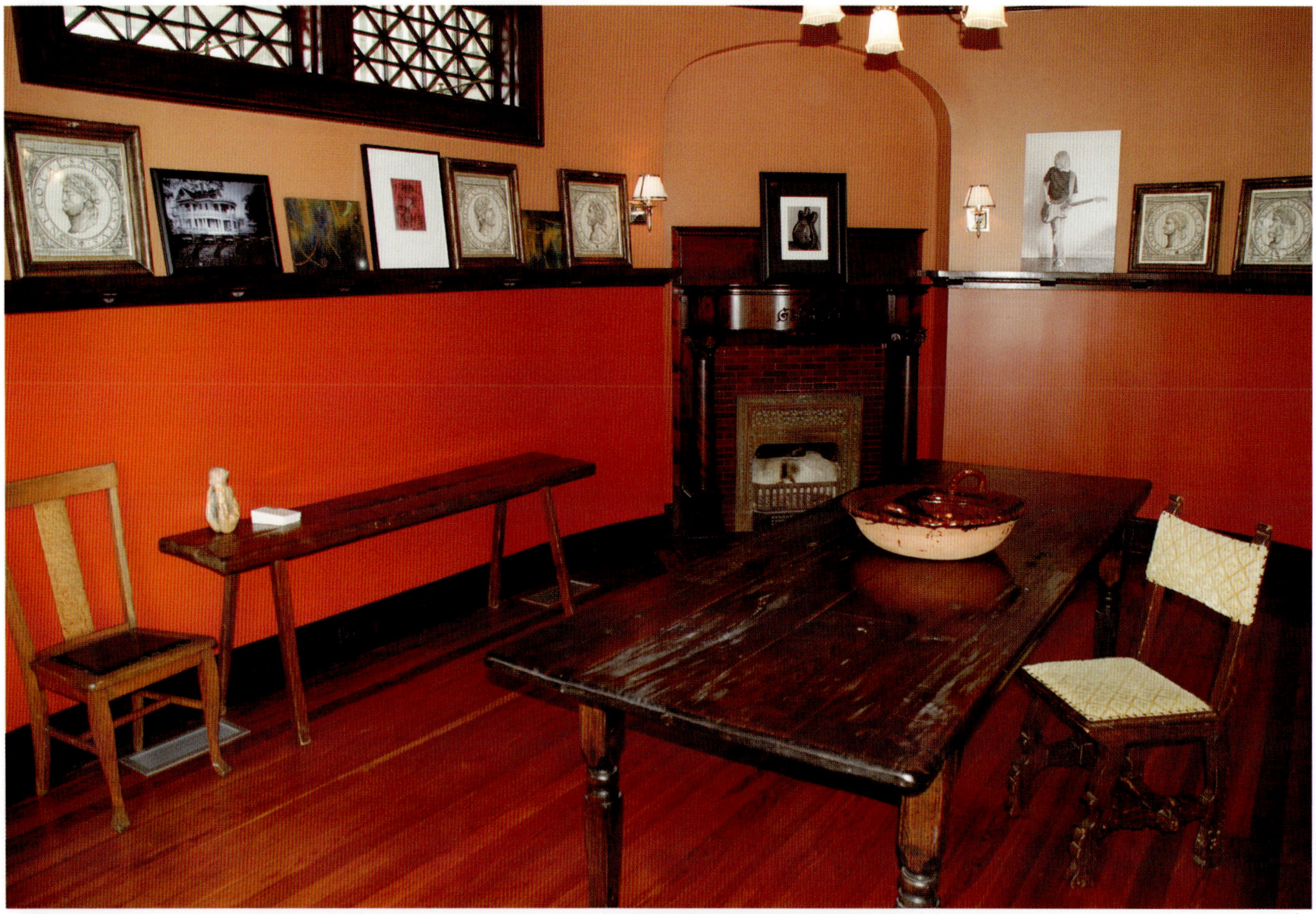

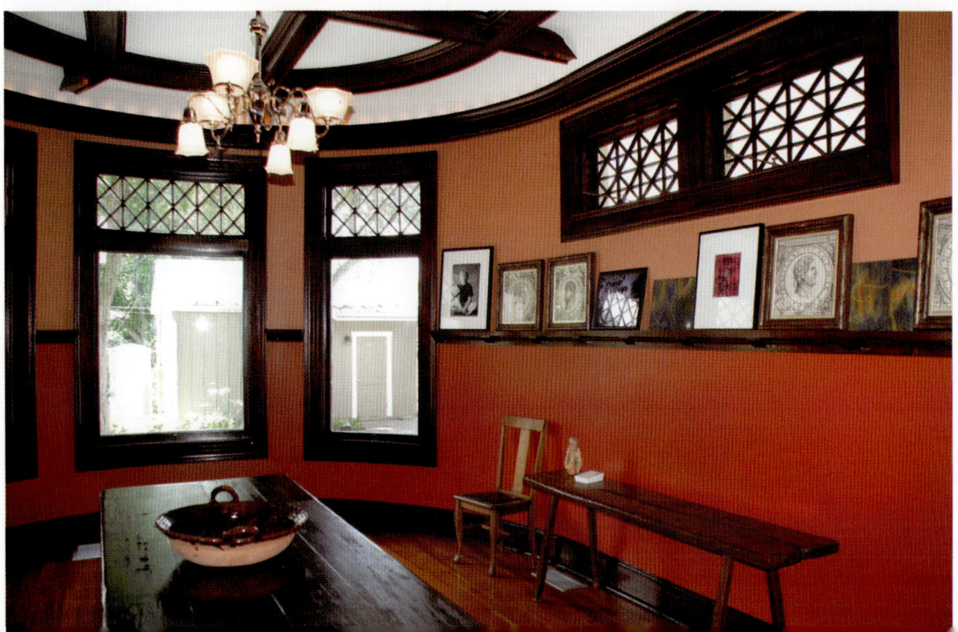

Large windows at one end and a fireplace at the other create an inviting dining room. Overhead, dark wood trim creates a tracery pattern.

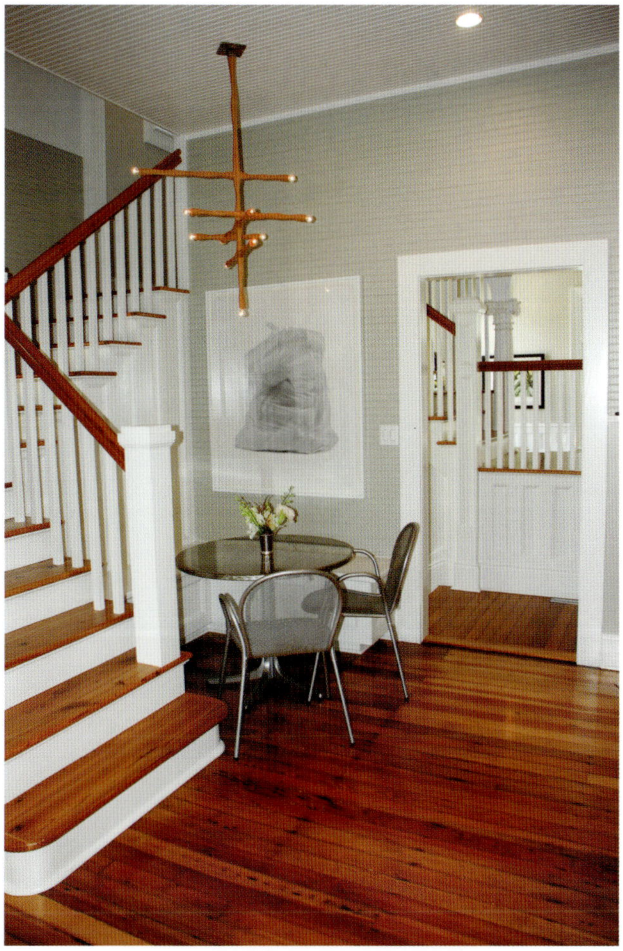

A passageway between the entry hall and dining room contains a butler's pantry and space for a breakfast table.

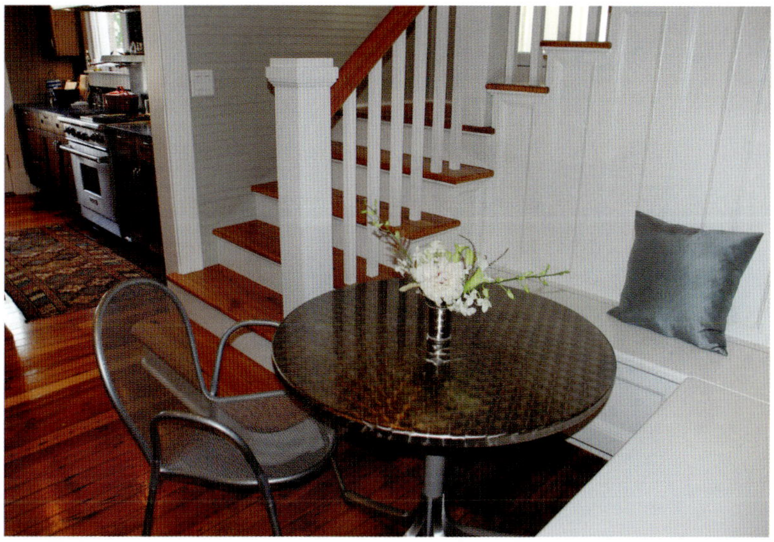

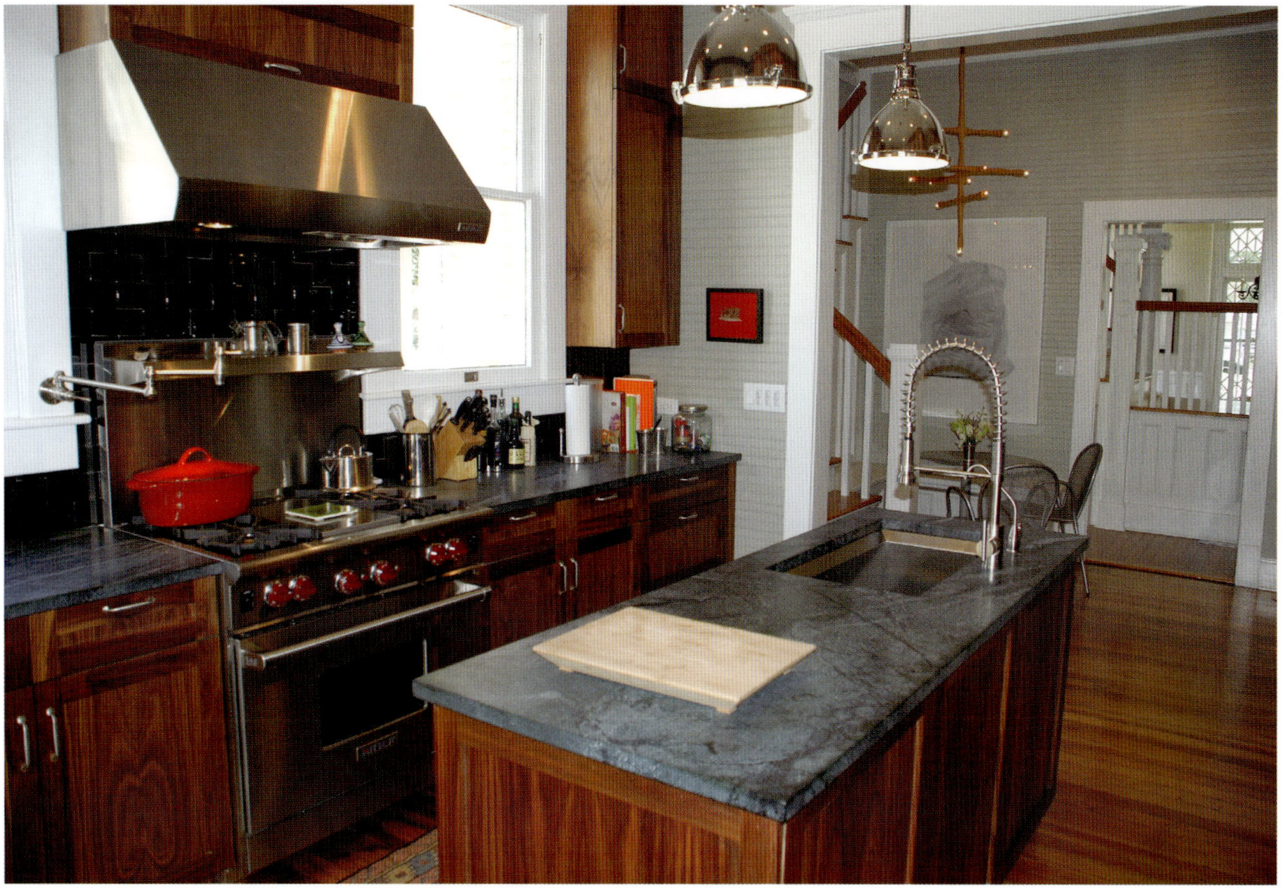

The kitchen was remodeled with up-to-date appliances and furnishings.

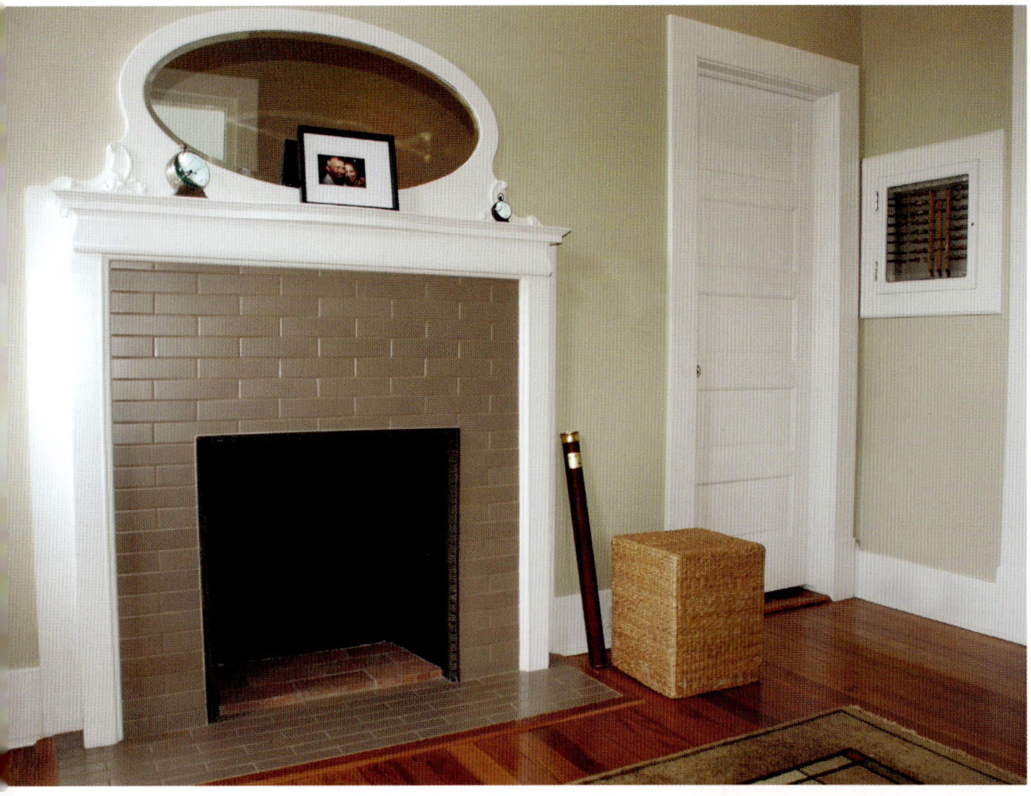

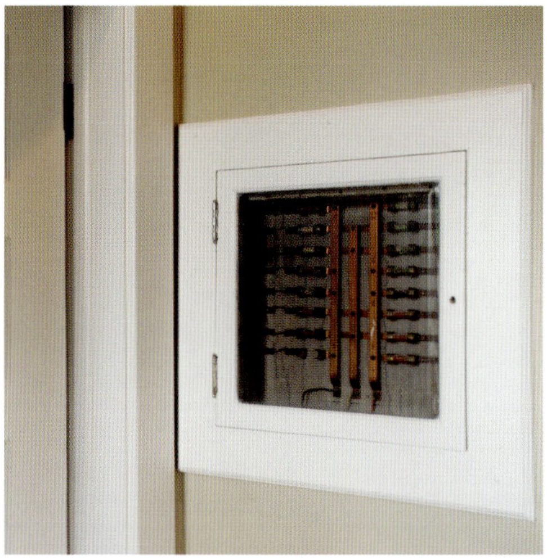

A bedroom on the second floor has its original fireplace and the old fuse box is treated now as an art object! Double sliding doors open into an adjoining sitting room.

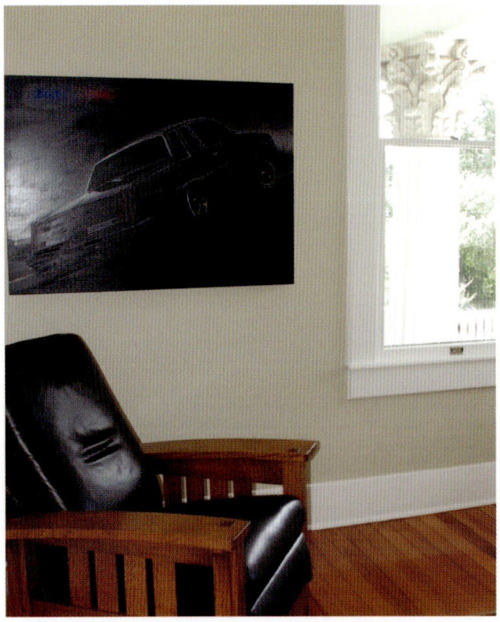

A Craftsman-style chair is juxtaposed with contemporary graphic artwork.

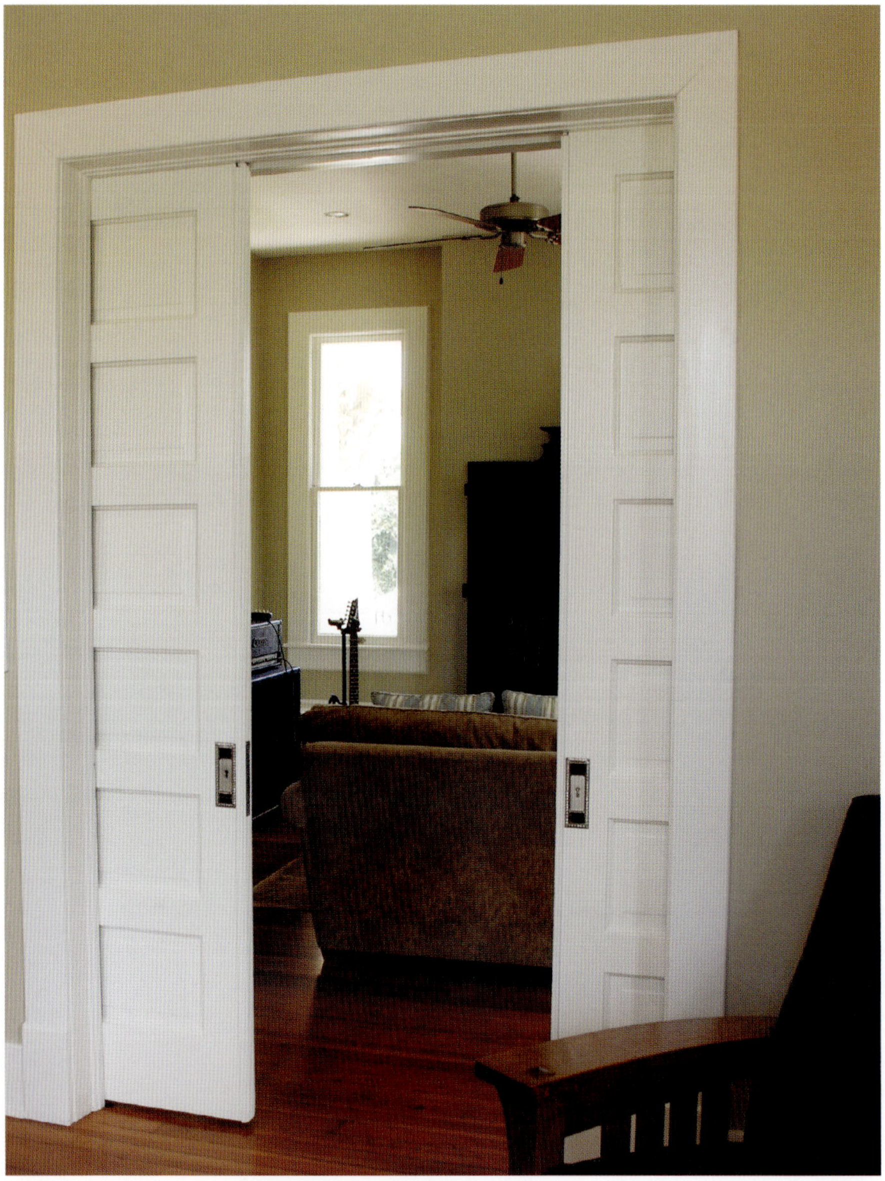

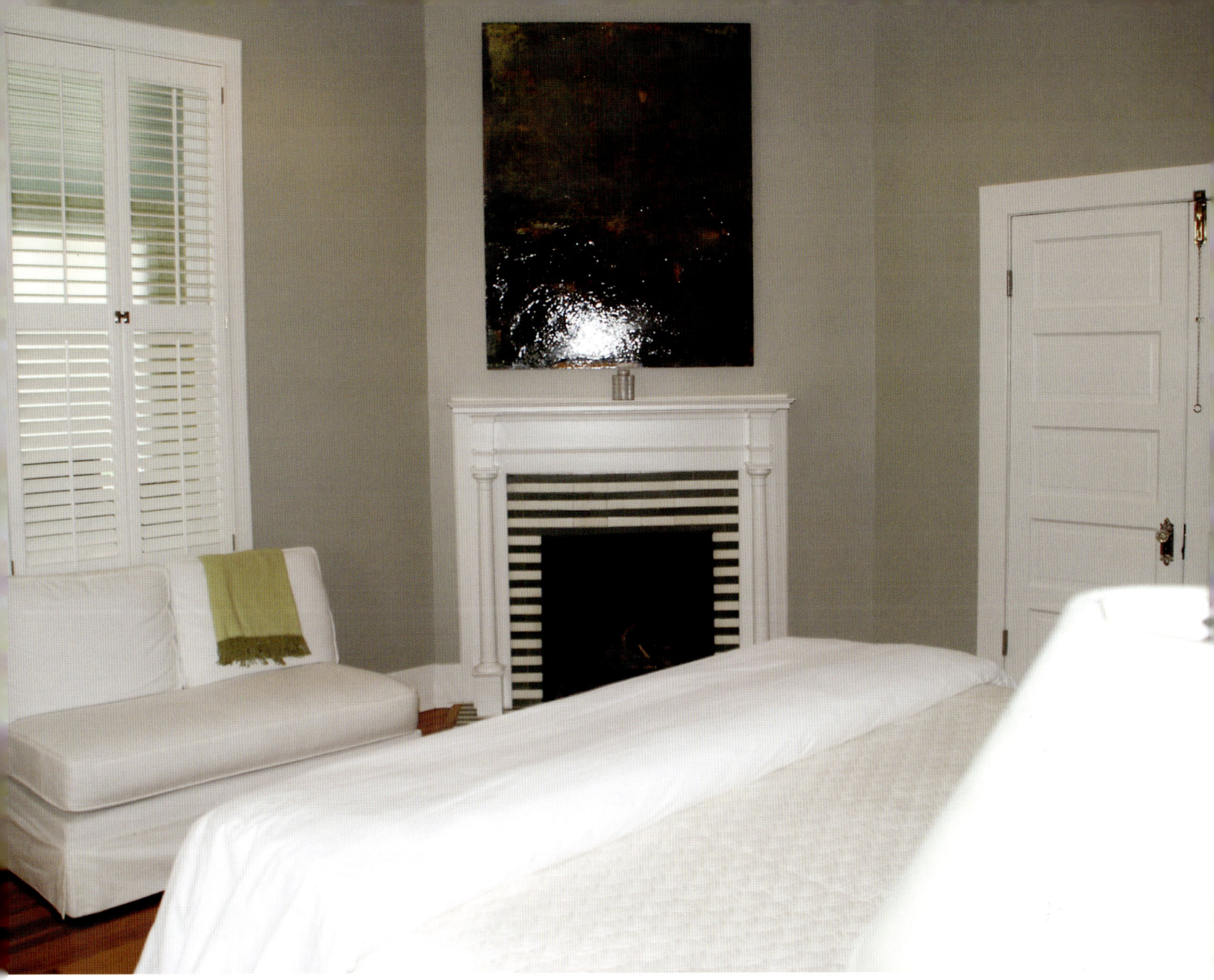

In the master bedroom, original tile enhances the fireplace, making it a graphic focal point.

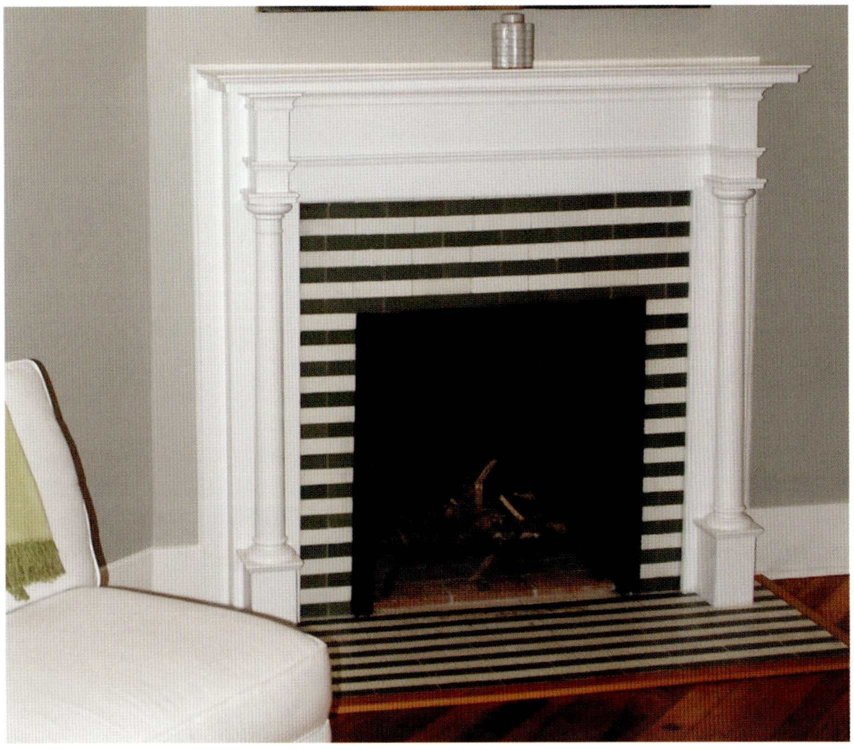

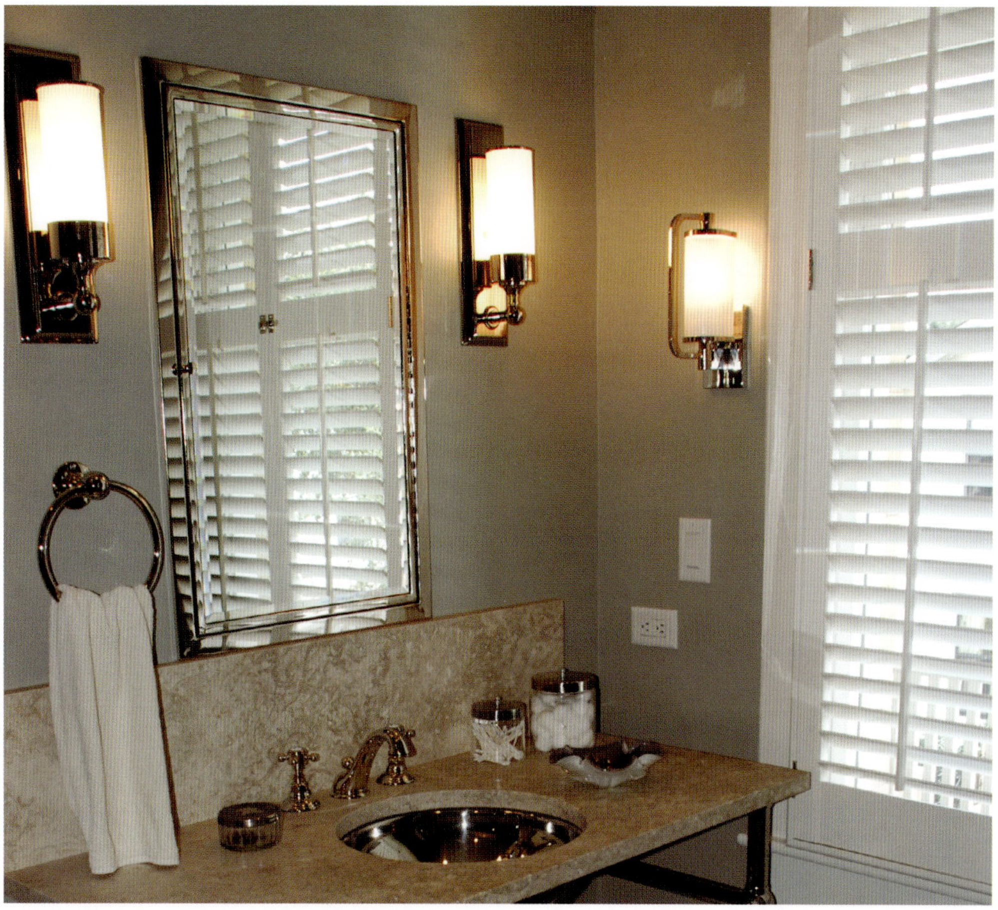

The master bathroom design includes back-to-back his-and-her lavatories, a state-of-the-art steam shower stall, and built-in storage shelves and cabinets.

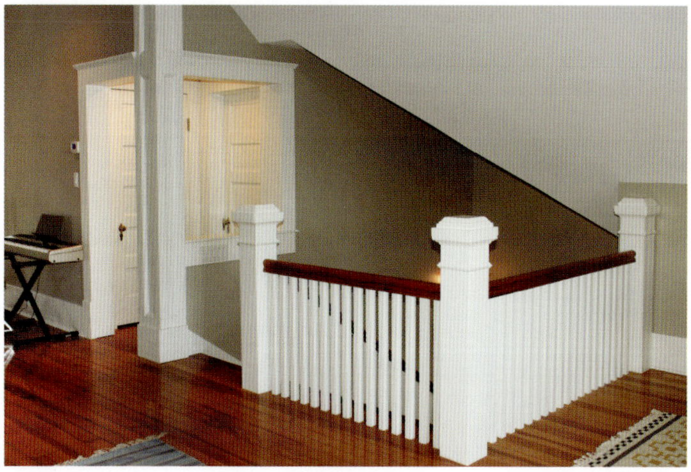

Stairs lead to the third floor, a handsomely finished full-footprint space that is a studio guest suite.

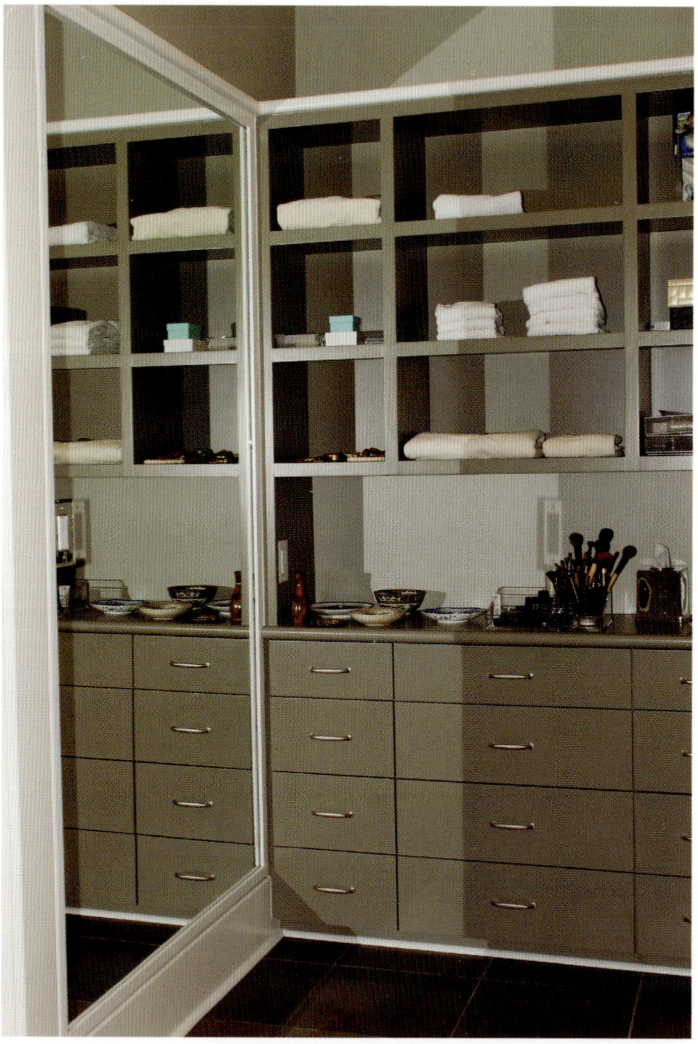

A handsome doorway leading to the balcony has a Greek-temple façade.

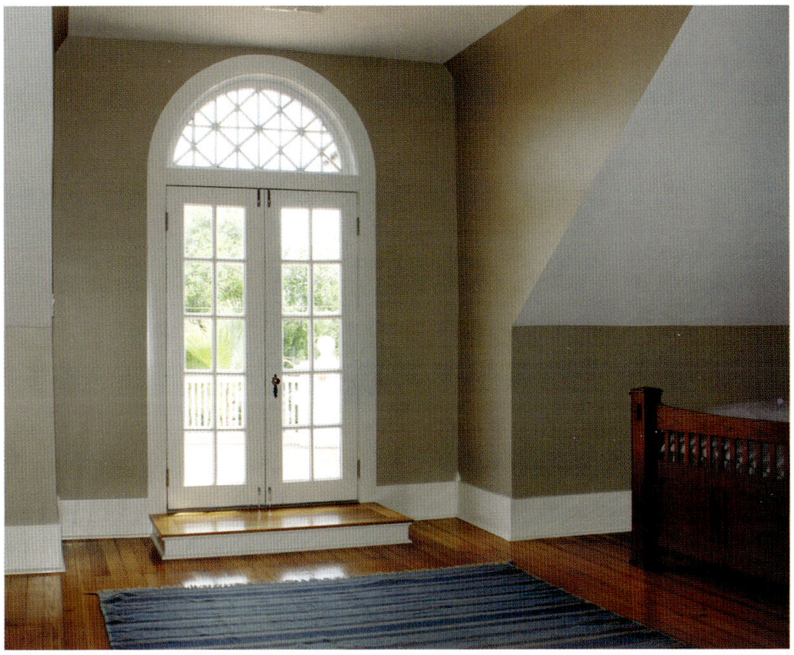

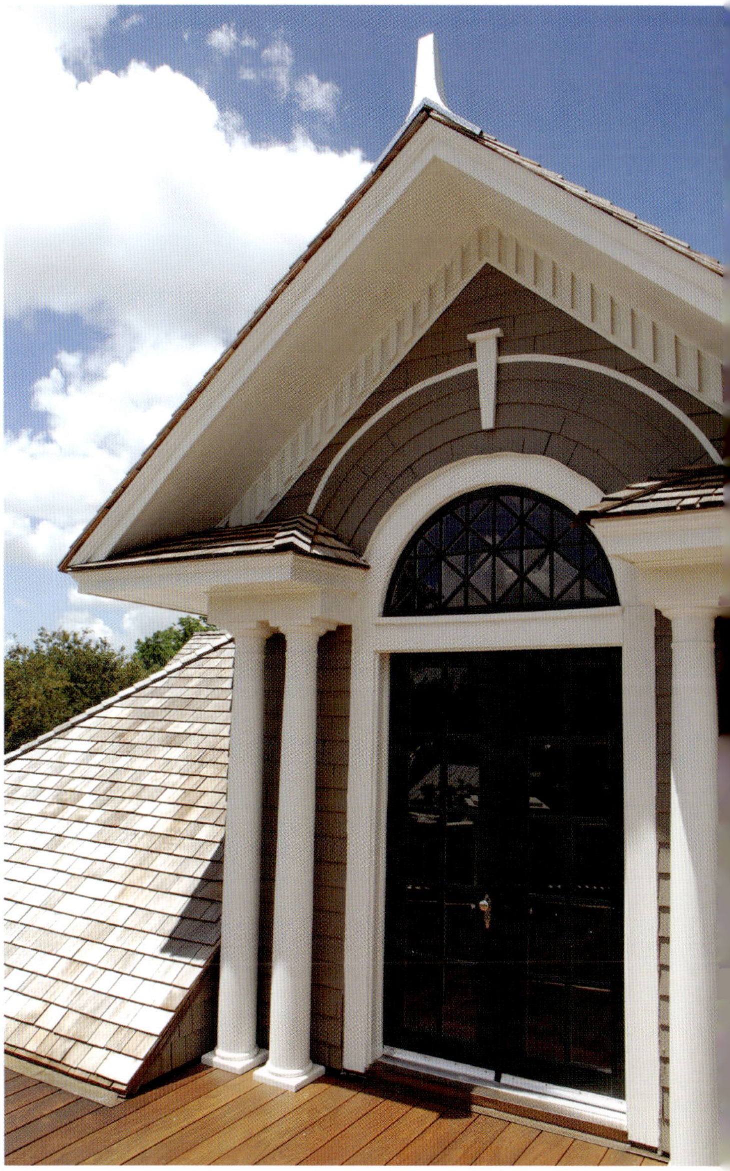

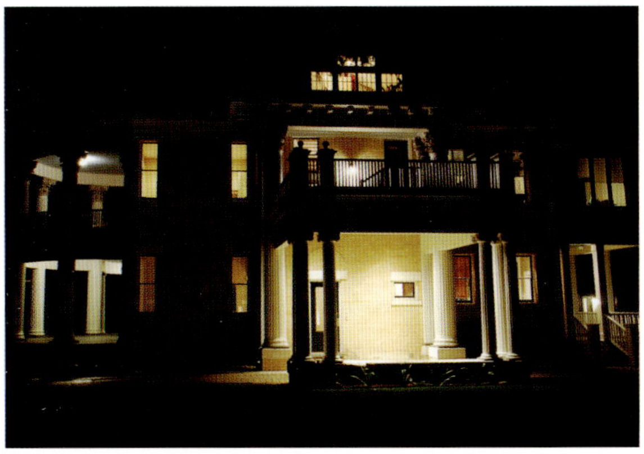

At night, the lighted home—once an eyesore—is now a beautiful beacon.

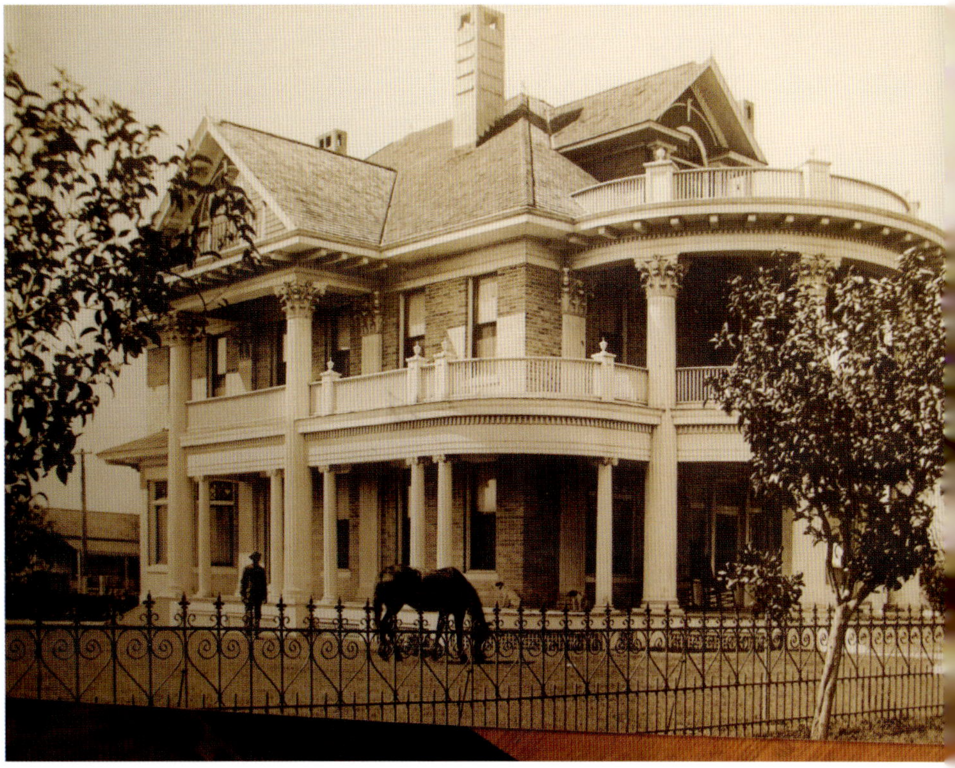

It is difficult to believe that the Luby family kept horses on the great lawn.

7
The Meerscheidt House

"From 1995 until Fall of 2010, my husband, Rex Stone, and I lived in the Otto Meerscheidt House on Adams Street," says Jay Hall, who knows a bit of the history of the imposing house. "It seems that brothers Axel and Paul Meerscheidt developed two parcels of land in this area, and Otto was their banker. According to King William Association records, in 1888, Axel and Paul purchased fifteen acres of land and another eighteen acres in 1890. Following their land acquisitions, they entered into a business arrangement with C. A. Stieren, a lumberman, to offer buyers the option of buying a lot or a lot with a house."

The house built for Otto and his wife, Nellie, in 1907 is a 5,300-square-foot structure in the imposing style that borrows from the Greek Revival style. A large attic, spacious basement, verandas, and decks add to the monumentality of this building. Like all houses in the King William area, it has a checkered past. "At one point, it was a Masonic Lodge," says Hall. "Some of the stained glass doors on the second floor opened to offices and are fitted with brass-rimmed mail slots. But, eventually it was restored to single-family occupancy and was listed on the National Register of Historic Places in 1980."

When Hall and Stone bought the grand house in 1995, especially appealing was the impressively scaled entry with graceful staircase and the large-scaled rooms. To the right of the oversized entry door with beautiful stained glass side- and over-lights is the large 18-foot by 18-foot living room. Adjoining the living room is the spacious formal dining room (20-foot by 18-foot). "What caught my eye in this elegant room was the large, extraordinarily beautiful built-in china cabinet and beautifully detailed coffered ceiling," says Hall. To the left of the entry door is a generously sized family room (17-foot by 18-foot). Behind that is a 17-foot by 16-foot kitchen designed for serious cooks. Called a "gourmet kitchen," it features a large granite-topped island, six-burner commercial stainless steel gas stove, and Subzero refrigerator. Of course, like all grand old houses, there is a butler's pantry (*sans* butler, it is now fitted out as a wet bar). The downstairs also has a "bonus" room and a convenient powder room.

The second floor contains three bedrooms, a home office, two full baths, a library/study, and a very large and airy sunroom. And, of course, there is that very large covered veranda with classical columns and beautifully detailed railings. The veranda extends into a demilune shape above the entry steps—a highly distinctive element in the design of the façade.

Throughout, 12-foot high ceilings and beautiful wood floors are grace notes much envied in contemporary housing. A large central air conditioning unit is zoned for room-to-room climate control on the ground floor. Two units provide cooling for the second floor.

The second story sunroom overlooks the rear deck that was added by Hall and Stone in 2004. Other outdoor amenities added by the couple include a hot tub/spa with deck, gazebo, and privacy fencing. New landscaping included installation of a water feature loved by birds, a sprinkler system, and lighting. Mature pecan, citrus, and other fruit trees create a beautiful oasis surrounding the main house and the detached cottage at the rear—an oasis in what was once farm land, then a development, and now a truly urbane urban area.

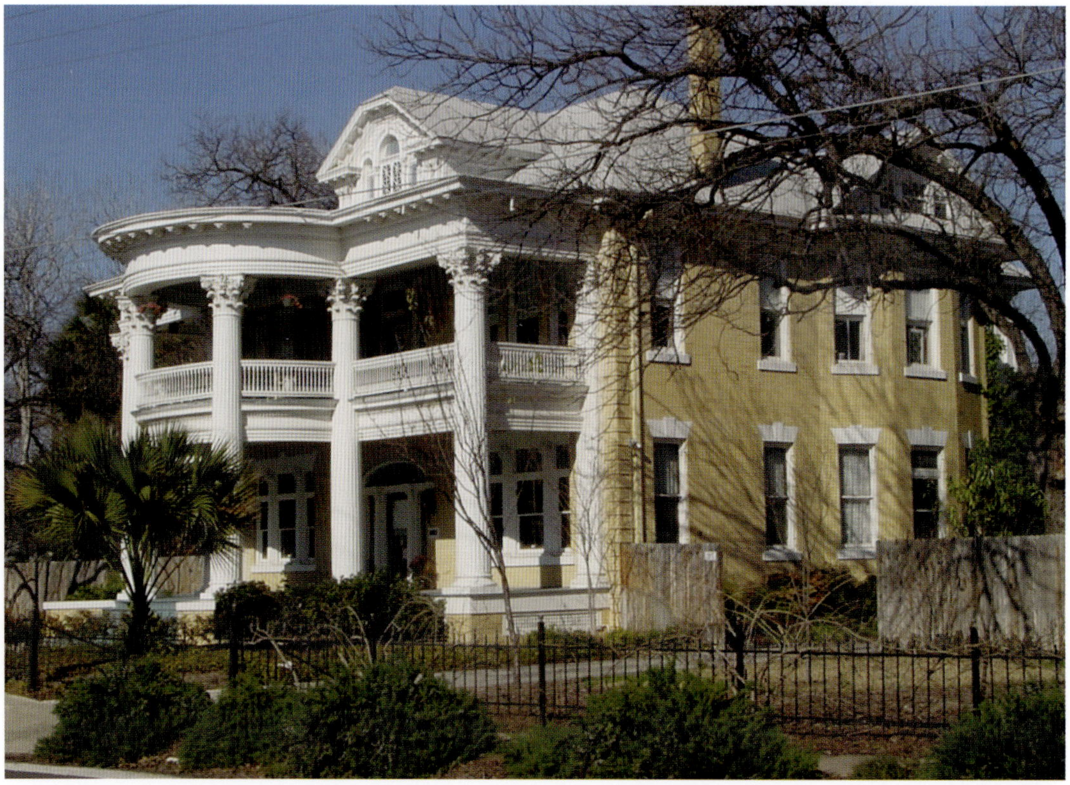

Built in 1907, the Greek Revival Meerscheidt House was placed on the roster of the National Register of Historic Places in 1980. A gracious demilune veranda distinguishes the street façade of the grand house. *Photographs by David Strahan, AIA*

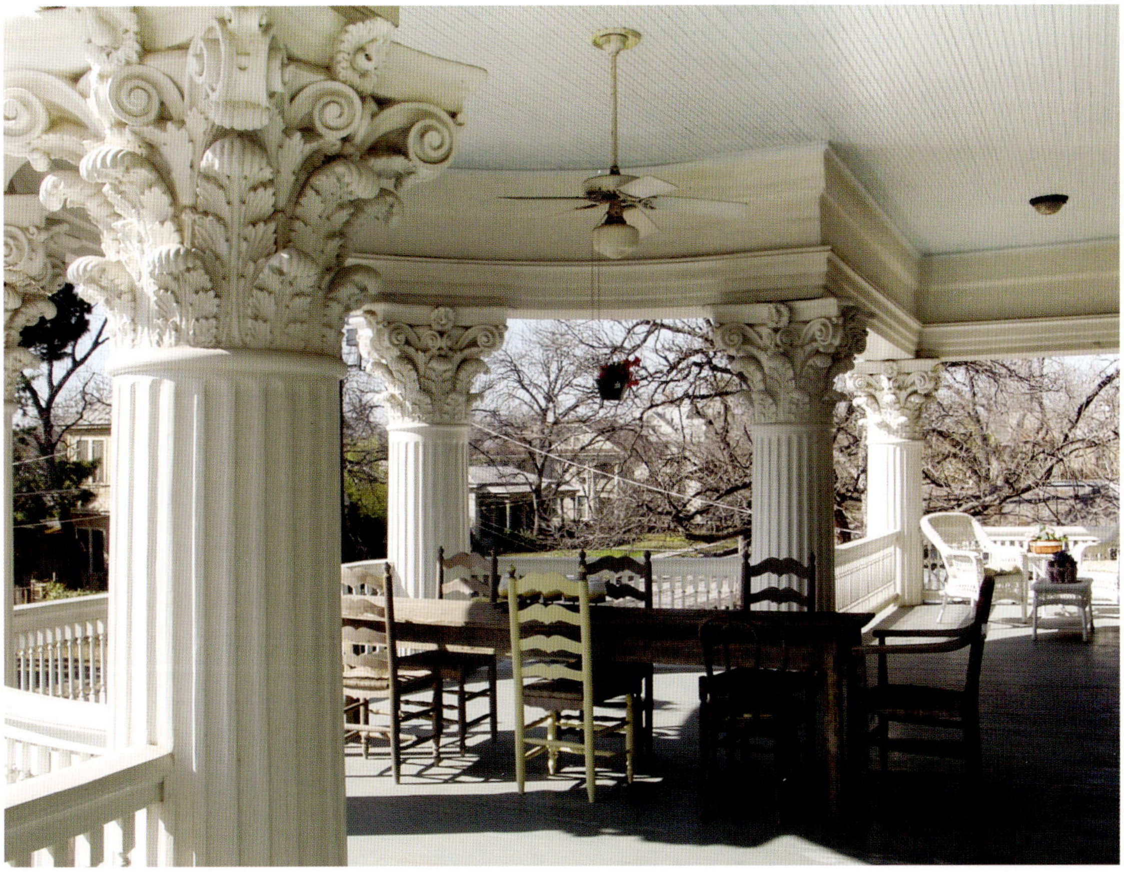

Classic Greek architectural elements are evidenced in the Corinthian-inspired columns and decorative elements beneath the overhang.

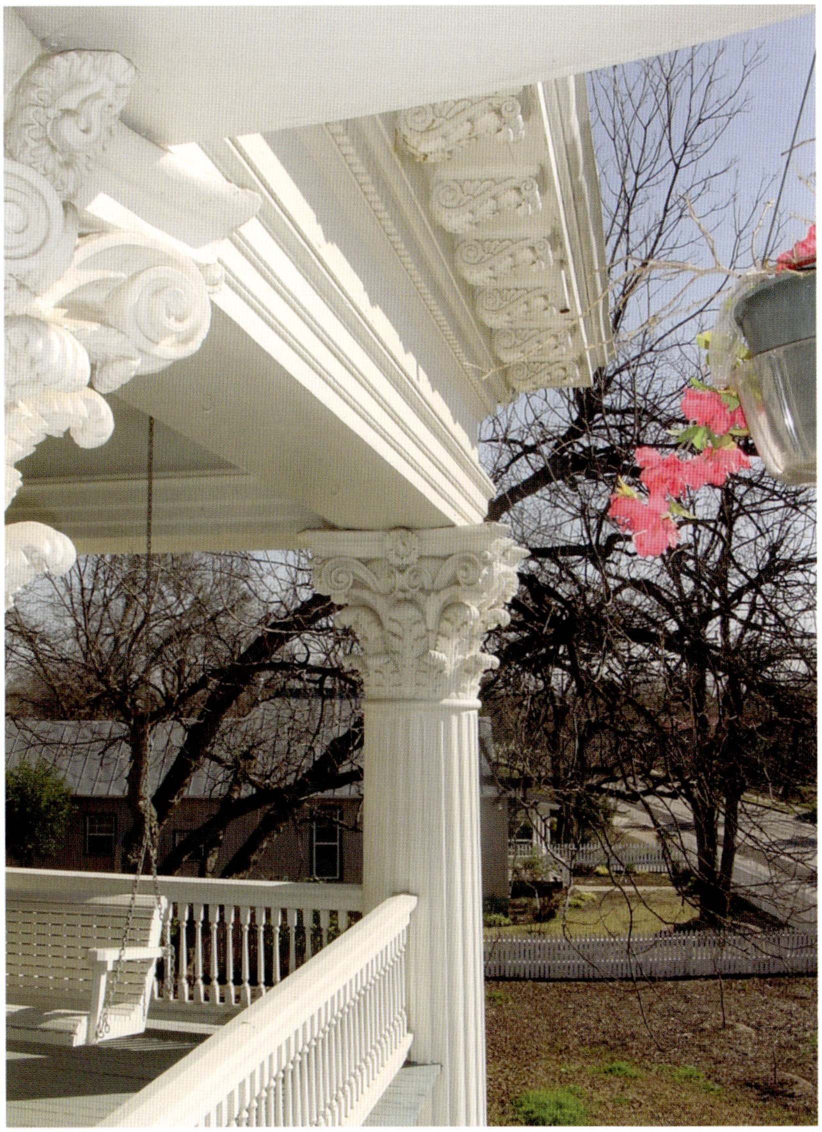

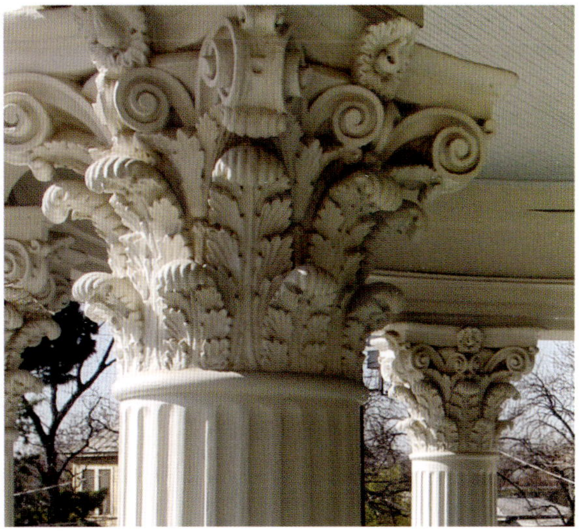

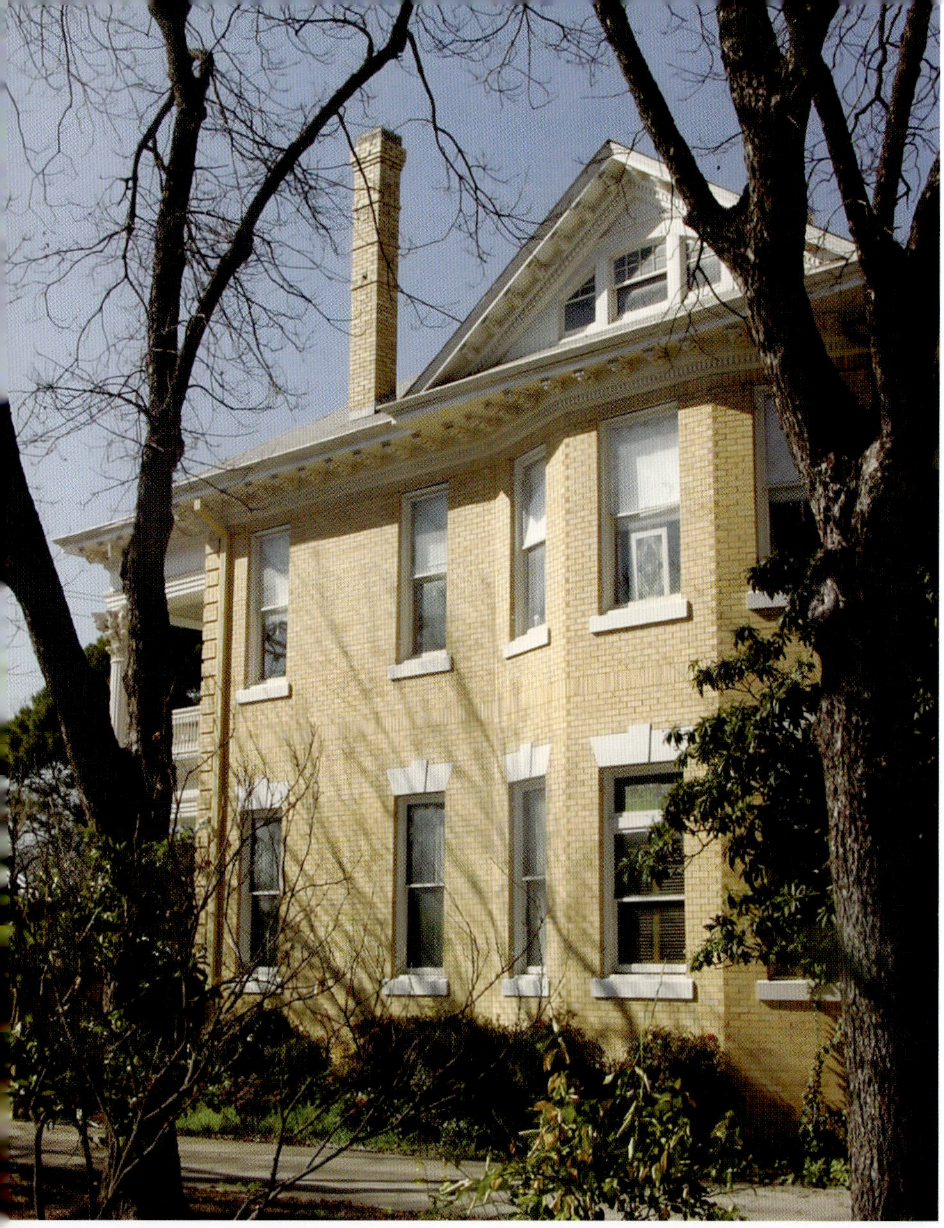

Meerscheidt House's side elevation features classic rhythmic placement of windows with keystone surrounds. Carefully planned brickwork includes subtle features such as a horizontal banding or stream courses that distinguishes individual floors.

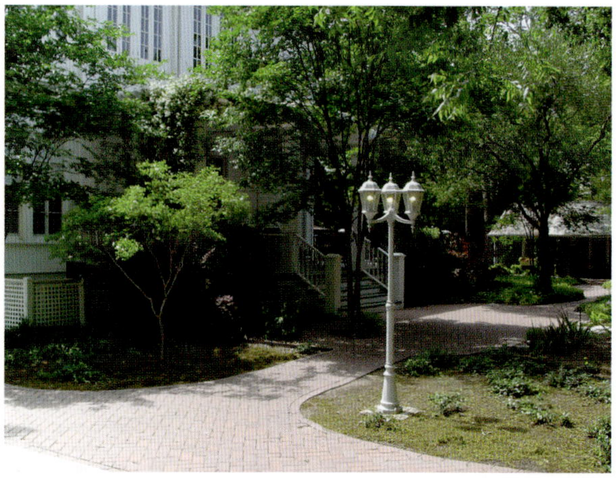

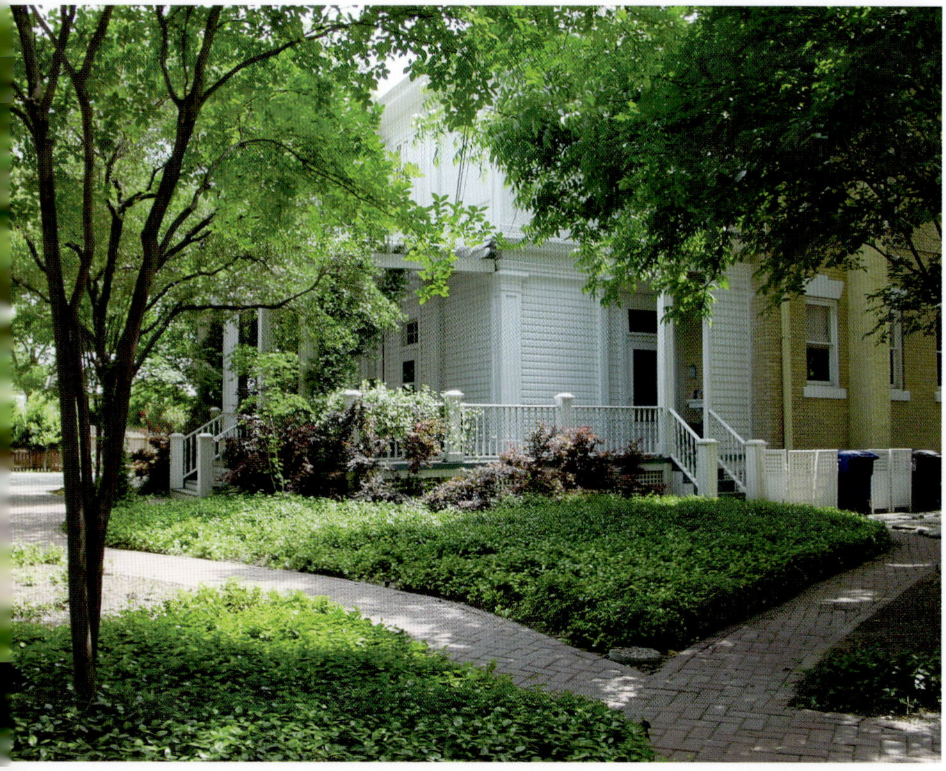

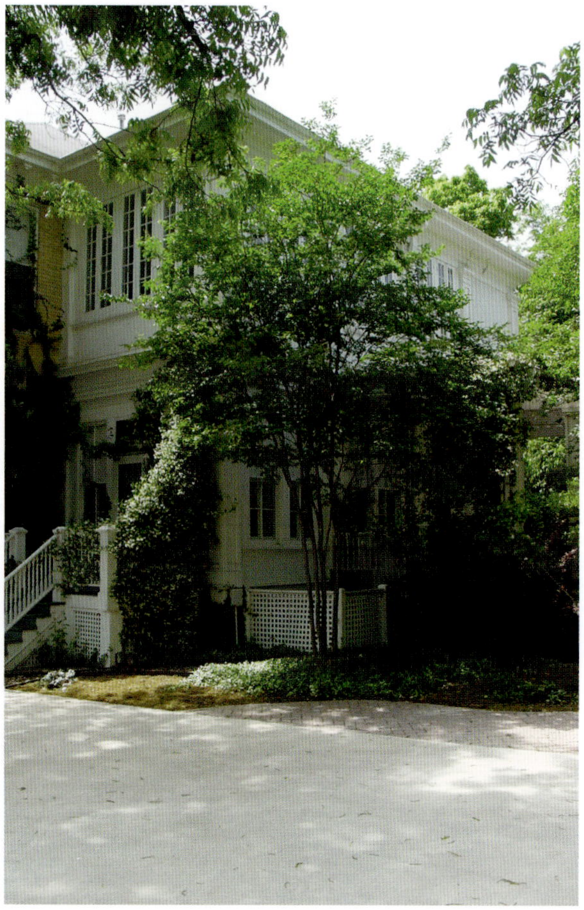

A recent addition at the rear of the house includes a porch and second-story sunroom that respects the history of the house while updating it to meet the owners' lifestyle. Lush new landscaping features abundant foliage, gazebo with hot tub-spa, vintage-look lamppost, water feature, and a guest house.

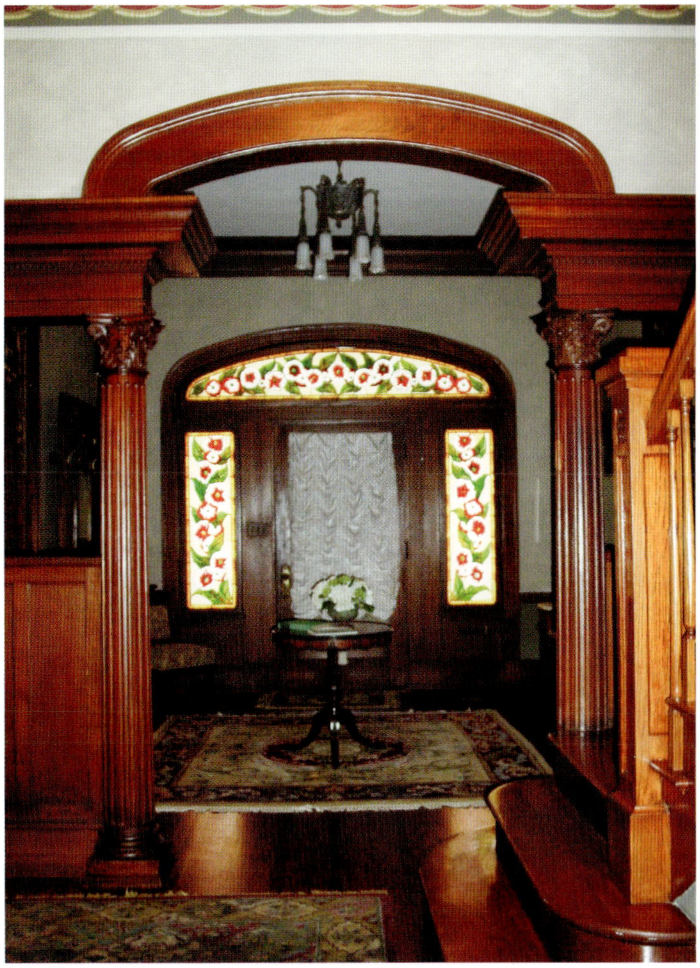

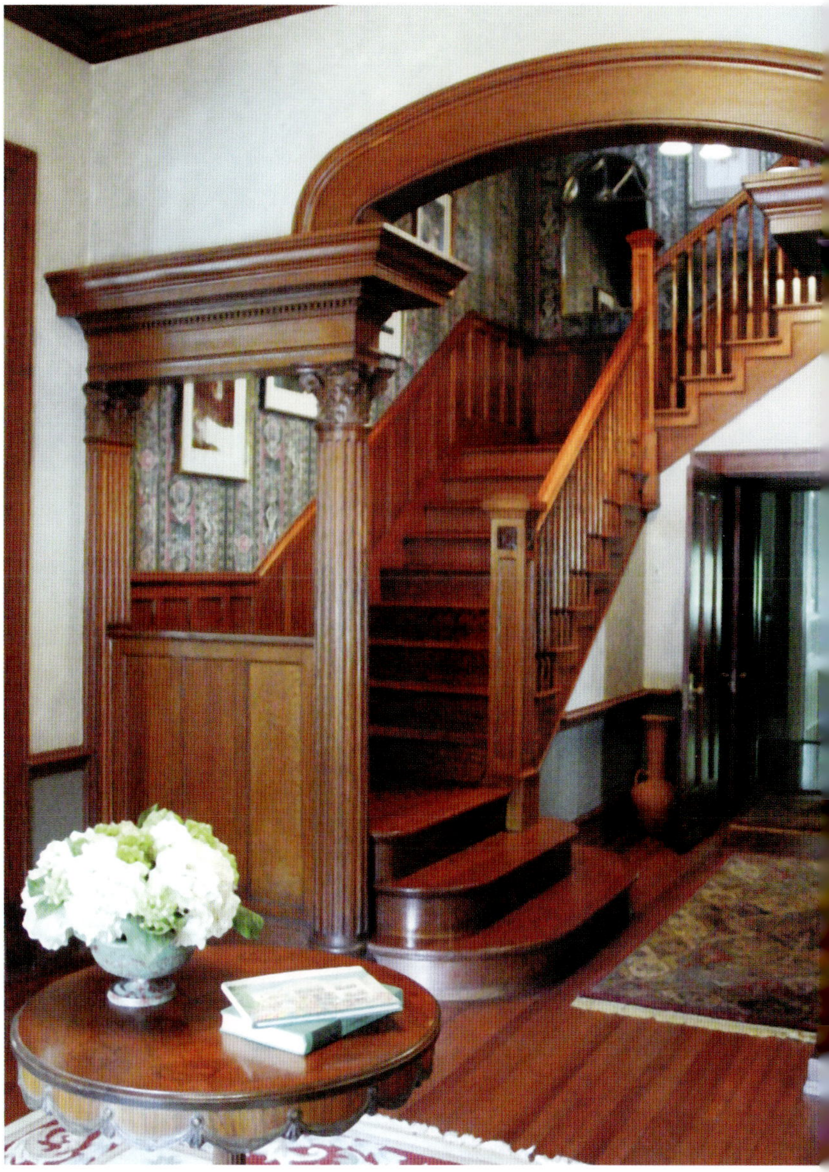

A Tiffany-inspired, morning glory-theme stained glass surrounds the entry door. Corinthian style columns and dark wood-trimmed arches repeat certain Greek Revival elements of the exterior. Curvilinear metal grille work associated with the Victorian era accents passages from the entry hall into various rooms. Floral wallpaper in the stairwell recalls the Victorian love of large-scale pattern and strong color.

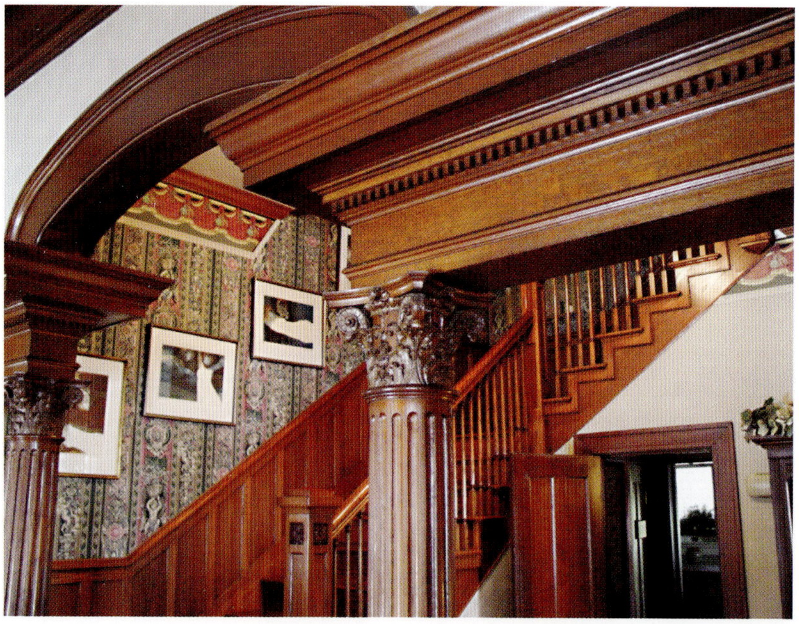

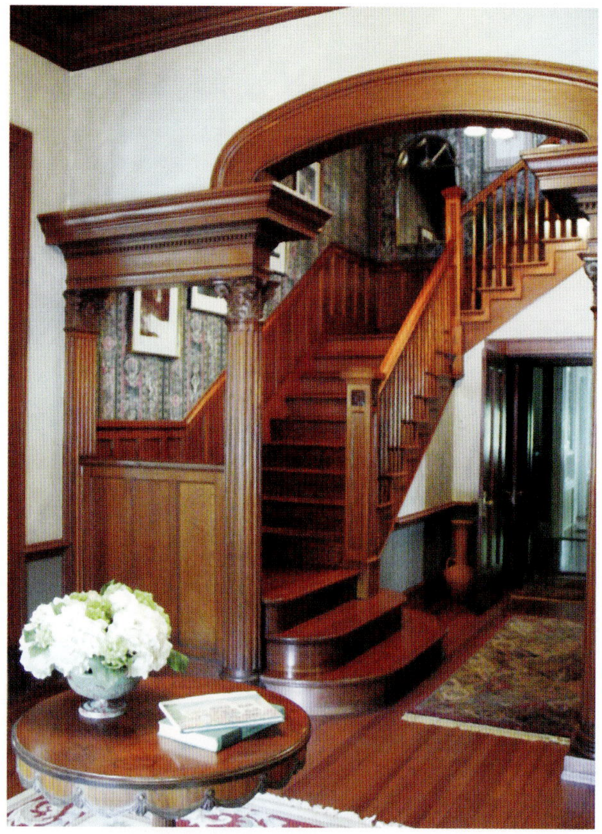

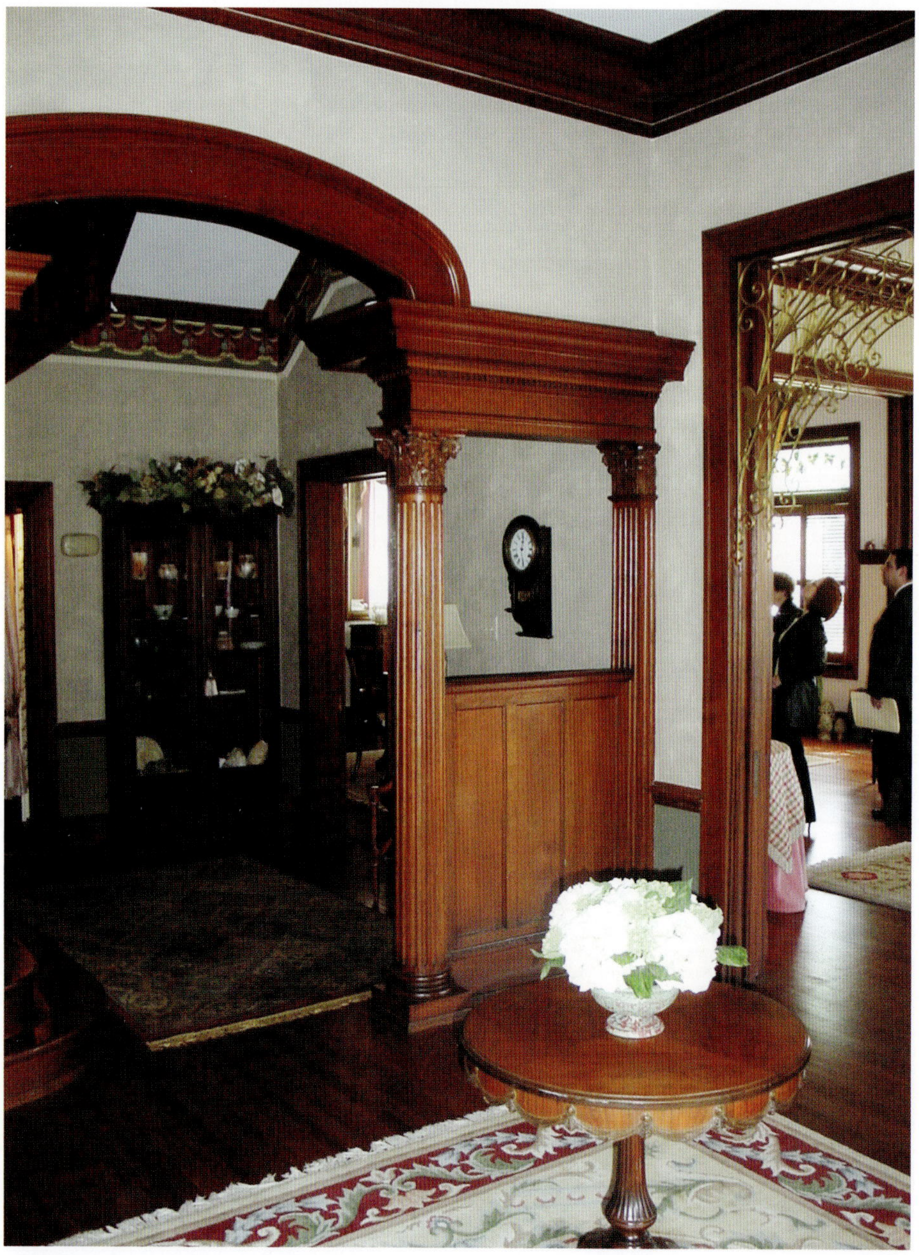

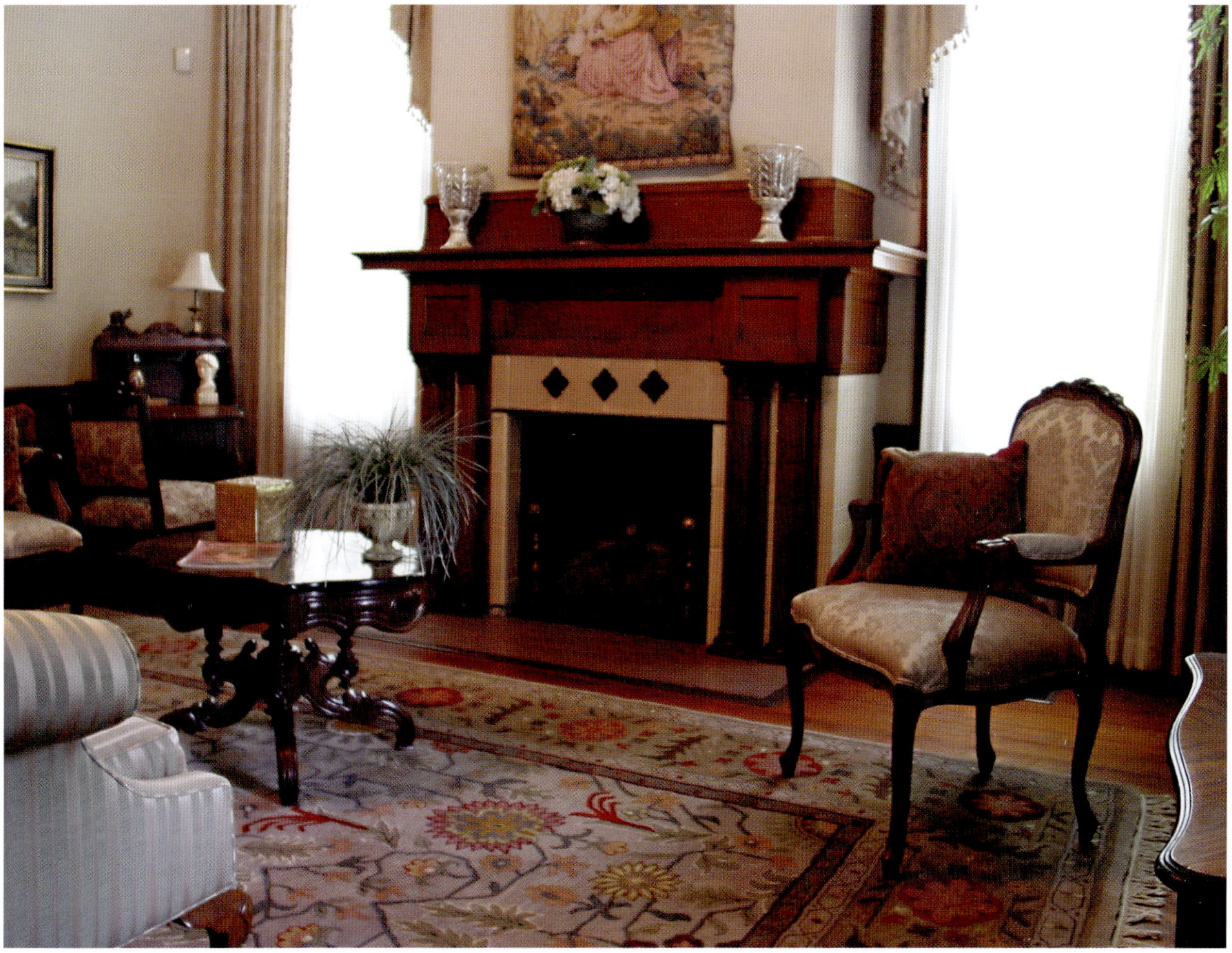

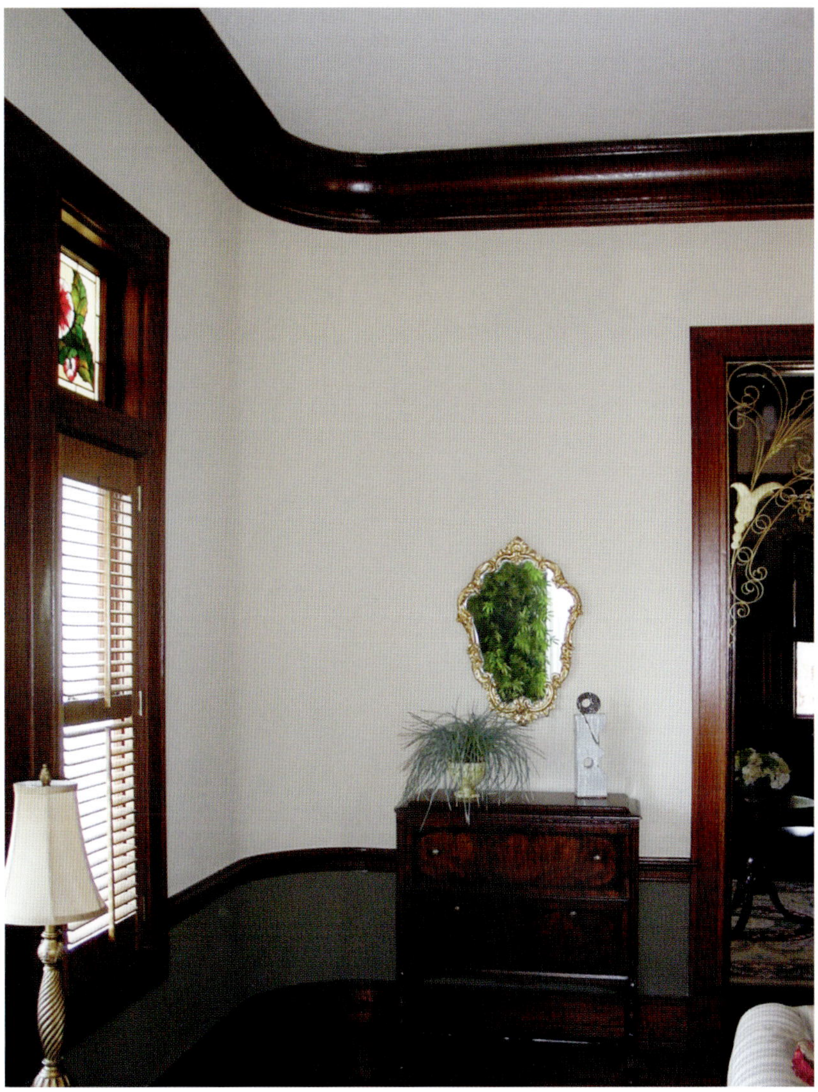

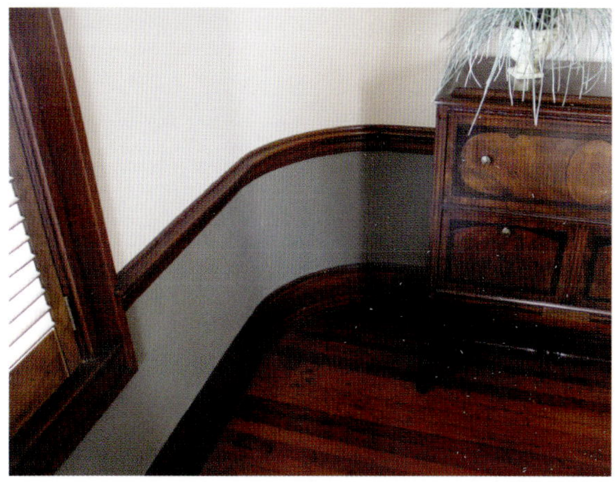

A mainstay of the parlor, the carved fireplace mantle creates a focal point for upholstered seating. Rich wood, original to the house, is used for flooring, chair railings, and ceiling molding. Double-hung windows are elegantly elongated with stained glass over-lights.

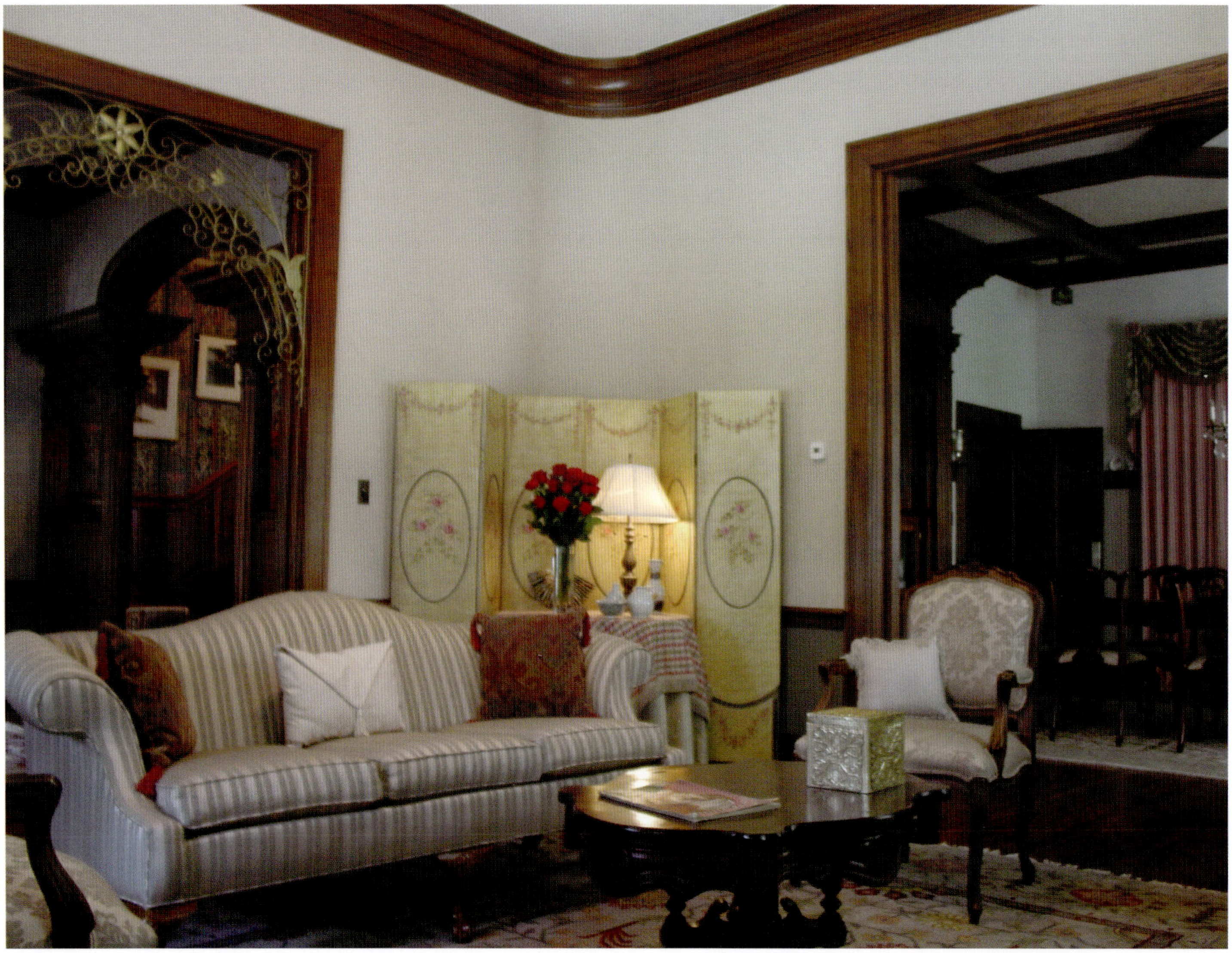

Decorative Victorian touches, seen in the standing screen and carpeting, evoke the spirit of the time. Through the parlor's wood-embellished passage, the warmly elegant dining room is easily accessed.

By design, the magnificent carved china cabinet is integrated with the wood-trim that creates a distinctive pattern on the dining room ceiling. A picture- or plate-rail displays collectibles.

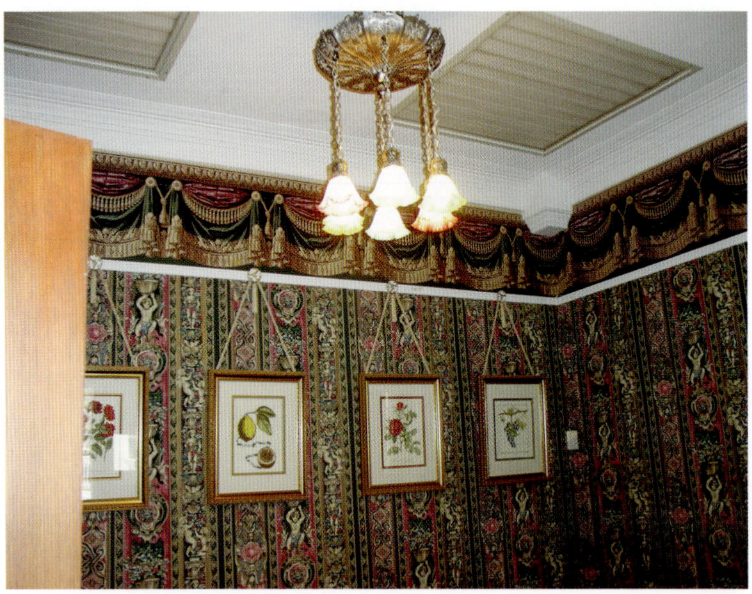

Wallpaper provides a background for crisp, white-matted art hung from a picture rail.

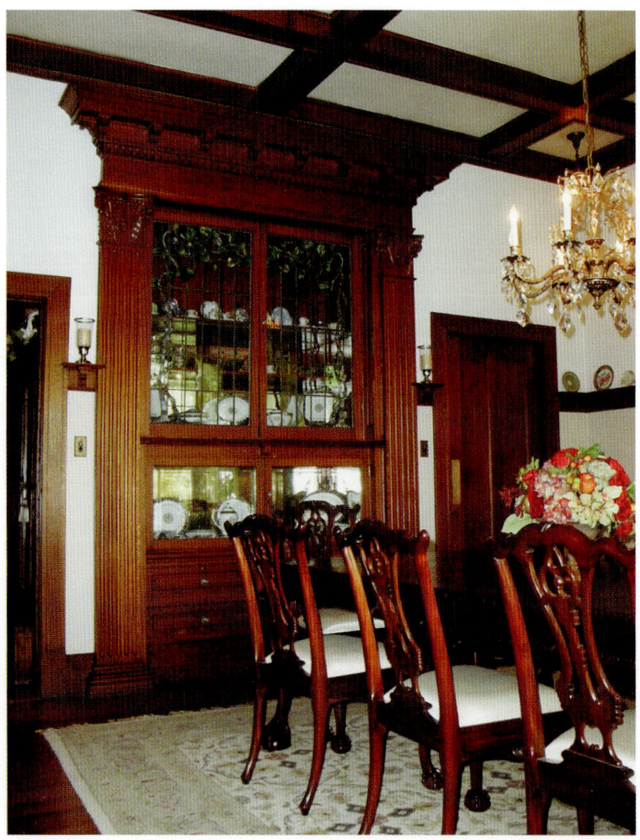

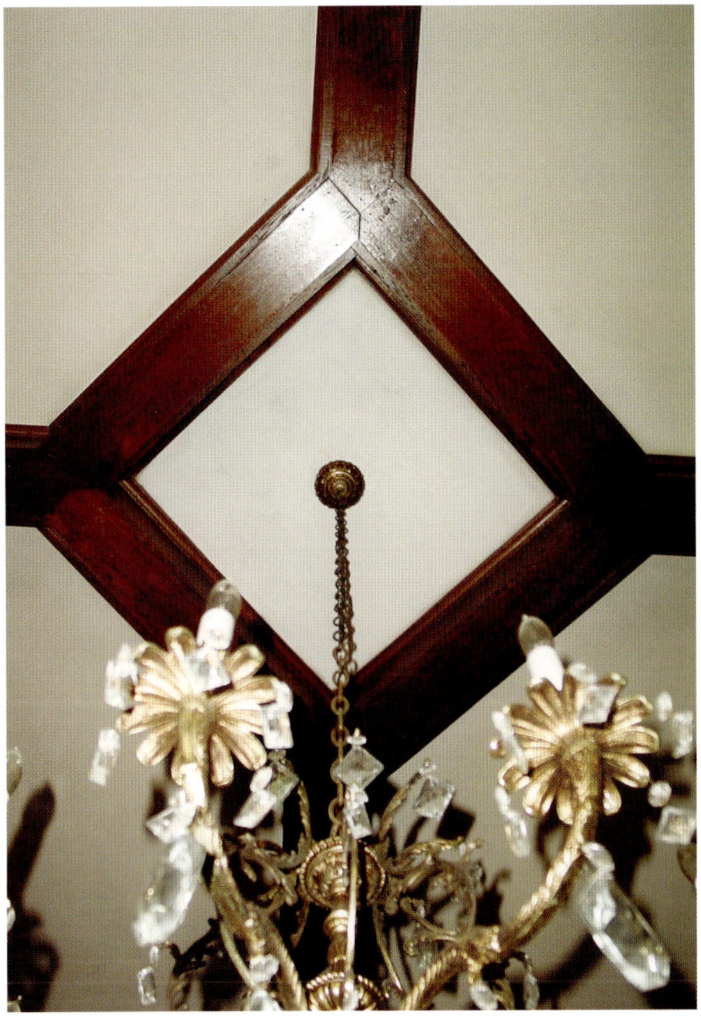

Applied dark stained trim create a decorative focal point for the chandelier that is original to the house.

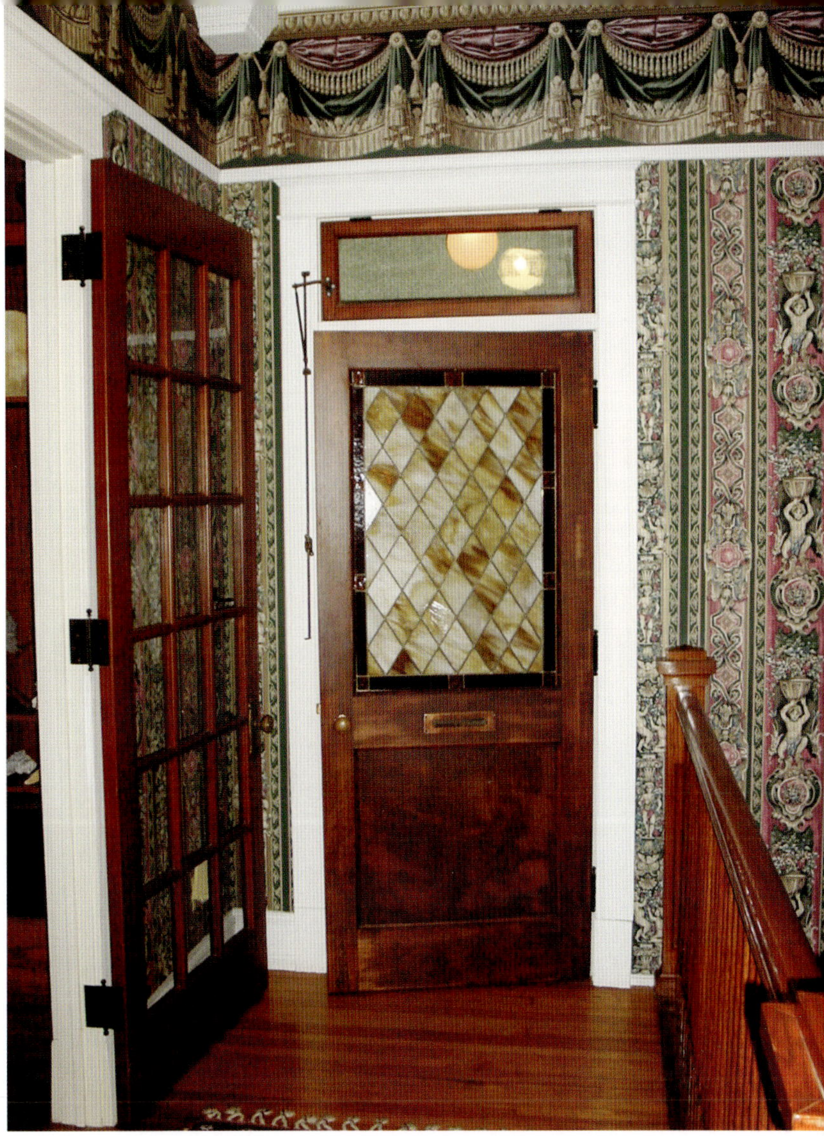

This house was once owned by the Masonic Lodge, who used it as an office. Some second-floor doors were fitted for privacy with stained glass panels and brass mail slots.

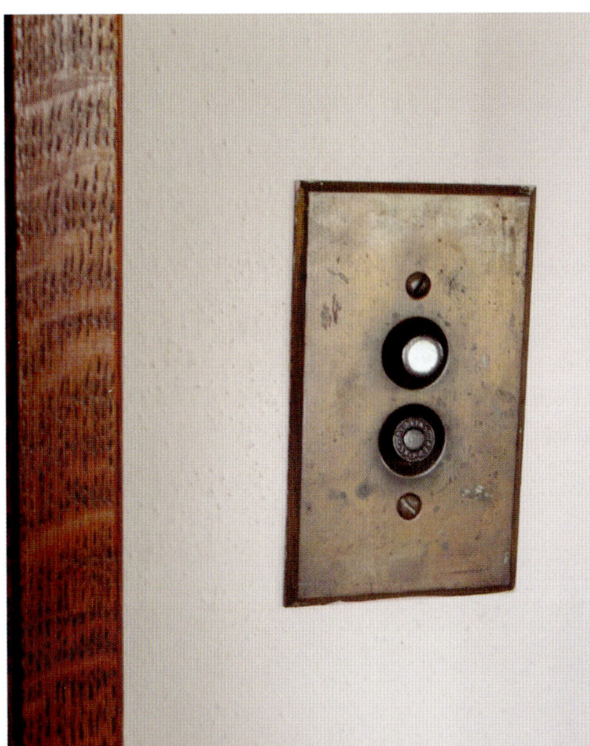

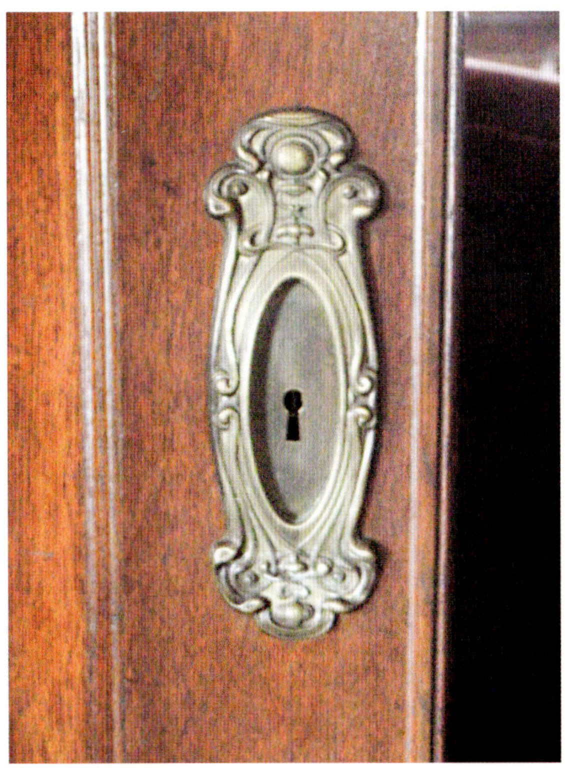

Fortunately much that was original to this house, including hardware and electric light switches, has been preserved by various owners over the years.

8

Combs House

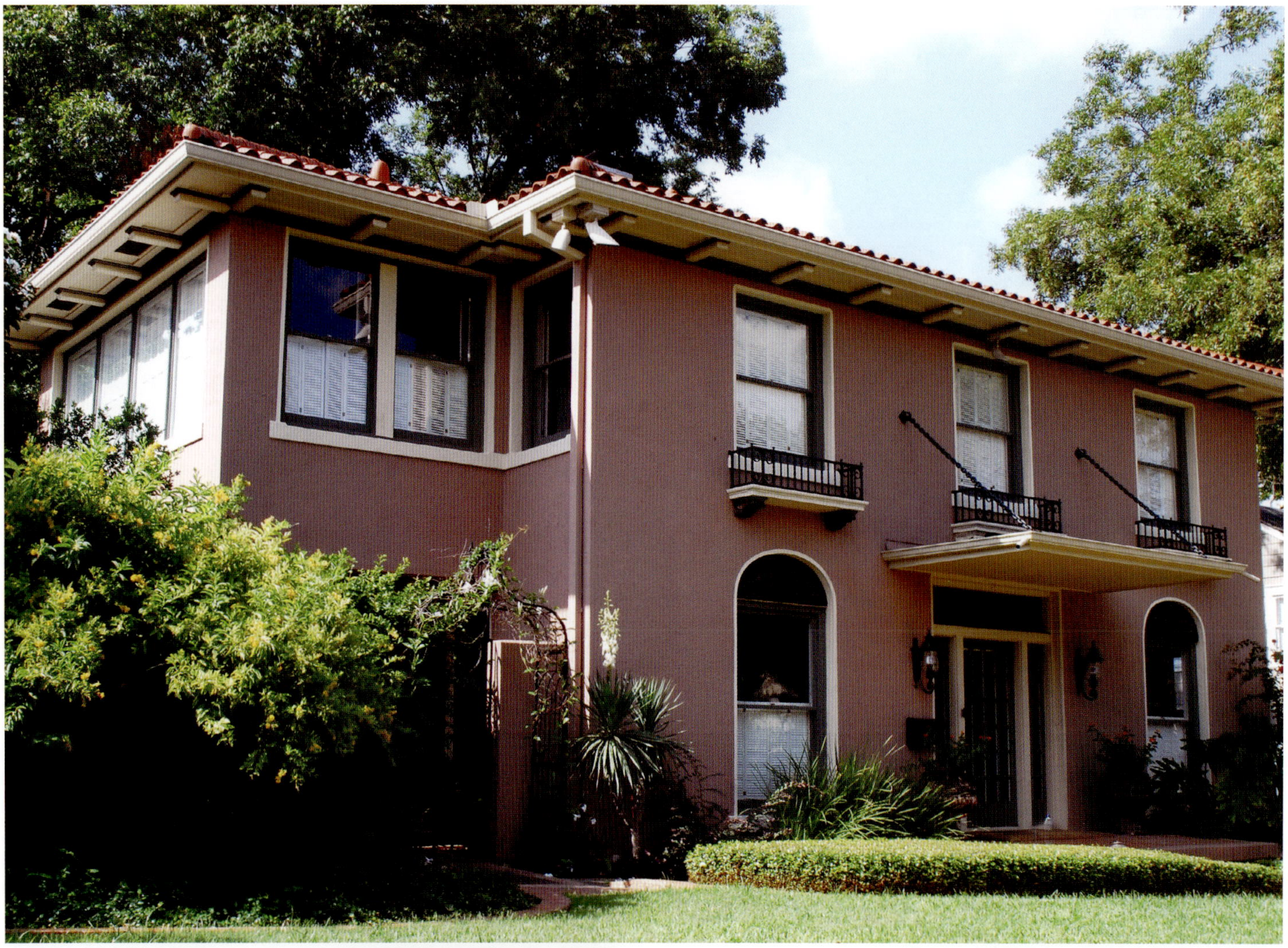

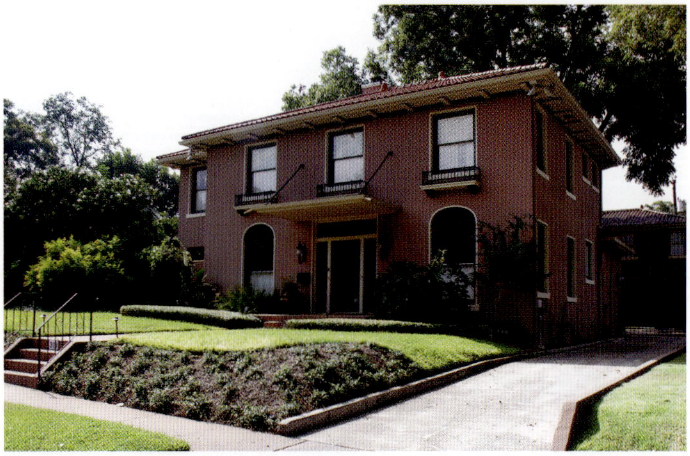

A Tuscany-inspired color enhances the Italianate style of the Combs residence. A pair of rounded arched windows and series of balconied windows encourage an easy visual flow between interior and exterior, the hallmark of contemporary living. *Photographs by Barbara Justice*

The handsome house on Summit Street in the historic Monte Vista district may rightfully be considered "old," since it was built in 1922. But, it is difficult to think of this Italian Renaissance style structure as "vintage," because the classic architectural design gives this structure a timeless quality and always-fresh appeal. The absence of the typical multi-storied tower associated with the Italian Renaissance style contributes to the more modern or contemporary look of this house. So do pane-less windows and greatly restrained use of decorative exterior trim.

The house might conceivably meld into the environment, were it not for its vibrant exterior color reminiscent of Tuscany—both ancient and *au courant*—that distinguishes it from more conventional neighboring houses. Inside, strong jewel-like colors add dash and panache to interior walls and inject a certain vigor that marks this as the home of its lively, involved owner, Cynthia Combs. The decorating style—clean

A Texas Lone Star highlights the access to the garden, casita, and guest house. Lake-Como-blue colored trim accentuates the French doors. *Photographs by Barbara Justice*

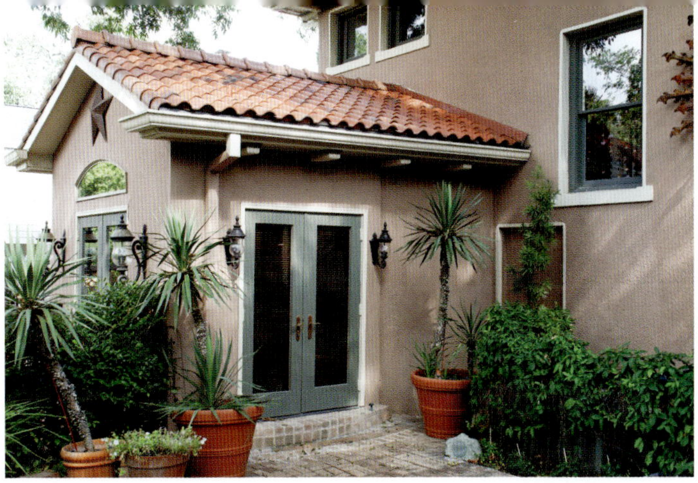

lined, without clutter, and gracious—adds to the unique atmosphere of serene readiness.

"The house was constructed by builder Ernest Schrivener for Ed Fitch, founder of the Fitch Insurance Agency on McCullough Street," says owner Cynthia Combs. "Over the years, there have been some changes, but many original elements remain. These include the windows, interior French doors, a charming frieze above the fireplace mantel, and the walled gardens." She also points to a very small (150 square foot) garden casita located at the back of the property. "The original owner's long-time family maid lived there," she says.

Important changes to the house include updating the upstairs bath and remodeling the kitchen. These remodeling efforts are discreet and non-invasive so that there is no sense of retrofitting. Instead, it seems that these modern amenities were always in place.

Like kitchens in all the historic houses featured in this book, the Combs' updated kitchen is designed for current lifestyles. The inviting kitchen features a convenient island, ample storage cabinets in a rich warm-colored wood, and state-of-the-art equipment. This is a kitchen designed to work efficiently for a small or large family. It also works well for serving a small crowd, like the group of women gathering well in advance of an upcoming election to meet political candidates—a fitting role for a house on Summit Street.

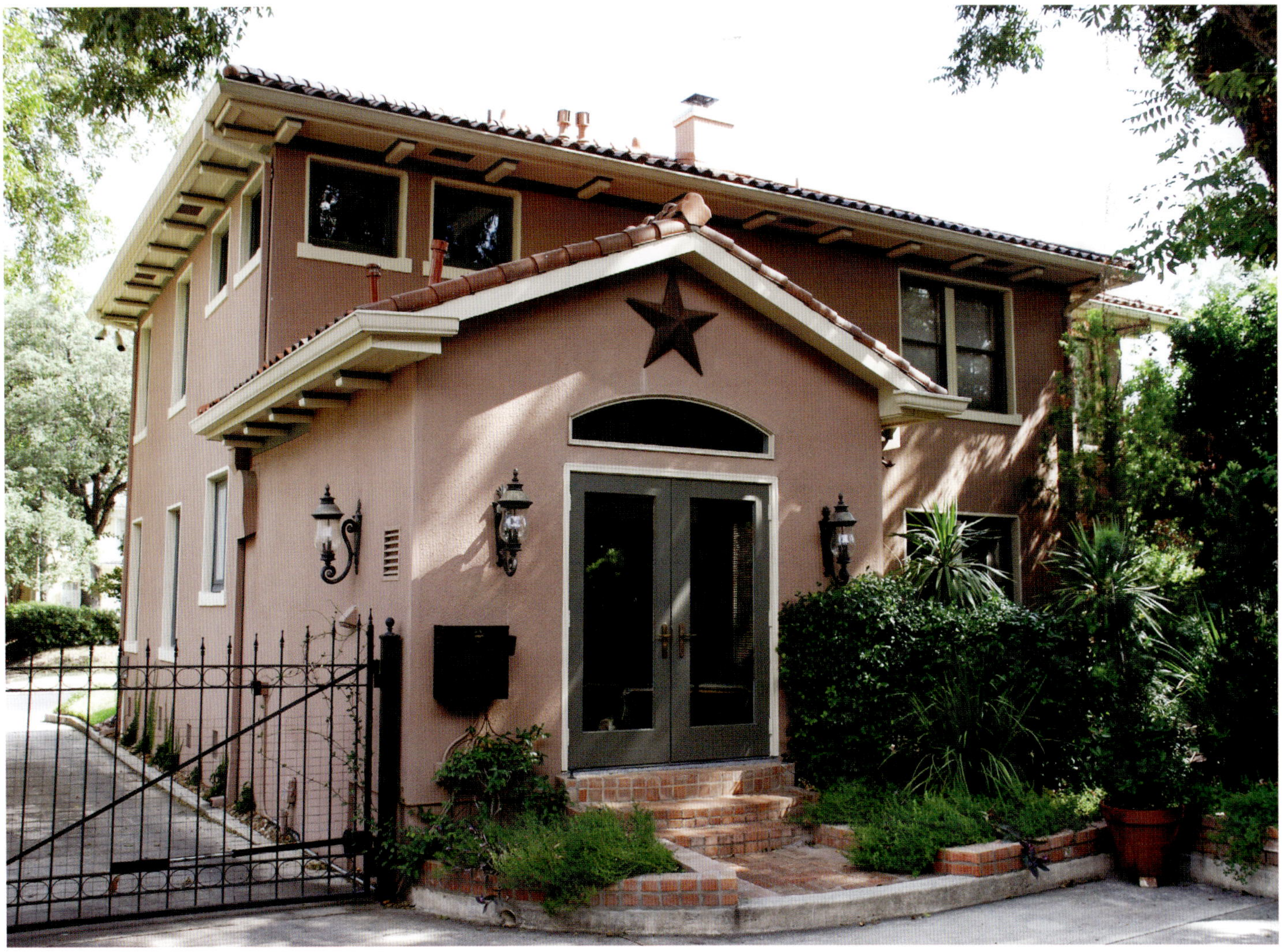

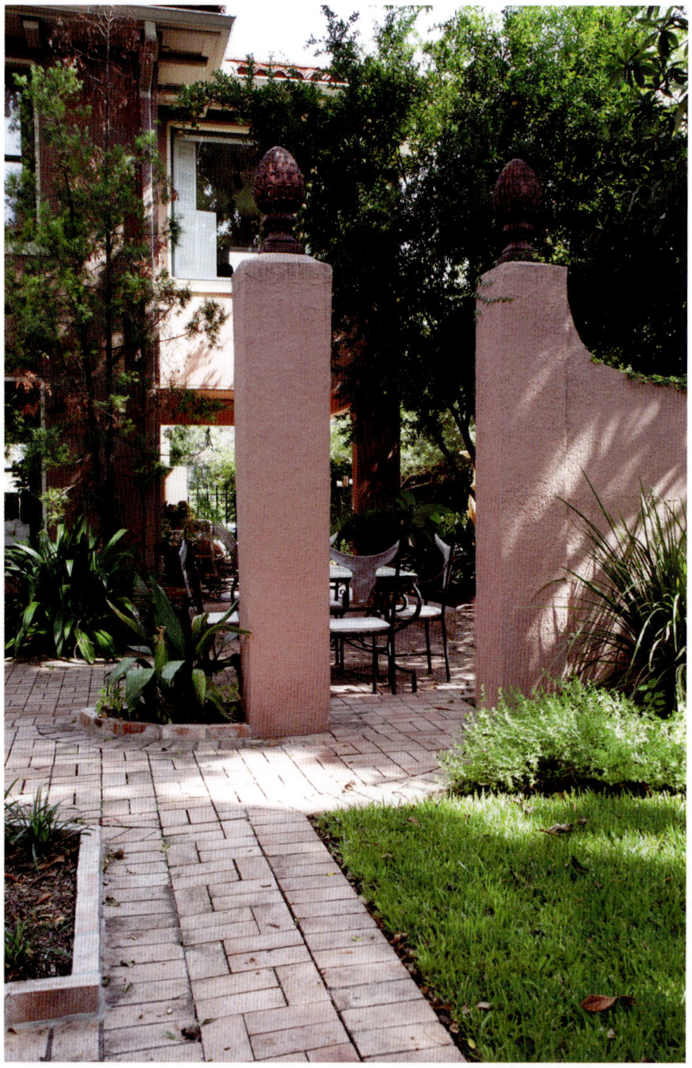

Classic finials delineate entry into the Eden-like gardens that seem a world away from the world outside these walls.

A graceful bronze figurine commands the courtyard.

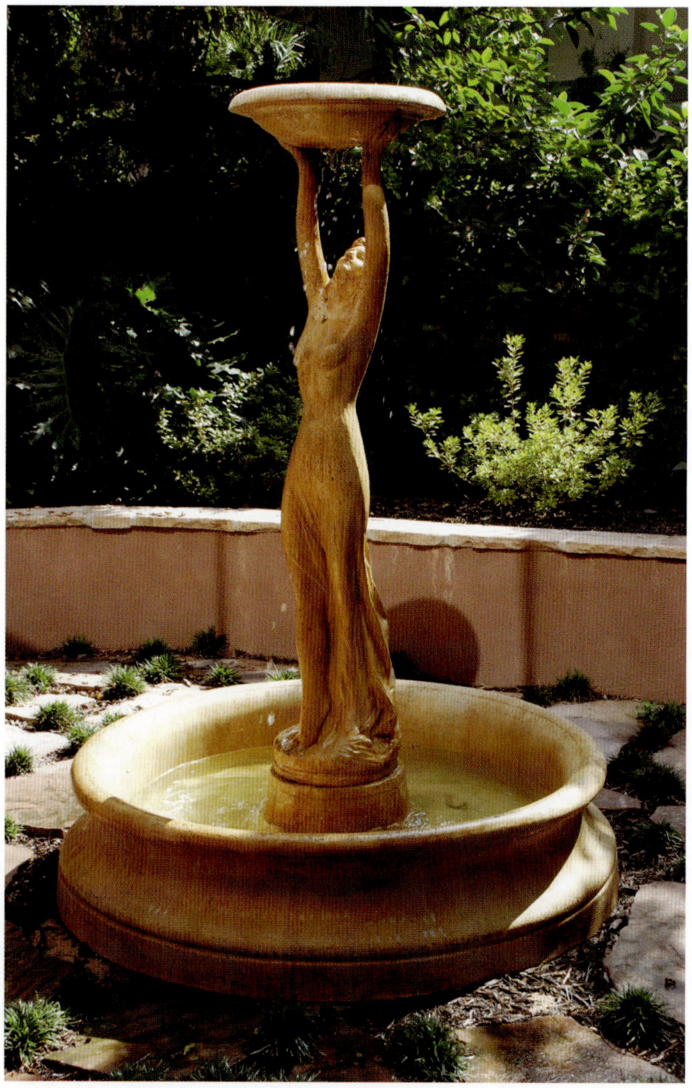

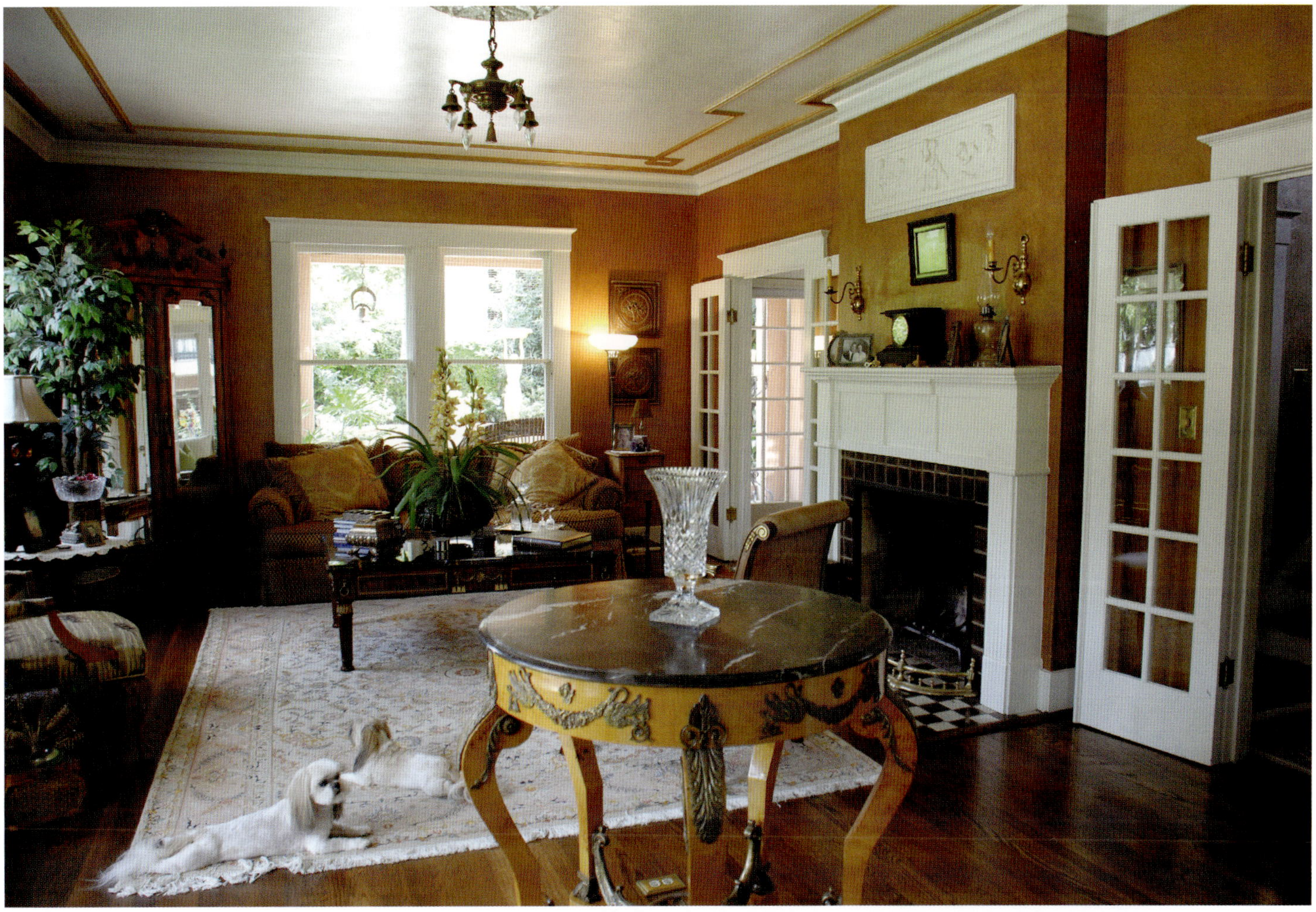

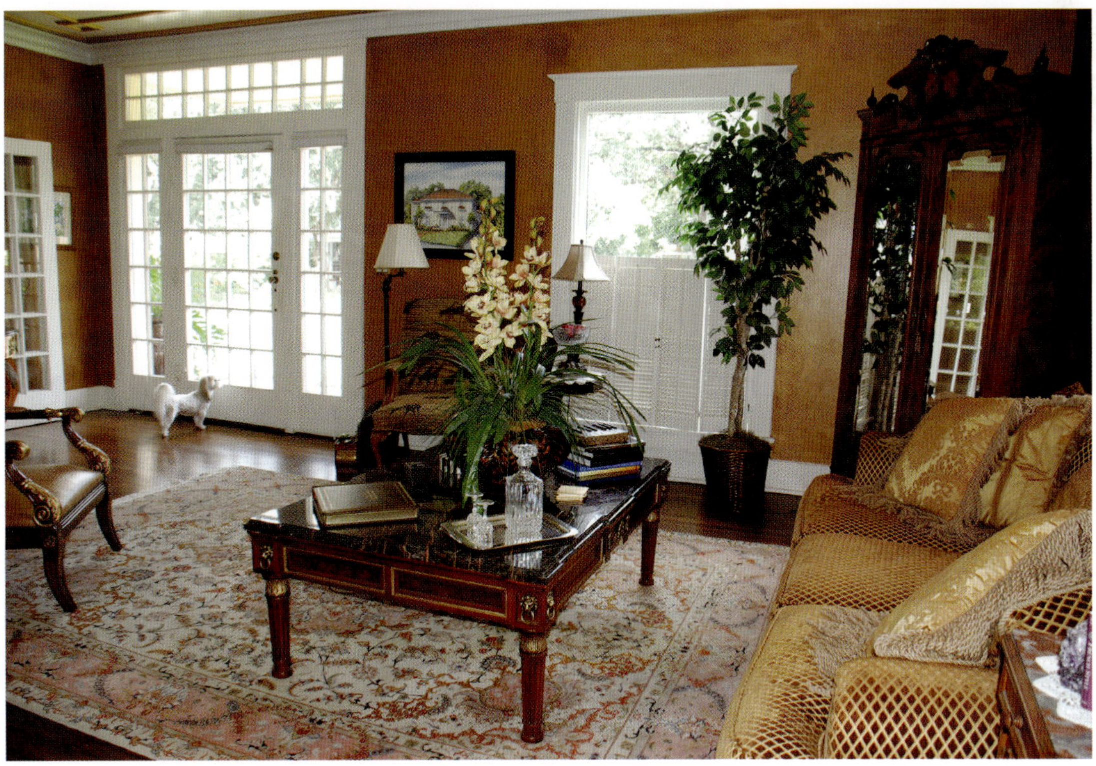

Venetian-inspired gold walls, accented with sparkling white trim, create a rich backdrop for the living area. Decorative gold trim enriches the ceiling. Original neoclassic tiles of the fireplace's hearth were restored. Expansive windows and doors allow for an easy flow between interior and exterior.

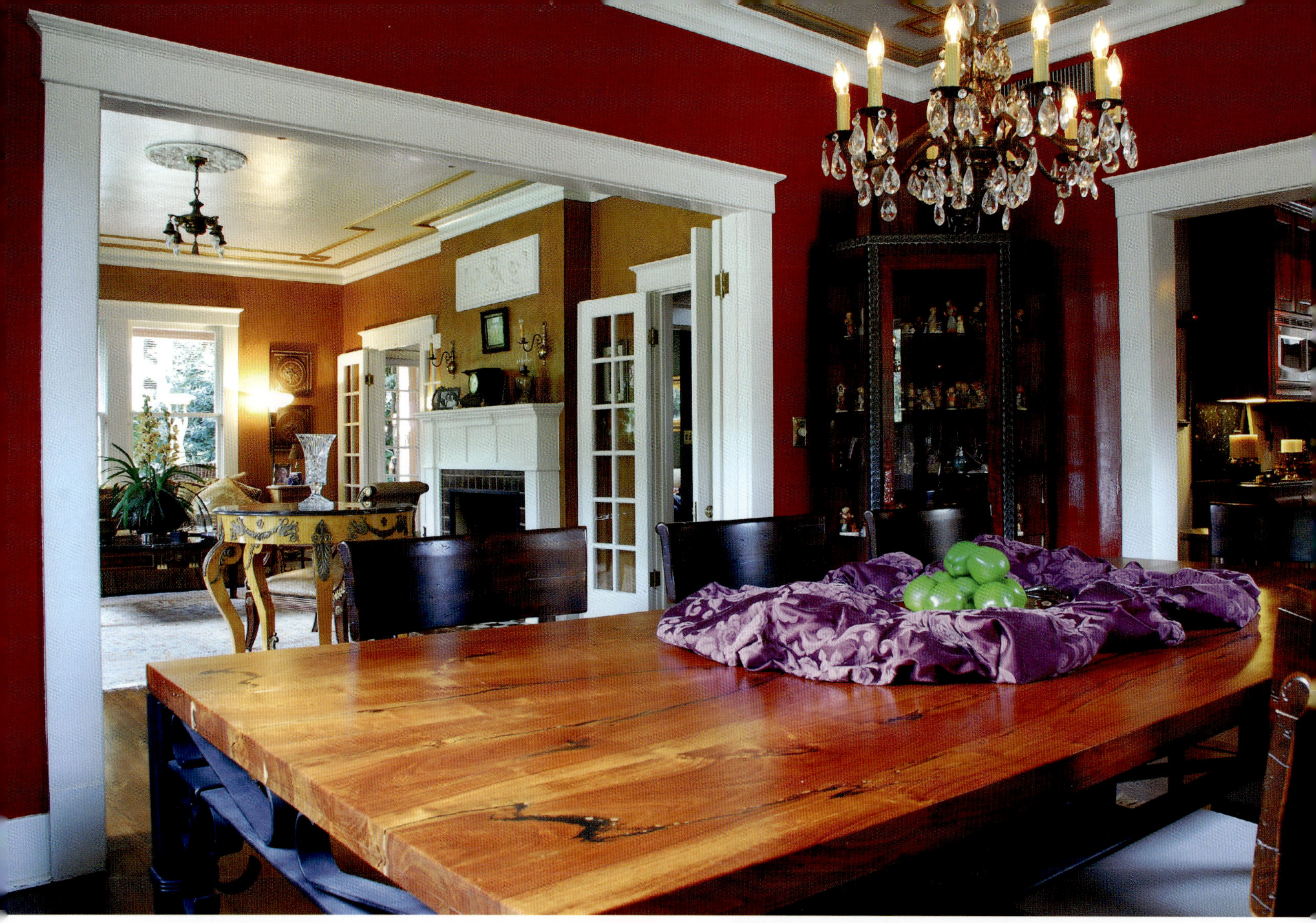

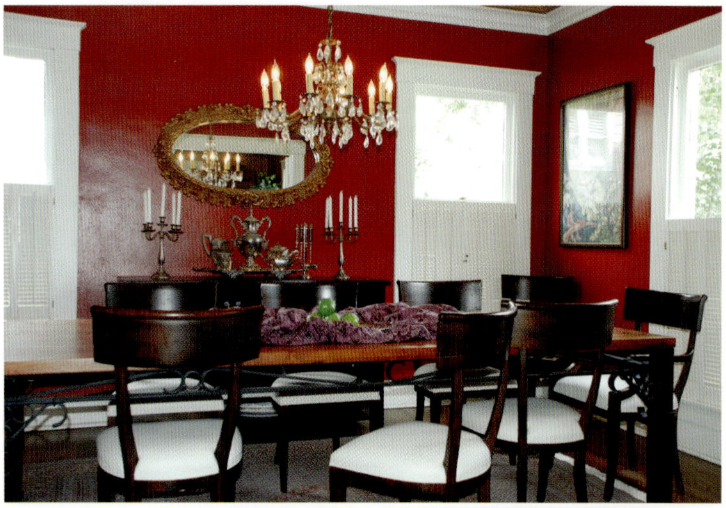

Deep Tuscany-red walls and trim at ceiling add verve to the dining room. White trim unites the dramatic colors of living and dining spaces. A chandelier provides a striking focal point and brilliant illumination.

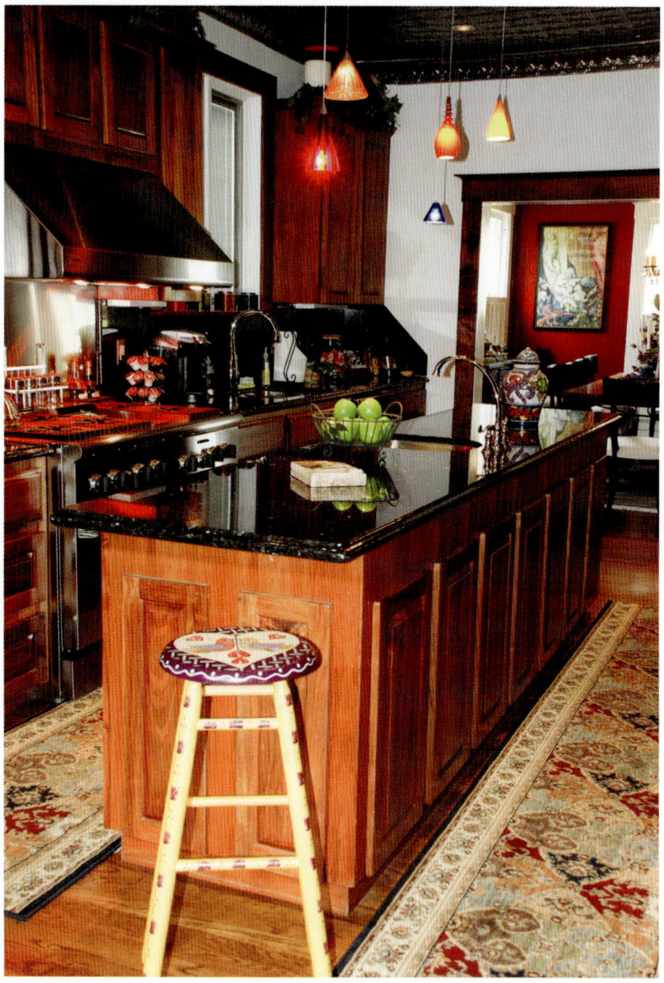

A remodeled kitchen is the singular modern note in residence. A collection of spirited colored glass pendant lights sparkle against the deep-hued wood cabinets, black granite counters, and stainless steel appliances.

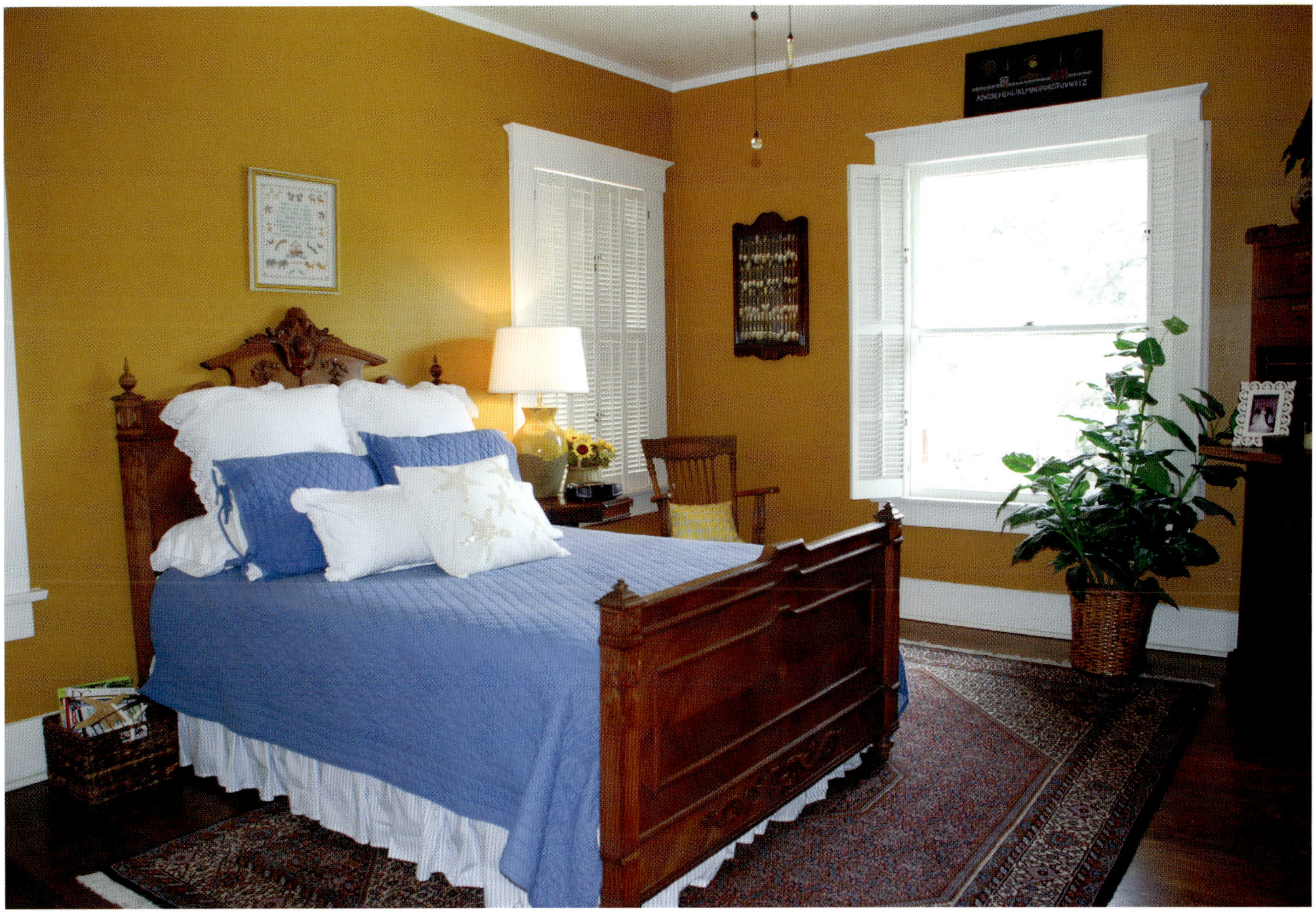

The guest bedroom is furnished with a handsome antique bed and other antique and vintage pieces. White shutters filter sunlight and view.

9
Lavaca House

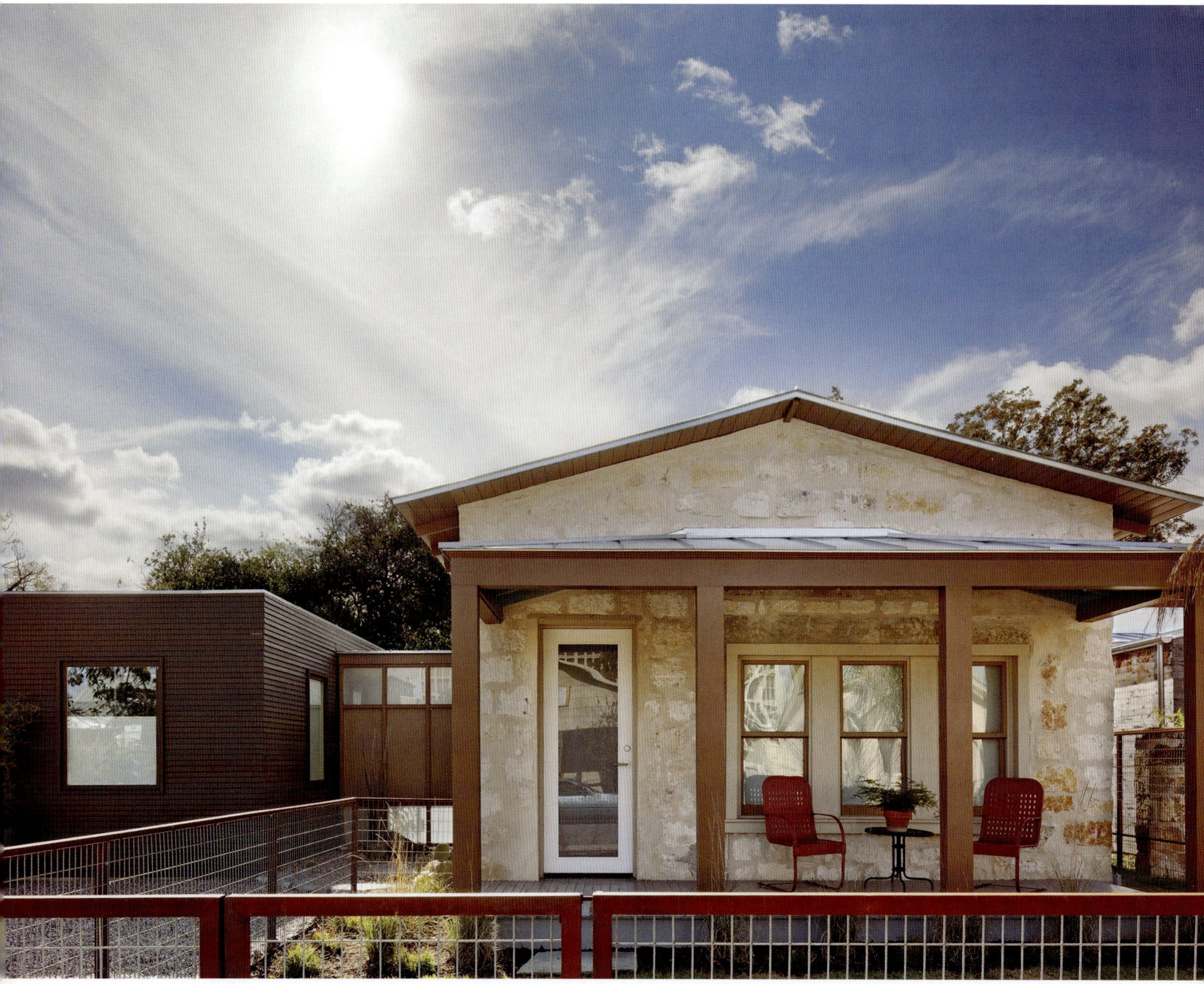

Simple rectilinear lines and dark wood trim contrast with the soft matt texture of native Texas caliche stone in an updated Lavaca cottage. *Photographs by Chris Cooper, courtesy Poteet Architects*

Realtor Julie Hooper knows a great deal about houses—especially San Antonio houses—and the people who buy them. Most house-hunters—even those interested in turn-key new construction—are looking for some special quality. So was Hooper. What she was looking for—nineteenth century caliche block construction that insulates naturally—is not usually found in new construction. And old caliche block structures are far from move-in condition. When she saw the house in the downtown historic Lavaca area (near the famed King William historic district), she *thought* it was a caliche block house. But, who could tell for sure?

"Our clients purchased this home in a leap of faith," says Architect Jim Poteet. "The contractor/developer knew that there was an 1880s era masonry (caliche block) structure somewhere under several layers of shapeless exterior additions and interior partitioning. The challenge for this Yale-and Texas-trained architect, whose firm is noted for its skill in giving new life to old buildings, was to find, restore, and renew that vintage structure. Poteet says: "The caliche building (considered a landmark by the City of San Antonio, which has designated the Lavaca area a historic district) only became visible when all those layers had been stripped away." Once that was done, faith in the building and its purchase by Hooper and her partner, Jennifer Abad, was justified.

After inappropriate additions and partitions had been eliminated, a re-design that would respect history, create contemporary living space, and ensure a future for this building began. "Our approach was to use the vintage masonry structure as one undivided living space. We set the two new sleeping and bathing areas (master and guest suites) apart in separate wings. These wings are alike in their formal simplicity. New materials defer to those of the older main house; but new exterior claddings necessarily differ from the existing materials and from each other (the master bedroom is stucco and the guestroom has painted wood siding)."

Poteet's design adds new wings at right angles to the existing main house, creating a courtyard—an ideal place, he points out, for the small dipping pool. "The design both respects the historic structure and creates a small compound which accommodates a modern, urban way of life," says Poteet.

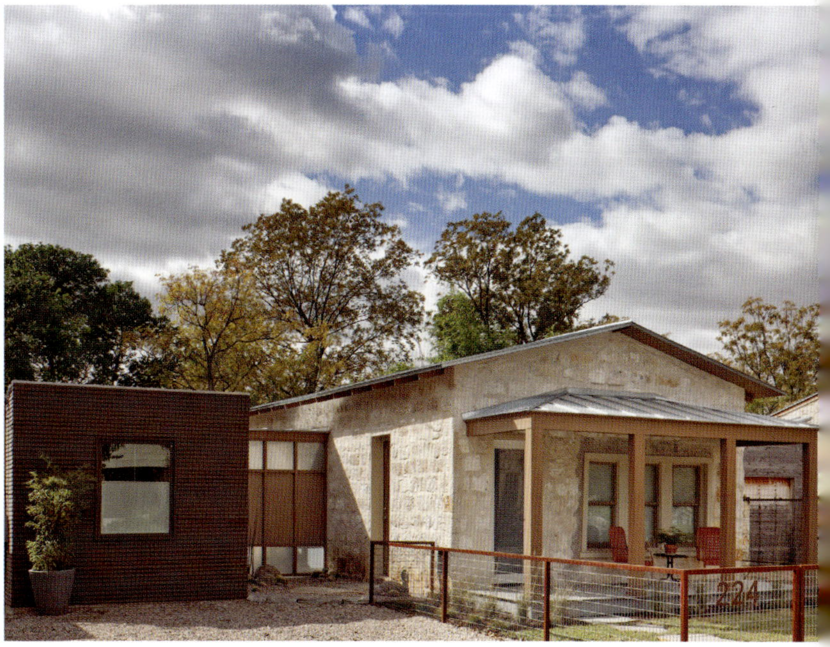

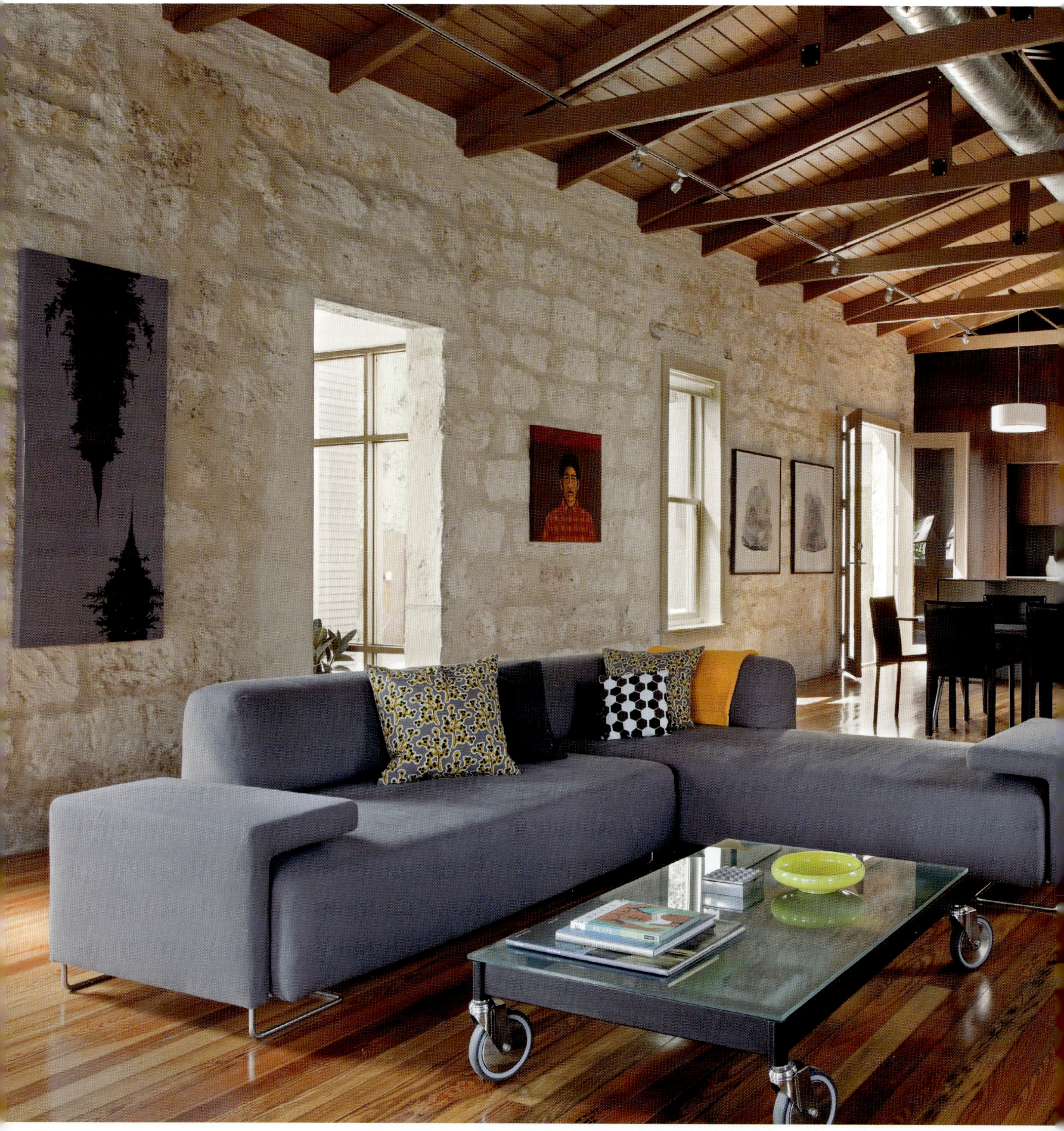

Removing partitions and the ceiling created a large, open, and airy living space. Contemporary track and pendant lighting and furniture enhance the contemporary mood.

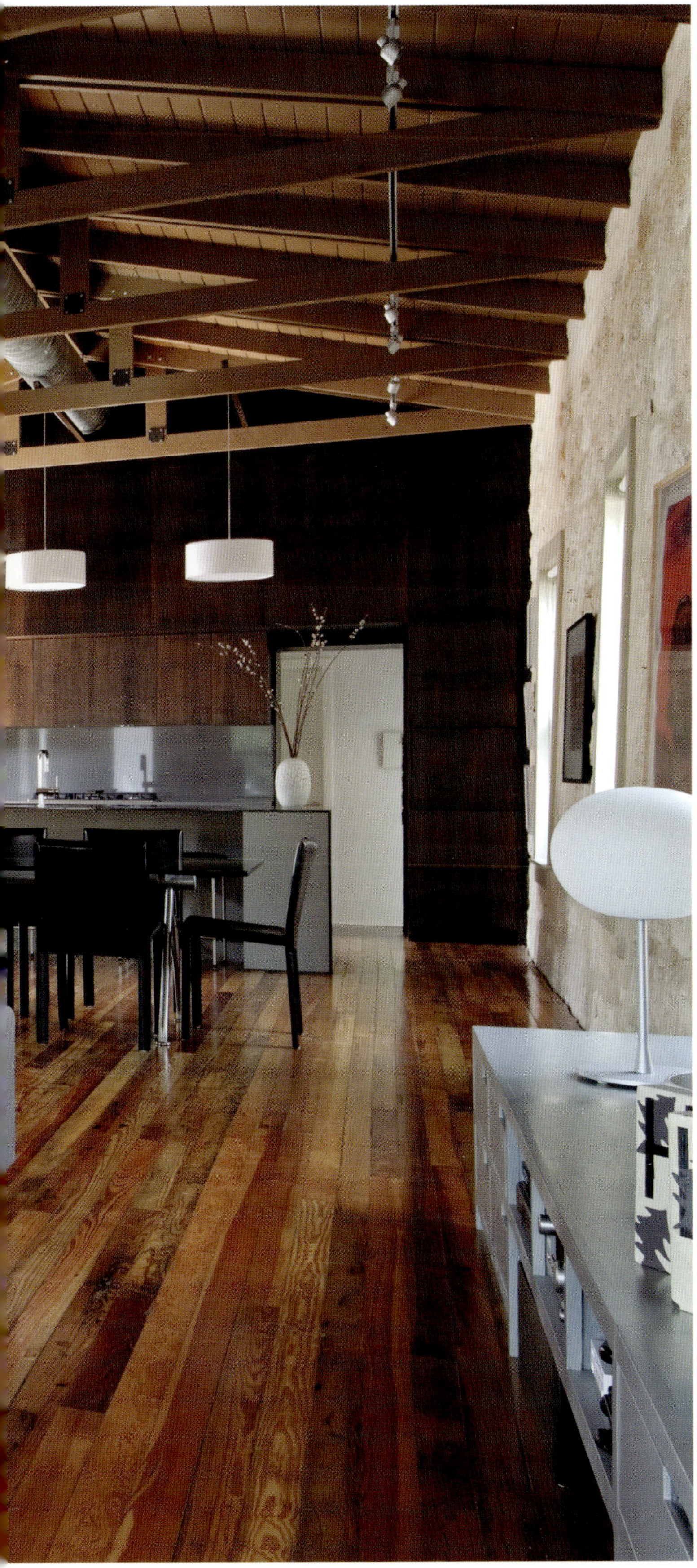

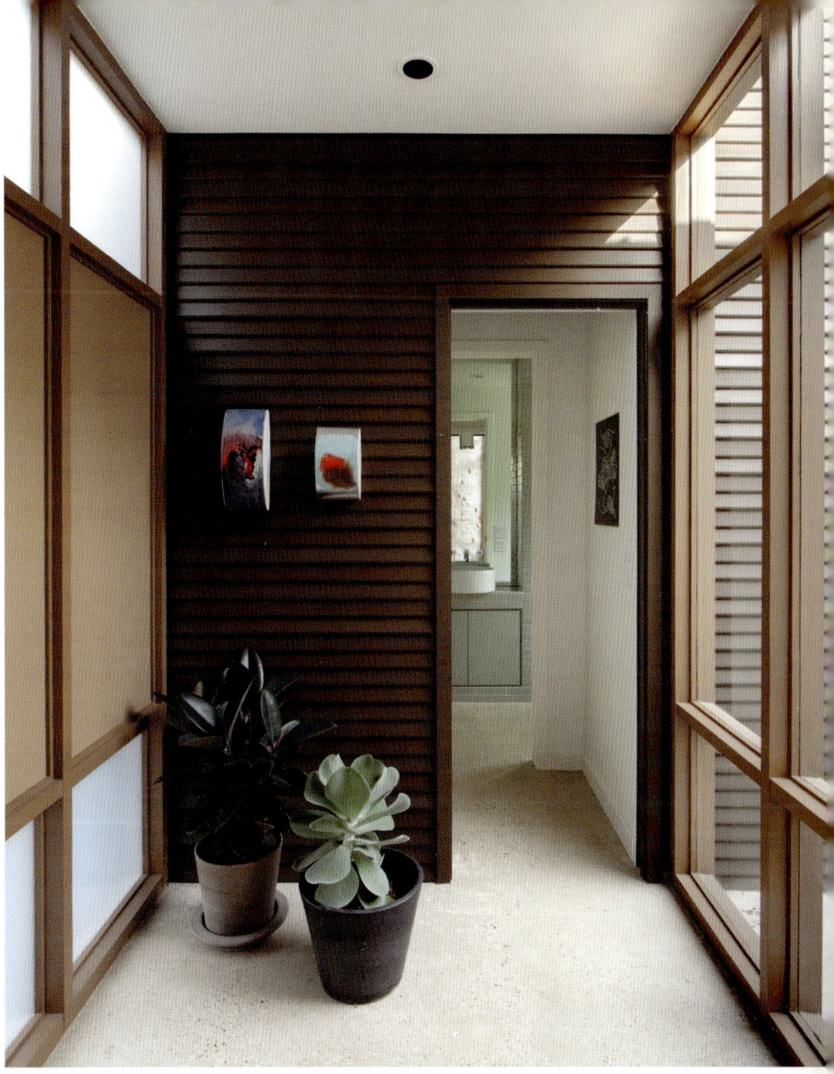

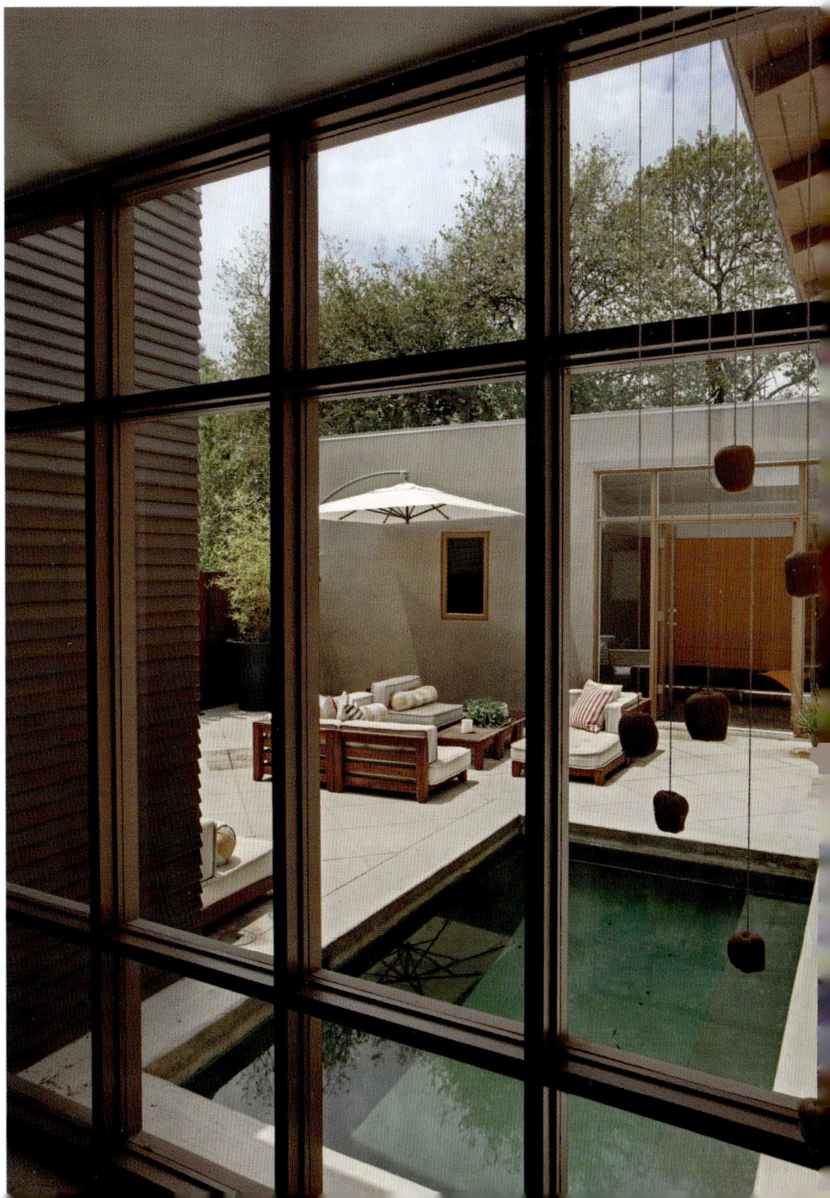

A small hallway links the existing house and a new guest suite. A window wall in the hallway overlooks the new paved courtyard.

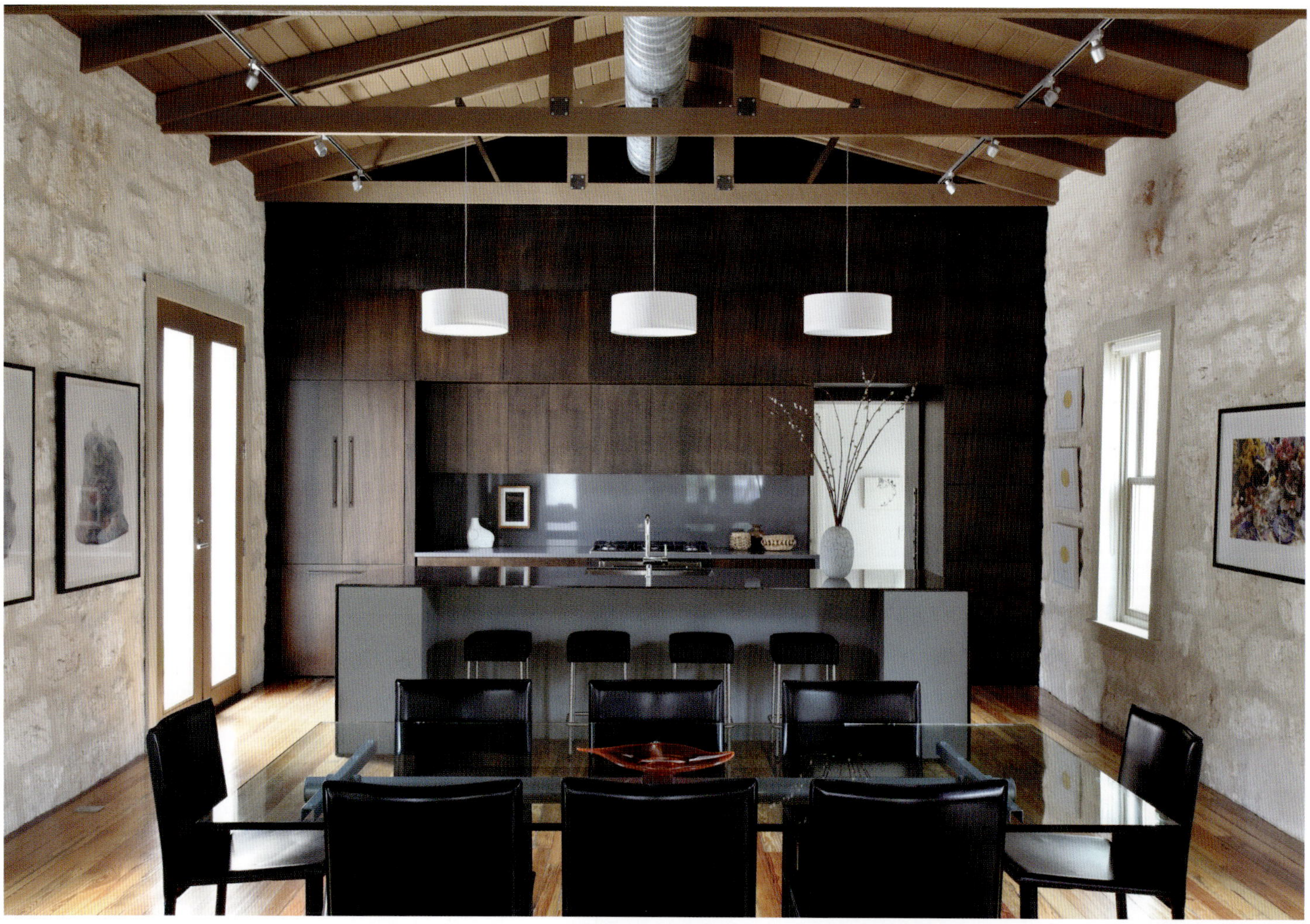

Sleek cabinetry adds dignity and formality to the open kitchen.

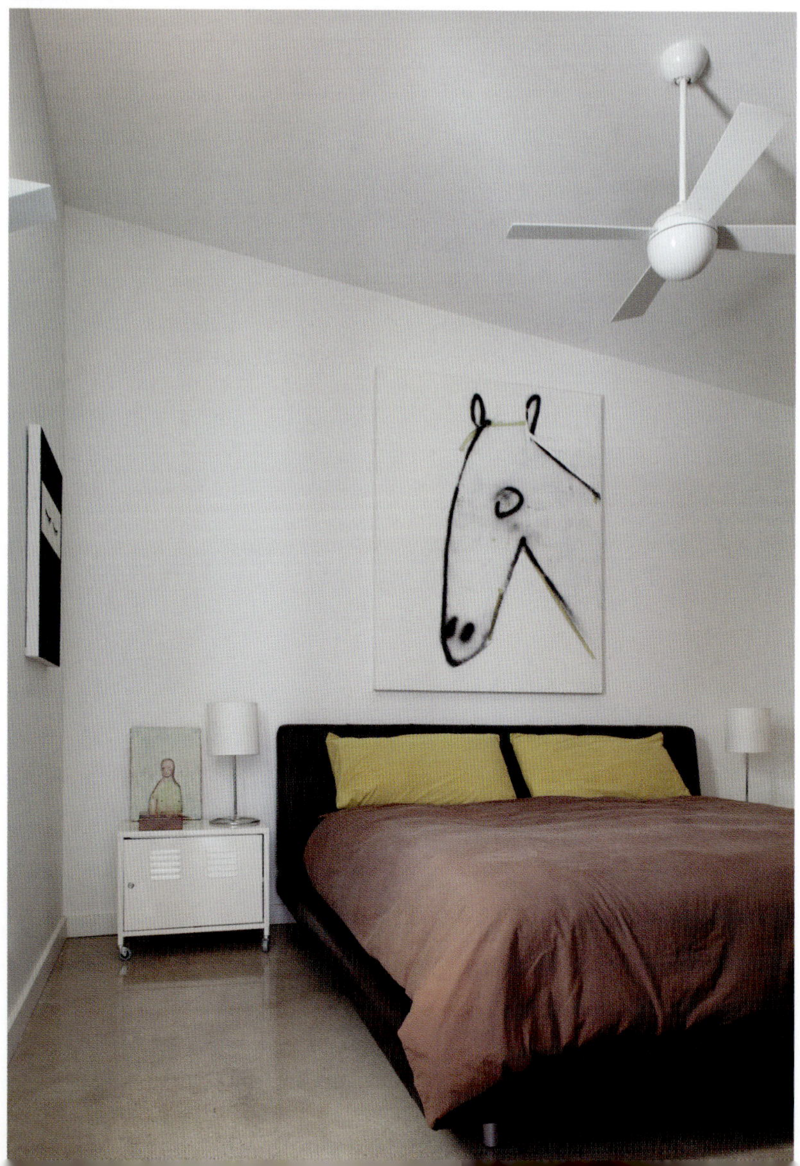

Simple furnishings and muted neutral colors keep a small bedroom looking large.

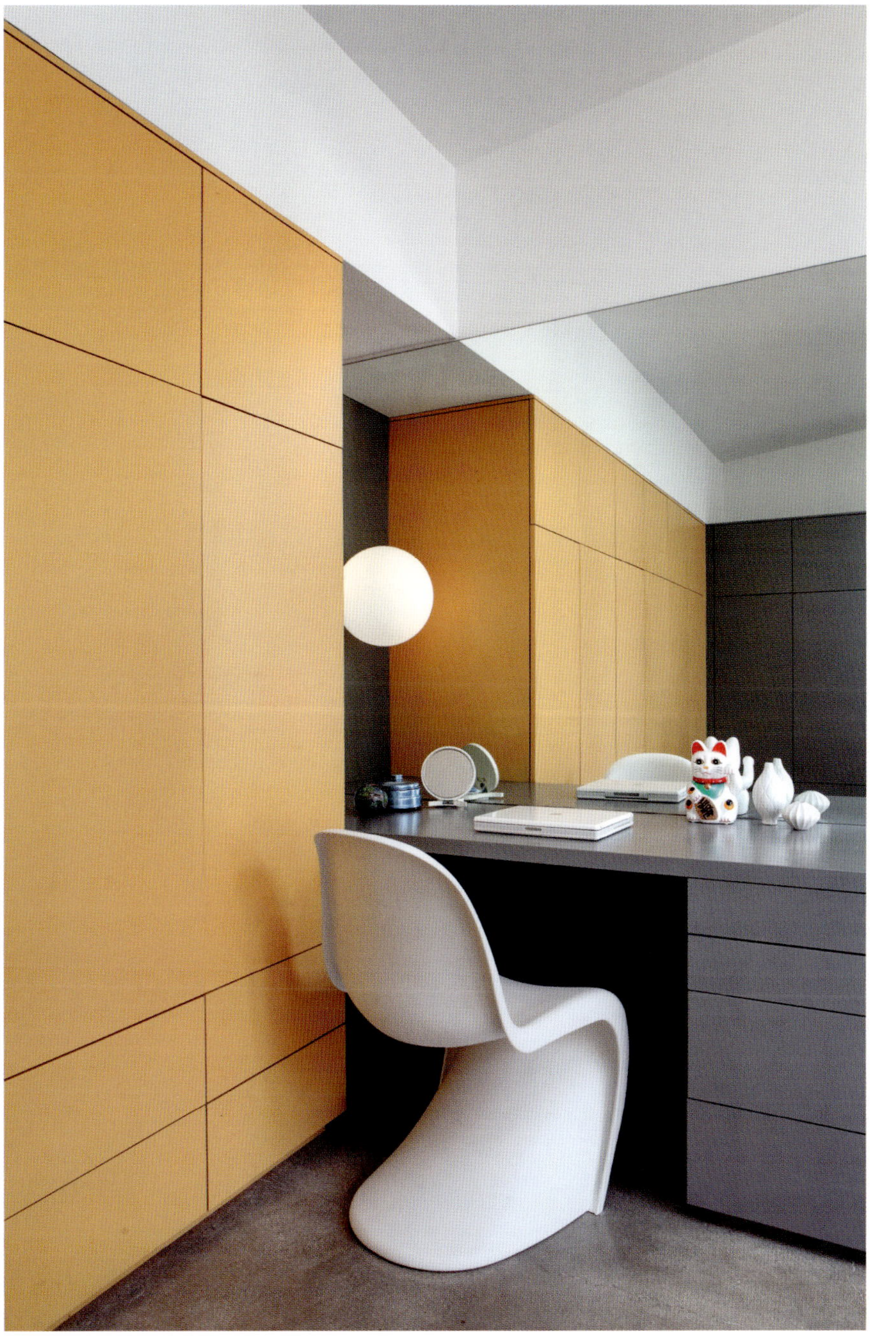

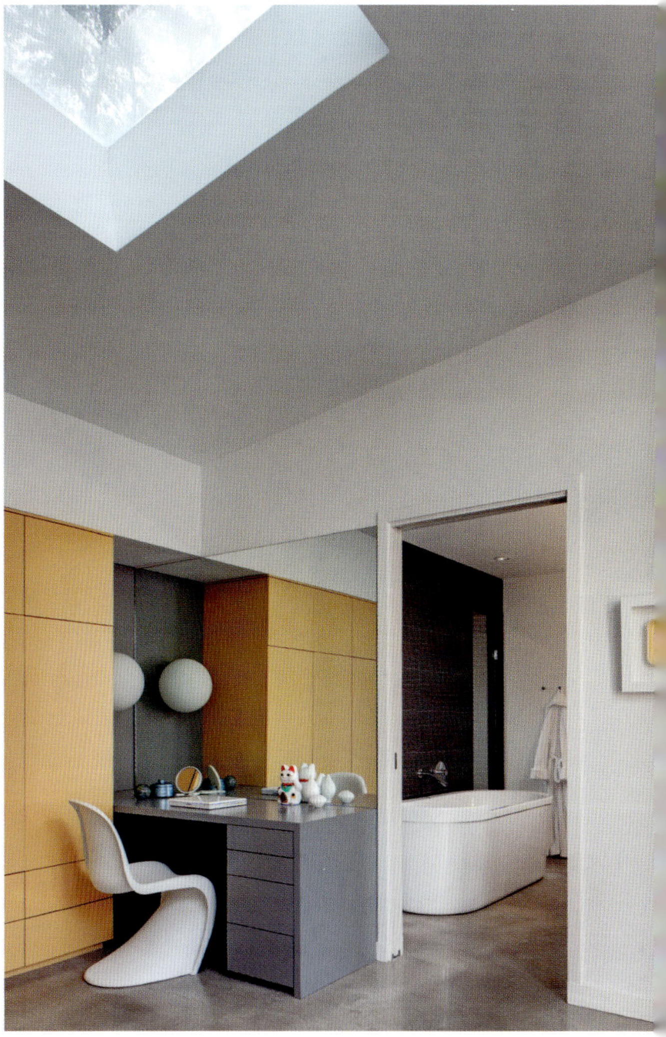

In the master suite, a skylight admits light and adds interest to the ceiling design. Cabinets, built-in dressing table, and bathtub have clean-lined contemporary design.

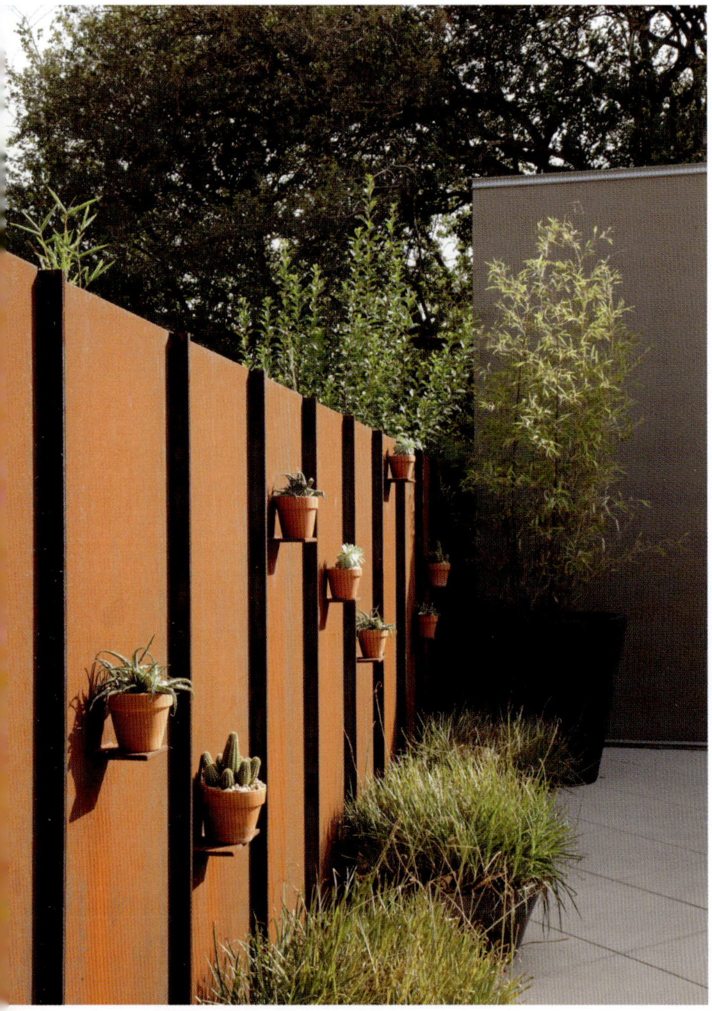

A planter pocket at the foot of the fence offers visual relief to the paved courtyard.

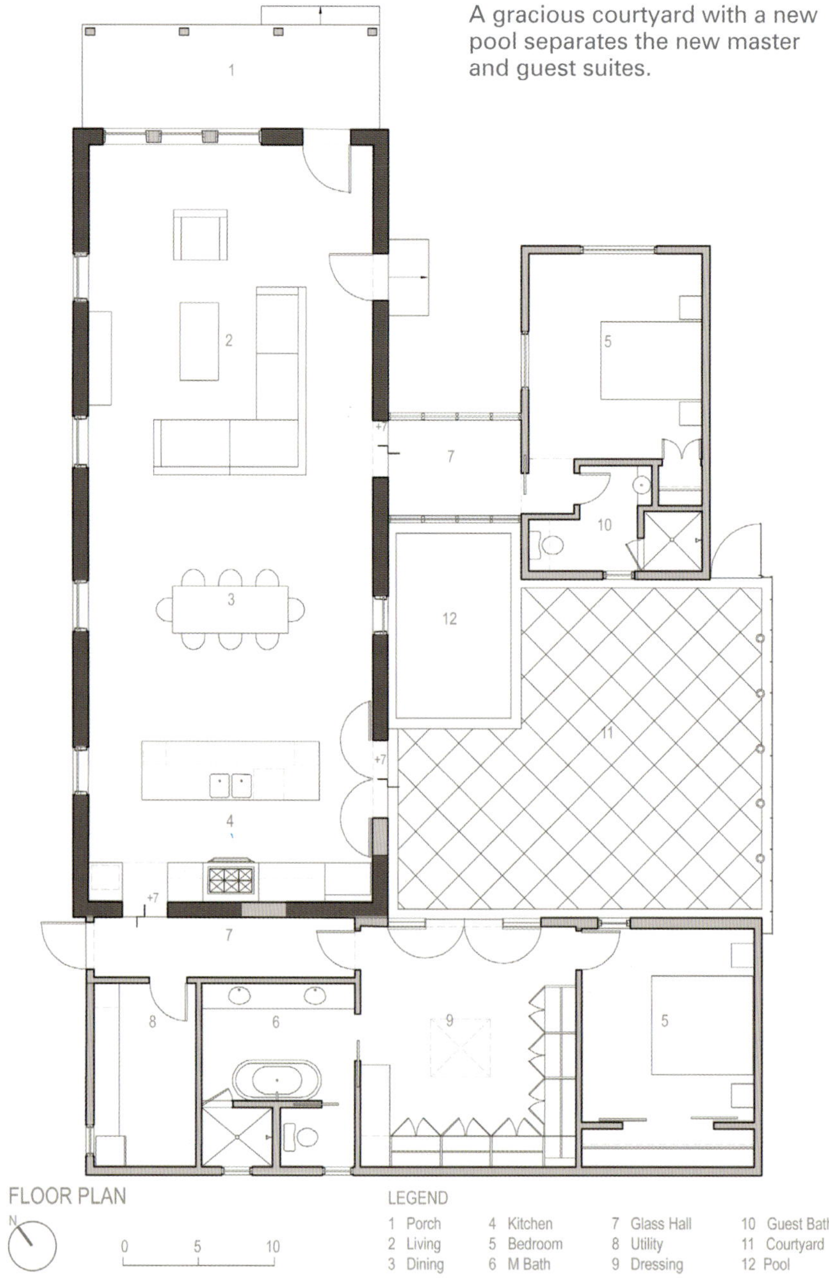

A gracious courtyard with a new pool separates the new master and guest suites.

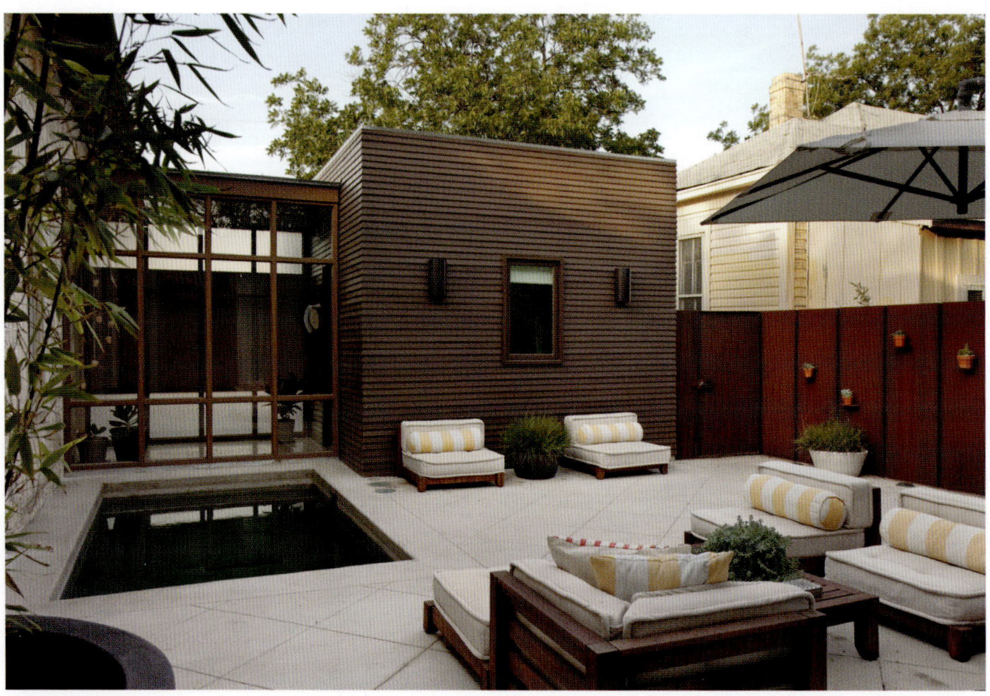

Walls of windows permit seeing through from the courtyard across to the main building.

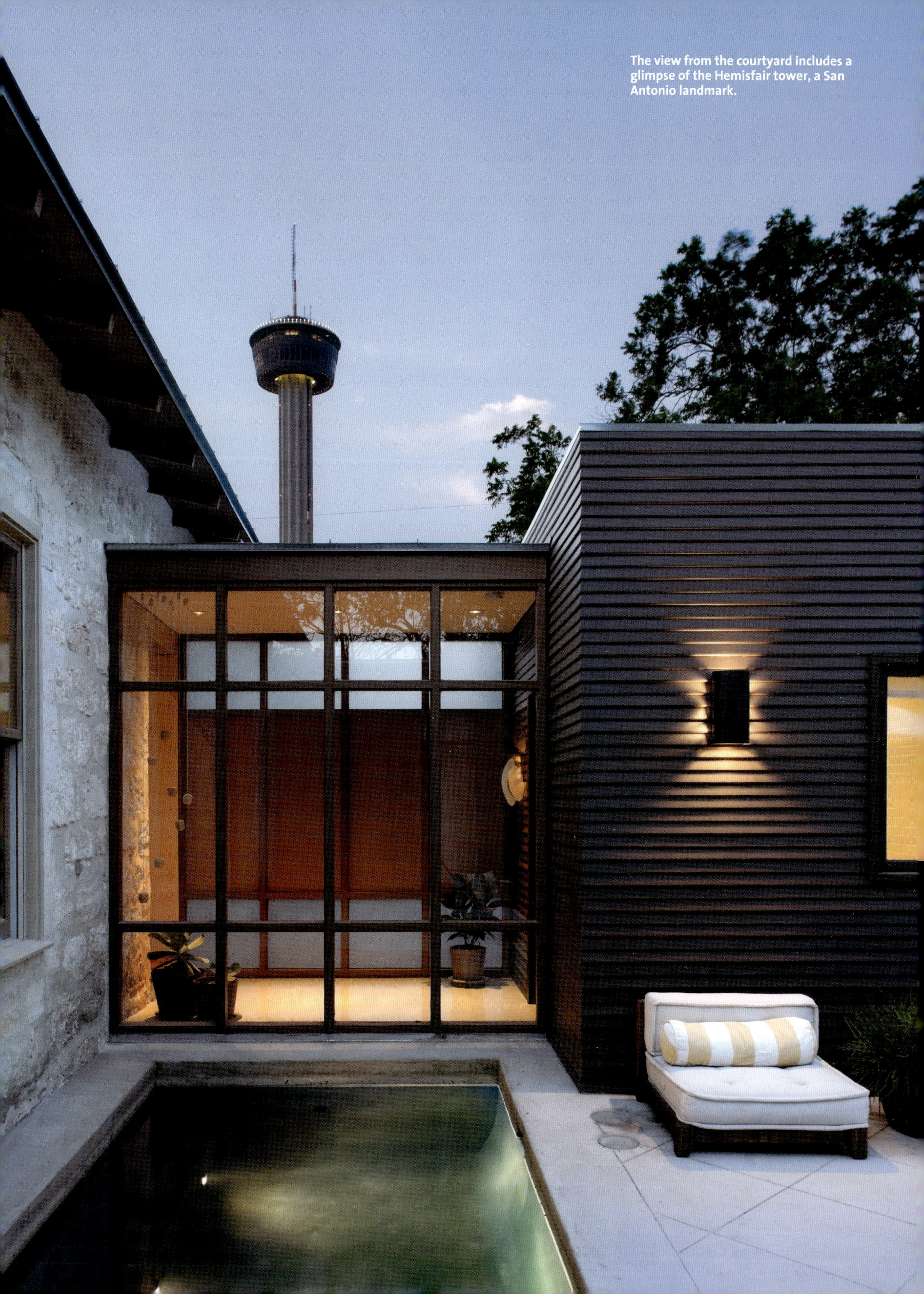

The view from the courtyard includes a glimpse of the Hemisfair tower, a San Antonio landmark.

10

El Picoso

In the 1990s, a powerful windstorm came through Southtown, San Antonio's art-district neighborhood in which Architect Darryl Ohlenbusch lived. "It destroyed the porch, brick parapet, and much of the roof of an old building at 1802 South St. Mary's Street. As I drove by, I remember saying to myself: 'Some poor soul is going to have to rebuild that place'. Well, the poor soul turned out to be me," he recalls.

Ohlenbusch did not base his decision to rebuild the structure he calls *El Picoso,* which means "the spicy one," on any rational expectation of return-on-investment. "That 1924 building is such a crucial piece of the neighborhood that I couldn't imagine it being torn down," he says. "The original owner, who built it, created a two-story mixed-use two-tone brick building with a decorative parapet. The ground floor was for commercial use. A wrap-around second-floor porch was accessible from the second-story residence in which the owner and his wife raised their four children."

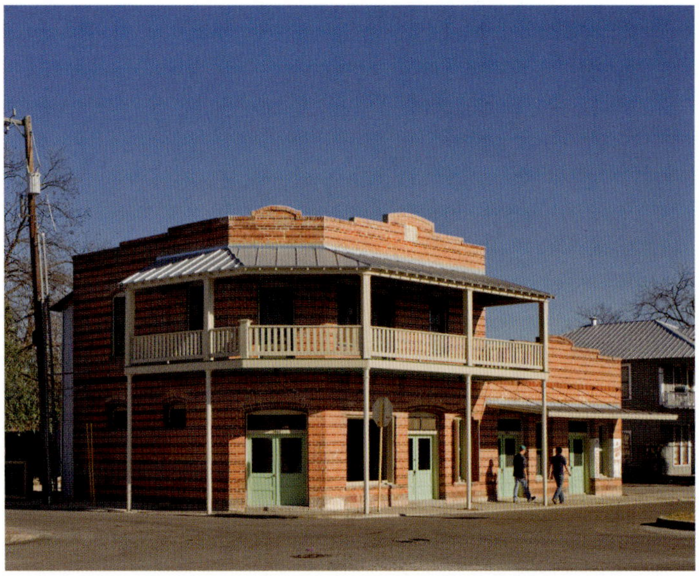

Ohlenbusch says, "The children sold the building to me and a business partner. At the time I bought it, the structure had not been occupied for about twenty years. The collapsed roof and parapet along with the second-floor porch had allowed water to penetrate the interior, causing extensive damage to the interior framing."

Undismayed by its appalling condition, Ohlenbusch set about rebuilding the all-but-destroyed structure. "I used salvaged brick from the original parapet and some new brick to reconstruct the upper part of the parapet that was knocked off during the windstorm," he says. His advice for anyone interested in preserving a similar old mixed-use structure is to keep as much of the original materials as possible, even if there are defects or signs of wear. "Don't try to make everything look new! Treat historic brick gently: no sand blasting, or even high-pressure washing."

Rehabilitating *El Picoso* meant remodeling the second-floor residence to bring it up-to-date and compatible with contemporary taste. "Upstairs, several existing walls were removed to 'open' the space. All new electrical, plumbing, and central air conditioning systems were installed. As part of the rewiring, recessed ceiling fixtures were installed in the second floor apartment. As for insulation, the original exterior brick walls were not insulated, so no new insulation was installed in the walls. We did insulate the ceiling (where greatest heat loss occurs). I reused existing beadboard from the original structure to clad walls of new rooms upstairs," he says. "We only needed to scrape and paint it."

Flooring on the first floor is a new poured concrete slab. On the second floor, original longleaf pine flooring was sanded and sealed. "About twenty percent had rotted out and had to be replaced," he says. "For the bathroom floor, we used linoleum sheet flooring, which is made from linseed oil, a rapidly-renewable material."

This labor of love was expensive. Were there any tax credits from the city, price breaks or help from the utility company? "No. We did receive a grant from the San Antonio Conservation Society for rebuilding the porch, and a grant from the City of San Antonio Operation Facelift program for restoration of the ground floor storefront windows and doors," says Ohlenbusch.

All work was approved by the City of San Antonio Historic and Design Review Commission. The completed project received a Preservation Award from the San Antonio Conservation Society in 2008, and in 2009, an AIA San Antonio Citation Award.

Once again, *El Picoso* is a vital, vibrant part of a lively neighborhood. The second-floor is home to a resident. On the street level, a busy ice cream shop attracts customers who have a sweet tooth.

Since his successful preservation of *El Picoso*, Ohlenbusch says, "I've done a couple of other remodels/additions in the general Southtown area. In addition to preservation projects, I've done about a half-dozen new projects—mostly residential—in this historic neighborhood where I live and practice. The City of San Antonio designated *El Picoso* a Historic Landmark long before I purchased the building," says Ohlenbusch. "To me, the *designation* was not important, the building was and is very important."

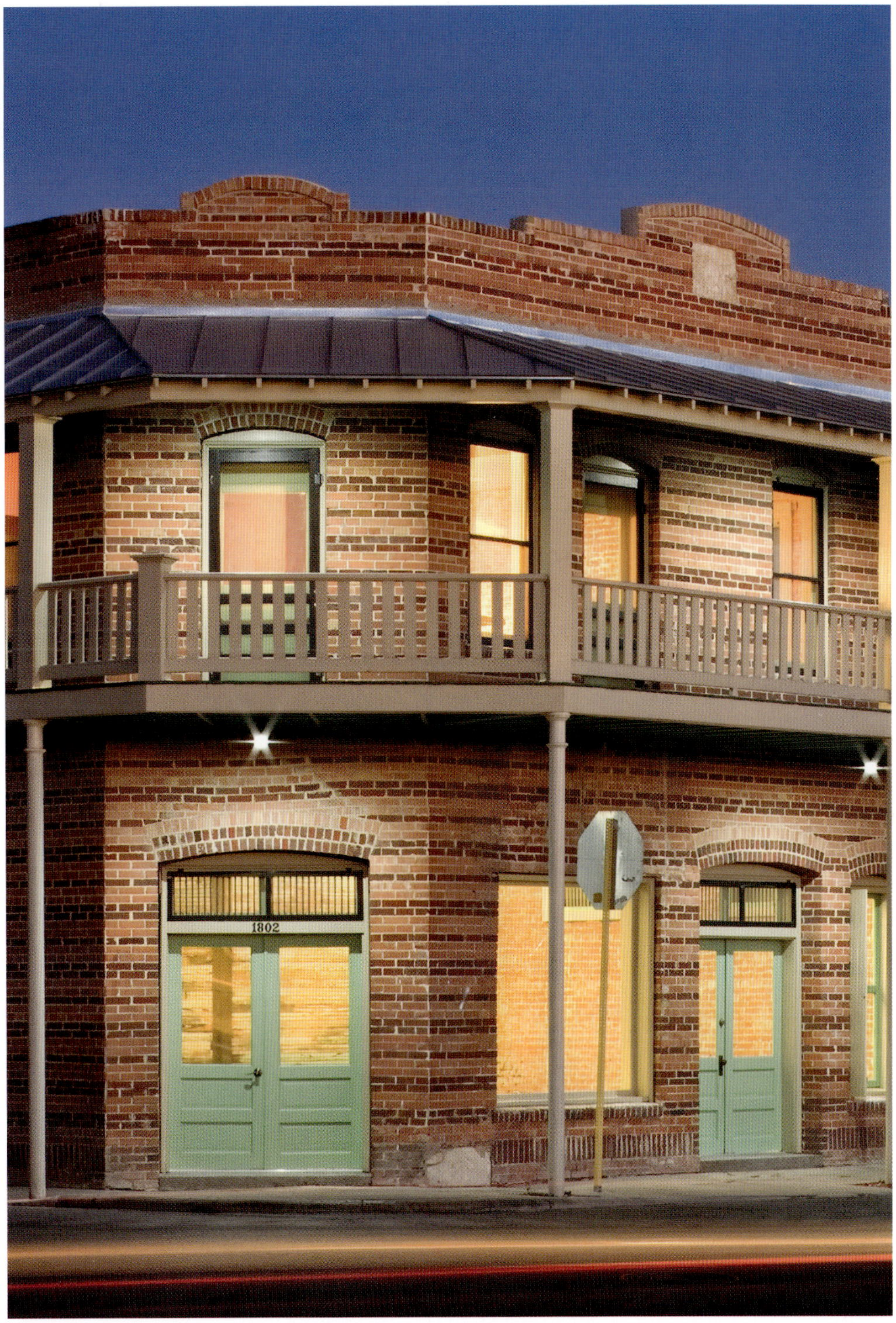

Architect Darryl Ohlenbusch, a long-time resident of the Southtown Art District, rescued the nearly destroyed El Picoso from the wrecking ball. *Photographs by Chris Cooper, courtesy Darryl Ohlenbusch Architect*

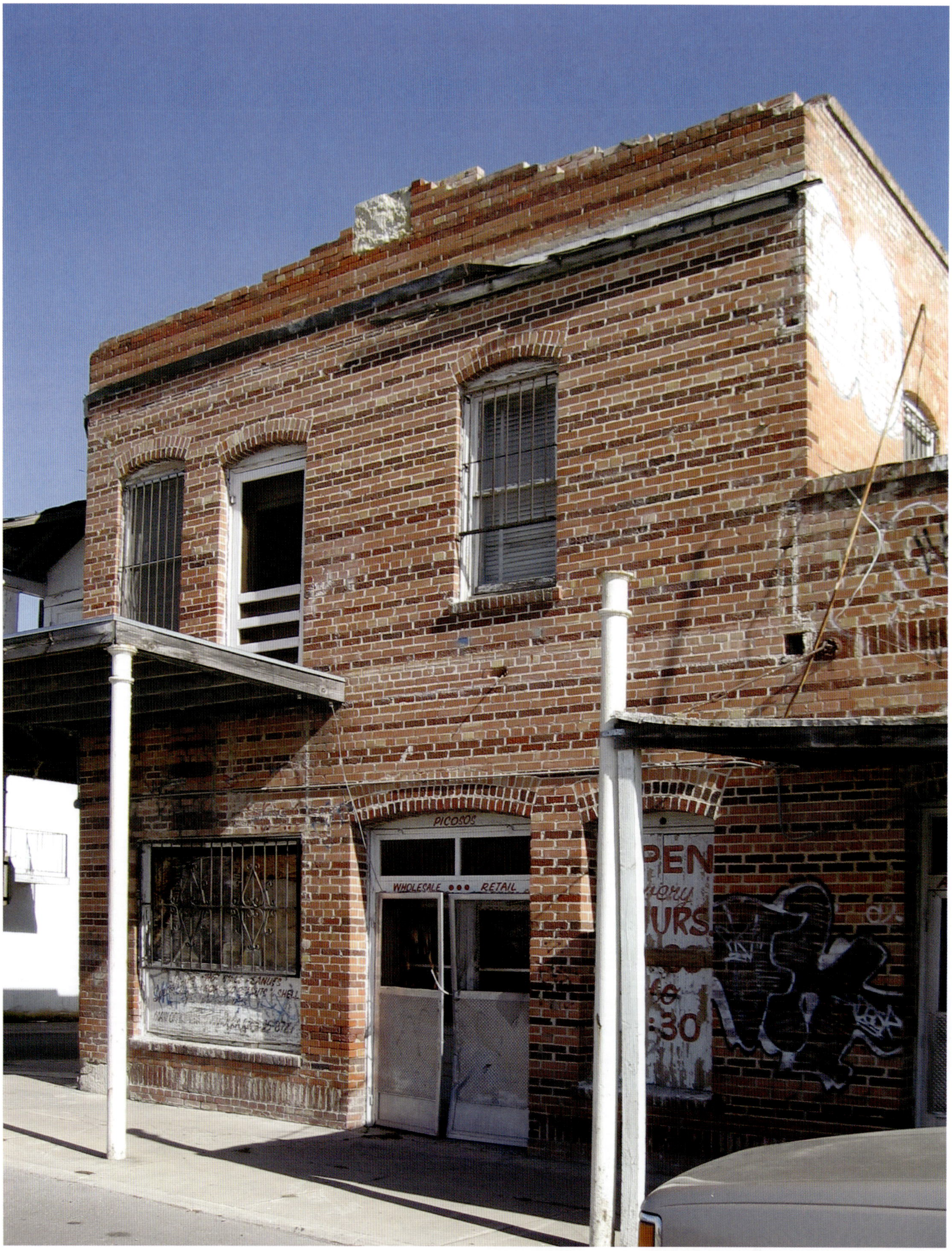

Before heroic restoration efforts by Ohlenbusch, years of neglect and a major windstorm had caused extensive damage to the two-story porches, the parapet, and the interior of the historically designated building.

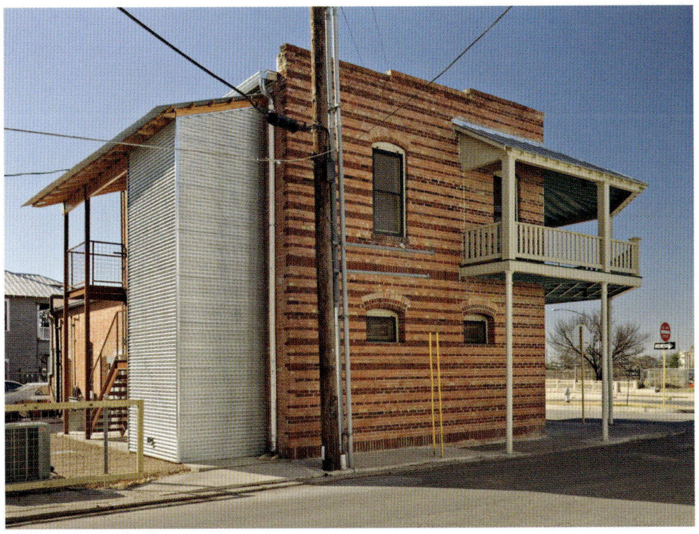

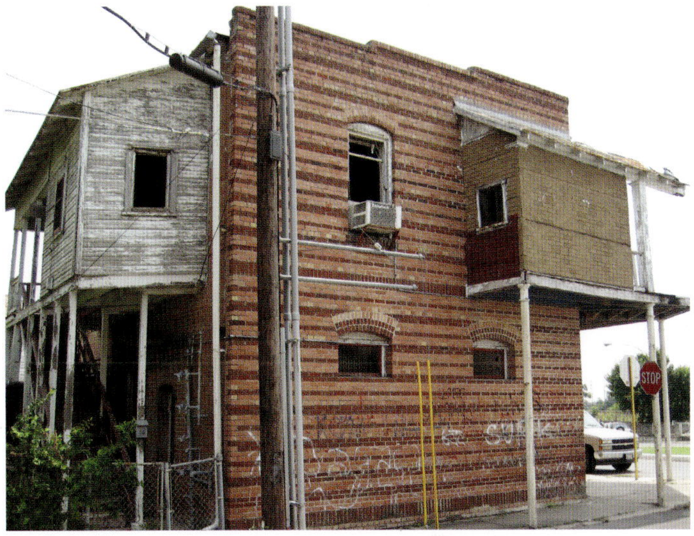

A new porch replaced the dilapidated one. The restoration retained the flavor of the building and incorporated contemporary elements such as a two-story industrial-style rear entry and roof to replace the rotted originals.

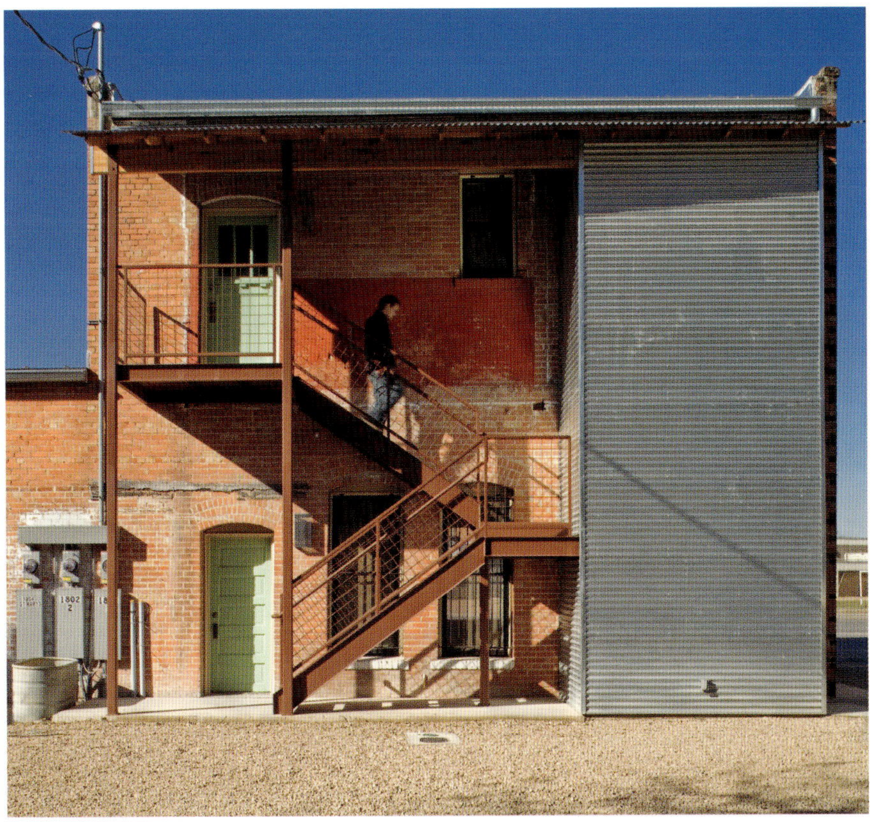

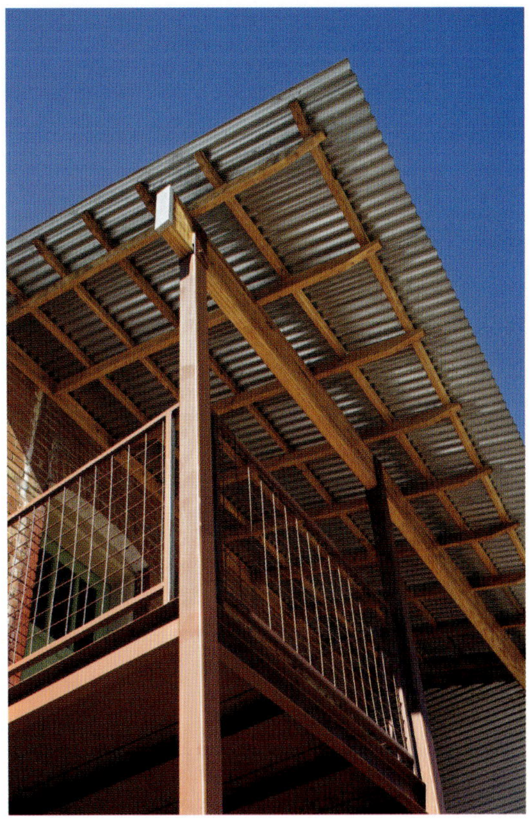

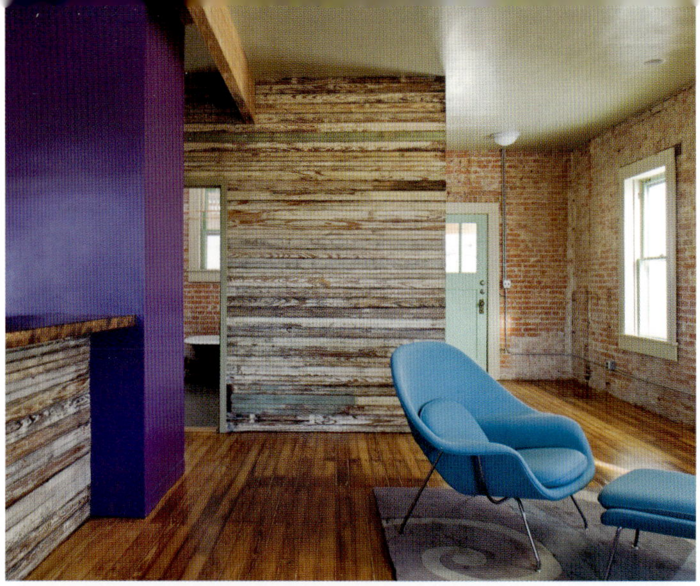

Bold color and modern furniture contrast with the original exposed brick, salvaged hand scraped beadboard, and restored wood flooring. Bright green reveals frame the views from the windows, creating a sense of dynamic, living art.

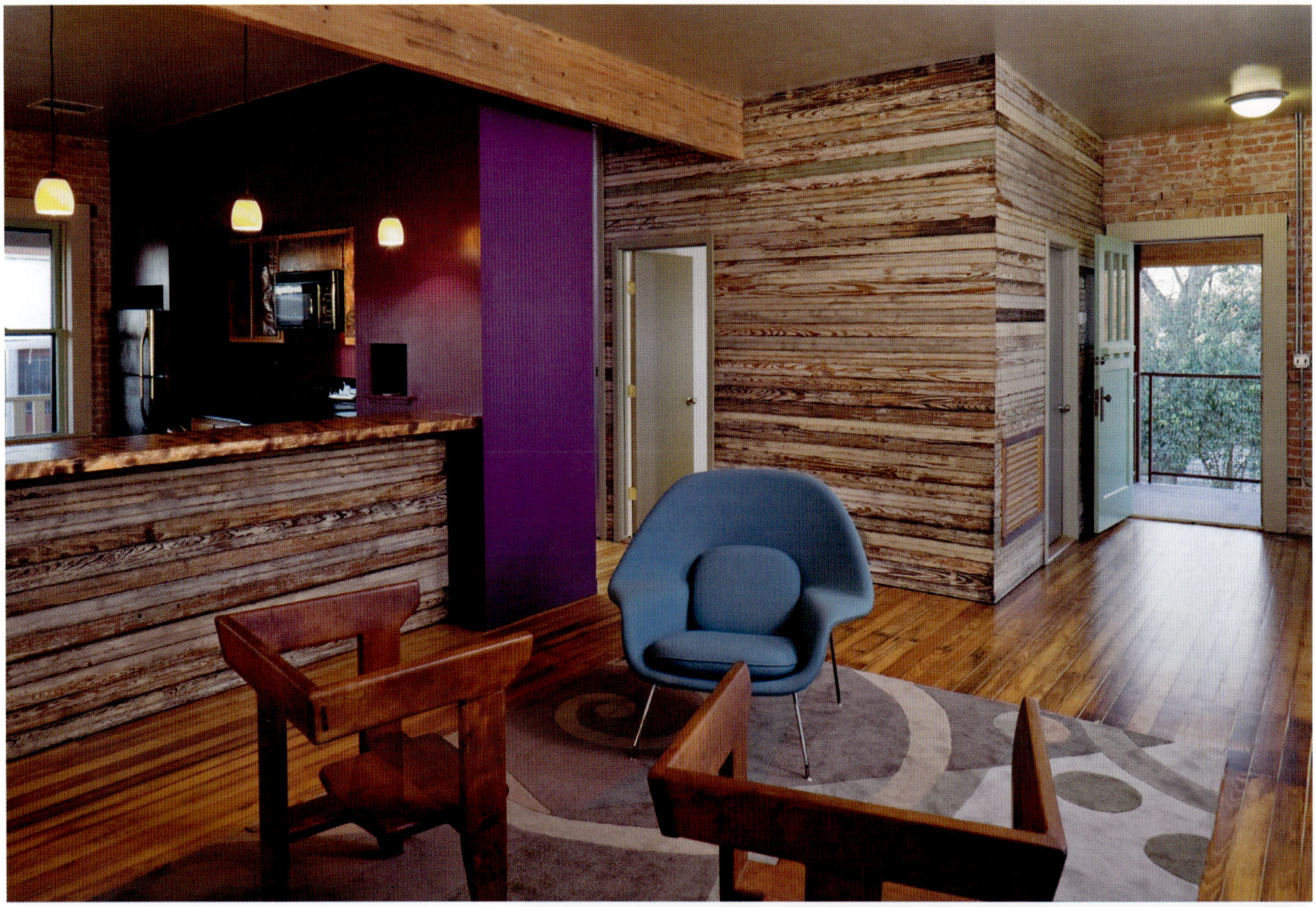

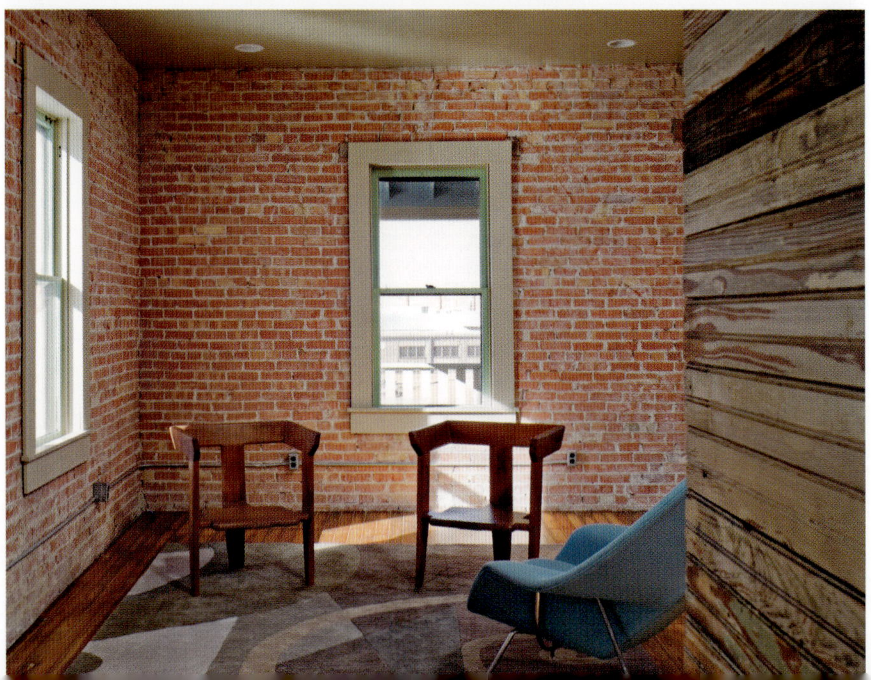

Ohlenbusch's fearless contrast of strong hues carry on, thanks to ghostly remains of colors found in salvaged beadboard.

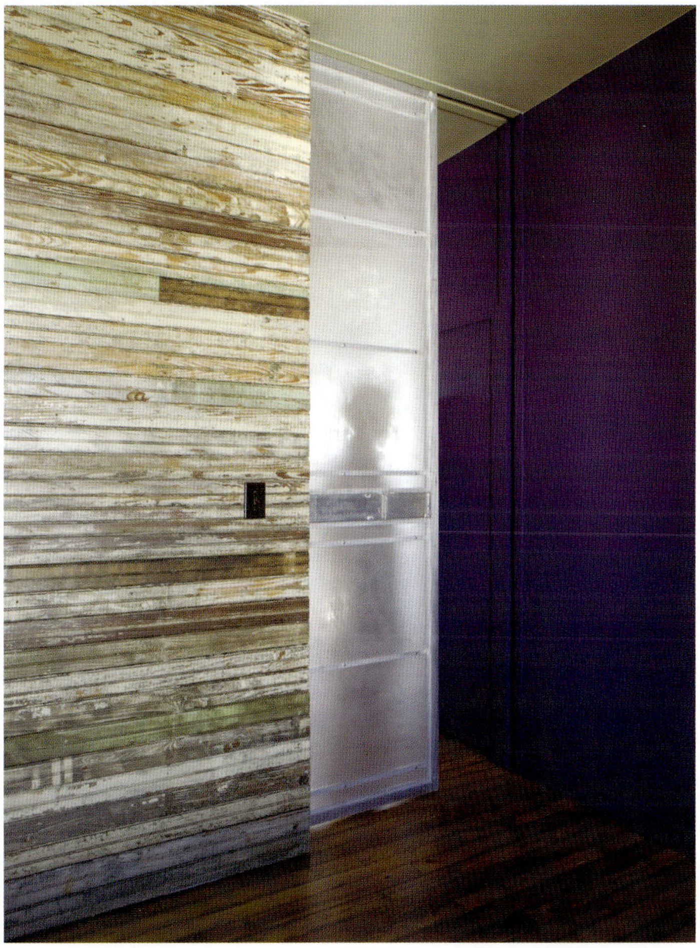

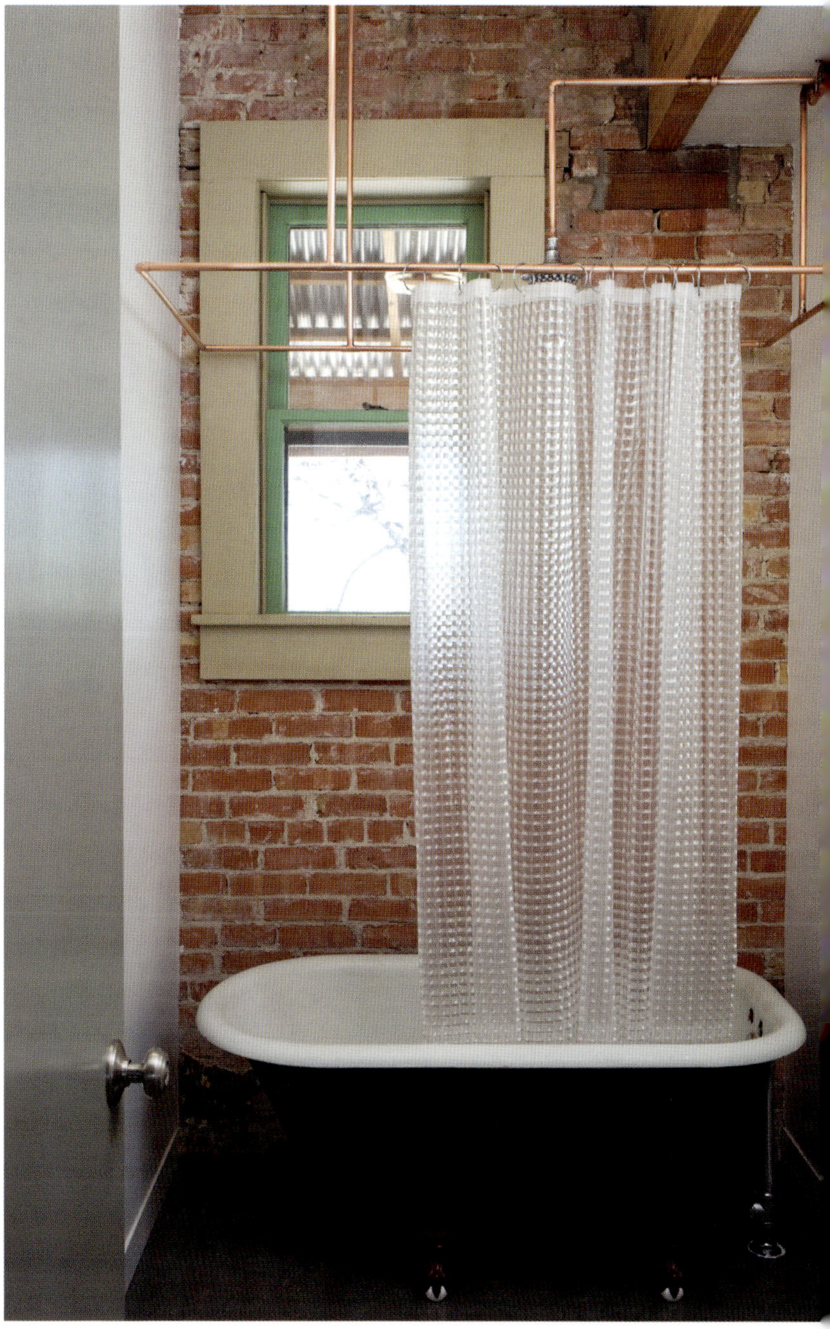

A claw and ball bathtub, a staple of homes of an earlier era, is modernized with a black finish and contrasting purple and white feet. Exposed pipes add a sense of deconstructed contemporary style.

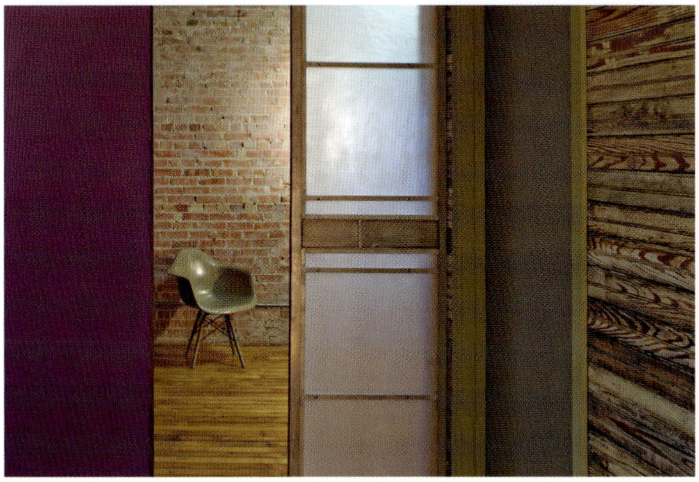

A translucent door delineates private from public space.

11
Dog Team Too Loft, A Downtown Hacienda

Fire broke out mid-way through construction to transform an old downtown industrial complex into a urban dwelling, destroying the original wood roof structure of the planned living space. Some saw a ruined structure. Undismayed, owner Jill Giles (head of her own renowned graphic design firm), and Ted Flato, FAIA, principal of Lake/Flato Architects, saw new design opportunities.

"My own design philosophy is about reuse, keeping waste to a minimum," says Giles, regarding the decision to retain the brick walls. "We replaced the wood roof with a 'light steel' north-facing roof with a saw-tooth silhouette seen on industrial buildings. The metal roof structure stabilized the free-standing brick walls. The saw-tooth design permitted clerestory windows that admit great light into the living area," says Flato. "When you walk into the living space, you see nothing but sky. The new roof structure makes the house come alive," says Bob Harris, AIA, Lake/Flato project architect. Giles declares the fully realized re-design that trades the old 11-foot-high ceiling for one dramatically 20-feet-high "so much better."

Phoenix-like, the sophisticated complex that Lake/Flato calls *Dog Team Too Loft and Studio,* recycles three original 1920s structures. The loft-like structure, once home to Petty Geophysical Laboratories (replete with a blasting chamber at one end), is the new living space. The building that was a work area was reborn as a studio. An old shed simply shed its walls to become the new courtyard pavilion.

Street-front walls, originally a hodgepodge of remodeled store fronts, were given design continuity. "Exterior glass-front openings were in-filled to a certain height with cement panels. Above the cement panels, frosted glass windows admit light," says Flato. This treatment provides privacy and security—increasing urban concerns and *musts* in an inner-city location.

"The overall layout of the 9,000-square-foot complex on a 0.5 acre site is similar to that of a hacienda," says Flato. "The former alley between the two larger structures is now a partially-covered 'outdoor entry hall' secured with a high steel gate. The passageway with alternate concrete/slate pavers leads past what Giles describes as an 'artfully sandblasted' wall. It terminates at the new walled courtyard, once a parking lot. Here, the pavilion and a raised 'water trough' create an oasis-like setting" that seems at once open and sheltered.

The ground floor of the main building—a two-bedroom residence—on the left side of the alleyway is vast, compares interestingly with the typical 3,000-4,000 square foot suburban home in a gated community. Actually, there is no comparison! The dining room (once the blasting lab) is gargantuan, yet it occupies only a corner of the loft-like space. The main living space is enormous. Then there's the open-plan grand cook's kitchen. The openness accentuates the grandeur of this awe-inspiring space. Fittingly, the bedroom opening off of one side has been described as chapel-like. As heavenly as it all is, Giles, who has renovated seven or more structures over the years, is down-to-earth in her design approach. "Two coats of crankcase oil give the concrete flooring in this building its distinctive coffee color," she says. Understandably, Giles Design attracts clients who, like Giles herself, are interested in an innovative approach to design.

On the right side of the alley is the wider second building. It serves largely as studio *cum* rumpus room. There is also a guest room for those fortunate enough to be invited to glimpse surely the most creative adaptive re-use design in San Antonio ... Texas ... the nation ... or, anywhere. Like Rome, which was not built in a day, this re-do of these vintage structures from commercial venue to private residence took awhile to complete—six years from purchase to perfection. Not such a long time, perhaps, for giving splendid new advantages to once terribly disadvantaged vintage buildings.

Jill Giles' "industrial hacienda" features a contemporary Great Room—an open living space that combines living, cooking, and dining. Clerestory windows suffuse the living area with light. Polished concrete floors were stained a rich dark hue with used crankcase oil. *Photographs by Chris Cooper, courtesy Lake/Flato Architects*

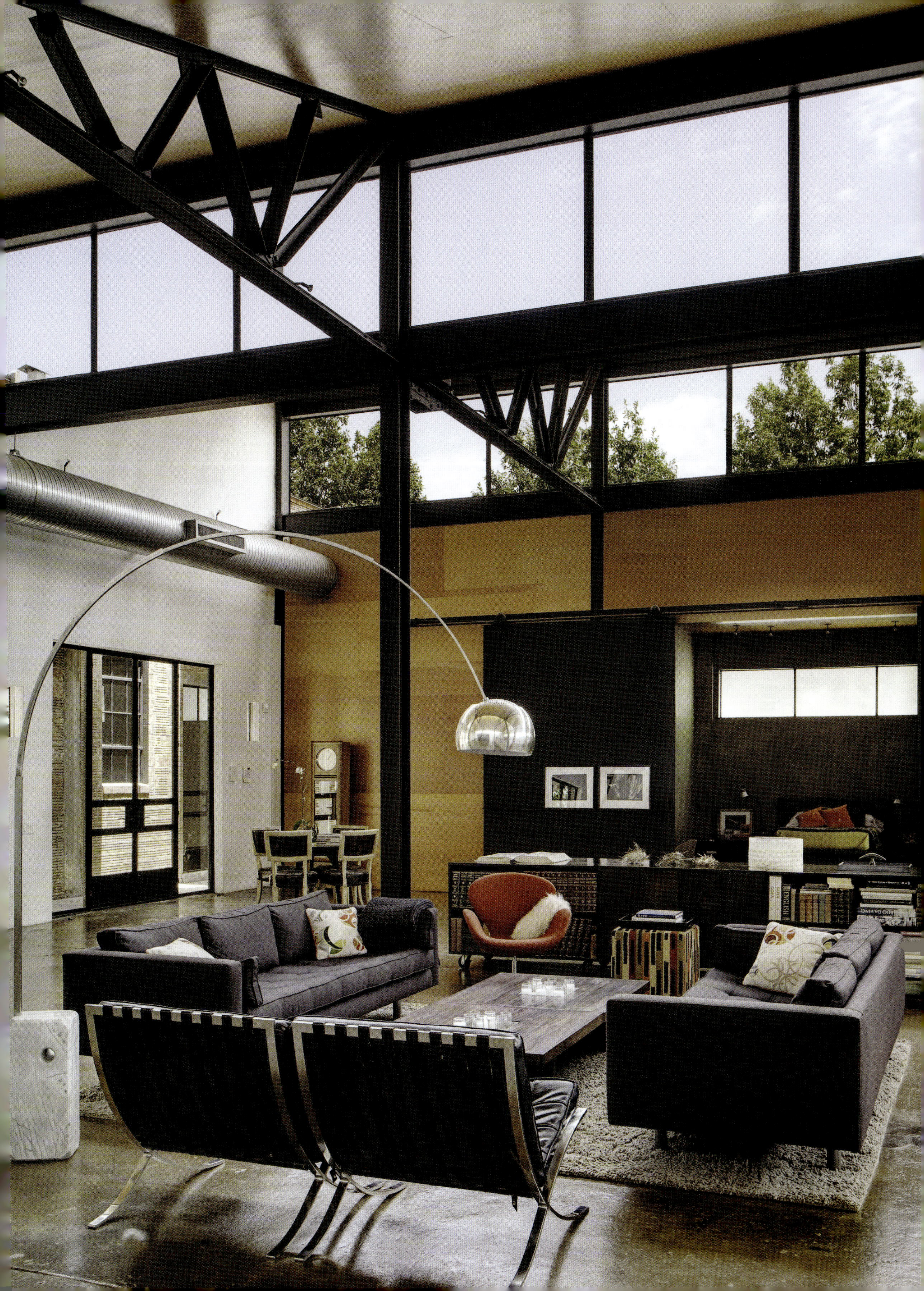

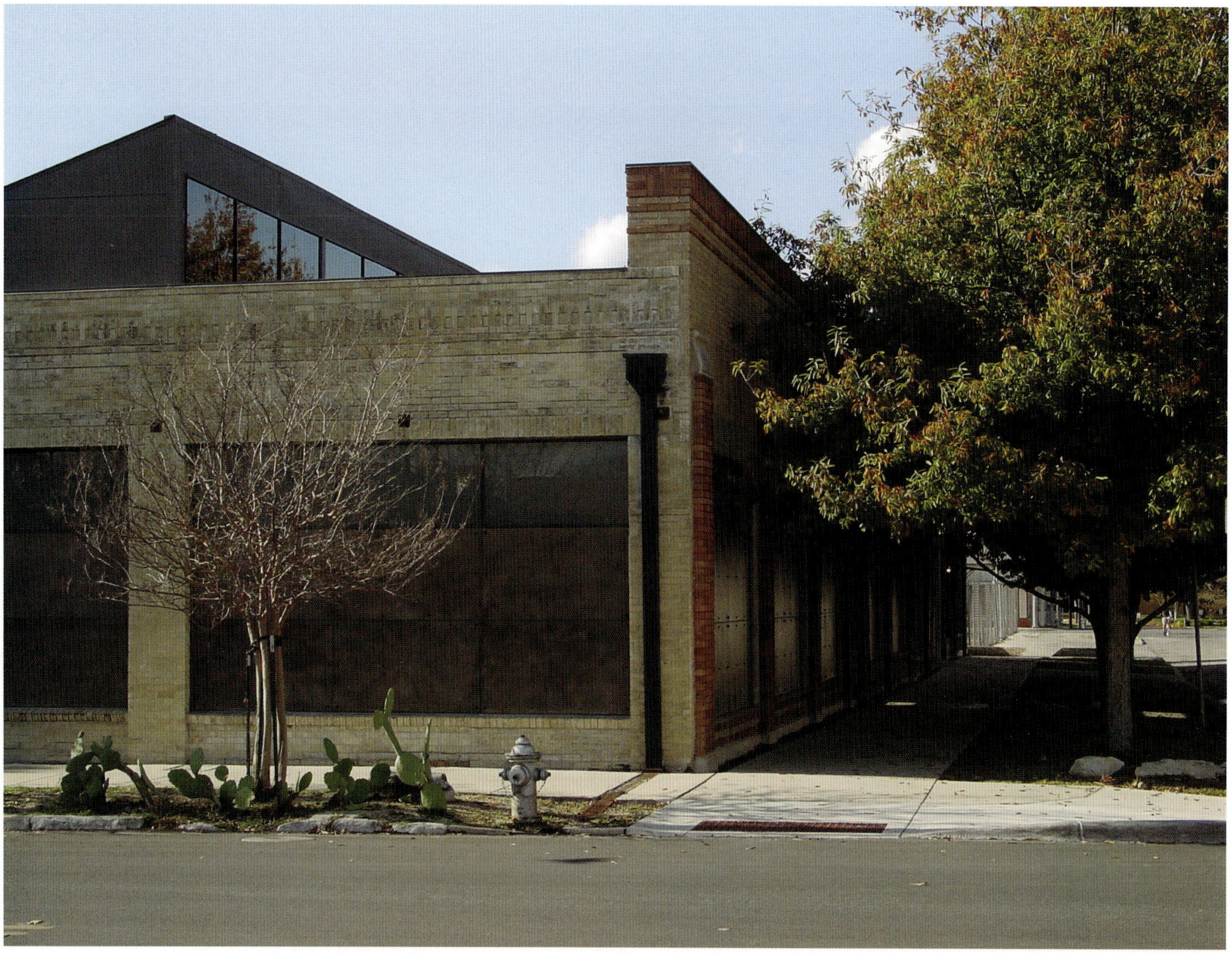

The expansive loft-like space incorporates a compact work space. Artwork rests upon the modernist take of a chair/picture rail.

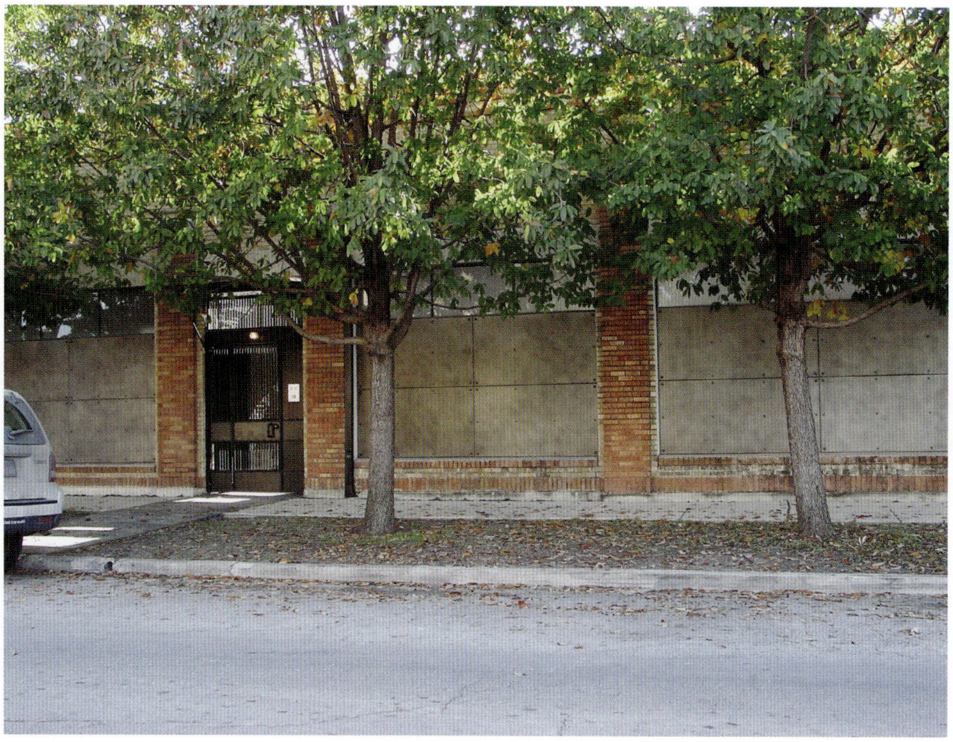

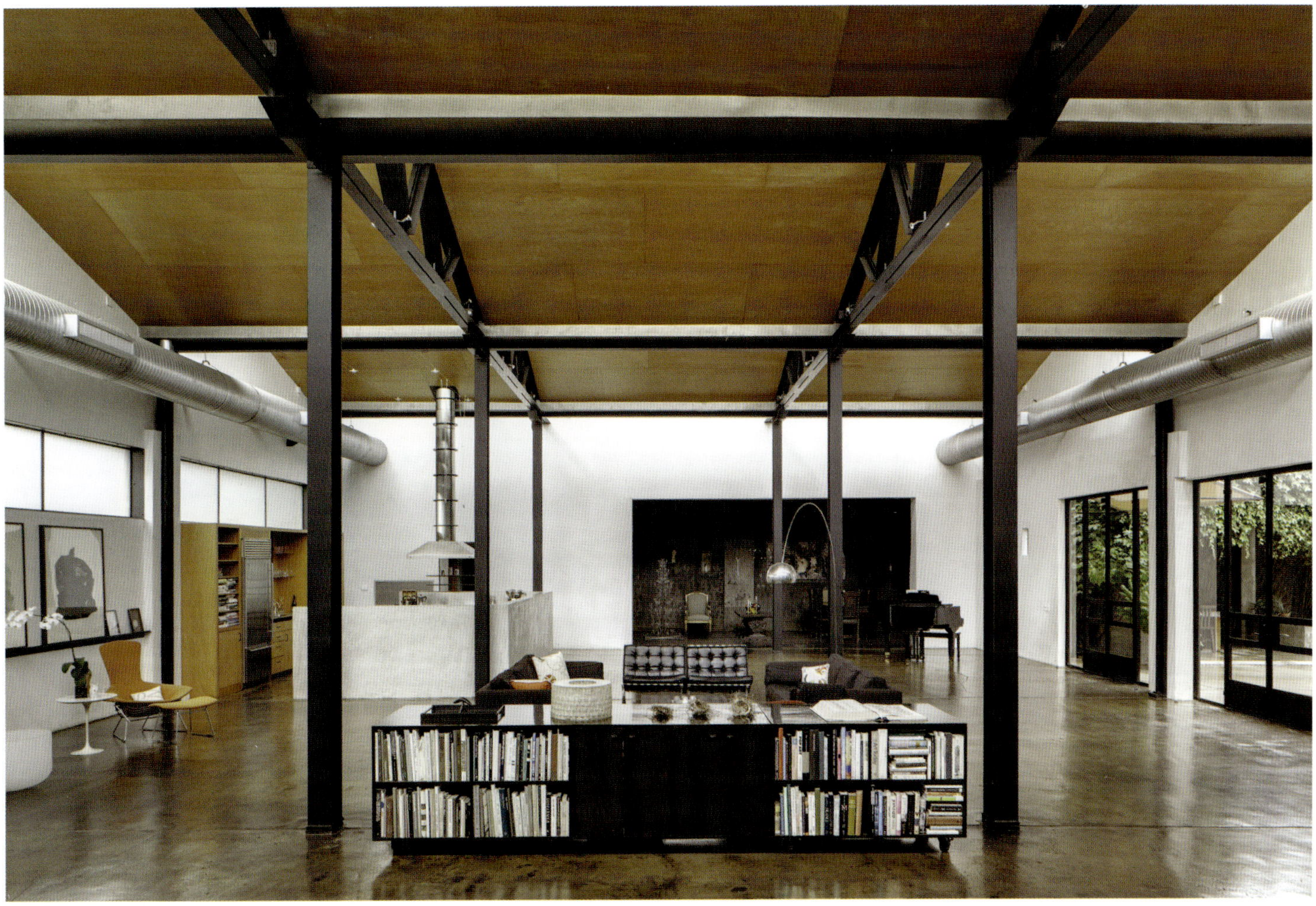

Visible from the living area, the palatial dining room with its dark plaster-finished walls rose from the ashes of the burned out blasting room of this former industrial building.

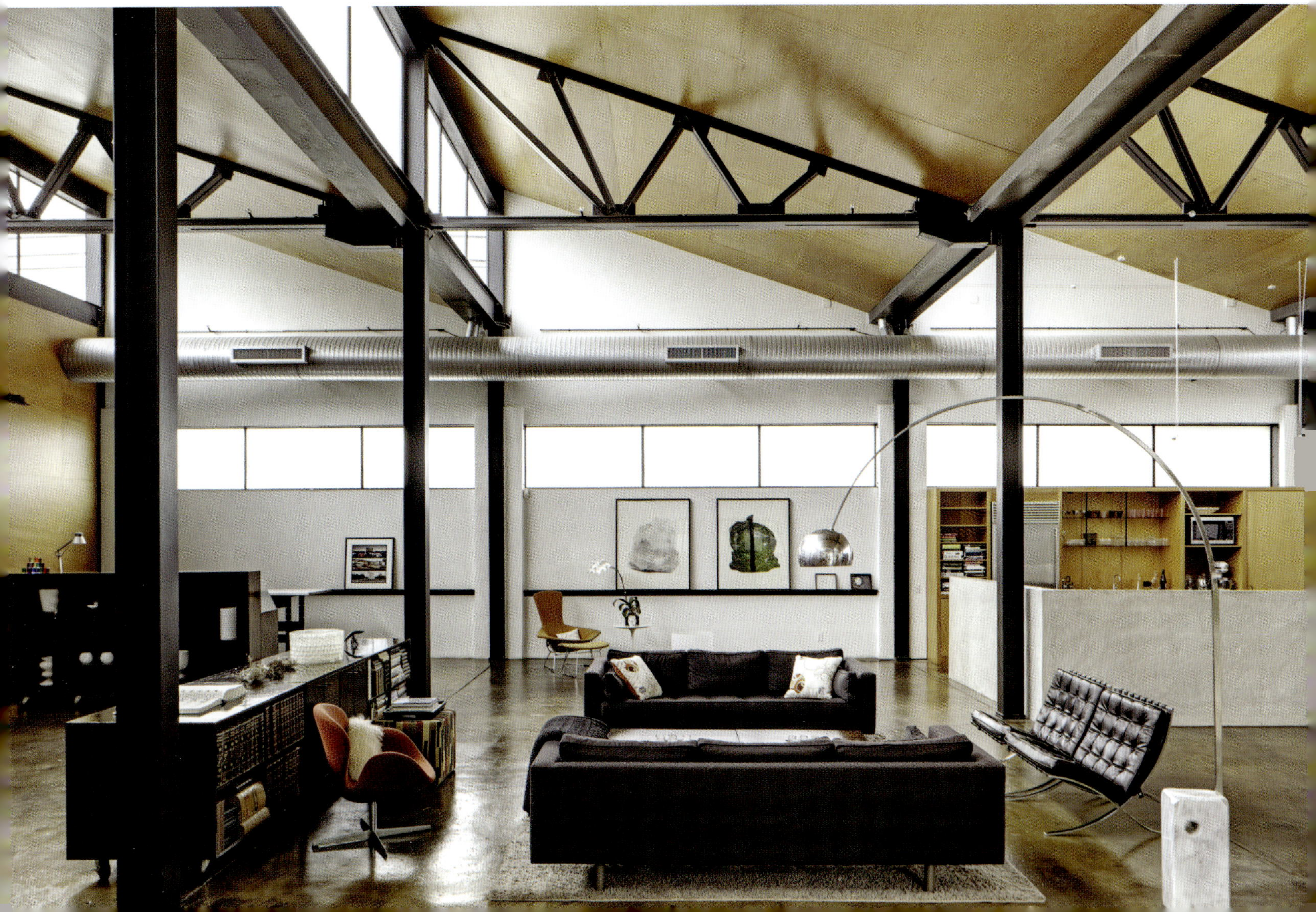

12

Casa Finale

Not all *historic* houses are *vintage* or antique (100 years old). Innovative architectural styles are historic the moment they come into existence—because they are *new*. The mid-twentieth century house at 102 Downing Drive in Bel Meade was a new style—the architectural response to changing societal values and democratic cultural norms that were new, dramatic, and historically significant.

This one-story, ranch-style house—and many similar homes in builder-developed sub-divisions across the United States—offered air-conditioned comfort, modern labor-saving appliances, and privacy at an affordable price to a large segment of society. Increasing automobile ownership made it possible for developers to place these houses on individual suburban lots, usually in municipal sub-divisions called "developments." These new-style shelters acknowledged the importance of the family car by integrating the garage, no longer hidden behind an impressive façade but visible from the street.

While architectural critic Colin Rowe dubbed them "ranchburgers" (he said they were proliferating like hamburger joints), these houses needed make no apologies then or now. They provided essential elements of shelter: comfort, convenience, and privacy. Today, new generations of homeowners, including young couples and empty-nesters, are discovering these mid-century marvels and remodeling them to meet the ever-changing idea of home.

In 2005, a super talented team, architect Frederick Williams and his interior designer wife, M. Robbins Black, with an expert eye toward easy maintenance and their own near-future semi-retirement, discovered the 1953 house at 102 Downing. Recognizing its potential and without a backward glance, they moved from a much larger house in another part of town. They set about to transform the "ranchburger" into a *casa—Casa Finale*—customized to their demanding specifications and tastes.

Black and Williams found their new 2,400-square-foot house on a well-landscaped corner lot on a quiet cul-de-sac in front of a lovely city park. Behind the main house (unusual for a ranch-style design) was a garage with an apartment—an ideal location for Black's design office.

The location—near to a grocery, dry cleaner, auto service center, and medical facilities—was ideal; the house was not. It was, as Black states, "a *real* challenge," even for these skilled pros. They met the challenge handily.

Changes to the exterior began with repairing the foundation (not uncommon in an area where alternating rain and drought create shifts in the clay soil). Next they replaced once popular vinyl siding with beautifully textured cedar shingles similar to those used throughout the neighborhood. The cosmetic change was immediate and remarkable.

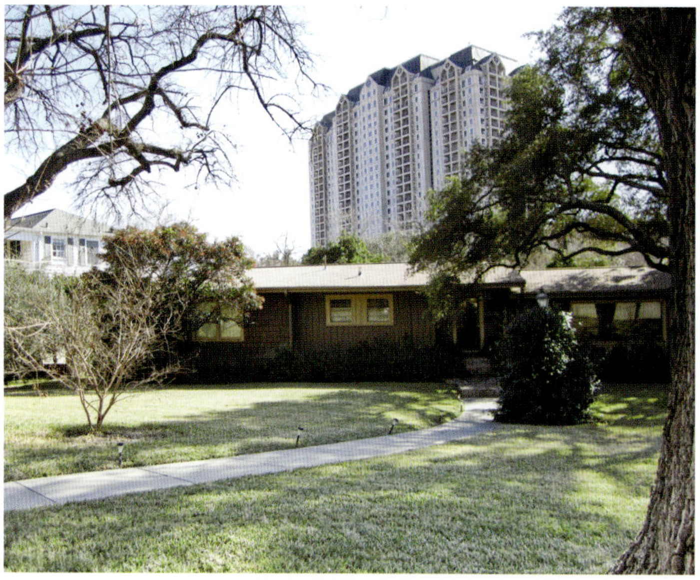

Affordable, practical mid-century ranch-style houses, which quickly captured the nation's fancy, are once again in vogue. *Photographs by David Strahan, AIA*

Solid-panel entry doors were exchanged for five-light insulated doors. Replacing small windows and doors with 3-foot by 6-foot 9-inch five-panel glass doors added a more sophisticated look to the exterior and lightened and brightened the interior.

Updating the interior. Changes to the floor plan included removing walls, enlarging doorways, and including a new wheelchair-accessible bathroom door. The new floor plan allows traffic to flow easily, beginning at the small but gracious entry and passing though rooms and spaces that never seem confining. Intelligent, elegant organization of space—physically opened with wider doorways and windows—creates a sense of spaciousness that seems entirely original.

The most dramatic change to the interior is the re-design of the long, narrow galley-style kitchen. On the long exterior wall, Williams replaced two small over-sink windows with four windows ganged to create a wall of light. "This new window wall let in glorious sunlight and opens this space to views of the yard," says Black. On the opposite wall was a door into the dining room. Williams relocated the door to a once-confining dead-end wall, where the new opening admits more light into the kitchen. Along the newly-open interior wall, Williams added a long run of new stainless-steel base cabinets. (Old wood cabinets were donated to Habitat for Humanity's re-sale store.) The backsplash is matte-finished glass tile. Above the new Jerusalem limestone countertop is a new bar-height counter. "Friends gather there while I cook," says Black.

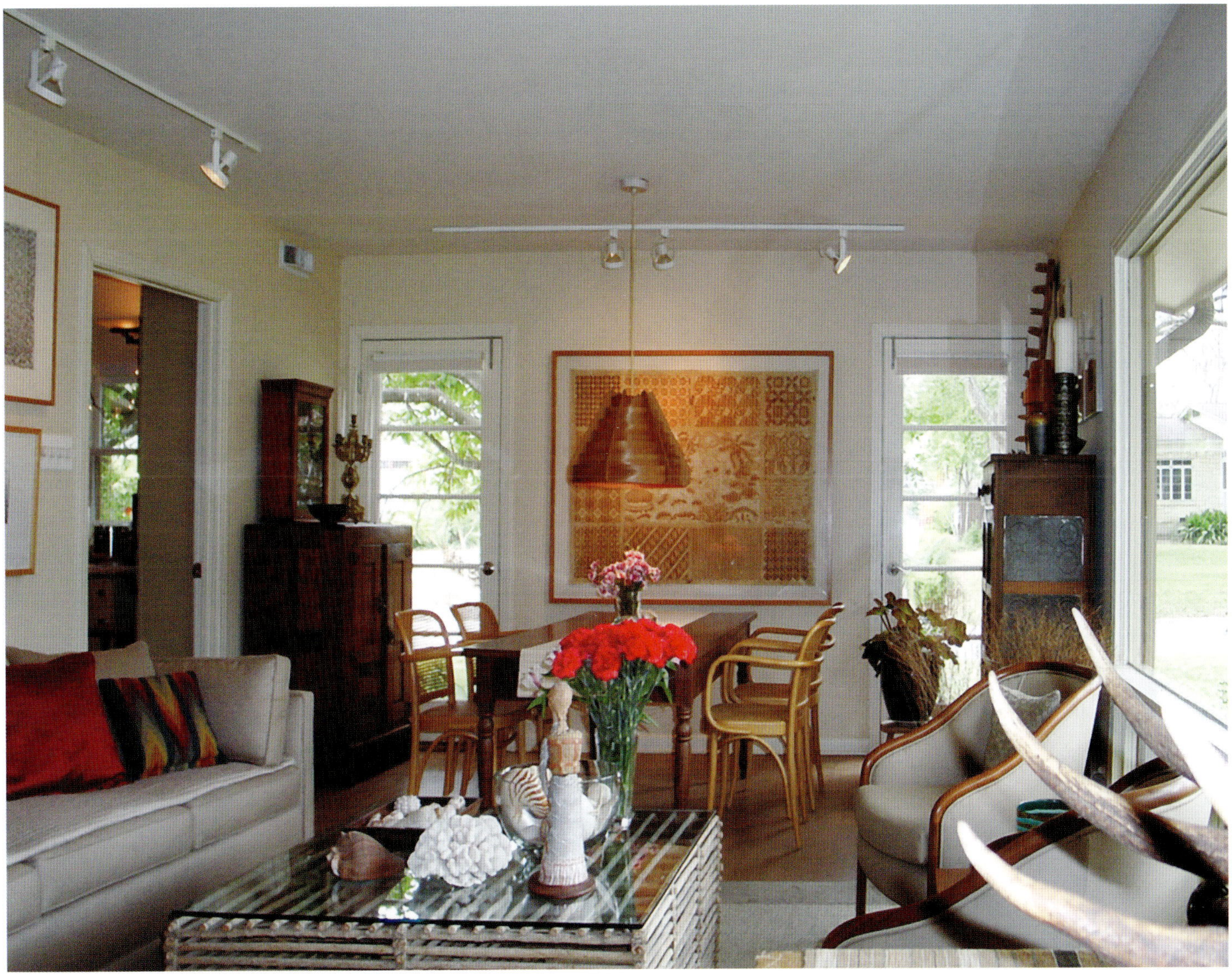

Architect Fred Williams and his interior designer wife, Robin Black, smartly replaced small windows with elegant full-length glass doors.

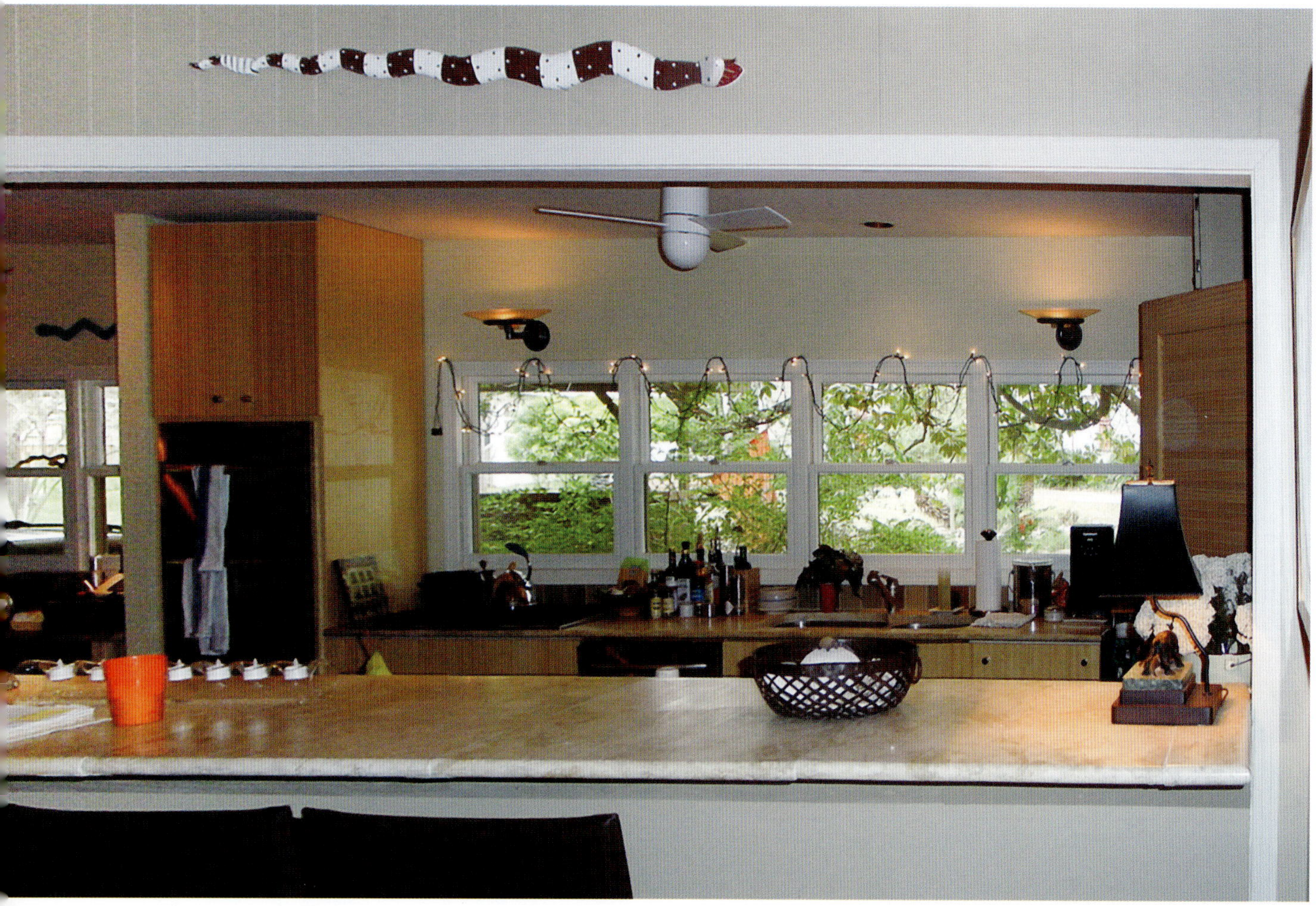

A two-level eat-at kitchen counter replaces an old doorway into the dining area. A new door was placed at one end of the Pullman-style kitchen. Above the sink is a new wall of windows.

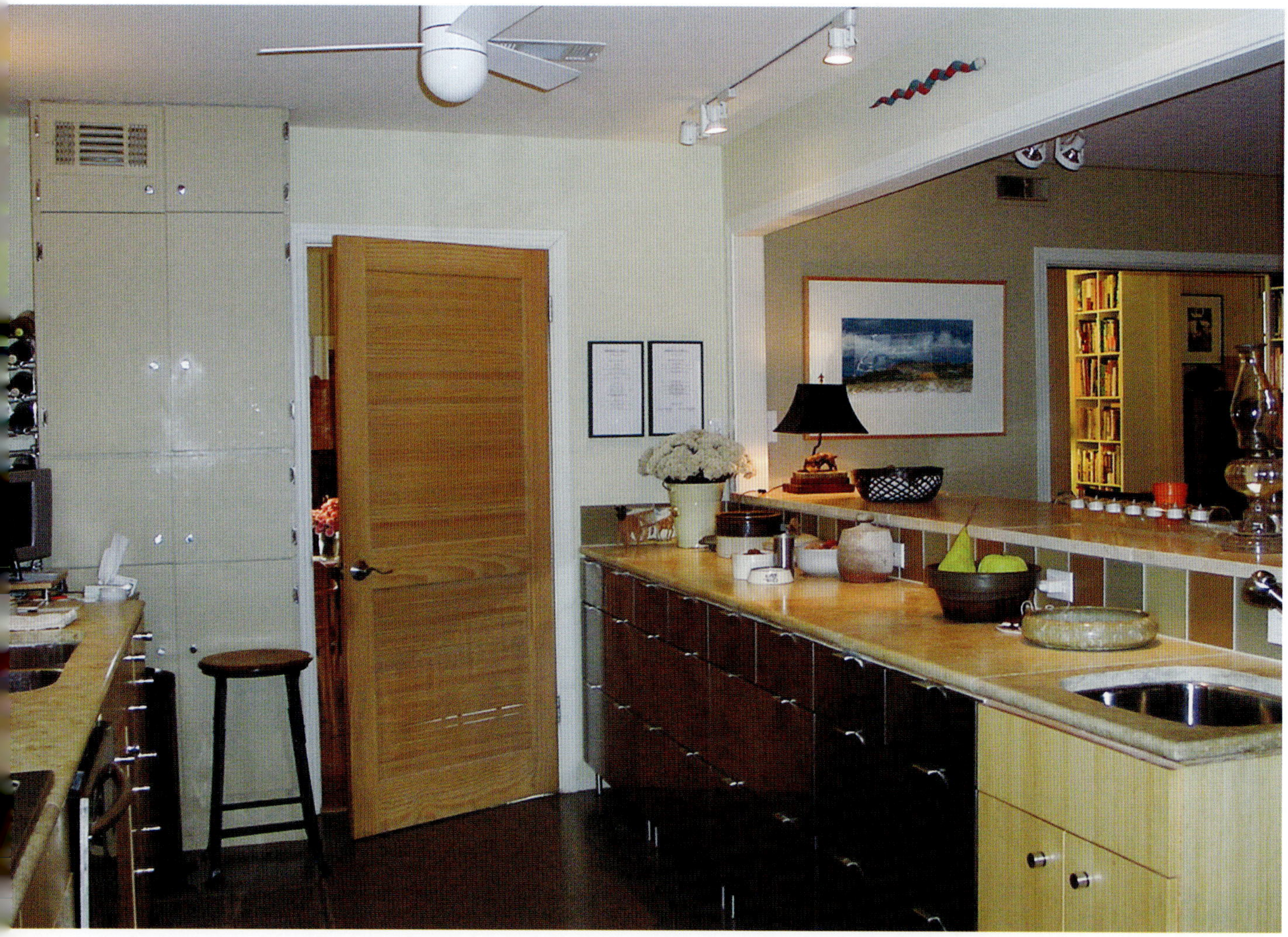

Outmoded kitchen cabinets were donated to charity and replaced with new ones in a contemporary style.

The "after" floor plan shows the artful simplicity of Architect Fred Williams' re-design.

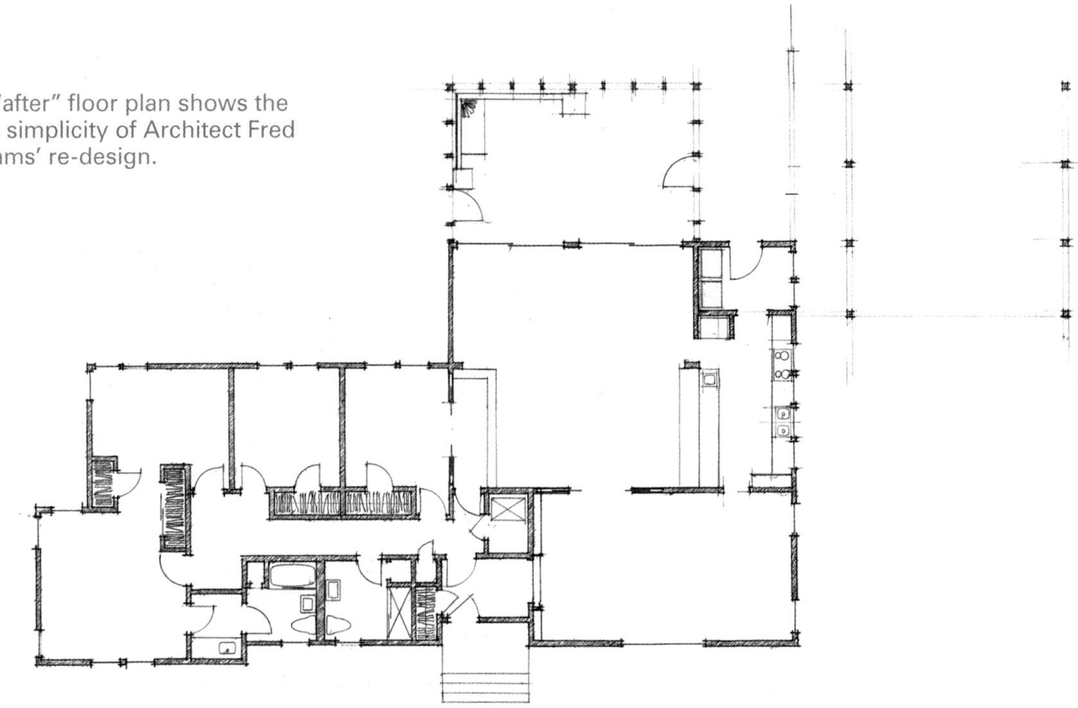

At the end of the hall leading to bedrooms, Williams altered a wall to create a charming mini-foyer in front of the guestroom on one hand and the master bedroom suite (which contains a sitting room, bedroom, and bathroom) on the other.

Going green. Black and Williams kept sustainability in mind by recycling materials removed from the house that once would have been sent to a landfill. Included were siding, doors, windows, and carpeting (all new floors are white or red oak). They also used recycled materials, including handsome fully-louvered doors—purchased from Habitat for Humanity at the tremendous savings of $50 per door—which replaced solid doors, allowing better ventilation throughout.

New plumbing involved bringing the hot water in compliance with code by relocating it away from the furnace. They installed low-flow toilets, and exchanged the tub in the hall bath with a ADA-compliant walk-in shower fitted with a Euro-style hand-held shower wand and a convenient bench.

The clean look of windows without curtains adds to the modern mood of updated interiors. Timeless, classic Venetian blinds provide light control and privacy. "Existing wood blinds were cleaned, refinished, fitted with new tapes, and re-hung," says Black.

Creating an All-Season Porch. Porches were not part of the ranch-house style vocabulary, but this house had a covered concrete-slab back porch that Black and Williams deemed useless. To make it a multi-seasonal space, accessed via glass sliding doors from the family room, they dressed up the slab with Arkansas River stone, screened it to keep insects at bay, and added ceiling fans for cooling in summer. A new raised-hearth corner fireplace takes the chill off during cooler weather and serves as a focal point for gatherings in this newly convivial space.

Williams and Black gave their *Casa Finale* a new beginning.

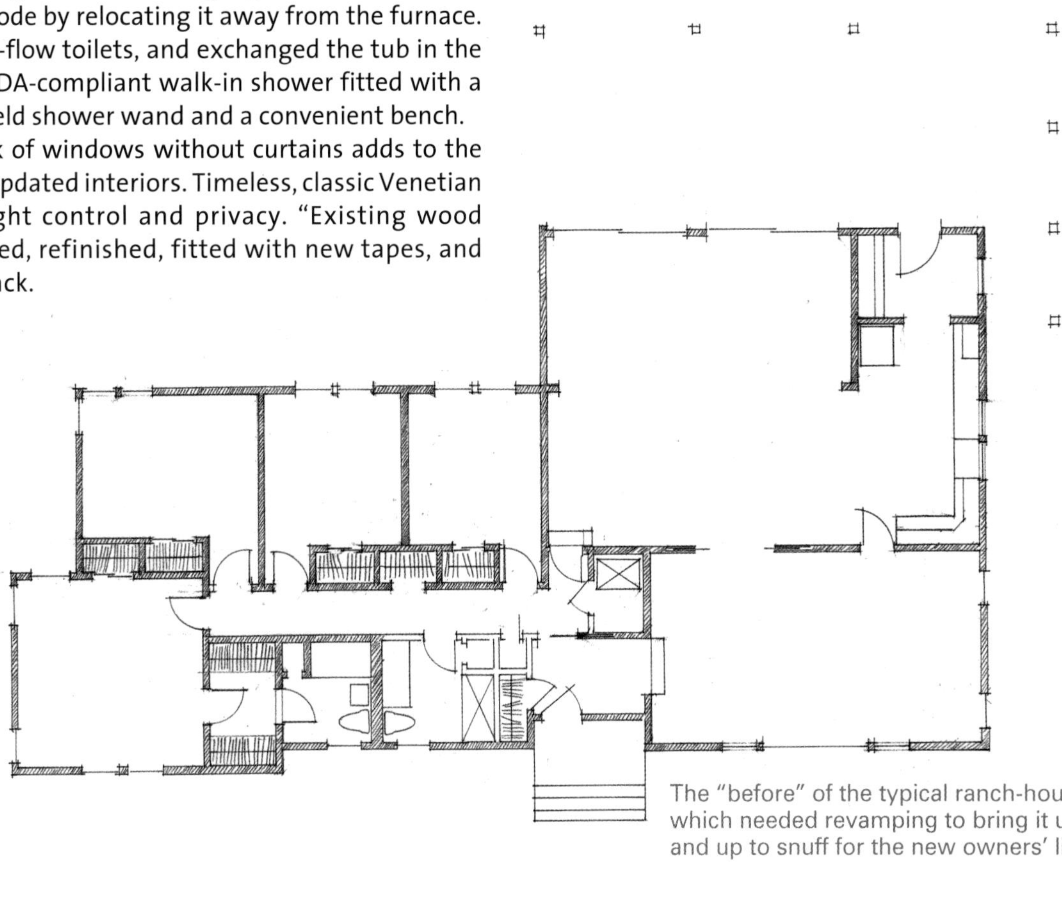

The "before" of the typical ranch-house interior, which needed revamping to bring it up to code and up to snuff for the new owners' lifestyle.

13
Northrup, Koenig-Reford House

"The realtor's brochure called this the 1885 Northrup House," says Mark Reford, current owner with wife, Lisa Koenig, and their daughters, Emma and Saskia. "Our landscape architect told us that the architecture is Victorian Stick Style." What distinguishes the Stick Style from other Victorian era architecture are the members or trim that look like "sticks" on the façade. They often also feature fanciful lace-like "carpenter's Gothic" milled trim that accentuates walls, gable ends, and porch pediments. Some houses feature this millwork indoors, and in the Koenig-Reford's King William district home, turned millwork connects columns that accentuate an arched doorway between the entry hall and the living room.

The term *Victorian* refers to the long reign (1837 to 1901) of Queen Victoria of England, and is used as a blanket term covering a multitude of architectural "looks" that borrow from the Queen Anne, Richardsonian, and Shingle styles. Whereas classic architecture is symmetrical, these romantic styles feature asymmetrical massing of component blocks. Other features they have in common are towers (some rounded), arched windows, porches, and balconies—capped with chalet-like pitched rooflines that create deep eaves. The old Northrup house has many of these features.

A house as old as this one at 401 Adams Street in the historic King William district is bound to have a fascinating history. "The house has had some very colorful characters live and work under its roof," says Reford. "For decades after the second World War, a prominent local art dealer lived in the home with his wife. She was a French duchess who had fled the austerity of postwar Europe." Reford heard that other past occupants include a renowned author. "I was told that for a few years, the world-famous San Antonio and King William district writer, Sandra Cisneros, author of ***The House on Mango Street***, lived here." Like all the houses in the once-elite King William area, this one suffered from the economic decline that caused them to be divided into units. "Neighbors tell us that the house was split into separate rooms for lodgers. At various times, a group of young men lived here; then, a group of nuns were housed here," says Reford.

Fortunately for this house, in 2008, Jim and Charlotte Crowley moved to San Antonio from San Francisco, a city famous for its restored Victorian homes known as "painted ladies." "The chance to renovate a beautiful old Victorian in such a charming part of King William was irresistible. They worked closely with a local contractor, David Lopez, owner of DSL Construction, who has an intuitive and deeply respectful feel for the integrity and beauty of the antique," says Reford.

"The goal was to restore the old longleaf pine floors and woodwork to their original beauty without stripping them of 100 years of character. Paint covered the wonderful wooden staircase and columns and trim around the arched doorway into the living room. It was carefully stripped away by hand by Charlotte and David, who also stripped paint covering the beautiful old glazed tiles surrounding fireplaces. The house was meticulously restored," Reford explains.

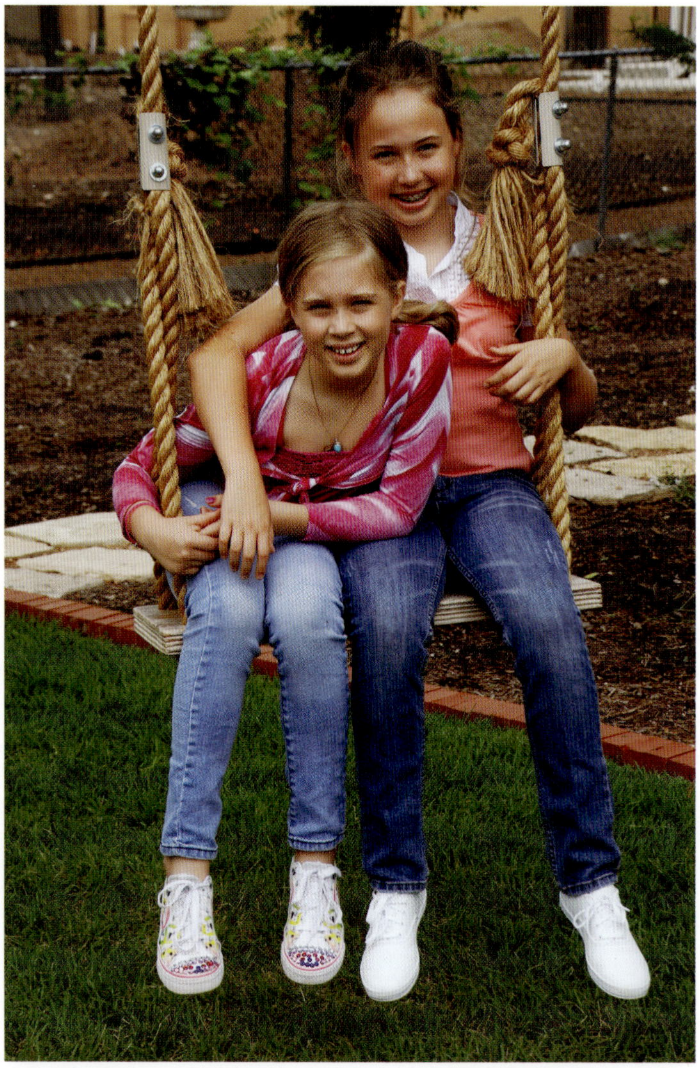

A new swing for Emma and Saskia signals that the restored 1885 Northrup house is home to young San Antonians.
Photographs by Barbara Justice

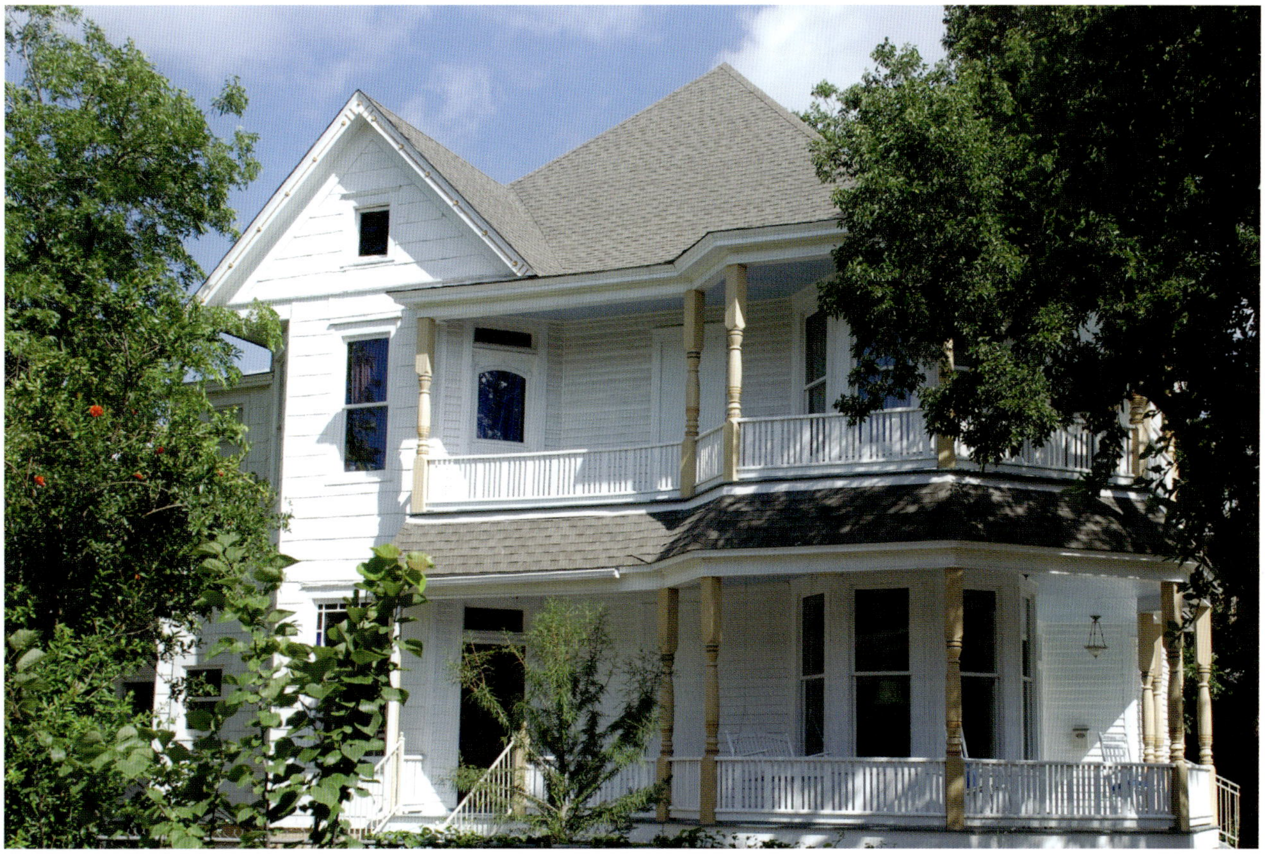

A variety of sidings (including novelty shingles), turrets, carved embellishments, and verandas (porches) are typical of the many-angled Queen Anne style, one of several favorite architectural styles during the Victorian era.

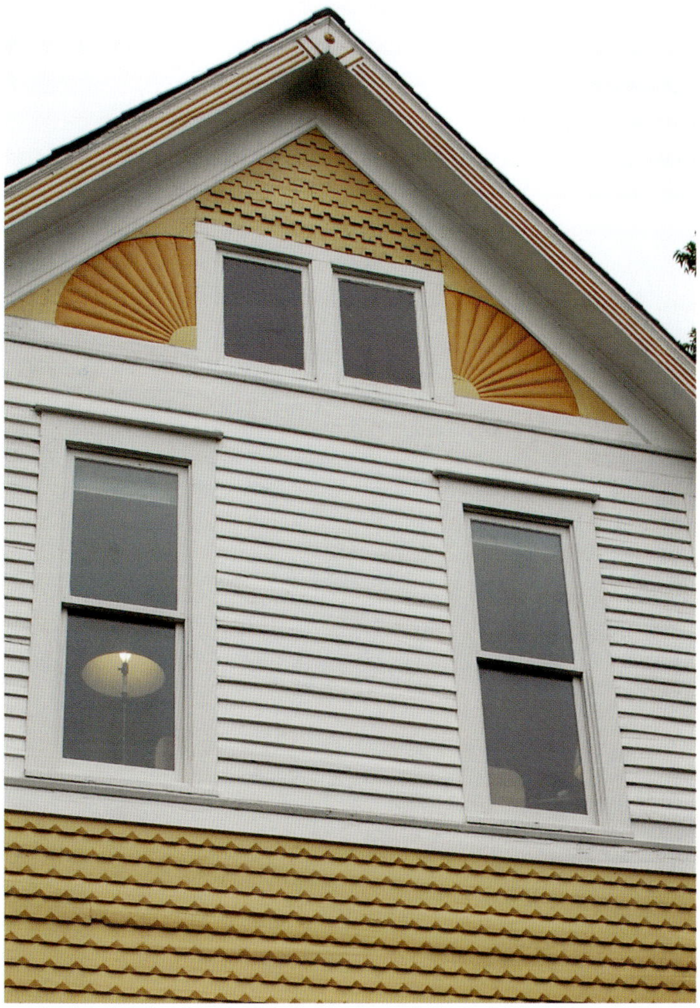

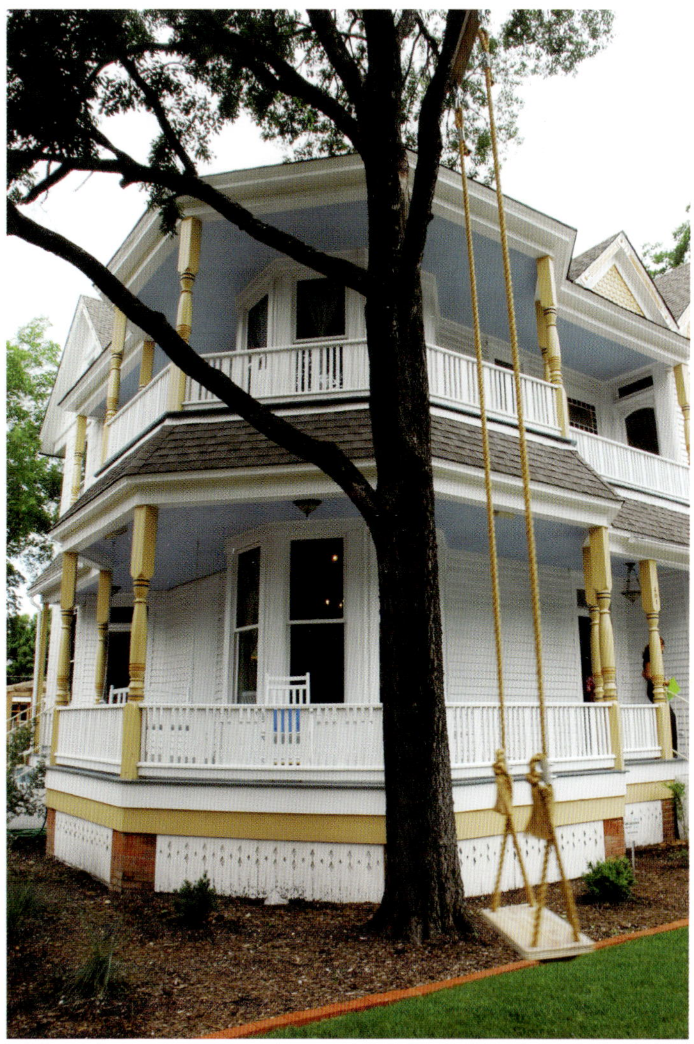

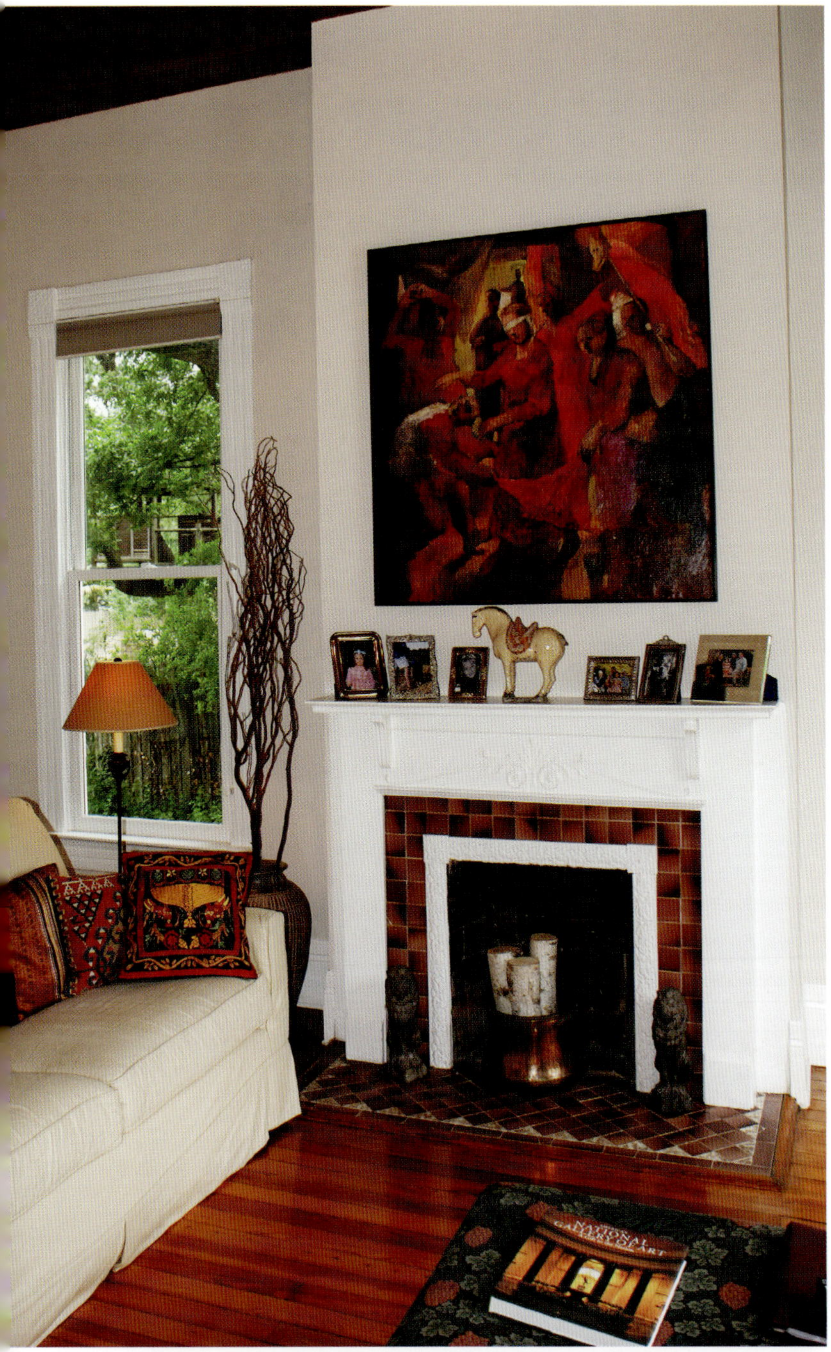

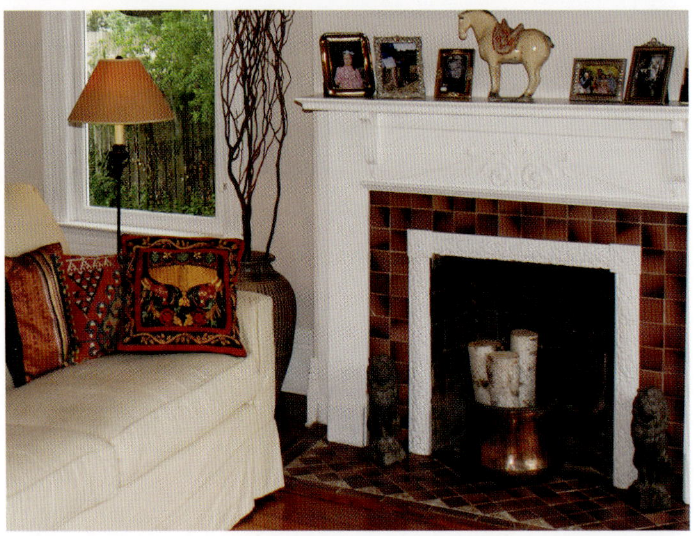

Fireplace tiles in the living room and throughout the house had been painted, but were cleaned and restored.

Notoriously, old houses have few or no closets (perhaps because for tax purposes they were counted as rooms). "Victorian houses often lack storage space," says Reford's wife, Lisa Koenig. "When we moved here, we had David Lopez add closets and bookcases. He wonderfully incorporated them into our rooms."

The house had been brought into the current era with a new kitchen that suits the Koenig-Reford lifestyle. "We adore this kitchen with its huge island. We spent lots of family time in this room, which is the work of David Lopez. It's modern, but designed to feel like a Victorian kitchen. The large space was created by removing partitions from several small rooms. Enclosing and incorporating a porch transformed one end of the kitchen into an inviting sun-drenched spot. We read there and enjoy the garden," says Koenig.

Like the new closets, new landscaping is the contribution of Koenig and Redford. "There was no landscaping when we arrived—only a bare lot. Landscape Architect Sarah Westkamper Lake designed a stunning *Texas* garden using native and adapted traditional plants. The plan emphasizes the geometric and historic elements of the house. Lake also designed the white picket fence and arbor, both constructed by Lopez. New curb appeal is more than cosmetic. "The landscaping totally changed the property—the adults can entertain under the shady arbor and porch, while the kids play on the lawns with their tree swings and zipline," Koenig says.

"In every way, we tried to keep with the original feel of the home and the neighborhood," says Reford, who moved with his family to San Antonio from Washington, D.C., when he accepted a position as Head of St. Luke's Episcopal School. (In Washington, Koenig was the award-winning Senior Producer for George Stephanopoulos' news program.) "We were drawn to this neighborhood because King William has a flavor all its own. Generations of inhabitants have protected the architectural heritage, and in doing so have created a neighborhood that is rich in stories, gracious homes, and interesting characters. Our home in particular is an ideal combination of the old and the new. Ceilings are twelve feet high. The staircase is a unique piece of carving done especially for this home. Rooms are large and, unlike those in so many Victorian homes, flooded with light from the endless array of floor-to-ceiling windows. The kitchen is contemporary. More than that, our house is set on a very private level lot—huge by King William standards. Surrounding homes create a series of serene views."

There are advantages to living in this historic area. "We love living downtown. We can walk to great restaurants, the River Walk, art galleries, and so on. We think it is great for us and for our daughters."

Would Reford recommend that others consider purchasing an old house? "Yes, indeed," he says. "Our joy in living in our home is beyond our expectations. The house has great warmth and character. The garden is interesting and eventful twelve months of the year. And the porches are large, welcoming, and private—an ideal outdoor space, even on a rainy day." As for the house, he points to features that appeal strongly to both of them: "The quality of the space, the workmanship, the sheer feeling that comes from being surrounded by something well-made and long-cherished—that is just different from the mood created by drywall mass-produced in a Chinese factory."

"Our daughters know that living here puts them smack into the history of the city, yet they have all the modernity they could ever want," concludes Reford. In a real sense, he speaks for all owners of updated historic San Antonio homes—they, too, are smack into San Antonio history, with all the modernity they could want.

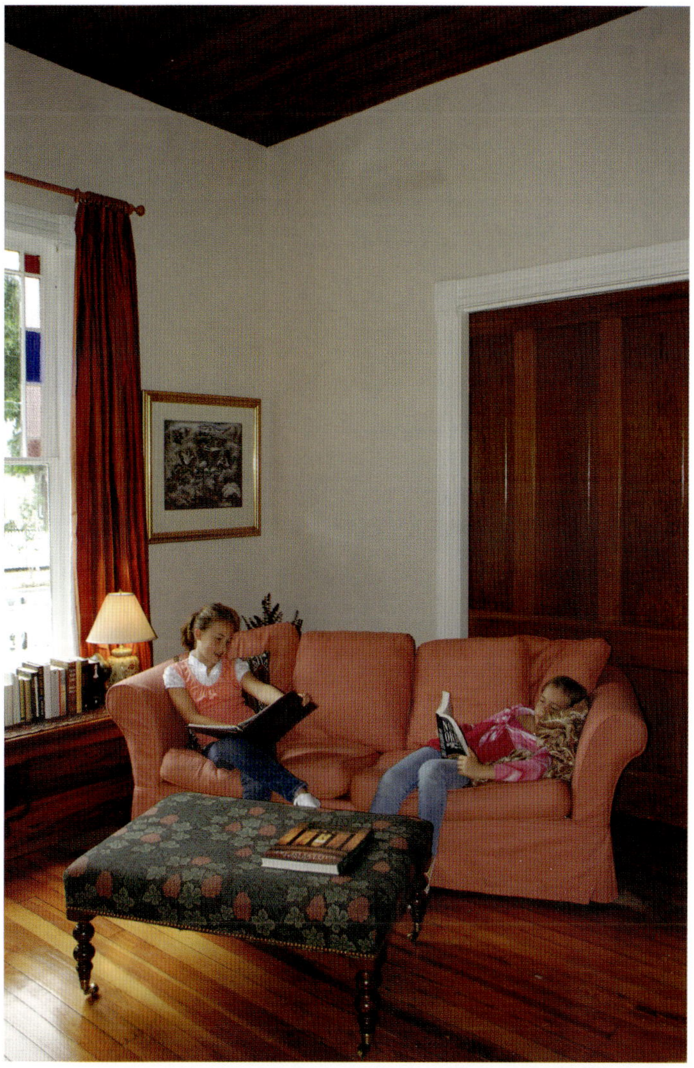

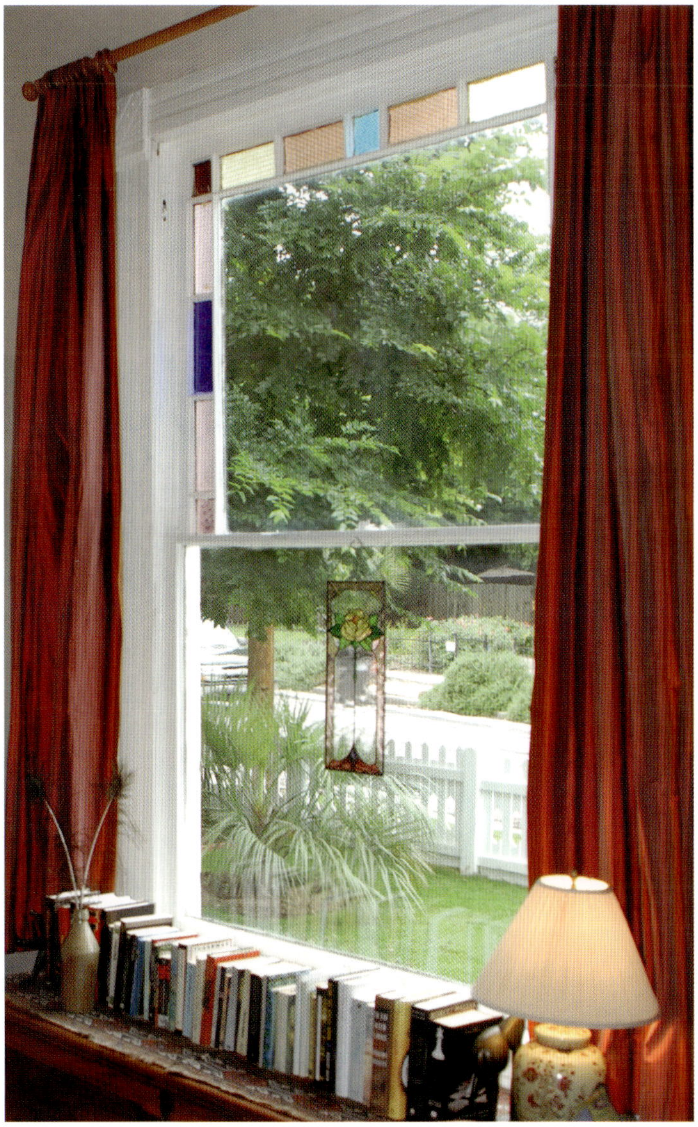

Stained glass panes accent living room windows.

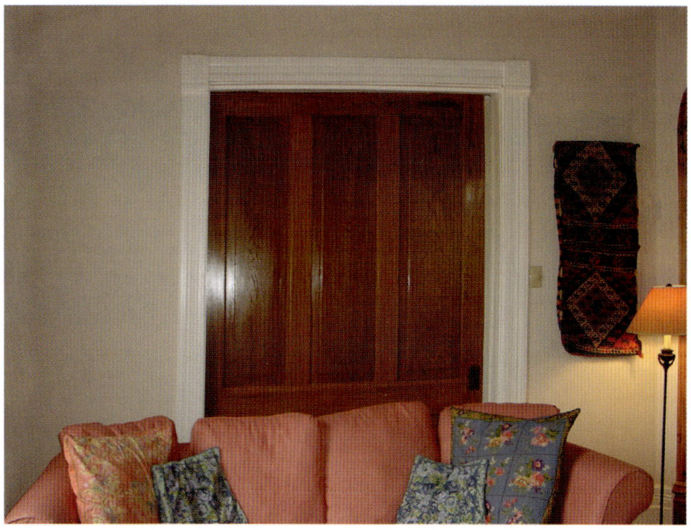

An unusual double-wide sliding door opening into the entry hall provides privacy for the living room.

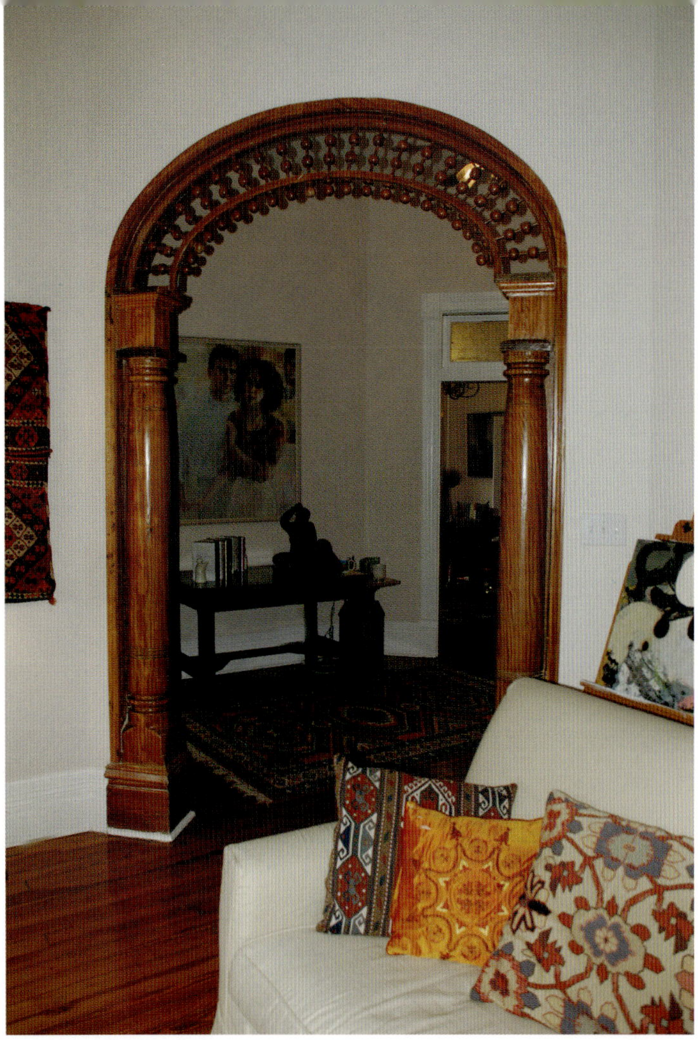

Rich wood trim, cleaned of white paint, decoratively delineates the doorway opening into the stair hall.

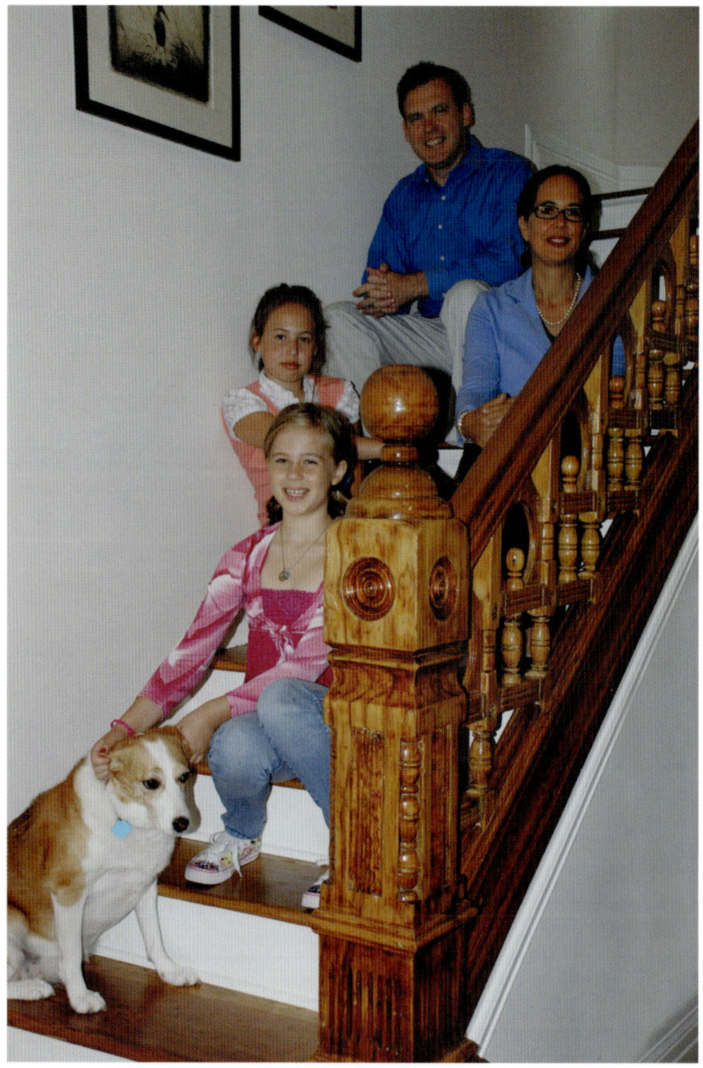

Lisa Koenig, her husband Mark Reford, and their daughters Emma and Saskia appreciate the fact that white paint was removed from wood stair railings, revealing beautifully grained, naturally stained wood.

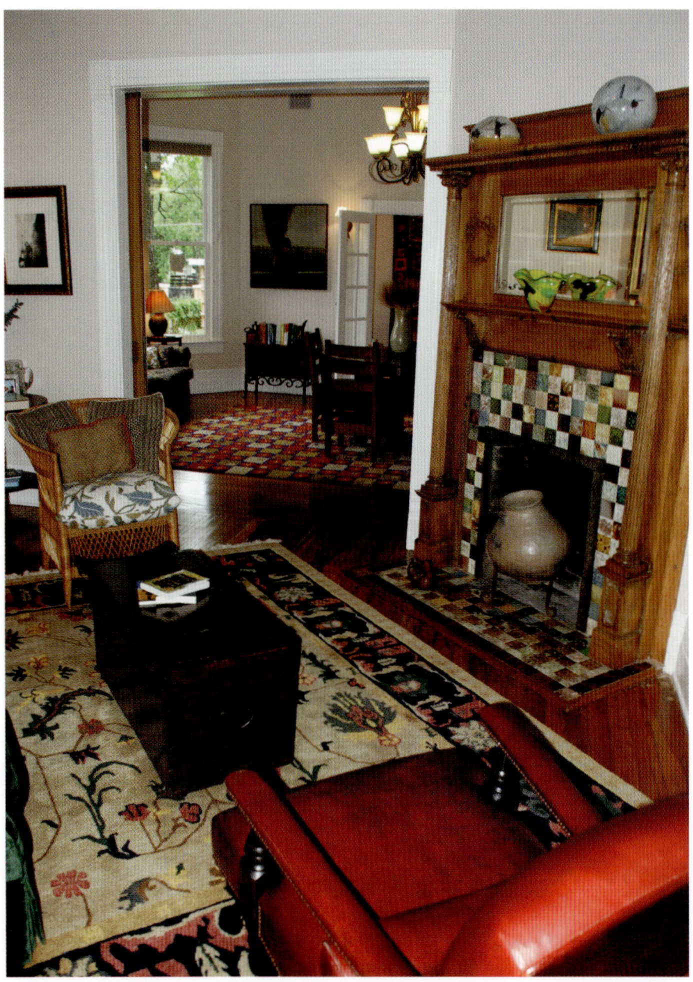

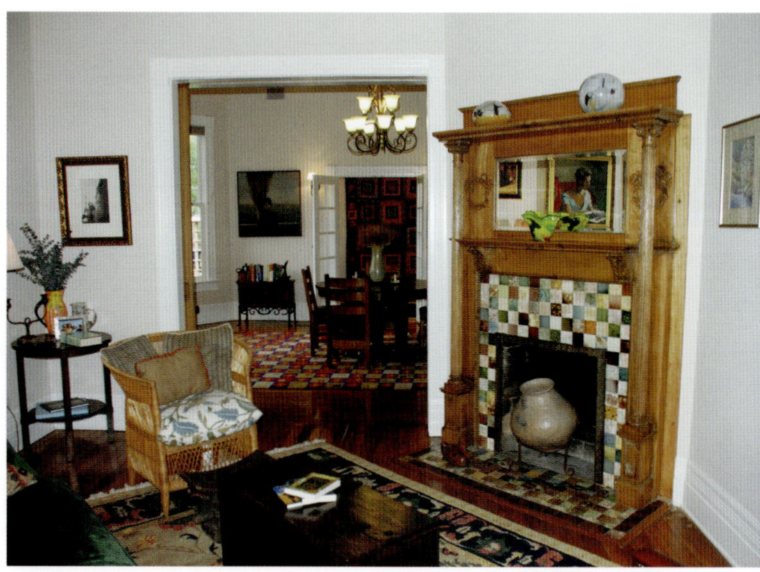

The patterned rug in the adjacent dining room repeats the pattern of the art tile fireplace surround in the parlor sitting room.

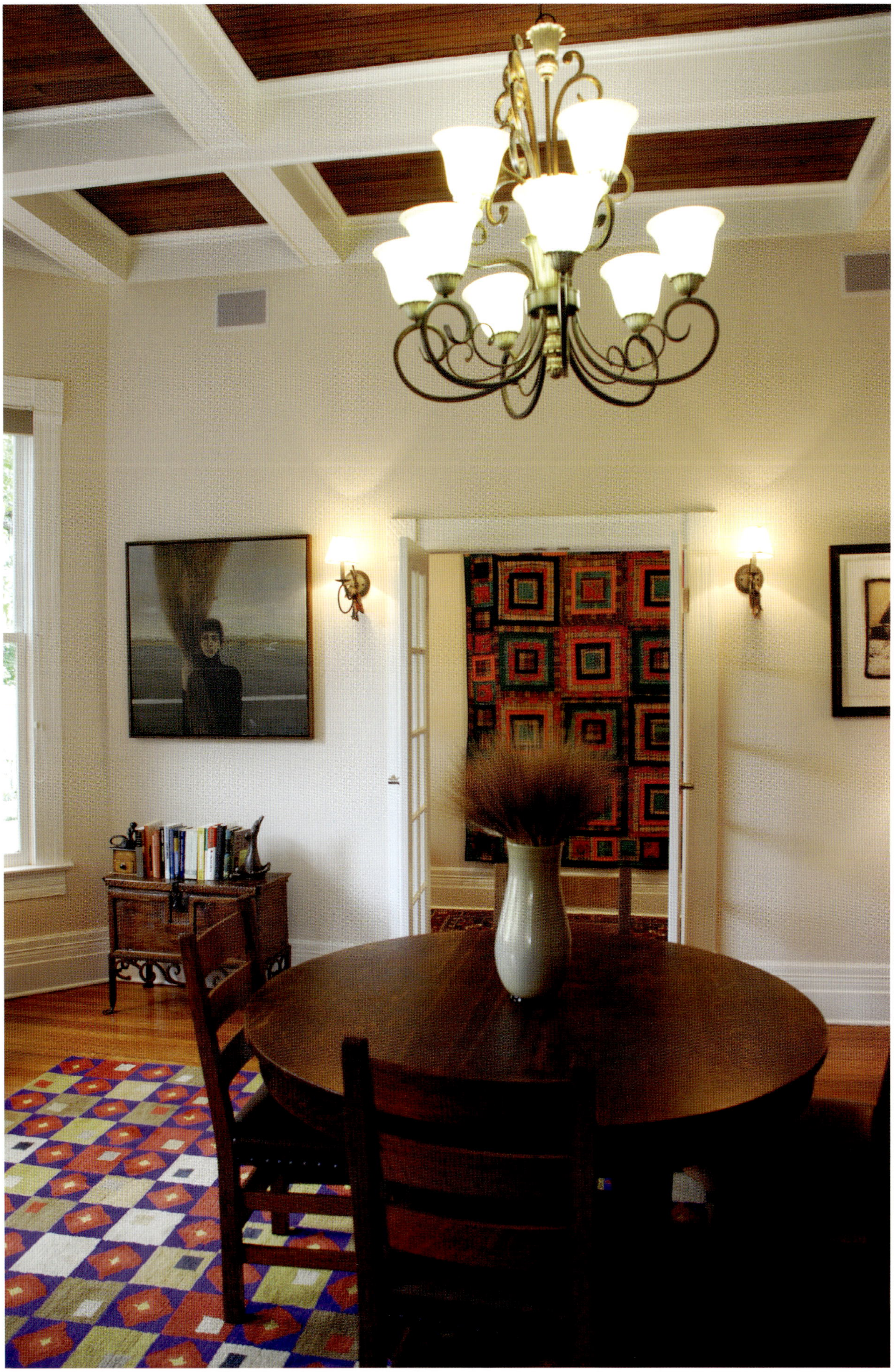

Coffering adds interest to the expansive dining room ceiling.

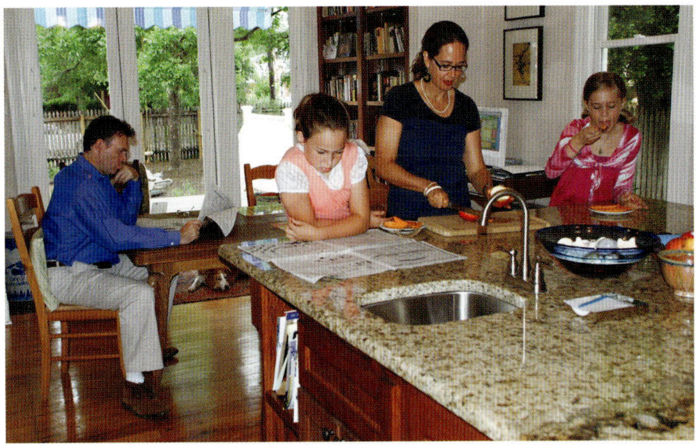

Not just for cooking, the remodeled kitchen is a favorite room for family activities.

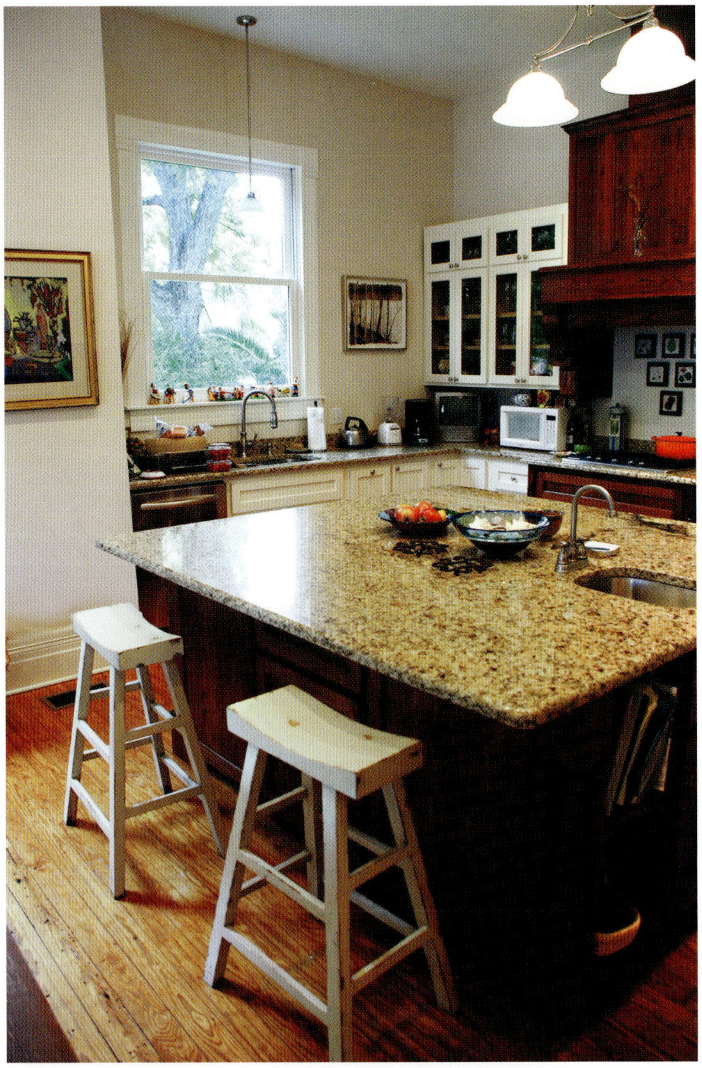

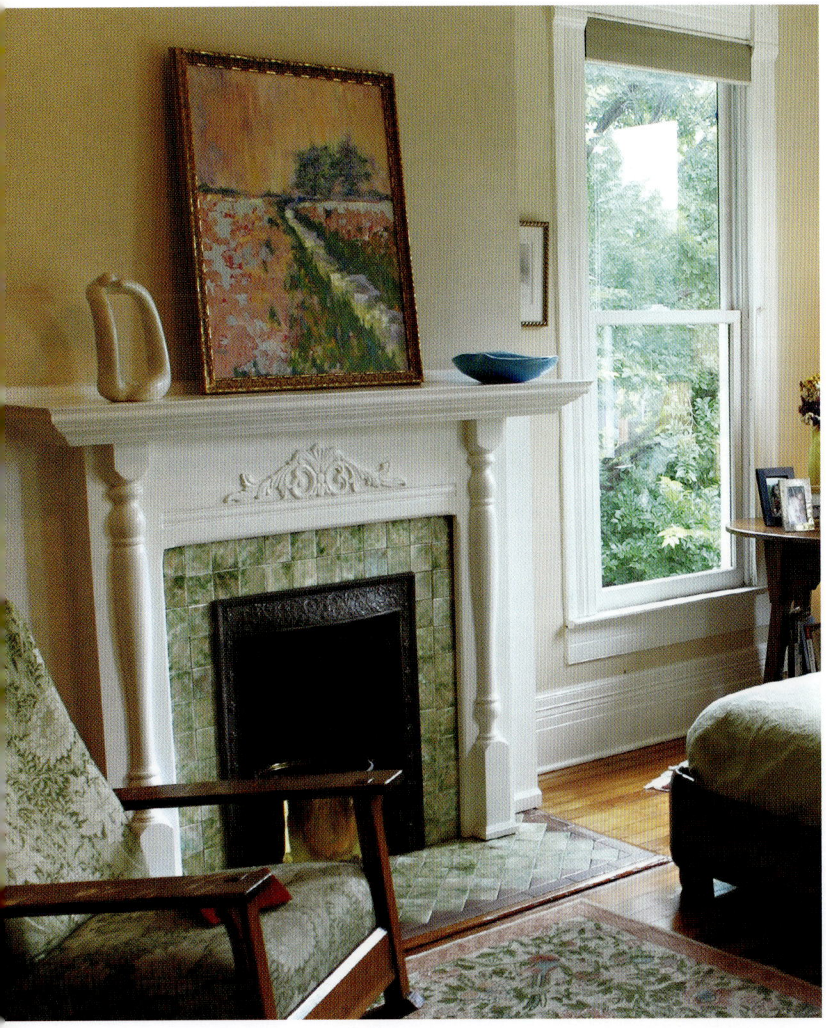

A fireplace is the cozy focal point of the master bedroom.

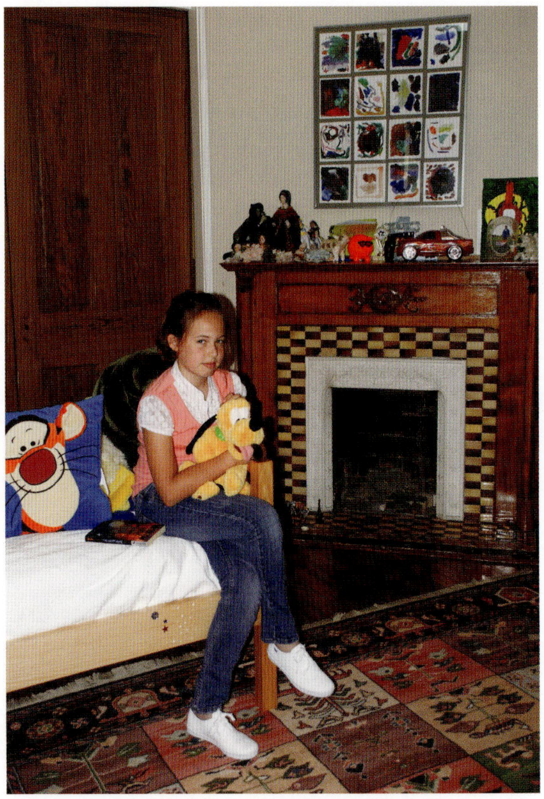

Emma in her bedroom with its handsome fireplace featuring a beautiful art-tile surround.

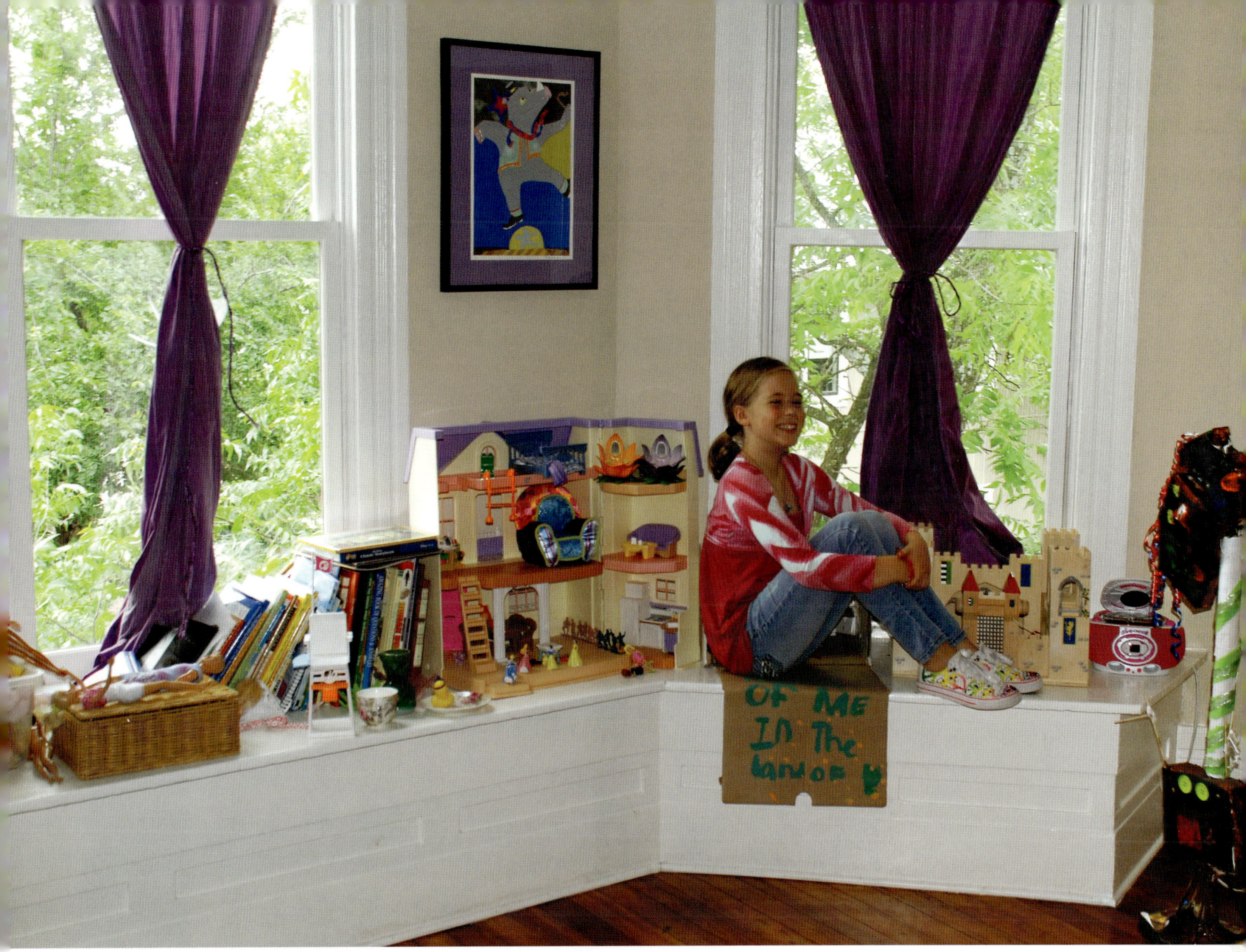

Saskia at home in her bedroom with an expansive toy-laden window seat.

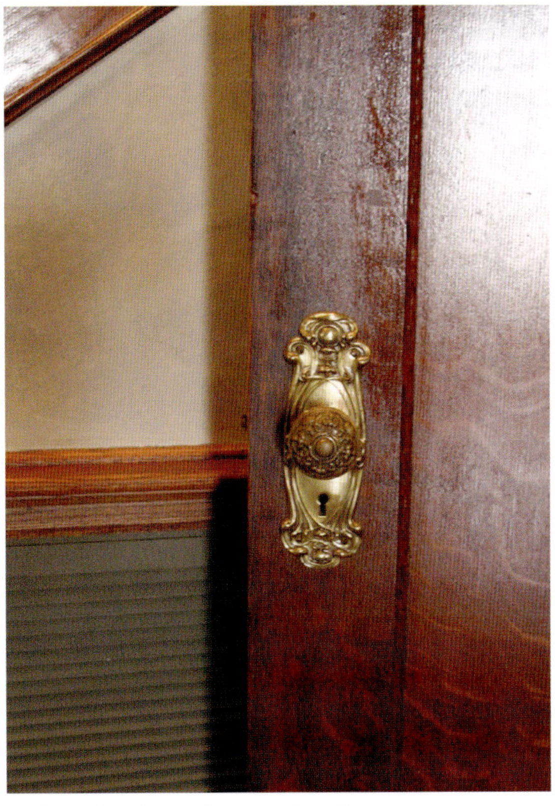

Antique hardware is an authentic accent.

14

Capps House

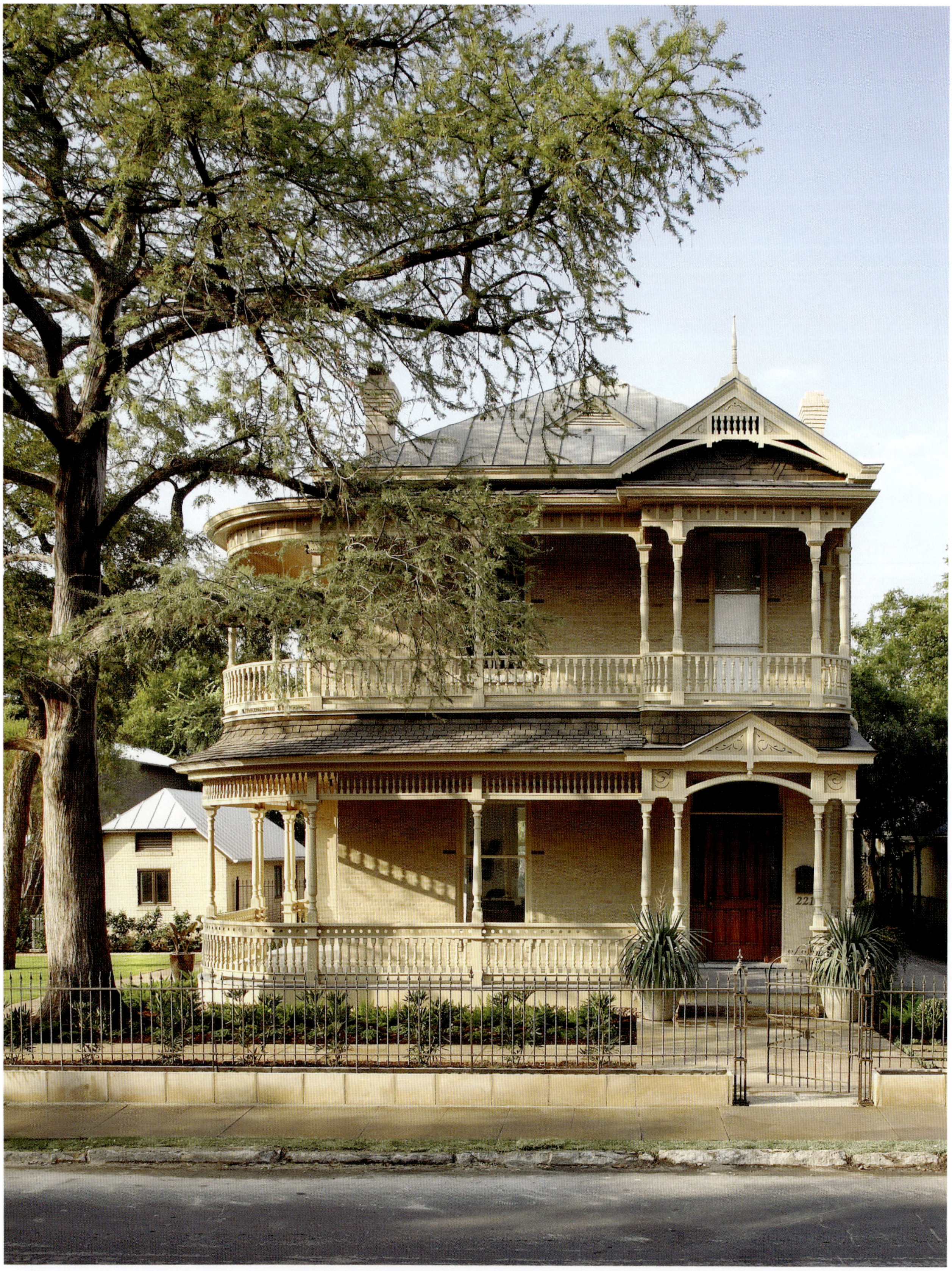

An elegant monotone paint scheme adds sophistication to the exterior of a vintage home in the Queen Anne style popular during the Victorian era. *Photographs by Ryann Ford, courtesy Poteet Architects.*

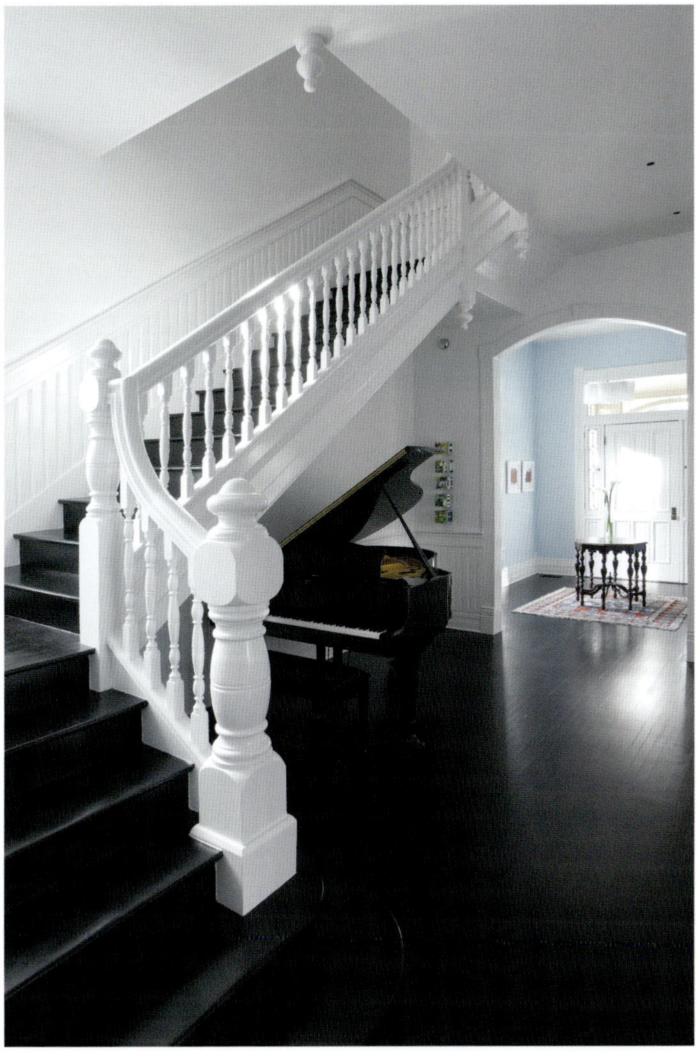

Ebony flooring and gallery-white walls throughout much of the interior create a dramatic backdrop for the owner's serious collection of contemporary art.

"The wrap-around porch was rotted and sagging," says Architect Jim Poteet. The grounds were equally neglected. "The large lawn and river front were overgrown," he says. The grand old house at 321 East Guenther Street in the historic King William district, continuously occupied since its construction, was suffering from what Poteet gently describes as "a good deal of deferred maintenance." Travis Capps and Lee Anthony were not dissuaded. They purchased the 1896 building, one of several distinctive masonry homes in King William that had been designed by German Architect Albert Beckman. Then, Capps engaged Poteet Architects, a firm well known for its restoration and preservation work.

The owners' charge to the architect: "To tailor the house to their needs, without sacrificing the historic character its prominent site demanded," says Poteet.

Work began first on the carriage house. "It was to be the owners' home during the rehabilitation," says Poteet. "The carriage house now contains a living space with a small—and very orange—kitchen on the lower level and bedroom and bath above. A small, highly stylish salon was installed in the brick pool house."

Poteet approached the exterior of the main house as a full restoration. "That included a painstaking reconstruction of the wrap-around porch by General Contractor Rubiola Construction. At the rear of the house, a 1970s era addition was removed. We replaced it with a new two-story addition in the same footprint that contains the kitchen on the first floor, and a new master bath above," he says.

While the exterior of the restored house remains historic, the interior is *au courant*. "The interior of the home was transformed to support the lifestyle of the new owners," Poteet says. "Capps and Anthony are avid collectors of contemporary art. They open their home for entertaining and large events on a regular basis. The interior design supports these passions by unifying the restored plaster walls in white and ebonizing the floors. The museum quality lighting that was installed throughout is controlled by a 'smart house' system that also operates the audio visual and security systems."

Poteet says that the personality of the owners is most clearly expressed in the new kitchen and master closet and bath. "Kitchen walls are sheathed in honed Carrara marble that forms open shelves which span the banks of windows." Never mind the shortage of overhead cabinets. "Kitchen storage is extended by a butler's pantry, which is tucked into the basement access of the old residence." On the second floor, above the kitchen, the new master closet and bath are merged into one flowing space. "Dominating this area is the black closet island and the large glass-tiled steam shower in four colors of blue," says Poteet.

"To keep the white palette fresh, bold color surprises are interjected at intervals," notes the architect. These include robin's egg blue in the foyer, "Rorschach" damask wall paper in the downstairs powder room, magenta "L" cabinetry in the upstairs office, "black on black" wallpaper in the guest bath, and the four blues in the shower. "These colors reflect the owners' love of color and visual sense of humor," says Poteet.

Poteet points out that just as Capps' and Anthony's art collection is international in scope, so are the new materials and furnishings. "The design team found wallpaper from Scotland. Decorative light fixtures are from Germany, Italy, and the Netherlands. Fireplaces are from Australia. Plumbing fixtures are from Germany and Spain. Marble installed in the kitchen is from Italy. The glass tile for the master bath is from Canada."

Thanks to Capps, Anthony, and Poteet Architects, this elegant house, once down-at-the-heels, is now kicking up its very chic heels. And will be for years to come.

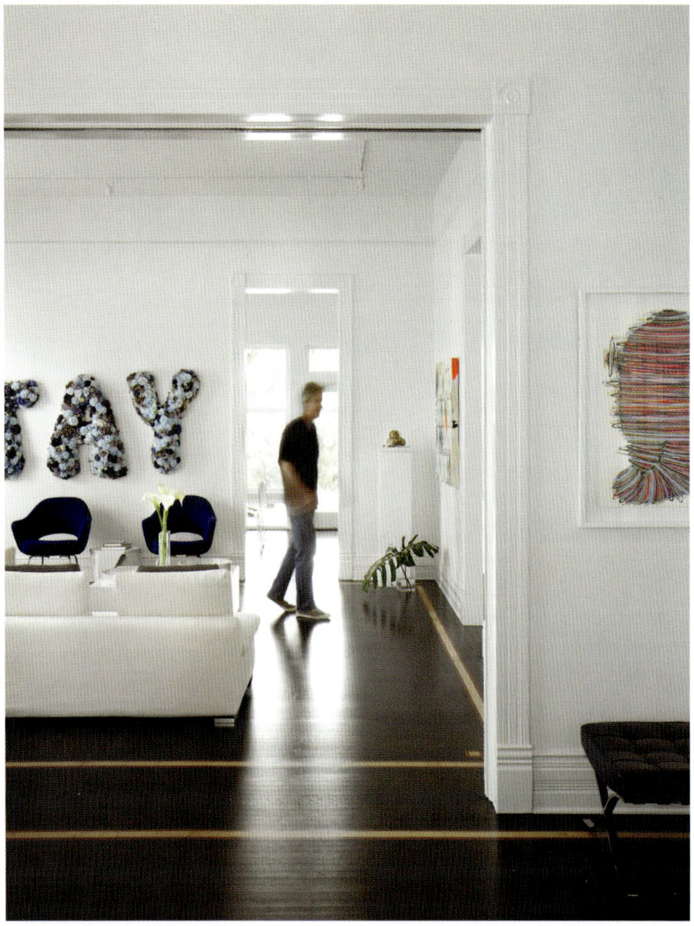

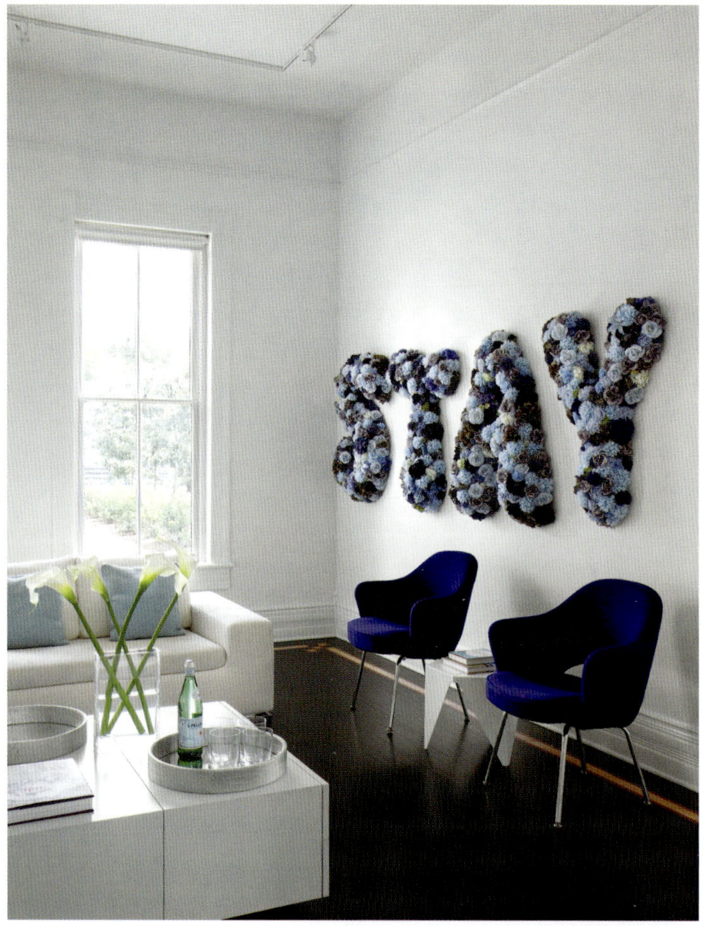

Contemporary art and furniture contrast vividly with period architecture, bringing a once-dated structure into the current era.

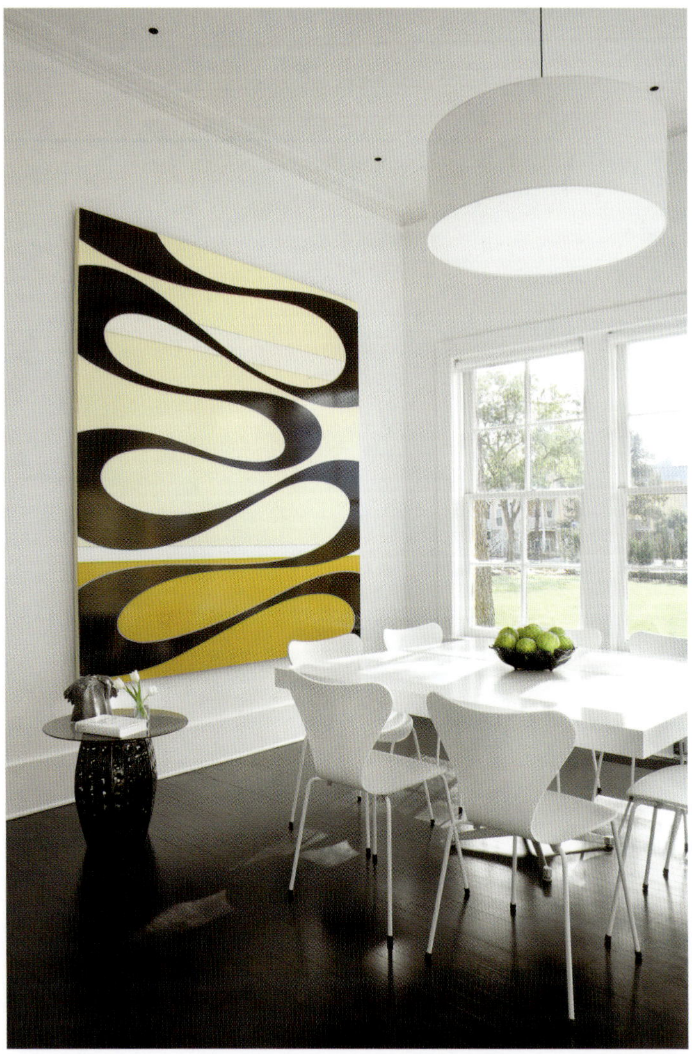

In the dining room, a striking work of art makes an eloquent style statement.

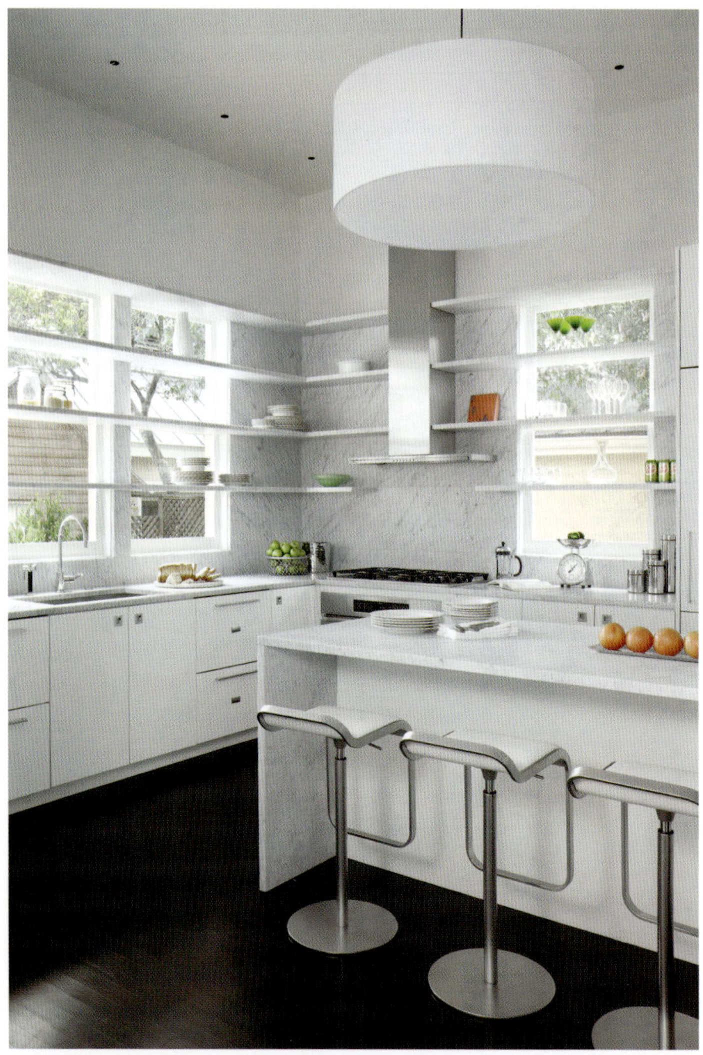

Carrara marble shelves span kitchen windows and eliminate the need for wall-hung cabinetry.

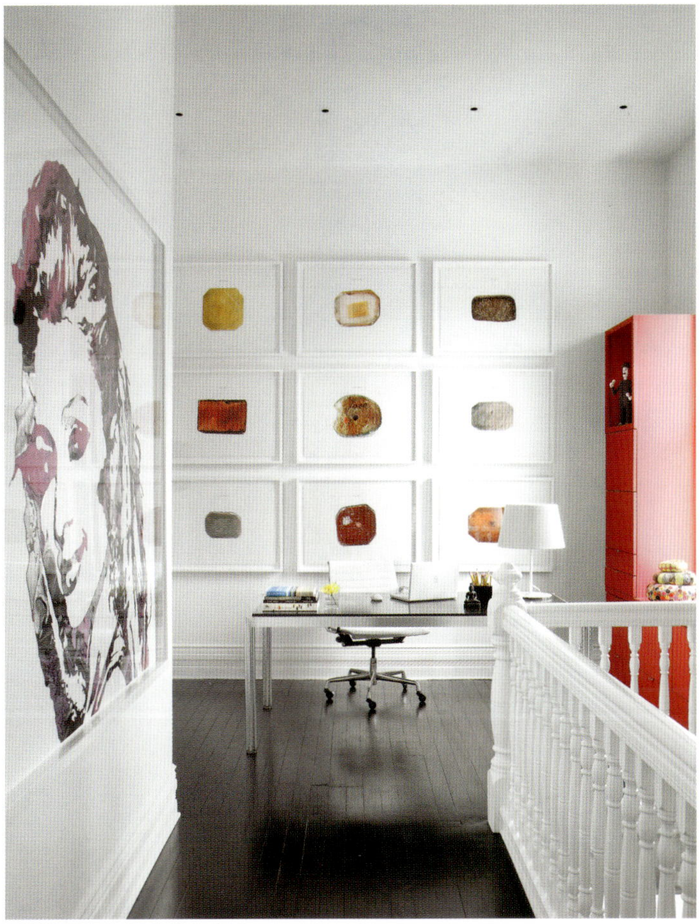

Bold, bright artwork adorns walls at the head of the stairs.

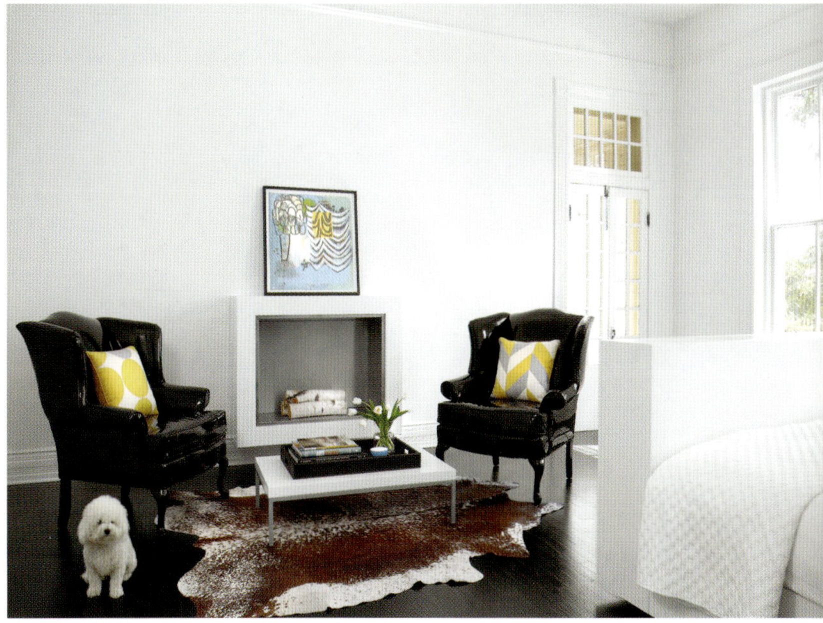

Shiny black upholstery makes traditional wing chairs timely.

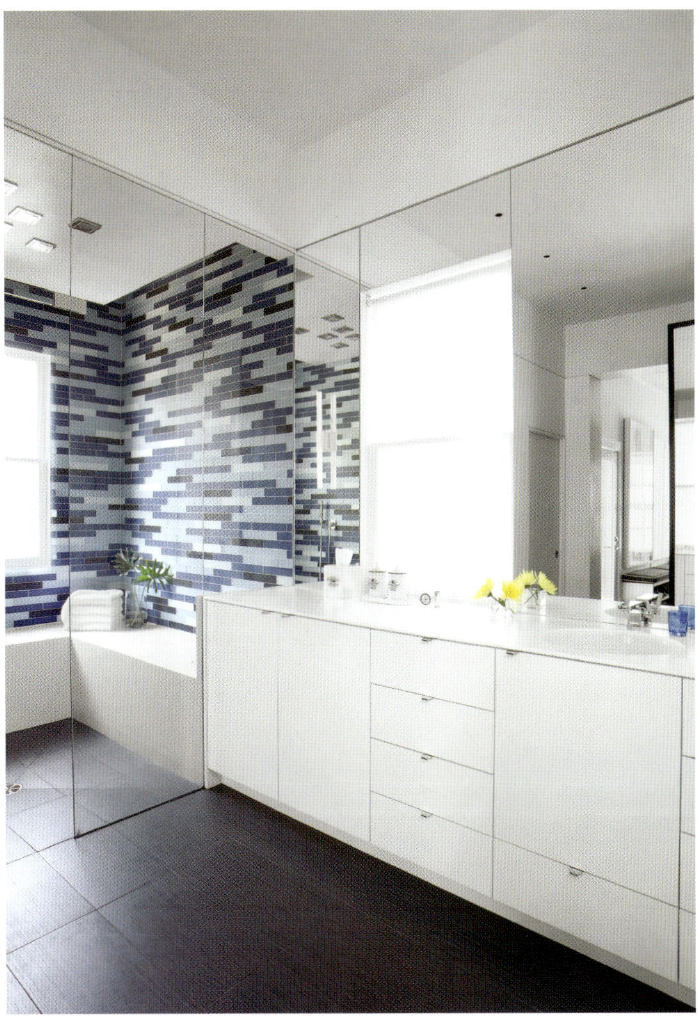

Architectural glass tile refracts the light, creating both random graphic patterns and light-play in the updated bathroom.

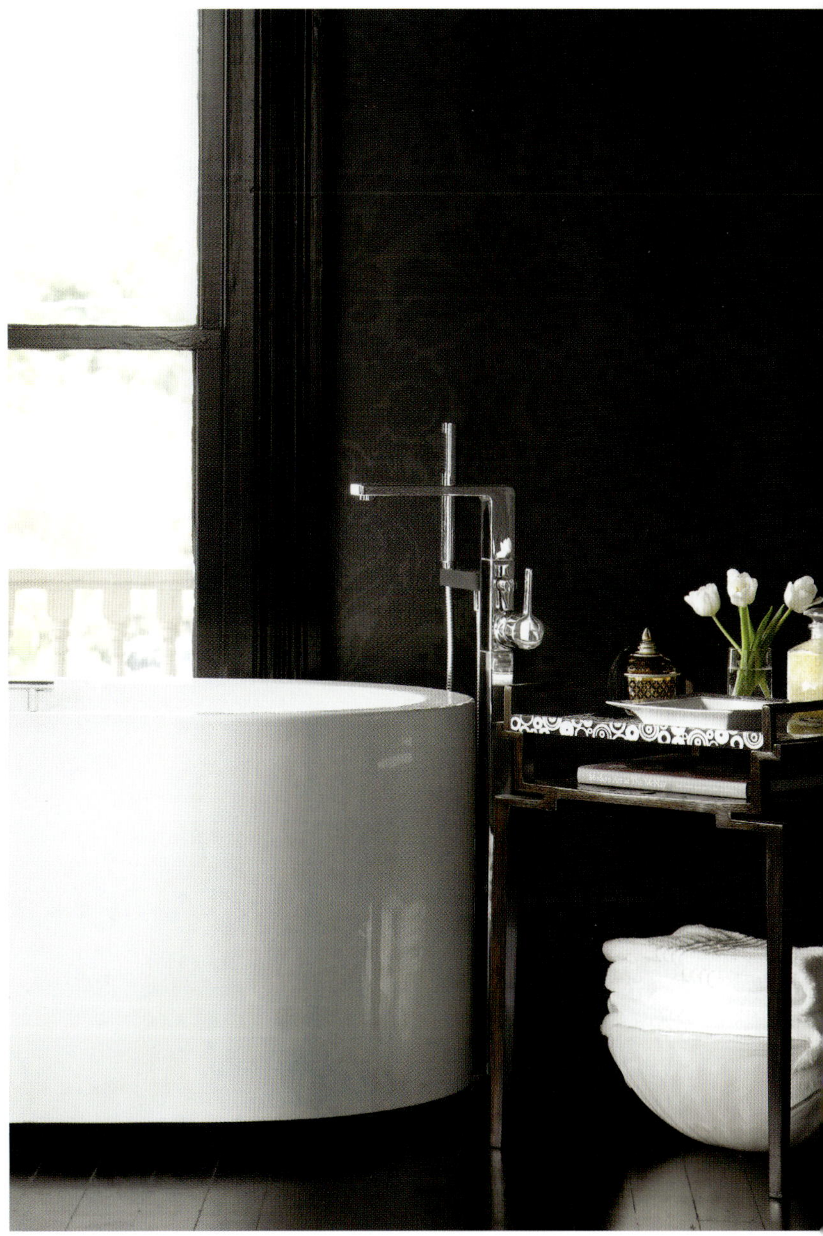

Black-on-black patterned wallcoverings and black trim for the window add impact in the bathroom.

15
Hill Porch House

The home on South St. Mary's Street is a wonderful example of creative rehabilitation and conversion—the transformation of an old commercial building in historic downtown San Antonio into a residence. "Shortly after completing the adaptation of a small warehouse building at the south edge of downtown San Antonio into a family home, we were asked by our client to create a screened outdoor living space," says Architect Jim Poteet, head of a firm noted for excellent redesign of old buildings.

A gazebo might have come to mind, but the architect envisioned something more compelling. "The project became a small outdoor room, with both screened and open spaces. Sited adjacent to the converted warehouse, it provides shade from the South Texas sun and shelter from South Texas mosquitoes, both potentially devastating," says Poteet.

The new outdoor room does exactly what its owners asked. But, the skillful design does a great deal more. "We saw that the structure could serve several functions. In addition to its contribution as living space, it signals the entry to the main house which is near the rear of the property, facing sidewise away from the entry walkway. The new room also remediates between the house itself and the urban garden space beyond," explains Poteet.

Excellent design is also practical in the time-honored waste-not, want-not manner. Poteet points out that the L-shaped enclosure is built around and makes the most of a concrete parking pad left over from the warehouse's previous incarnation. It is constructed of reclaimed pine timbers fastened together by mortise and tenon.

Detailing throughout mark this as a carefully designed and constructed addition to a unique San Antonio home. "The roofing is detailed to be all but invisible from outside. On the inside, the roof seams are hidden by the cedar roof framing. The theme of quiet detailing is carried through to the electrical wiring which is channeled into the timbers themselves," says Poteet.

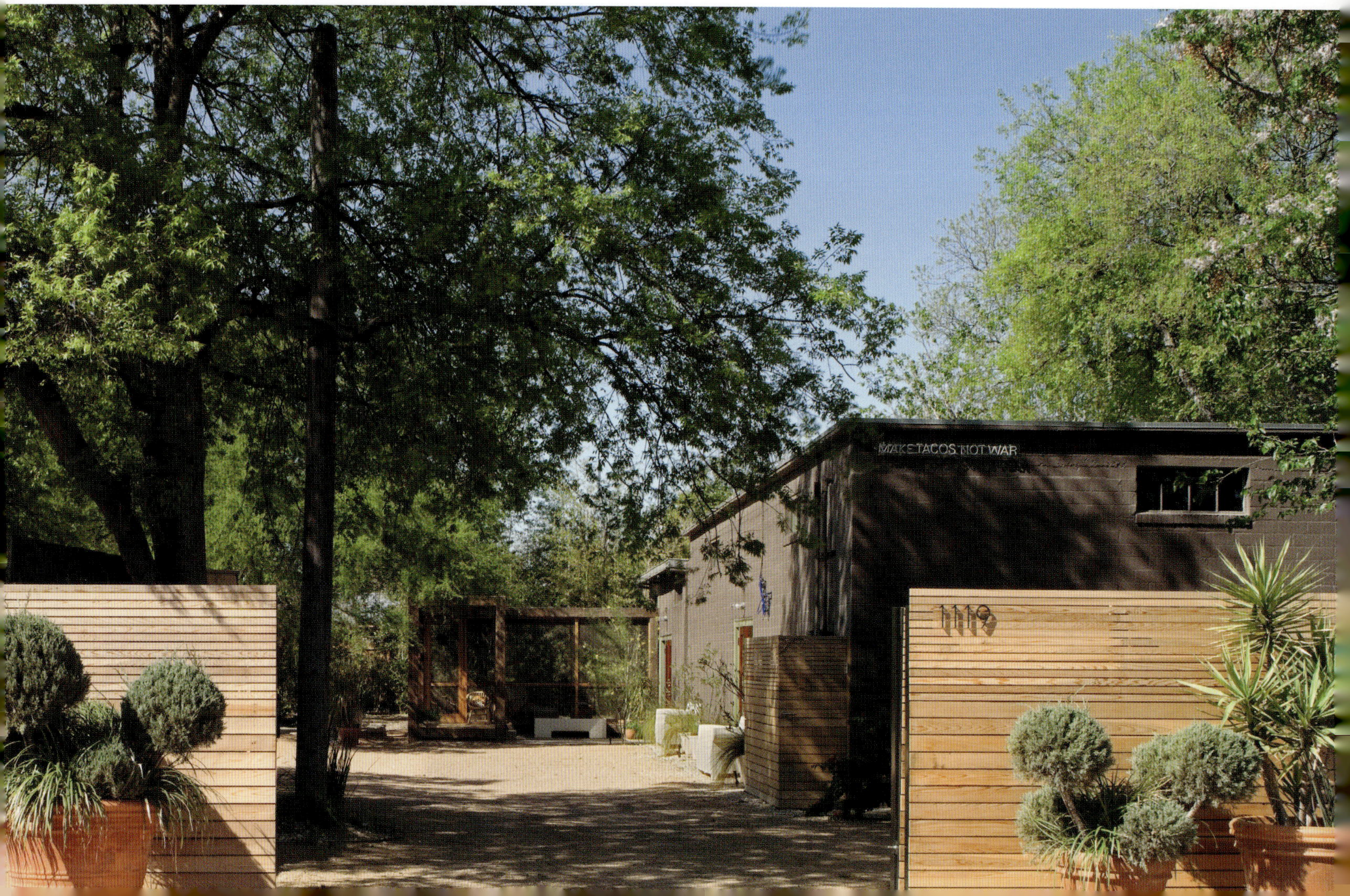

A wall/fence adds a sense of protection to a new two-part outdoor living area added to the rear of a commercial structure renovated earlier as a dwelling. *Photographs by Chris Cooper, courtesy Poteet Architects*

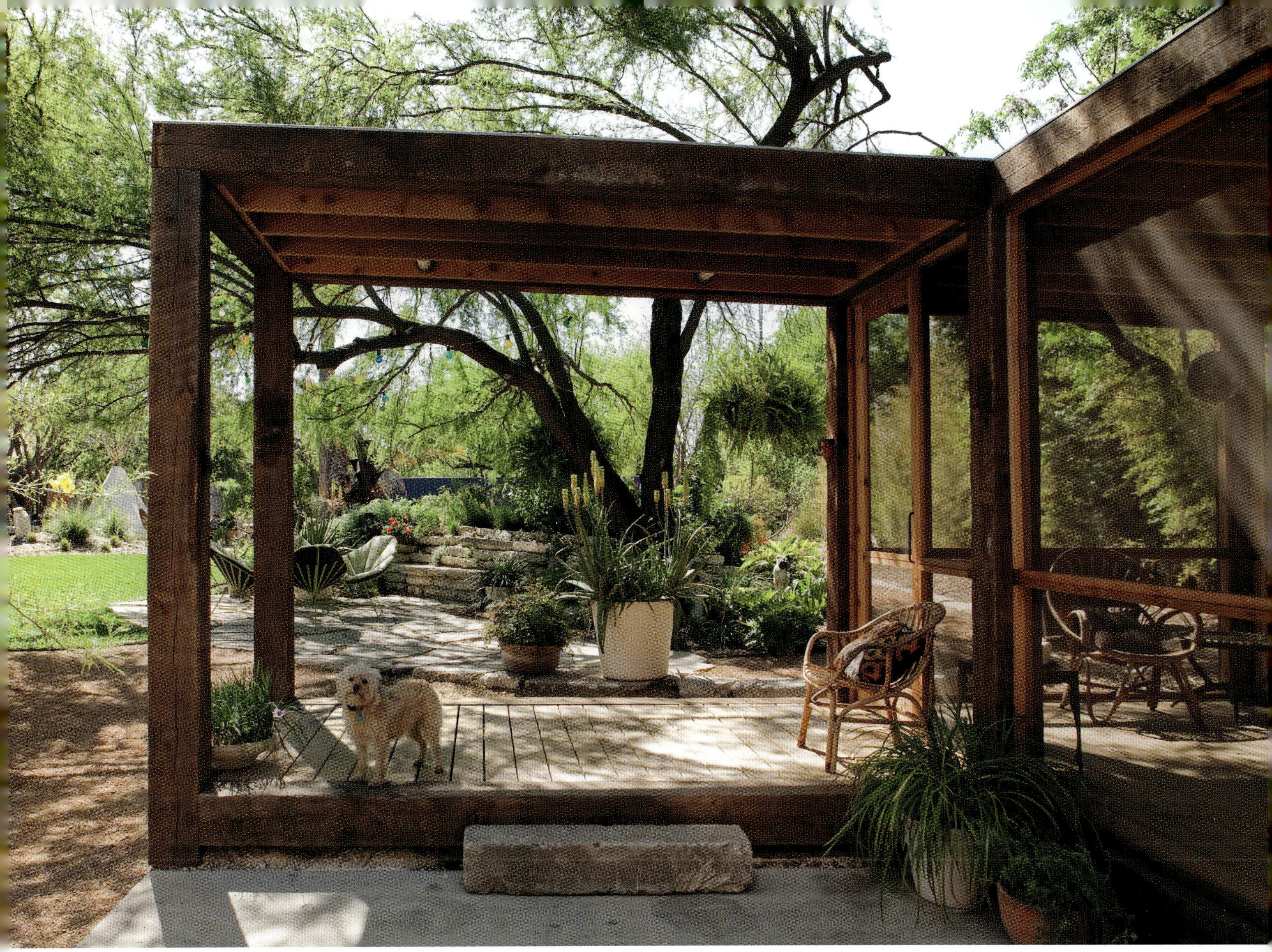

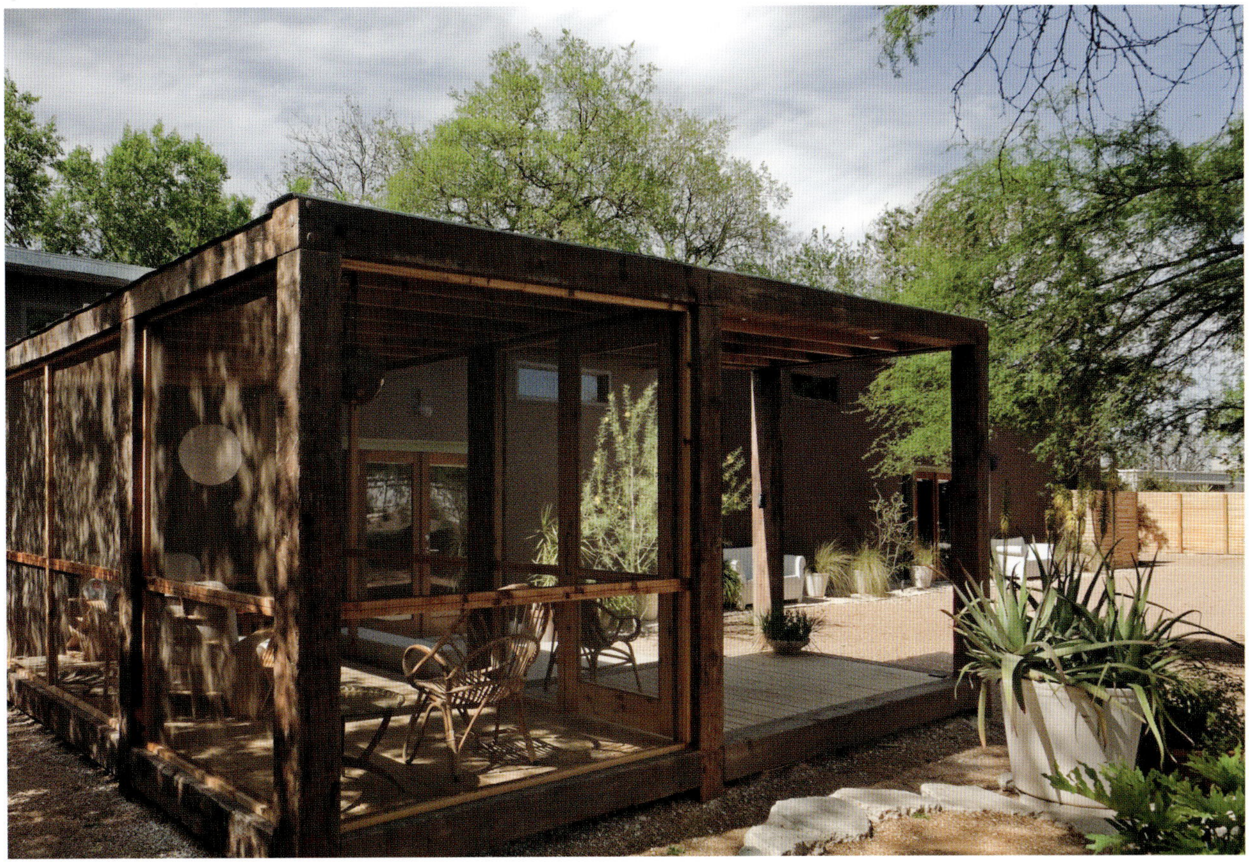

The two-part addition by Architect Jim Poteet features both open and screened areas.

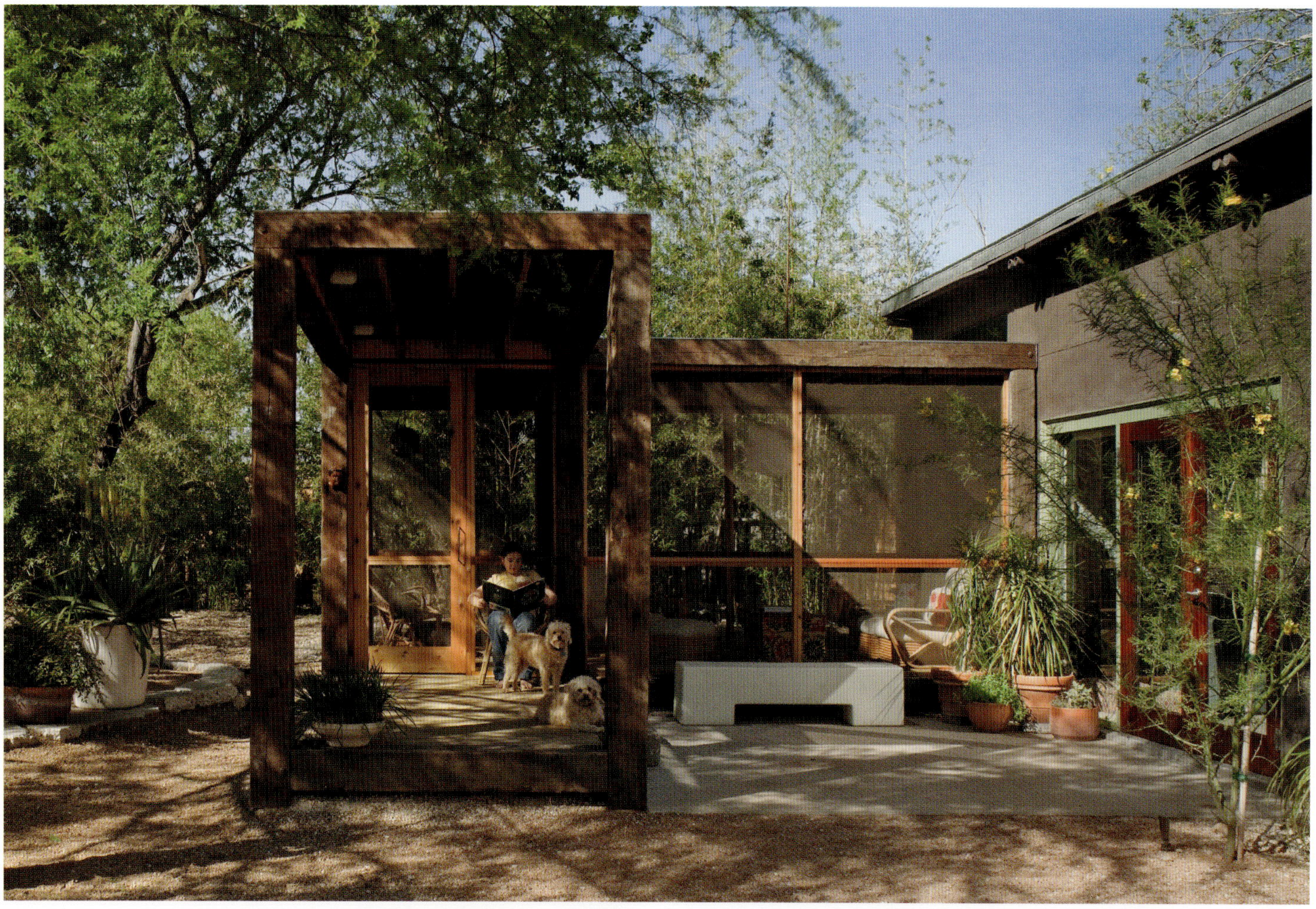

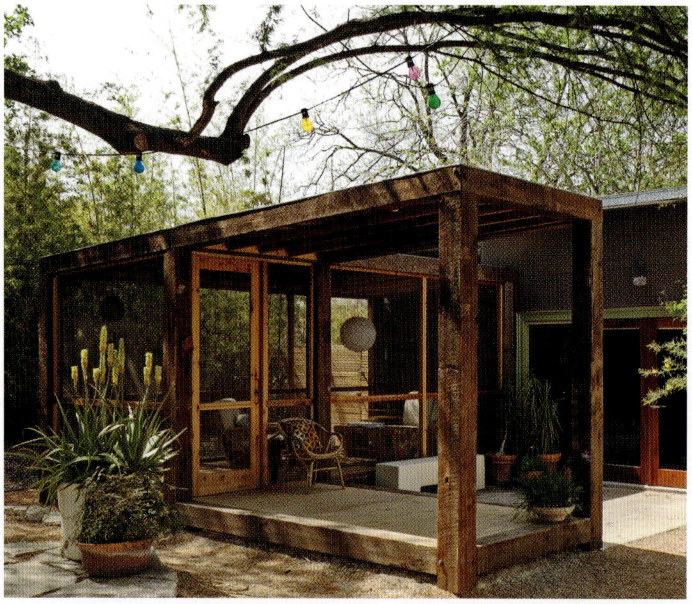

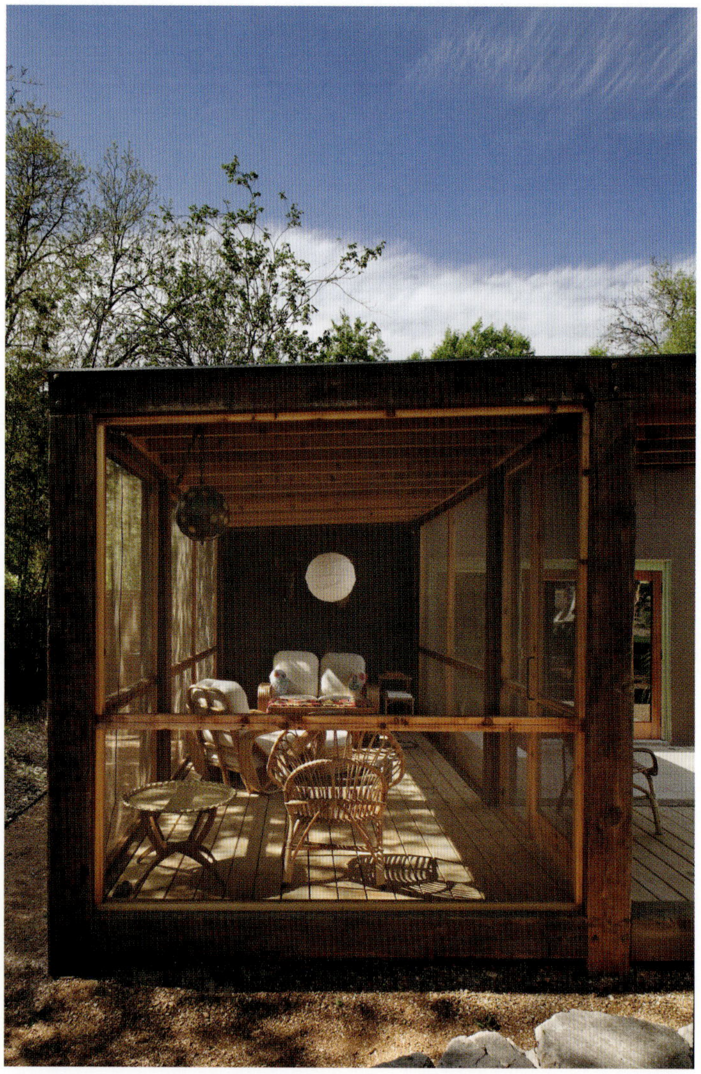

The existing house and open porch that extends at right angles to the screened porch form a U-shape that draws attention toward the entry to the main structure.

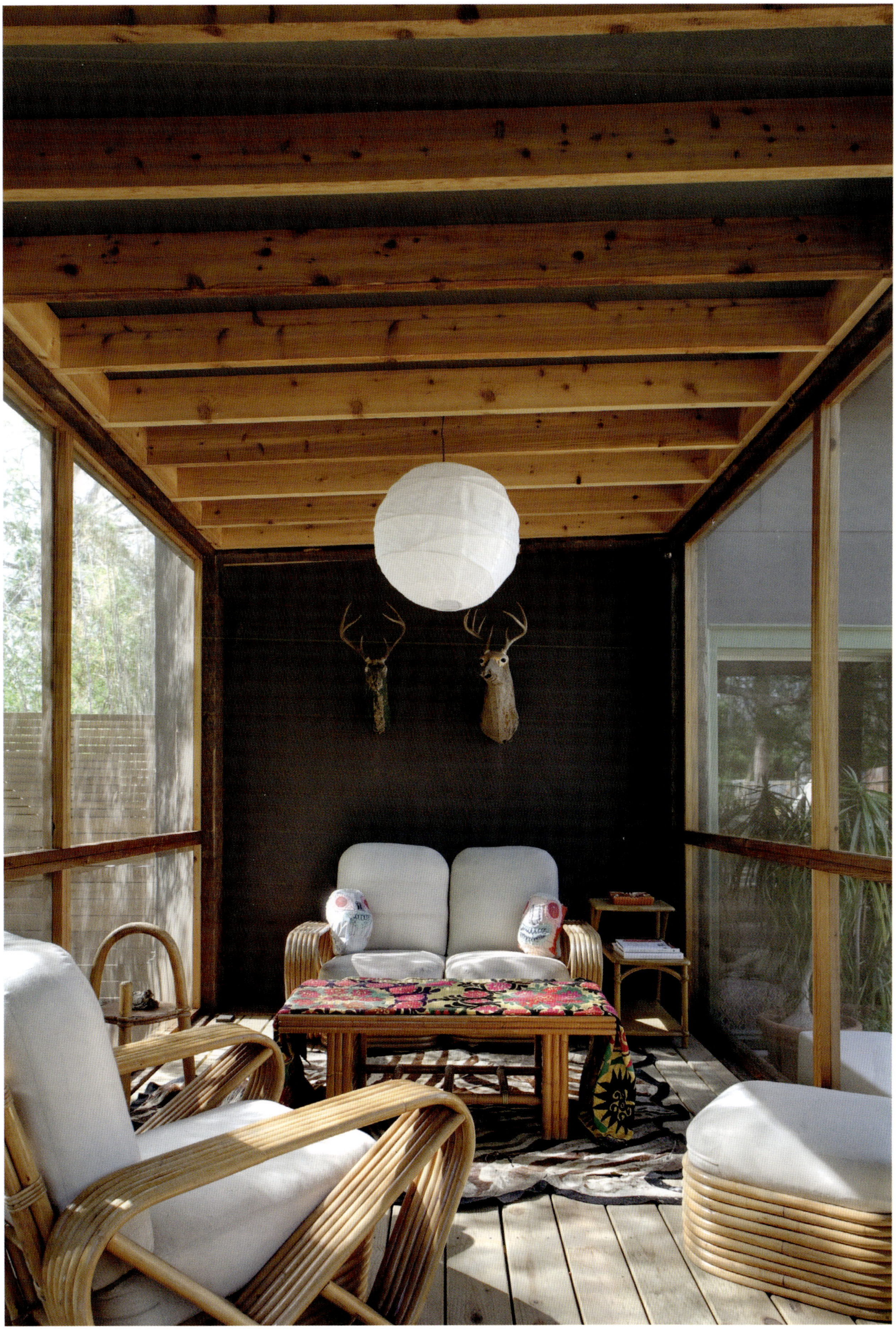

The comfortably furnished screened porch serves as an outdoor sitting room.

16

Tree House

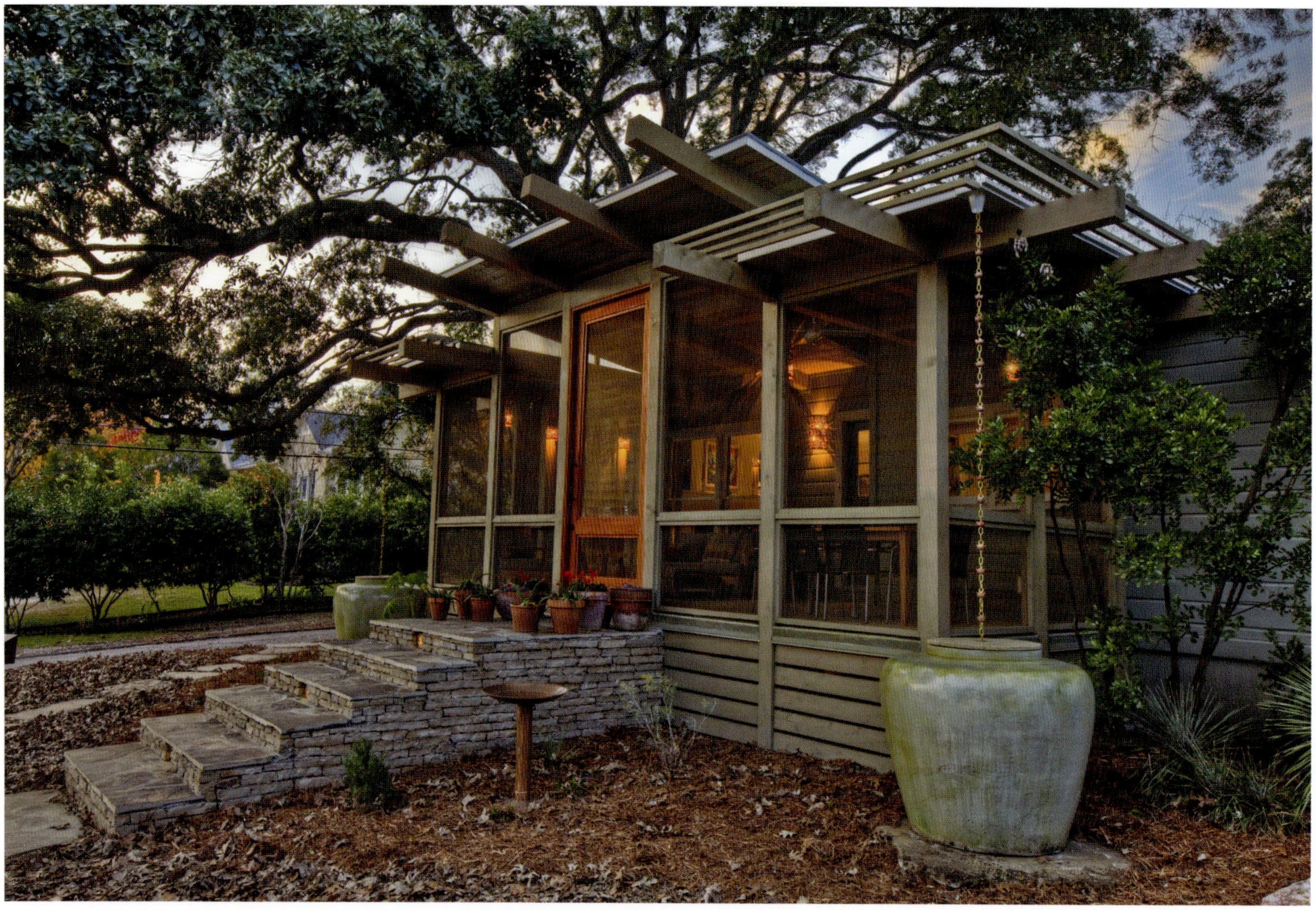

A new projecting porch and cascading steps were carefully designed by Architect John Grable. They seem to reach out and embrace the neighborhood. *Photographs by Chris Cooper, courtesy John Grable Architects*

The house in Terrell Hills was not ancient, just old. Actually, it was only sixty years old—retirement age for a human, but hardly so for a house. What makes this 1950s house noteworthy, and in a real sense historic, is Architect John Grable's redesign of the façade that realizes a shift in social consciousness—a new awareness of neighbors near and far.

It seems fair to say that generally speaking, houses along any given street in the United States do not relate. Individual, often of wildly dissimilar architectural styles and periods, materials, and design messages, no house speaks to its neighbor. Surrounded by a manicured lawn—today's moat—houses in these situations remain aloof, often with hard-to-see entries that deprive them of what architects call a *ceremonial sense of arrival*. Such houses are unwelcoming, if not actually unfriendly in their "look, don't touch" state.

The owners of this Terrell Hills house decided that it needed what Grable describes as "front entry definition," and new (less moat-like) landscaping to complement that of neighbors. Homeowners of the Terrell House also liked the idea of a porch—a back porch came to mind. But Grable says, "What the architect's eye sees is very different from what the homeowner sees." After walking around the grounds and studying the structure, Grable saw a *front* porch.

"Instead of a north-facing backyard porch, my design flips the porch to the south, so that the new porch faces the street," says Grable. This seemingly simple concept resulted in an extraordinary change for both house and grounds.

"The new timber-framed addition—a sort of shadow box that enriches the older existing structure—synergizes with adjacent public space interior rooms for future expansion.

Rain chains direct rainwater from the roof to large storage jars that stand, sculpture-like, at either corner of the porch.

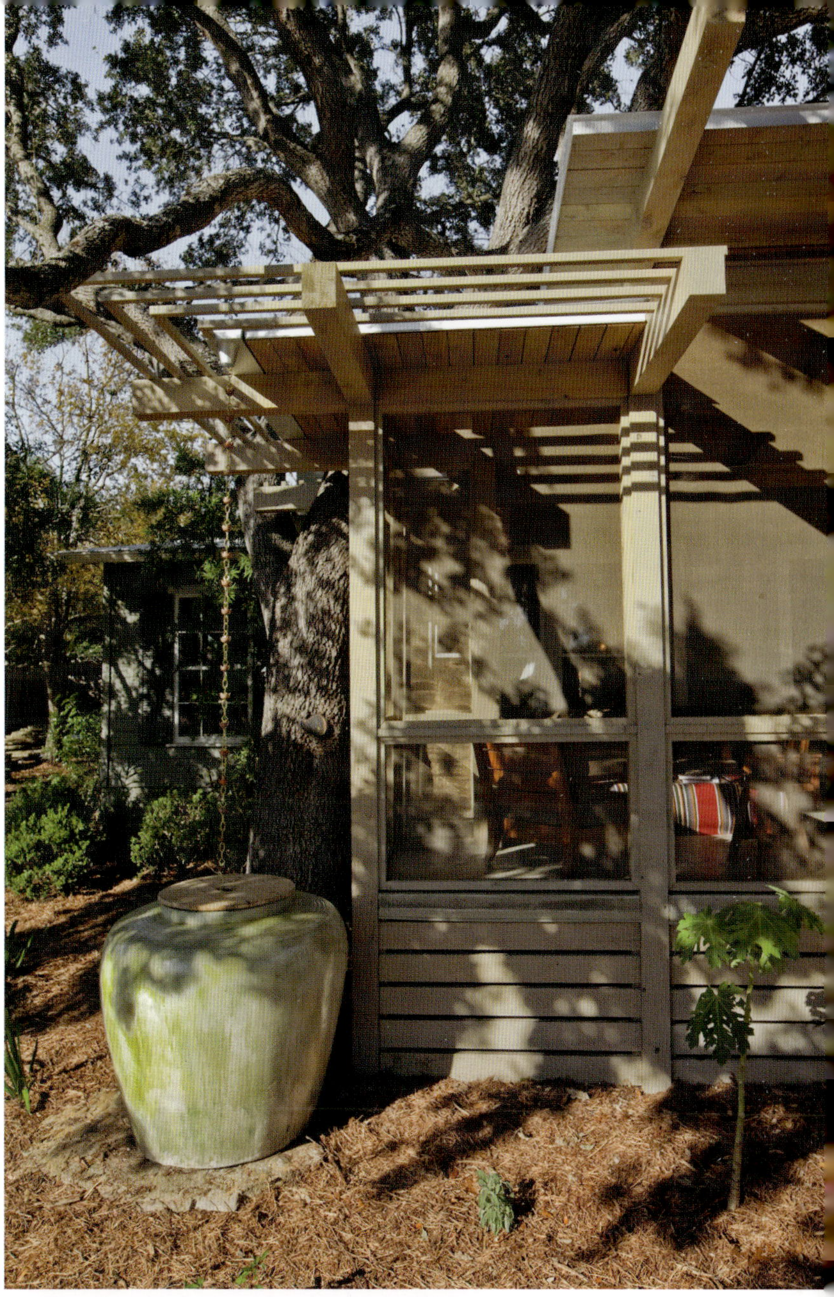

Stone materials enhance the façade change, adding a sense of permanence to the existing stick frame residence," Grable notes. "The result: a dramatic façade, with emphatic front-entry definition."

Not incidentally, the new porch transforms a staid structure into a young-at-heart, up-to-date, forward-looking home. Its tree house look is visually arresting and inviting. But, there is more than merely a socially-aware *look* involved in the transformation. Grable's architectural plan addresses increasingly vital eco-conscious issues of concern worldwide. "Locating the porch on the south side of the house enables this space to capture prevailing southeasterly breezes that cool the house in the spring and summer. The structural concrete metal pan floor section serves as a thermal mass for low southern winter sun angles, which helps heat the home in the fall and winter months," says Grable, whose firm is well known for sensitive, eco-aware architecture.

The new structure works hand-in-glove with new landscaping planned for its semi-desert locale. "The timber frame structure with 2x6-inch T&G (tongue and groove) roof decking/concrete floor provides warm interior spaces that serve as a collection point for a new rain water collection system. The 2x2 lattice roof edge detail is a metaphor for 'rain water capture ripple' that vectors toward a rain-chain down which rainwater flows for storage in ornamental concrete jars. This arrangement provides rain water storage, gravity feed irrigation for new zero-scape gardens," Grable notes.

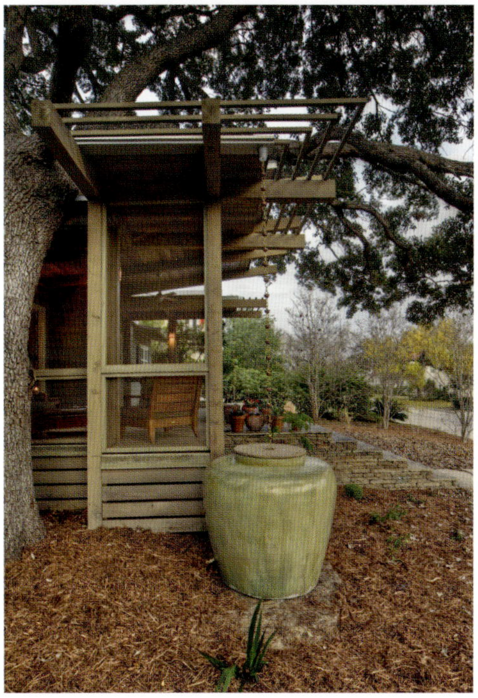

"The social connection—the sense of responsibility to the neighborhood—is reinforced with the new cascading stone garden-entry walk. It serves as a 'welcoming arm' to the heavily pedestrian-traveled street," Grable states. This sense of welcome, in an age of increasing isolation made possible by technology, seems to signify a shift in perspective for residential architecture—architecture that reaches out to the immediate neighborhood and responds responsibly to global concerns.

Proof of project success was the owners' final comment, "Thank you for providing us the house of our dreams without our ever having to move."

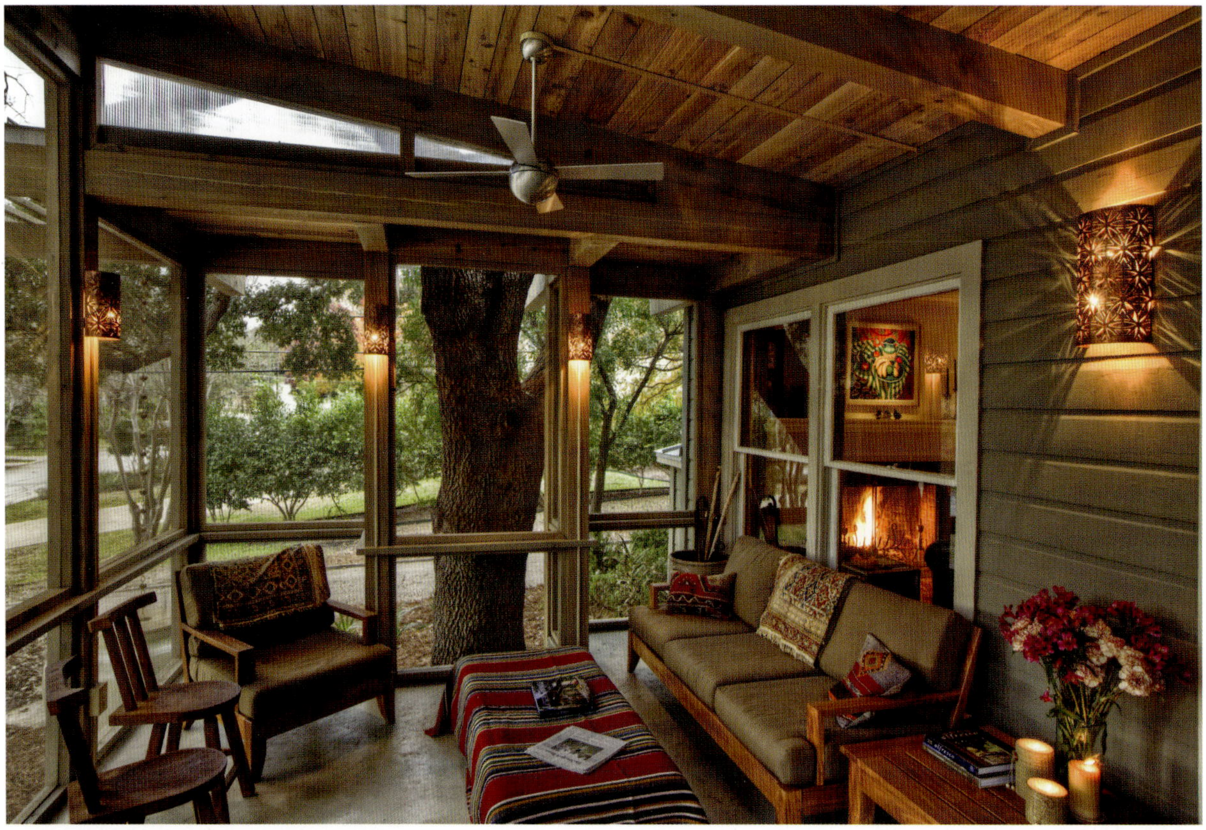

The large porch is designed to capture breezes that make it a pleasant living space. Screens keep out insects and add a sense of privacy.

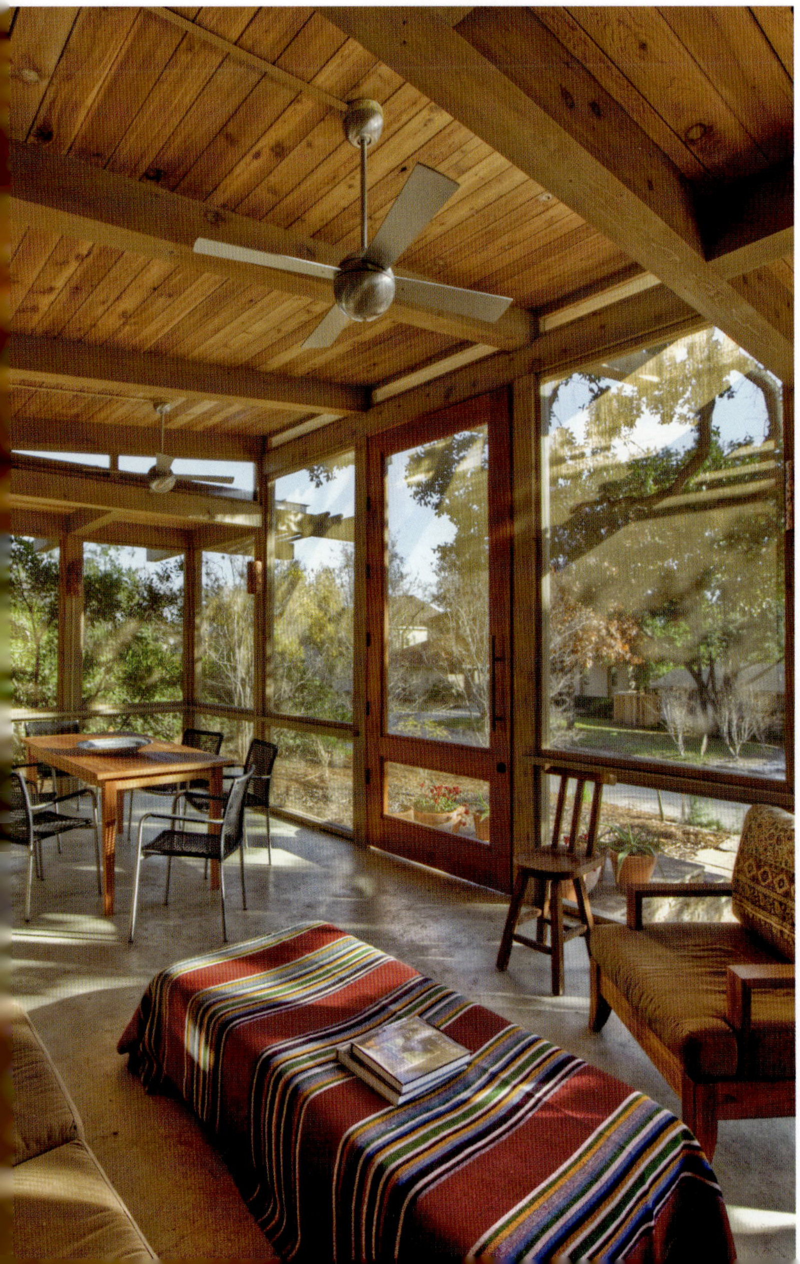

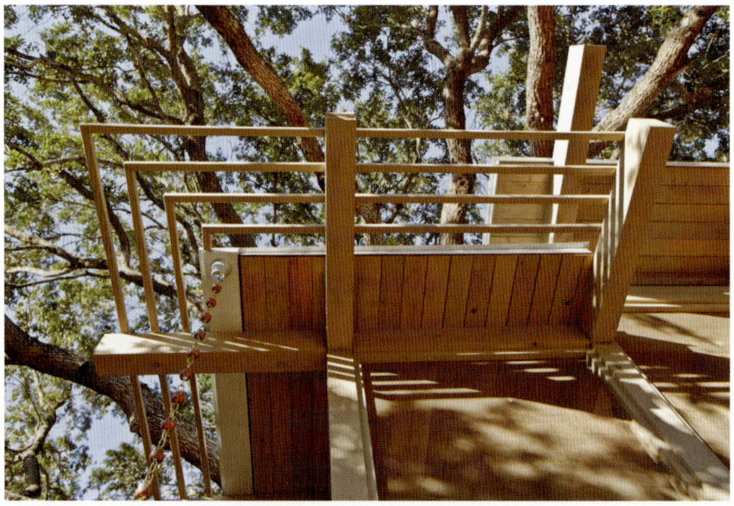

Overhead trellis adds interest, character, and dimension to the porch façade.

Careful integration of ceiling beams and vertical supports create a pleasing rhythmic pattern, while the natural colored wood adds sophisticated warmth.

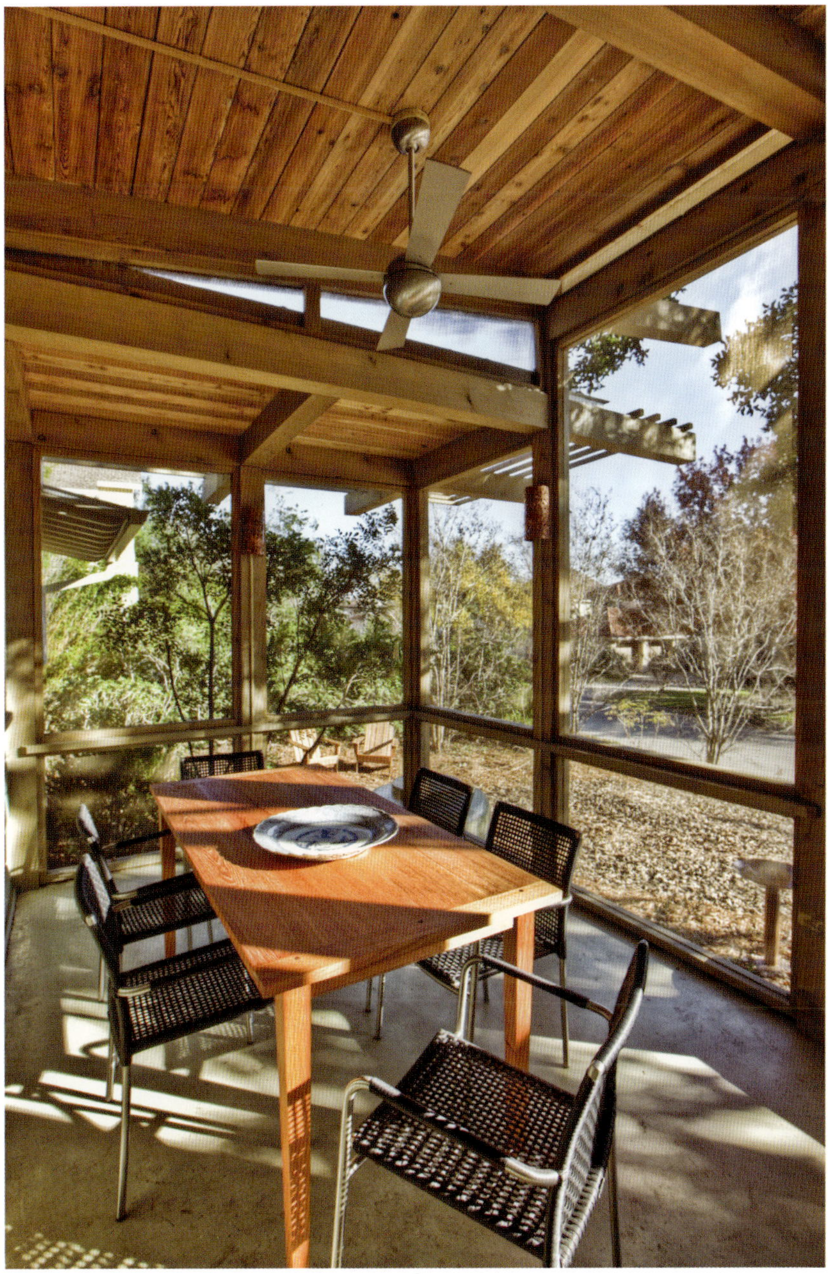

The large multi-functional porch has upholstered seating for lounging and a table and chairs that double for dining or games.

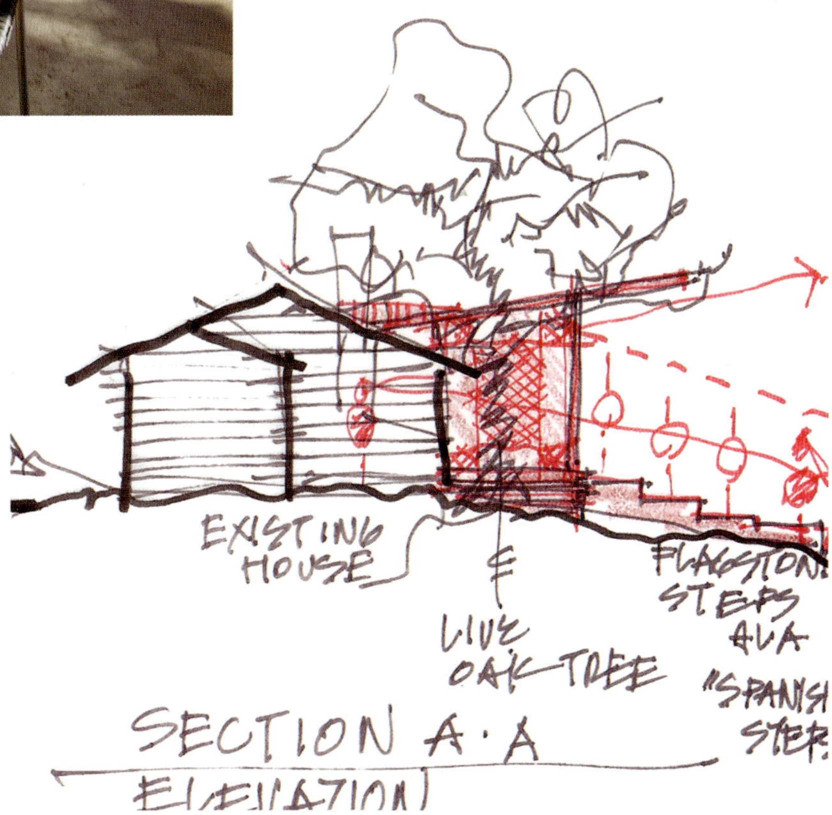

John Grable's original sketch shows how the porch integrates with the existing structure to create a façade-enriching shadow-box effect.

17
Lantern House

Excellent older structures demand a certain respect from the contemporary architects called upon to bring them successfully into a radically different era. That can be seen in so many houses in this book. The 1930s cottage that architect John Grable, FAIA, and head of John Grable Architects, now calls the Lantern House, is an excellent example of resolving specific issues beautifully.

"I was commissioned to double the size of the house to accommodate a growing family. I was also asked to maintain the integrity of the original linear stone box. I necessarily took note of the site—a long, thin corner lot on a street that meanders, without street lights, through a park-like area of a highly desirable part of San Antonio," says Grable.

"Located near the historic Alamo Quarry in Alamo Heights, this small cottage was constructed of limestone acquired from this site. The house is prized as a famous 'Thorman built home'. Thorman was a highly skilled contractor who constructed many of the original homes in the developments of Olmos Park, Terrell Hills, and Alamo Heights neighborhoods in San Antonio," says Grable, whose office is also located in Alamo Heights.

Needed were a formal dining room and a master suite. "I took my design cues from the old house—a spare, simple structure. With no trim around the steel casement windows and light oak floors, the interior already looked modern. My new design, book-end like, adds a single-story glass room to opposite ends of the house. At one end, a new glass room houses the formal dining space. At the other end is the new glass-walled master suite, built over an existing subterranean garage," says Grable.

The concept—adding two glass rooms—sounds simple, but there were issues. Scale of the additions was a key consideration. "Keeping the scale of the expansion from overwhelming the original house or neighboring houses, meant stepping the second story addition back from the front façade. By doing this, it seems to retreat into the surrounding canopy of live oak and elm trees. As a result, the upstairs bedroom feels secluded and protected among the treetops. On the opposite end of the house, the dining room expansion quietly overlooks a meandering street that flows like a creek through this old park-like San Antonio neighborhood," says Grable.

Combining new with old materials was another challenge handily met by Grable. "Masonry chimneys and stone trim for each of the new glass rooms relate to the limestone exterior of the original house, tying old and new structures together in perfect unity," he says.

No street light on the street where this house is located explains why the remodeled structure shines like a beacon in the night. "At night, when lights are on in both the glass box-like dining room and master bedroom, the house serves as a light fixture—a lantern—for this sylvan neighborhood," Grable says.

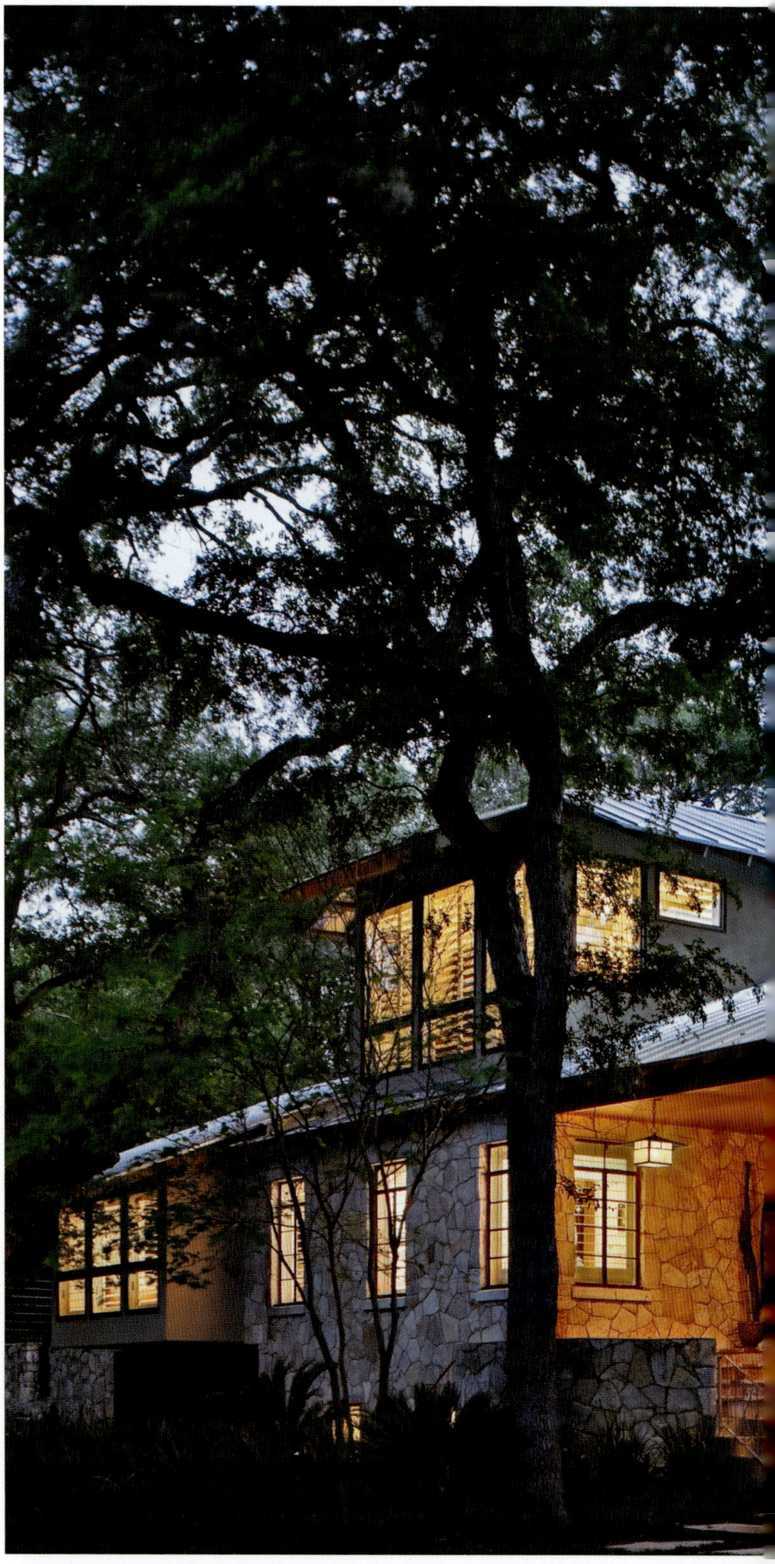

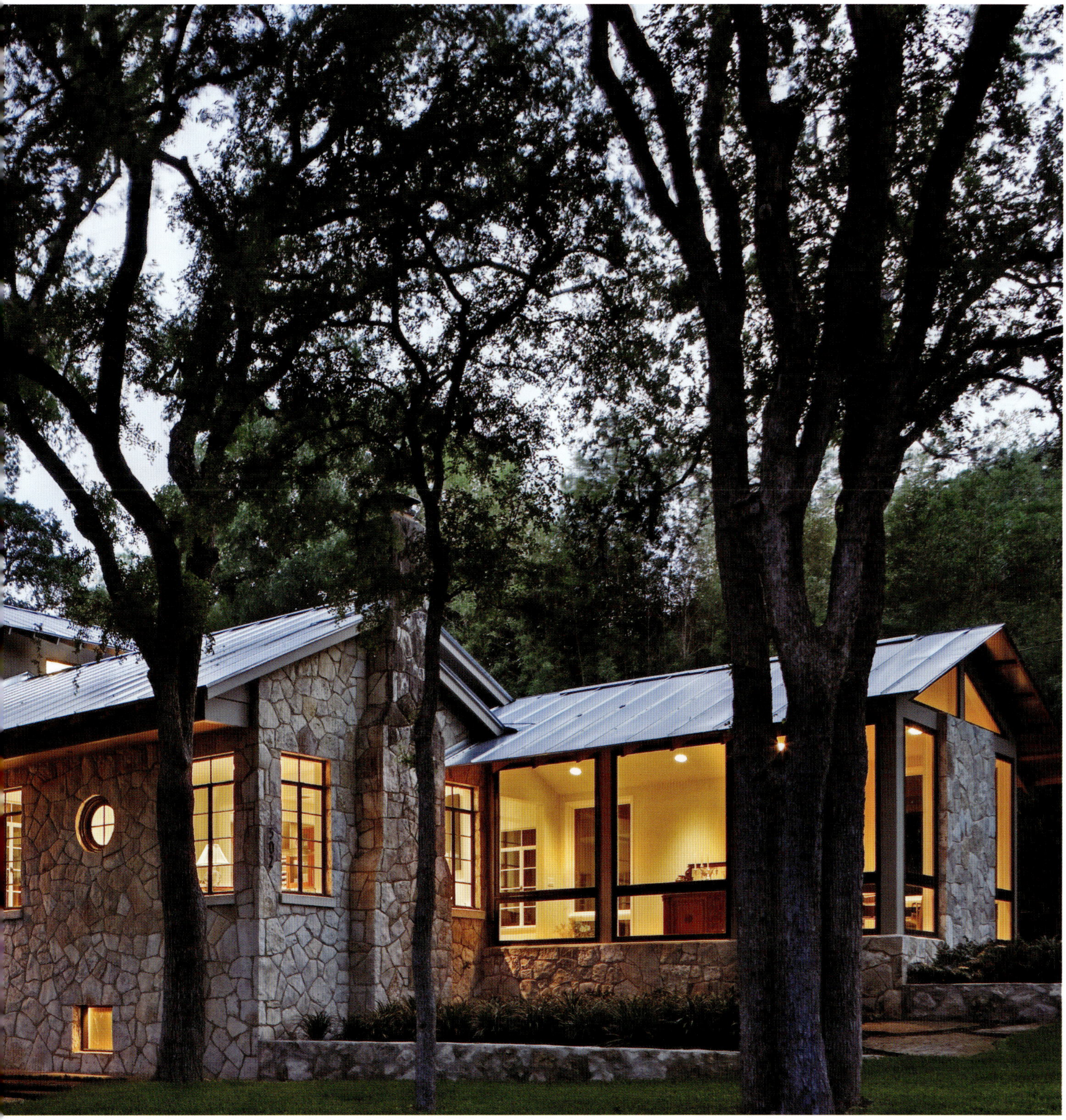

Additions at each end of the original stone cottage—glass boxes, Architect John Grable calls them—glow like lanterns in the night.
Photographs by Chris Cooper; courtesy John Grable Architects

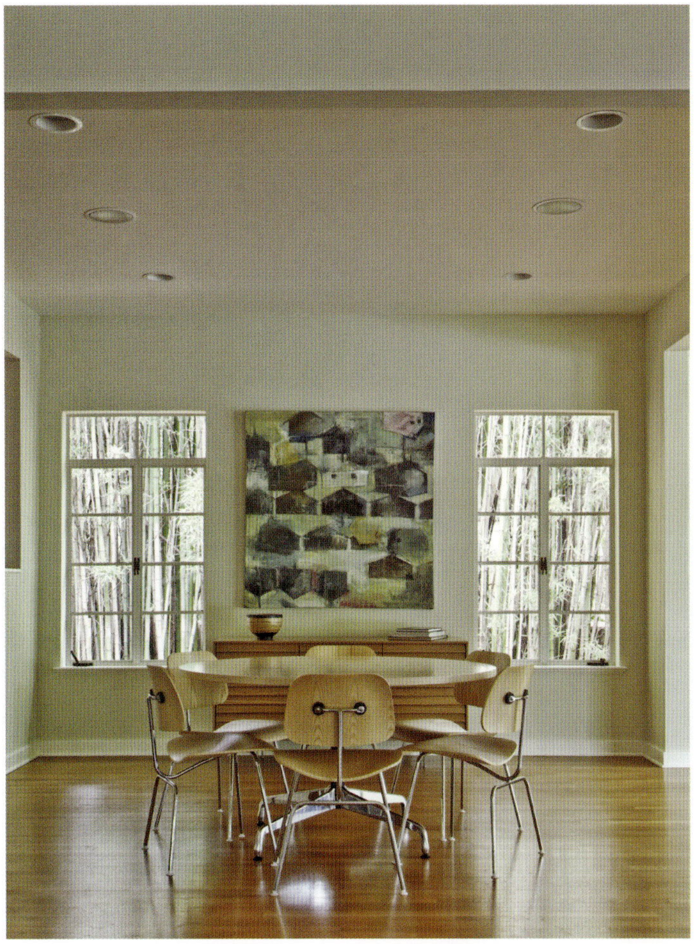

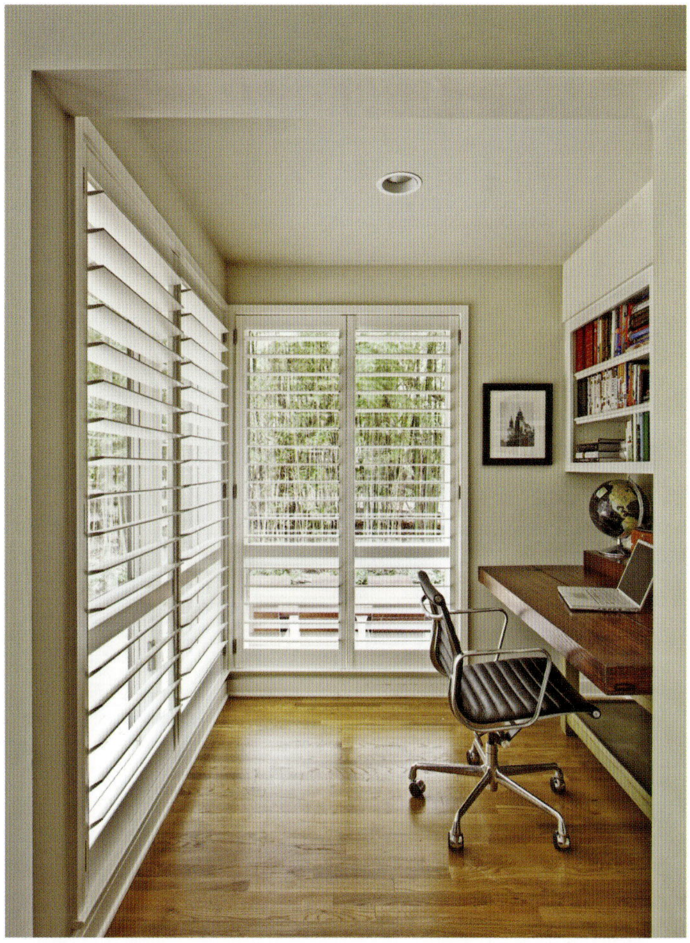

Light-colored wood floors, museum-light walls, and contemporary furnishings create a fresh, modern mood that is consistent throughout the house.

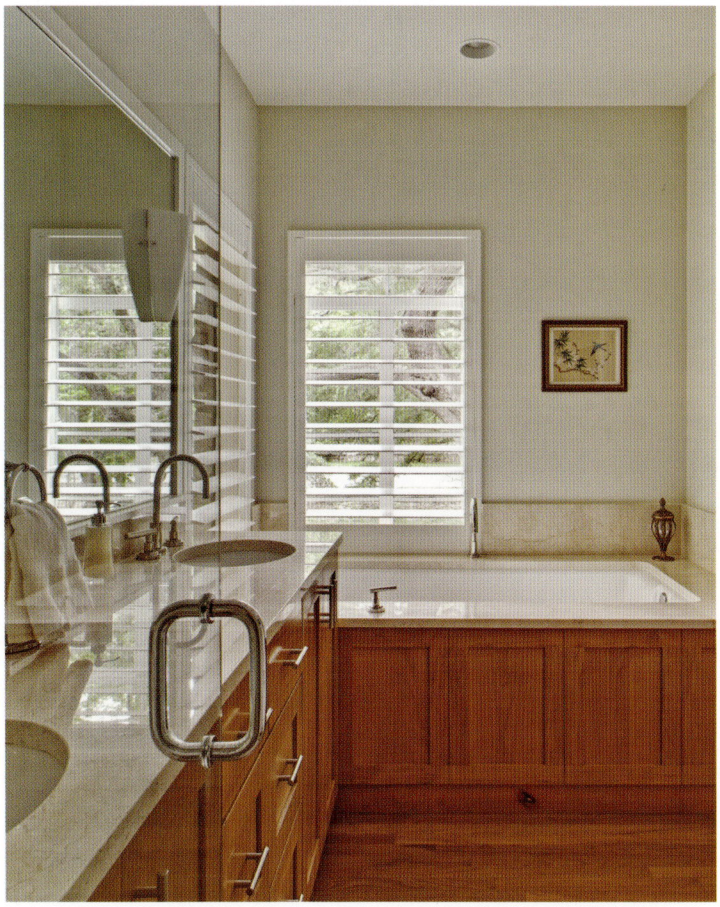

Identical window treatments unite a study area and bath.

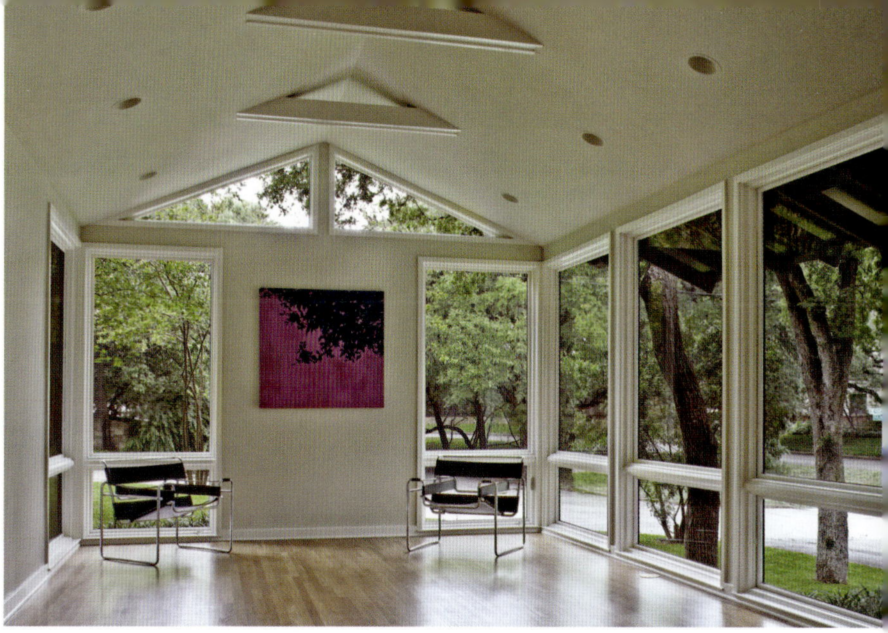

Thorman's, the builder's, signature round window in the original living room is perhaps the only clue that it is not as contemporary as the new Grable-designed dining room and master suite.

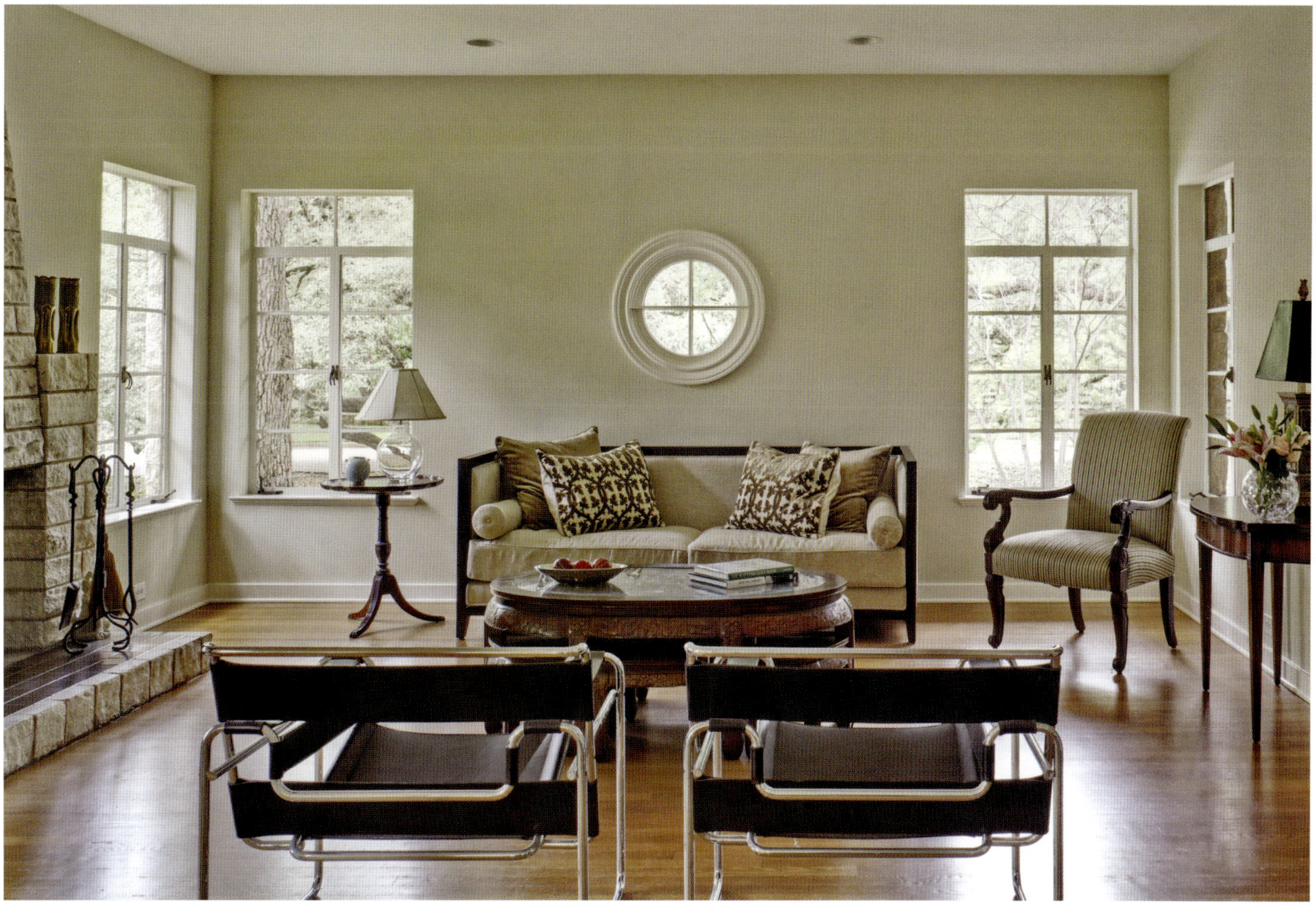

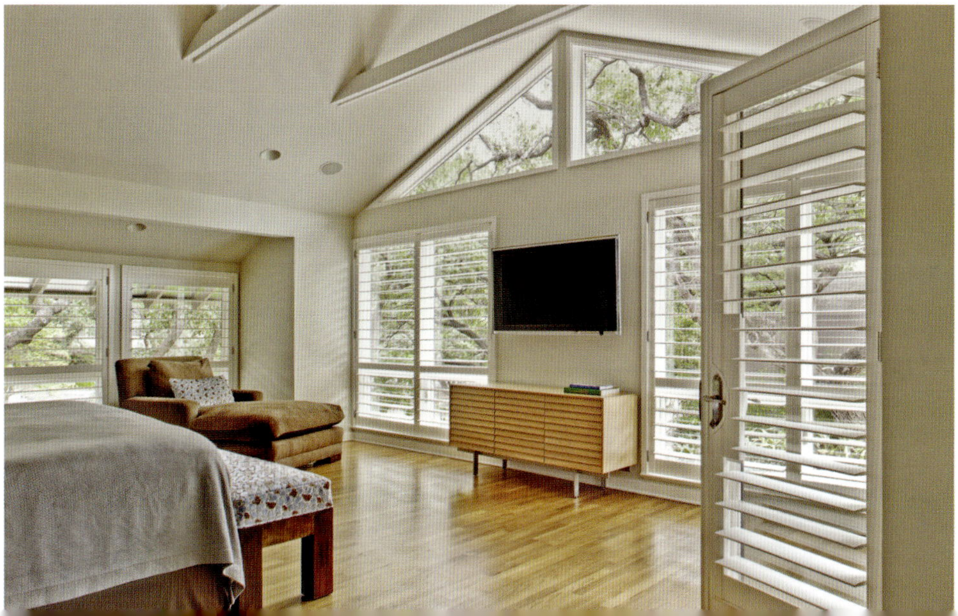

18

Camp Street Residences

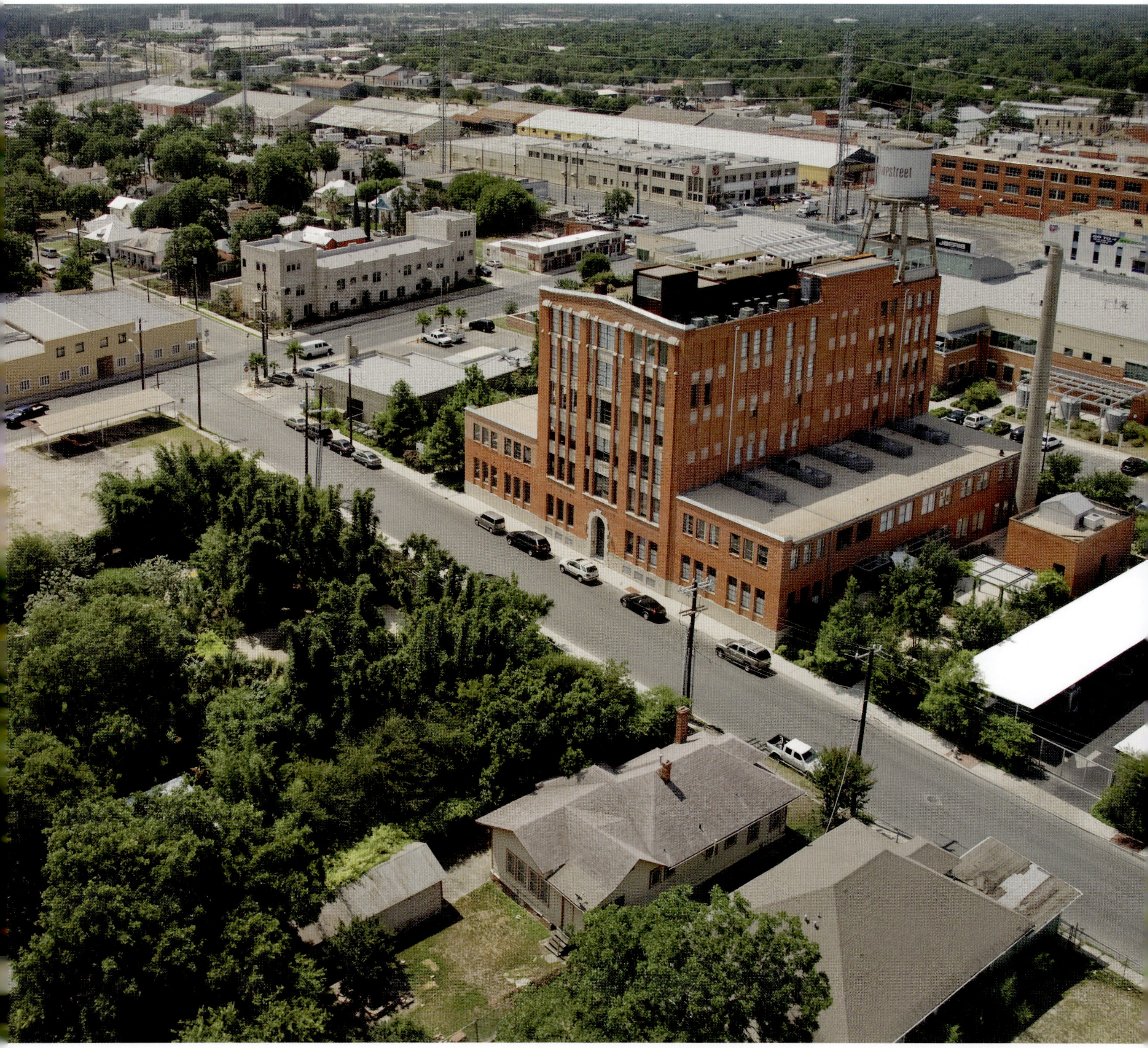

Not all historic homes in San Antonio were originally designed for residential use. In fact, some of the most sophisticated were originally commercial buildings. Among the most fascinating adaptive re-use examples is Poteet Architect's CAMPstreet/CHRISpark project. Architect Jim Poteet succinctly describes it as "the rehabilitation of a 1920s factory and its grounds near downtown San Antonio." What Poteet and his firm, Poteet Architects, did was transform the 1926 Duerler Candy Factory by Herff & Jones Architects into handsome loft residences, realizing the new-use vision of the building's owner, noted artist and art patron, Linda Pace, founder of Artpace San Antonio.

"The Lofts were sold in shell condition for the buyers to finish out," says Poteet. "One of the challenges of the project was bringing systems (HVAC, wiring, plumbing, etc.) to each unit in a way that respects the building fabric and maximizes the flexibility of the finish-outs." The Cicconi loft, he notes, is just one example of options in finishing a shell space with concrete floors and ceilings to suit the owner of that unit. Pace made the fifth floor her own residence, and placed an art gallery on the top floor of the six-floor building.

"We divided the 88,000-square-foot structure into twenty loft-like units. Additionally, the redesign of the building provided for indoor common areas, including an exercise room, community art gallery, and basement parking," says Poteet.

Poteet's design approach was to recognize the former factory as "a beautiful building" and to "get out of its way." Indeed, care was taken to retain the original appearance of the façade, still some changes were necessary. "Over 100 steel windows were added to the building's refurbished façade. On the exterior, new concrete and steel porches and balconies are bounded by outdoor garden and courtyard spaces," Poteet explains.

"The interior public spaces were treated as a backdrop for art in all media, since the developer, Linda Pace, was a nationally known contemporary art collector," says Poteet.

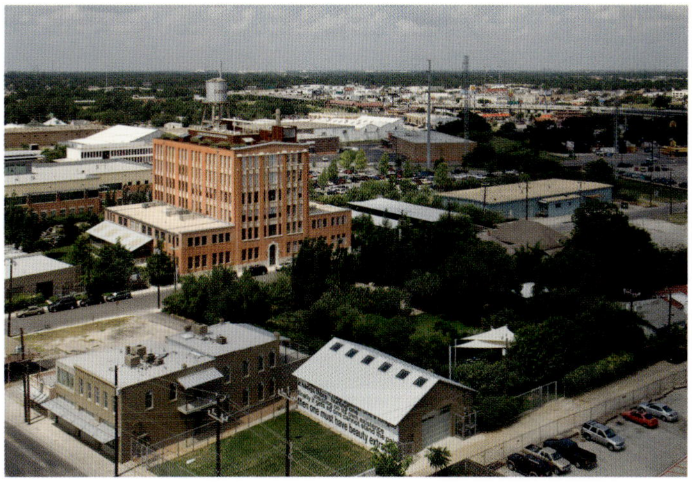

Aerial views show the six-story Camp Street Residences, Chris Park directly across the street, and (adjacent to the park) Linda Pace's studio (with skylights), now the offices for the Linda Pace Foundation. *Photographs by Chris Cooper, courtesy Poteet Architects*

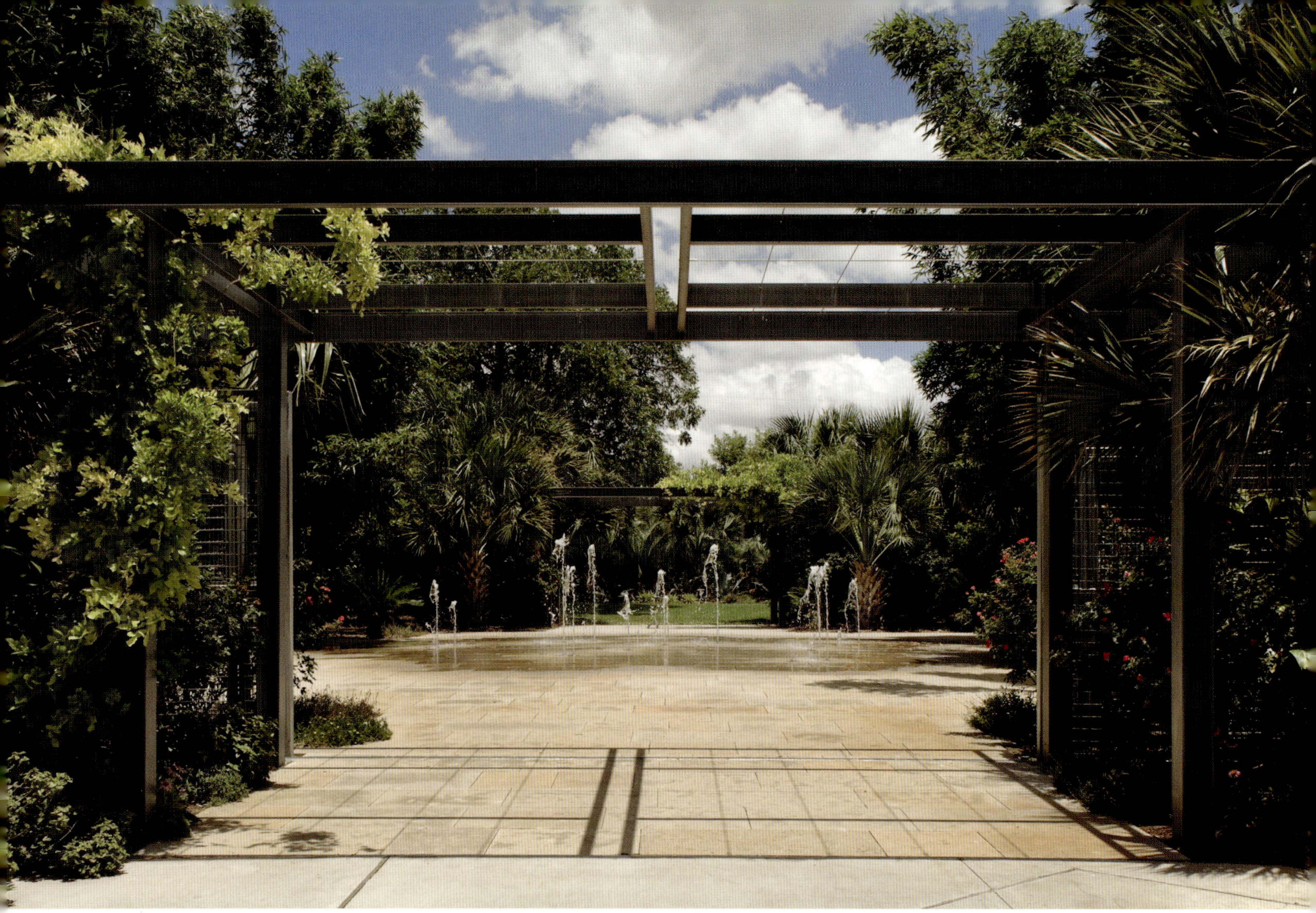

The view into the park when standing in front of the Camp Street Residences is one of an animated water feature.

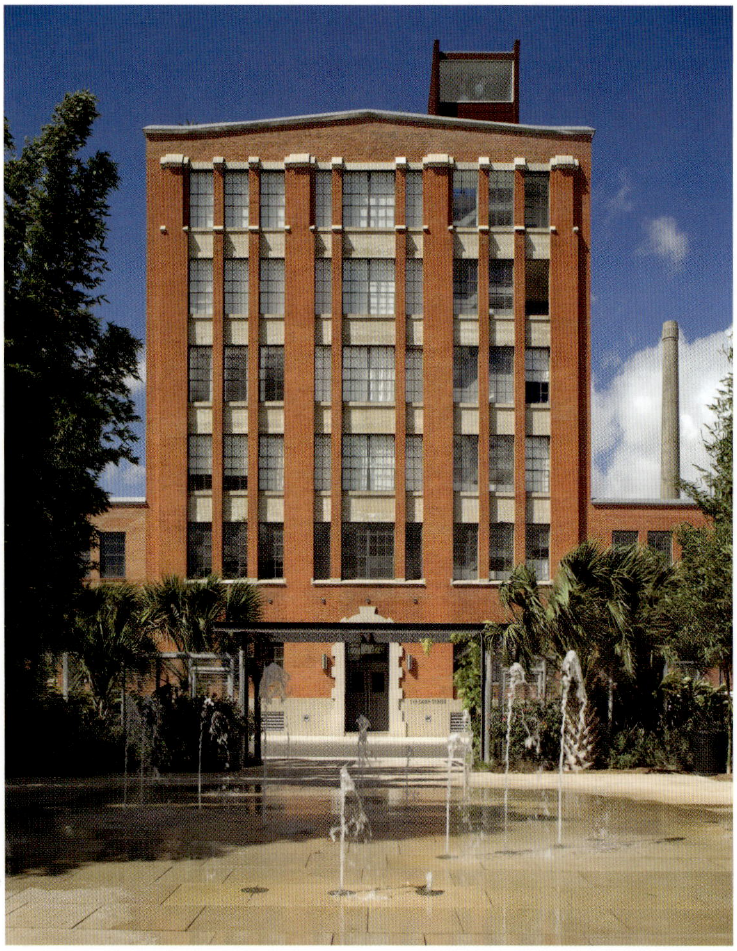

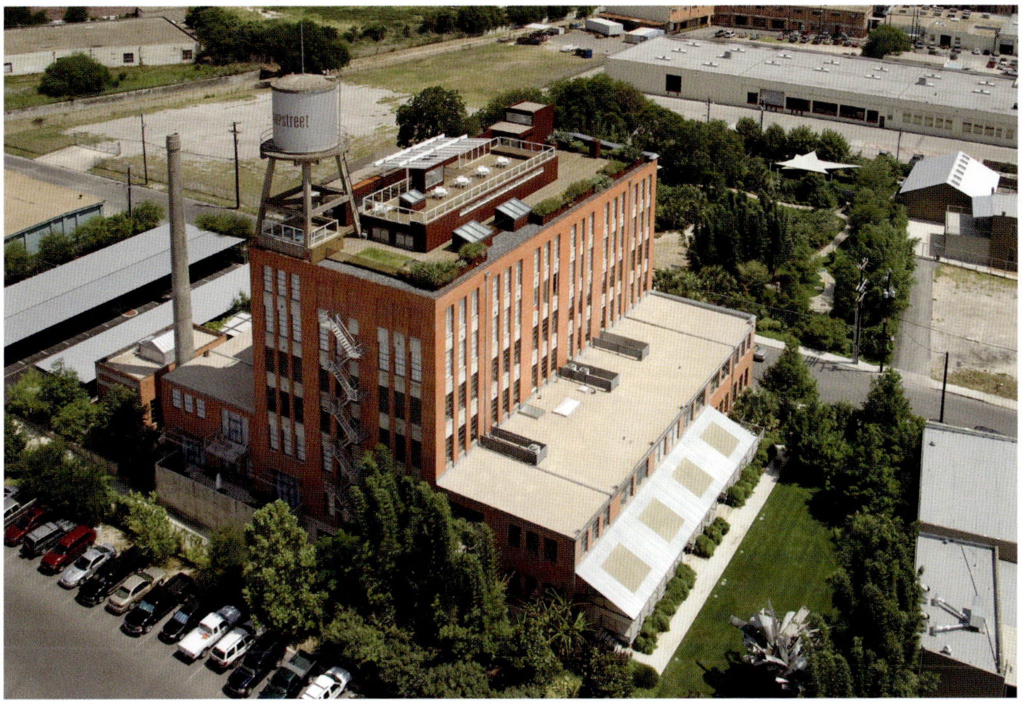

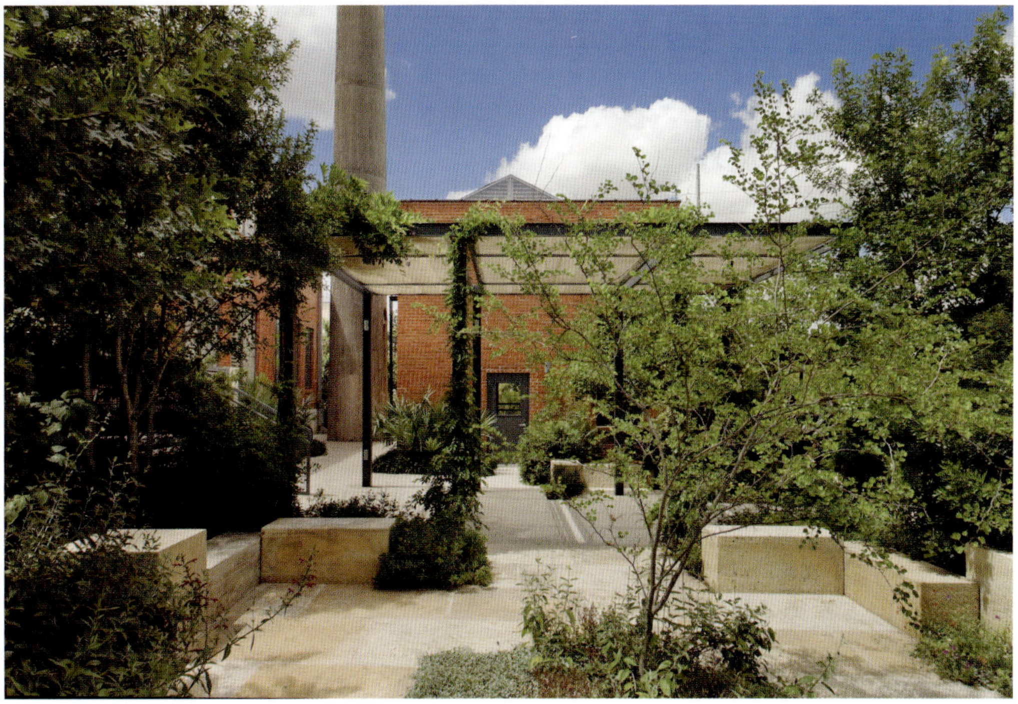

An aerial view shows rooftop lounging, dedicated parking, and a beautifully landscaped garden.

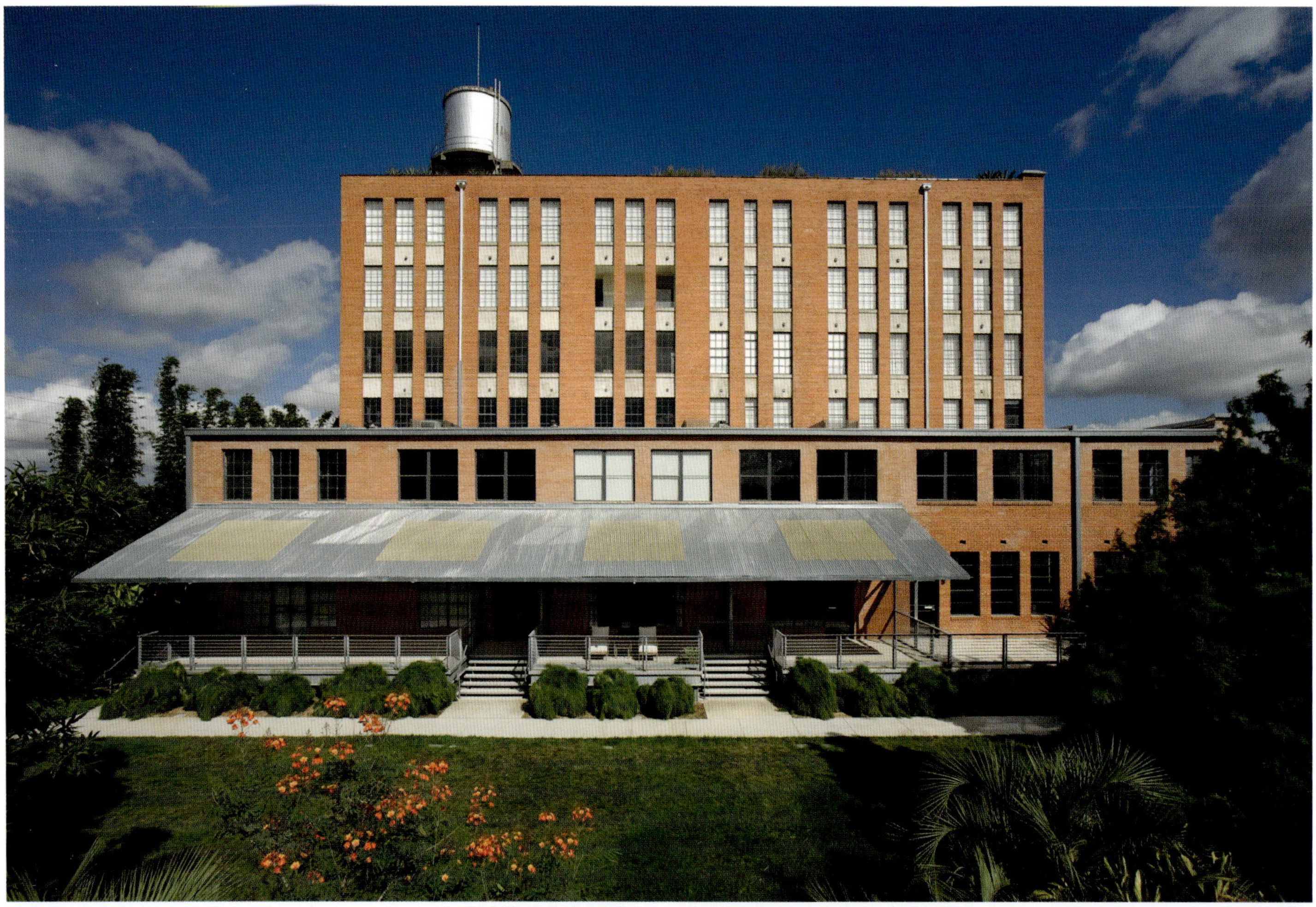

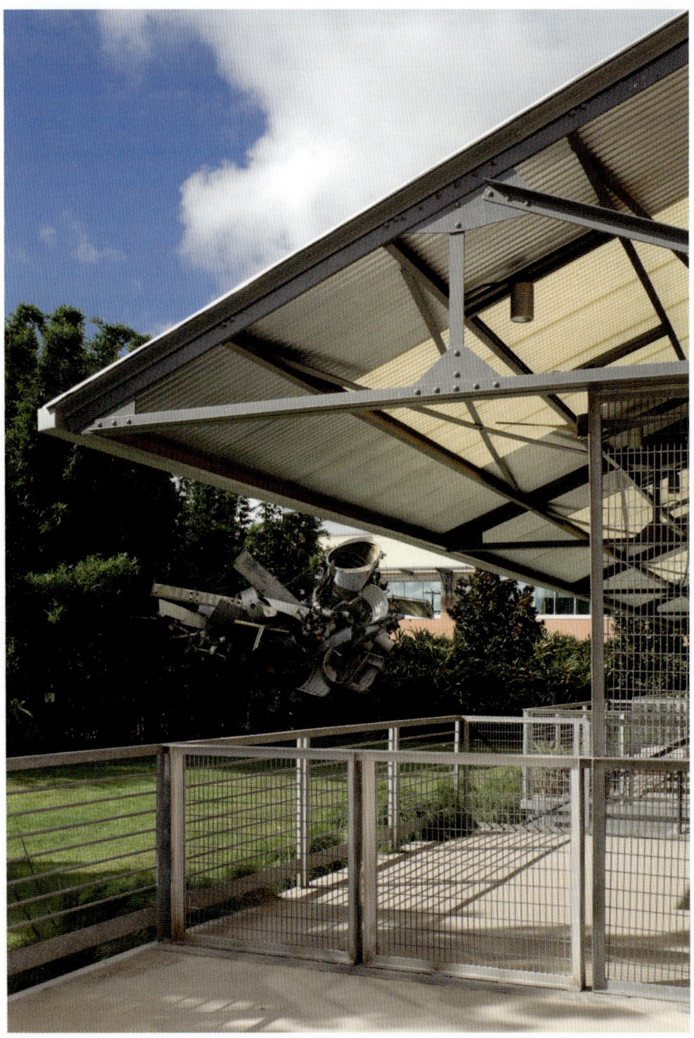

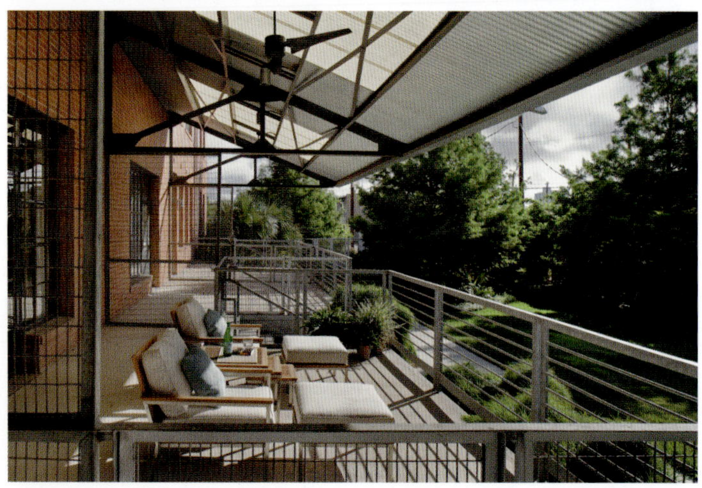

Most loft residences have balconies; but, the Cicconi apartment has an expansive terrace with a view of the garden and its monumental sculpture.

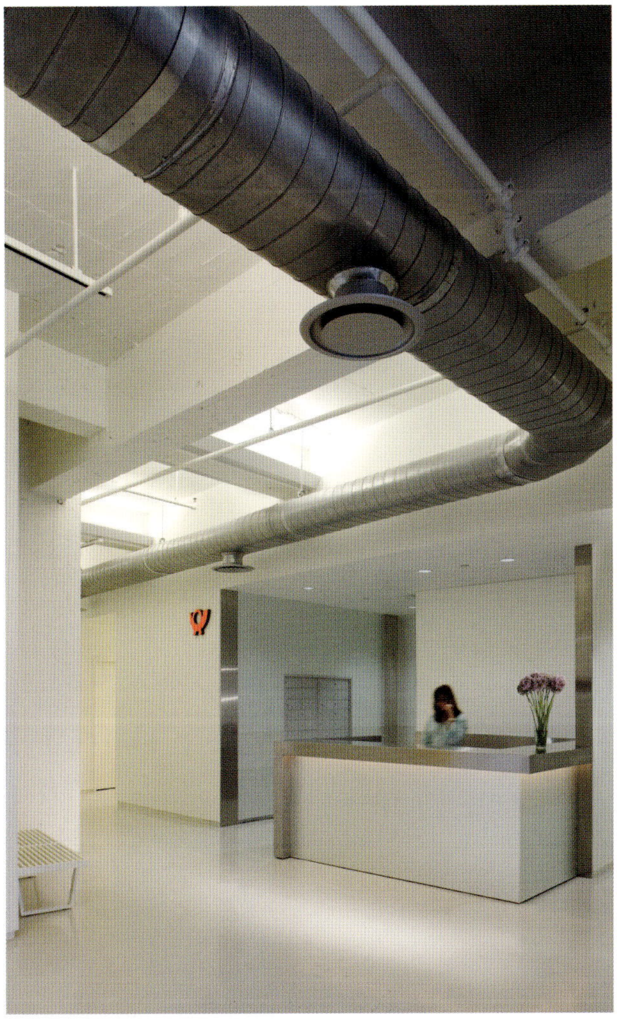

Public areas are treated as though they are an extension of the gallery on the top floor of the six-story building.

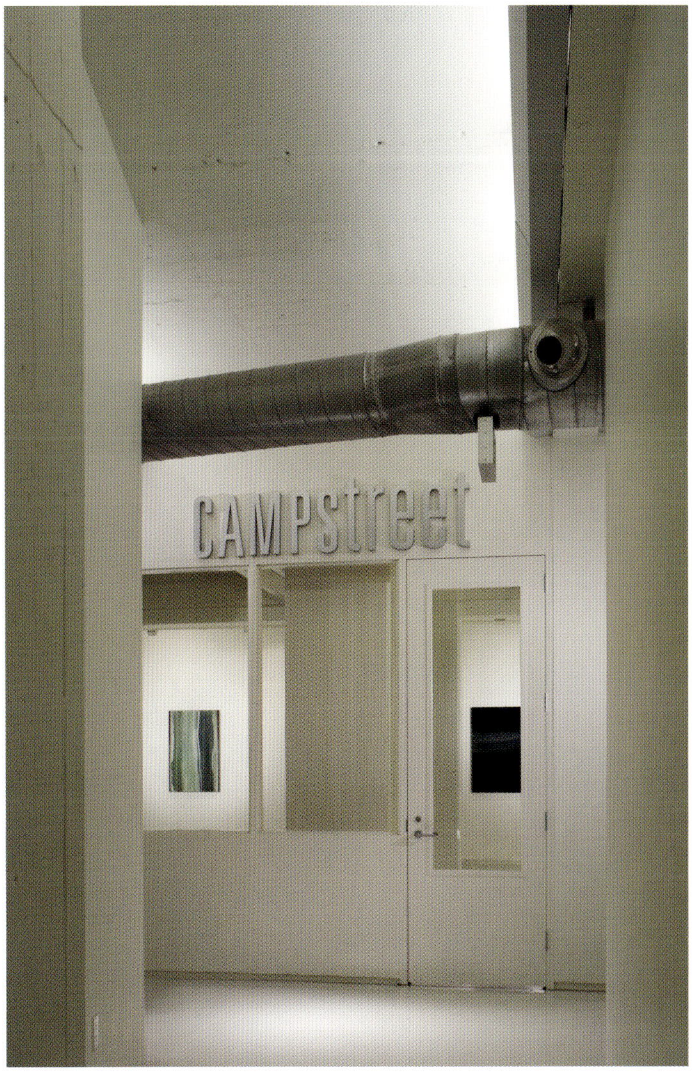

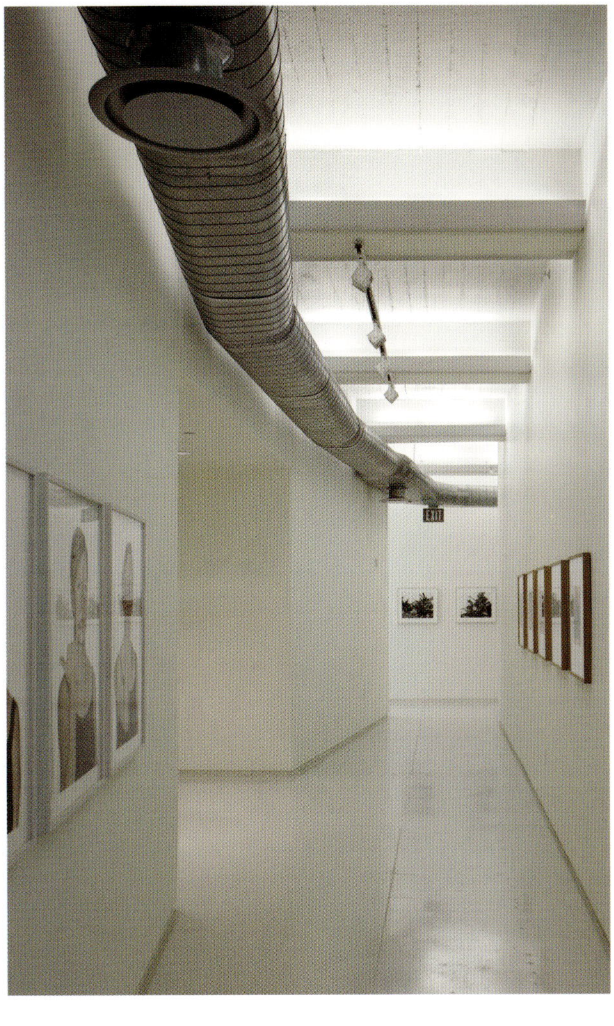

Cicconi Loft

"Number 103 at the Camp Street Residences—the Cicconi Loft—is the finish-out of a raw 2,258-square-foot shell," says Poteet. "The loft's owner, a Washington, DC-based executive, retained Poteet Architects to create a home with the quality of a retreat that he could enjoy while conducting regular business in San Antonio."

"The lower level consists of spaces for entertaining—the kitchen, bar, living, and dining areas—each distinct, but open to one another. On the exterior, a large covered deck overlooks a lush garden and a striking sculpture by Los Angeles artist Nancy Rubins. "It was once the building's loading dock," says Poteet.

Poteet says that the owner wanted a true loft—one that took full advantage of the warmth and materiality of the old building. "To that end, on the lower level, red brick walls and the concrete floor and ceiling were repaired, cleaned, and left exposed. The existing concrete floor was polished to achieve a terrazzo effect. These original materials are supplemented with Brazilian cherry on the stair and walls, and dark stained walnut and chocolate-colored limestone in the kitchen and bar," Poteet explains.

Not all units are two-story, but the Cicconi loft's focal point is an unusual, visually arresting open stair that allows light to flow from a large overhead skylight through the upper level and down to the lower level. The skylight-lit stair begins on the lower level as a block of rich Brazilian cherry wood. As the design (and the stair) moves upward, a change of materials transforms the stair into a light steel structure suspended by slender steel bars. "The sculptural stair marks the transition from public to private spaces," says Poteet. And changing light underscores the awareness of movement from space to space, affecting mood en route.

While the lower level is rich and dark, "On the upper floor, a lighter (but still warm) palate prevails," Poteet points out. A quick tour shows that in the skylight-lit master bath, Texas limestone countertops, honey-colored glass tile, and painted cabinetry create a soothing ambience. "The secluded media room/office, tucked into the masonry shell of the old building, reprises the materials mix of the lower level."

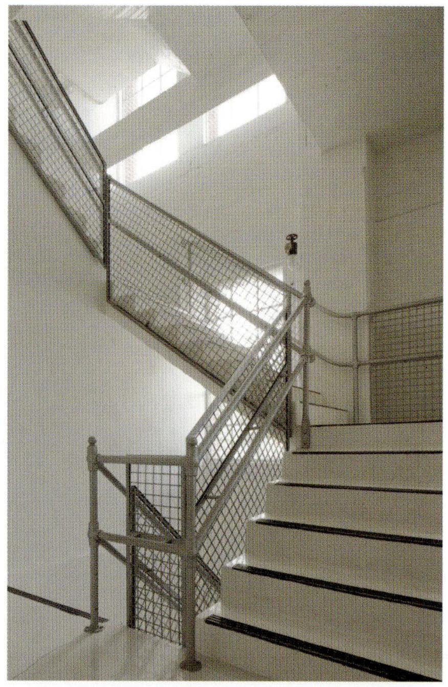

Loft-like apartments were sold as shells, then finished to suit buyers. Materials for the staircase in the two-story Cicconi loft include dark paneling on the first level, then switch to metals somewhat similar to those used elsewhere in the building.

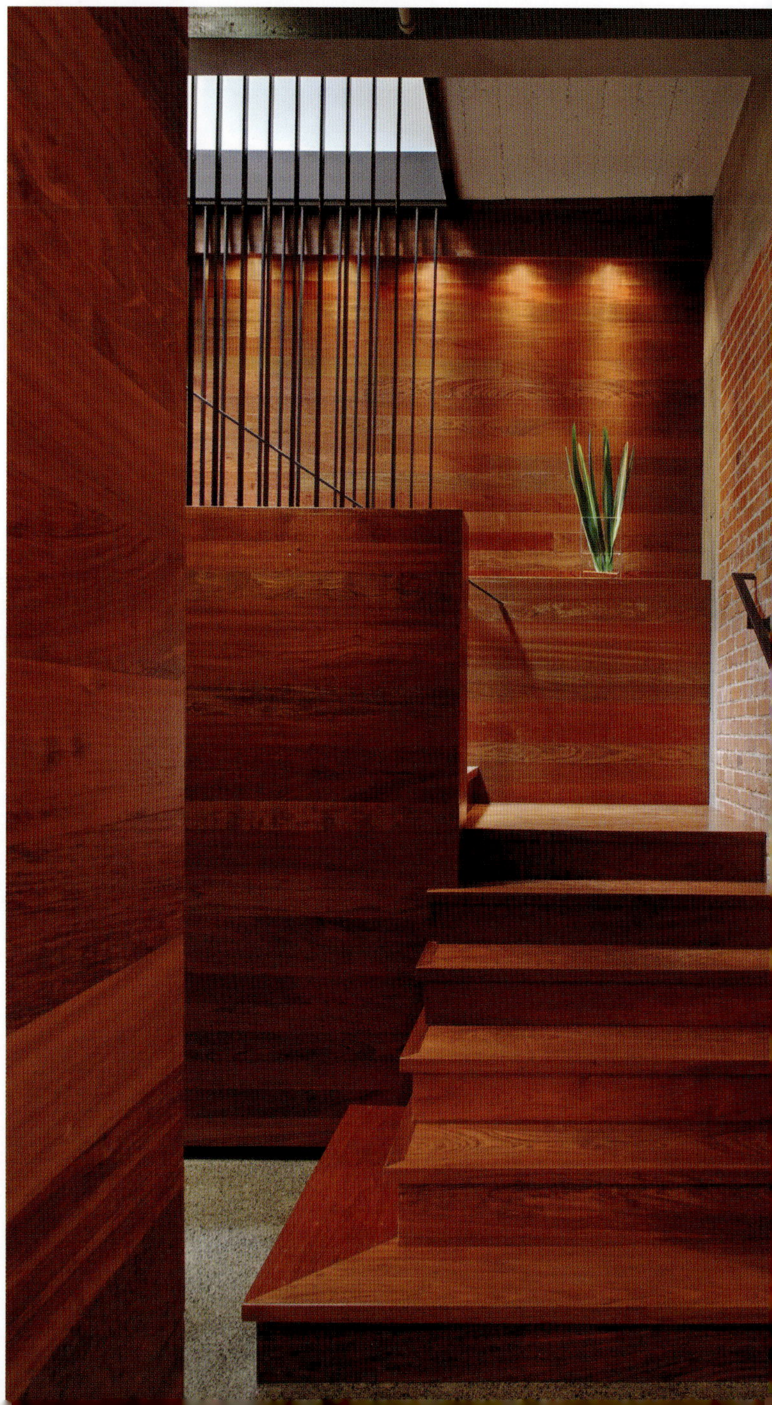

Architect Jim Poteet's design of the Cicconi loft uses the original brick wall as a textural and pattern foil for luxurious wood paneling.

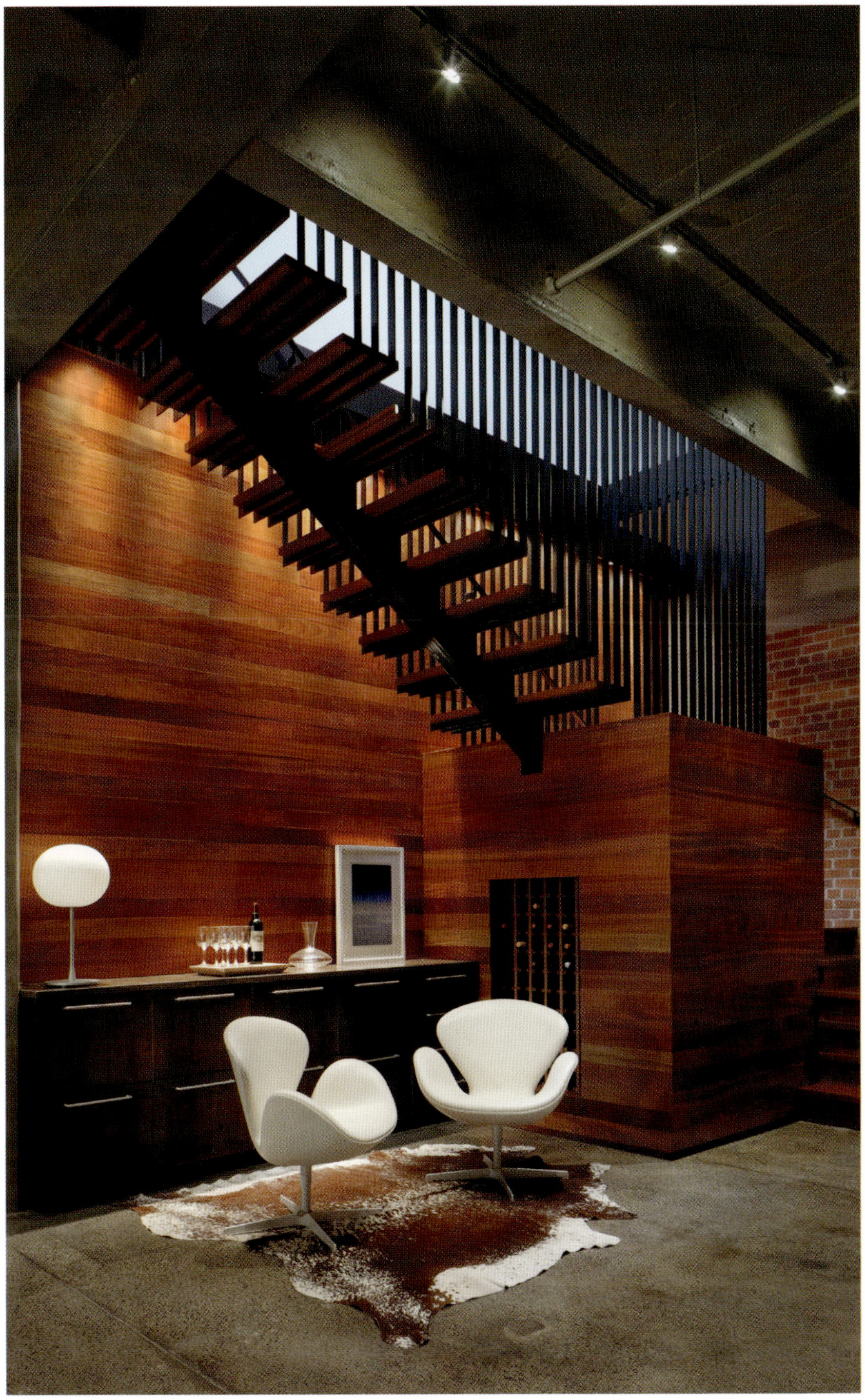

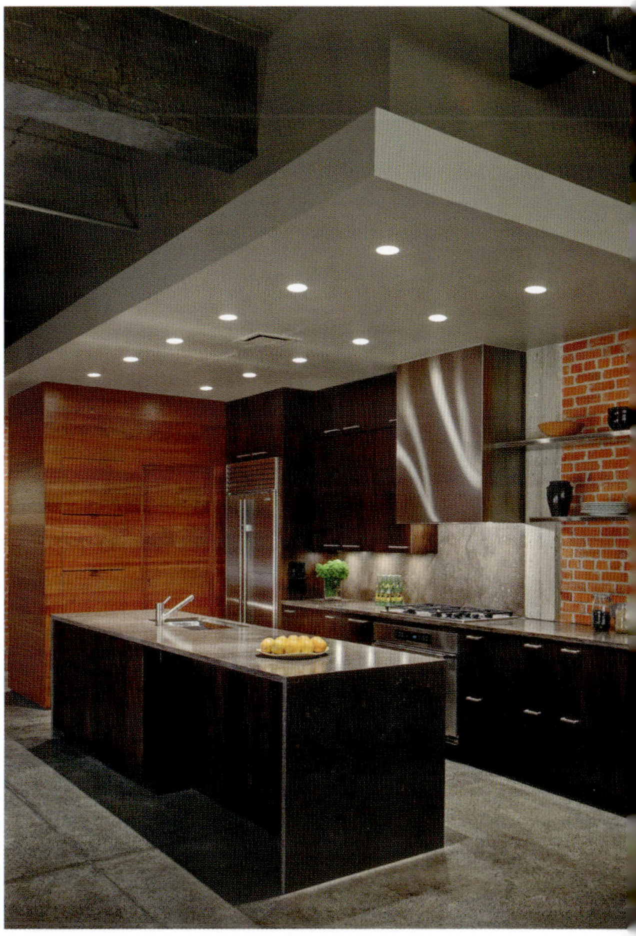

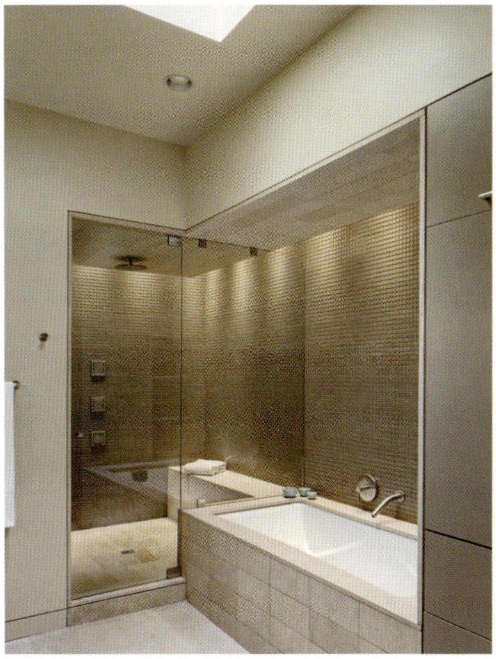

The spa-like bathroom in the Cicconi loft is state-of-the-art and a subtle study in glamorous textures.

19
Artpace Apartment

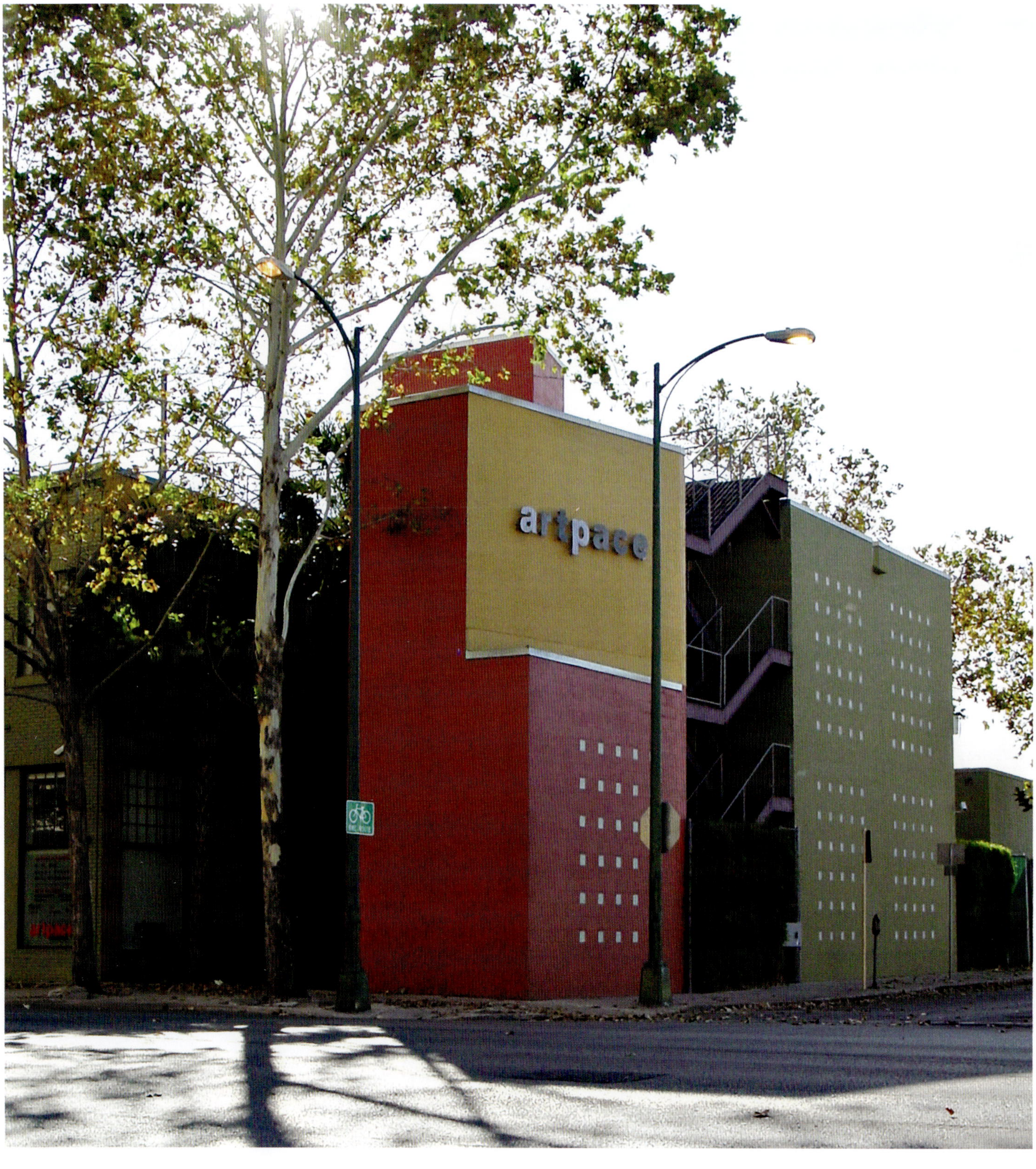

Increasingly, historic San Antonio homes include adaptive reuse of vintage commercial structures as exciting contemporary living quarters. Some, like the apartments for artists-in-residence at Artpace at 445 North Main Street, are temporary homes, but nonetheless homes and important both to the artists carefully selected to reside there and to San Antonio as a cultural center.

Artpace, a unique art center, was conceived as a creative laboratory—a place where resident artists would (over an eight-week stay) live, create artwork, and exhibit that work. It is part of the large legacy of Linda Pace, who was artist, collector, philanthropist, and developer—a leader in the adaptive reuse movement in San Antonio.

Pace, who founded the Linda Pace Foundation before her death at age sixty-two in 2007, served in various capacities with such major art institutions as the Whitney Museum of American Art and the Dia Center for the Arts in New York City, and the Tate Gallery in London. Her name alone would have promoted adaptive reuse. But her personal and financial involvement, and the *results* achieved by the teams that she organized to assign new roles to venerable buildings were proof positive of the viability of adaptive reuse in a forward-looking city that treasures its history.

Three high-profile, *tres chic,* Pace-initiated transformations demonstrated vividly just *how* old buildings large and small could be revitalized.

- The 1926 Duerler Candy Factory which architect Jim Poteet transformed into the Camp Street Residences (chapter 18) is an excellent example of factory *cum* loft homes.
- Poteet changed a 25,000 square foot 1920s automobile shop into a studio where Pace might create her large-scale artworks, and following her death redid the space as headquarters for The Linda Pace Foundation.
- Lake/Flato Architects recast the 18,000 square foot 1920s Hudson automobile showroom on Main Street as Artpace. According to spokesperson Matt Johns, "The most recent update to Artpace was completed in November 2009, by Julie Thornton, designer of the three similarly-furnished loft-like apartments."

Each of the three similar apartments is private, with its own kitchen and bathroom. Multifunctional living areas are fully furnished with a Murphy bed, desk, upholstered seating, and television. Laundry facilities on the same floor as the apartments are shared. The artists create in spaces provided for work and exhibition within the Artpace building.

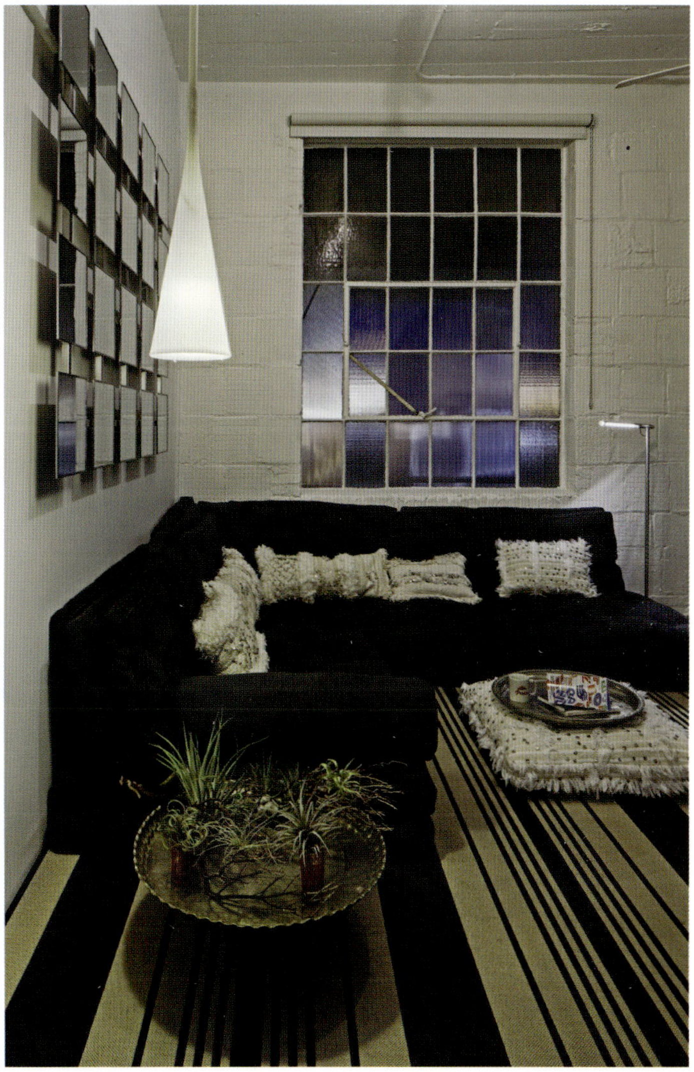

Comfortable seating fills one corner of the living space in each of three similarly furnished apartments at Artpace. *Photographs by Chris Cooper, courtesy Artpace*

Artpace has exhibition space but is not a gallery per se, nor is it a collecting institution. Instead, departing artists take their work home and are free to exhibit it where they will. Johns says, "In this way, the influence of Artpace is diffused globally." Three times each year, at the end of their eight-week residence period, the three visiting artists (one from Texas, another from the U.S., and the third from a foreign nation) vacate their temporary homes. Then, new resident artists move in with fresh ideas for contemporary art that keep the concept of Artpace ever green—a unique recycling on so many levels.

Desk/work tables in each sitting room provide in-quarters work areas for resident visiting artists.

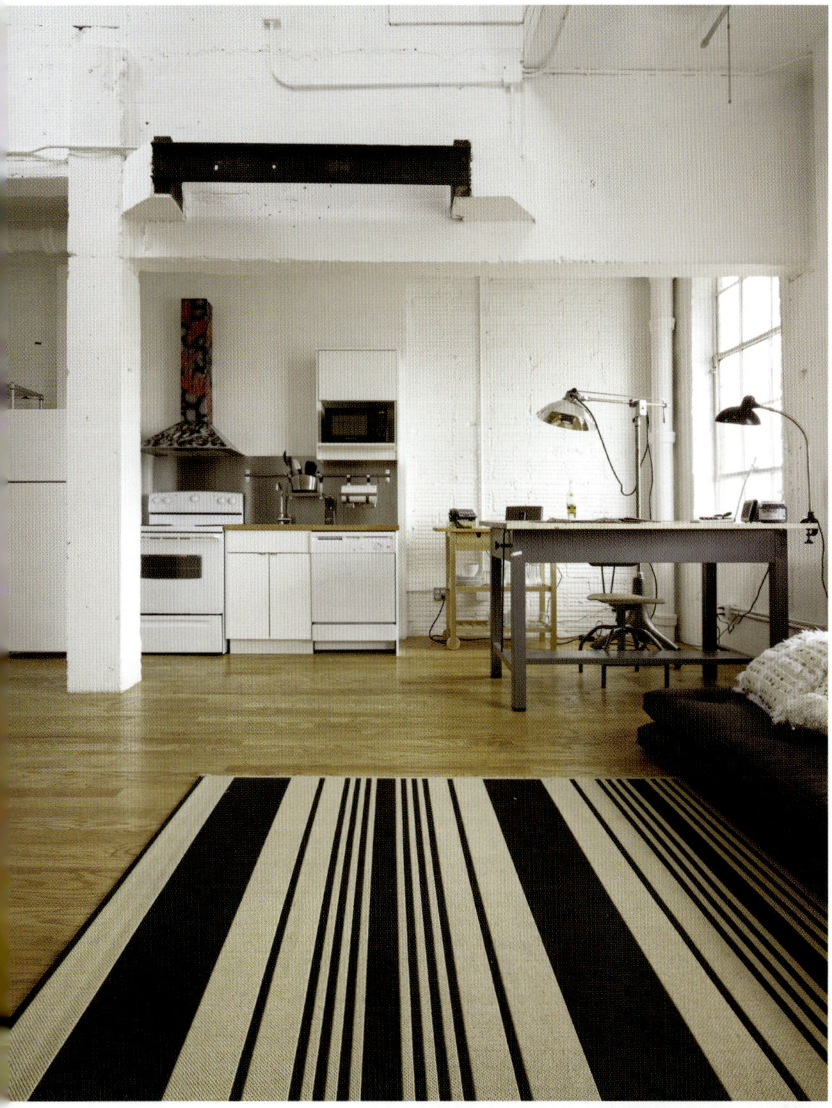

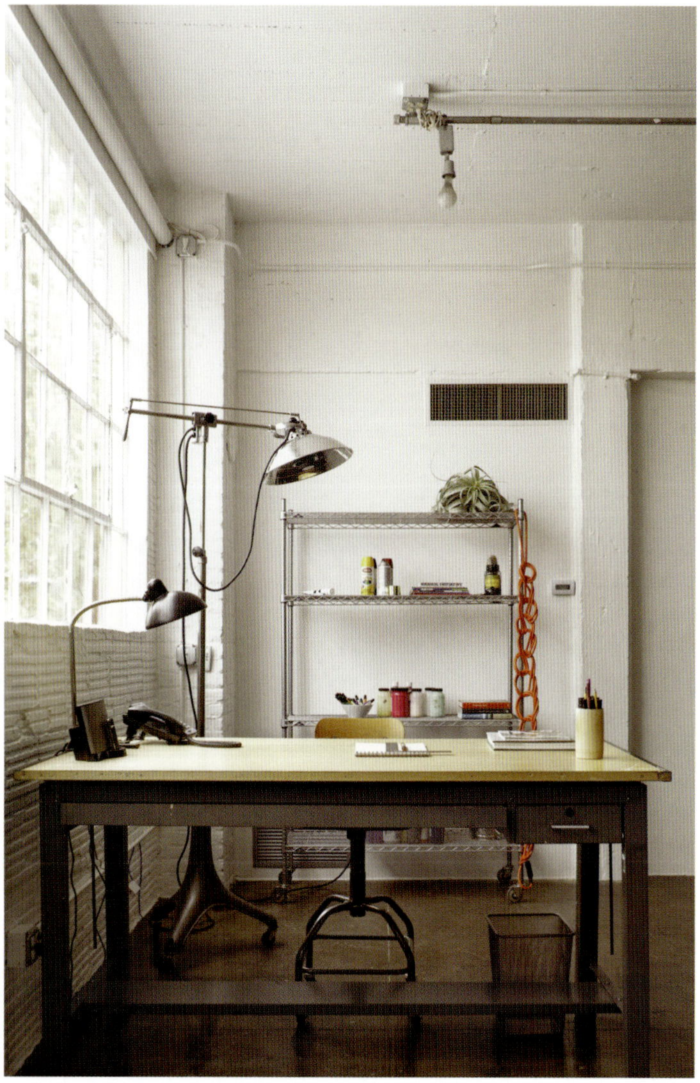

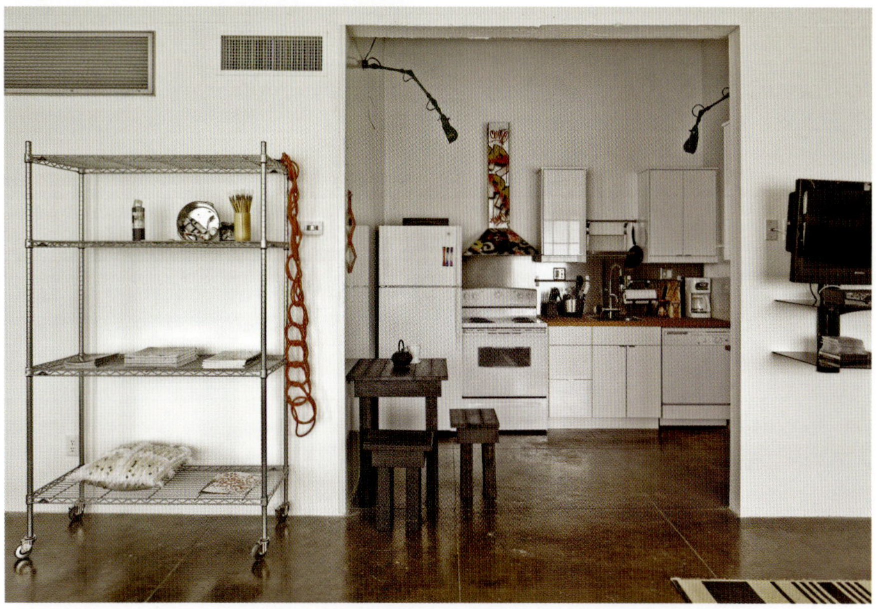

In one apartment, a high tech rolling shelf contrasts with the rustic breakfast table and benches in the kitchen which is just around the corner.

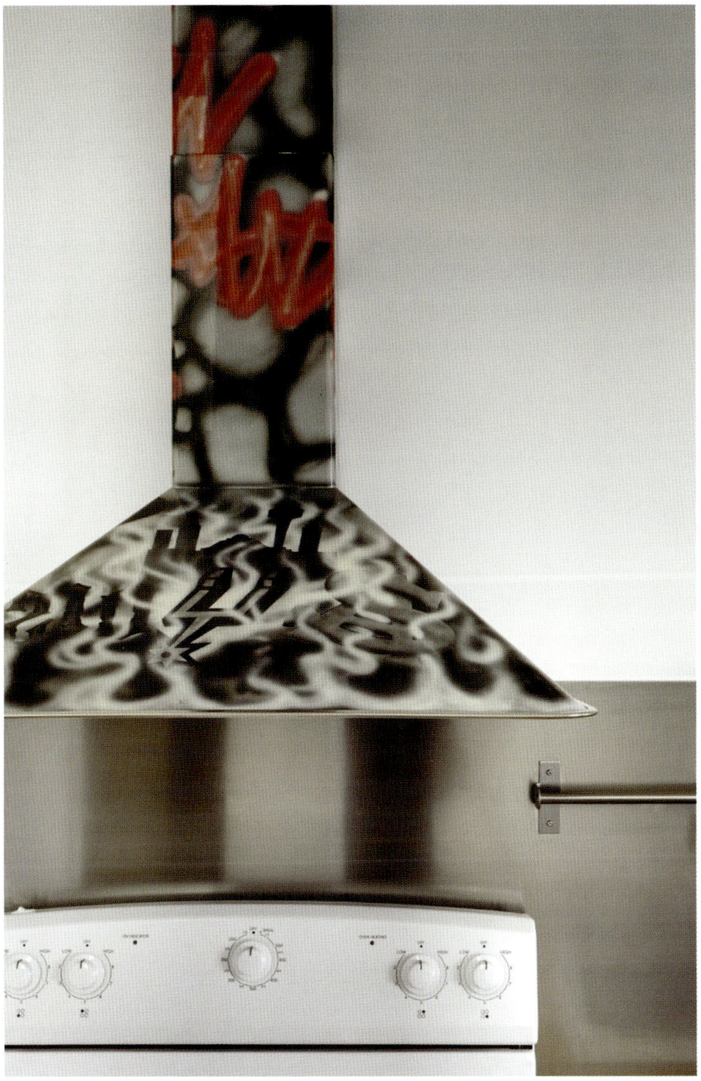

The kitchen vent hood in each apartment was treated to a custom paint job, so that each is a unique work of art.

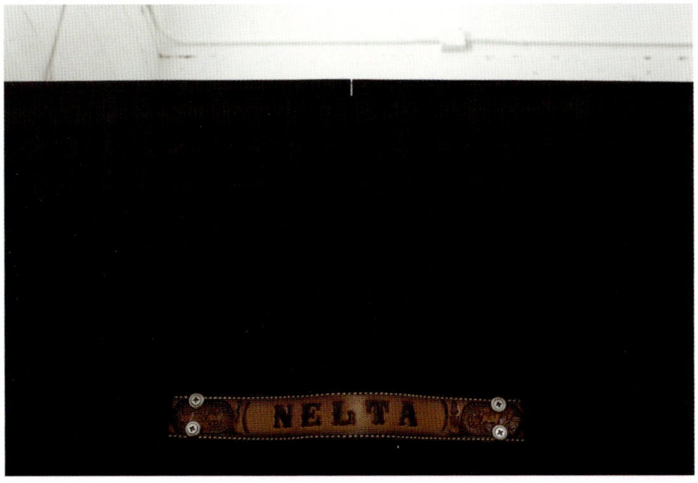

In each apartment, a hand-tooled leather strap is the pull for a Murphy bed that transforms the sitting room into a bedroom.

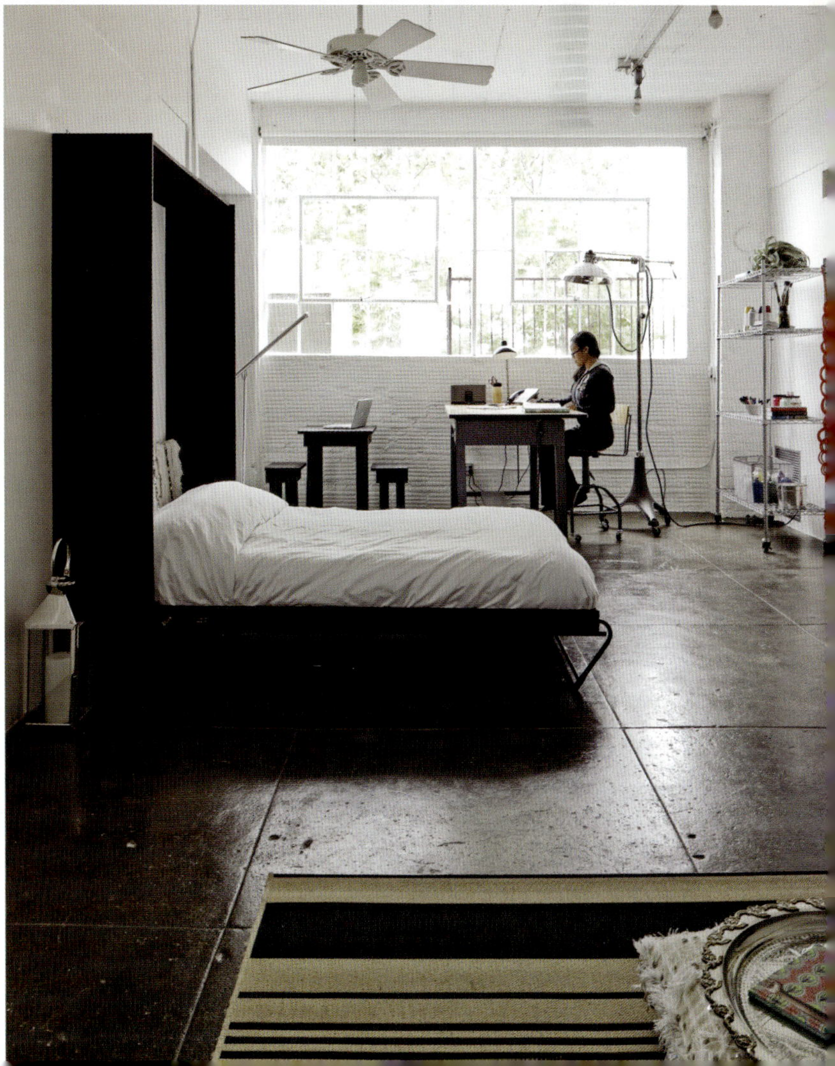

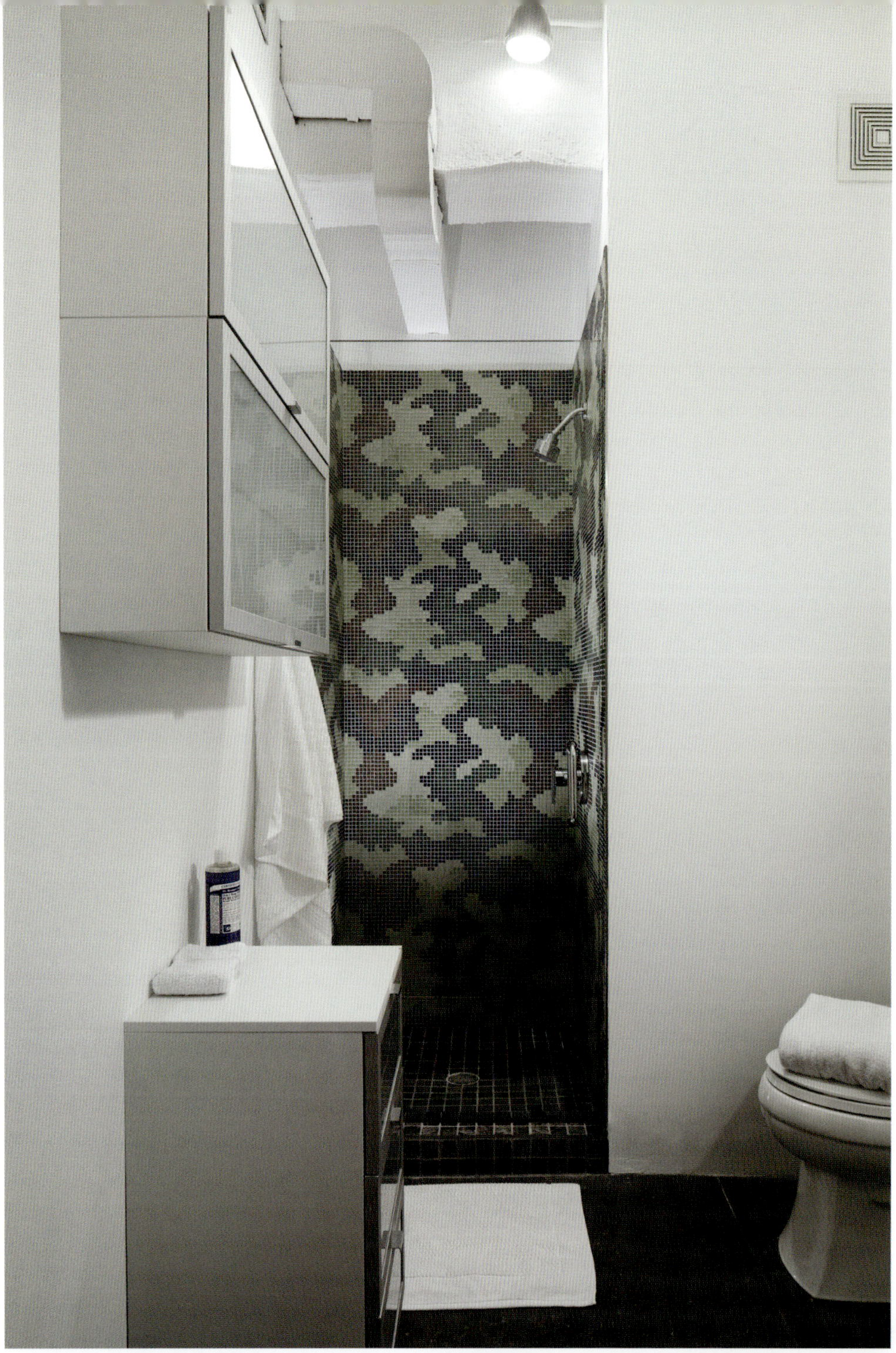

Mosaic patterns in architectural glass tile distinguish the compact bathrooms in each apartment

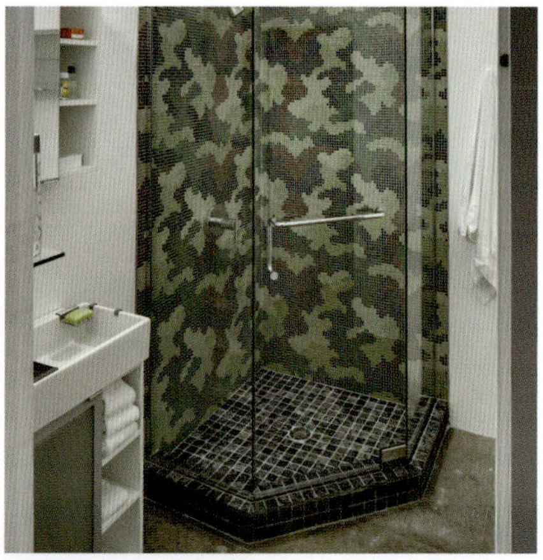

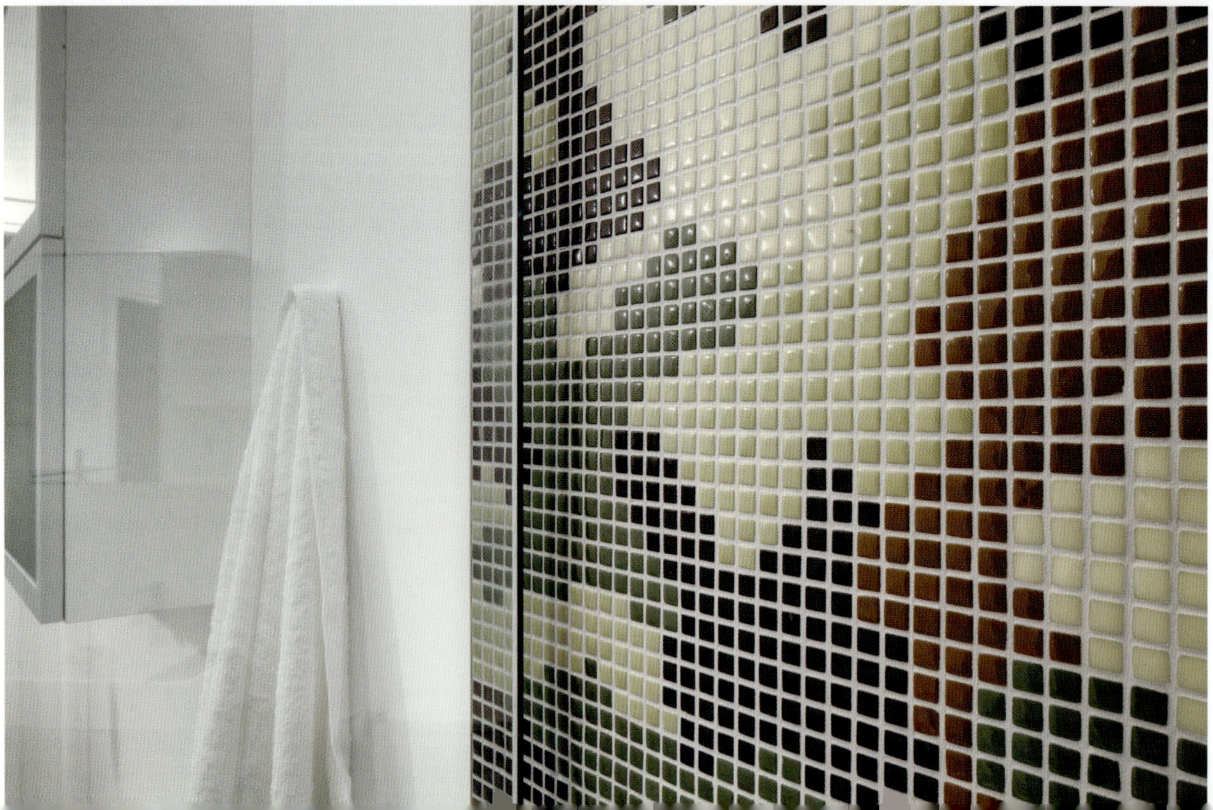

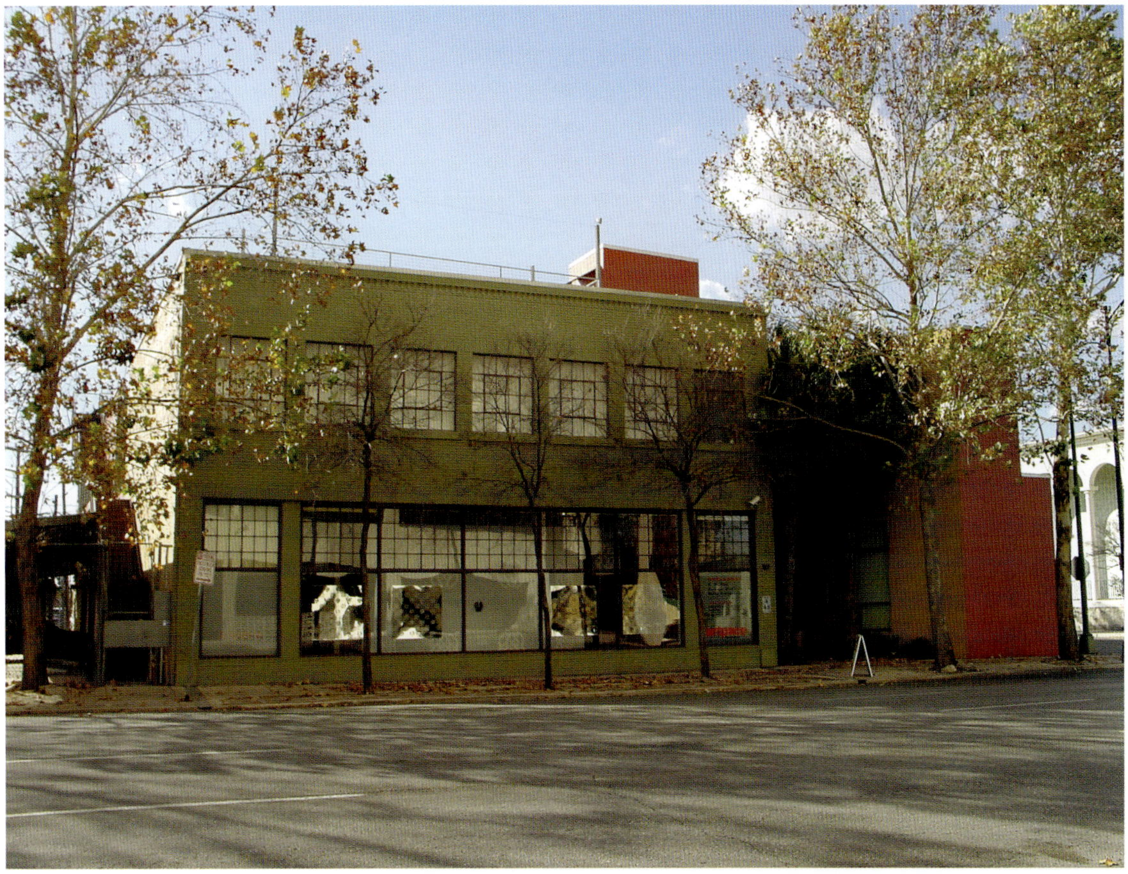

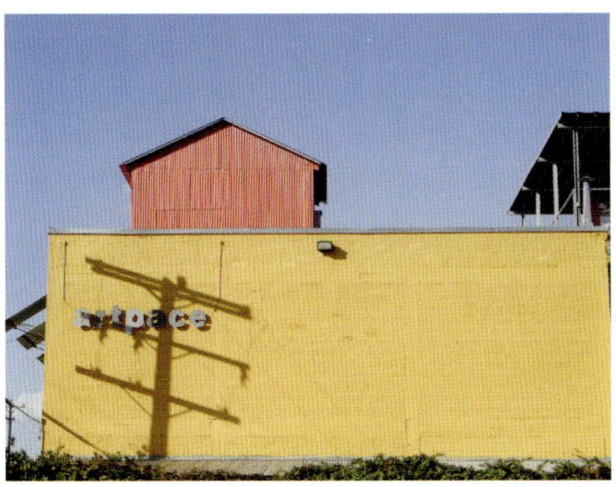

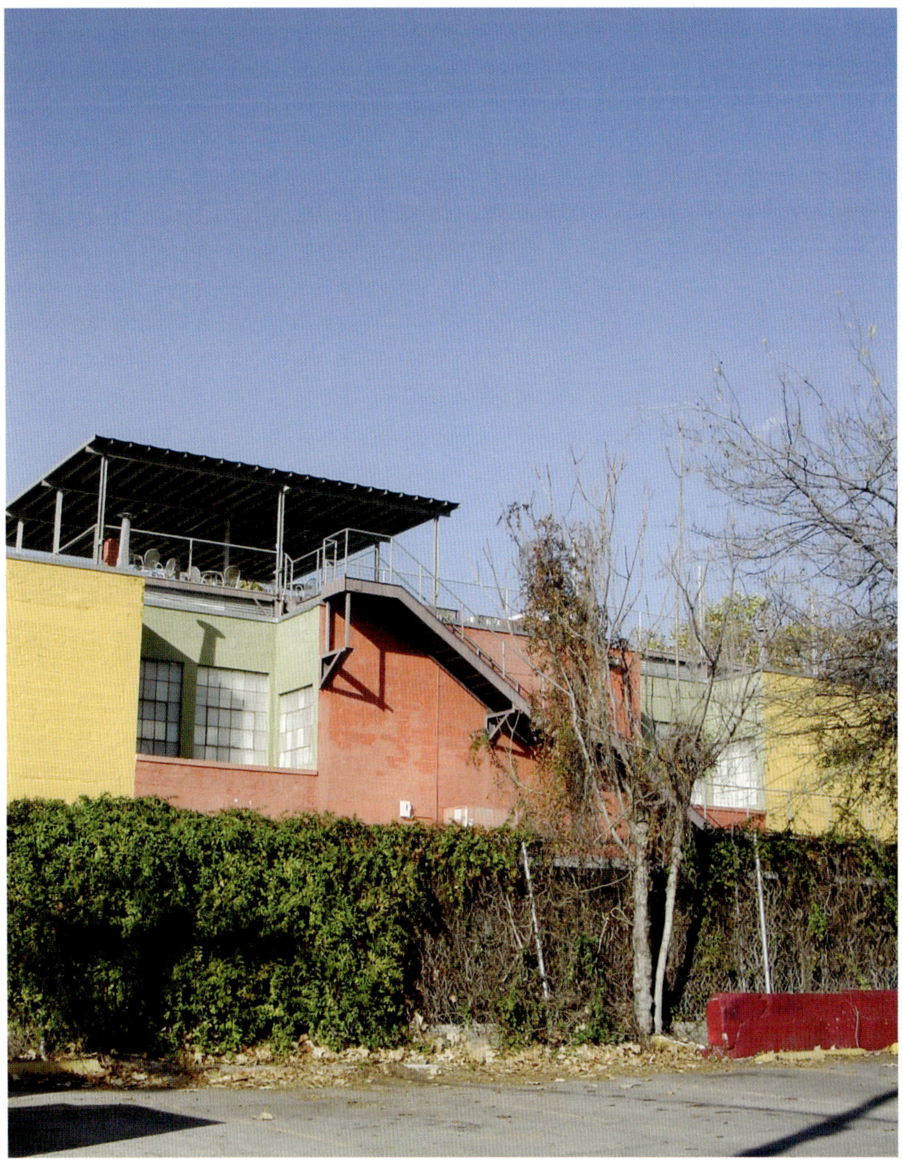

From any angle, Artpace makes a strong statement for contemporary art and architecture. *Photographs by David Strahan, AIA*

20

Casa 218

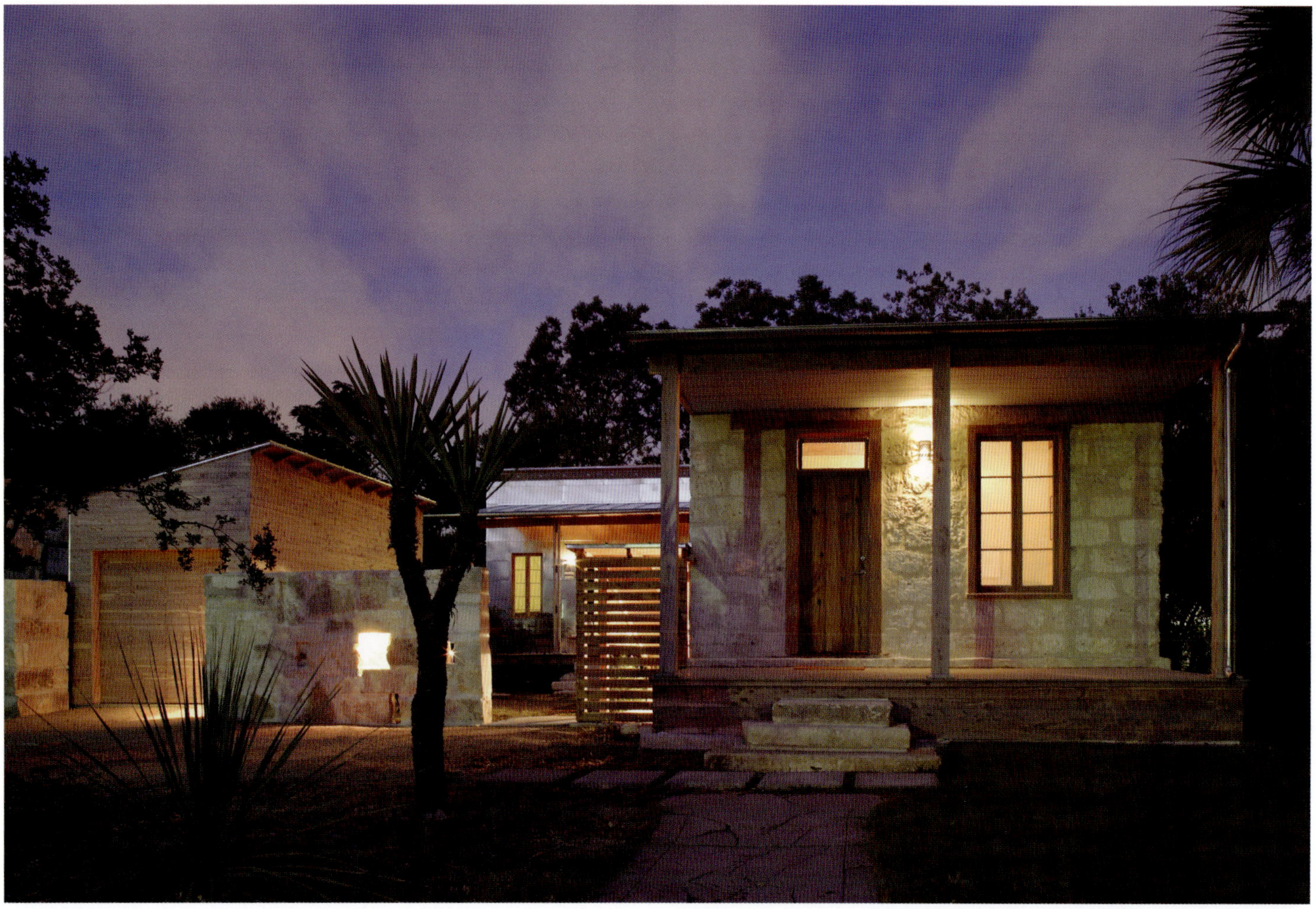

San Antonio is blessed with a number of original nineteenth century small cottages constructed of caliche. This light-colored native limestone with a soft matte finish is especially beautiful in the bright south Texas sun. This stone gives simple structures great dignity and timeless appeal. Current owners of many of these historic homes have lovingly brought them into this century without losing one scintilla of original charm. If you've seen one updated caliche cottage, you definitely have not seen them all.

Architect Candid Rogers updated a caliche cottage in Lavaca, an area with strong appeal to artists, architects, realtors, and those interested in the arts. The increasingly popular area is adjacent to the historic downtown King William area and Blue Star, a thriving complex of galleries and studios. "Casa 218 was built in 1873," says Rogers. "The original volume of the two-room limestone residence was little more than 500 square feet, with a 500 square foot basement. Then, the basement," he explains, "was the owner's living space. Today, it is the owner-architect's studio."

"A 960 square foot addition to the original structure includes a kitchen, two bathrooms, and two bedrooms,"

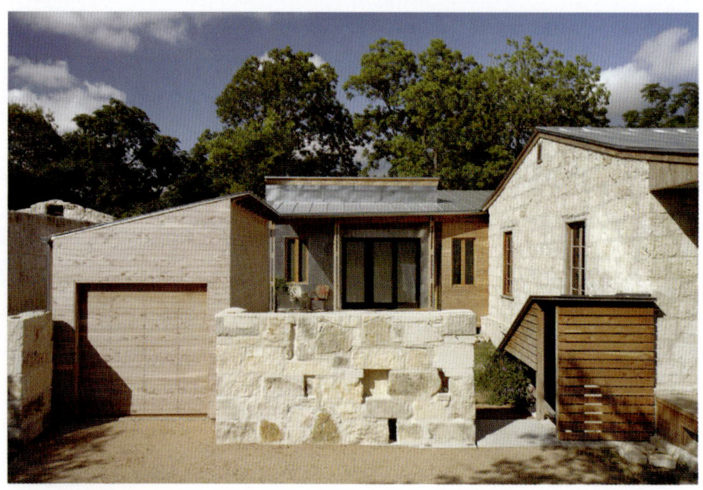

A decorative stone wall and garage add new horizontality to Casa 218.

says Rogers. "My design sets the new addition in back of the existing residence, sensitively connecting the new structure to the rear of the old. Doing this allows uninterrupted place and undisturbed siting for the original building." Placing new

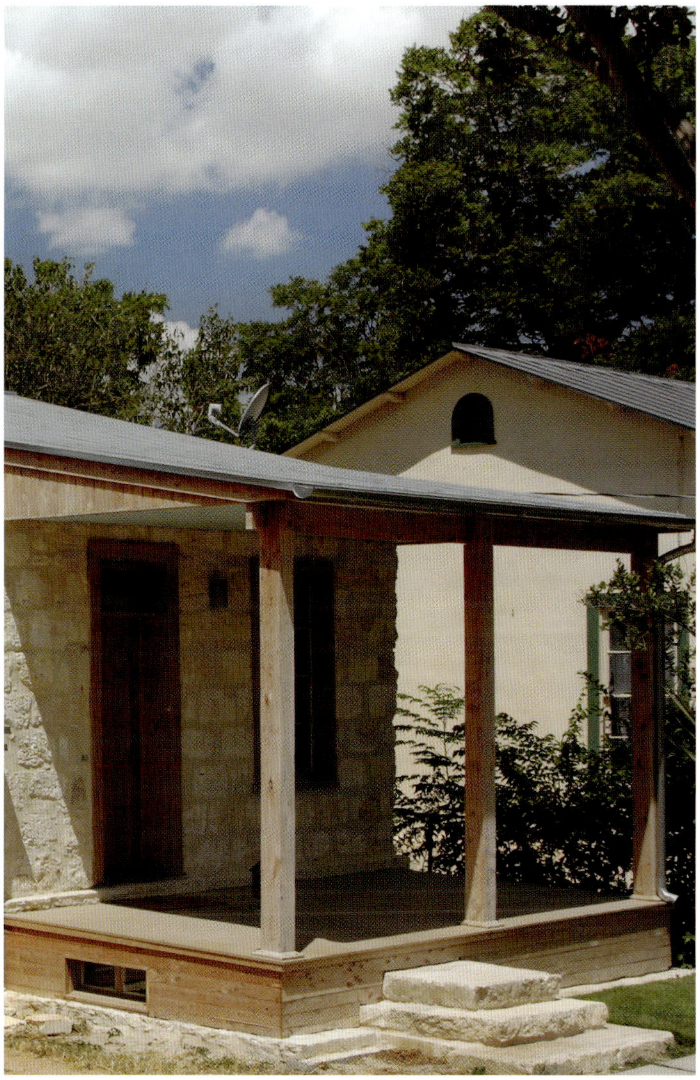

Deep porches thematically unite the existing cottage and a new rear addition.

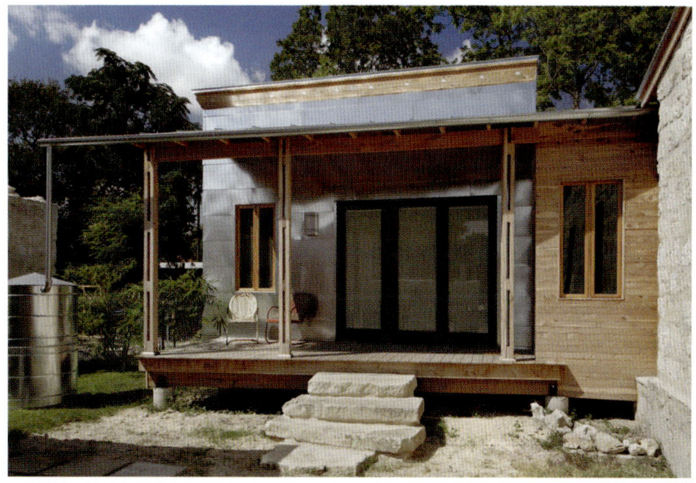

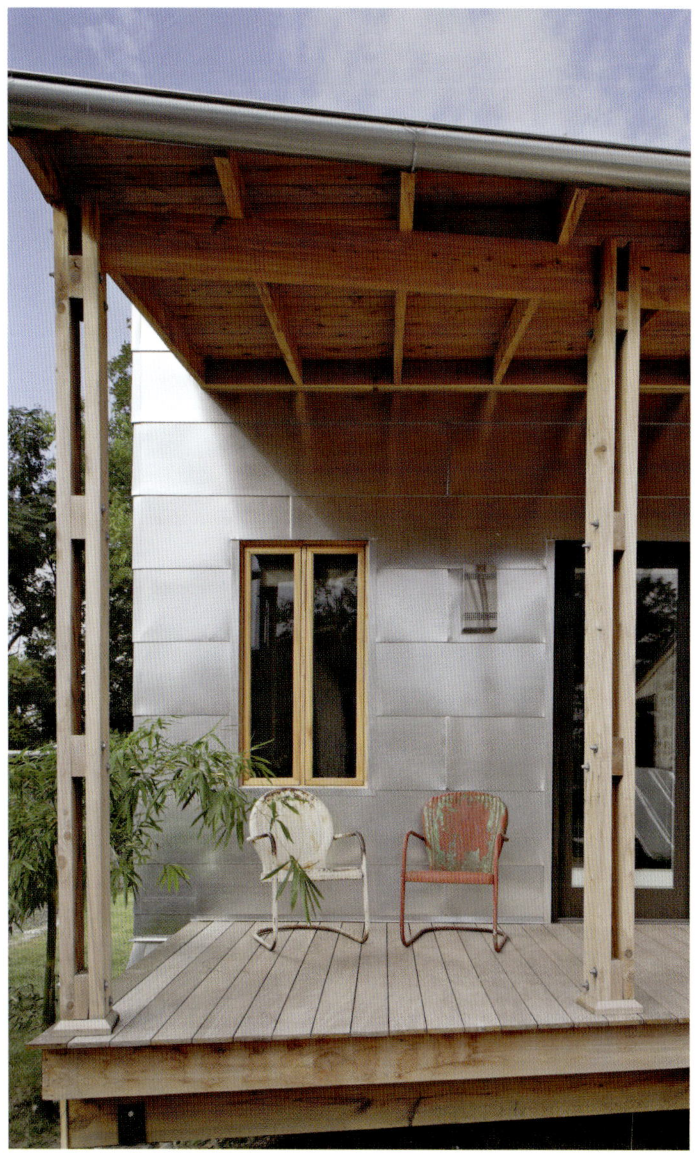

bedrooms and baths in the rear of the house, away from the street, also thoughtfully provides privacy and greater quiet for these areas. A bonus is the sheltered courtyard created between the existing house, new garage, and the new addition—a feature especially welcome in the inner-city. The courtyard offers a private outdoor space.

Rogers chose native Texas cedar siding and galvanized wall and roof panels for the new addition's exterior. "These materials, which have a long tradition in Texas vernacular architecture, are complementary to the original stone house," he says. Interiors feature painted walls and natural cork tile floors. The electrical and mechanical system were updated throughout with the addition. New rooms sizes remain intimate and customary of the period. Ceiling heights vary between nine and ten feet.

Changes to the original structure include removing the ceiling to expose existing timbers and create a dramatic new vaulted ceiling, expressing the original wood structure. A layer of insulation was added above the roof deck. Old longleaf pine floors and wood trim were refinished.

There is an increasing effort by architects and others to make San Antonio a "green" city. "This project features passive climatic design," says Rogers. "There is a rainwater collection system and the new landscape uses native plants." With this sophisticated, sensitive architectural design, Rogers has given Casa 218 a new lease on life in a city that values its history and cares for its historic homes.

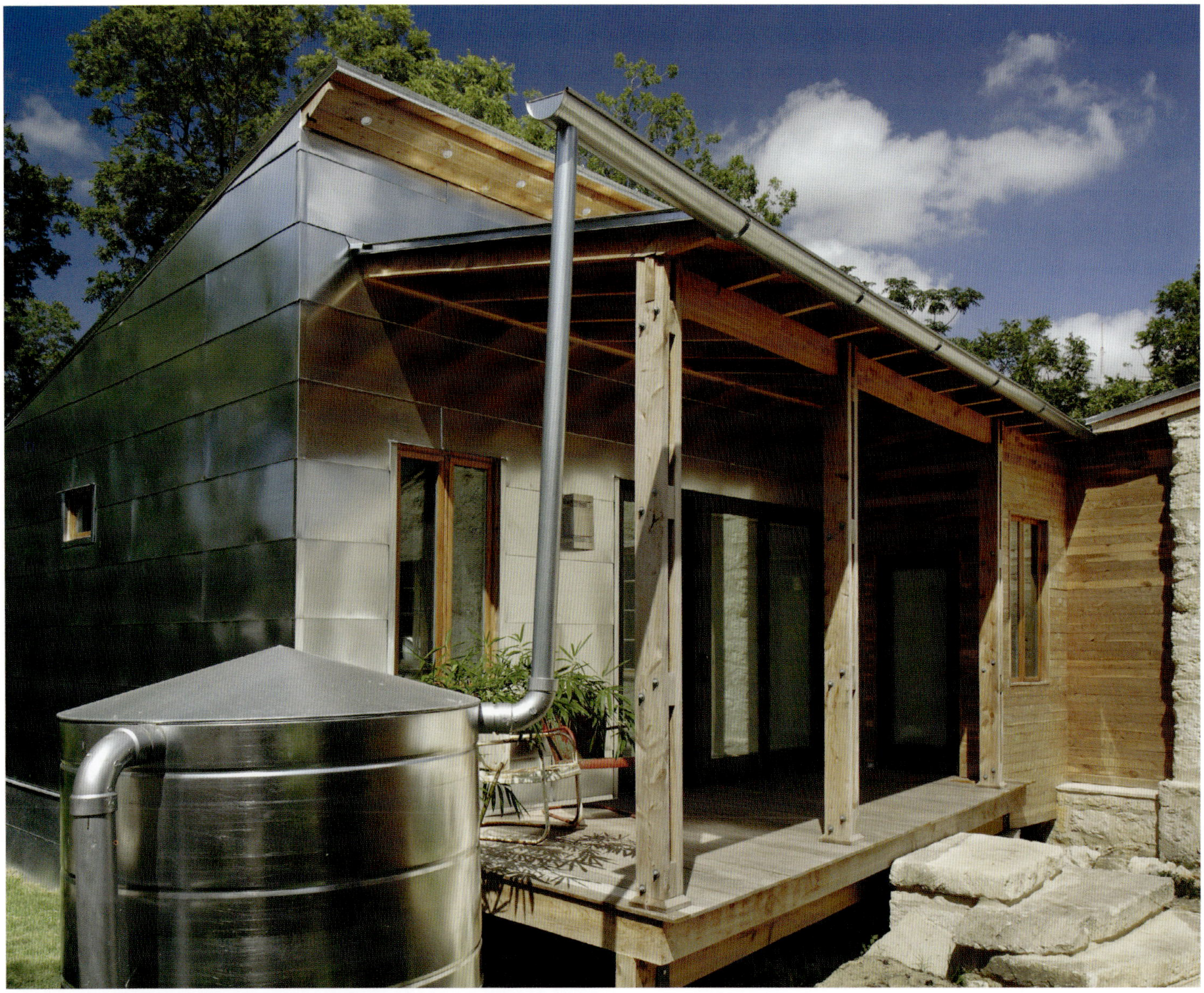

Gutters direct rainwater into a galvanized storage tank.

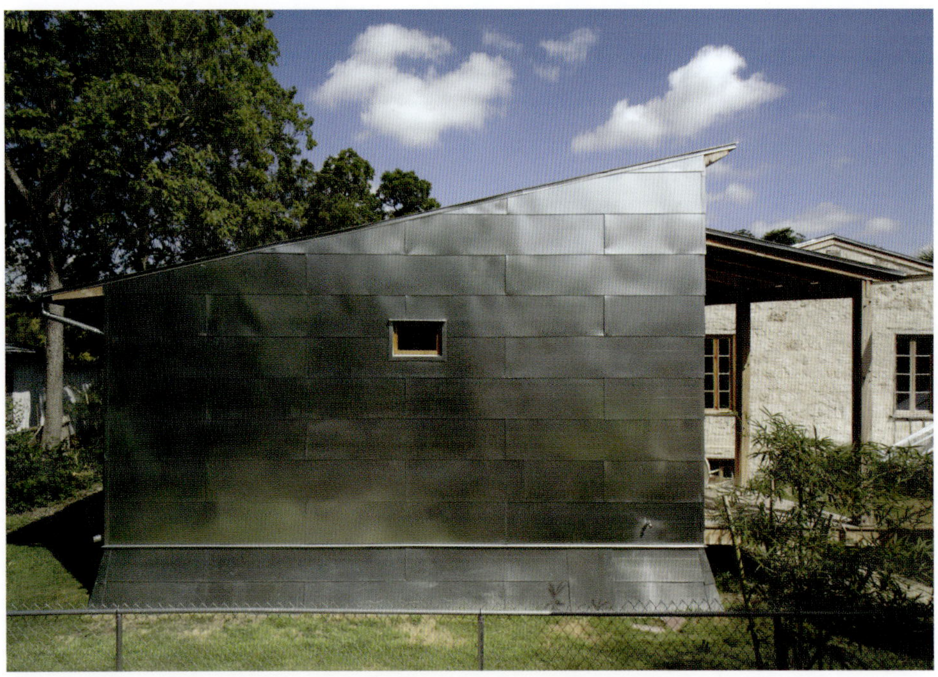

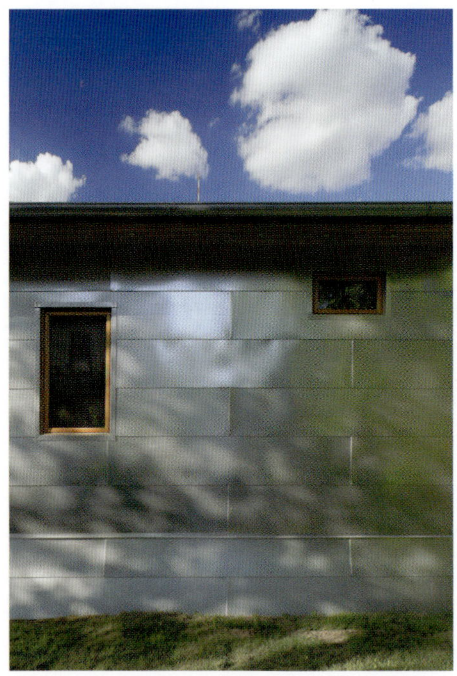

Galvanized metal panels clad the exterior of the addition.

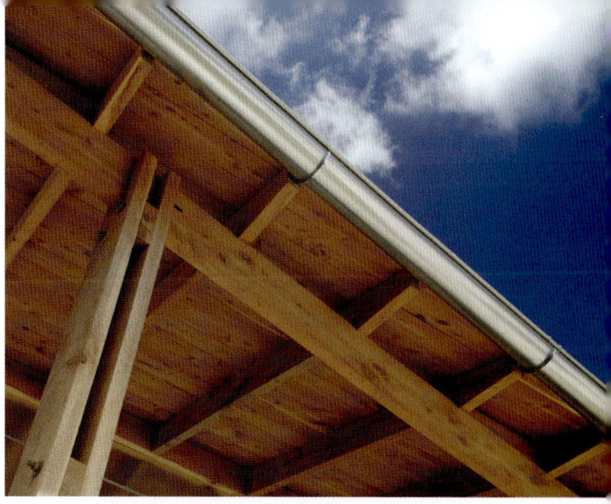

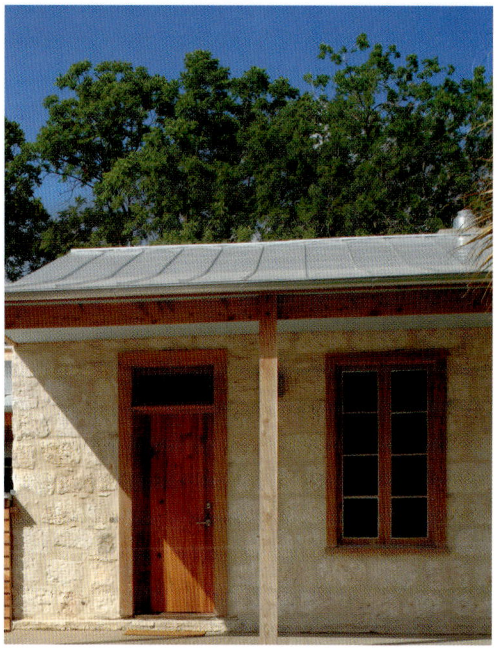

Restoration of the original residence used original materials, while materials for the new addition include native Texas cedar.

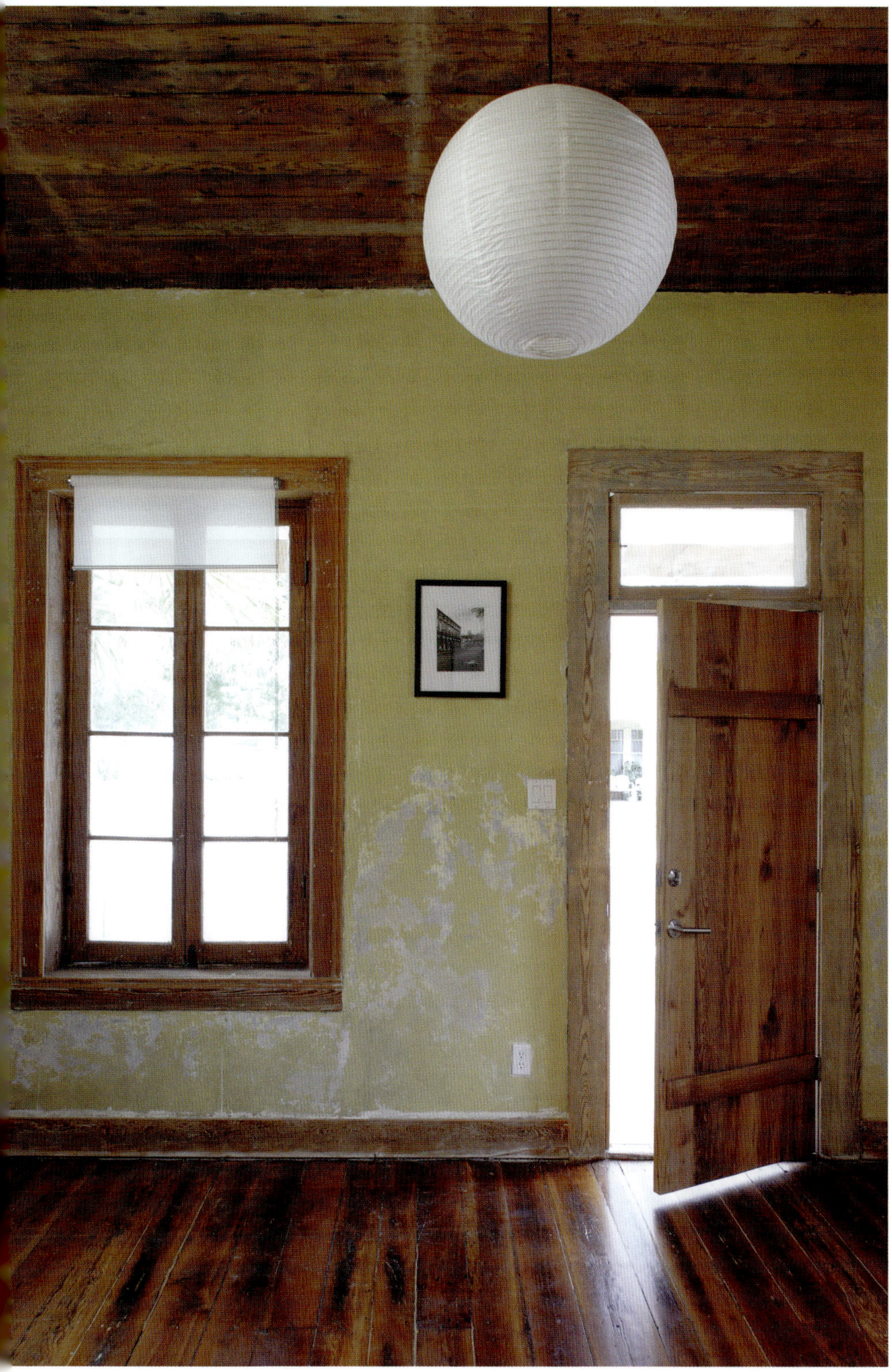

Deliberate design simplicity places great emphasis on the unique qualities of caliche stone and rugged native timbers throughout the restoration and renovation.

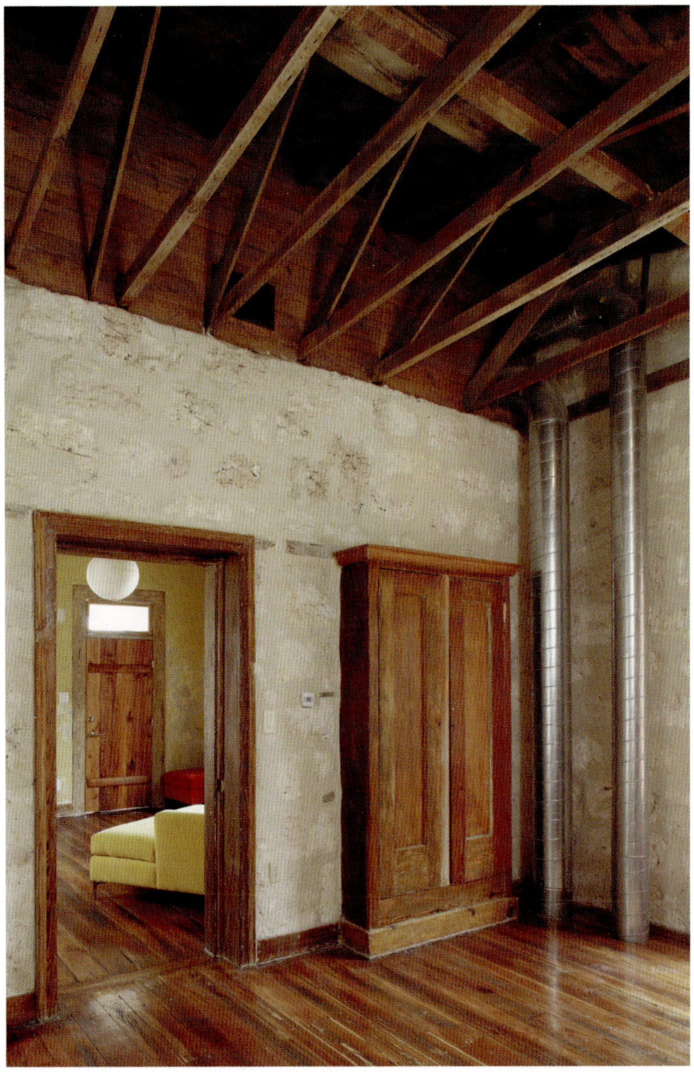

Removing the low ceiling and exposing ceiling timbers add height and visual interest to the entry.

A stairway leads to the original basement, home of early owners and now an office for the owner-architect.

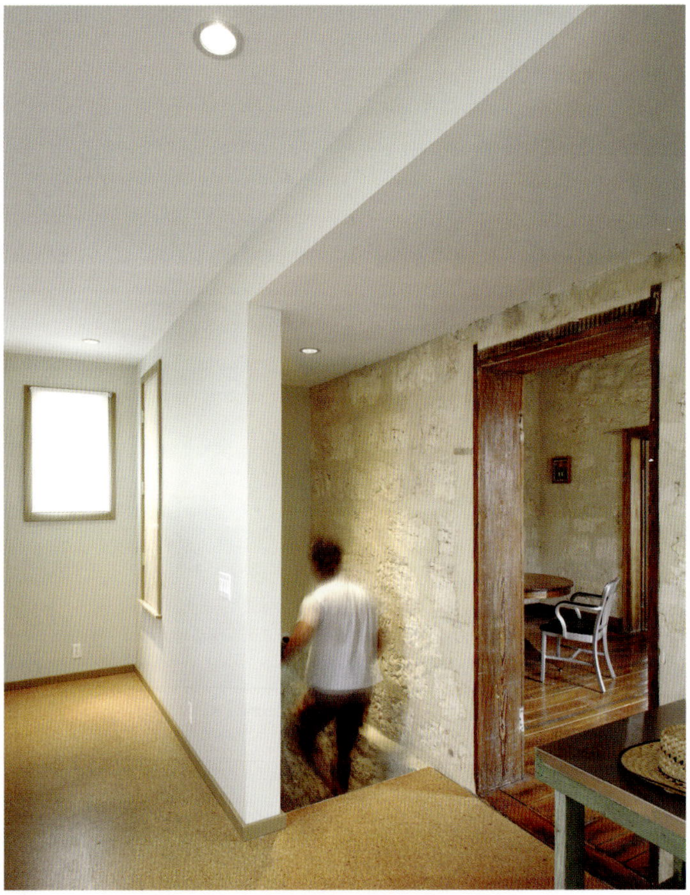

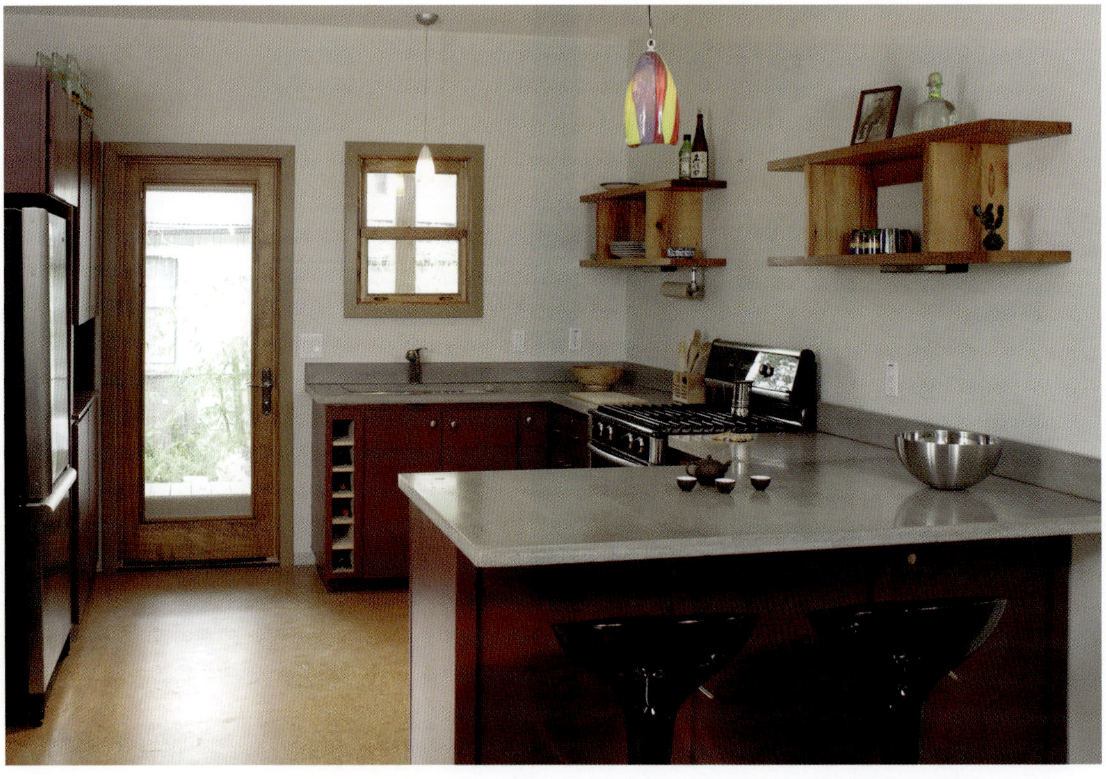

Using only base cabinets creates greater sense of space in the renovated kitchen.

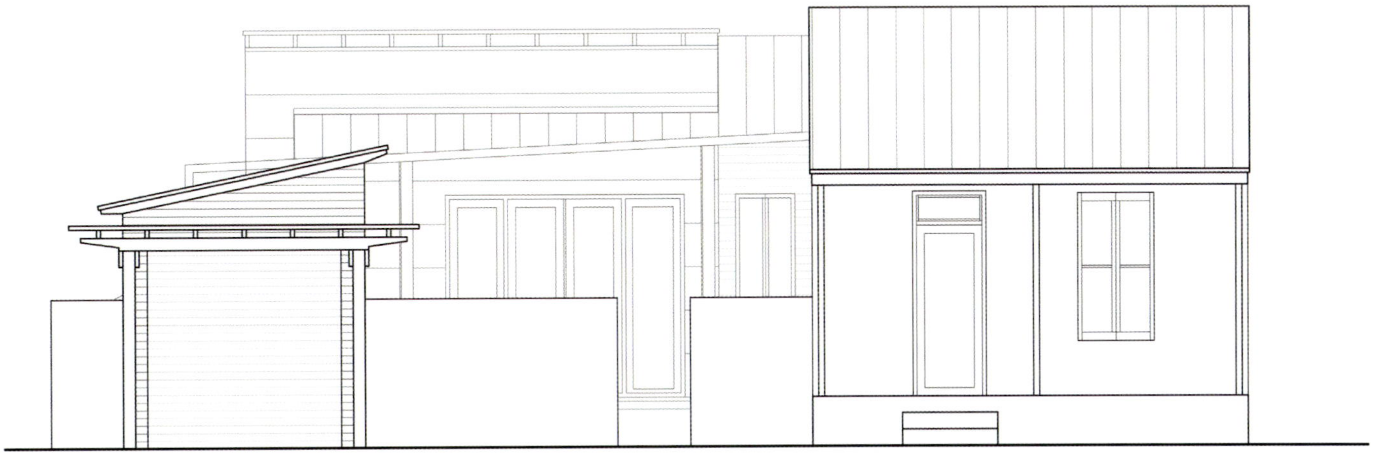

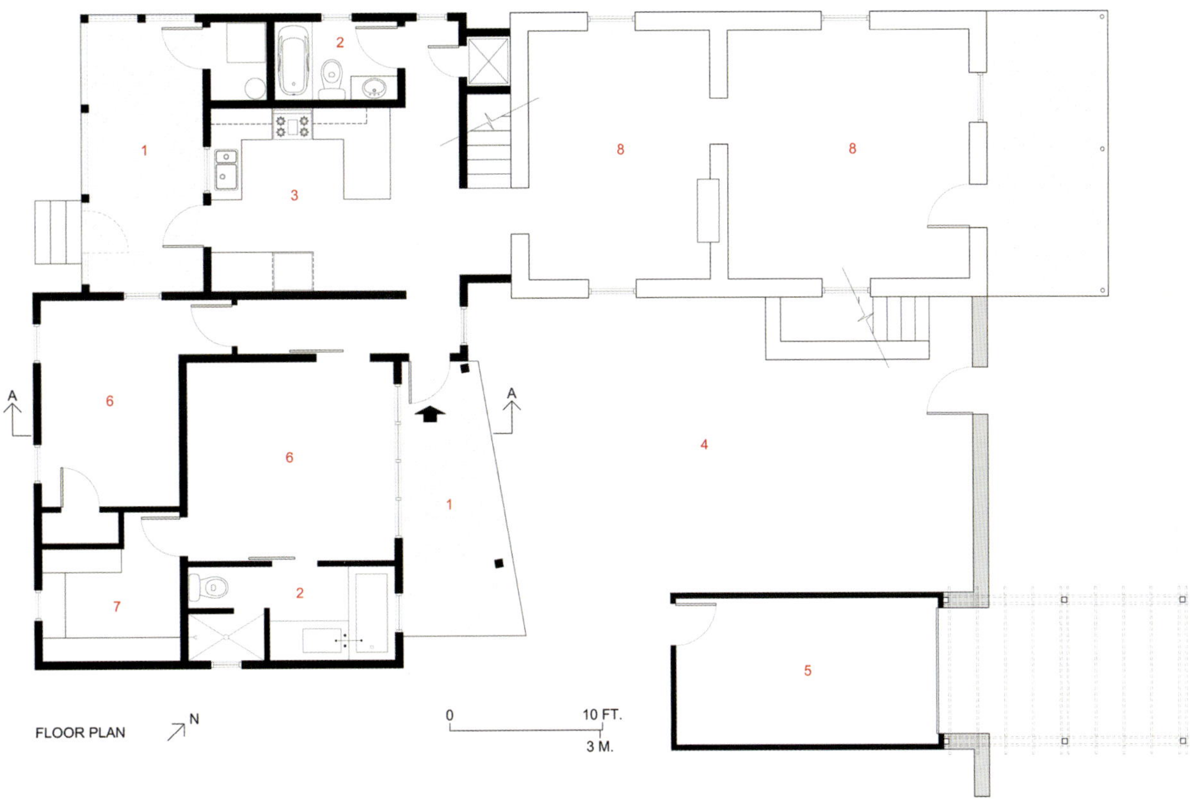

1 PORCH
2 BATH
3 KITCHEN
4 COURTYARD
5 GARAGE
6 BEDROOM
7 CLOSET
8 EXISTING

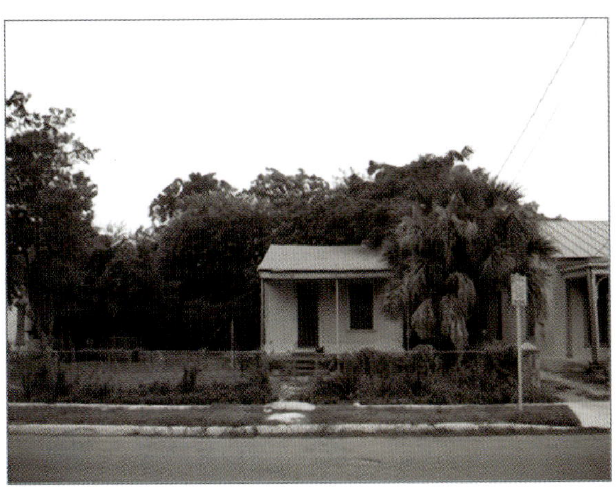

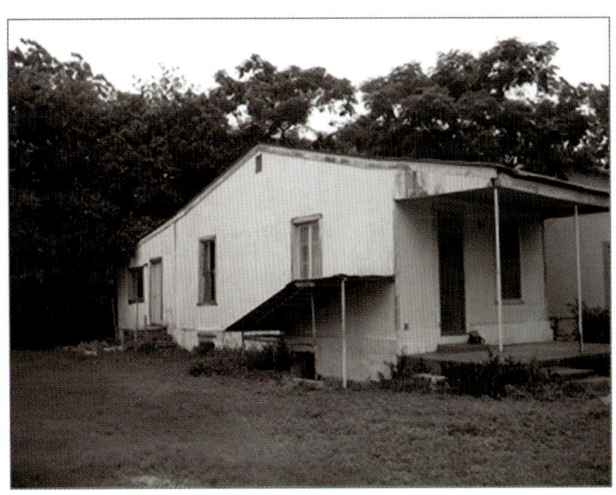

Before: front and side views.

21
Dos Diez

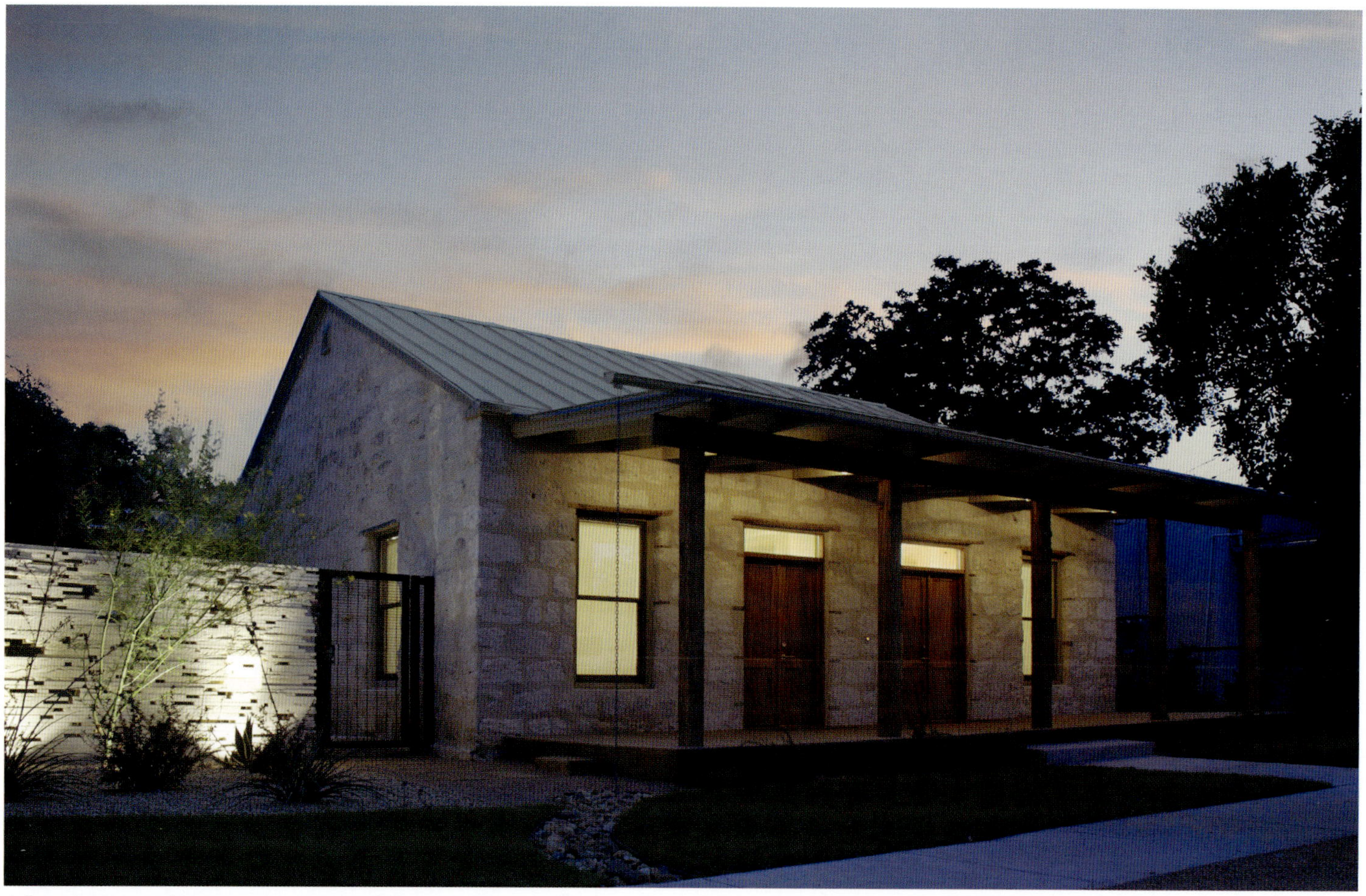

A handsome wall creates a courtyard that screens sophisticated additions and provides privacy for outdoor living.
Photographs by Bailey Porter, courtesy Architect Candid Rogers

This sophisticated, art-filled dwelling—originally a 1,000-square-foot cottage built in 1871 and known as the Bippert-Judd House—was hiding behind a chain-link fence, overgrown yard, and whimsically painted trim. Still, those who love native Texas limestone structures and are ready for a downtown lifestyle with its nearby art galleries could recognize its real potential. And, they could appreciate its Lavaca location. In 2009, new owners called on Candid Rogers, a San Antonio architect well versed in the restoration and redesign of caliche (limestone) cottages, to transform this house from eyesore to eye-popping.

"Through the years, changes had been made to the property," says Rogers. "In the 1970s, a 560-square-foot addition housing a kitchen, dining room, and bathroom had been added. In 2004, a secondary structure consisting of a two-story garage/studio was built at the rear of the site." Rogers new design provided 2,300 square feet of new living space.

Restoration and remodeling began by removing the inappropriate 1970s addition. "A new 1,606 square foot addition was planned for placement at the rear of the site. This allowed a sensitive connection between the original cottage, the redesigned garage (new bedroom wing), and the new kitchen/dining space that links those two structures," he says.

The existing cottage remained as the main entry. Two home offices with sliding barn doors flank the entryway, which opens into a large, open main living area. Following the living area is a transitional space with polished cement floors and a window wall that looks out at the new courtyard created by placement of the new addition and redesigned garage. Beyond the transition space, the kitchen leads to the modern addition, which houses a ground floor master bedroom and two second-story guest bedrooms.

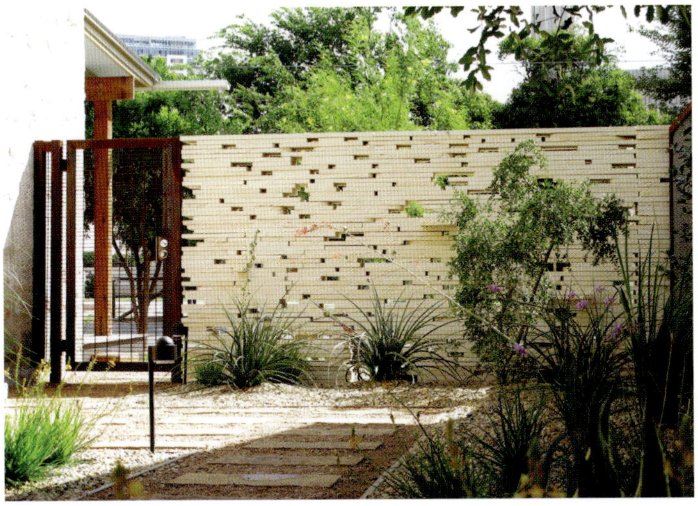

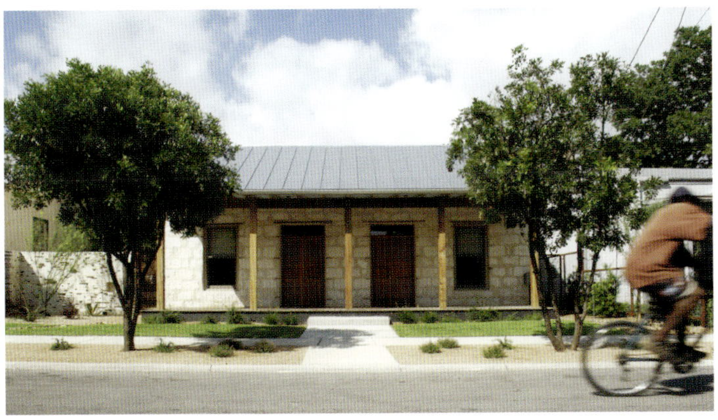

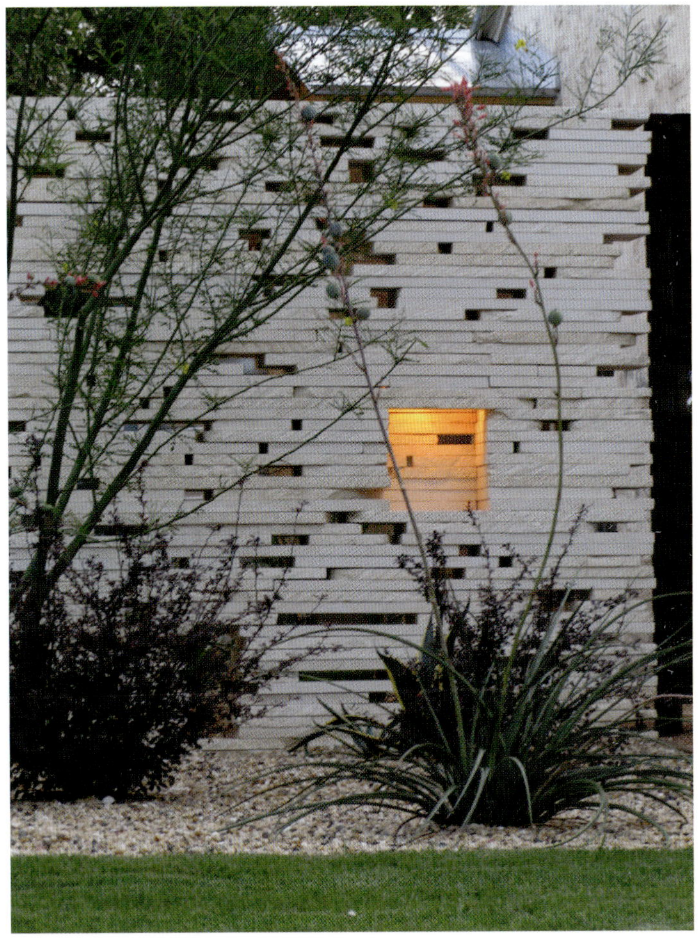

"The house now centers around a southeast-facing courtyard fitted with a pool, fire pit, 400-gallon rainwater cistern, and an herb garden near the kitchen. The courtyard maximizes breezes and minimizes western sun exposure—a result of principal passive climatic techniques employed in the design. The site orientation minimizes solar heat gain and catches prevailing breezes. Shading devices provide welcome respite in outdoor spaces. Two 400-gallon rainwater collection cisterns supplement pool evaporation and are used to irrigate the landscape," Rogers explains. As for new structural materials, he says that western red cedar was chosen for its sustainable qualities and to accentuate the local native limestone.

An unusual eco-conscious gesture was the harvesting of an on-site ailing pecan tree. "We used this fine lumber to create a new dining table and bed frame for *doz Diez*," says Rogers.

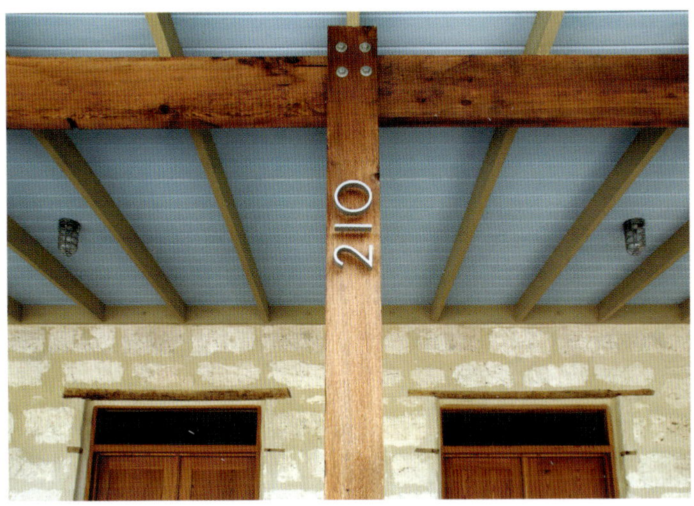

The restored façade of an 1872 caliche (limestone) block house keeps secret the interior renovations and contemporary additions by Architect Candid Rogers. *Photographs by Bailey Porter, courtesy Candid Rogers Architect*

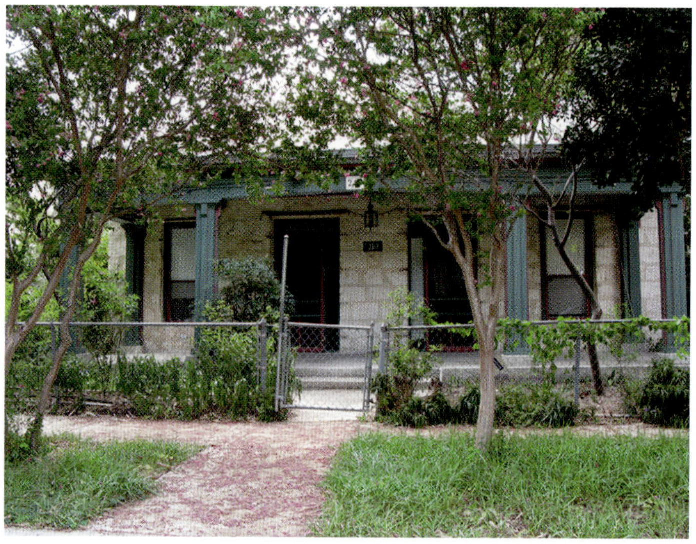

Before, Front.

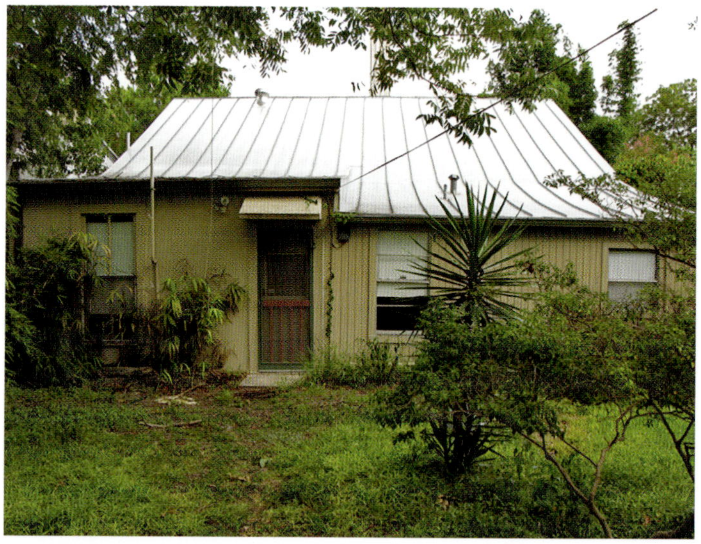

Before, Rear.

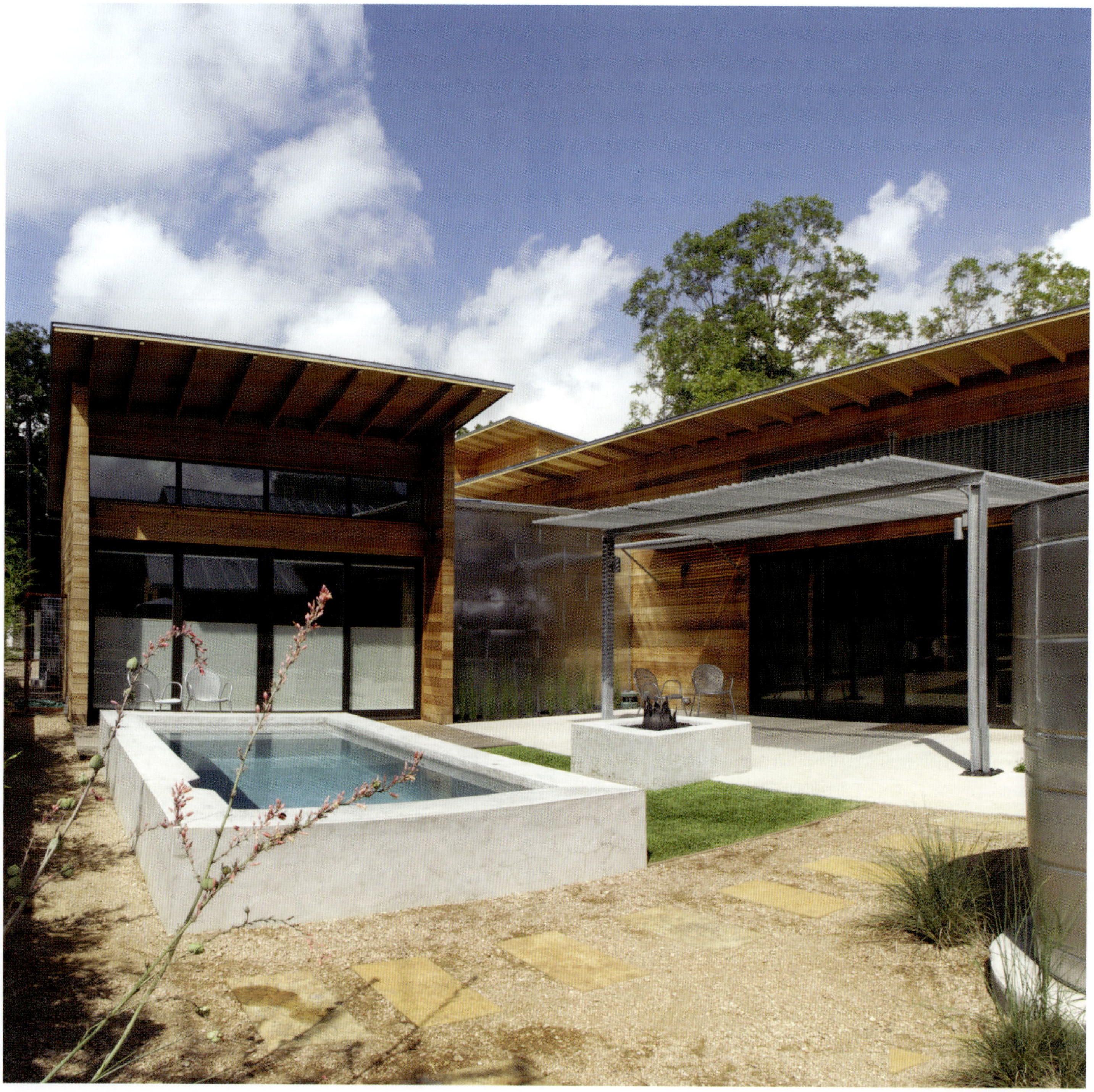

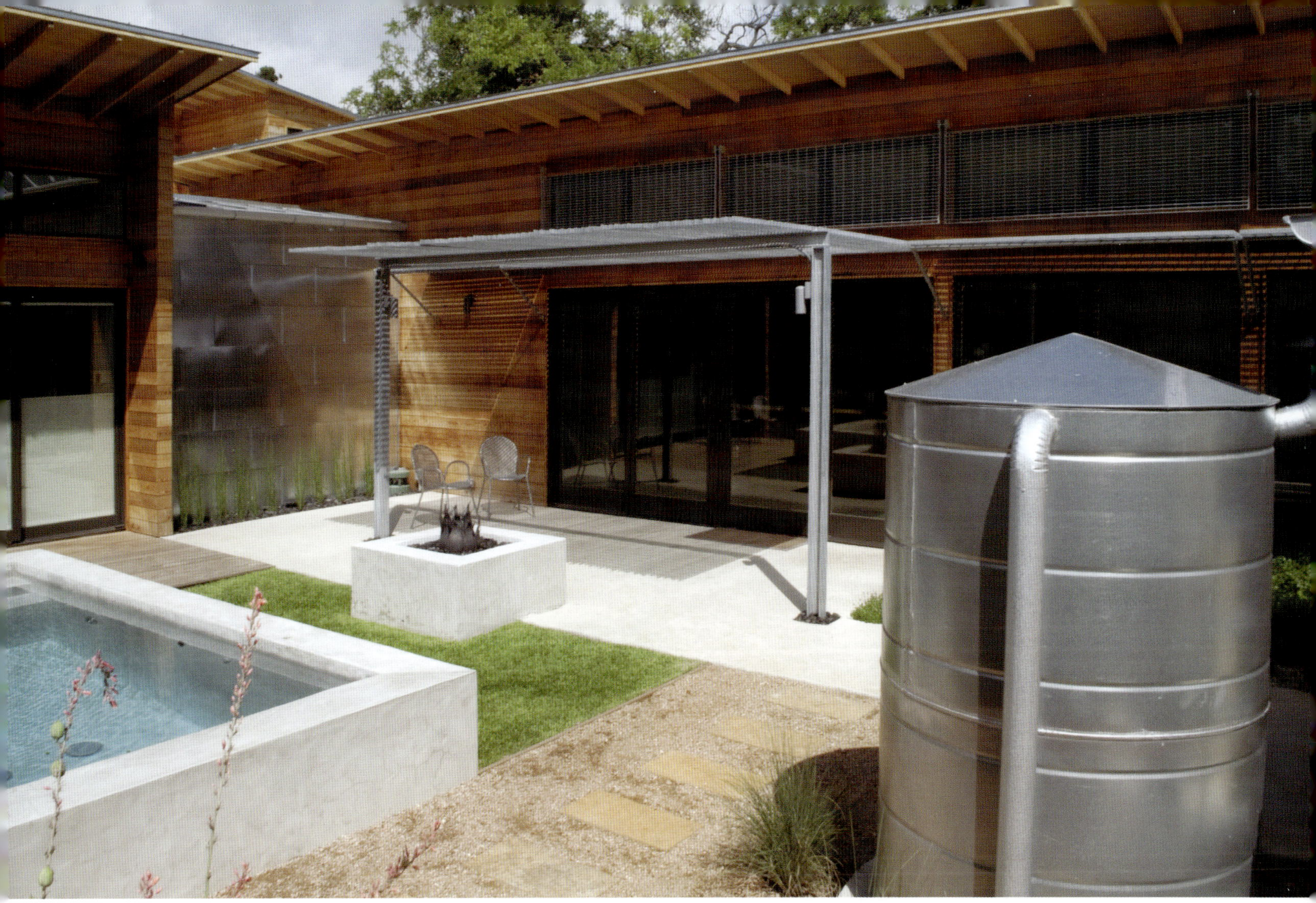

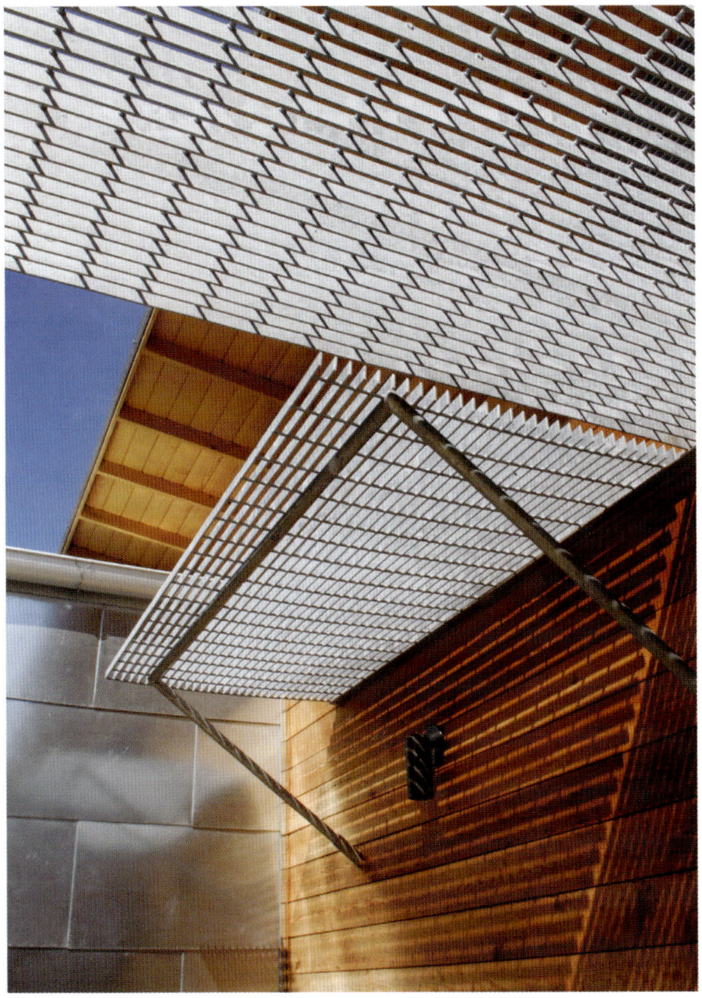

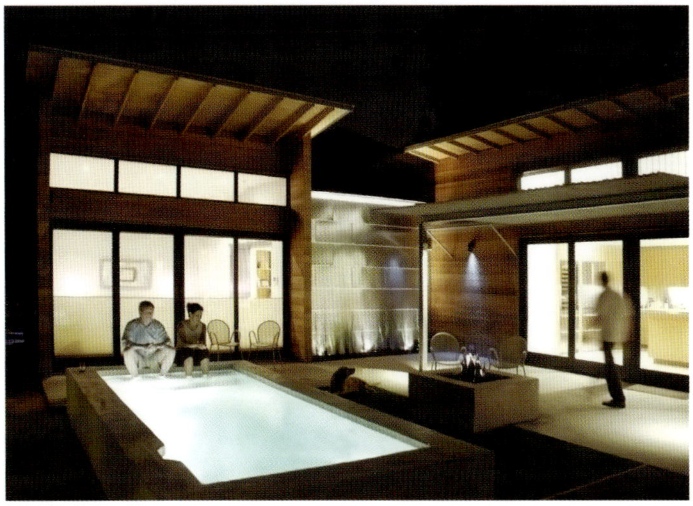

New covered patios, pool, and landscaping transform the newly formed courtyard into an oasis for entertaining, day and night.

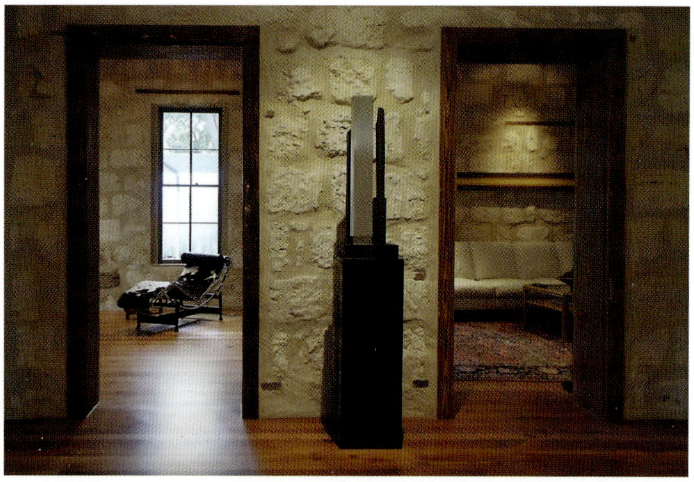

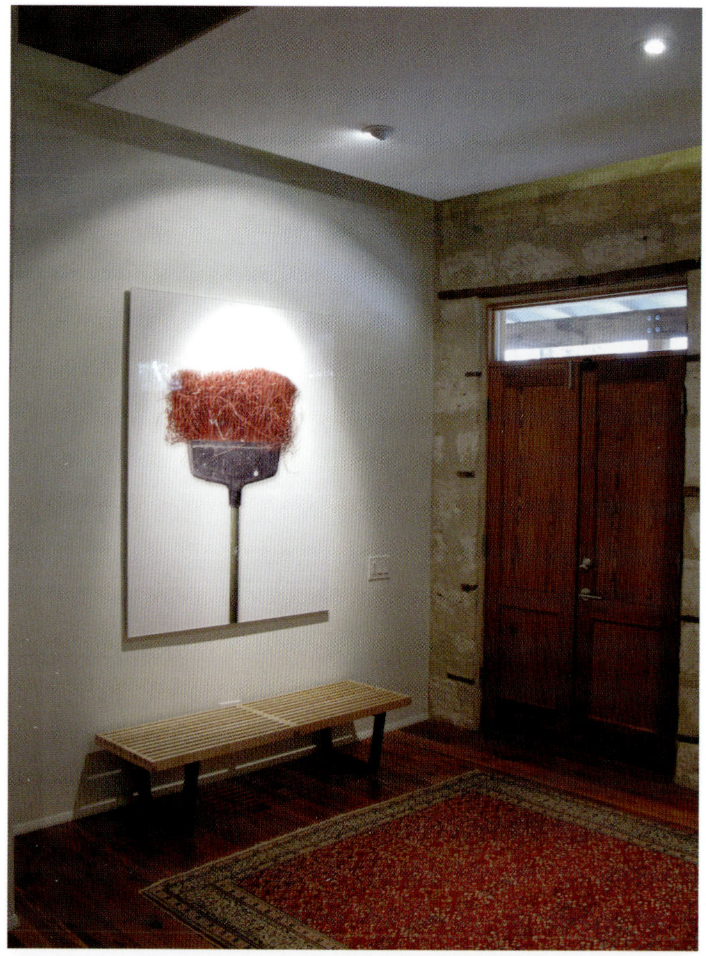

Twin doors open into a glamorous entry hall featuring freestanding large scale sculpture and wall-hung art by San Antonio artist Chuck Ramirez from his "Broom" series.

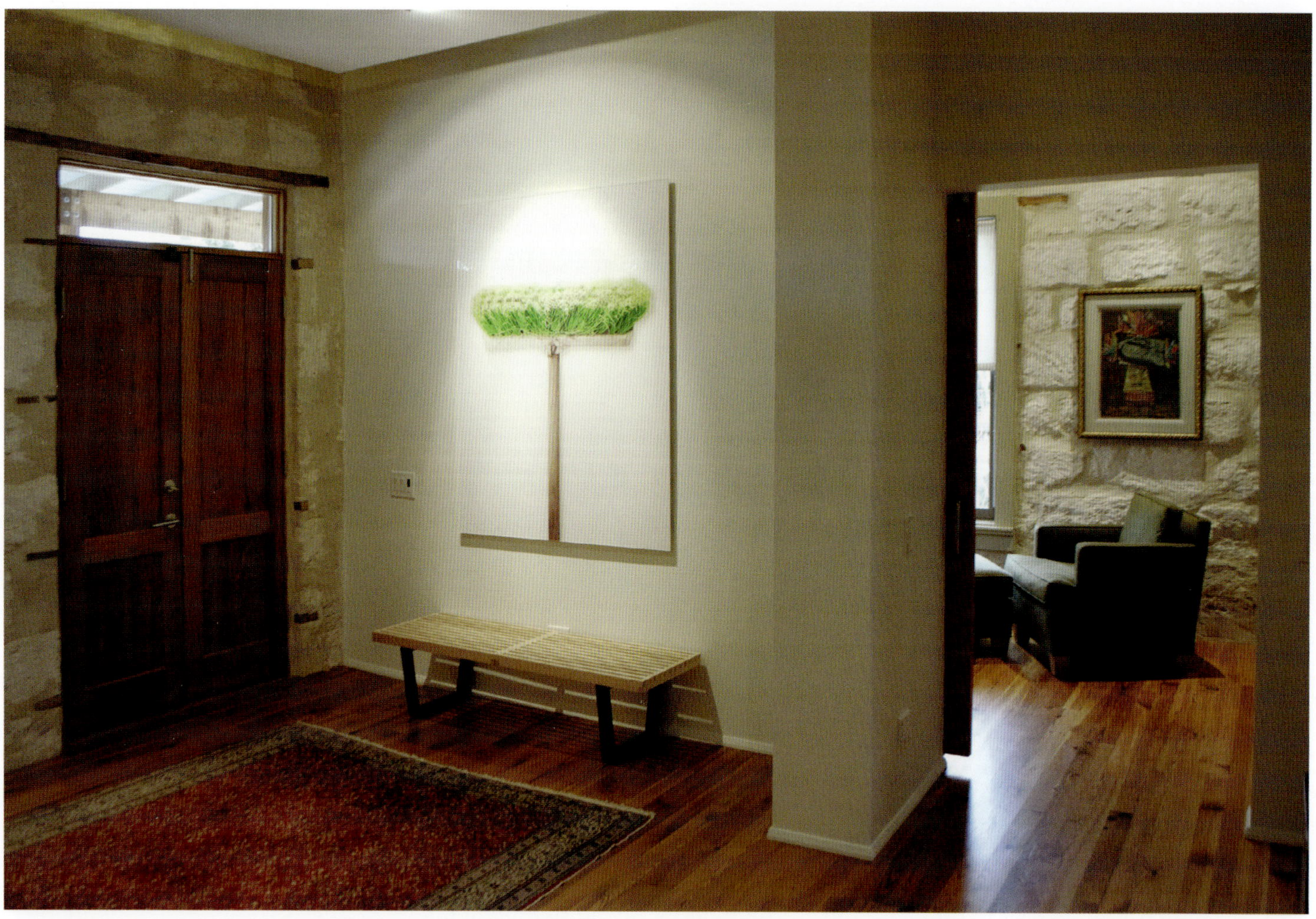

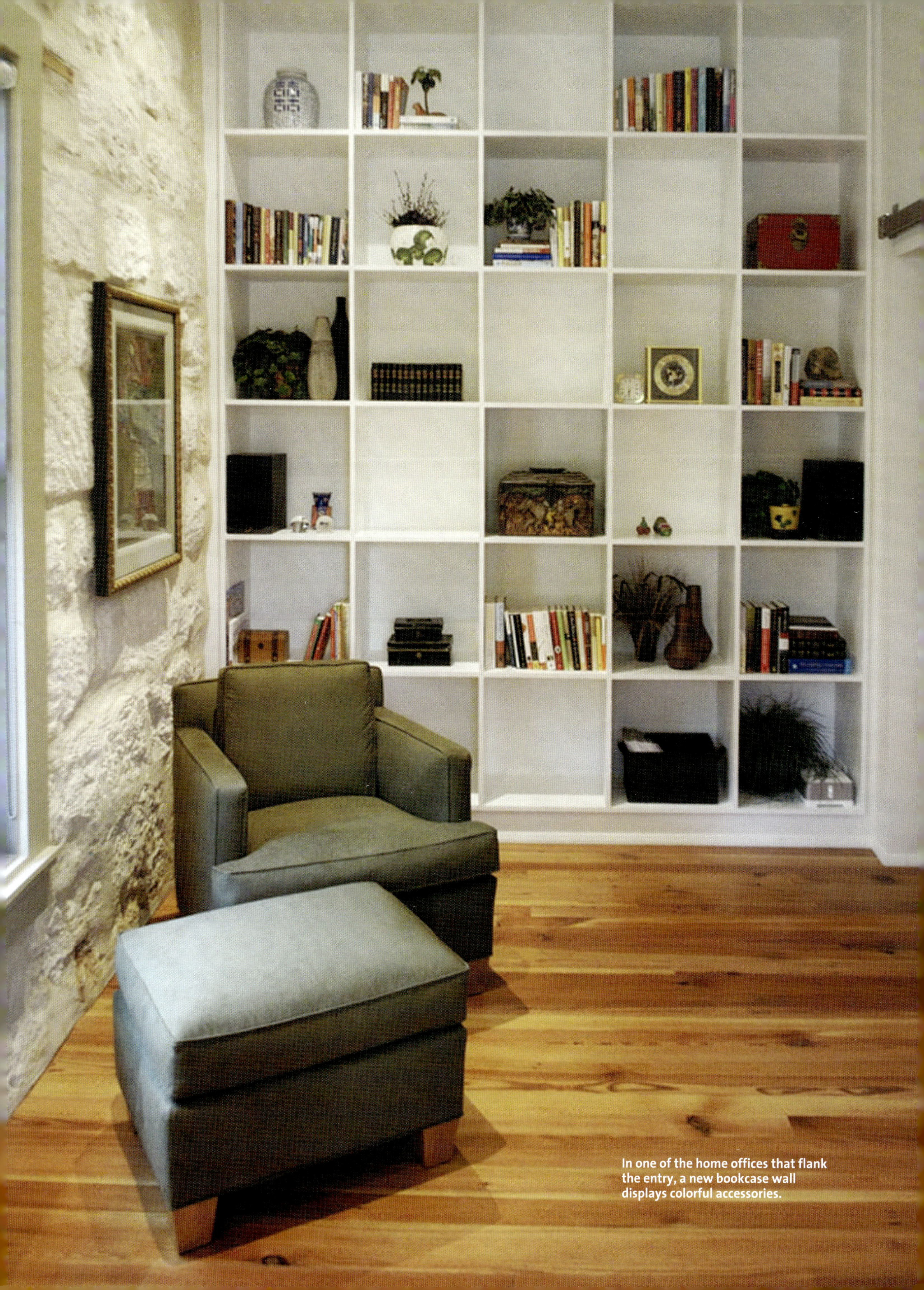

In one of the home offices that flank the entry, a new bookcase wall displays colorful accessories.

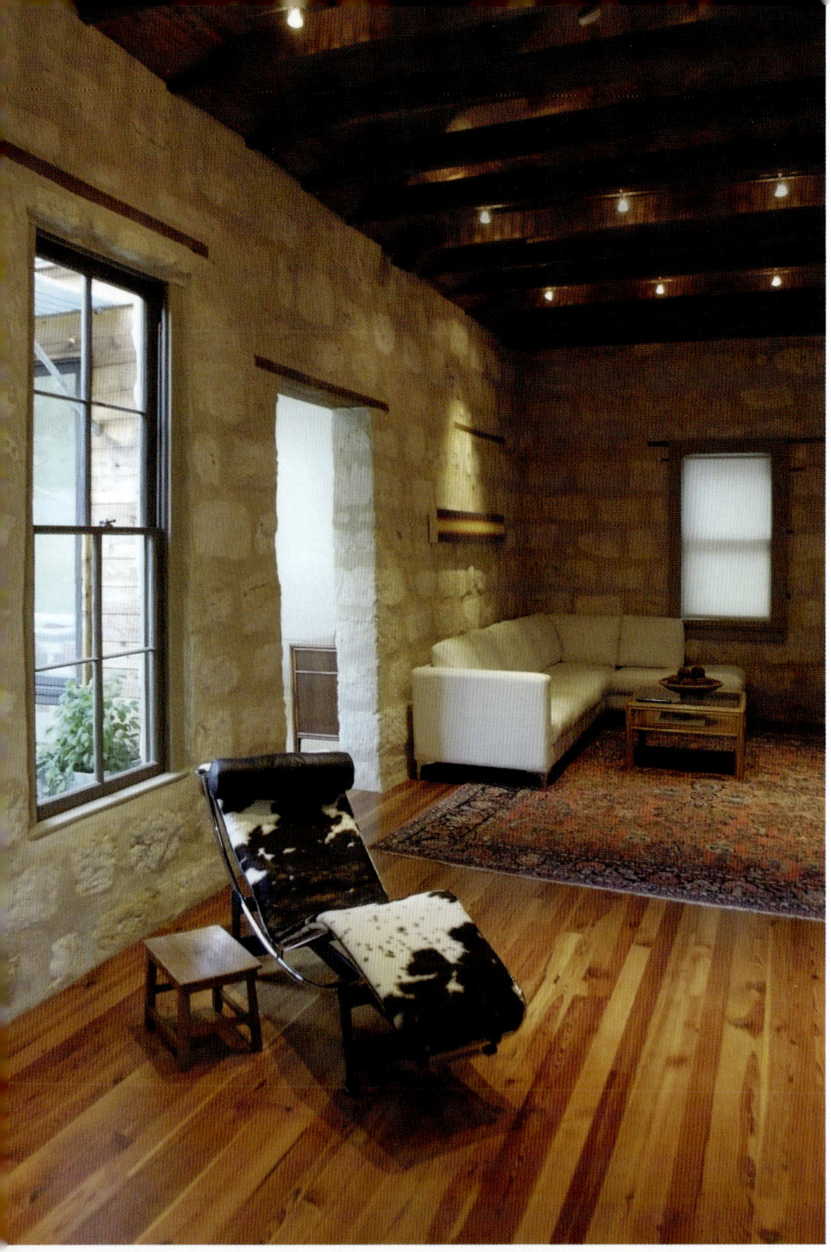

Adroitly the artful simplicity of the living room design lets the natural beauty of the caliche block and original timbers star.

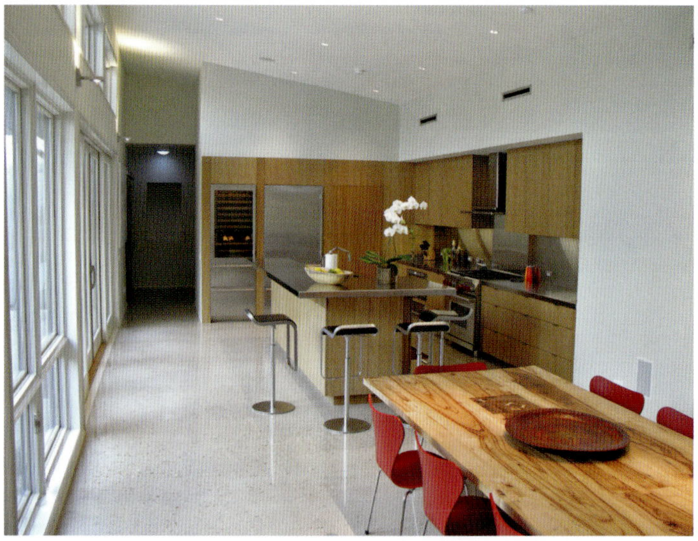

Polished cement flooring and light cabinetry underscore the contemporary mood in the renovated kitchen. The table was custom-crafted by artisan Peter Zubiate from a dead tree on the property.

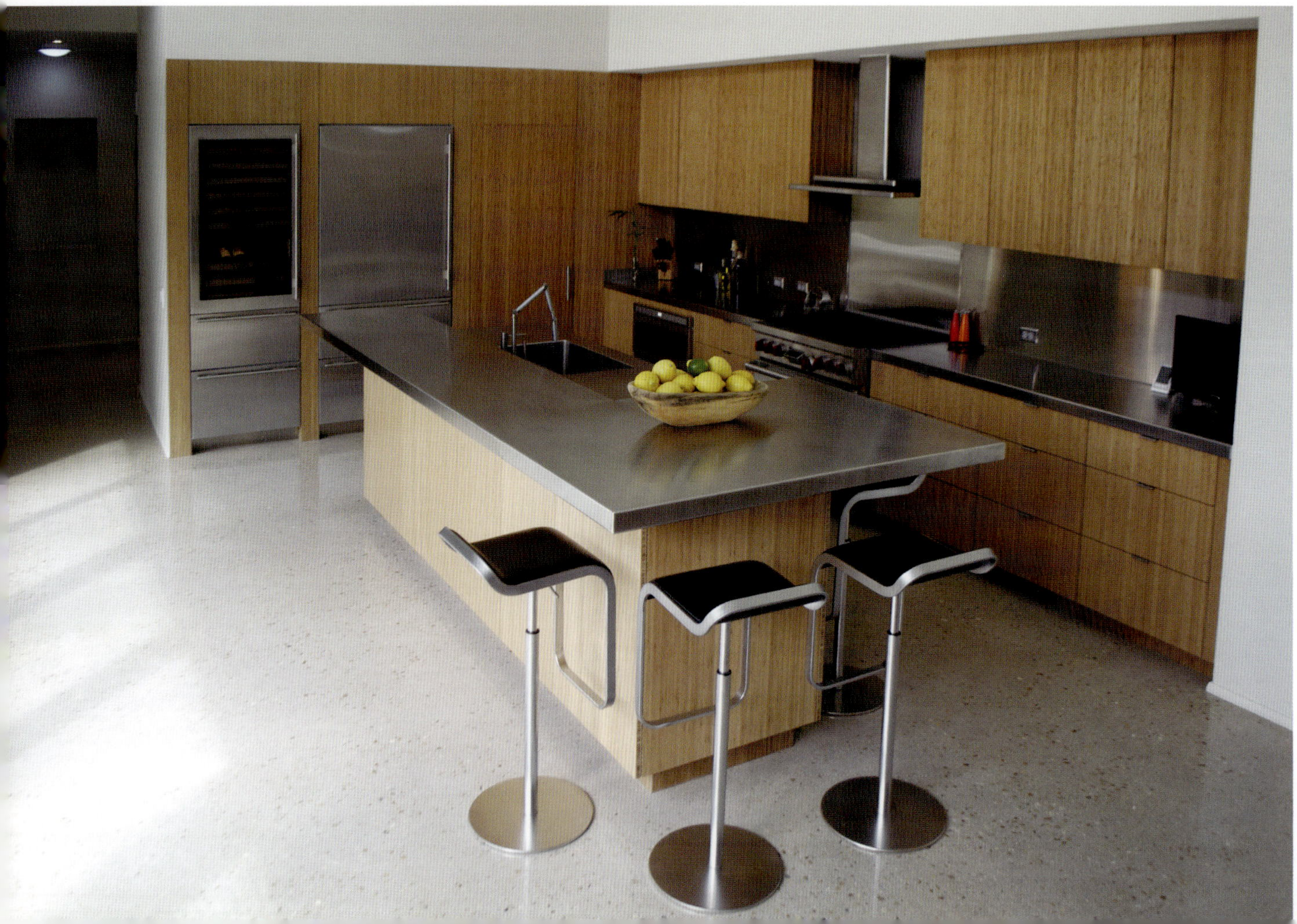

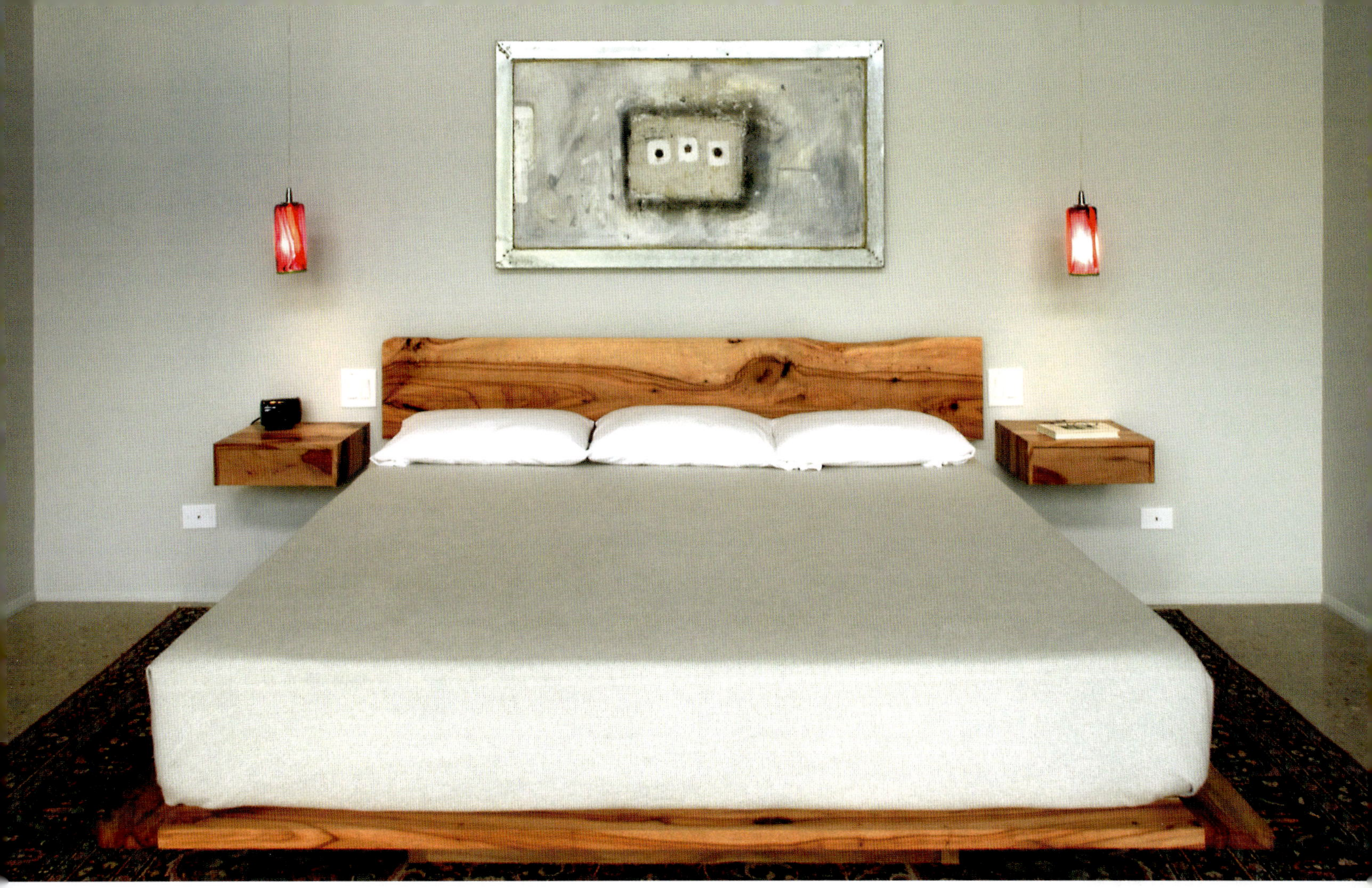

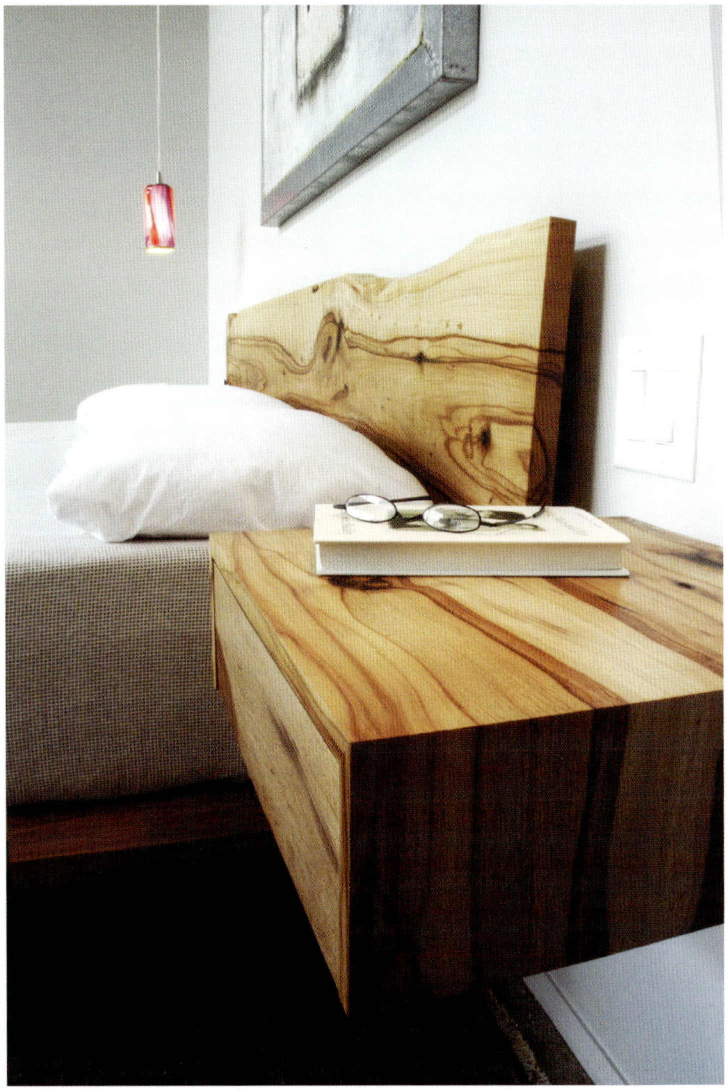

The master bedroom has a custom bed and nightstands crafted from the dead pecan tree found on the property.

22

Cooper House

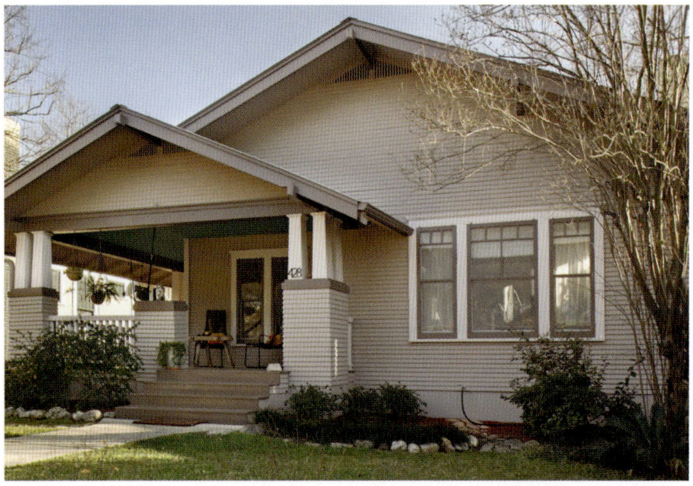

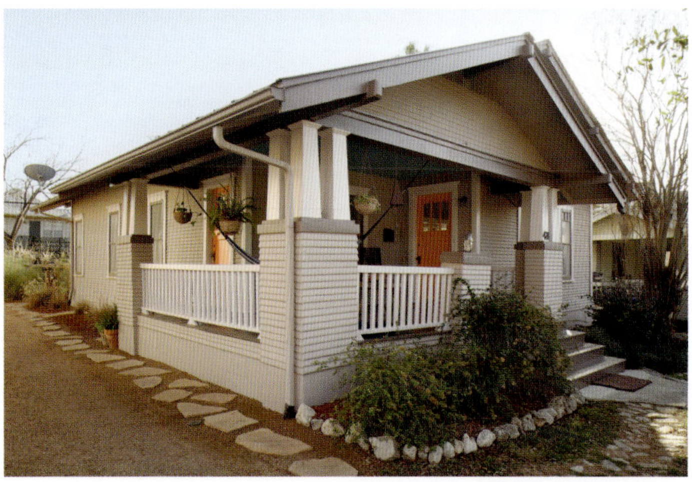

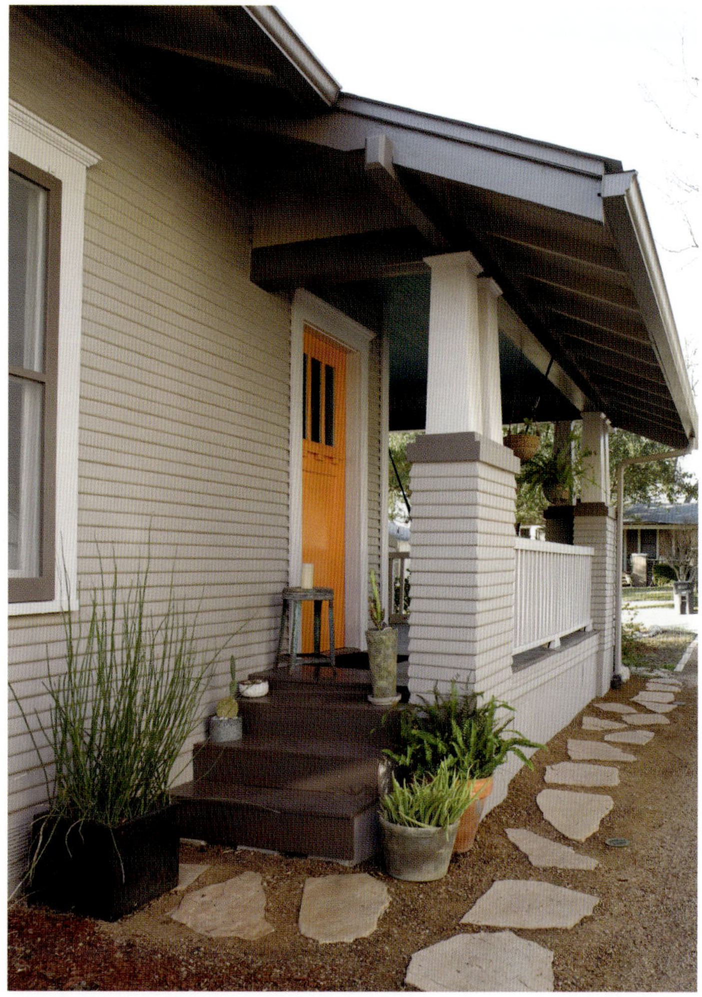

Frank Lloyd Wright's early 1900s plain-spoken Prairie Style architecture spread across the country like wildfire. Its influence is seen in this 1911 San Antonio house with its strong horizontality, low-silhouette roofline, strip of windows, and short support columns resting on solid square pedestals. *Photographs by Chris Cooper*

"The house we bought in the Fall of 2001 was structurally in very good shape, considering that very little had been done to it since it was built in 1916," says noted architectural photographer Chris Cooper. "The previous owners had remodeled the kitchen and bathroom, updated the wiring, sheet-rocked the interior, and added a metal roof. We installed a new HVAC (heat, vent, air conditioning) system." But, it is the redecorating by the Coopers in their own personal style that brings this house, that owes its architectural origin to Frank Lloyd Wright's Prairie Style, into contemporary focus.

The grounds needed new, more than merely cosmetic curb appeal. Cooper says, "We corrected some bad drainage issues by raising the grade around the house and installing underground drains and rain-gutters. We installed a crushed granite driveway and back patio." Then, the Coopers redesigned the garden areas. "For new landscaping, we used xeriscape plants and clumping bamboos. As an architectural photographer, I am influenced by the minimalist landscapes that I document regularly. Adapting this style, I chose not to 'busy' things up with a lot of competing plant types. Instead, for a particular planting area I used just one type of plant. The result is a clean minimal look that creates a Zen-like mood." Color was important outside and well as indoors. "The selection of the paving stones, granite, and house and plant colors were all deliberate choices. They give a relaxing vibe of complementary colors."

Nothing updates any house, especially an old house, faster than a new color scheme. The bright orange front door signals new life for the 1916 house. "The house was in more or less its original configuration," Chris says. "We repainted the exterior and interior, choosing earthy colors for the larger

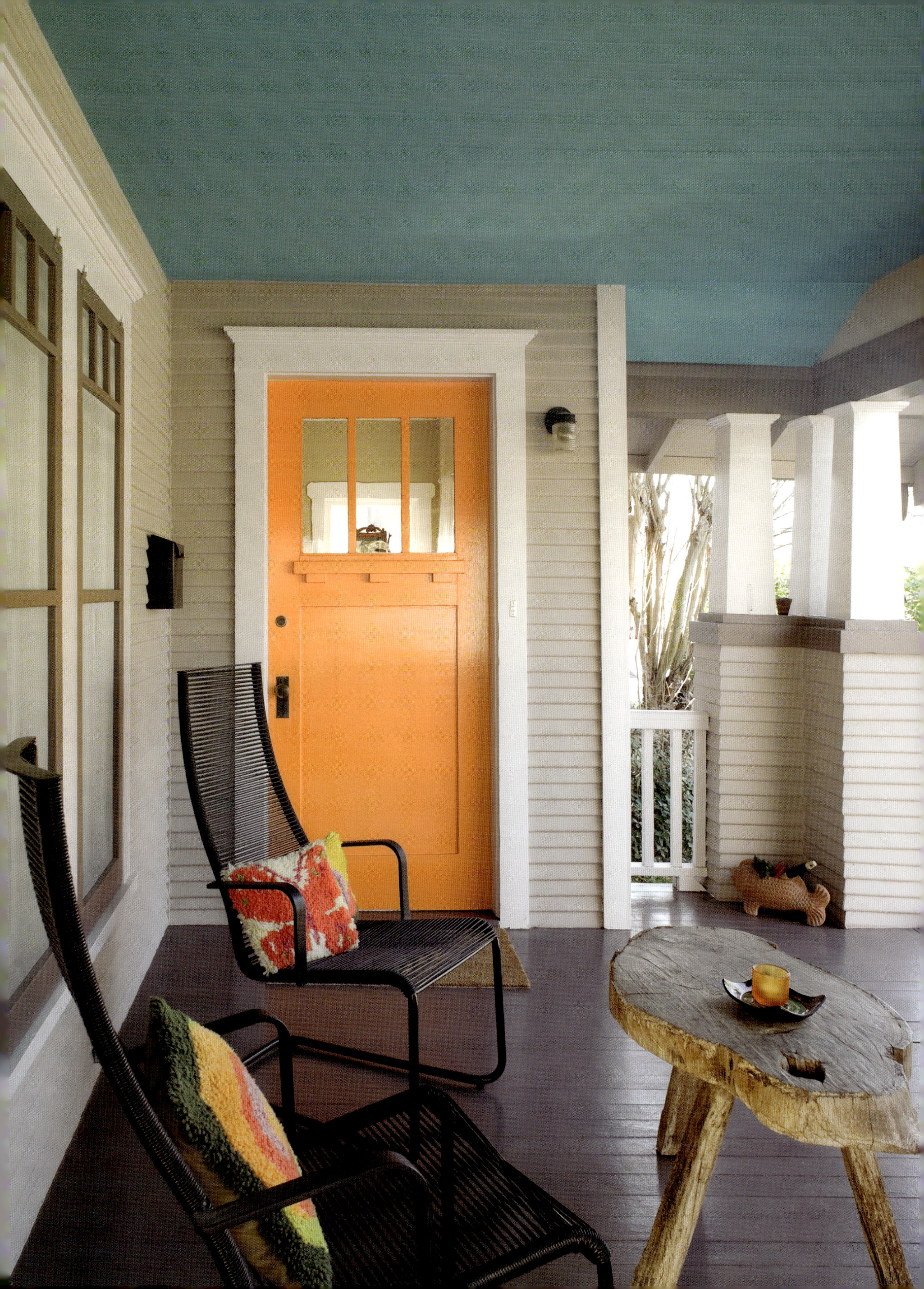

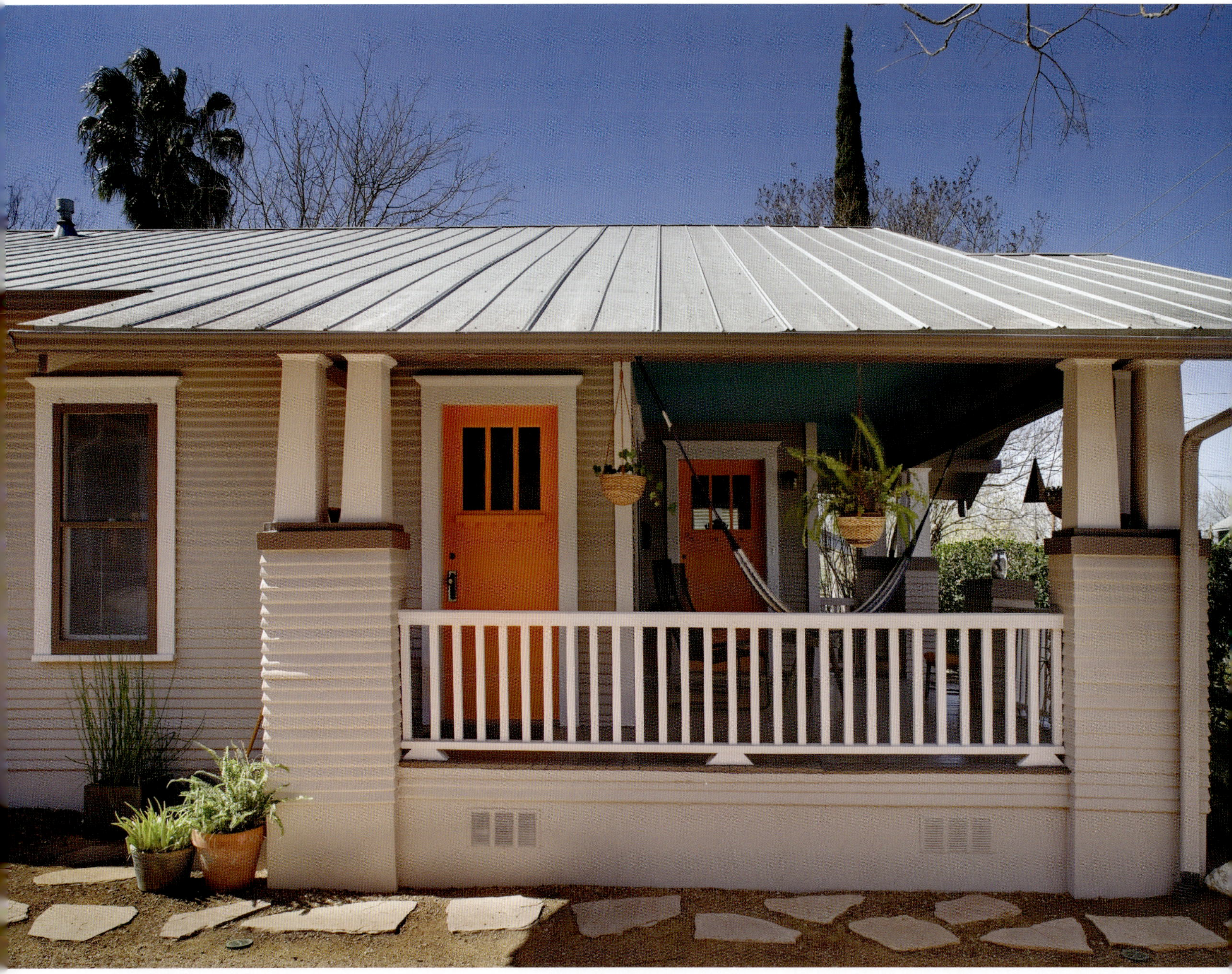

Characteristic of the Prairie Style, deep roof overhangs extend beyond the walls, adding shade and design-enriching shadow.

areas (on the outside and indoors). Pops of bright color accent areas like the front door." He points to what he calls "little hidden surprises" of color: "An example is the front porch ceiling. It is a bright turquoise that is seen nowhere else and not discovered until you come up the steps. My wife, Carina, is Swedish, so her touch is reflected throughout the interior with pops of bright colors and eclectic furniture."

Buying a vintage home in a historic district, similarly to buying a house anywhere, is a matter of location, location, location. "I can't think of a better location. It is just minutes from Highway 281, downtown San Antonio, and the airport," says Cooper, who also has a New York City apartment and who is constantly on the go to photograph locations across the country. Location, of course, involves more than convenience. "I think it is great to live in a historic neighborhood—there is a sense of community among neighbors who are proud of their homes and what they are doing to restore them. More importantly, it connects you with the history of the city. A neighbor had lived in the area since the 1940s." Cooper points out that in the right economy, a house in a historic district that appeals can be a great investment in both property and self. "It feels good to be part of positive change," he says. Rightfully, the Cooper's home is now the Cooper House.

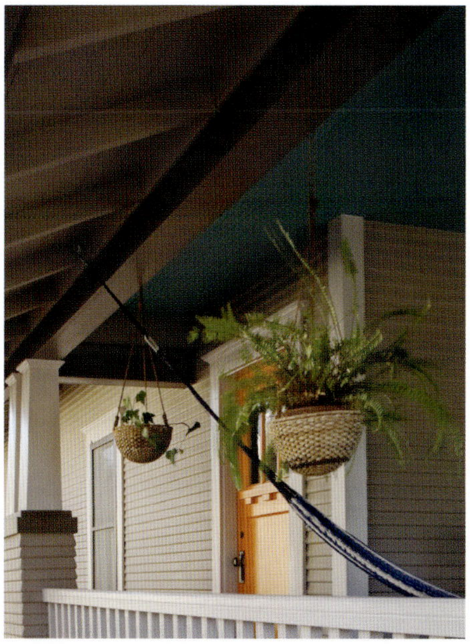

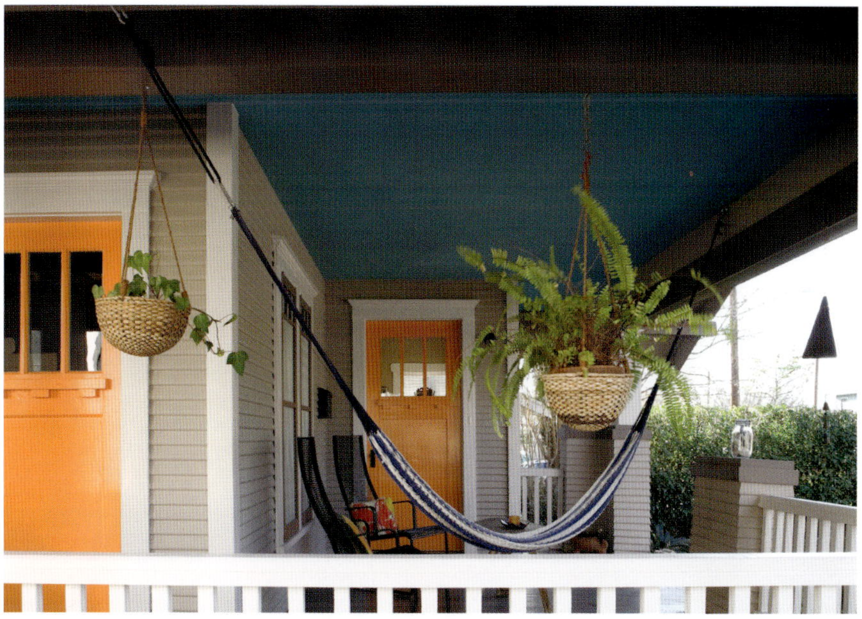

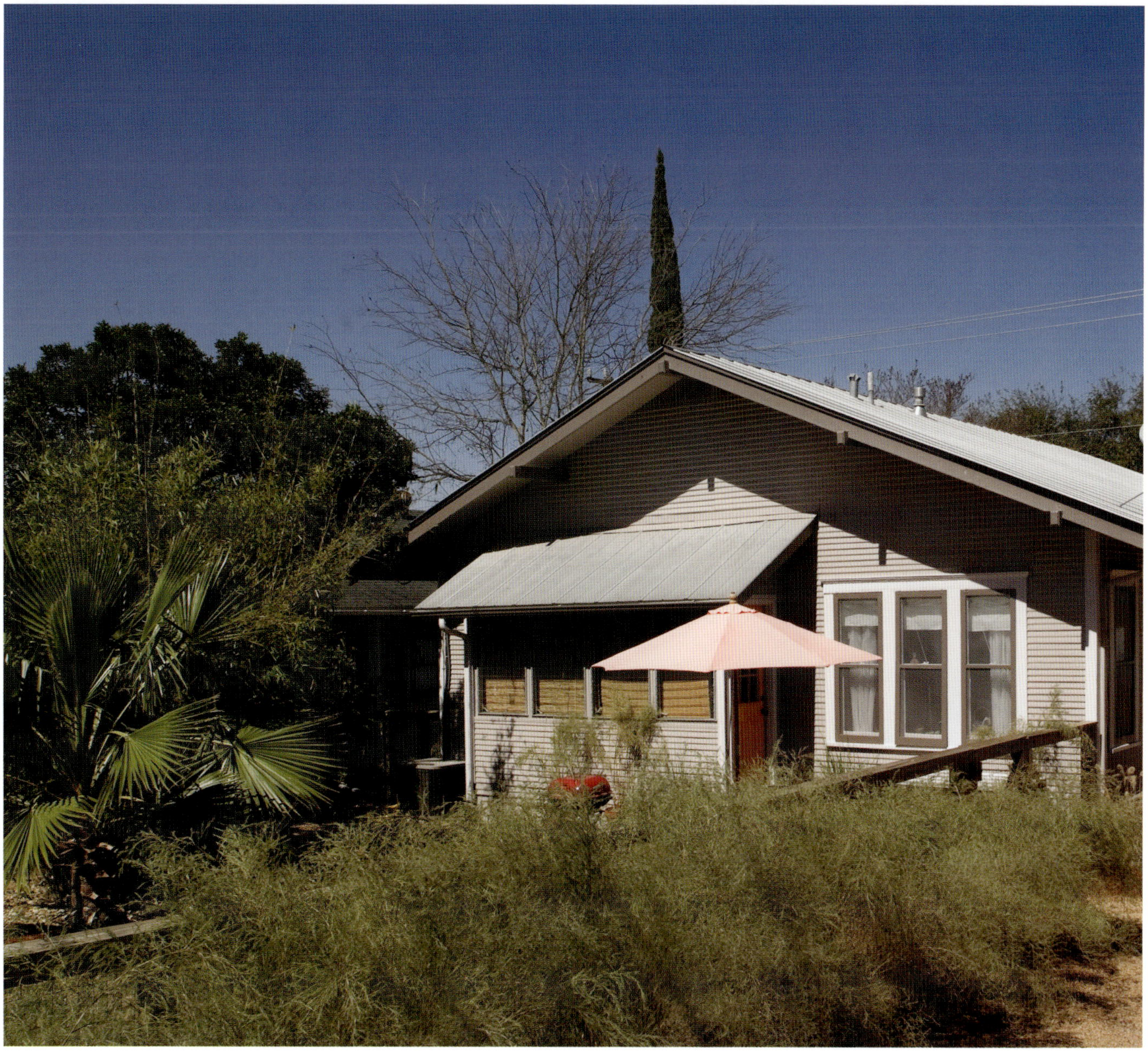

A neutral sand color gives the house a sense of dignity, but surprise punches of bold color add zest.

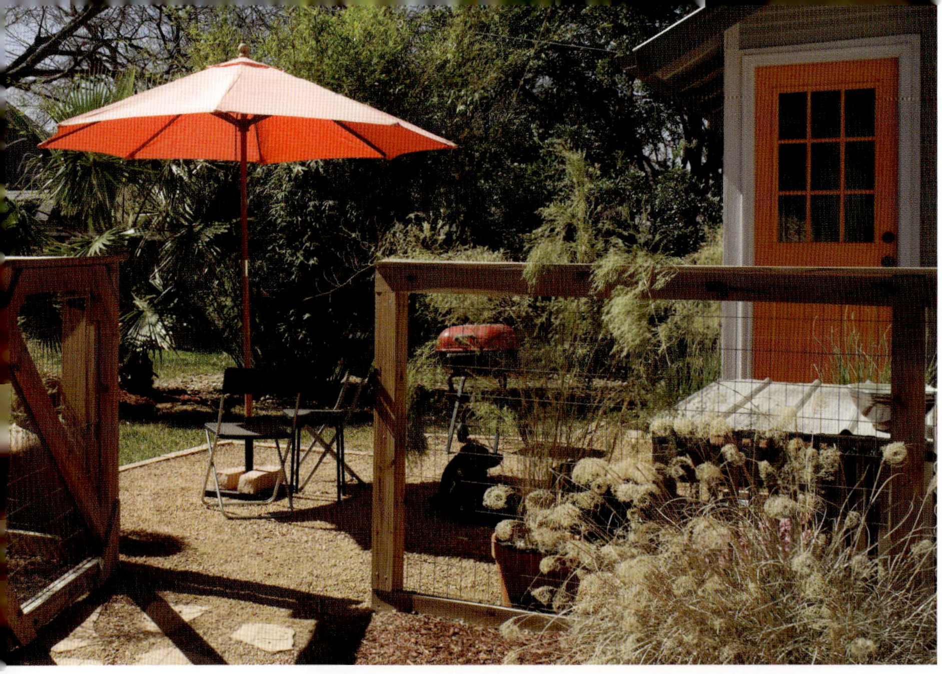

New natural-style landscaping transforms the once-barren backyard into an oasis.

A room with a built-in captain's bunk *cum* sofa does double duty as sitting and guest room.

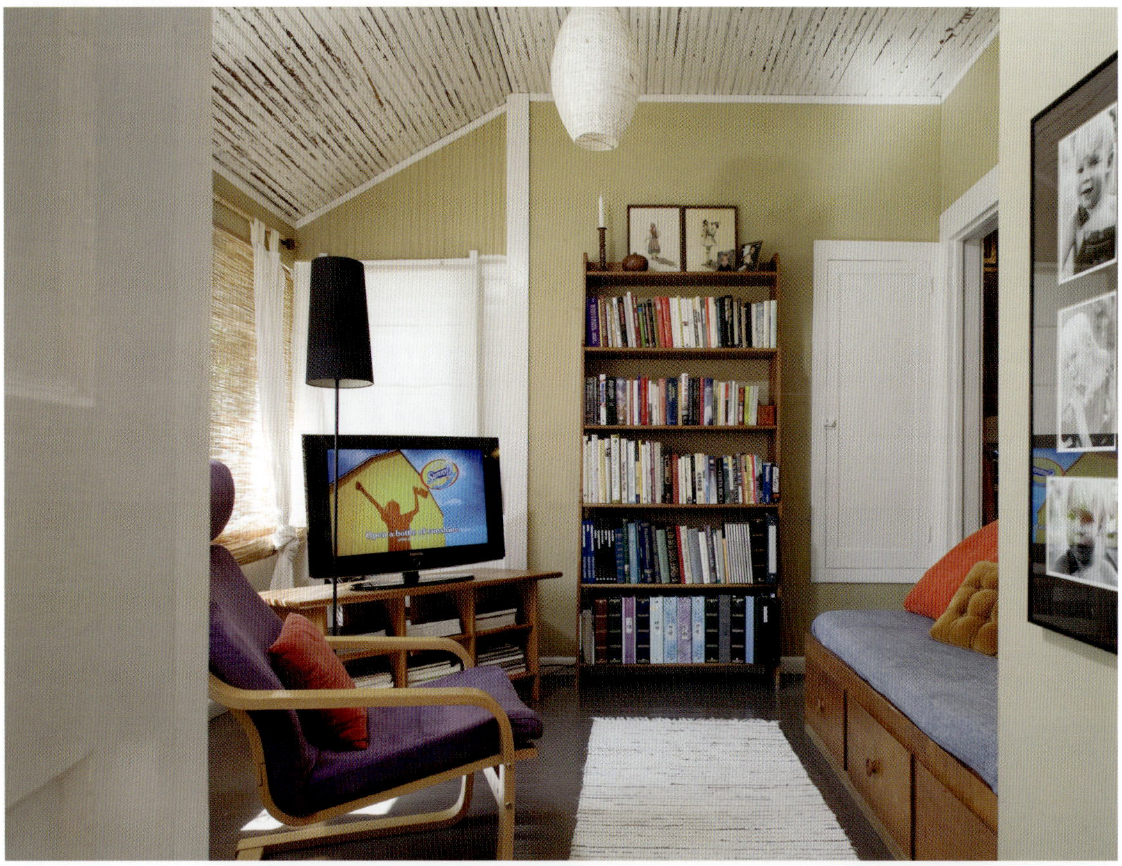

Built-ins surround the fireplace, creating an inglenook effect. Painting trim a crisp white and adding bright accent colors keeps the period architecture in tune with the times.

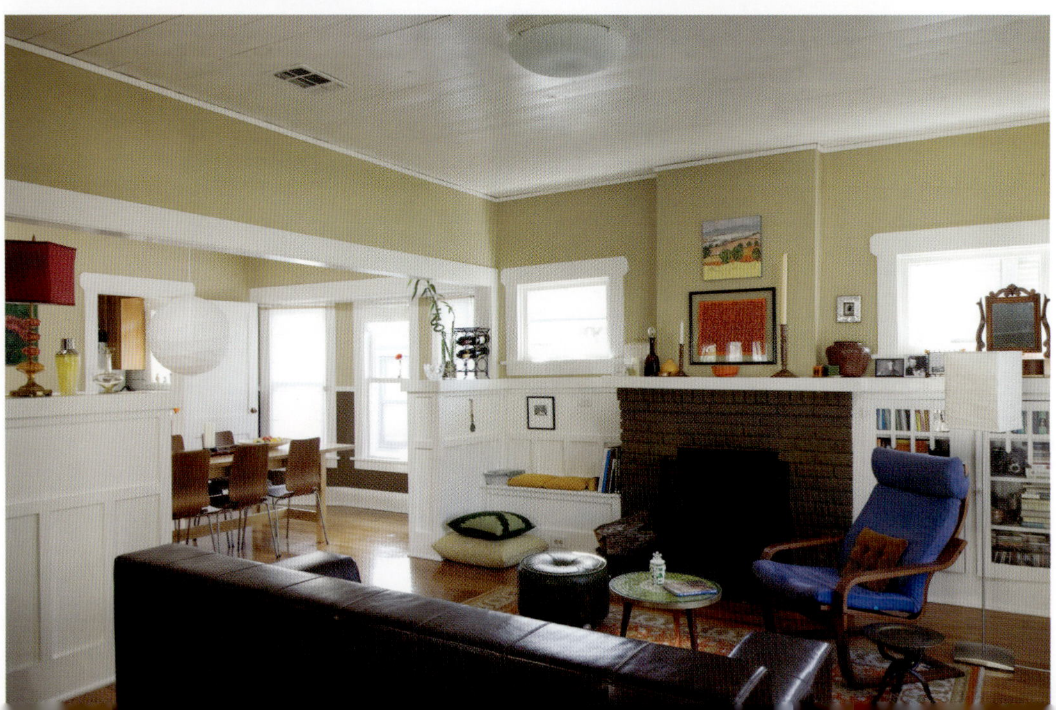

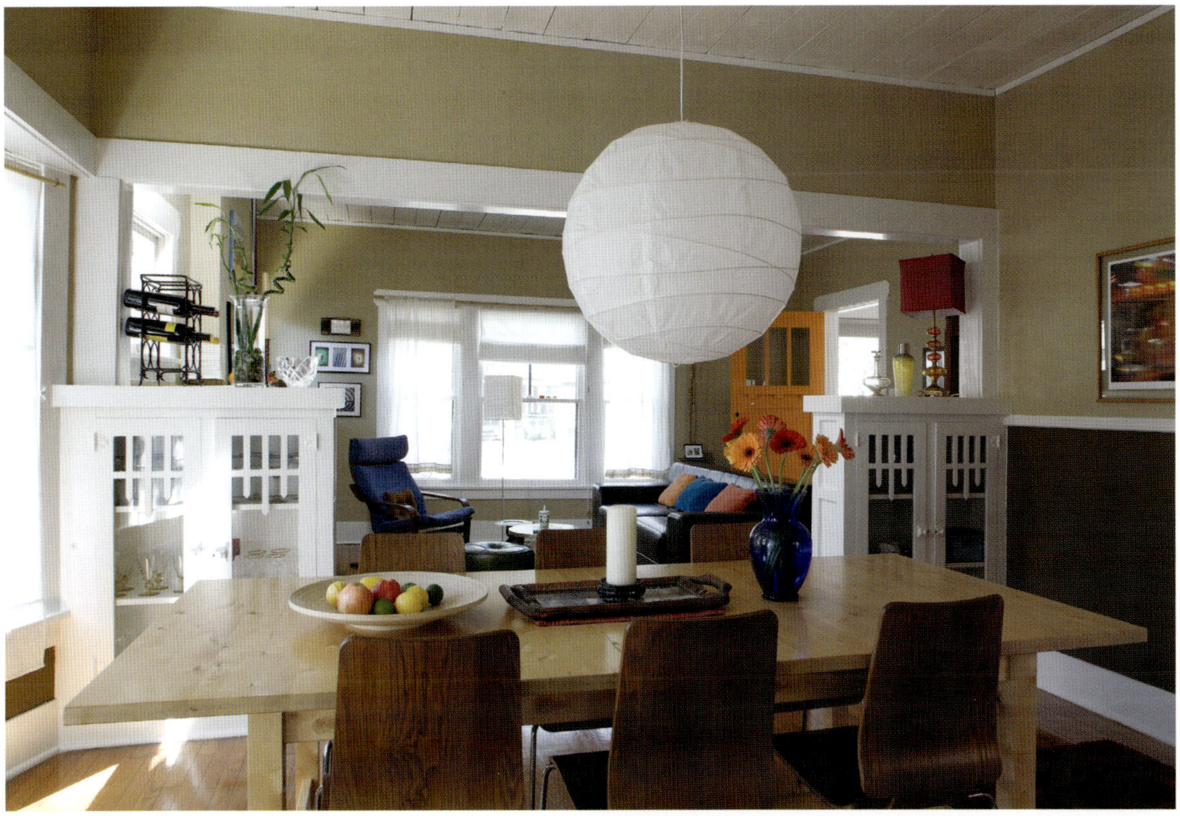

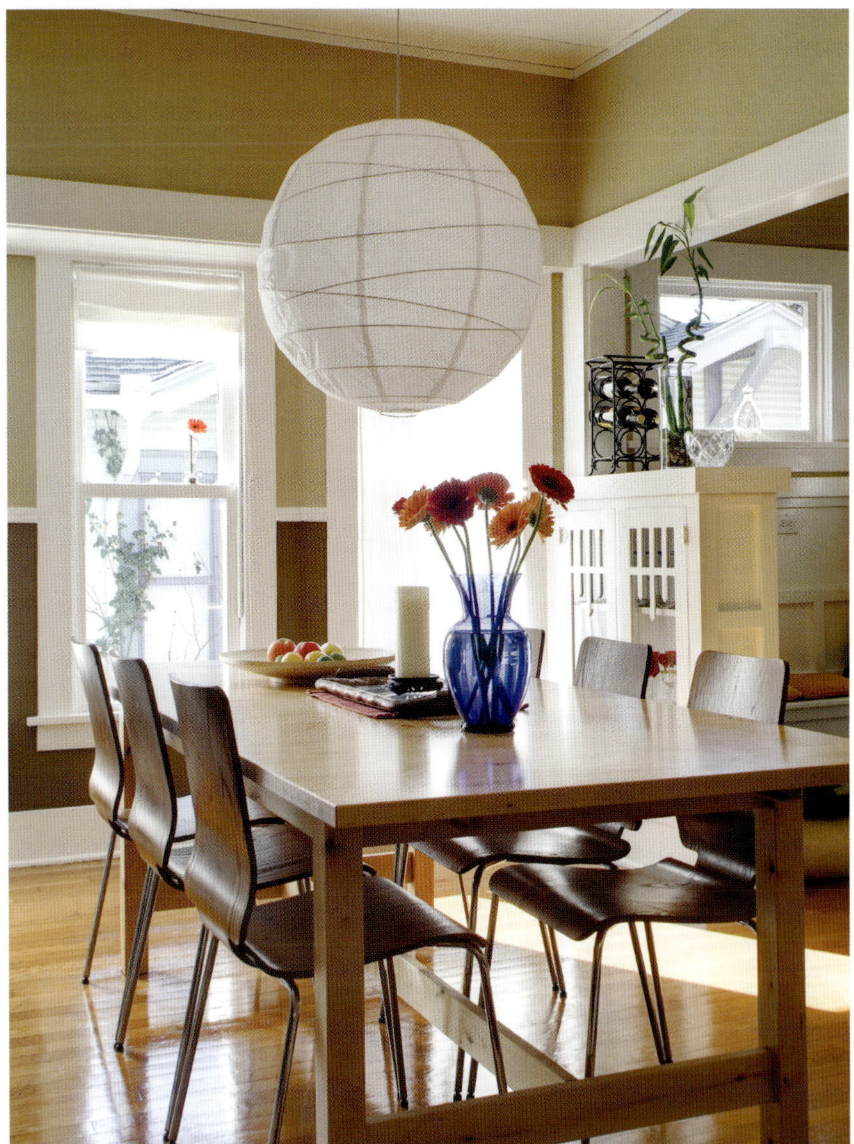

Modern furniture and light fixture affirm the contemporary spirit of the living and dining room.

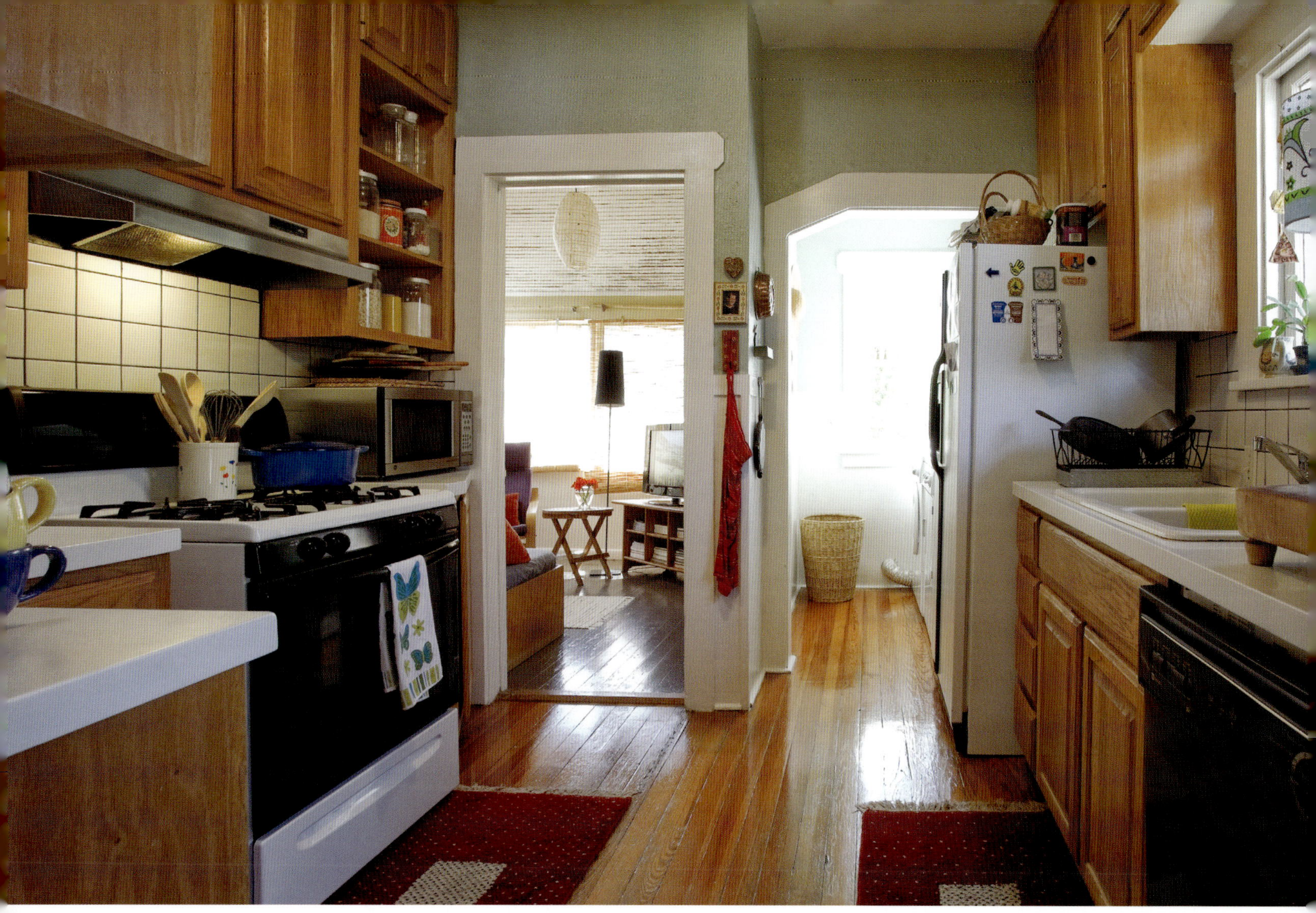

Natural wood cabinetry and flooring add warmth to the remodeled kitchen.

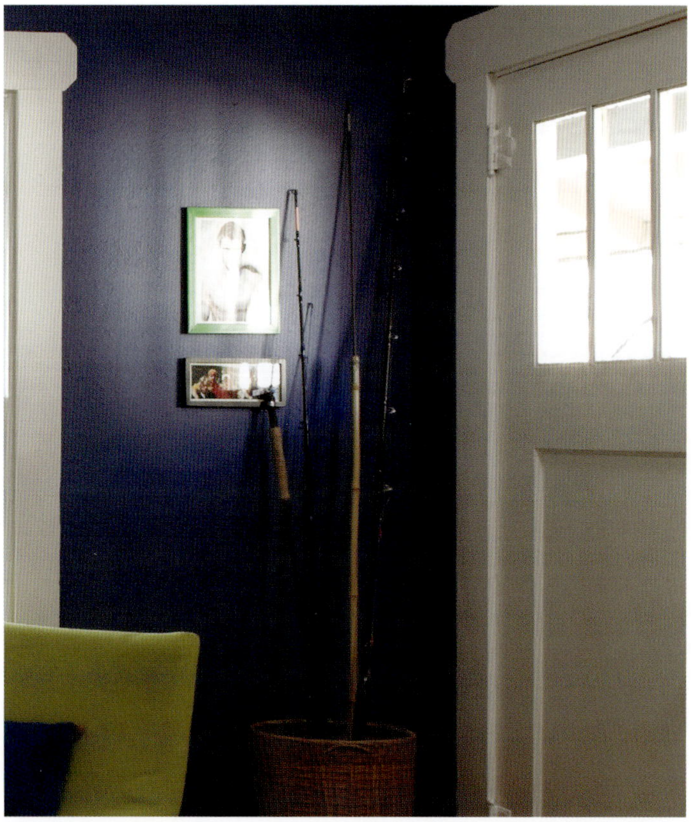

Bright blue walls add depth to bedroom *cum* study.

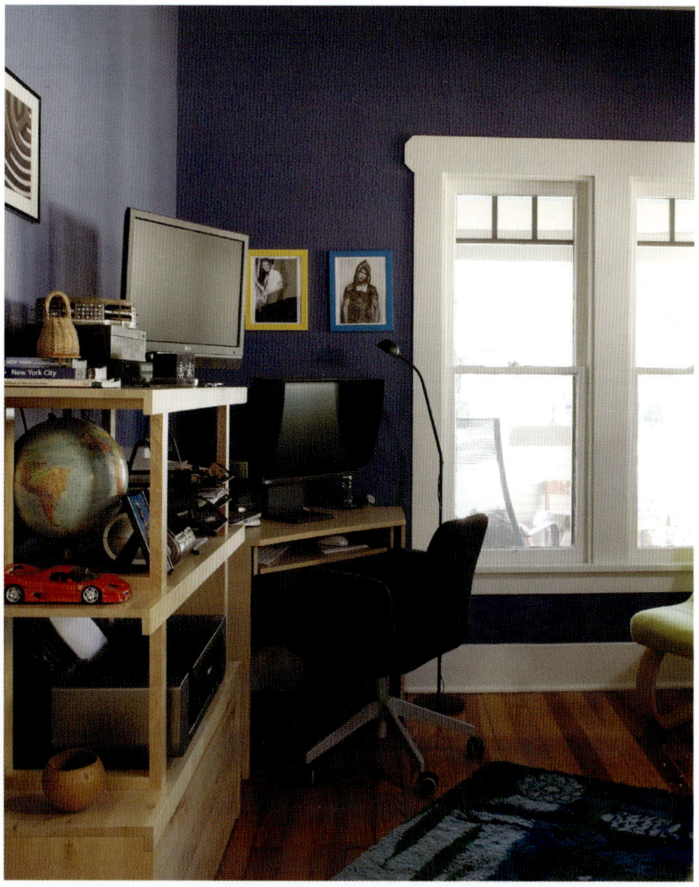

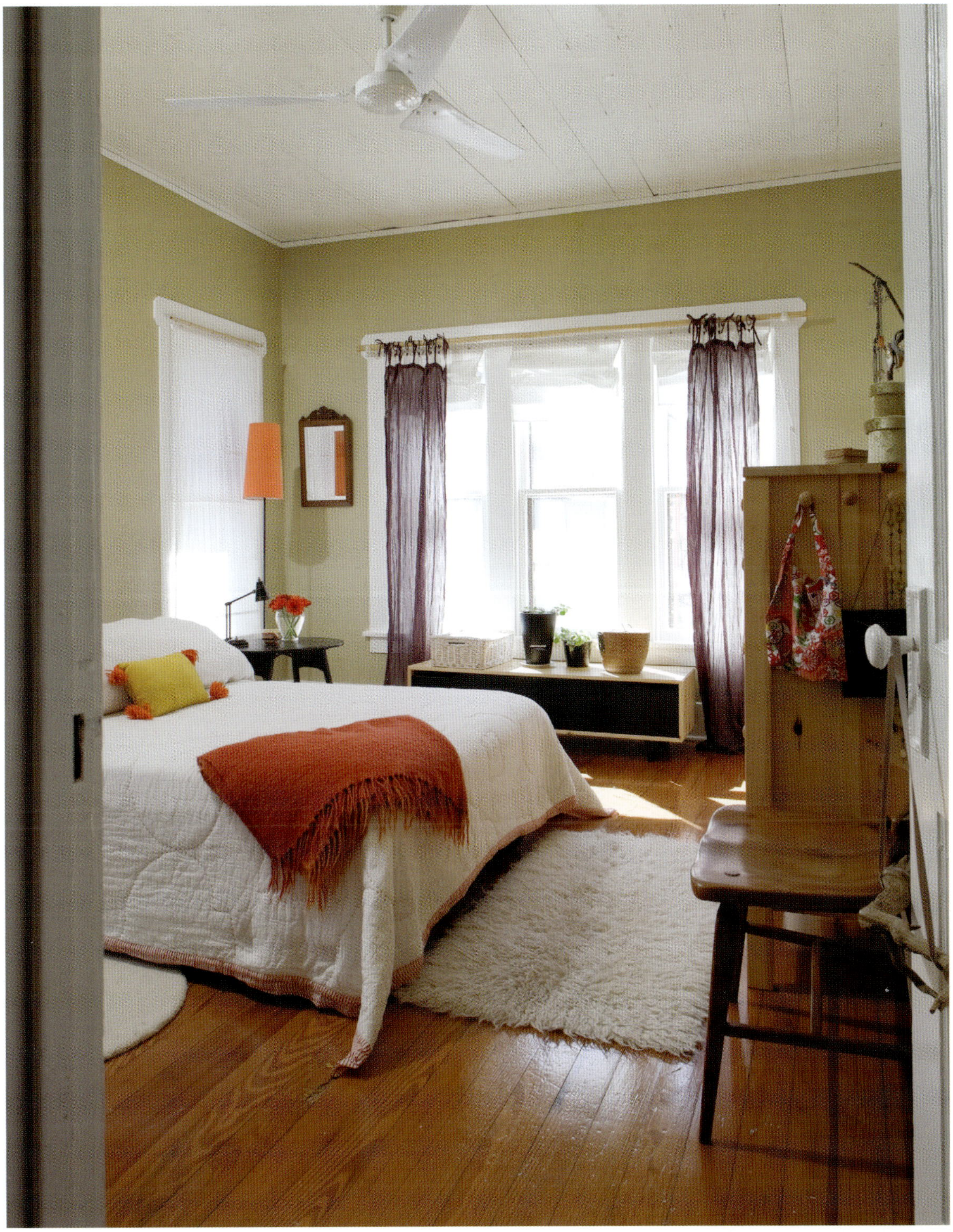

Sophisticated furnishings in the master bedroom and bathroom, including the mod ceiling fan, lamp, and accents of bright orange, are refreshingly contemporary touches that make an older house young again.

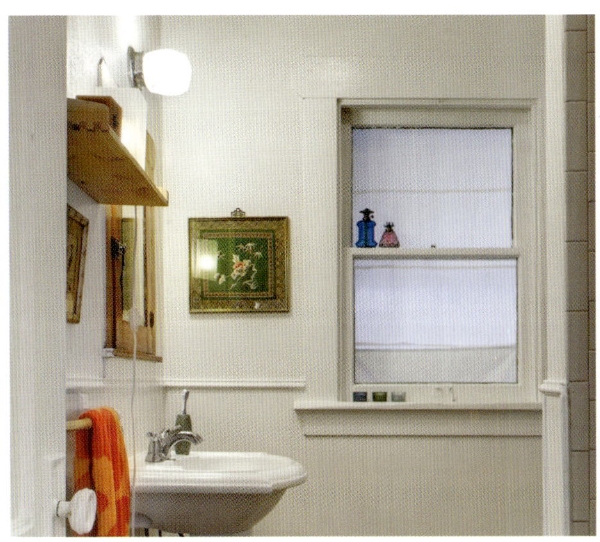

23
Daniels House

Few old house owners in San Antonio know as much about the history of their homes as Michael Daniels, a realtor known in his industry as "the old house lover." "Our home on West French Street in the Monte Vista Historic District is listed on the National Register of Historic Places," says Daniels. "Designed by Architect Atlee B. Ayres for Builder/Developer W. D. Syers in 1911, this grand old house was first occupied by Bishop and Mrs. W. T. Capers in 1914. It remained in the ownership of The Bishop and Standing Committee of the Diocese of West Texas of the Protestant Episcopal Church, U.S.A. until 1962. Then, it was sold to Benancio and Hugette Juarez and to her sister, Mrs. Claude Rideau. The Juarez family owned the home until 2000, when it was sold to a subsequent owner who attempted to capitalize on the property's commercial zoning with little success."

In December 2005, Michael Daniels, a successful realtor, and his wife Linda, a retired attorney—long time Monte Vista residents and architectural preservationists—purchased the house. "Our goal to restore the property to its original grandeur and make it our homestead," says Daniels, who planned to use part of the spacious structure as a home office.

Michael and Linda Daniels describe their house as a vertical "prairie style." "It's mostly Arts and Crafts, but there is a melding of more traditional architecture with the newly emerging Arts and Crafts movement of the time. This is evidenced by the horizontal decorative brick bands coursing around the exterior of the body, and by the style of the woodwork and trim work inside the house," says Daniels. He points out that the living room's ornate fireplace with turned columns and beveled glass is out of character with the rest of the interior's design. "It may have been included to appease the first homeowner, whose taste may not have been thoroughly in keeping with 'new age' design."

The 5,200 square foot house on three levels has what is probably rare in San Antonio—a full basement. "One basement room has 10-foot-high ceilings," Daniels says. (There is a three car garage. A detached cottage was probably the original garage, he surmises.) Elegant ceiling heights throughout are impressive. Ceilings are 11 feet high on the first floor, 10 feet high on the second, and 9 feet high on the third floor.

Daniels points out that the house has unusually large 8-foot-tall windows, capped with Atlee B. Ayres' distinctive snowflake motif transoms. "This house was built in an era without air conditioning, high on a hill overlooking the City, with huge windows to catch the prevailing breezes," Daniels

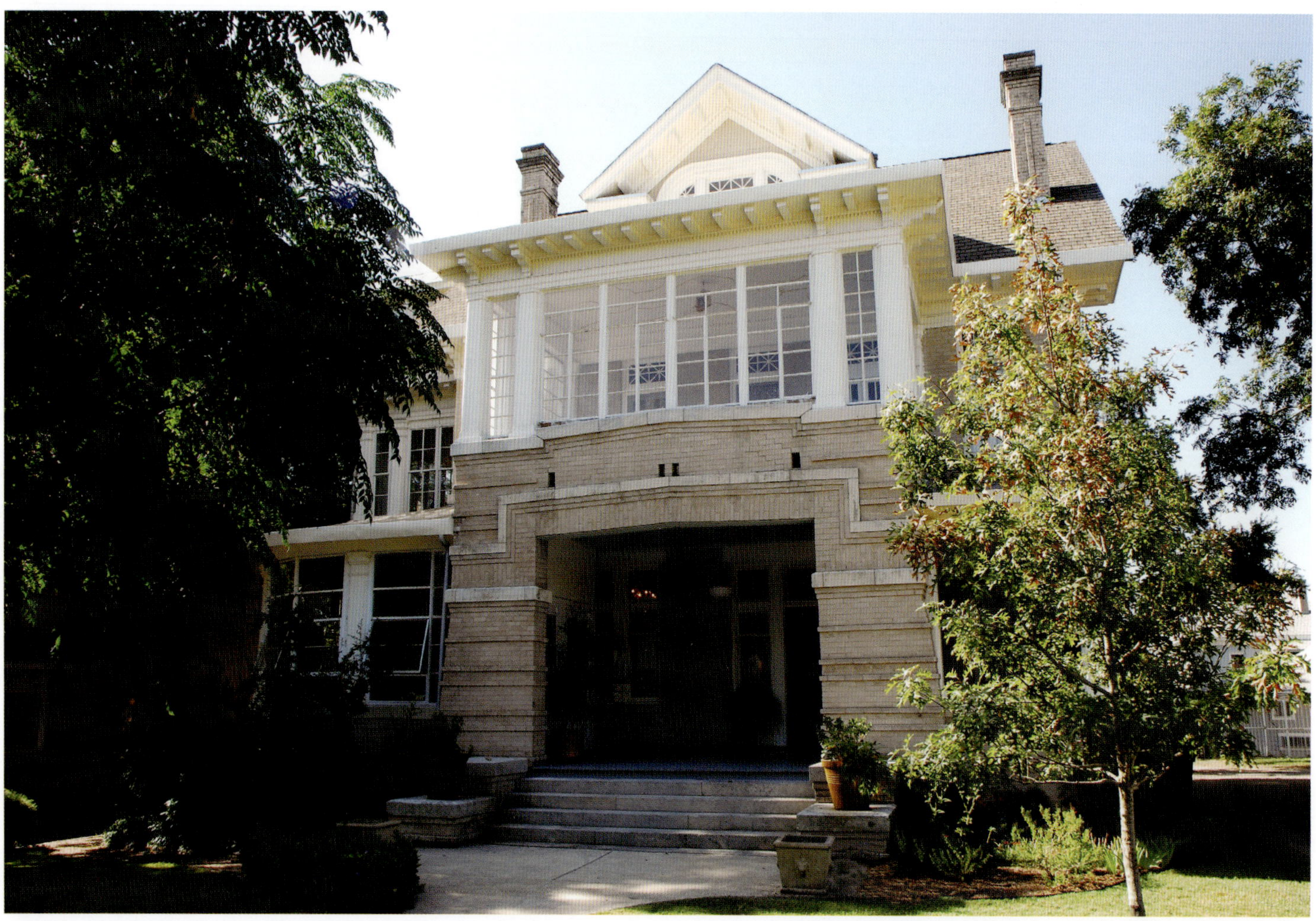

Famed Architect Atlee B. Ayers designed the Daniels House in 1911. *Photographs by Barbara Justice*

states. "The huge windows also provide one of the most unique features of this house—an expansive third-floor view of the San Antonio skyline."

Even the work of celebrated architects is subject to remodeling. In the case of an earlier owner, the objective was to generate income. "Mr. Juarez enclosed the sleeping porches with glass. A portion of the circular, wrap-around front and side porch was enclosed to become the Paris Beauty Salon run by the two owner-sisters. The family lived in the house, and rented out the third floor as an apartment," says Daniels.

"After the Juarez ownership, the interiors suffered serious abuse," says Daniels. "When we first looked at the home as a potential purchase, we discovered a fabulous coffered dining room ceiling hiding behind an acoustic tile dropped ceiling with a suspended commercial 'shop light' style fixture!" Finding the coffered ceiling was encouraging, but it was also an indicator that a great deal of work (and money) would be involved in restoring this grand house.

"We had long walked and driven by this house and admired its architecture and scale. When the acquisition cost fell to a level that supported a major restoration project, we were the first in line to make an offer on the property," says Daniels. "We began restoration and modernization in January 2006. Our goal was to create a finished product that looked as though all changes were original to the house," says Daniels.

"This was much more a restoration than a remodel; although we included a state-of-the-art kitchen and period-style, upgraded baths," says Daniels. The scope of the work was extensive. "The project included adding new zoned HVAC systems (one for each floor). The plumbing and wiring were upgraded. All missing decorative brackets on exterior soffits were custom-made to replicate those lost to time and neglect. Interior plaster was repaired and new paint now covers all interior surfaces and exterior wood. Newly milled decorative trim replaced missing pieces. Rotten windows were replaced with new windows made to match the old. Stained glass was repaired and reinstalled. Chandeliers replaced the sad assortment of light fixtures. Every square inch received TLC," Daniels recounts.

"Green" building/construction concerns were not as well publicized in 2006 as they have become. In a real sense, the Daniels led the movement: "We did not know we were being 'green' by scouring architectural salvage warehouses and antique stores for missing house parts. Every scrap of decorative wood that needed to be removed for some reason was carefully labeled, so that it could be put back in place. The condensate lines for the three cooling units water the garden. Rainwater is also collected," Daniels says.

Restoration efforts left the layout and floor plan just as Atlee B. Ayers planned them in 1911, except for the porch enclosures. "The only change *we* made was to remove a wall separating the original maid's room from the original kitchen space to form the large, modern space for our new gourmet kitchen. The new stove vent-a-hood tapped into the kitchen fireplace—the starting point for the kitchen design," says Daniels.

"We do our own remodeling work, and through the years, because of several prior home restorations, we have a group of craftsmen we can tap when we need them. When things got messy, I cleaned and fussed. When the painters didn't show

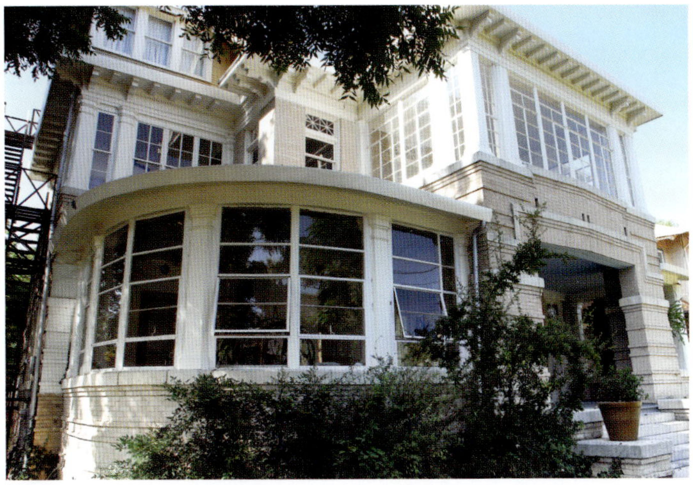

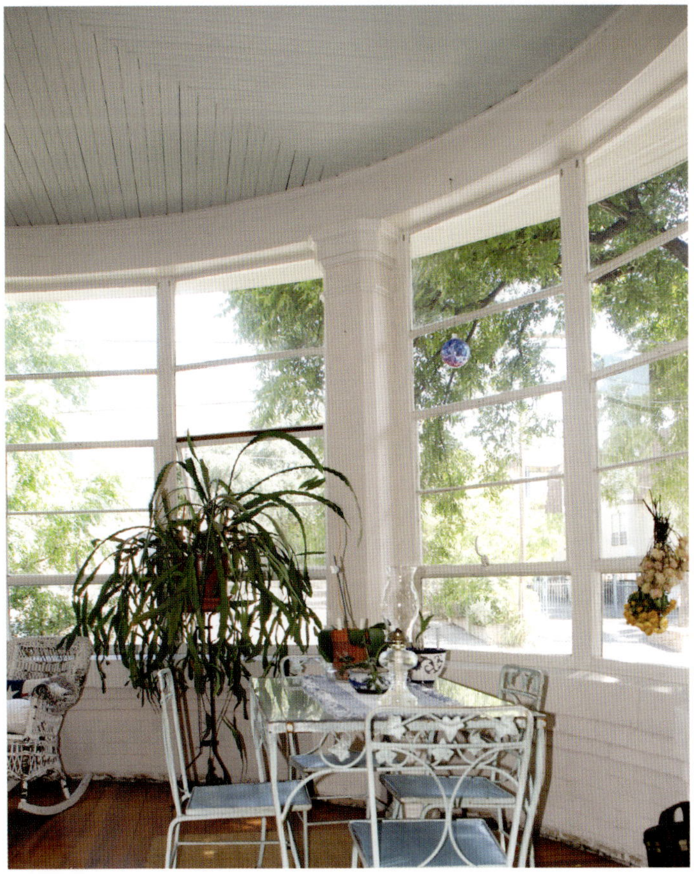

Earlier owners enclosed the curved porch, making it their Paris Beauty Salon.

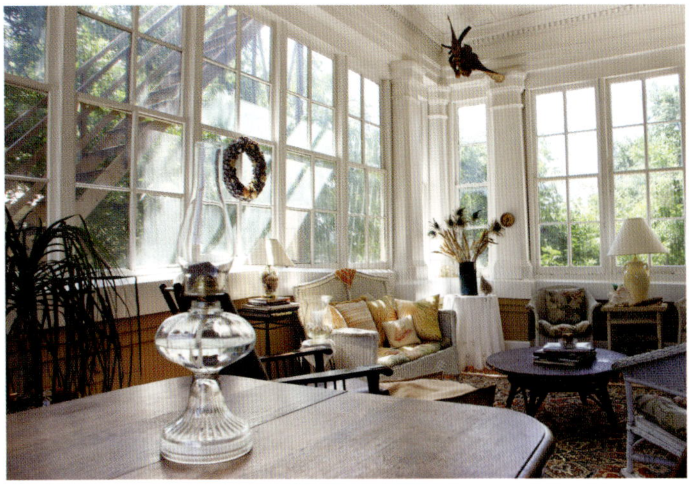

Second story sleeping porches were enclosed with glass for four-season use.

up, we painted. Michael was general contractor on the job, but often worked as a carpenter," says Linda Daniel. "We joke that the master carpenter, Dan Pentecost, was more family than family by the time the project neared completion," says Michael Daniel. Of course, he adds, "A house like this is never really finished. At press time for this book, we will still have projects to complete: replacing the original widow's walk railing to the third floor balcony, removing the wrap-around porch enclosure, repairing the section of balustrade that someone, for some reason, sawed off. The list goes on." And, thanks to the efforts of the Daniels, so does their newly elegant, revitalized house on French Street.

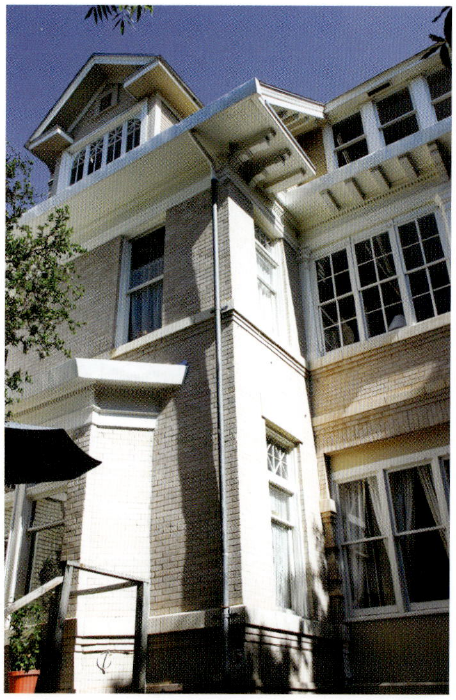

Three stories above a full basement create plentiful and varied living spaces in graciously-scaled rooms.

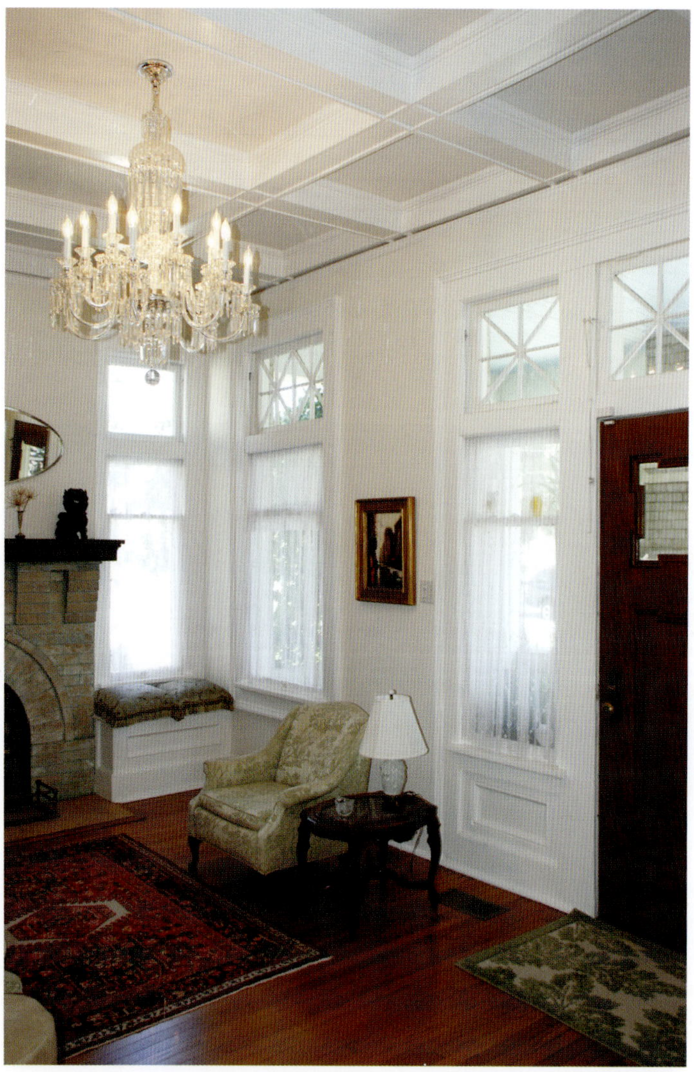

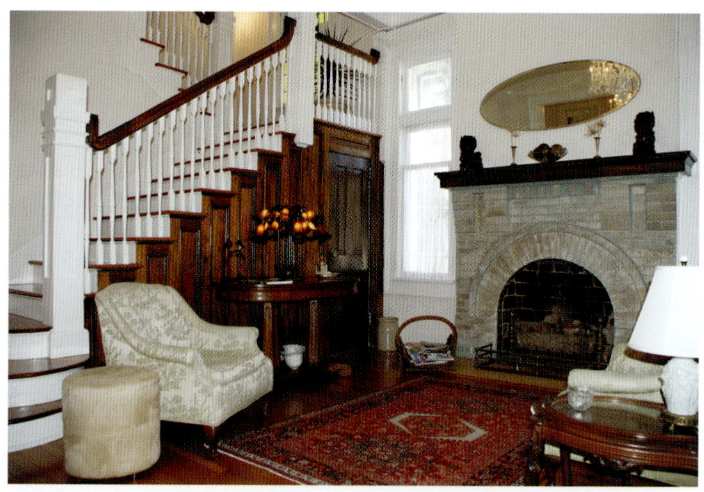

The entry, fitted with a fireplace, is a gracious reception area that dispatches traffic so that it moves easily throughout the large house.

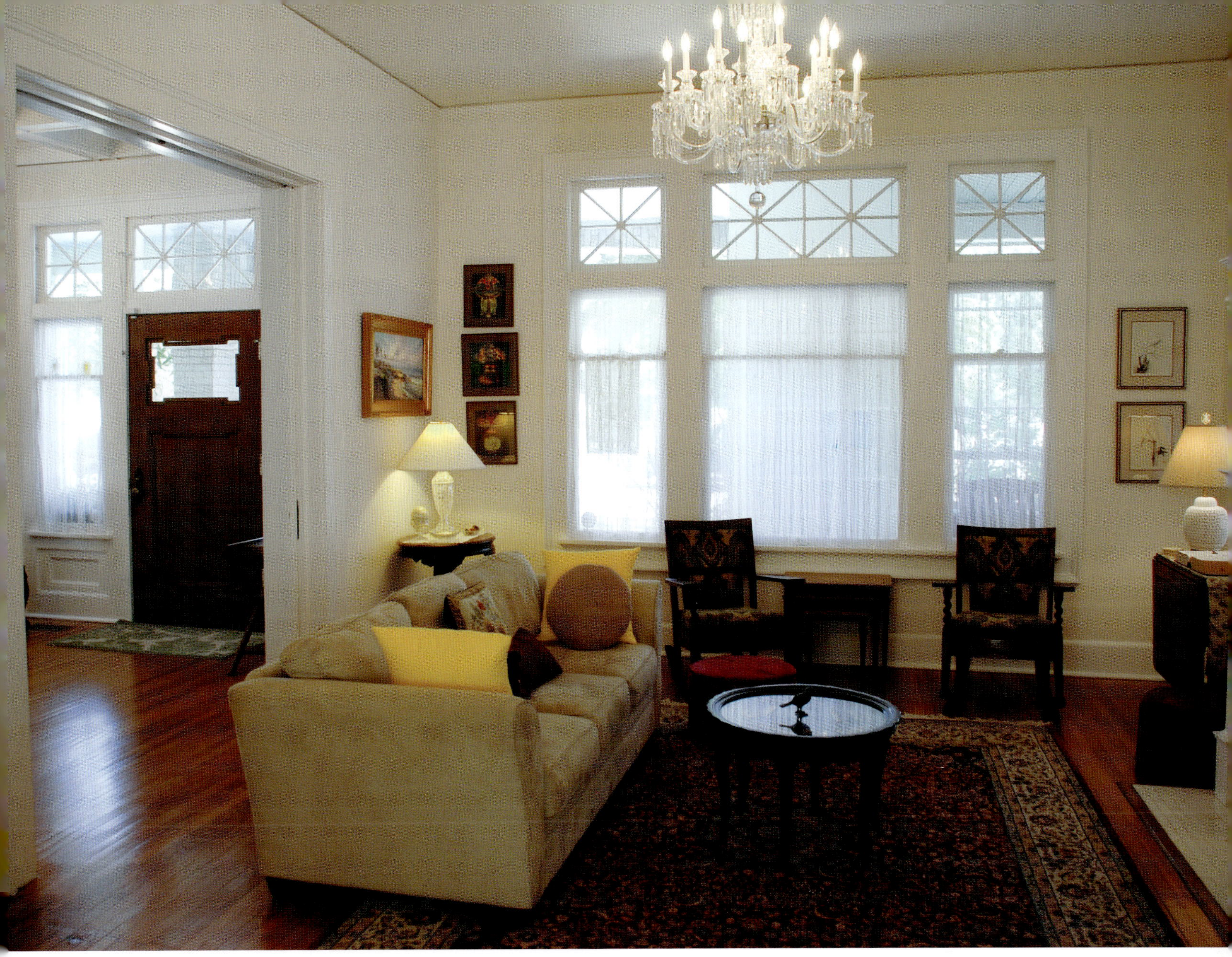

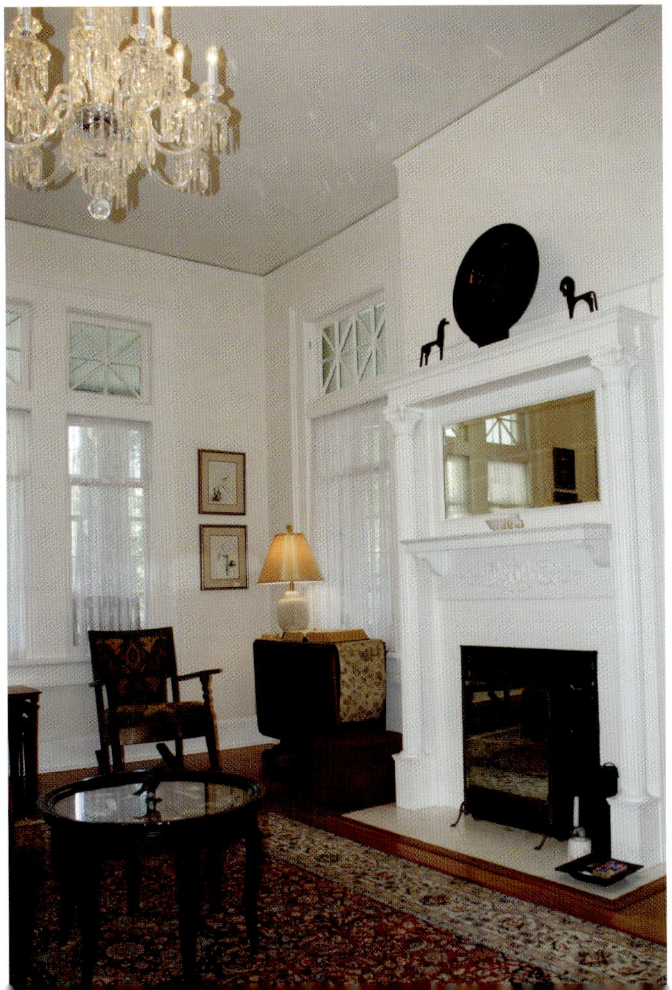

Elegant tri-part windows and a handsome fireplace are grace notes that lend elegance to the spacious living room.

Light-colored walls are a gallery-like foil for warm-wood furniture and gold-framed art in the formal dining room.

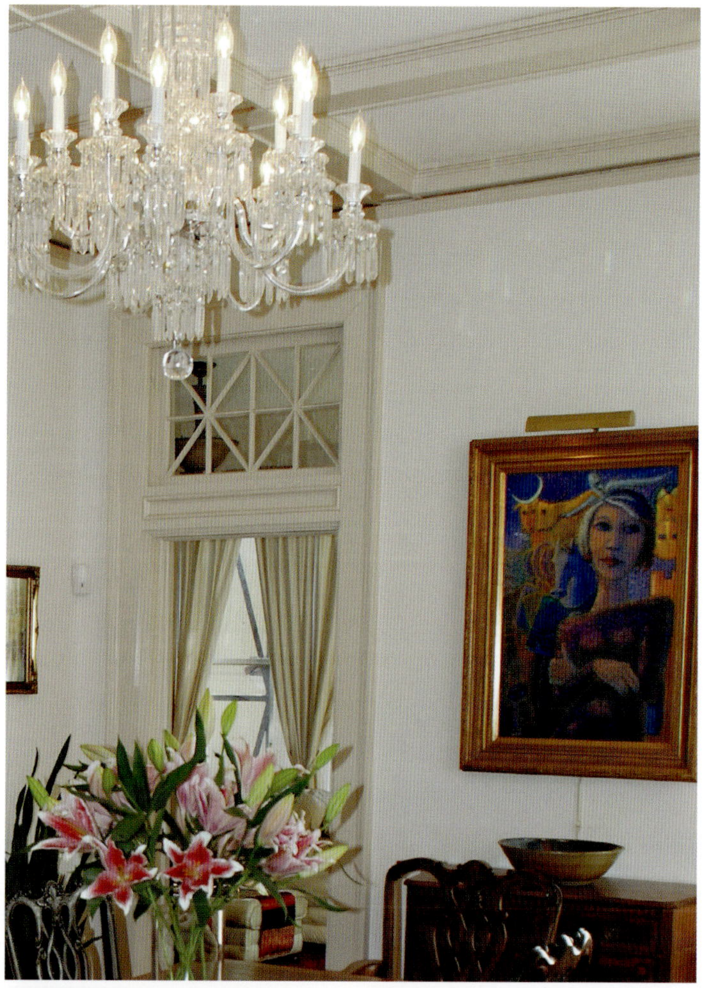

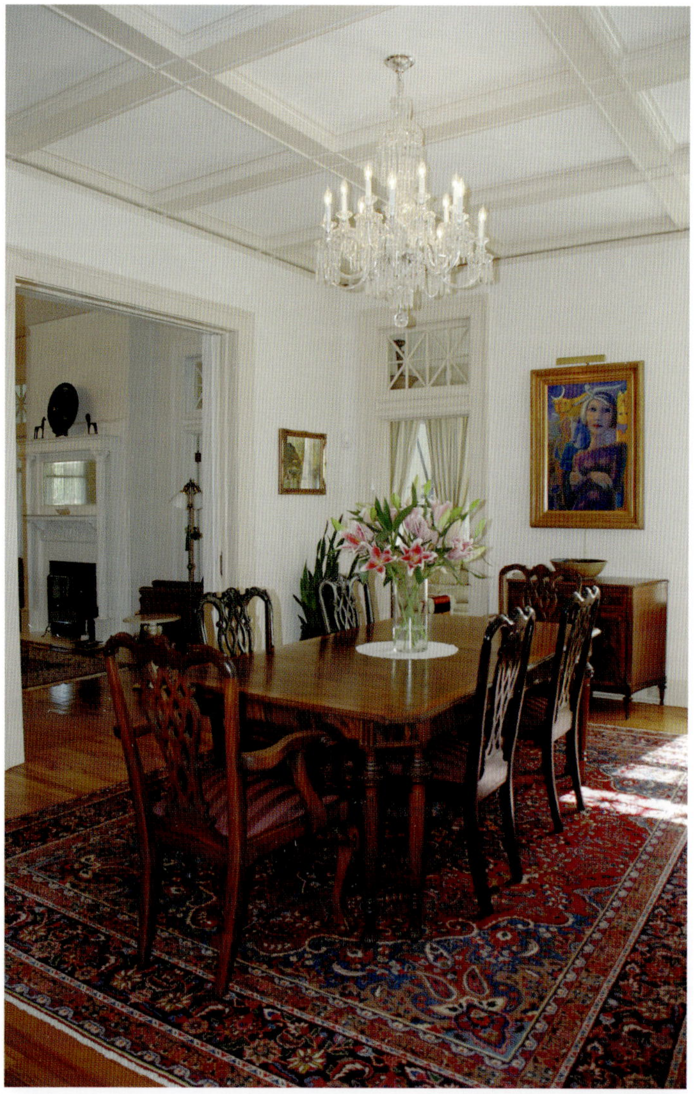

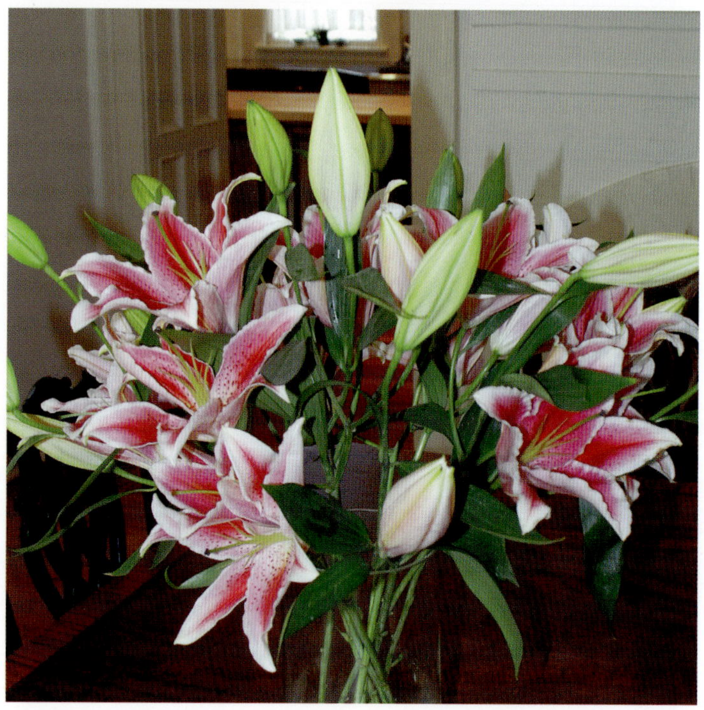

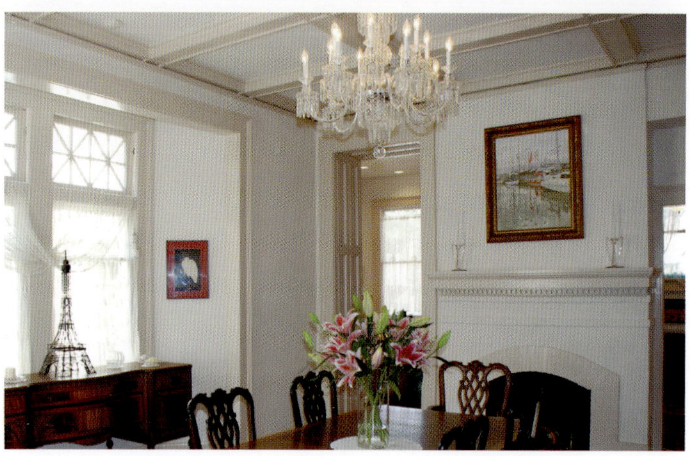

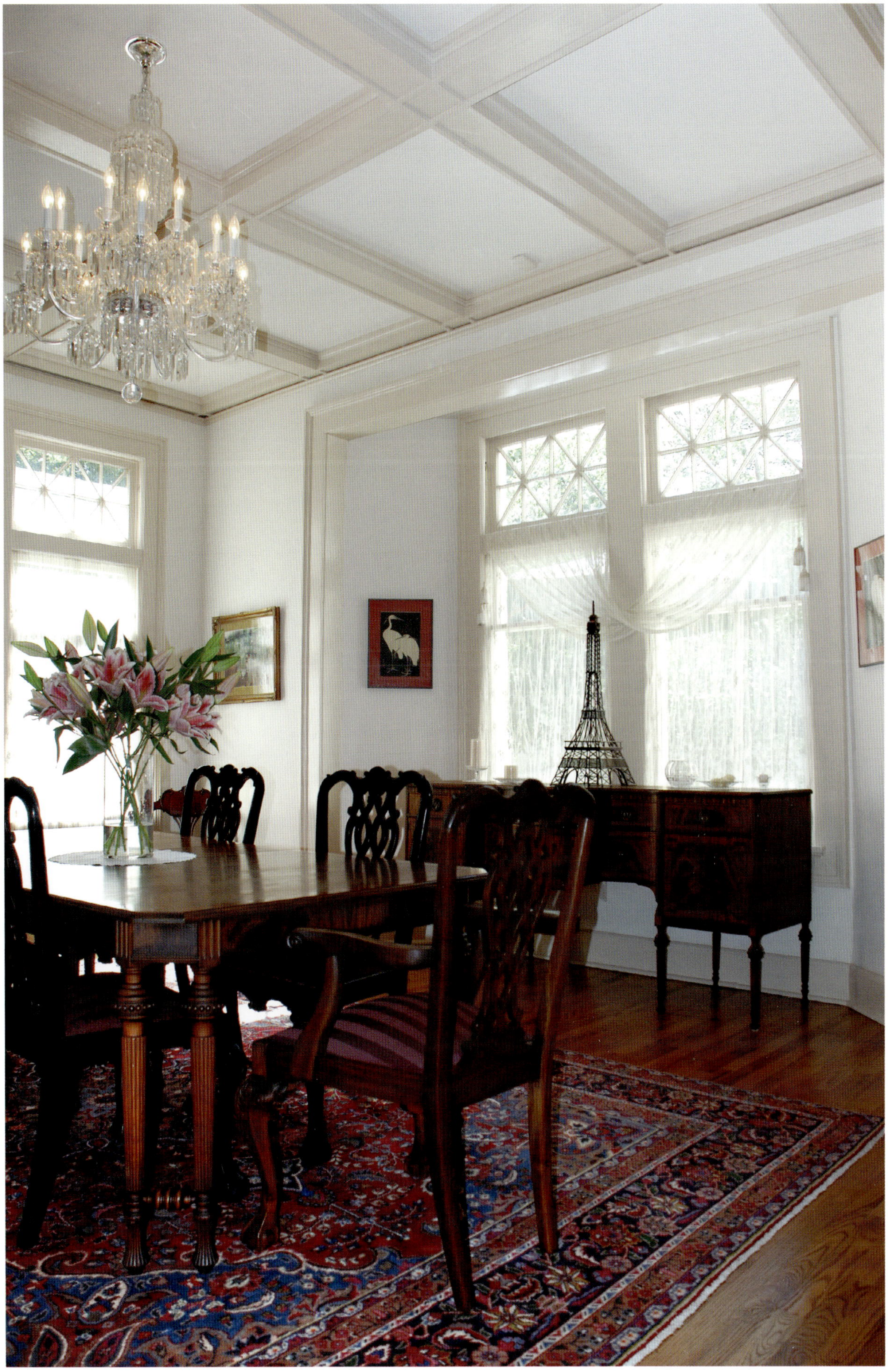

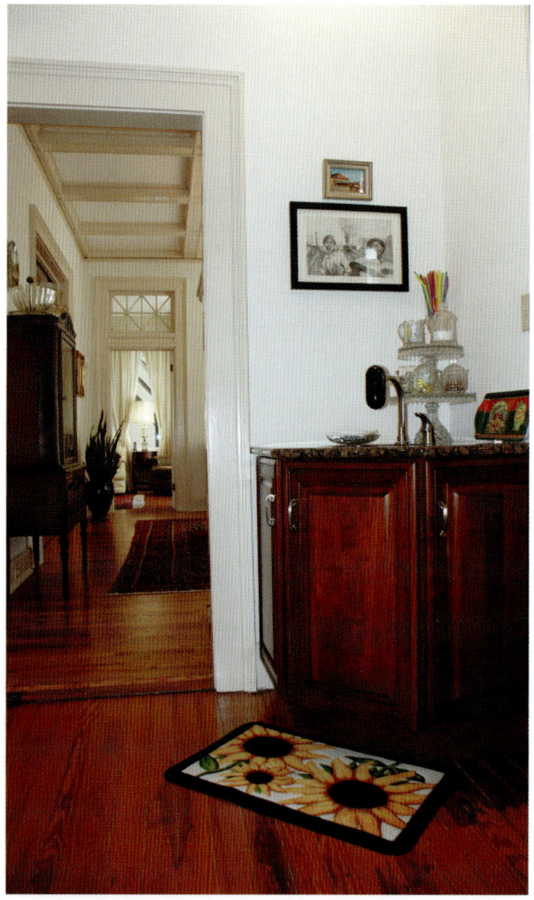

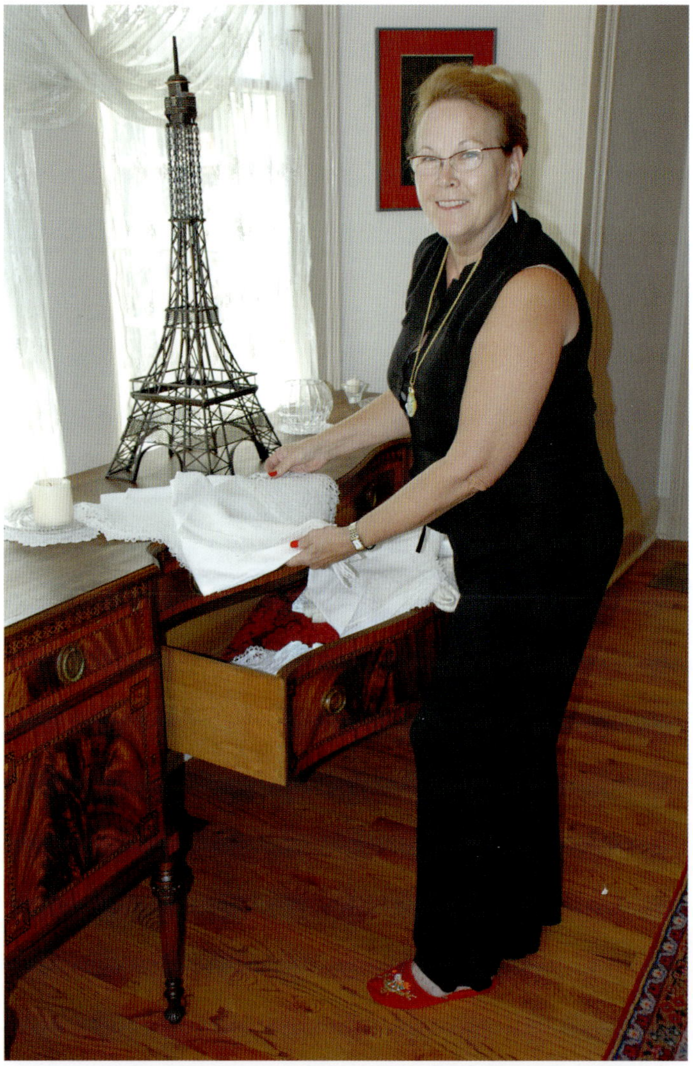

Linda Daniels, a retired attorney, collects beautiful antique linens.

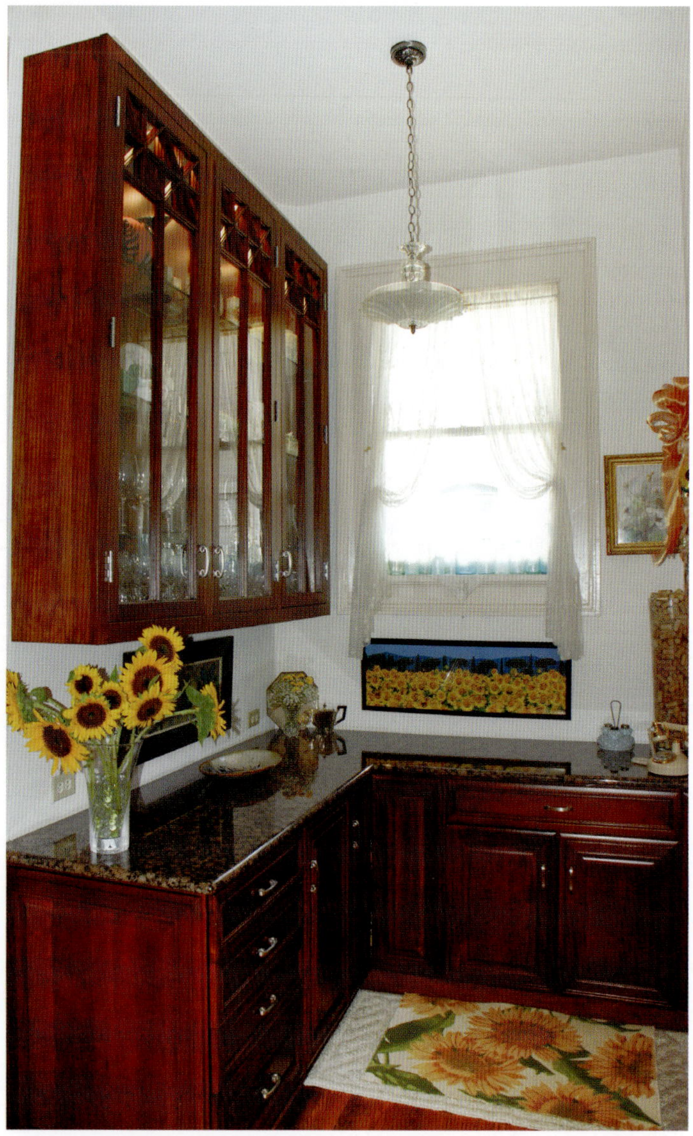

Sunflowers are a favorite motif for the butler's pantry and kitchen.

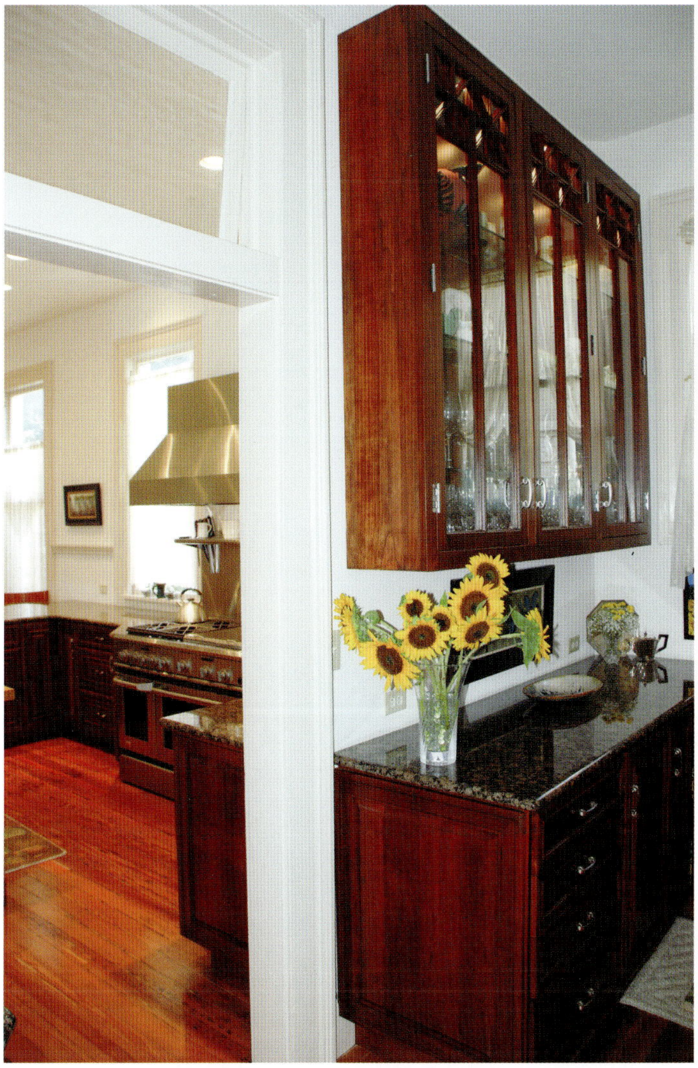

The butler's pantry adjacent to the dining room and kitchen adds welcome storage. Sunflowers are a favorite decorative motif, and rustic pottery a delightful accessory.

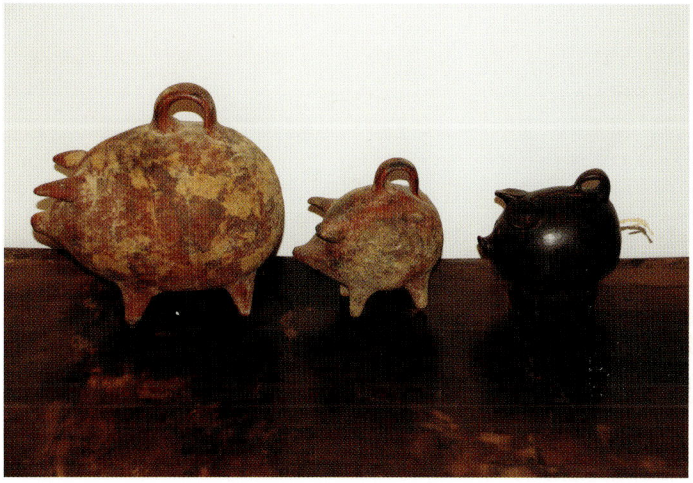

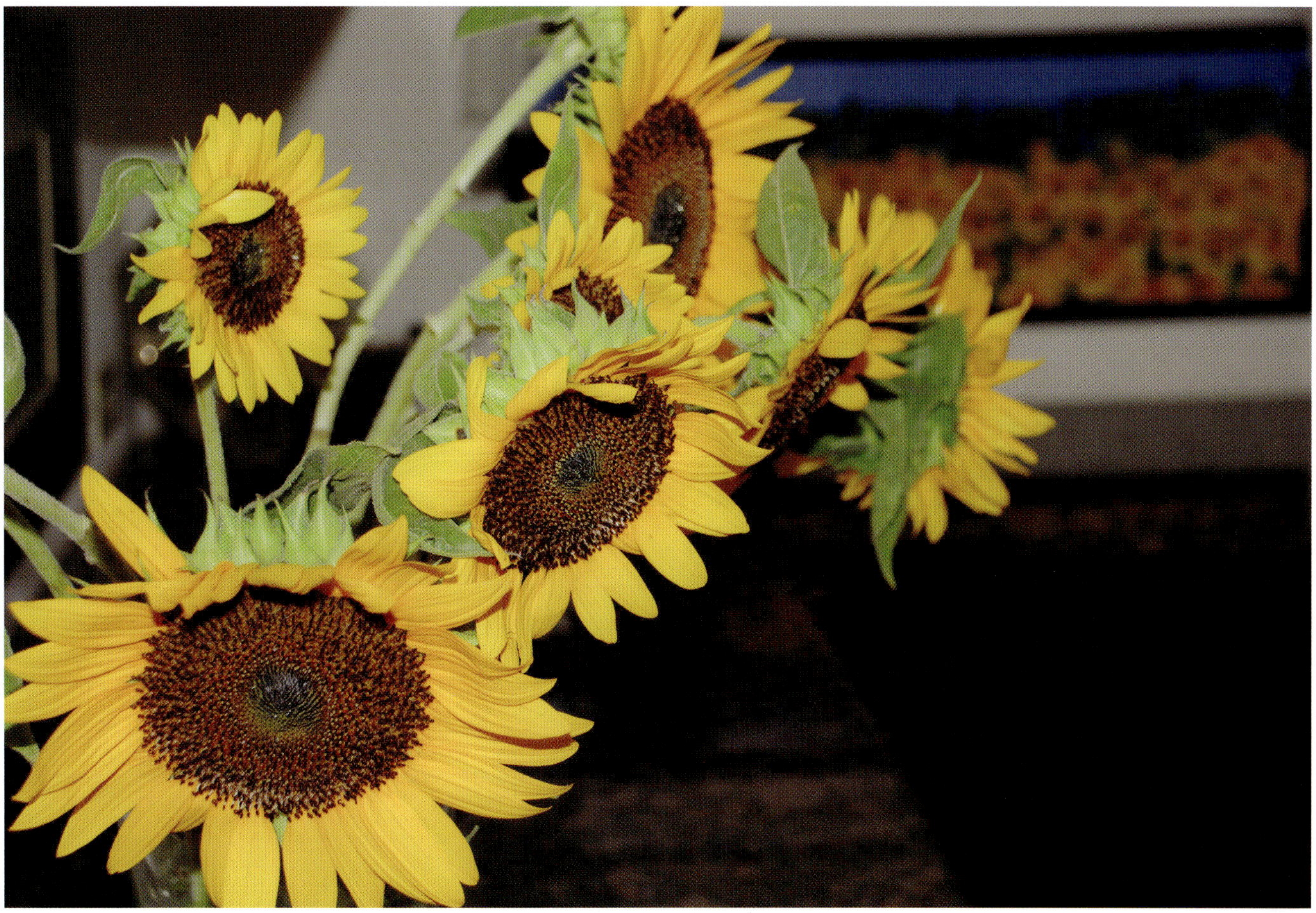

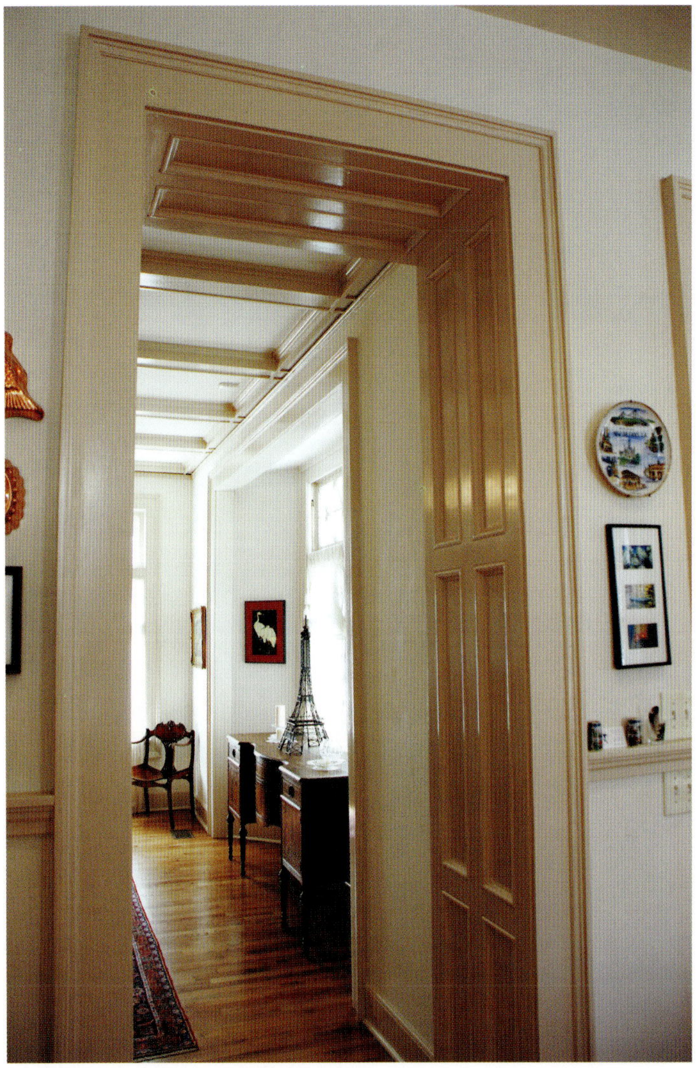

A narrow hallway is an elegant transition from the formal dining room to the adjacent kitchen.

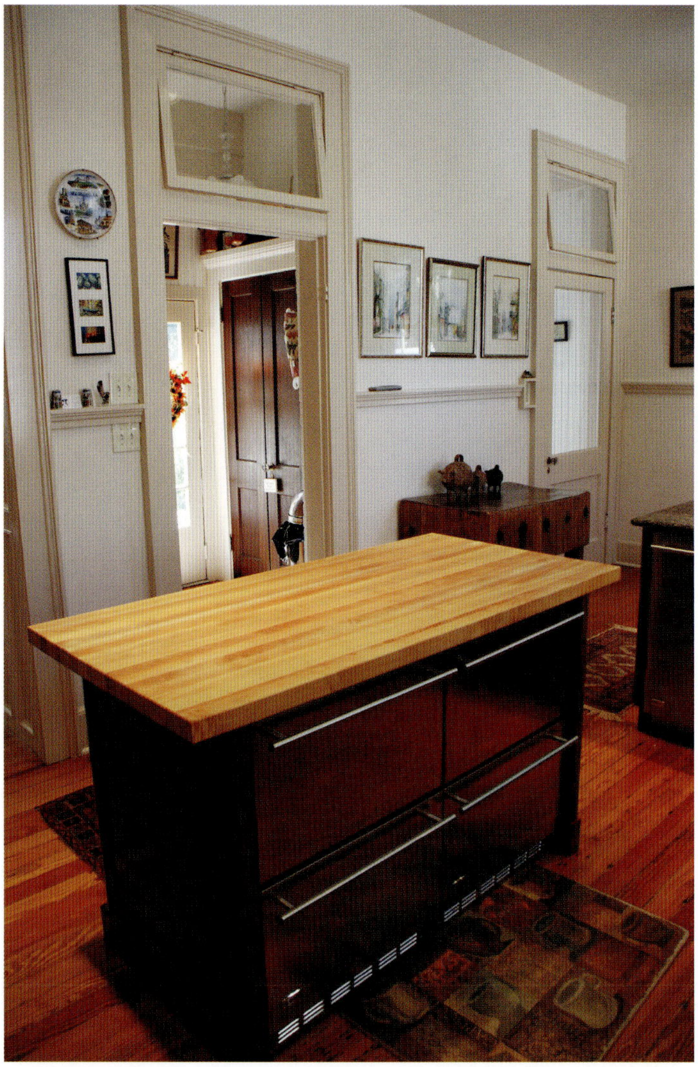

In the remodeled kitchen, a convenient island blocks the view from the dining room and defines the work area.

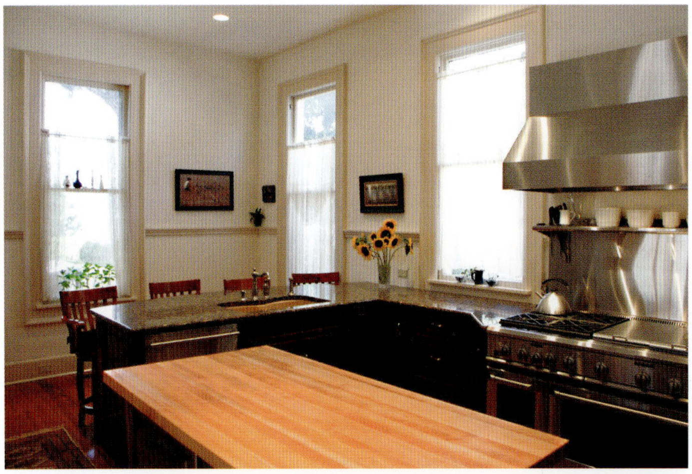

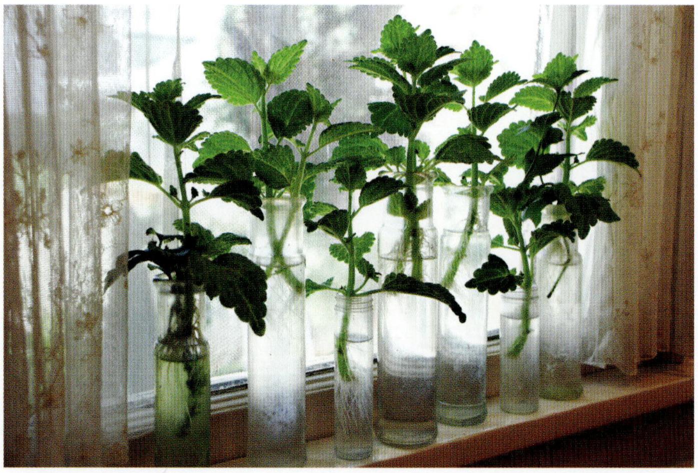

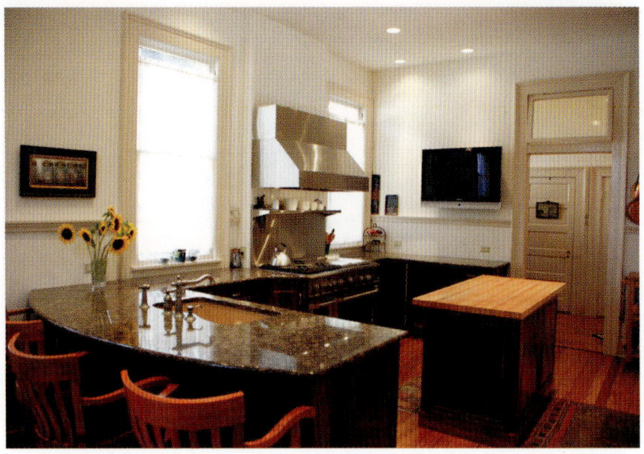

Wall-hung cabinets were omitted in the new kitchen design, calling attention to the beautiful windows where Linda grows plants in glass vials. A ledge added to the countertop provides for eating in.

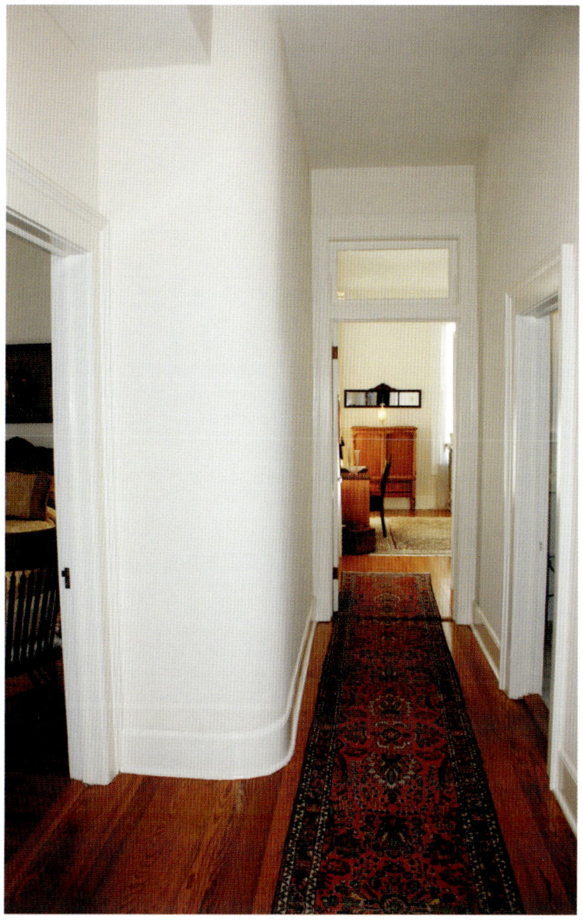

In the hallway on the second floor, a rounded corner softens the line and adds dimension.

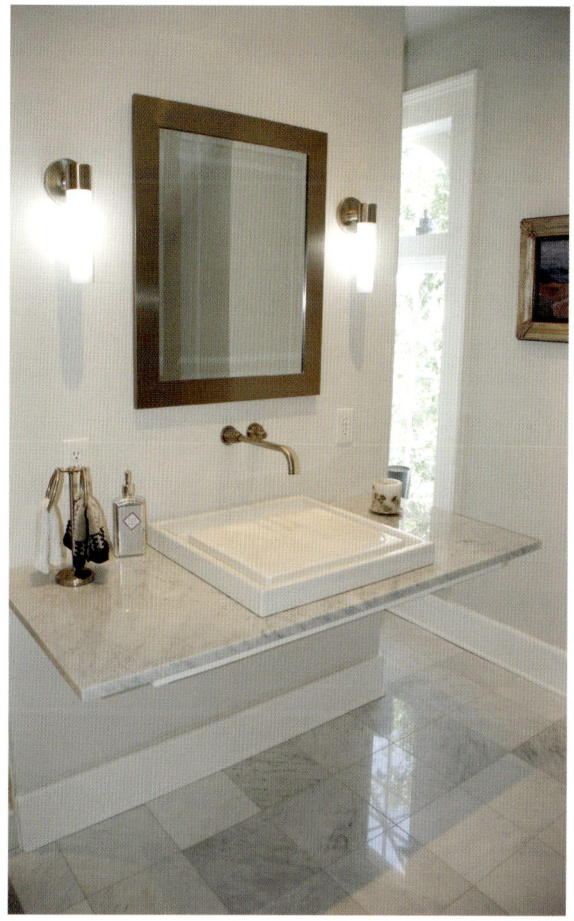

The Daniels remodeled the master bathroom to suit their contemporary lifestyle.

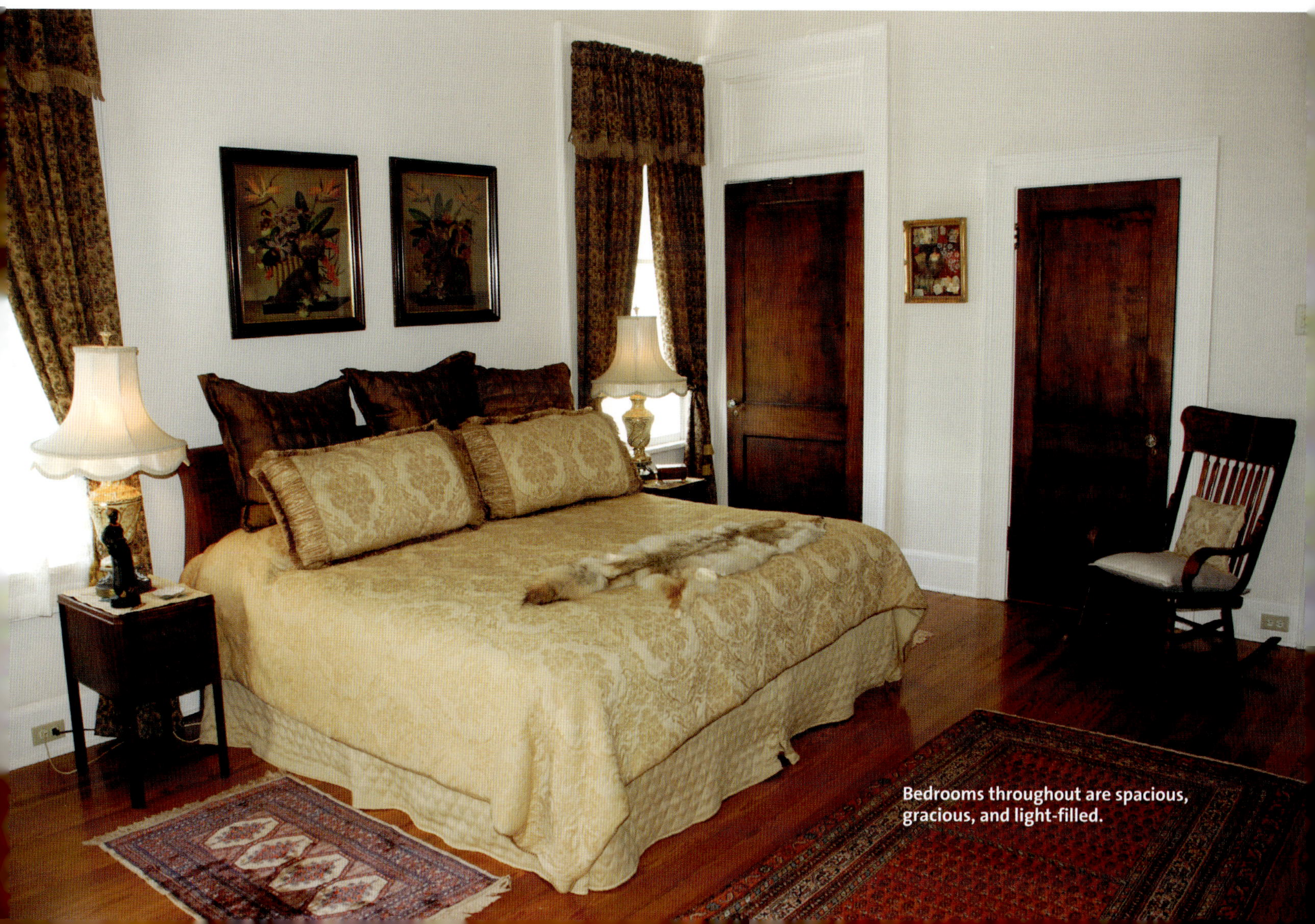

Bedrooms throughout are spacious, gracious, and light-filled.

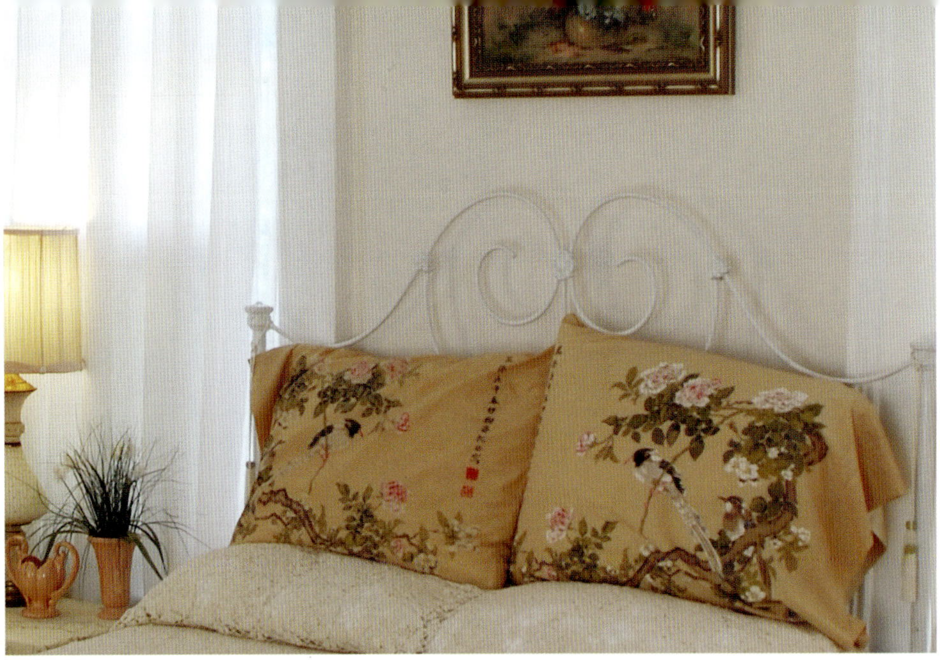

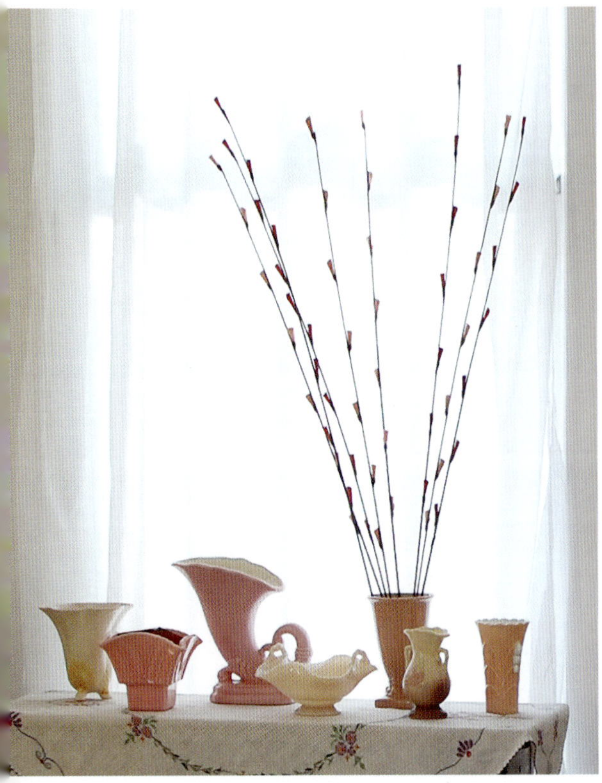

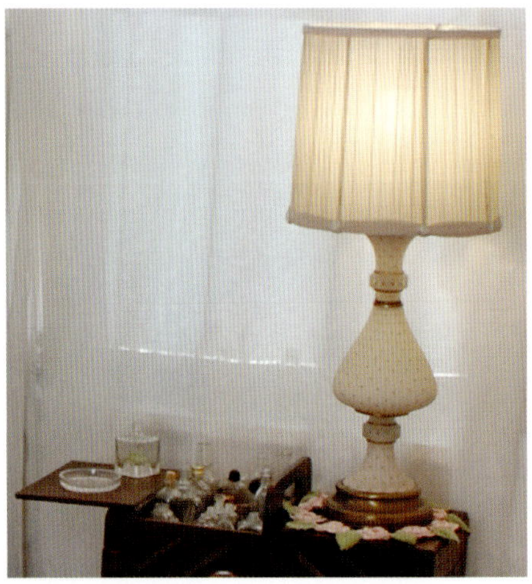

The guestroom in soft pastels is welcoming and relaxing.

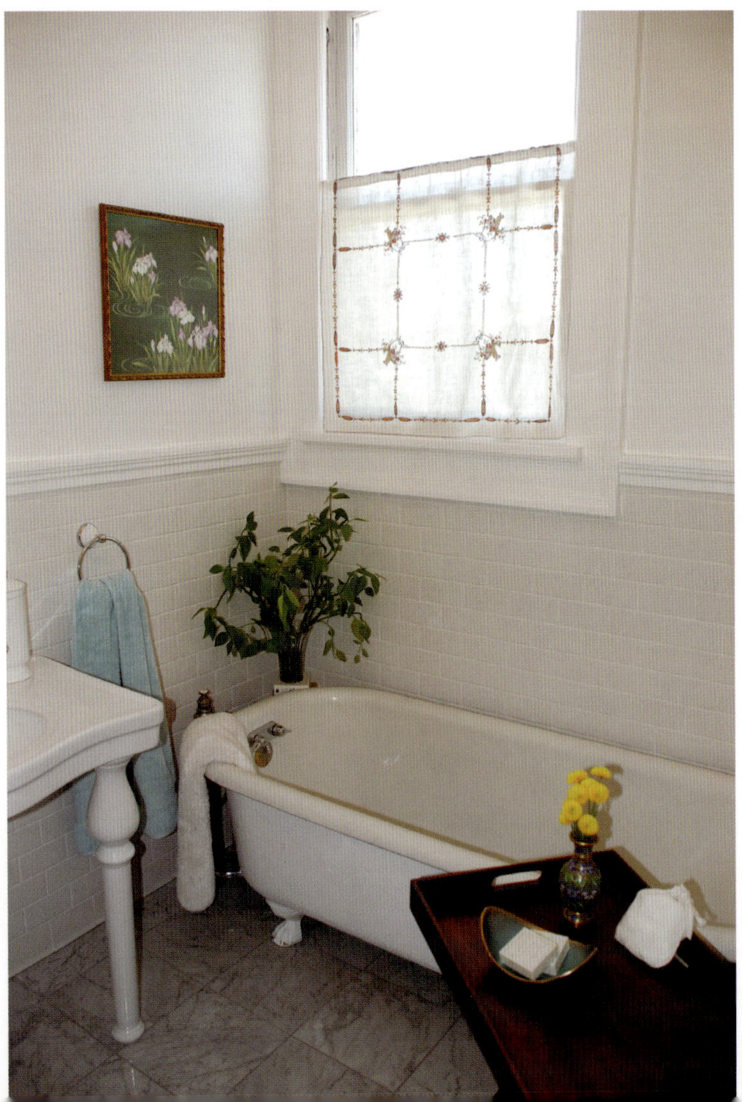

The guest bathroom retains the old clawfoot tub, but has a coat of fresh, light paint.

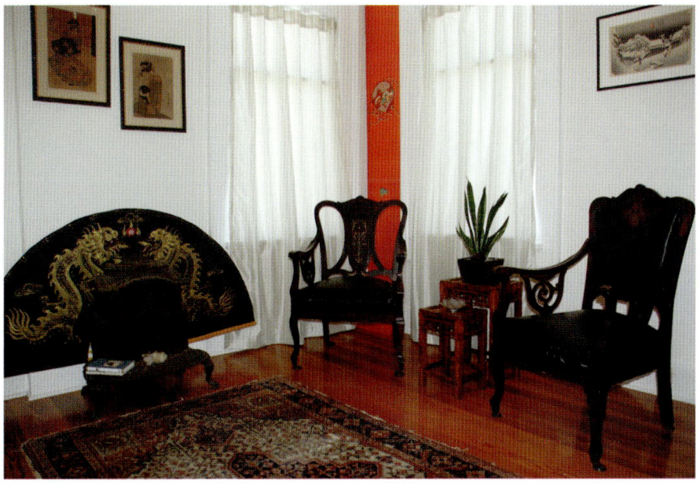

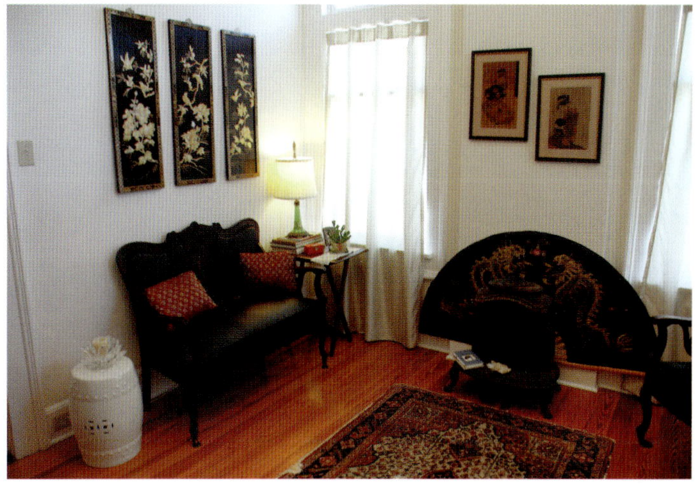

Linda Daniels devotes one second-story room to her collection of Orientalia.

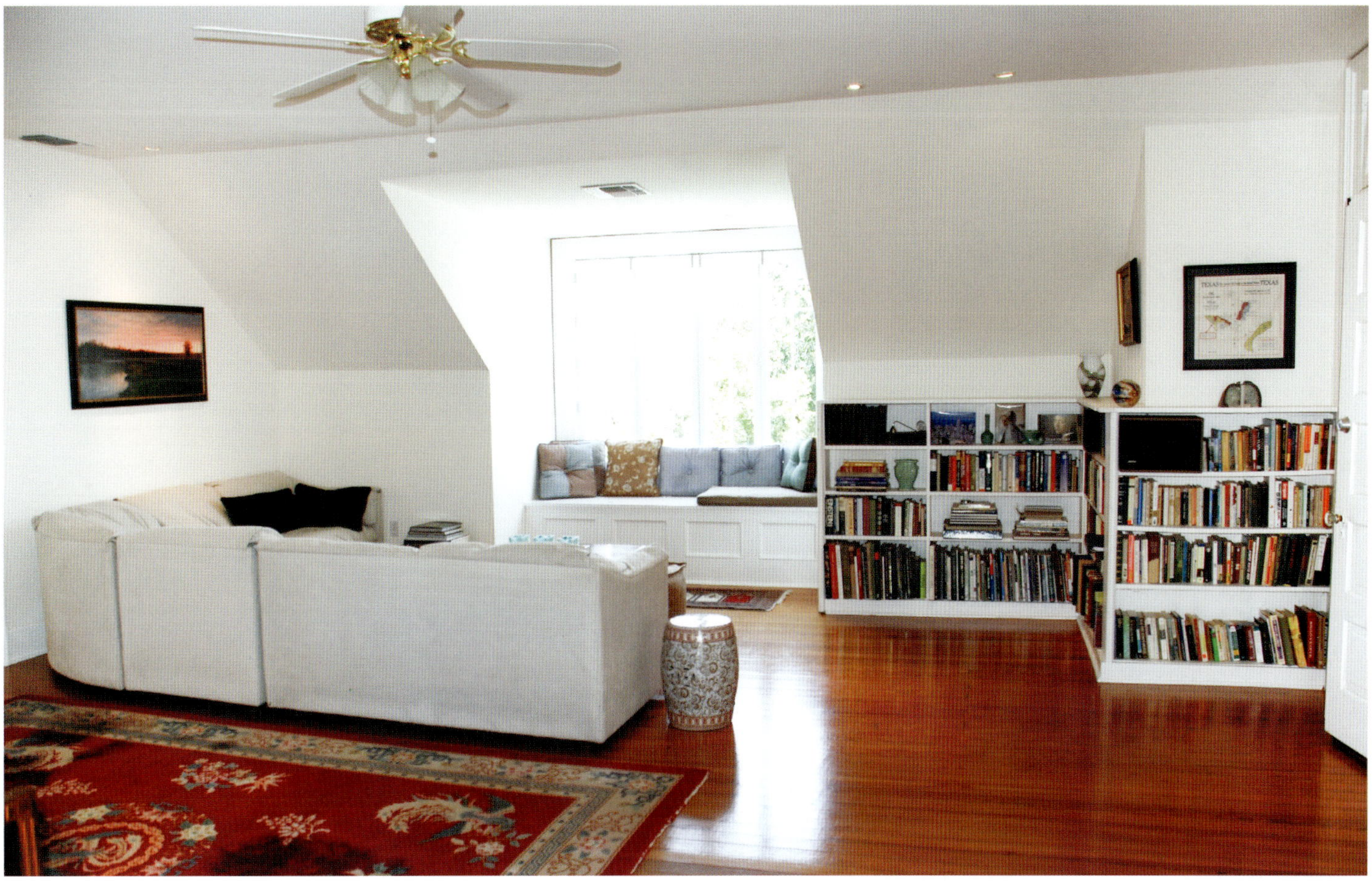

The third floor is a sweeping floor-through space with dormer windows on several sides. A south-facing window provides an excellent view of downtown San Antonio.

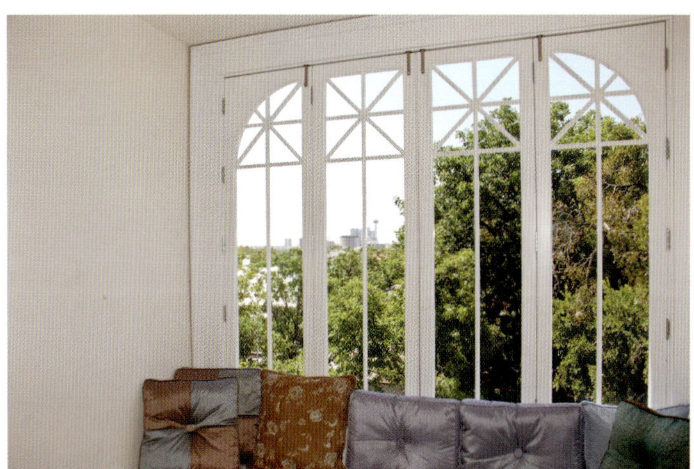

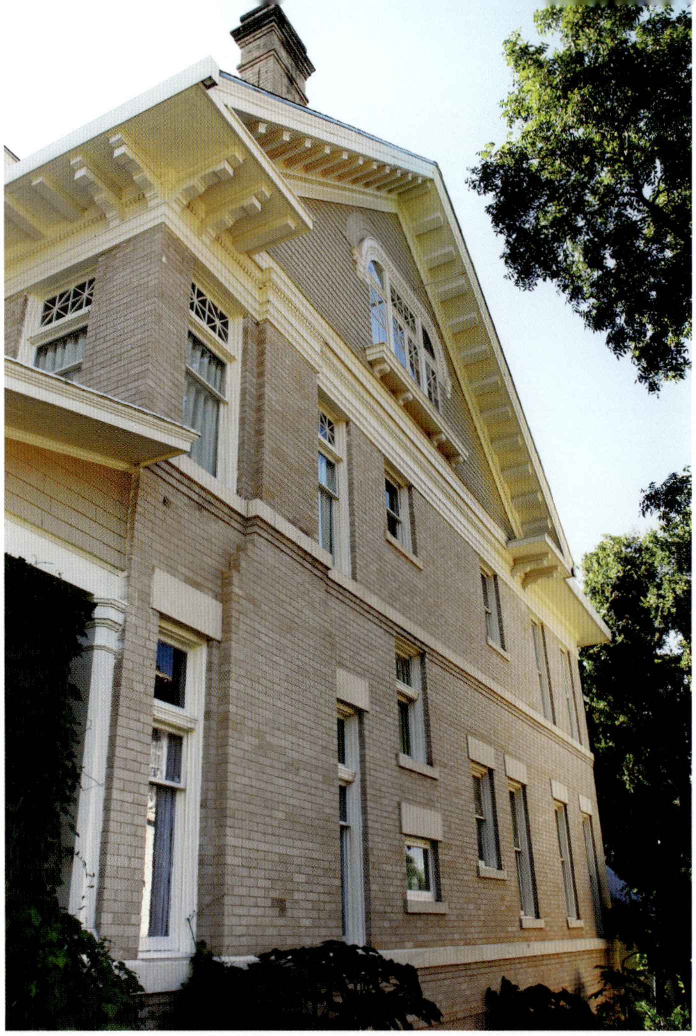

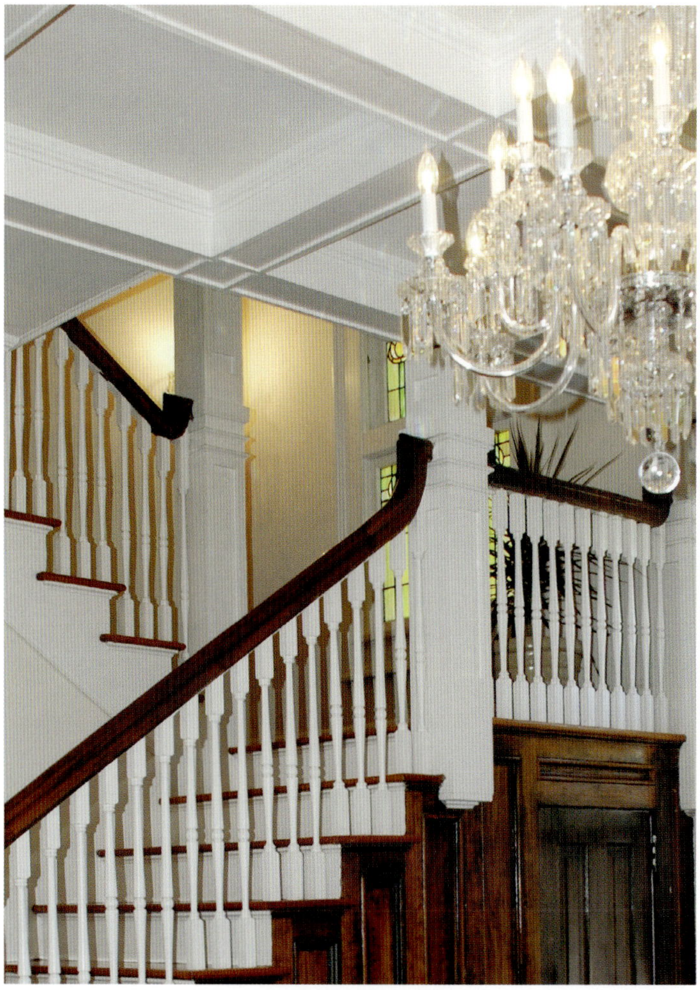

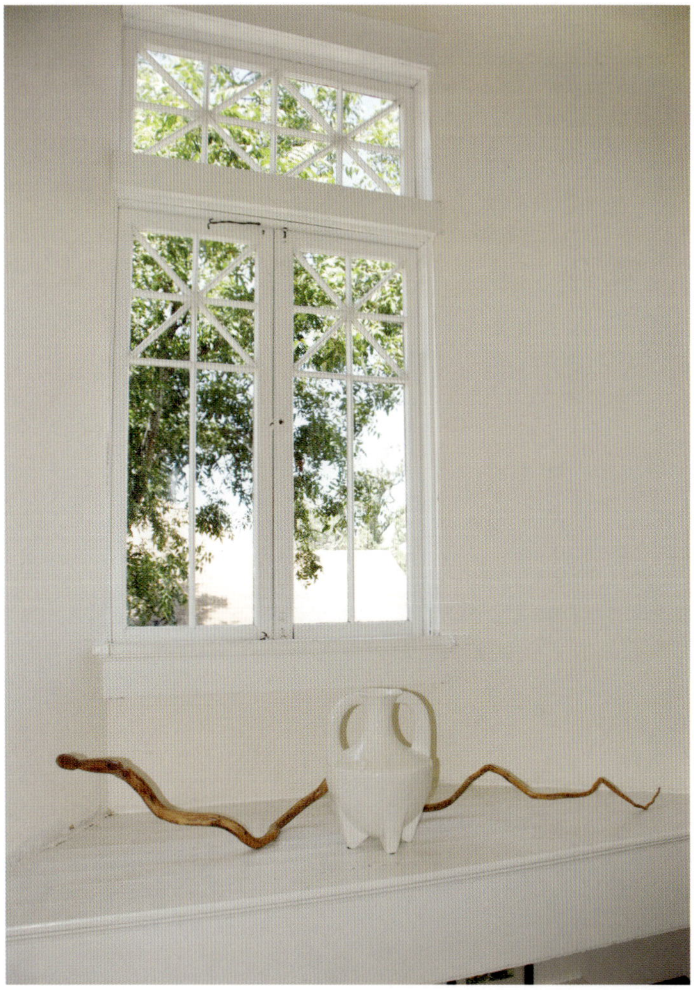

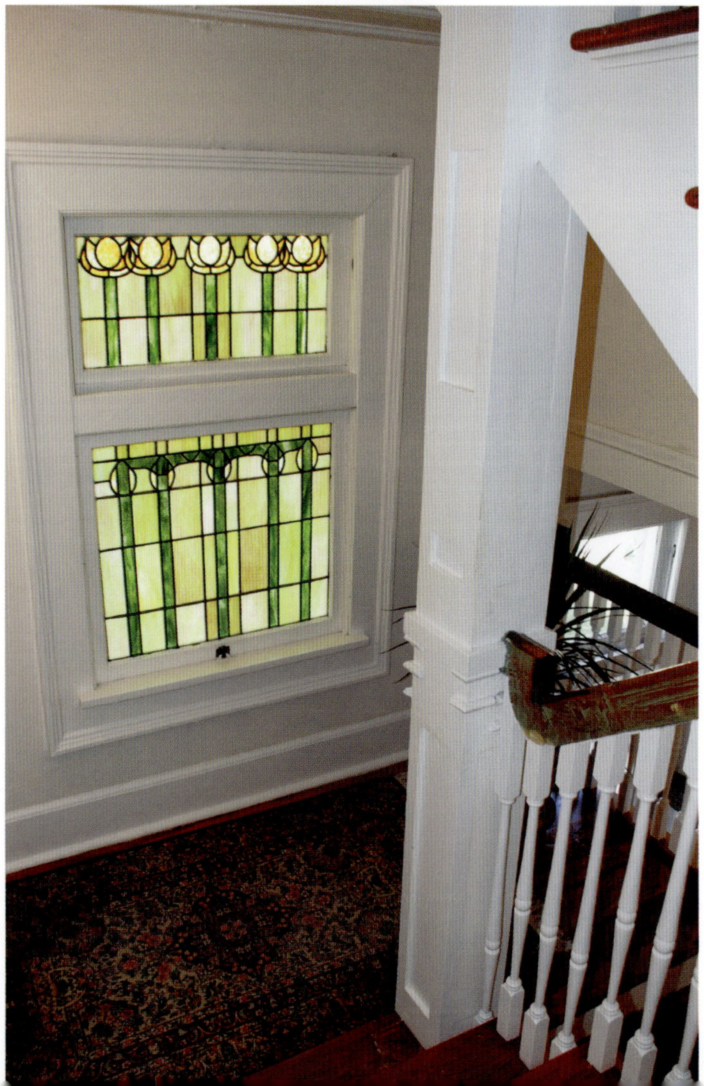

The Daniels Advise

Those who are contemplating re-modeling, restoring, and/or rehabilitating an old house may want to heed advice from Michael and Linda Daniels.

- Work within the parameters of the existing structural features; that is, situate new HVAC vents so as to avoid joists; create chases (in our case along bumped out chimneys and in closets) to hide new wiring and gas lines; and hang no upper kitchen cabinets that would encroach on existing windows.
- Do not tackle a project as large as ours without prior experience, because such a project will cost more time and money to complete than any well thought out budget projection.
- Make architectural salvage sources your best friend.
- If you're skilled, invest in equipment to mill your own custom moldings to match the original design so that replacements appear seamless.
- Find an "old school" master carpenter, who will prove as valuable as an architect and/or interior designer.
- Keep costs down by changing the floor plan as little as is necessary to accommodate your lifestyle.
- Carefully think through every phase of the project *before* doing any demolition. Spending time in the space getting to know it *before the project begins* will ultimately pay off in fewer, costly change orders.

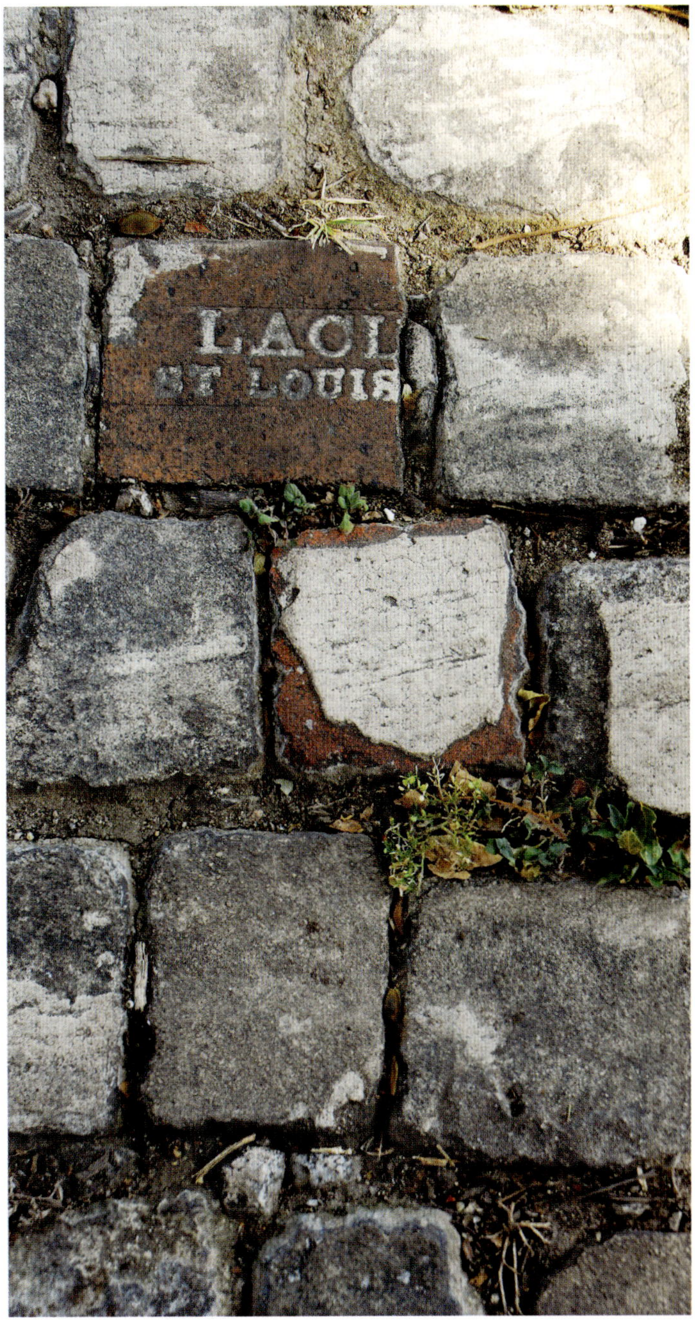

24

One of Twelve Originals

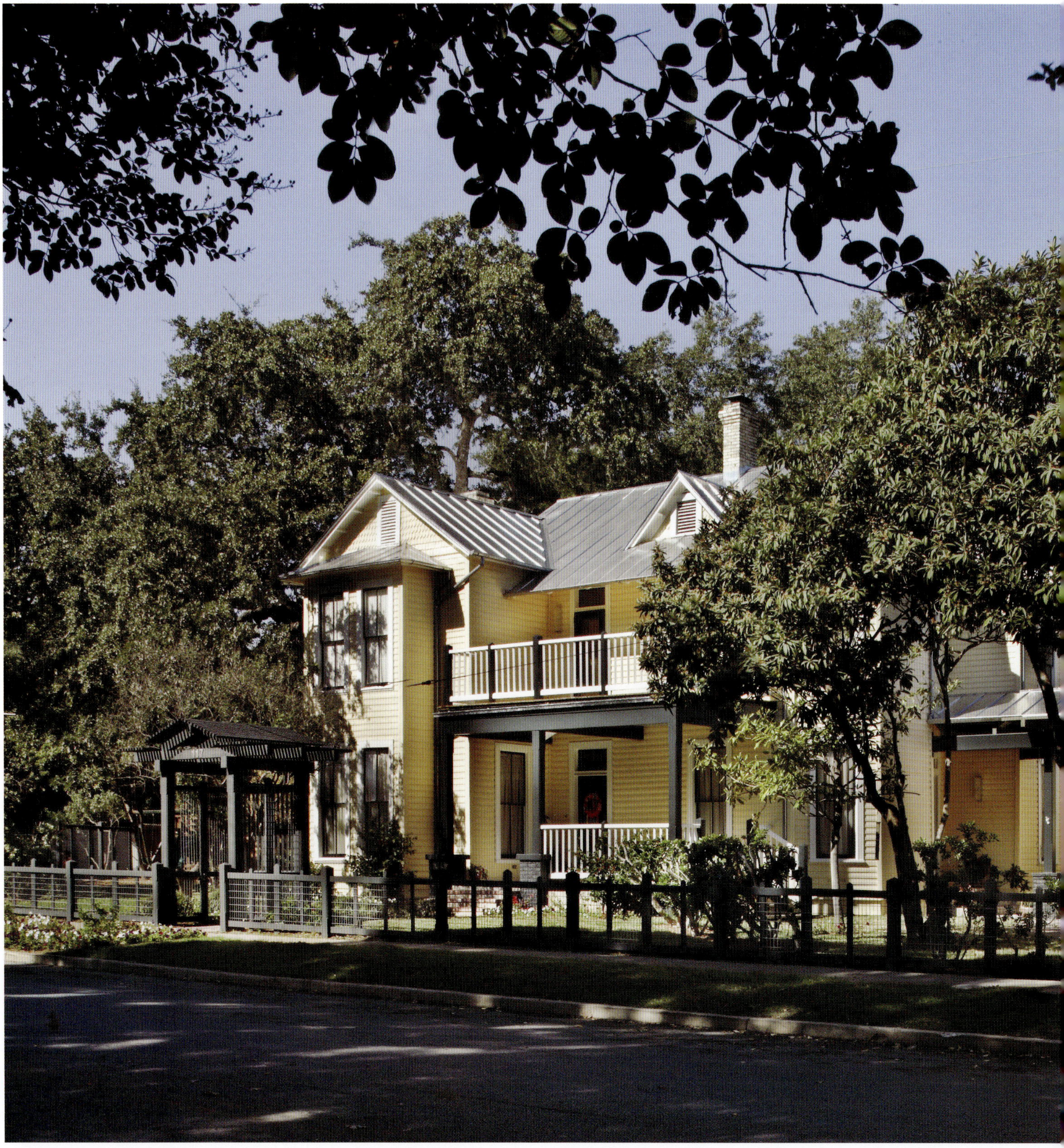

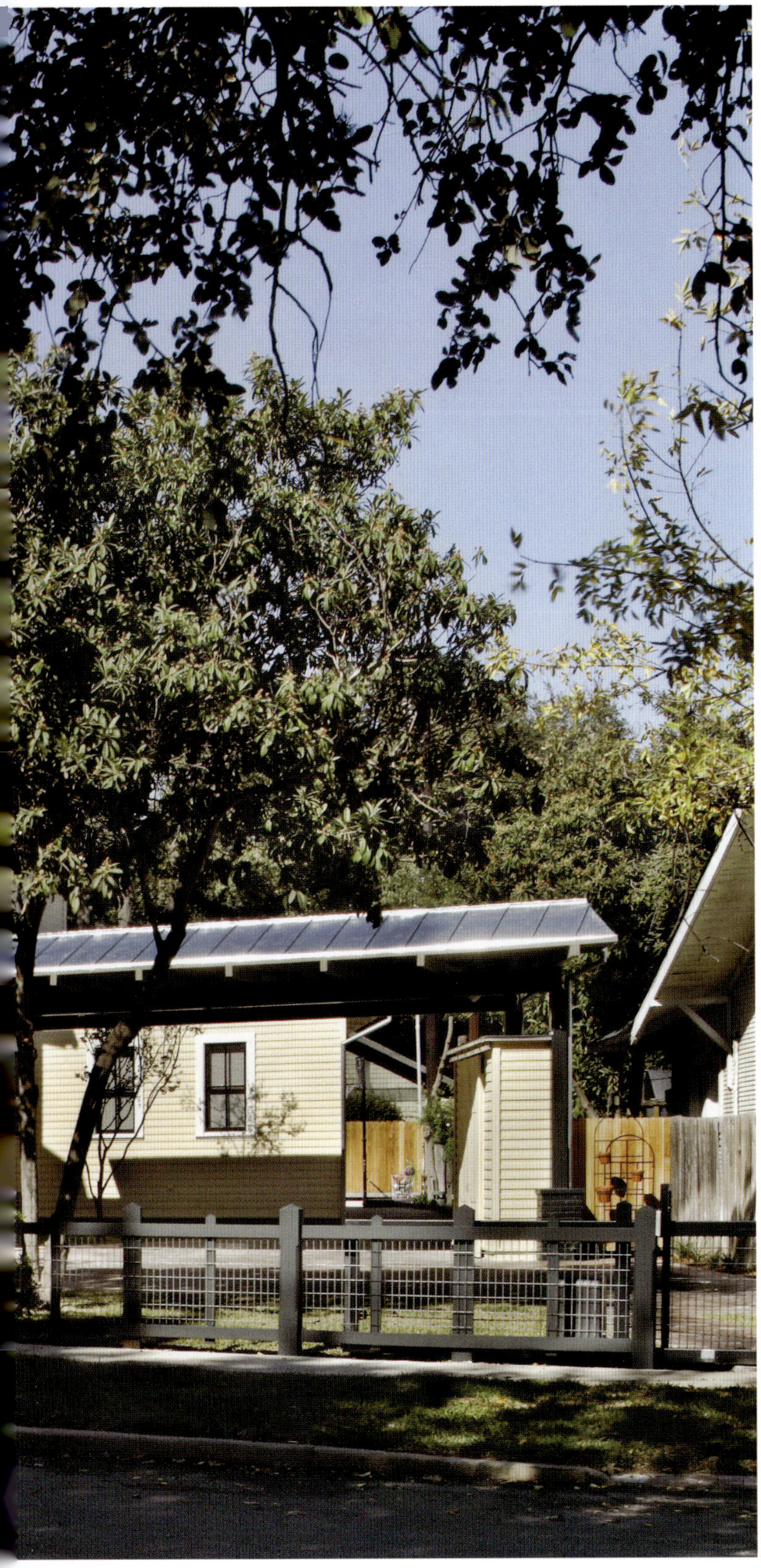

"We were restoring a piece of Texas history, one of the *twelve original houses in Alamo Heights*" says Architect John Grable in commenting on his redesign of a venerable old San Antonio home. "Careful renovations and new, open interior spaces revive the spirit of this historic 1885 farmhouse. This saved it from reincarnation as a McMansion."

Briefly, Grable describes changes to the ground floor. "A porte-cochere accesses the recreated traditional back-door entrance. Inside, the foyer links to the central hall via a gallery defined by relocated stairs adjacent to bright living spaces."

On the second floor, a gallery links bedrooms that open onto generous decks. "Here, the dense oak tree canopies create a tree-house experience," says Grable. "A new solarium looks out at a stand of live oaks. It functions as a sentry lantern, spilling warm light into the yard, the entry, and the road beyond."

"By re-establishing connections to the exterior and revealing its original character," says Grable, "I created a home that now is visually and contextually connected to its old San Antonio neighborhood."

The sense of neighborhood, and the protection of historic neighborhoods is a major concern of San Antonio, a very big city that maintains its legendary, traditional, small-town charm. Recognized as a major art center, this city appreciates its architects, whose genius extends the lives of San Antonio's original architecture.

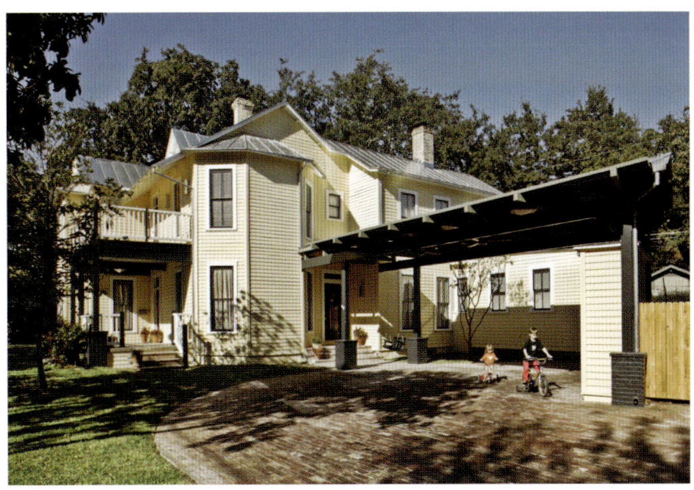

Architect John Grable romantically and emphatically integrates an old farmhouse to its site with handsome trellised structures at front and side entries and covering walkways. The trellis and other trim are called out dramatically with sophisticated *au courant* dark color, a bold contrast to the light-colored house. *Photographs by Chris Cooper, courtesy John Grable Architects*

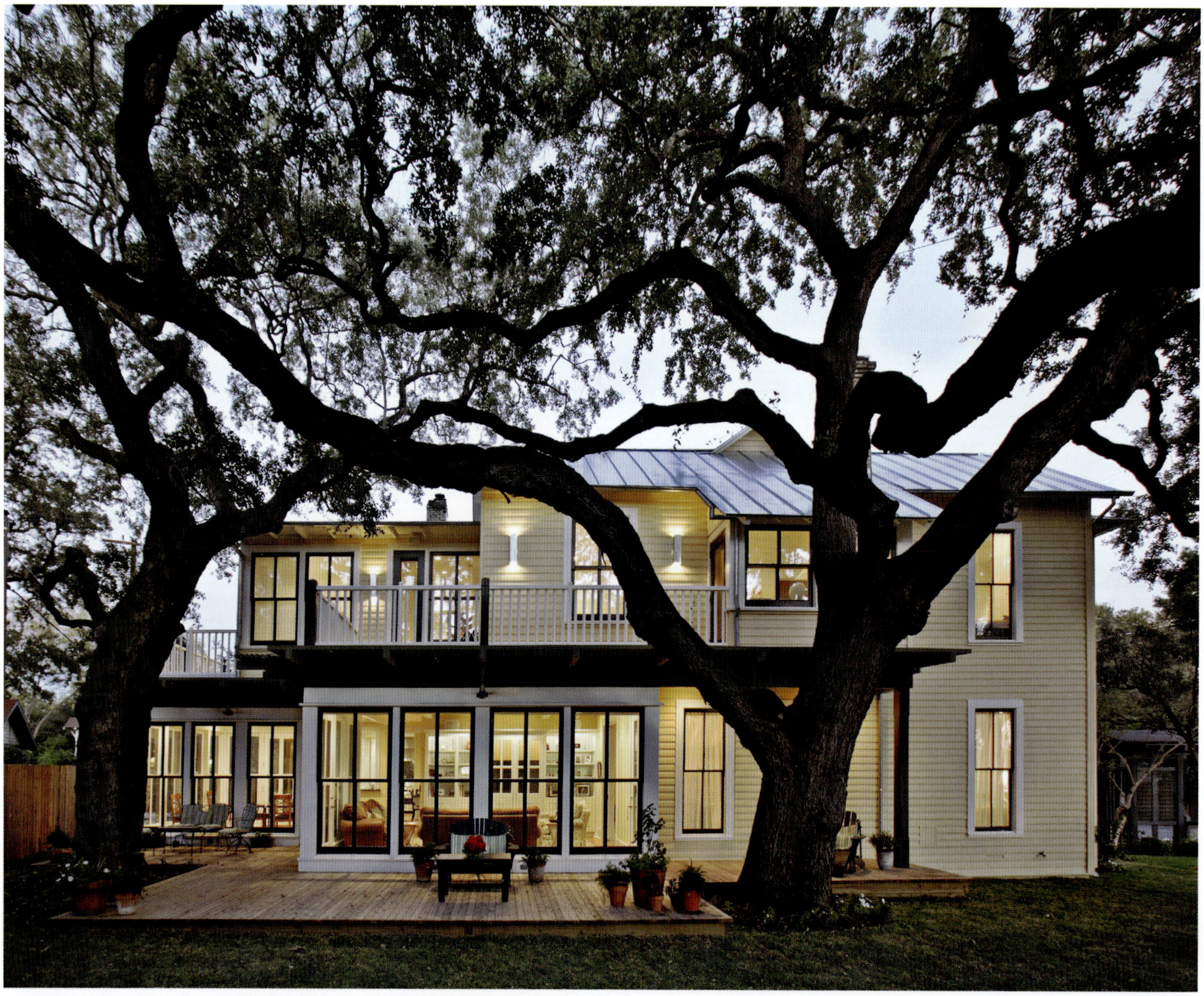

Interior-brightening window walls on one side of the house reveal outdoor views.

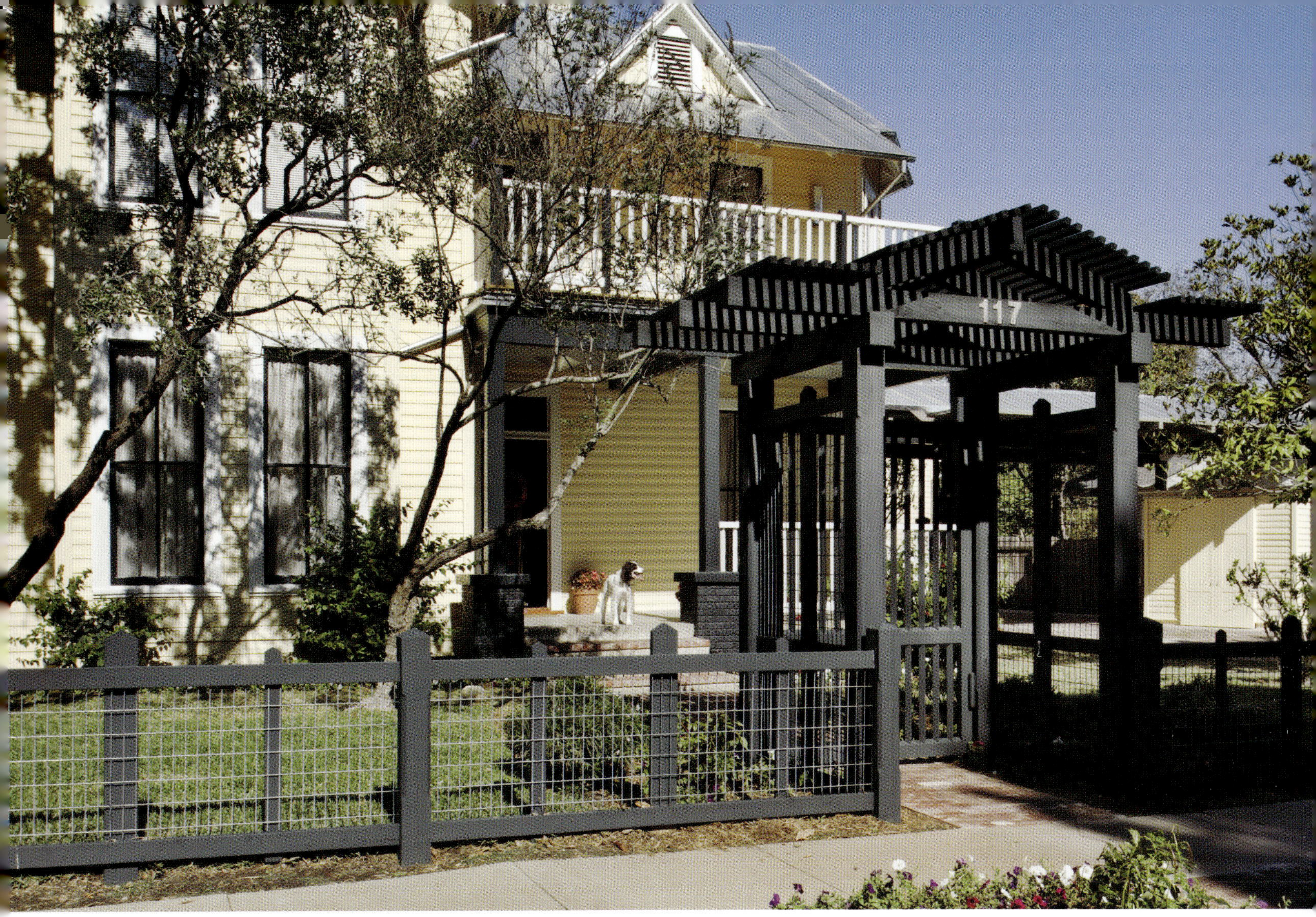

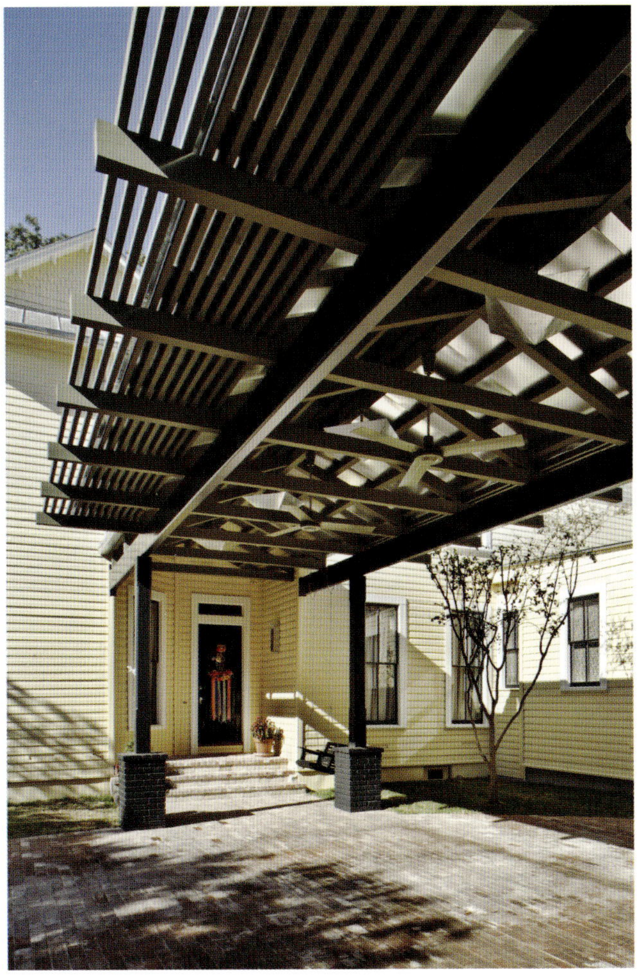

Beautifully designed and constructed trellis forms arbor-like entries and an overhead canopy for a walkway. An electric fan cools the brick-paved walkway that doubles as a play area.

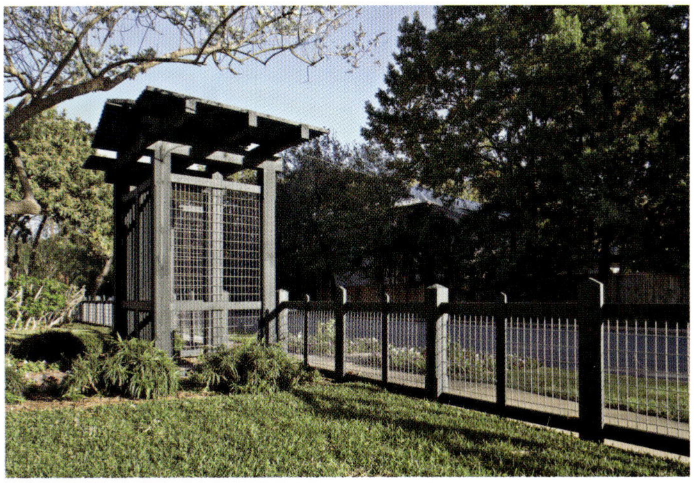

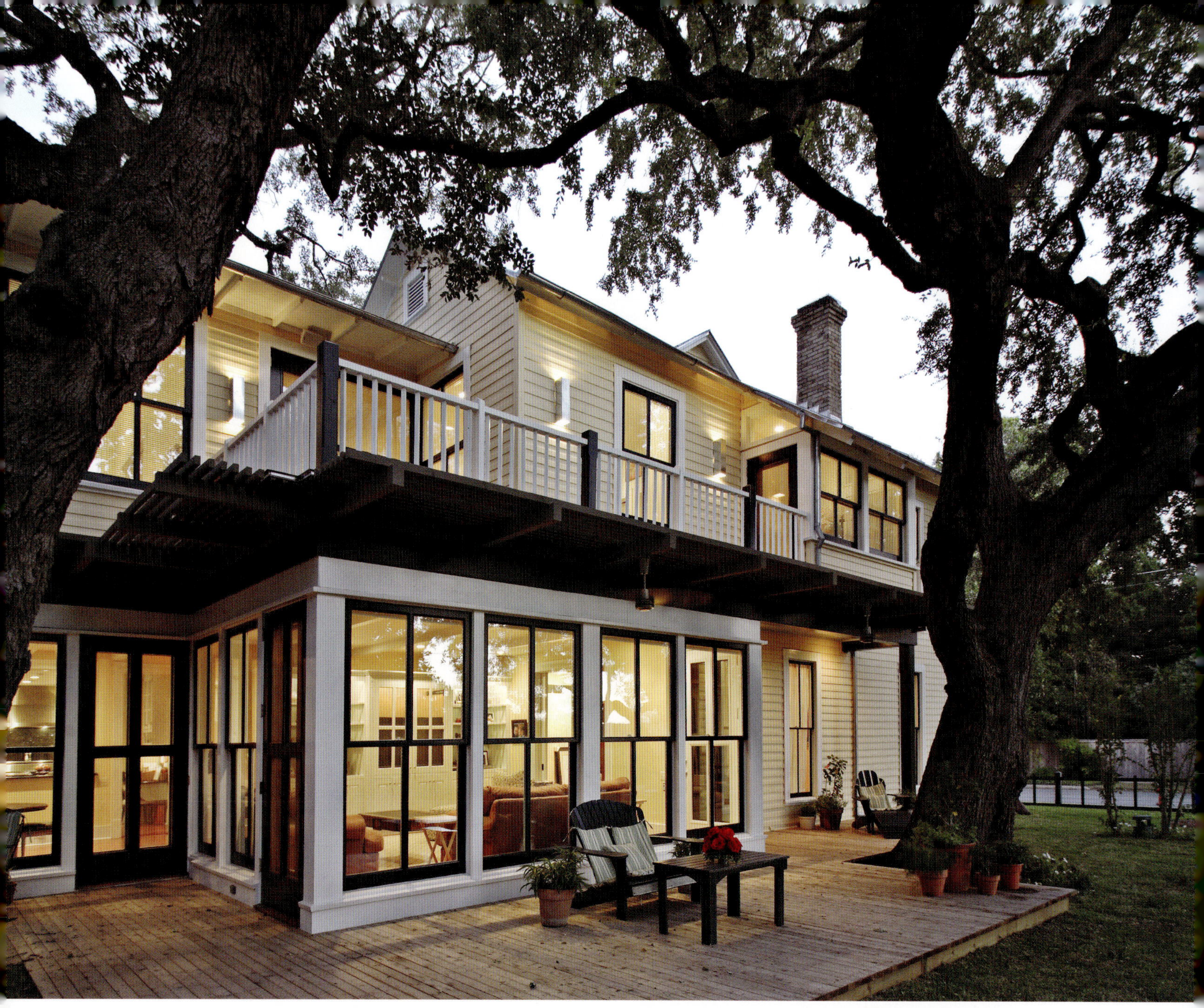

Doors lead from interior spaces to a new deck shaded by aged trees that provide a shady canopy for outdoor living.

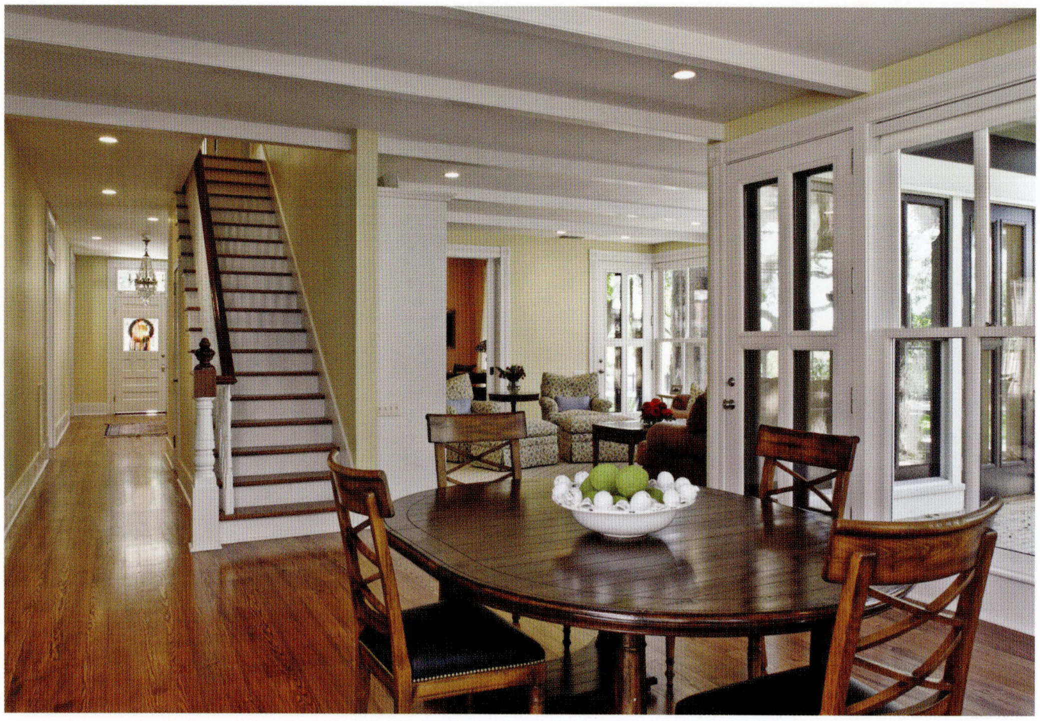

The open dining area creates an axis and passageway that permits traffic to flow easily indoors and to and from the exterior deck.

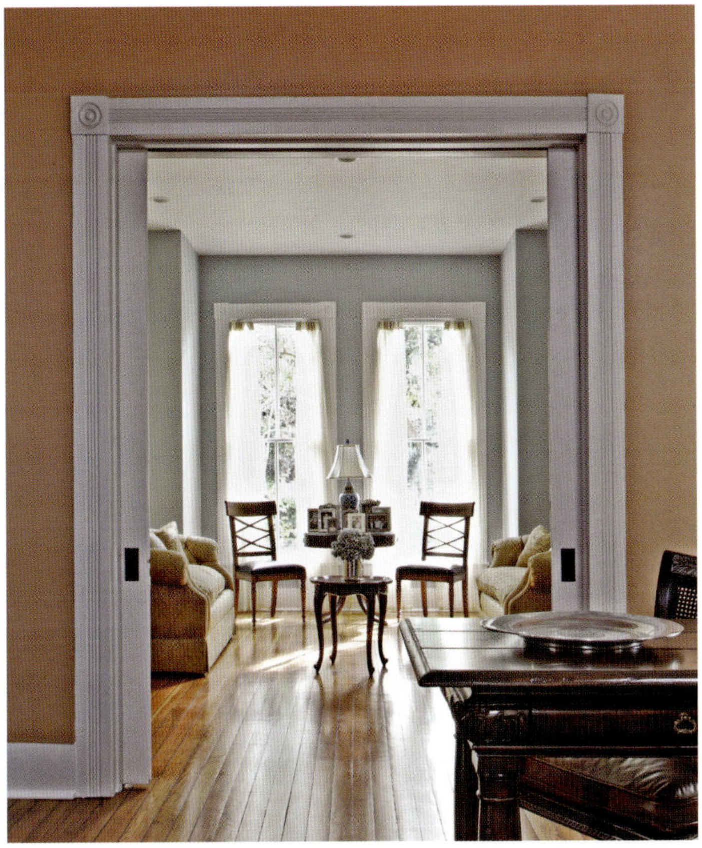

Clear lines of sight offer a sense of free movement, while bright citrus colors imbue the once tired-looking house with new vigor that seems young and tireless.

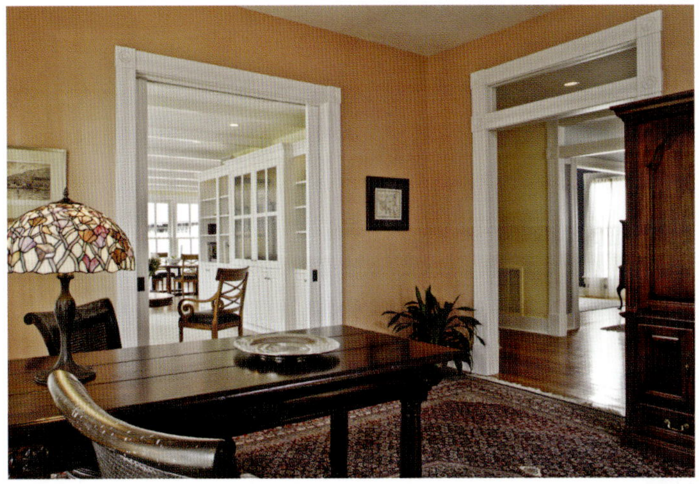

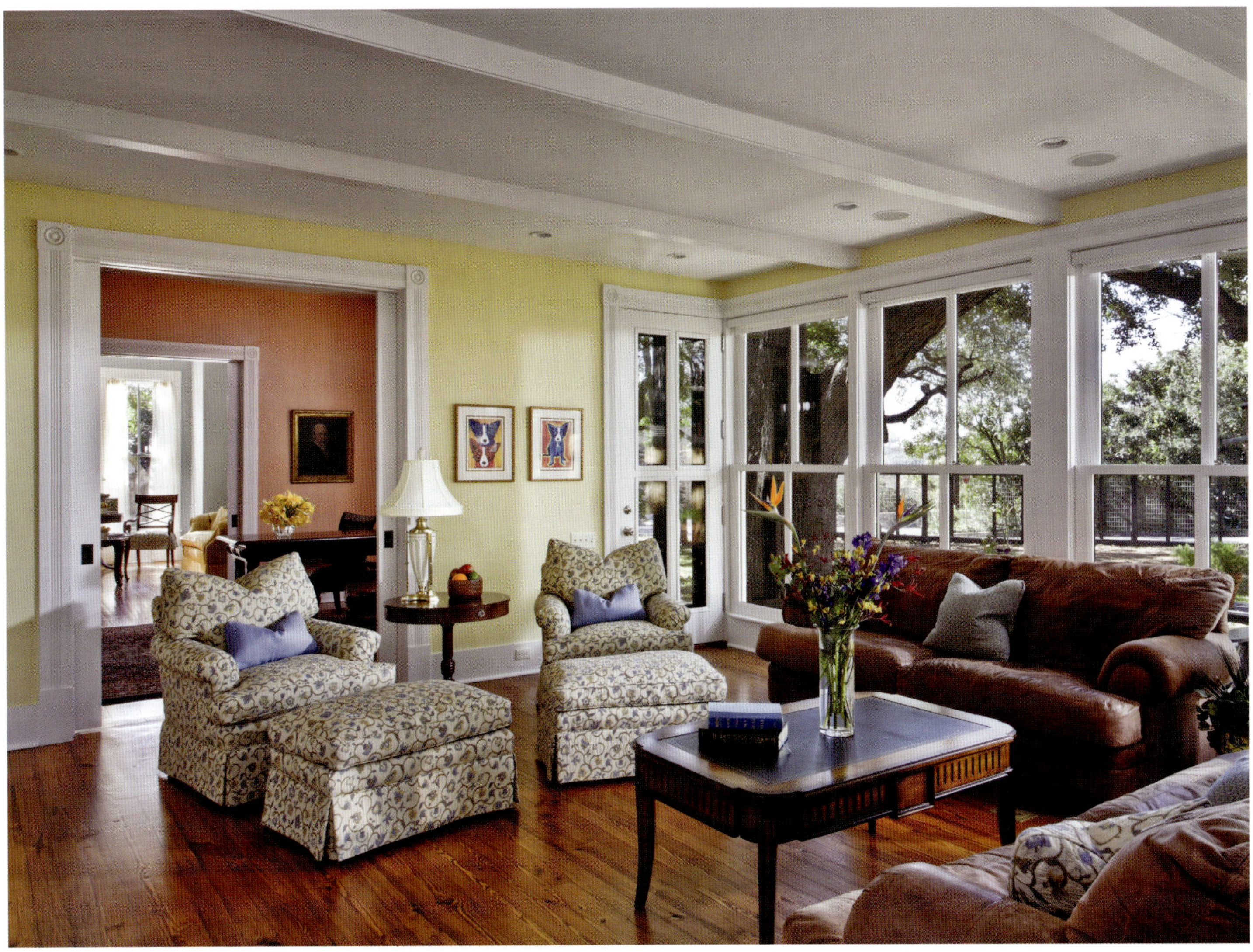

Openness and comfortable furniture add a sense of welcome to the seating area overlooking the new deck.

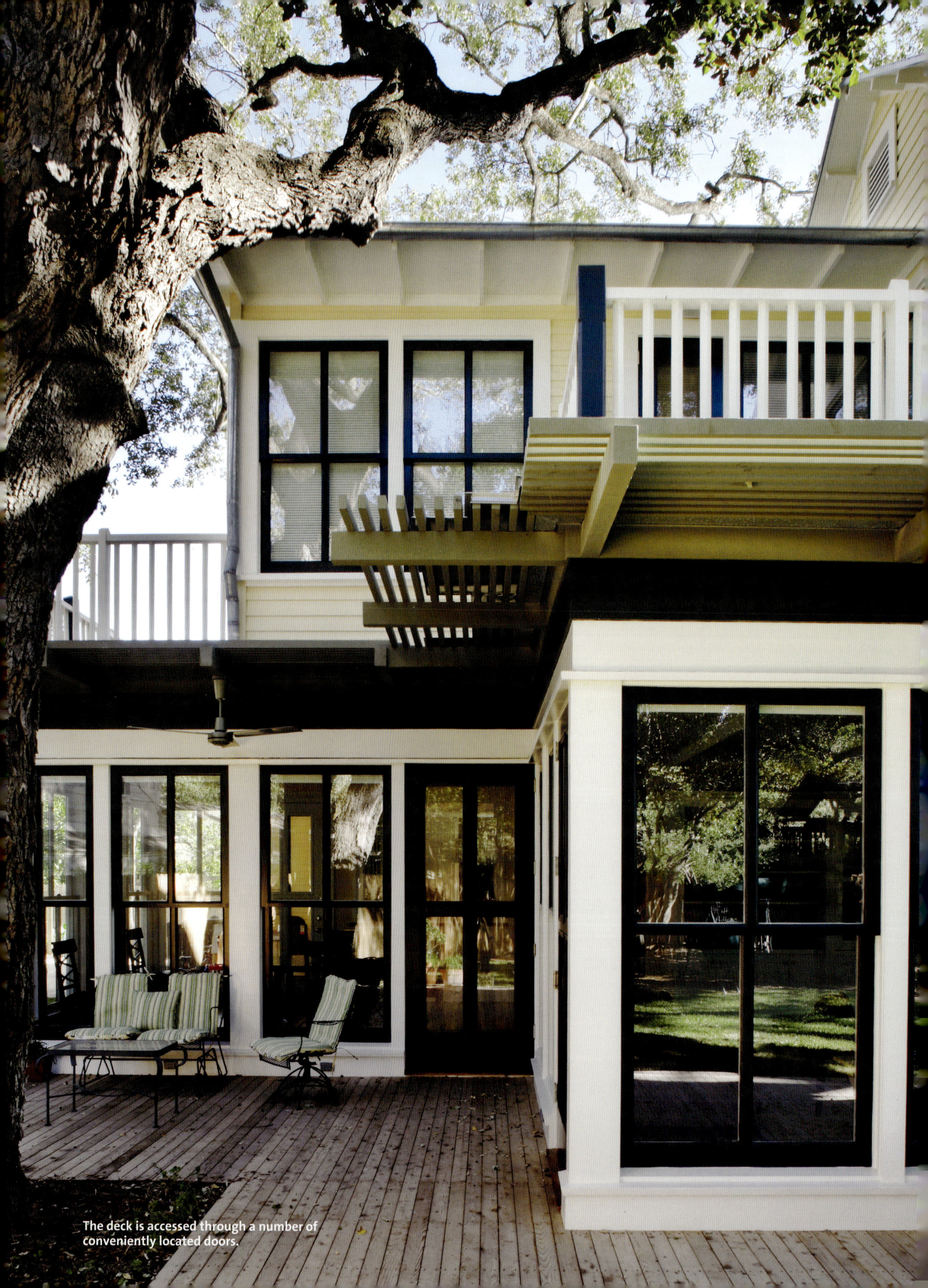

The deck is accessed through a number of conveniently located doors.

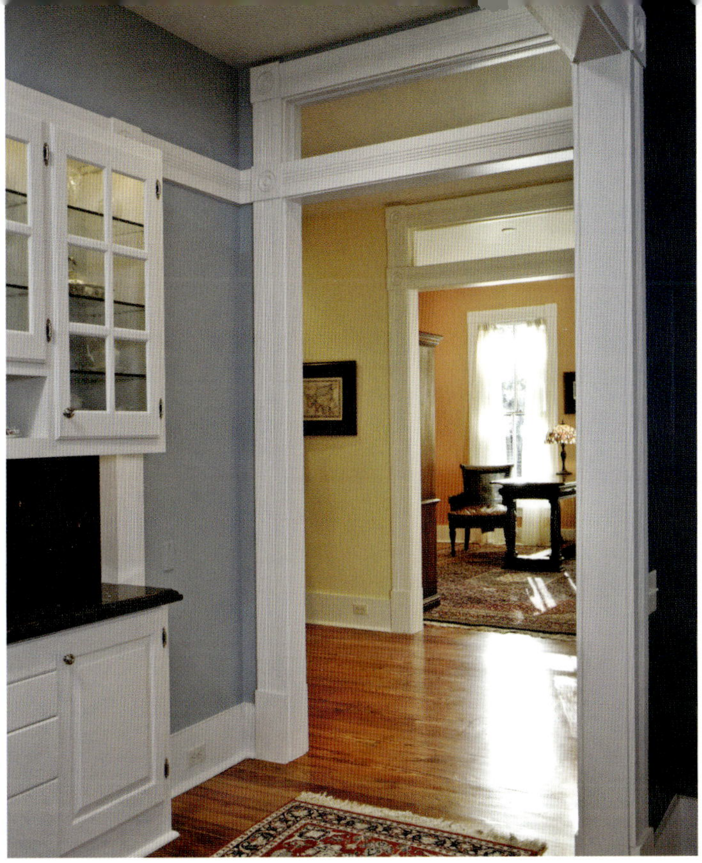

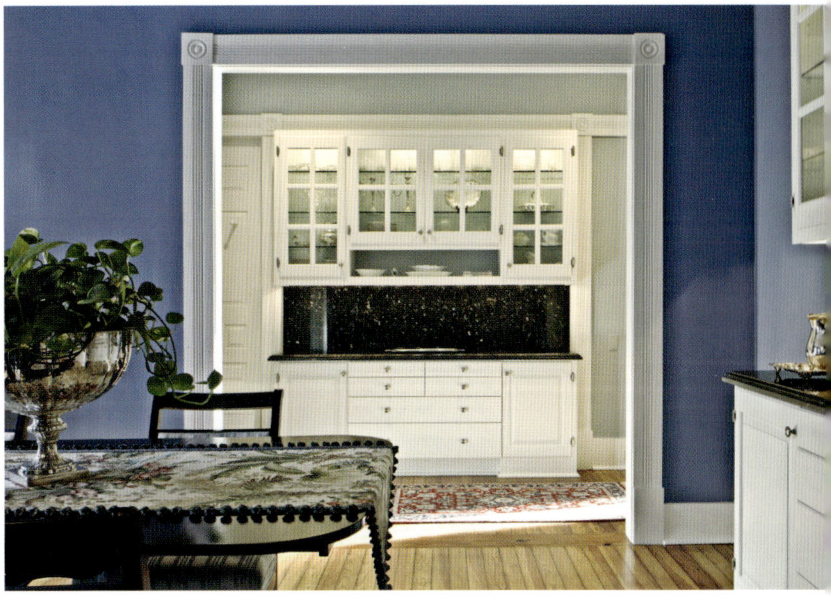

The newly up-to-date kitchen includes a handsome butler's cabinet, dining area, and a full complement of cabinets for ample storage. Wide open doorways and lots of windows admit interior and exterior views.

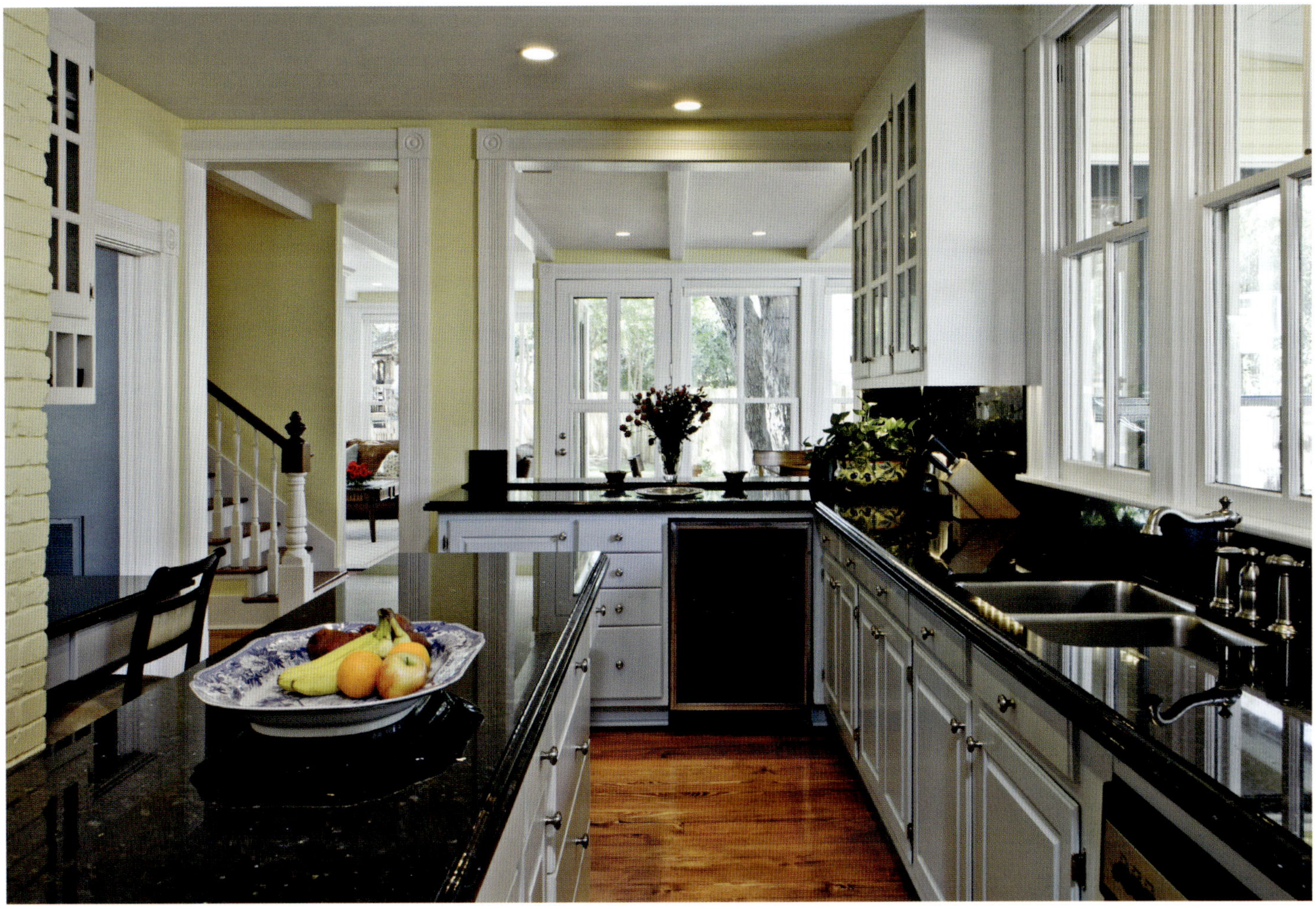

25

Terrell Hills House

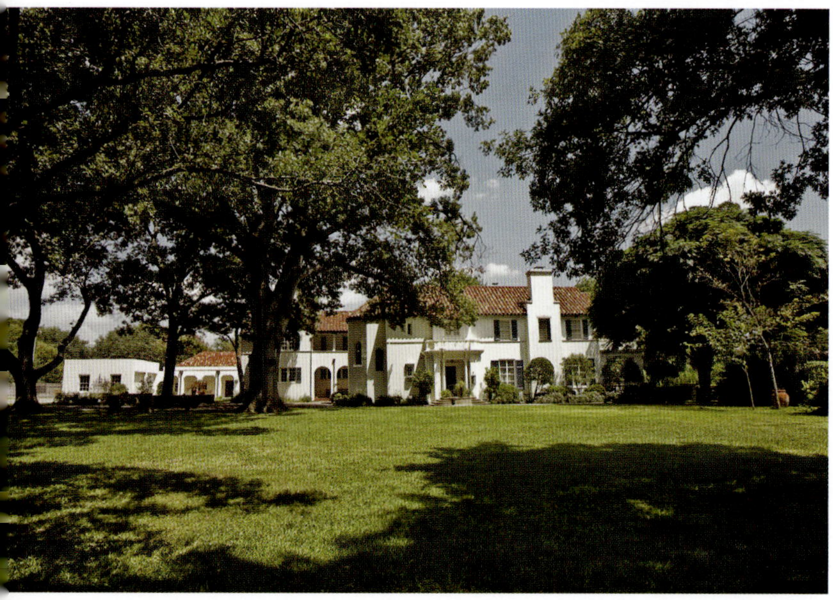

The façade of a new wing by Architect John Grable looks original and adds contemporary livability to a splendid old-now-new Terrell Hills house. *Photographs by Chris Cooper, courtesy John Grable Architects*

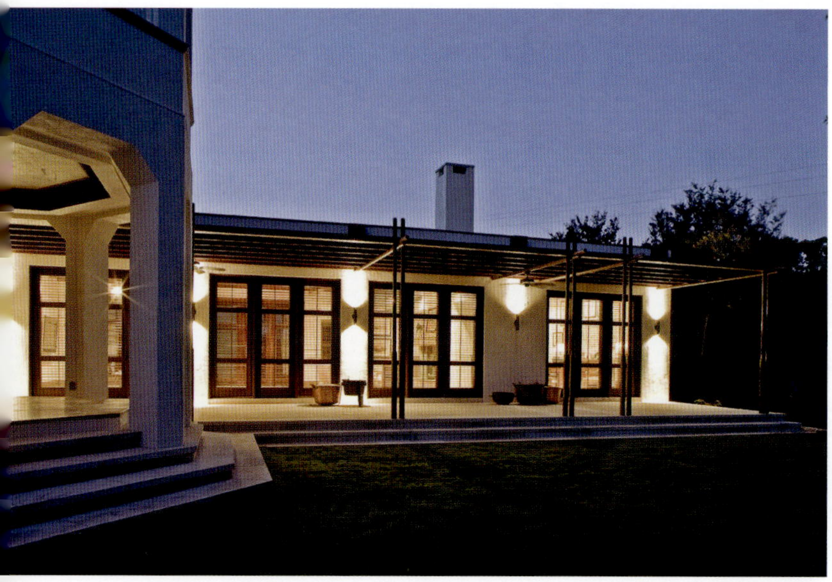

Damage by weather, changes wrought by owners over the years, and changing lifestyles can mark even a once grand house as ready for a redo. "Perched on a promontory point that provided sweeping views of the city to the southwest, the once grand old 1930s house by Architect Bartlett Cocke, Sr. had been home to a prominent San Antonio family," says Architect John Grable. "A series of additions stymied those views and closed the house off from its beautiful site."

The owners called John Grable at John Grable Architects to transform the structure. "We were commissioned to renovate and expand the old house," Grable states. "We began by reclaiming its connection to the site. To reestablish the south lawn, we subtracted the inappropriate additions to the original house, which at this juncture were only one room wide. We then designed a wing—which could be described as a 'wall building,' or porch wing—with custom-built dramatic ten-foot-high walnut doors on each side, which bridged the gap between the original and best, most sensitive additions of the building." Custom walnut millwork flanked all interior openings, reinforcing the nondescript "wall-building" concept. On the north side of the wing, the elegant doors open onto a courtyard and sculpture garden. (This outdoor area is framed by a new two-car garage that doubles as a party pavilion and catering kitchen.) Doors on the south side of the wing open onto a new pool court/garden and the rebuilt south lawn.

For the new structures (wall wing and garage *cum* pavilion/kitchen), Grable reused all original longleaf pine in the framing and sheathing. "We recycled all existing door and window elements. Ceilings are paraffin-wax finished cypress. Floors are recycled quarter-sawn longleaf pine, as are floors in the existing building. The new walnut door and shutter system in the 'wall building' echoes walnut cabinets in the adjacent renovated kitchen, which now overlooks the pool garden," says Grable. Grable concludes: "The 'one-room'-wide additions recall the elegant proportions of the neo-Italianate structure, returning it to its former glory and solidifying the original strong linkage between house and site."

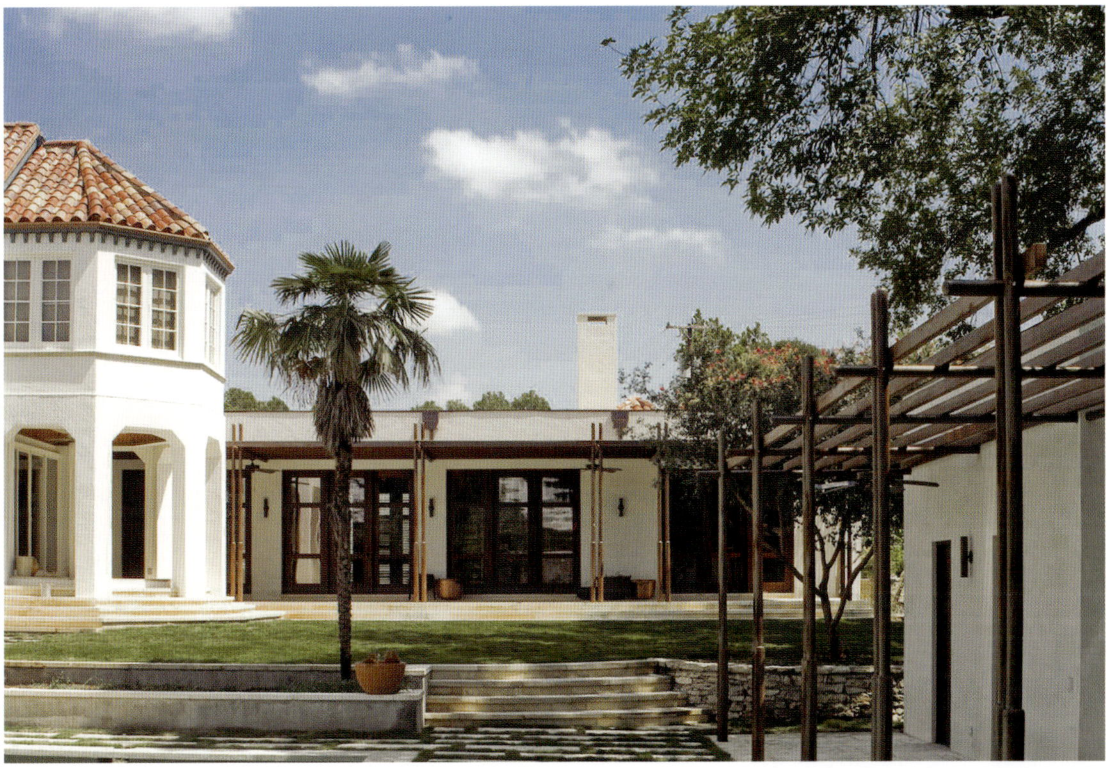

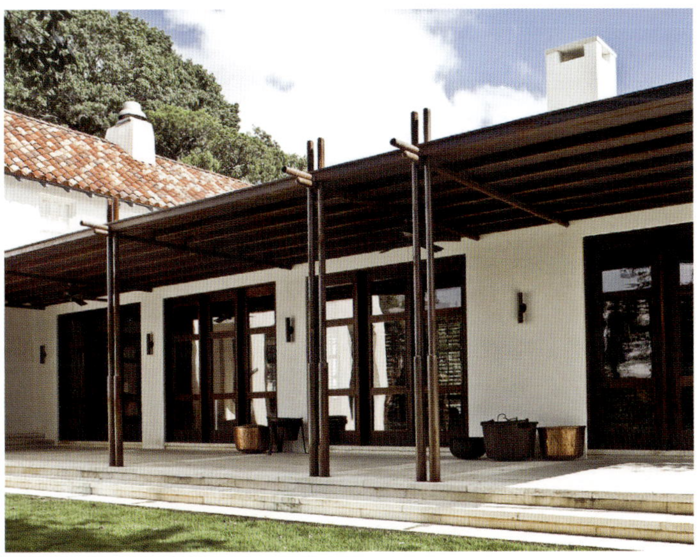

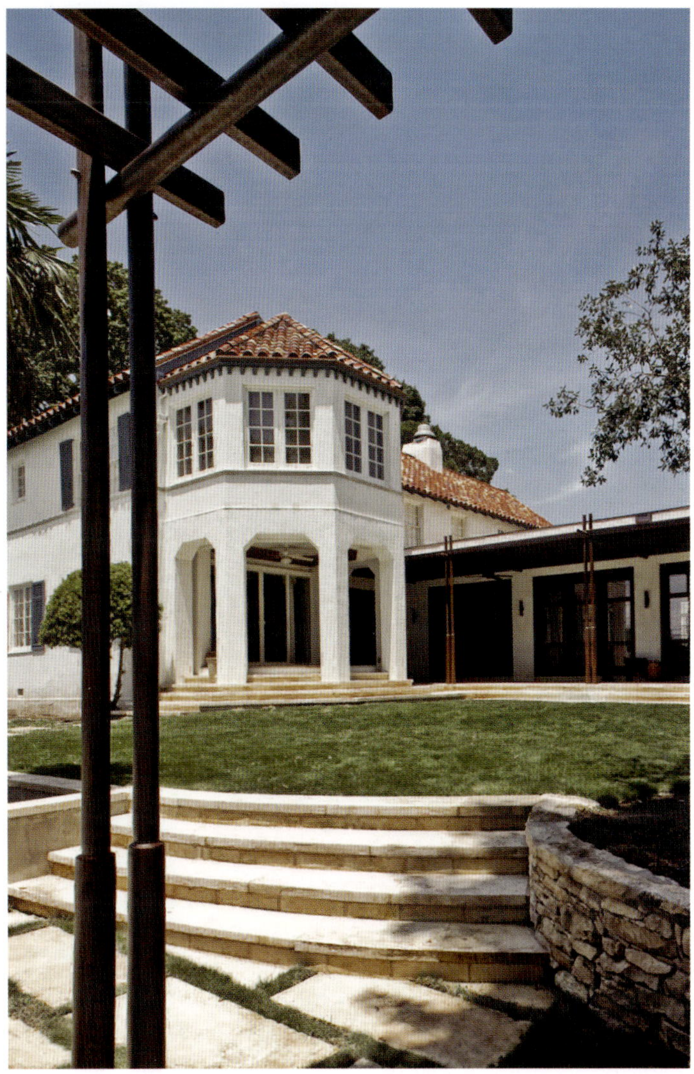

The new wing enhances the courtyard effect for the pool, an excellent vantage point for arresting night and day views of the veranda. Support members for the veranda roof (reminiscent of cedar pole supports for early Texas hacienda porches) are raw carbon steel finished to resemble copper. Paired supports cradle the roof rafter beam.

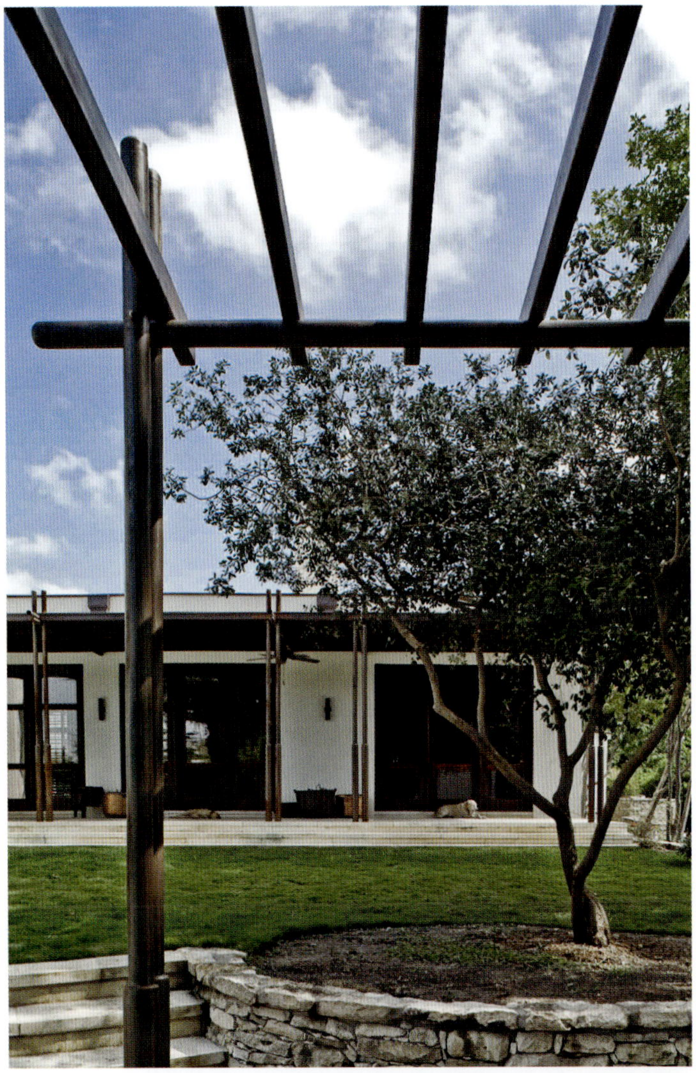

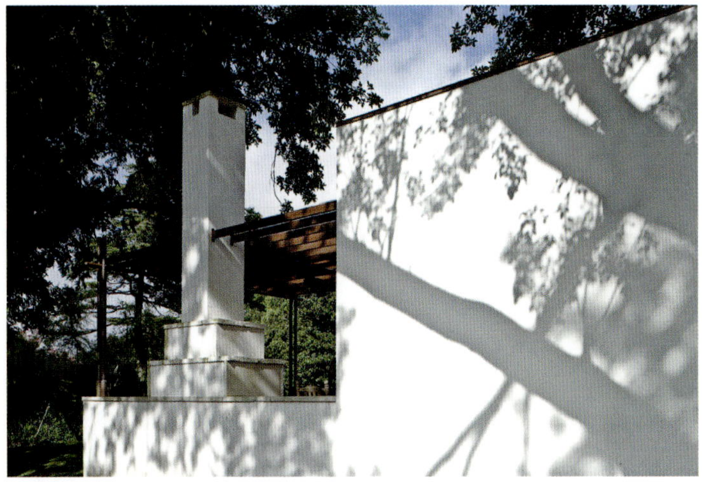

The handsome poolhouse reinforces the concept of courtyard and adds to the outdoor entertainment areas.

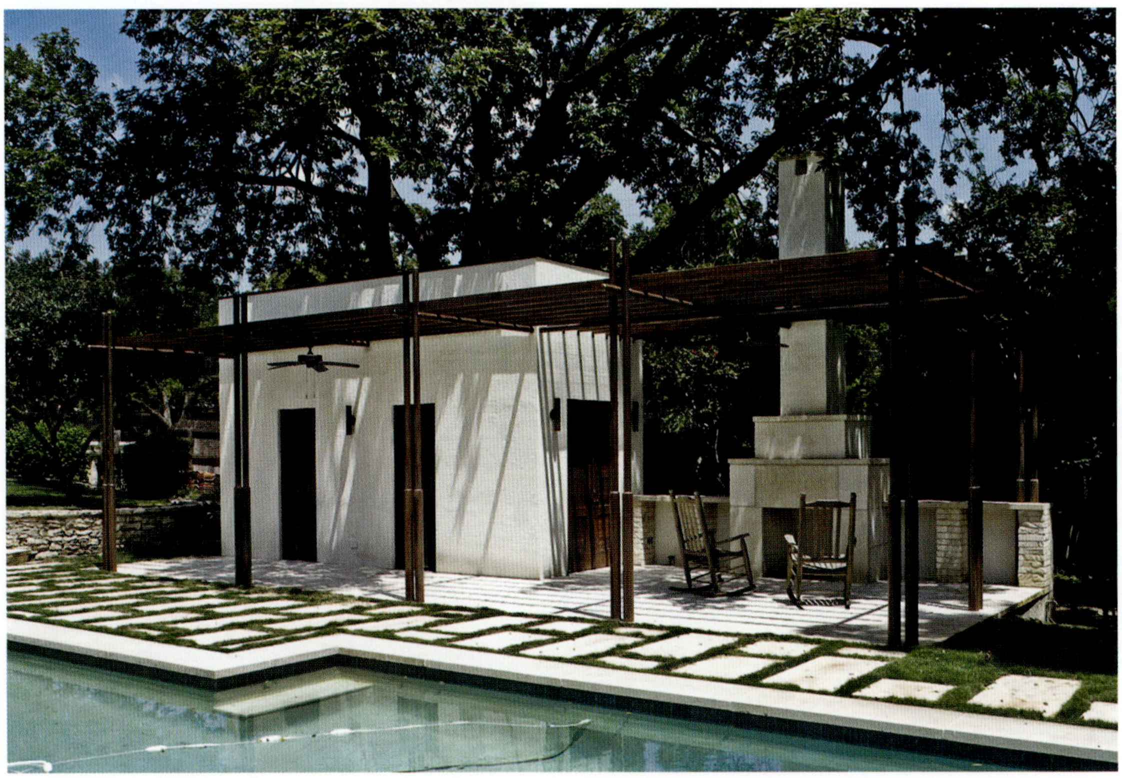

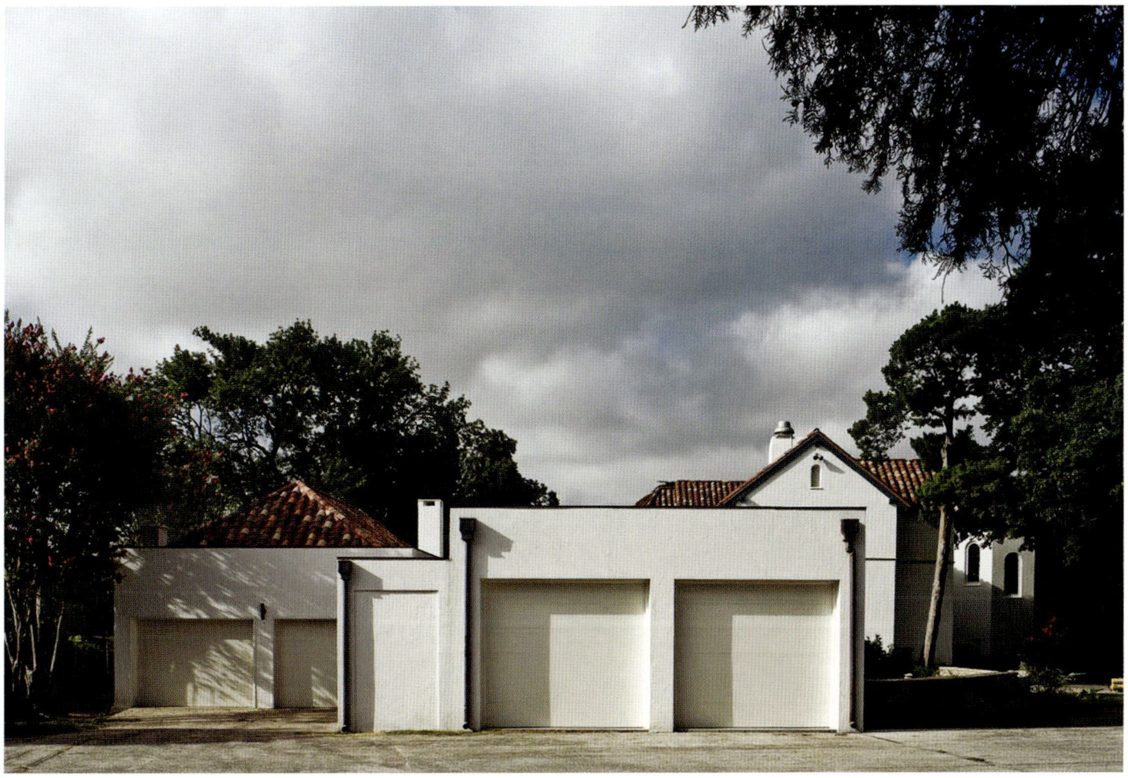

Identical materials and attention to design detail seamlessly integrates the new two-car garage.

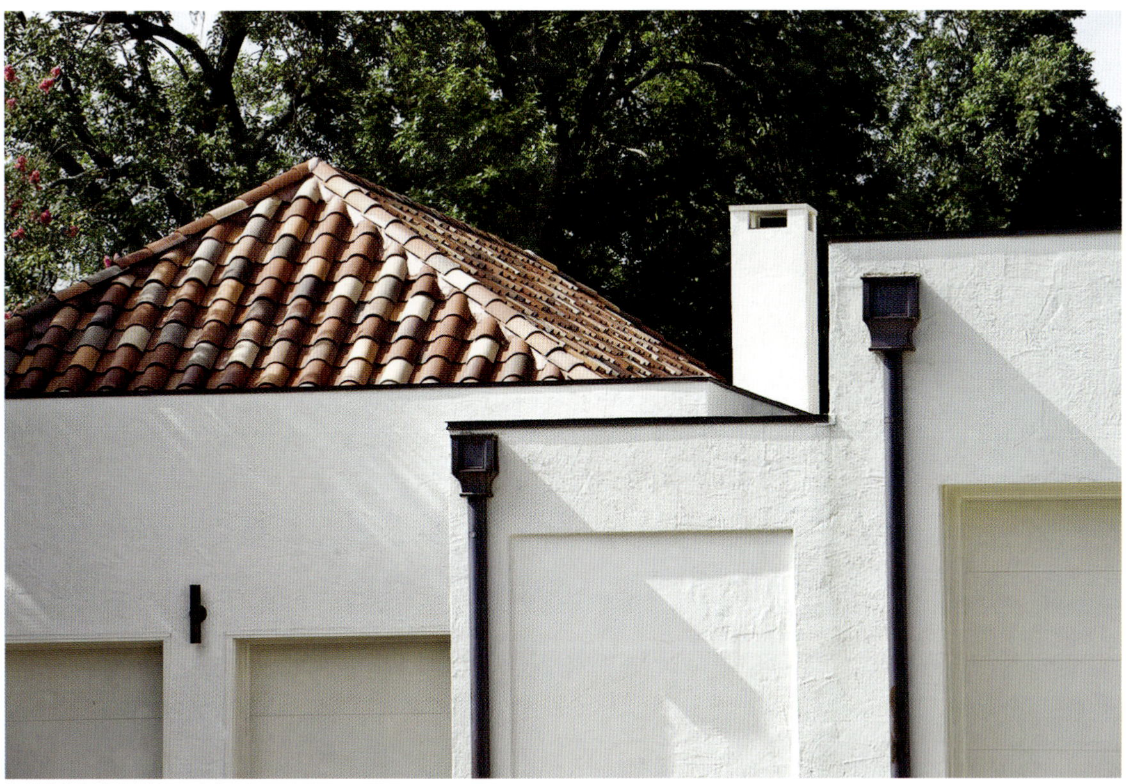

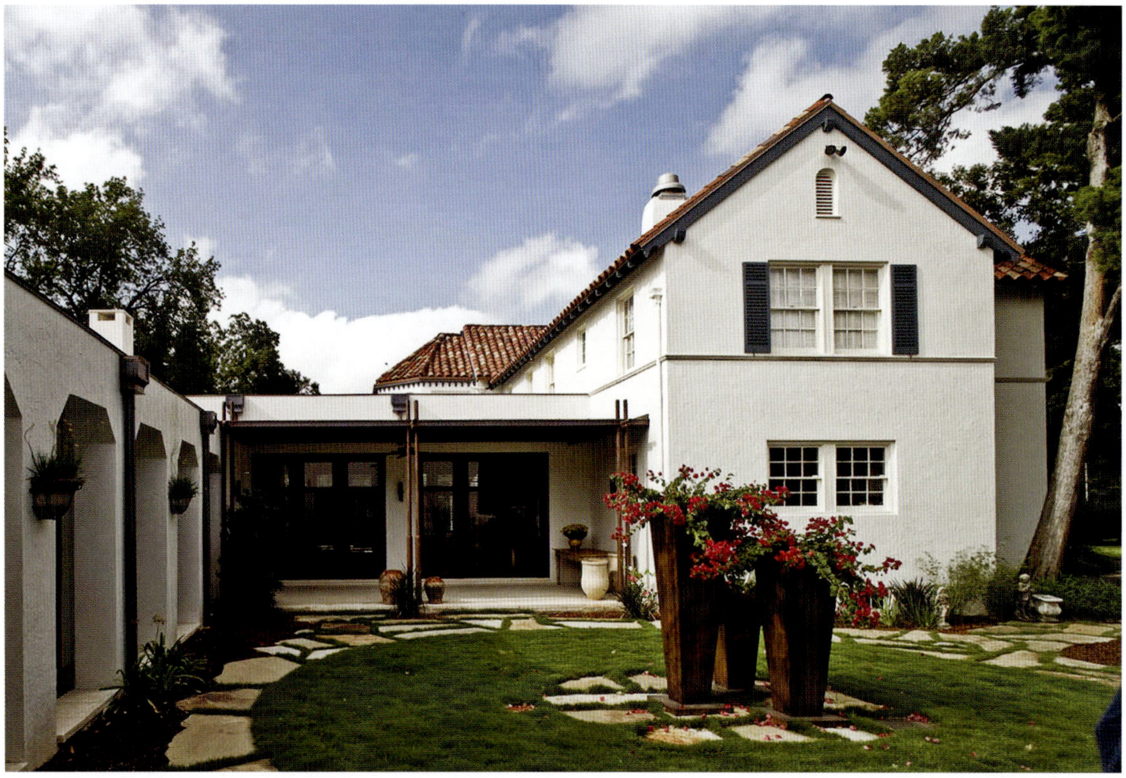

The new garage creates a courtyard sculpture garden.

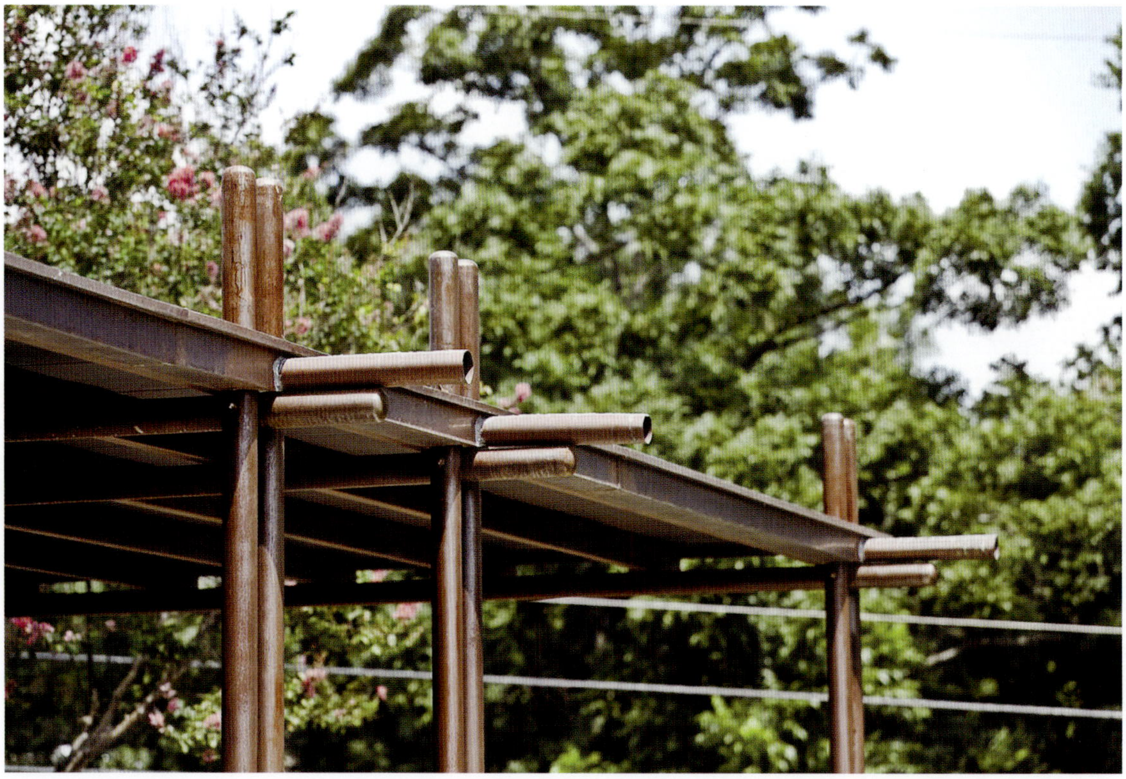

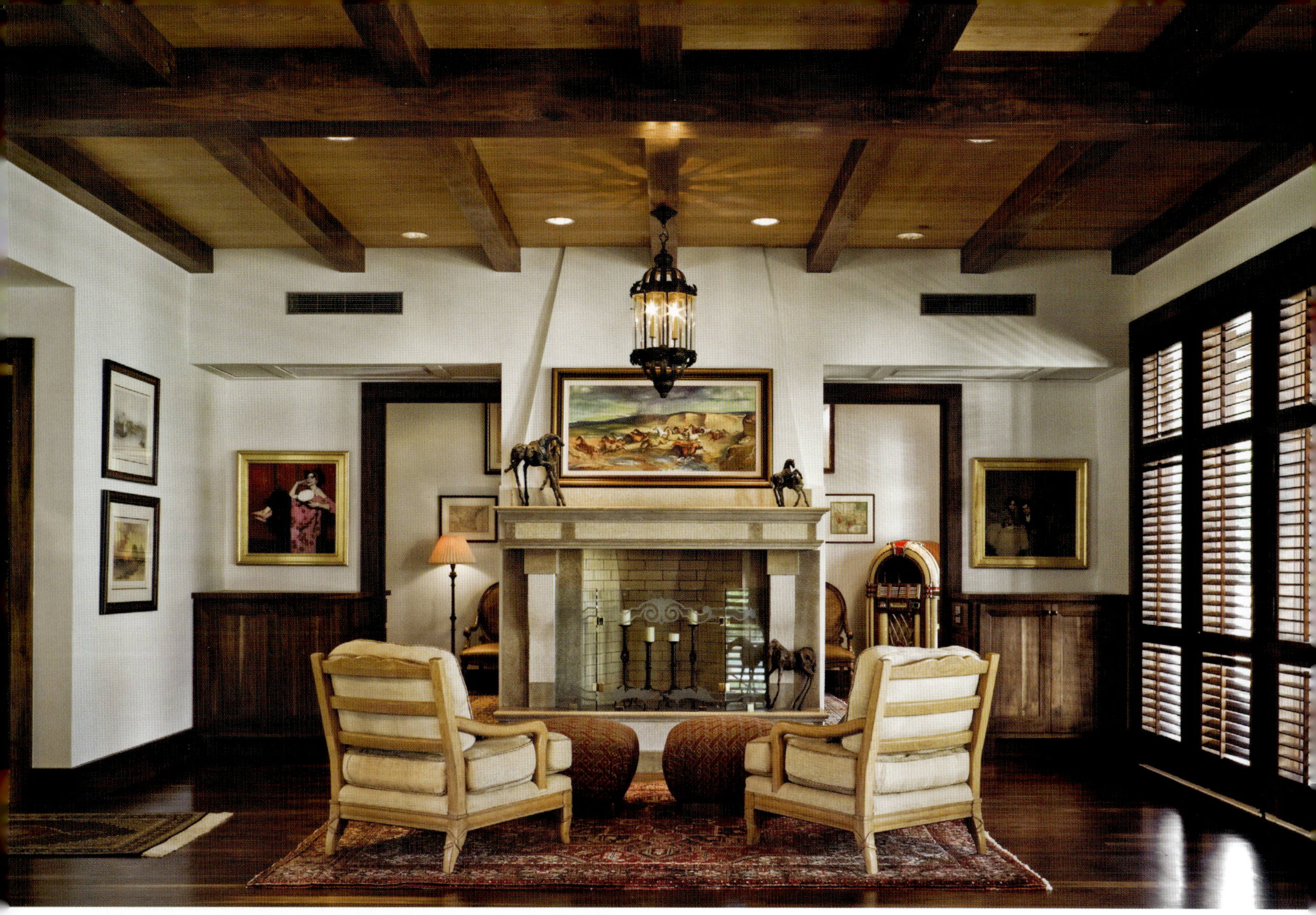

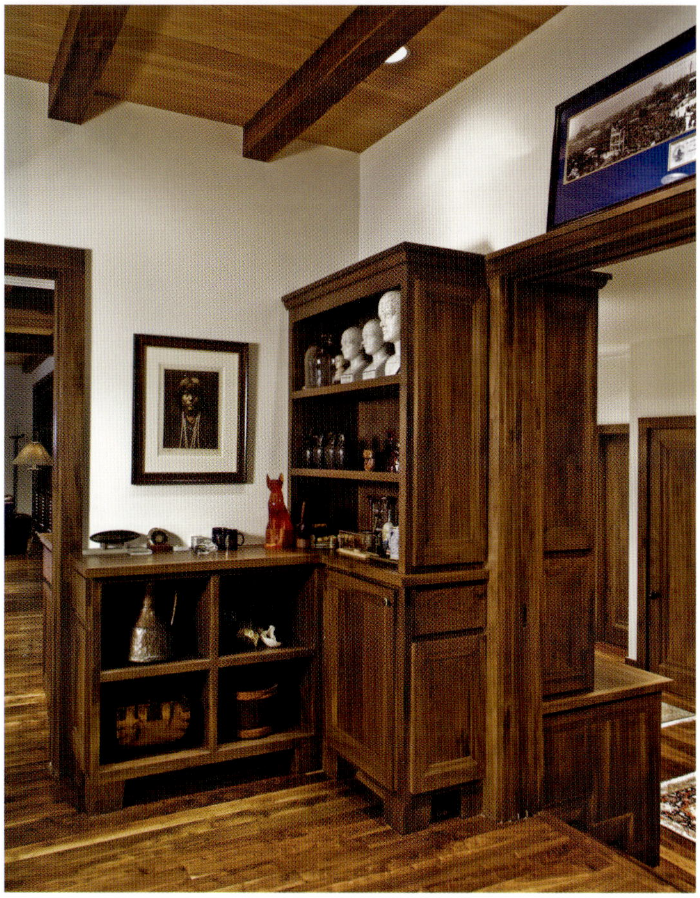

A new sitting room adheres to the generally Mediterranean (Spanish-Italianate-Moorish) mood underscored by the handsomely scaled stone fireplace and dark wooden ceiling.

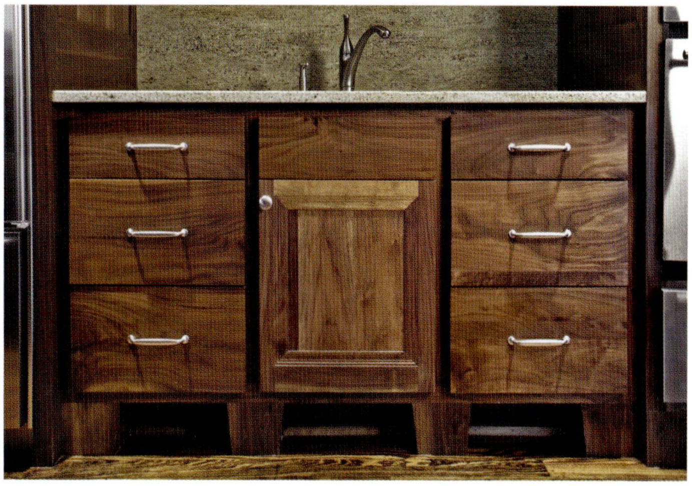

26
TERRELL-MCALLISTER HOUSE

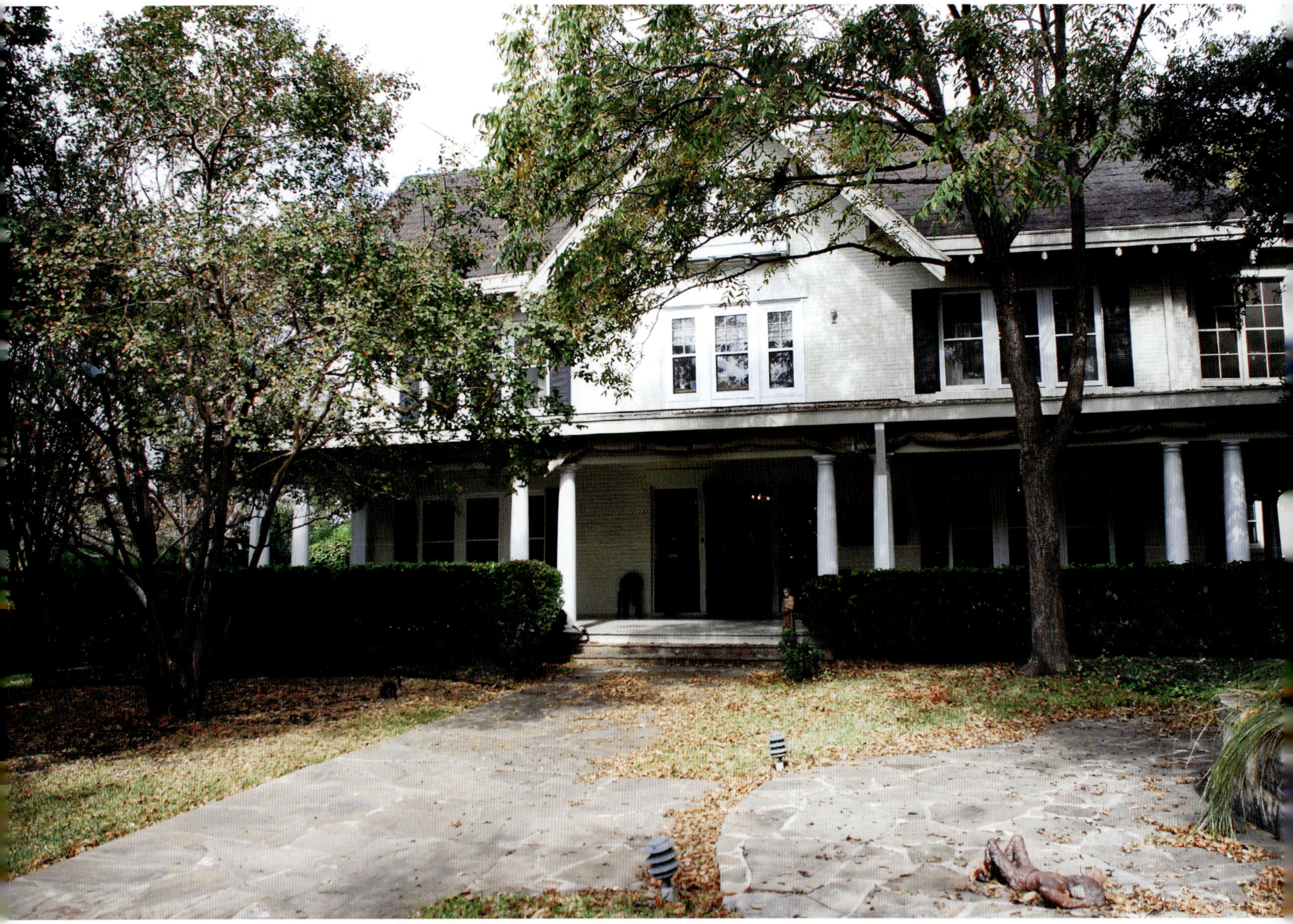

This was a new style in 1912, when Alfred Giles' designed a house that today seems timeless.

The Terrell House on Terrell Road in Terrell Hills was designed for the man whose father developed the area, Dr. Frederick Terrell. Dr. Terrell, a banker who served as San Antonio mayor in 1901, hired as his architect the famed Alfred Giles.

"This is not a typical Alfred Giles house," says owner Edith McAllister, who has lived in the house for sixty of her ninety-plus, extremely civically active years. A 1981 statement by the Junior League about the busy Mrs. McAllister is still appropriate: "It is difficult to name any major aspect of San Antonio's civic life in which our Volunteer Extraordinaire for 1981 has not been closely involved." The warm, witty, and very active Mrs. McAllister, with a sweeping gesture, continues, "I think Dr. Terrell had a great deal to do with its design."

Mrs. McAllister's insightful remark agrees with Professor Mary Jutson's statement in *Alfred Giles: An English Architect in Texas and Mexico* (1972, Trinity University Press, San Antonio). Jutson writes: "This *flow of influence* manifested itself in Giles' architecture, as indicated by *the variety of forms which he used* before 1900, forms known by the following designations: the Italian Villa style, High Victorian

Italianate, Second Empire, and Richardsonian Romanesque. His *various and ever changing solutions* to similar problems certainly stemmed from a desire to satisfy his *clients' demands for the latest fashion*."

Jutson attributes "the latest fashion" influence—which makes the Terrell House new and different from Giles' previous work—to Architect Frank Lloyd Wright and his new Prairie Style. She notes "similar well articulated forms" seen in the 1912-1913 Terrell House by Giles and Frank Lloyd Wright's design for Warren Hickox in Kankakee, Illinois, twelve years earlier. Today, a twelve year time lag seems considerable, but in the early 1900s, States beyond the Mississippi could lag fifty years behind the taste-making *avant garde* East Coast. A mere twelve-year span meant that Giles' Terrell House design was closing the gap between old hat and the latest architectural style.

Elements in the Terrell House design that Jutson cites as advanced include: "banks of windows, diagonal wings, projecting wooden galleries, and wide eaves"—considered "bold and positive features." Another bold feature (not cited) is the classically clean look of the façade. Virtually free of ornamentation, the structure ninety-eight years later seems somehow contemporary.

Even *the latest* fashion has some historic reference. That's true of the deep wrap around porch of this Terrell house. The façade-wide porch was a feature that was "suddenly everywhere" in the Western Hemisphere by 1750, according to Roger G. Kennedy in *Architecture, Men, Women, and Money in America 1600-1860* (1985, Random House, New York). He amends that to say that the porch/piazza/verandah was everywhere that West Indian traders reached *along the Eastern Seaboard*. The West Indian sugar plantation's Veranda Style was not everywhere in Victorian-era San Antonio. "Historicity" (the catch-all term for popular Victorian-era Euro-centric designs) reigned in the Alamo City. It is fair to say that in 1912 San Antonio, Giles' introduction and adaptation of the verandah for the Terrell House helped to make it "the latest," or as Jutson says, "... remarkably advanced for both the architect and the year."

In subtle ways it is clear that while style is important, function—the genius that puts the house to work for its owner (and not vice versa)—is the thing in a Giles design. Problems beg solutions. Cooling the San Antonio home was a problem in a pre-air-conditioning age. Giles designed solutions. In addition to that, the expansive porch, which shielded the vast interior from the sun's formidable heat there is a second-floor sleeping porch. "Before air conditioning, we slept very comfortably out here," Mrs. McAllister says, smiling at the recollection and glancing around the window-walled space.

On a walk through the house, she points to second-floor French doors and balconies and to copious groupings of spacious windows, designed for maximum cross ventilation.

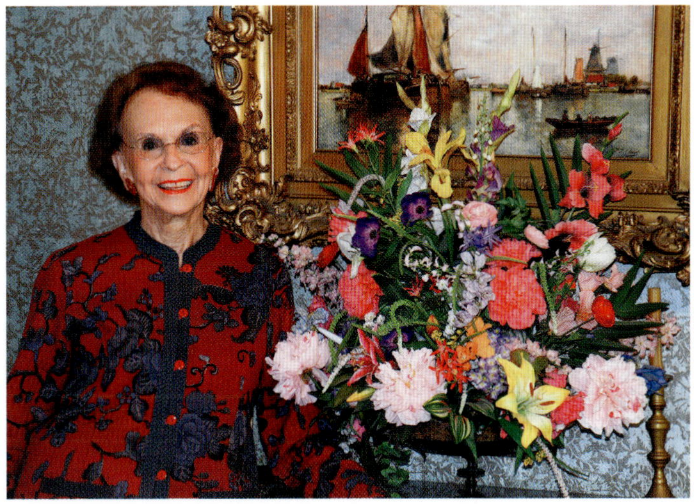

Edith McAllister in the entry hall with its walls covered in beautifully patterned paper in her favorite color—turquoise. *Photographs by Barbara Justice*

"There was no stained glass in any of the windows until I added it," says Mrs. McAllister, pointing to three on the stair landing. "The glass window designer asked about a pattern. I told her that I wanted trees and birds. She created a tree with birds for each of the three windows. I commissioned the over-scaled free-form sculpture of a bird atop a tall pedestal by Marshall Cunningham for its place near the window. I was told that it was too big to fit, but it fits. And I love it—every day I love it!" As for the French doors, early on Mrs. McAllister and her husband, Walter (head of the San Antonio Savings Bank founded by his father, Walter Sr.) removed balcony railings and sealed all but one set of the French doors. "Our kids jumped from that balcony to the roof of the carport," says the mother of four (Walter III, Taddy Jo Ellen, Reagin Scott, and Eloise Edith).

A vast attic, actually a high-ceilinged third floor spanning the entire footprint of the house, kept heat away from second floor bedrooms in the early days. It has undergone changes through the years. "This space was bare when we moved into the house. We removed a wall and finished the space to create a children's play area," says Mrs. McAllister. "Not too long ago, the clawfoot tub in the attic bath was removed at son Bo's insistence. In its place is a remodeled, modern shower that we call Bo's shower," laughs Mrs. McAllister. As the children grew, the attic space became guest space. "Once, Bo brought his entire fraternity from Austin. With existing beds and sleeping bags, there was plenty of space," she recalls. Later, a dormer area was walled in to house equipment when the house was air-conditioned. A half-wall (a cleverly designed closet/storage wall) replaced the whole wall that was removed earlier, providing privacy for a bedroom area. At the foot of

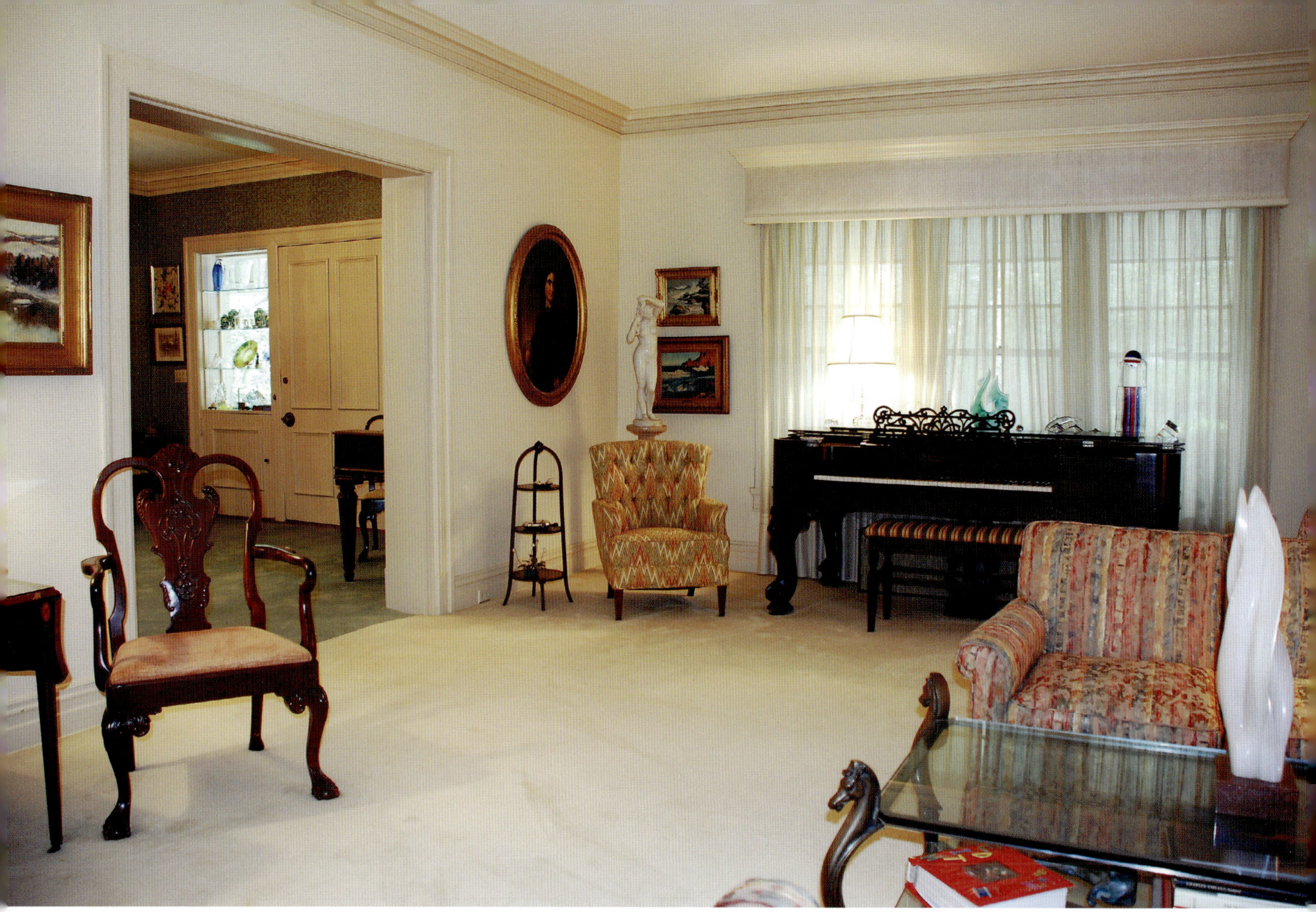

The large opening from the expansive living room offers a glimpse of the wide, welcoming hallway beyond.

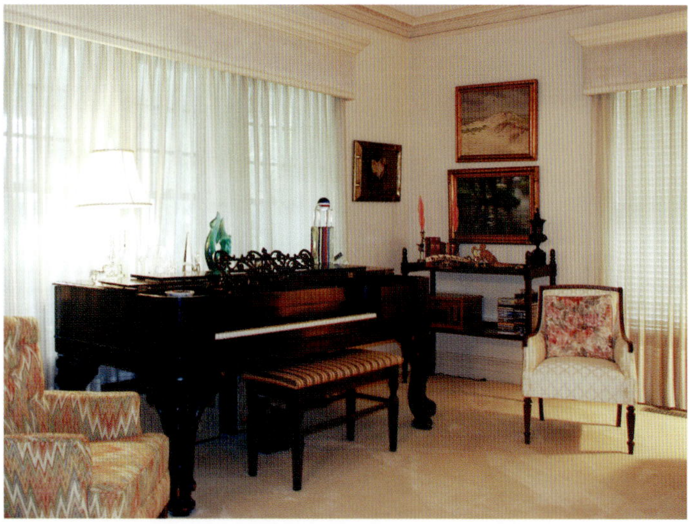

Gentle, neutral colors and groups of comfortable seating welcome visitors to the large living room that spans the width of the house.

the bed is a bench. "I never throw anything away," says Mrs. McAllister. "If you look closely, you'll see that the bench was once a radiator cover."

The floor plan for the Terrell House doesn't seem radically different, yet not many houses in San Antonio (or elsewhere) divide a 2,500 square-foot ground floor into only five rooms.

The entry hall is grand in its spaciousness, yet there is nothing pretentious about it. Furnished with pieces (heirlooms, actually) from several generations of family members, several seating areas make this a very inviting space. "We have Grandmother McAllister's furniture, including the Chippendale loveseat against the wall near the entry door. Our breakfast room furniture, which dates from the late 1880s, was her first dining room group. A member of Dr. Terrell's family, Jane, sent us a framed photograph of Dr. Terrell, saying that it belonged in this house. So it's there on the desk to the right of the entry door."

Opposite the over-scaled entry door is a beautiful stairway segmented by a landing above which are Mrs. McAllister's beloved three colorful stained-glass windows. A wide doorway on the left reveals a rectangular living room that runs the depth of the house. To the right, a door opens into a gracious dining room. Closer to the stair wall a doorway opens into a very large breakfast room (with Grandmother McAllister's dining furniture). Along one wall is a "back stair," a great privacy

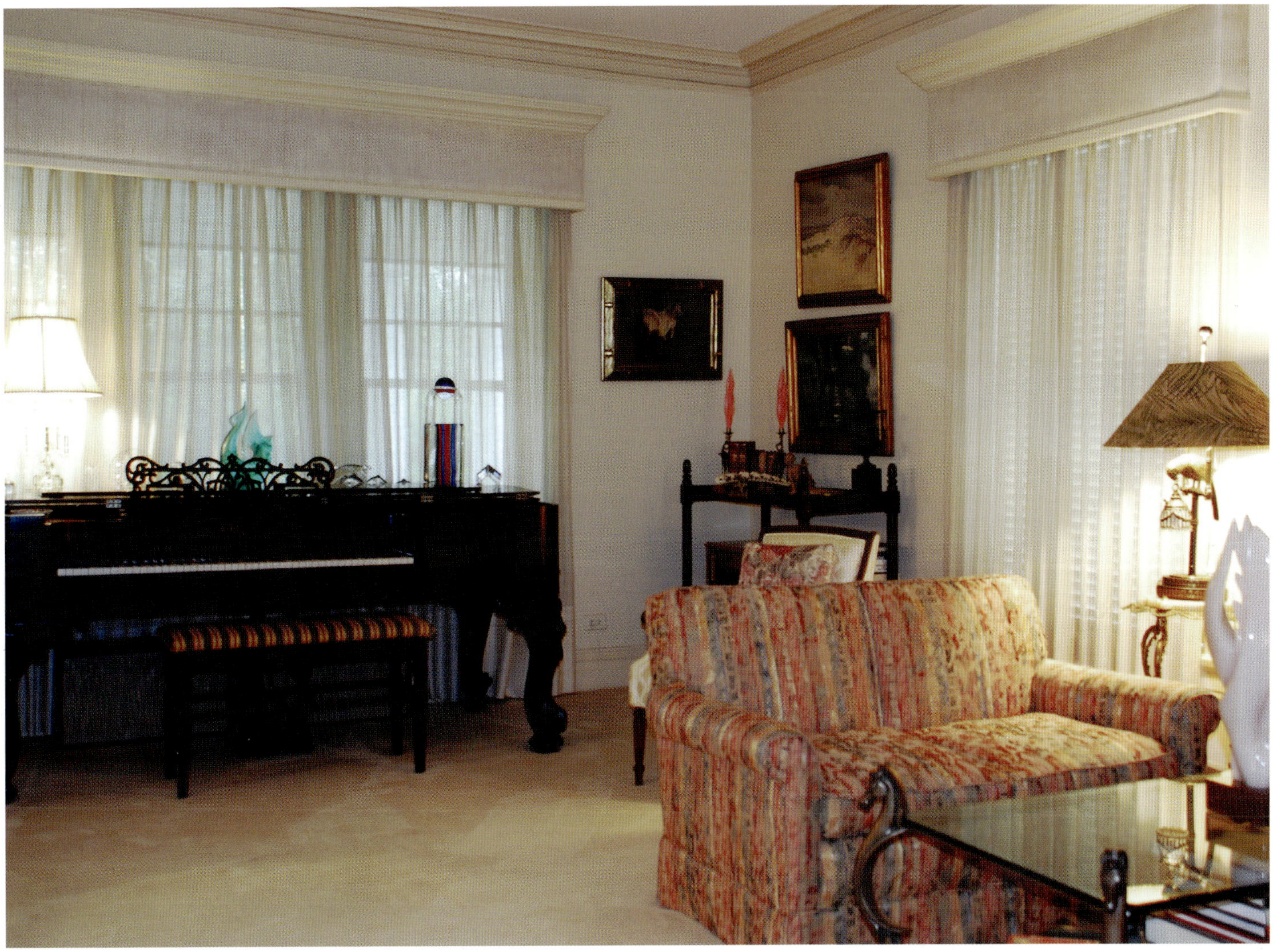

and convenience feature (not just for servants) found in older homes. Walls are covered floor-to-ceiling with a captivating variety of art and memorabilia. From the breakfast room entryway, the kitchen is visible.

Mrs. McAllister says, "We redid the kitchen—two times. The first re-do, sixty years ago, called for moving the sink from one side of the room to the opposite wall—its present position. We installed the latest cabinets—metal! Later, in 1990 when we decided the kitchen needed modernizing, we replaced them. And, we added an island."

The second floor is reserved for bedrooms. "In Giles' original design, each bedroom had it own lavatory, but not its own bathroom. We changed that. In one case, we took space from one large bathroom to create a second so that two bedrooms would each have a private bath. Bedroom closets were added where needed—in one case, a new closet was more important than the fireplace that it covers," she says.

"The second floor is where I live," says Mrs. McAllister, pointing out the bedroom that is now a home office—one of the latest feature in contemporary residential architecture. Carrying on the tradition of her late husband Walter, Jr., prominent in so many areas of San Antonio life, and her father-in-law, Walter W. McAllister, Sr., San Antonio mayor 1961-1971, Edith McAllister serves on as many as twenty boards and committees. Stacks of papers cover the desk and surfaces around the room, each stack a different and ongoing project for a museum, college, or some other civic organization.

Perhaps her most personal stamp on her historic home's interior is Mrs. McAllister's turquoise wallpaper. "Turquoise is my favorite color. Interior designer Orville Carr helped me select the paper, which we added to the entry hall walls shortly after moving in. The paper has aged beautifully—I just can't move any of the paintings," she says with a chuckle. Her love of turquoise—*the* color in year 2010—explains turquoise carpeting in the entry and a handsome tall turquoise buffet in the dining room. "It had a top, which my husband, Walter, and I did not like. We removed it, creating a very pleasing piece."

The latest, forward-looking, newsworthy thing that Mrs. McAllister has done to the Terrell House is to add solar panels to the top of the carport (the one her children used to hop across to). "After attending a solar fundraiser with long-time friend, Bill Sinkin, who founded Solar San Antonio in 1999, I decided that solar would help with my home's electricity usage. It's an investment in the planet," she says. Solar panels are also an investment in the Terrell House (now rightfully the Terrell-McAllister House), keeping this Alfred Giles-designed structure a vital part of San Antonio's continuing history.

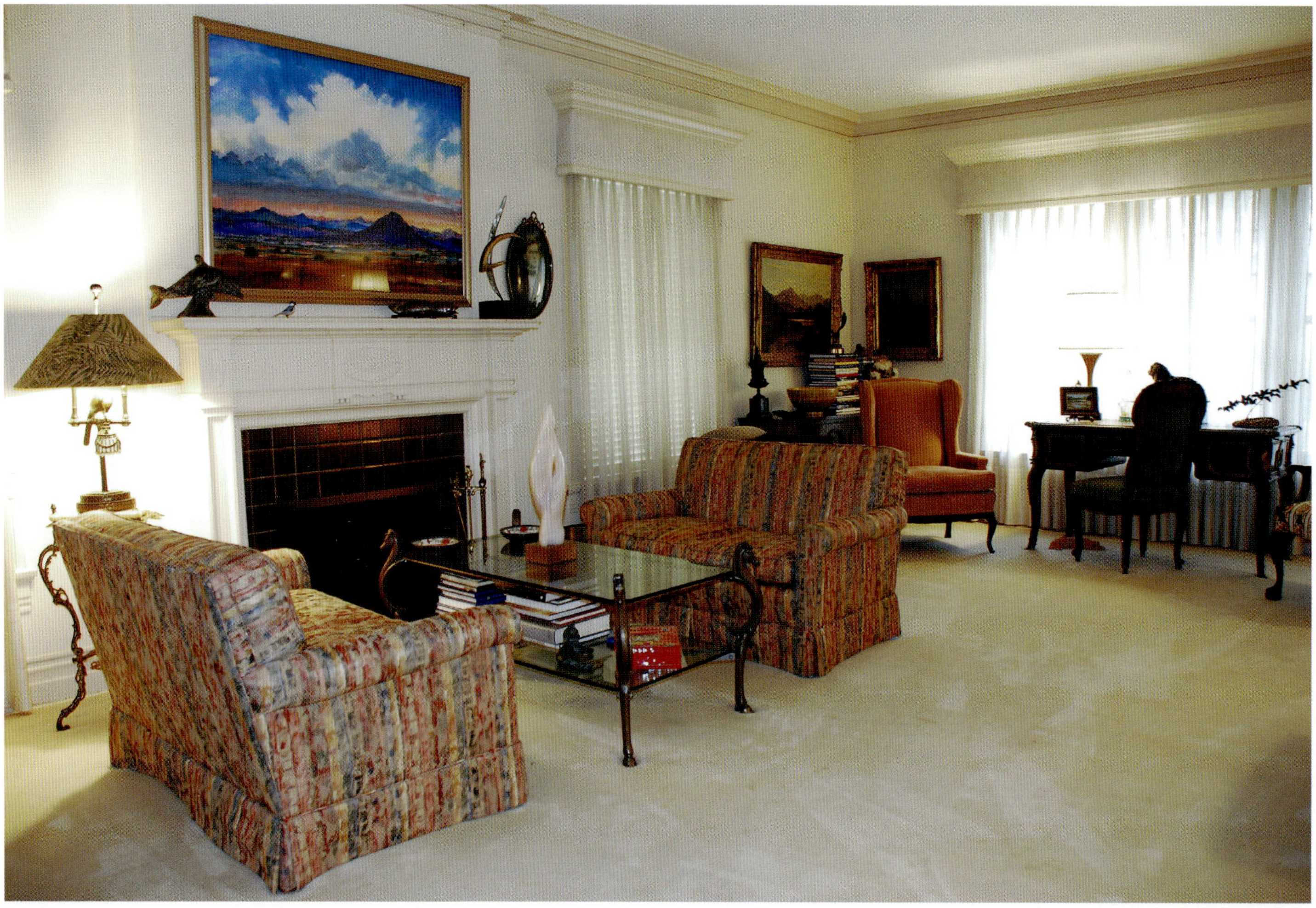

A piano at one end and a desk at the opposite of the living room mark this as a room thoughtfully planned for a multitude of purposes.

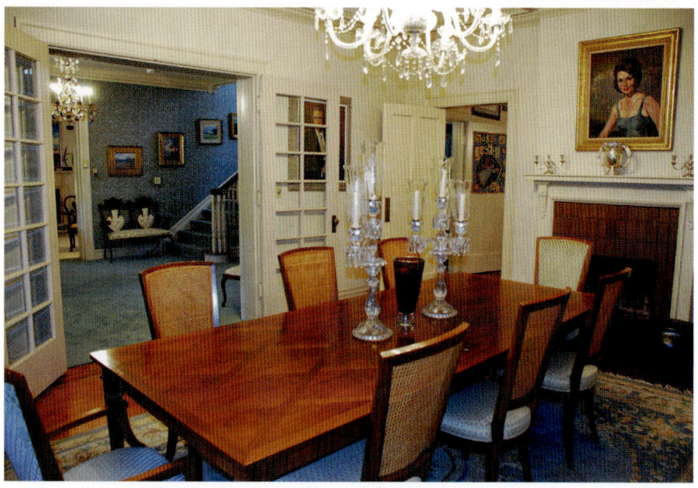

Family portraits hang in the formal dining room. A view is provided through the French doors of the spacious hallway and the living room beyond.

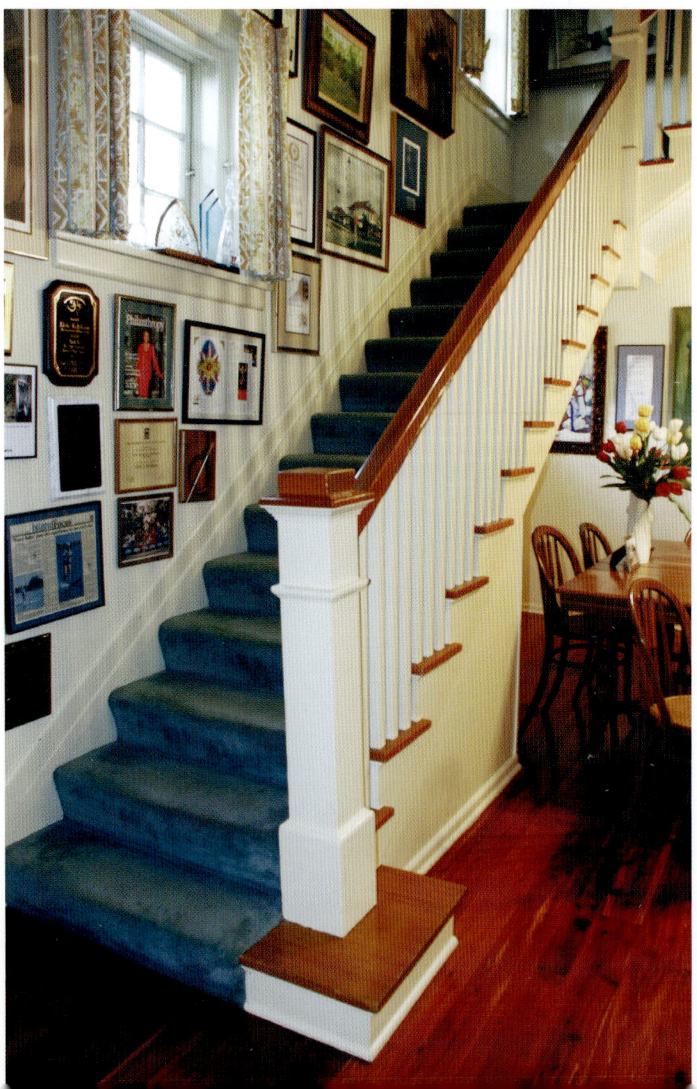

Family photographs and memorabilia decorate a lively "back stair" leading from the breakfast room to the second floor.

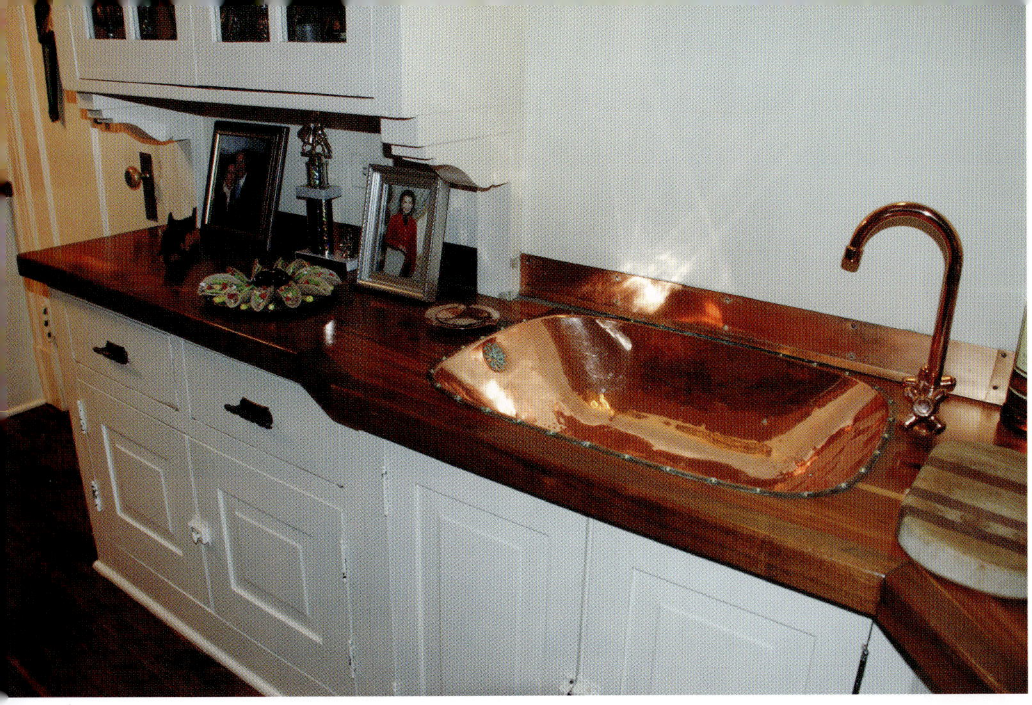

The sink in the bar area of the breakfast room is hand-hammered copper with nailhead trim and is original to the house.

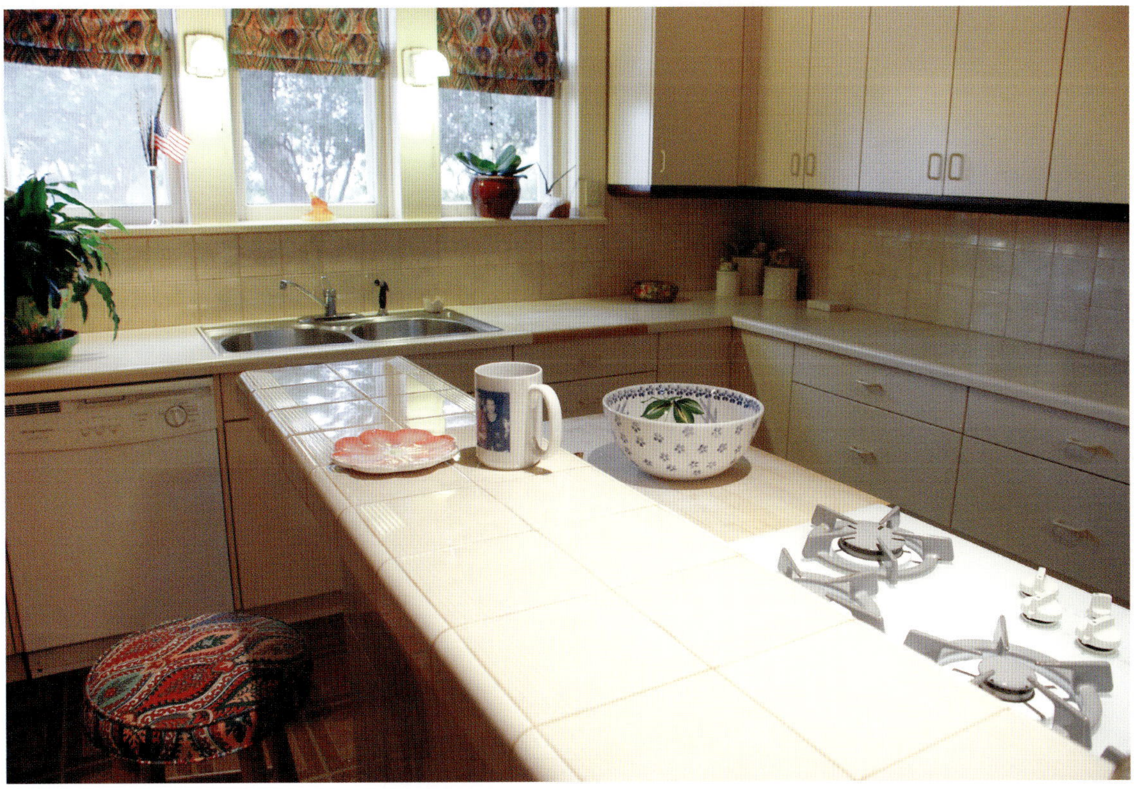

Two remodelings by the McAllister's during their long stay in their historic Giles-designed house have kept the kitchen up-to-date.

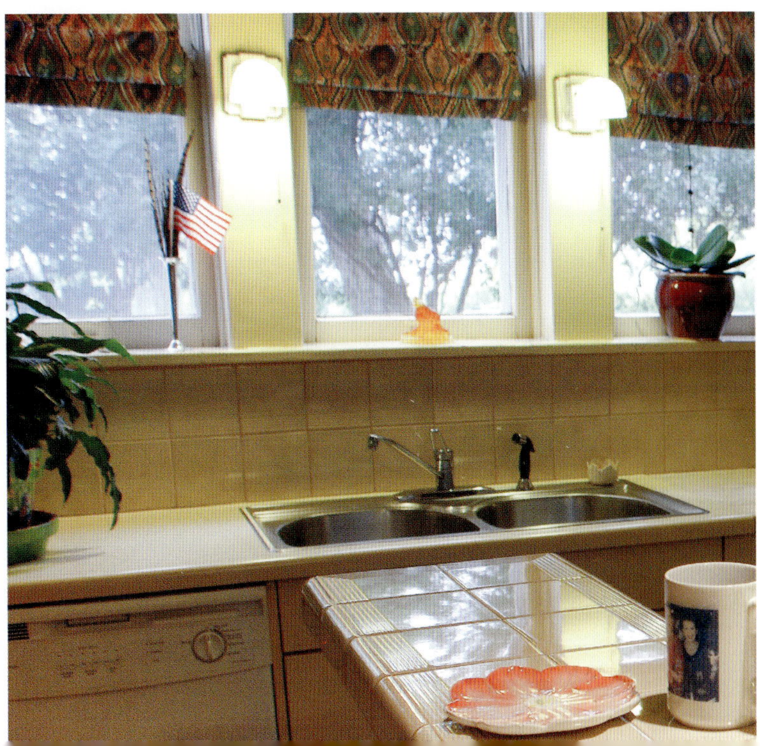

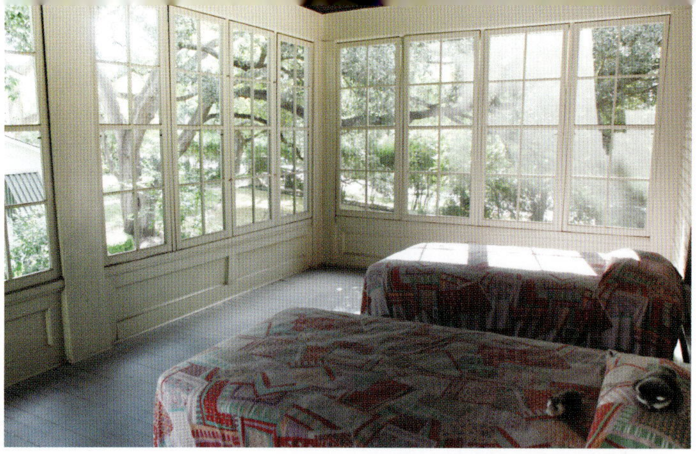

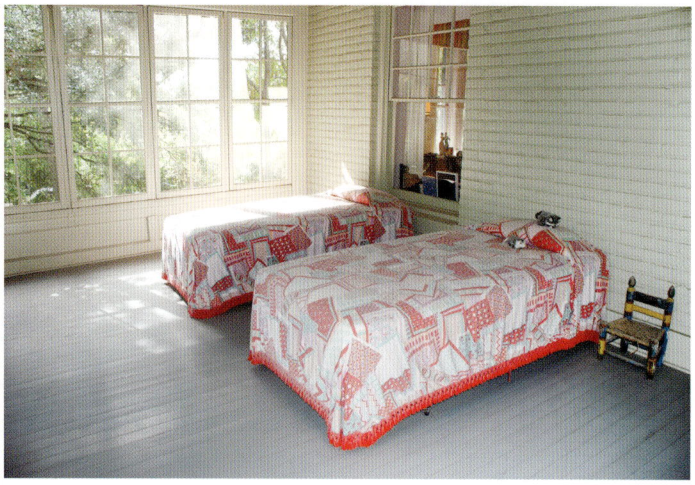

The sleeping porch was a welcome feature on houses built before the advent of central air-conditioning.

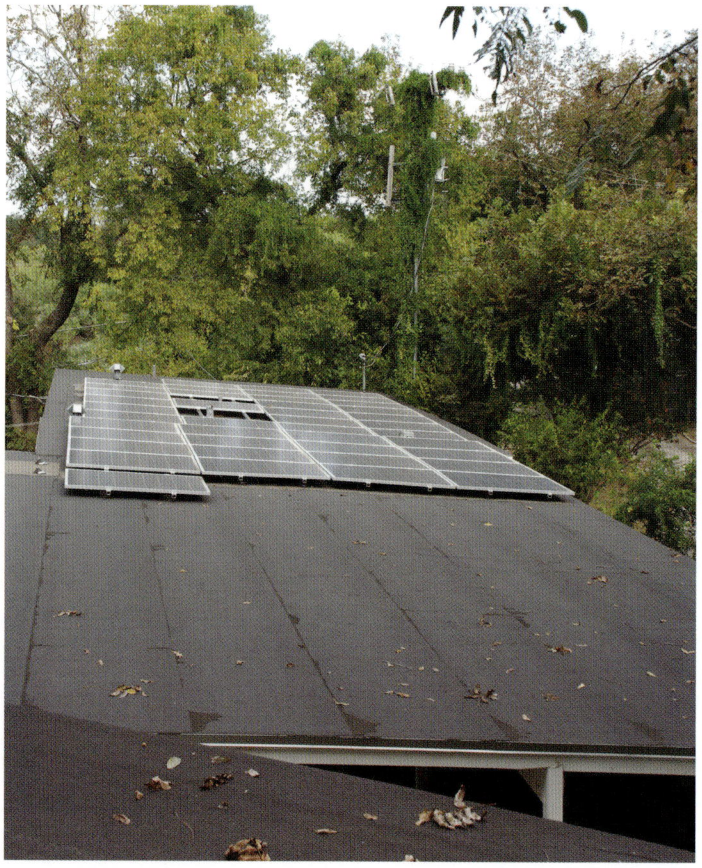

Solar panels added in 2010 keep the Alfred Giles-designed home *au courant*.

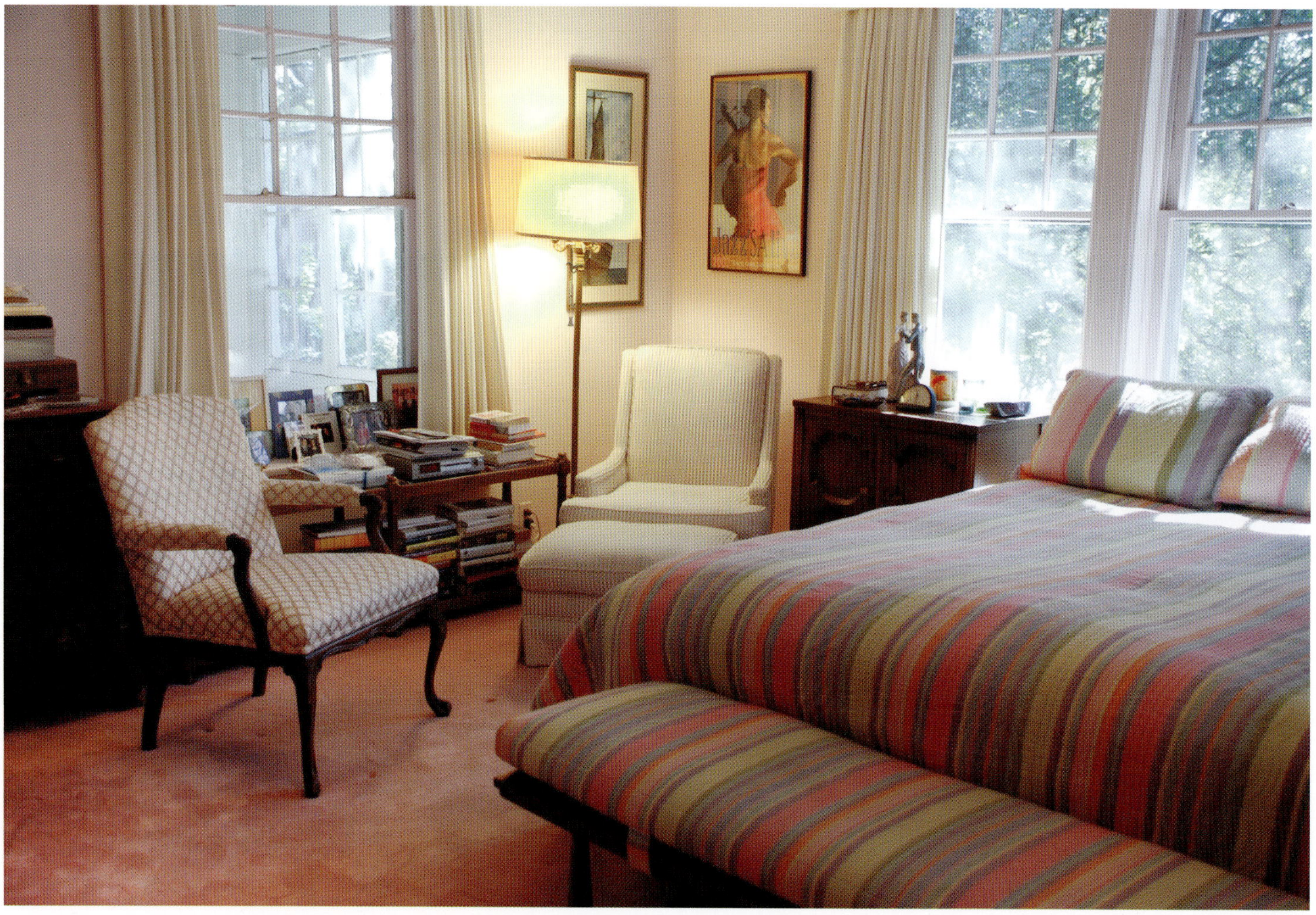

A corner of the master suite, which contained one of several original bathrooms, a forward-looking note of luxury when the house was built.

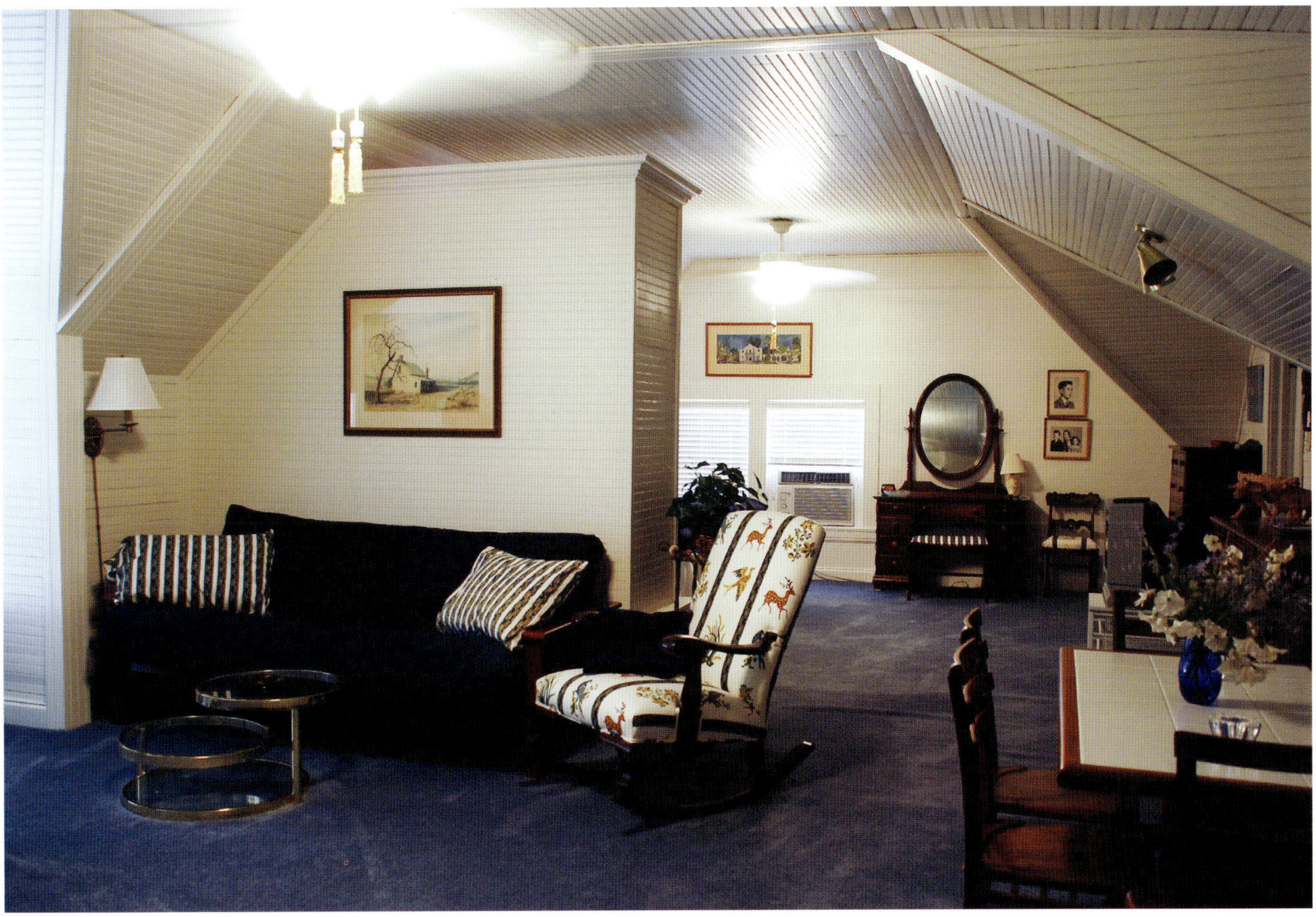

The spacious third floor has undergone several updates and has variously been the children's playroom and guest space.

Afterword

Omar Pachecano, Ph.D.

During a recent interview with Steve Thomas on the Discovery Channel's television program, ***Renovation Nation***, I was asked, "Can you teach an old dog new tricks?" My partner, who happens to be my son, interjected, "Yes, and that's priceless." I answered: "You see, I am old school and my son is new school. When we embarked on the restoration of Nix House I, in the King William district, it was a challenge, but we managed to achieve a balance between time-honored techniques and building innovation."

When my father arrived in this city, he came to build, following in the footsteps of a long line of masons stretching back 200 years to Mexico, Spain, and Italy. He came to San Antonio to build like the generations of immigrants who came before and flooded this country to toil, breaking new ground and being part of a continuum. Ours is the story of immigrant builders—lured by the promise to all who come and are willing to work to breathe free.

The oldest quarters in the oldest cities of the United States were built at the hands of immigrant sweat and labor—erecting, essentially, the most powerful country on the planet. When new ideas confront old ways, some things yield. Yet, I am hopeful that the promise we have found in these historic neighborhoods, is that our cultural assets are not disposable. Surely, what we leave behind shapes us even as we break the mold to create new environments.

Visiting my son on a recent trip, we were skipping across New York Harbor on the Staten Island Ferry one evening, and I couldn't help notice the Statue of Liberty in my peripheral view—a symbol of this country's inner spirit as embodied in Emma Lazarus' words, "I lift my lamp beside the golden door." In the end, it is up to us, individually and collectively, to open the door when opportunity arises. Like our ancestors, we must take up action with vigor and shrug off apprehension. In them, we see a dim reflection in the historic residue they left behind. In us, we see our faith in honoring their vision come alive.

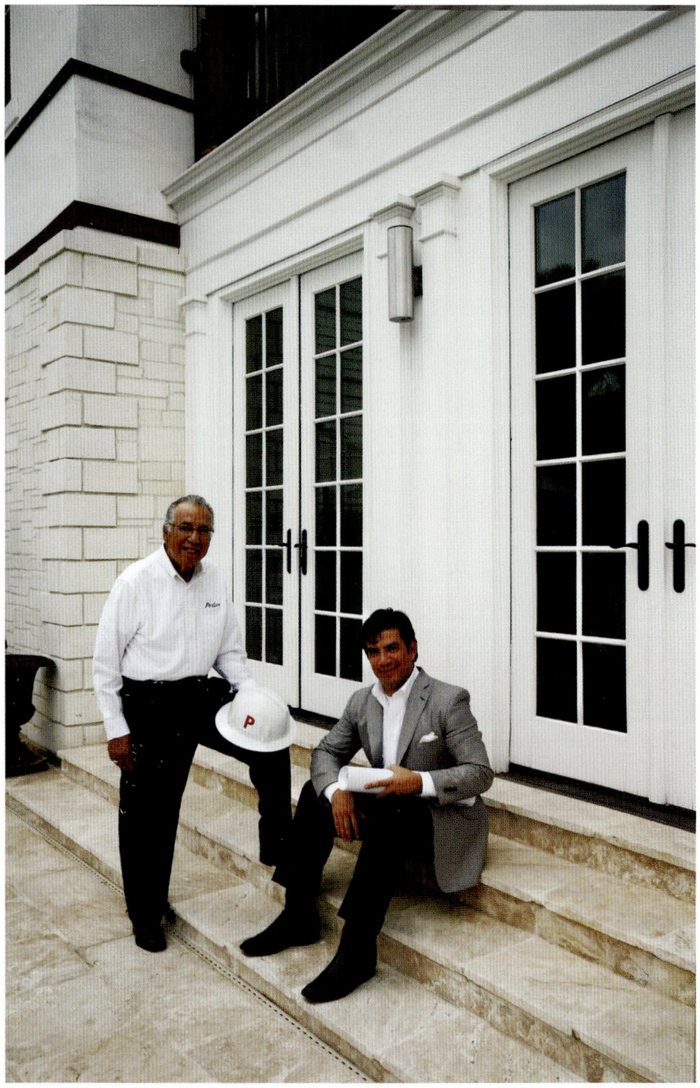

Omar Paachecano, Ph.D., left, and Roy Pachecano, AIA, right, in the Nix House Courtyard.

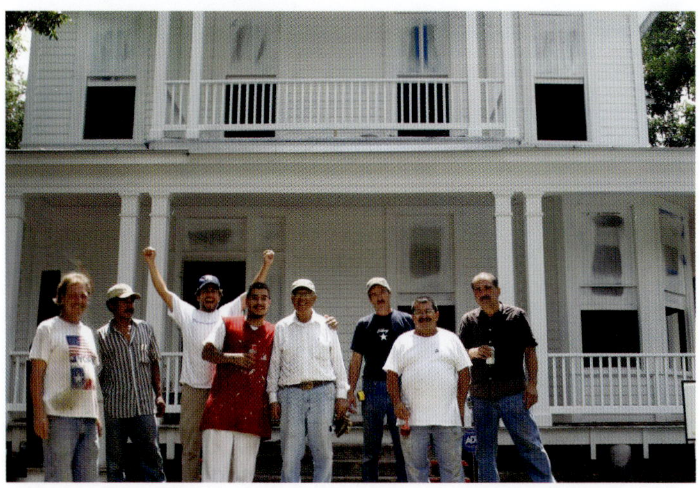

Omar Pachecano and the crew that restored the Nix House.

Sources

Architects

Black + Williams Design Studios
M. Robbins Black, RID, ASID, IIDA
J. Frederick Williams, AIA
102 Downing Drive
San Antonio, TX 78209
T 210-821-6631
F 210-821-6631
email: blackandwilliams@sbcglobal.net

Grable Architects
John Grable, FAIA, Principal
222 Austin Highway, #1
San Antonio, TX 78209
T 210-820-3332
email: jgrable@johngrable.com

Chris Hill, AIA
(Gallagher Ranch)
5111 Broadway
San Antonio, TX 78209
T 210-828-6565
F 210-828-1688

Lake/Flato Architects, Inc.
Ted Flato, FAIA, Principal
311 3rd Street, Suite 200
San Antonio, TX 78205
T 210-227-2335
F 210-224-9515
www.lakeflato.com

Mainstreet Architects
Sue Ann Pemberton, FAIA
133 W Mistletoe Ave.
San Antonio, TX 78212-4391
T 210-732-9268

Darryl Ohlenbusch, AIA
612 Labor street
San Antonio, TX 78210
email: darrylohlenbusch@me.com

Portico Residential, LLC
Roy Pachecano, AIA
315 Madison Avenue, Suite 901
New York, NY 10017
T 212-281-7444
F 212-957-1412
info@porticorei.com
www.porticoresidential.com

Portico Residential, LLC
Roy Pachecano, AIA
Po Box 830942
San Antonio, TX 78283
T/F 210-222-2268
info@porticorei.com
www.porticoresidential.com

Poteet Architects
James. E. Poteet, AIA
114 South St. Mary's St., #100
San Antonio, TX 78216
T 210-281-9818
F 210-281-9789
www.poteetarchitects.com

Candid Rogers Architect
Candid Rogers, AIA, Principal
218 Lavaca St.
San Antonio, TX 78210
T 210-224-6479
email: candidstudio@sbcglobal.net

David Strahan, AIA
PO Box 10004 Wurzback #331
San Antonio, TX 78320

Photographers

Chris Cooper Photographer
900 West End Avenue, NO. 10F
New York, NY 10025
T 212-380-6841
email: chris@cooperphoto.net

Barbara Justice Photographer
1509 Agua Fria
Santa Fe, NM 87505
T 210-573-2766
email: bjusticephoto@gmail.com
www.justicephoto.weebly.com

David Strahan, AIA
P.O. Box 10004
Murzback Parkway, #331
San Antonio, TX 78230
T 210-240-0618
email: davidstrahanAIA@gmail.com

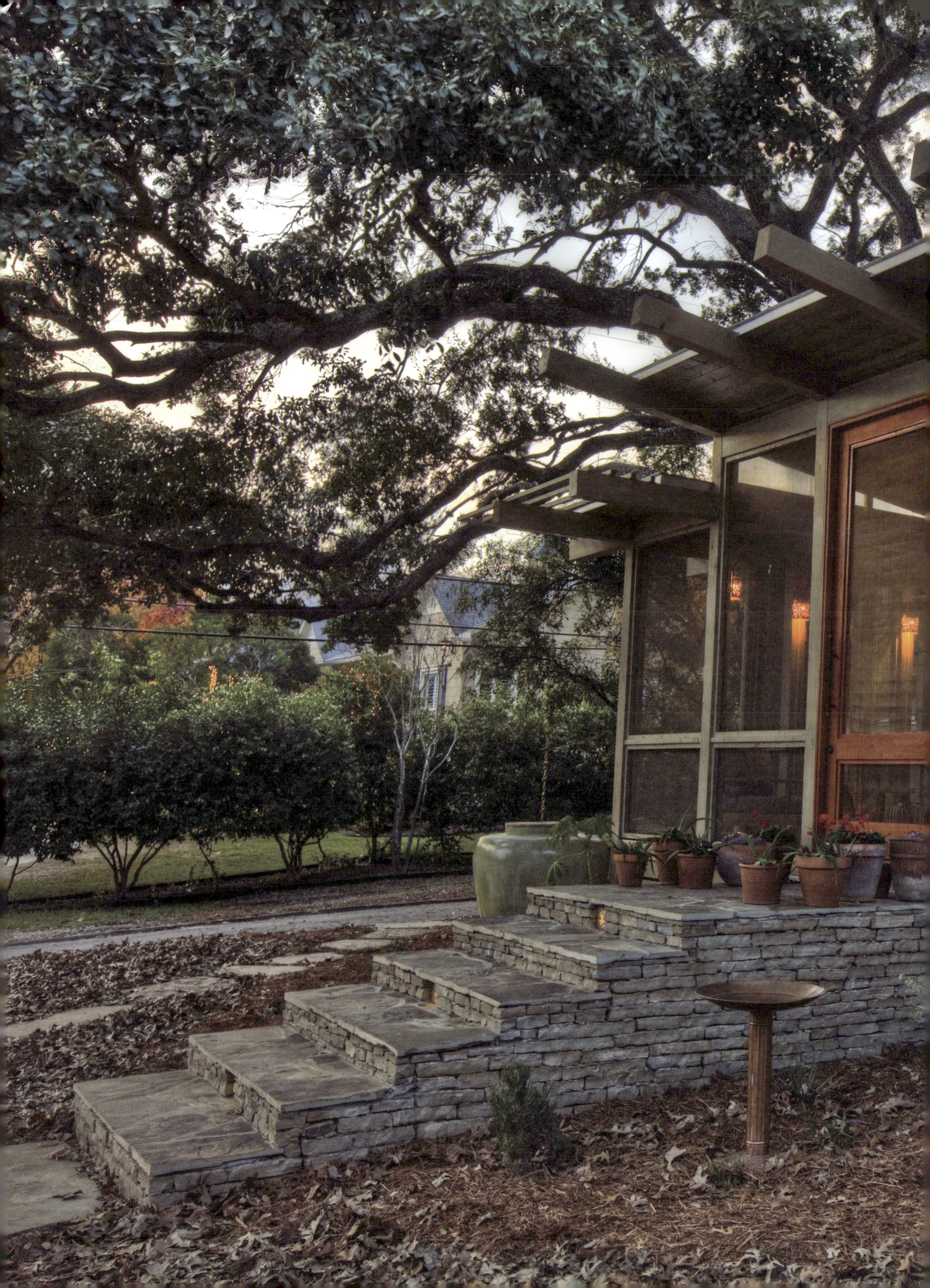